JULIAN ANDERSON

DIALOGUES ON LISTENING, COMPOSING AND CULTURE

JULIAN ANDERSON

DIALOGUES ON LISTENING, COMPOSING AND CULTURE

Julian Anderson
and
Christopher Dingle

THE BOYDELL PRESS

First published 2020
The Boydell Press, Woodbridge

ISBN 978 1 78327 498 7

The Boydell Press is an imprint of Boydell & Brewer Ltd
PO Box 9, Woodbridge, Suffolk IP12 3DF, UK
and of Boydell & Brewer Inc.
668 Mt Hope Avenue, Rochester, NY 14620–2731, USA
website: www.boydellandbrewer.com

A catalogue record for this book is available
from the British Library

The publisher has no responsibility for the continued existence or accuracy of URLs for
external or third-party internet websites referred to in this book, and does not guarantee
that any content on such websites is, or will remain, accurate or appropriate

This publication is printed on acid-free paper

Typeset by BBR Design, Sheffield

Printed and bound in Great Britain by
TJ International Ltd, Padstow, Cornwall

Contents

Contents

Illustrations

The authors and publisher are grateful to all the institutions and individuals listed for permission to reproduce the materials in which they hold copyright. Every effort has been made to trace the copyright holders; apologies are offered for any omission, and the publisher will be pleased to add any necessary acknowledgement in subsequent editions.

Foreword

Gillian Moore
Director of Music, Southbank Centre, London

In April 2002 I invited Julian Anderson to give a talk on Hungarian composer György Kurtág at London's Southbank Centre. His audience was an enthusiastic but non-specialist group of concert-goers, packed into an upper room in the Royal Festival Hall. 'How long do you want?' Julian asked as he was about to start, and I told him he had forty minutes to give an overview of Kurtág's life and music. He took his seat and, without notes and without a watch or a timepiece of any kind spoke, in a perfect arc – for exactly forty minutes. The talk appeared to be sponta- neous, as if he was just summoning things that he'd remembered on the spot. But there was a structure: a beginning, a middle and an end and, along the way, Anderson unpacked the essential details of Kurtág's intricate music and laid them before the Southbank audience with unflinching clarity. It struck me at the time that this talk was a particularly virtuosic example of a masterly composer's highly developed sense of how to structure time. I was also struck by his unrivalled ability to communicate with such clarity his prodigious knowledge of this particular music and its place in world history and culture. I knew that he could have done the same on any one of a huge variety of subjects across a vast range of music. It would be obvious, and a cliché, to say that Julian's knowledge of music is dazzling; but it never dazzles. It is generous, it makes us all understand better – it illuminates.

I've been lucky enough to benefit from many conversations about music with Julian over lunches, on the telephone, after concerts, and each one has left me feeling enriched, emboldened and looking at things in a different way than before. The gathering together into a book of such knowledge, such clarity of thought, such intellectual generosity is welcome and overdue. It's clear that Julian Anderson could be a major writer on music and culture, like Schumann or Schoenberg or Cage or Rameau. The fact that we have, to date, so few of his words about music in print is because he has dedicated himself to the hard labour of being a prolific composer of beautifully wrought and luminous music, as well as being a prized teacher of the next generation of composers. We can be thankful to Christopher Dingle for being midwife to this book; a stimulating conversation partner who knows Anderson's music and his musical world inside out, who is able to provoke, prod, lead, react and add further insights to Julian's. Christopher and Julian clearly enjoy each other's company; the conversation crackles and fizzes along. It took me several times as long as it should have to read the book – not because it ever drags, but because it's almost impossible to not to pick up on Anderson's enthusiasms and go off down rabbit-holes of listening to everything from Hildegard of Bingen to Ligeti, from Dufay to Messiaen, from Ruth Crawford Seeger to Haydn, from Shetland fiddle music to an Indian raga played by Hariprasad Chaurasia.

But this is much more than a book about the enthusiasms of an artist. Across all of the conversations we cumulatively form a picture of what goes into the formation, the training, the building of an artist from childhood through to maturity. Julian recognises that he had an intellectually privileged background – and he made the very most of it: his microbiologist father, his inspiring teachers at Westminster school, his time in France where he met Messiaen and where, even as a very young man, he was able to take an objective and critical look at the spectralist school of composers and take from it what he knew he needed. We also read about the role of curiosity and dedication. We learn that, when he was commissioned to write a major choral work, Anderson joined the London Philharmonic Chorus and learned about the great choral repertoire from the inside. And we find out that Anderson's was an education which took place, at least in part, rummaging through second hand record shops, listening to radio programmes and in conversations with like-minded and inspiring friends. One particularly moving chapter of the book is devoted to a conversation which took place on the day that Anderson had heard about the sudden death of his close friend and mentor Oliver Knussen. Christopher Dingle steps back and allows Anderson free rein just to talk about the quality of Knussen's friendship and the depth of his influence on himself and other composers. Like that Kurtág talk at the Festival Hall, it comes out as a perfectly formed and comprehensive tribute, spoken in the first shock of what must have been a very personal loss.

Most of all, in these conversations we see something of what goes into the painstaking, lonely and essentially mysterious business of composing music. I was specially touched to read about the years of revising, refining, paring back and making difficult choices which went into Anderson's breakthrough piece, *Khorovod*, first performed in 1994. The finished work is an exuberant and joyful, thirteen minutes of ecstatic whirling dances which seem to fly free of the formidable knowledge, study and technique which set them moving. *Khorovod* appears almost effortless but, in this book, we have a privileged glimpse into the skill, the effort and the breadth and depth of vision behind this and indeed all of Julian Anderson's music.

Acknowledgements

We are profoundly grateful to Michael Middeke at Boydell for his belief, support, encouragement and patience during the preparation of this book. We should also like to thank his colleagues Nick Bingham, Emily Champion, Elizabeth Howard and Megan Milan, as well as Ian Brooke, Chris Reed and Amanda Thompson, for their kind help. We are also grateful for the strong support we have received from Royal Birmingham Conservatoire and the Guildhall School of Music and Drama. We should also like to thank Sally Cavender, Sam Wigglesworth and all at Faber Music and Sam Rigby and all at Schott Music. Various friends (who know who they are) have kindly commented on aspects of the book. Particular thanks should go to Sophie Redfern for her dedication in checking the original transcripts and ferreting for various details as well as reading the draft manuscript. Thank you, also, to John Fallas and Oliver Rivers for their kind assistance. Special thanks goes to Chris's wife, Liz, and sons Wilfred and Nathaniel. Liz gave invaluable feedback, and all three showed tremendous patience and forbearance without which this book would not have been possible.

Introduction

This is a book rooted in conversations. It is an attempt to capture the kinds of dialogues we were having for some time before we thought to start recording them, and shall hopefully continue to have for a long time to come. They were informal, often by phone, would frequently last an hour or two and were unpredictable in nature, discussing not just a wide range of music, but much else besides. As befits the frequently serious subject matter, they were often punctuated by laughter. What follows reflects some of that spirit. Lest there be any mistake, this is a book about Julian Anderson's music and thought. There is plenty of the interview format that typifies books of conversations with composers, exploring Julian's life and works. Nonetheless, there are also passages that reflect the broader exchange of ideas and enthusiasms, ranging beyond Julian's music – indeed, beyond music into broader culture and society. Hence the term 'dialogues' since, while Julian is the focus, he is not merely responding to a neutral questioner with *ex cathedra* statements and, as a consequence, the conversations often take unexpected turns.

The conversations spanned several years, starting in early 2014, when Julian was completing his opera, *Thebans*. The overwhelming majority took place across the following two-and-a-half years, with a couple occurring after that. We set no time limit on our talks, allowing thoughts and ideas to progress as seemed necessary. The final conversation we recorded was neither planned nor expected: by chance, we happened to be meeting on the day in July 2018 that Oliver Knussen's death was announced. We took the opportunity to capture Julian's immediate reflections on a composer he knew personally for longer than any other.

Turning the more than thirty hours of recordings into the eighteen conversations in this book was not straightforward; the raw material was at times used merely as a starting point. Each conversation has its foundation in one or two of our sessions, and there have been several levels of editing. We have had no qualms about refining our phraseology. Material from some sessions is disbursed among several conversations. While some passages of conversation took place before or after a certain date, this does not mean that the entirety of that conversation occurred then. For instance, the opera *Thebans* understandably dominated significant portions of early conversations, ranging from the final stages of composition to the aftermath of the first production. It made sense to bring these varied perspectives together into a single printed conversation. Thus some comments refer to *Thebans* as an as-yet-unheard work, while others discuss aspects of the first productions in London and Bonn.

Inevitably, some works, ideas, anecdotes or issues arose on multiple occasions and, while some of these recurrences remain – in cases where they are approached from different perspectives – other repetitions were cut. Some material simply did not fit anywhere or would require a different mode of presentation from that used here.

The broad time frame of these conversations was dictated by the challenge of aligning our respective schedules. While that had its frustrations, it has also resulted in the kinds of insight rarely available from composers. For instance, in Conversation Sixteen, 'Quartets', Chris queries what Julian says about his approach to rhythm in the Second Quartet as it is significantly different from what was said about the relationship between pitch and rhythm in his music during Conversation Six, 'Composing (or not)'. Elsewhere in 'Composing (or not)', Julian talks through a sketch for the orchestral piece he was then writing for Sir Simon Rattle and the Berlin Philharmonic. In Conversation Eighteen, 'Partnerships', there is discussion of the completed piece, which departed significantly from Julian's initial conception.

In the broadest terms, the conversations follow the general sweep of Julian's chronology, from formative years to some of his most recent music, but a strictly chronological approach was avoided in the interests of liveliness. Although the final conversation discusses some of Julian's most recent works, it also stretches back around two decades. It is certainly not necessary to read the conversations in the order here presented. Even though there are links, parallels and follow-ups in all sorts of directions, each conversation is readable in isolation. Some have a clear focus on a specific topic, such as Julian's training or his relationship with dance, while others cover broader themes. Brief introductions are provided for each conversation to give some indication of the various paths to be explored. The overall order we have chosen provides a degree of contrast from one conversation to the next, as well as ebb and flow in subject matter and approach.

Aside from Julian's music, certain recurrent themes soon become apparent. Given our shared love of Messiaen's music, it is unsurprising that we return to this composer like moths to a flame. The obvious facts that Julian attended the Maître's summer course in Avignon in 1987 while Chris is a leading Messiaen scholar naturally prompted his frequent mention, but he would be an important point of reference even if this were not the case. Similarly, Stravinsky (especially *The Rite of Spring* and *Agon*), Debussy (notably *Jeux*), Janáček's *Glagolitic Mass* and Sibelius's Symphonies, to name but a few, are familiar friends across the conversations. We are both teachers so it may initially seem odd that there is not a conversation dedicated to Julian's pedagogy. The absence of a bespoke chapter on this subject actually reflects its importance generally in much of what is said throughout the book.

As this book is intended for the general reader, the main body of text does not include any musical examples, and we have not assumed the reader knows the ins and outs of either music itself or the musical profession. For these and other reasons, it seemed appropriate to compile a few extra items clarifying this and other background information: hence the inclusion of the Glossary of Musical Terms, a List of Personae and a Chronology of the composer's life. The Glossary of Musical Terms has been compiled by Julian Anderson alone and deliberately reflects the context of his understandings of music and culture, as he explains in his note heading it. We hope this aspect of these explanations adds another dimension to the dialogues contained in the main body of the book, as well as being of use to readers to whom some terms may be unfamiliar.

There is no fetishising of our first expression of each idea in these conversations. While they originated in recordings, the printed result at times differs substantially from the source materials, as is usual in such publications. Nonetheless, as Stravinsky said of the sources for *Pulcinella*, what is remarkable is how little we have changed, not how much. While every effort has been made to check facts and sources, in some cases this proved nearly impossible within the time frame of editing and publication. We apologise for any inadvertent errors which remain. We enjoyed ourselves very much with these conversations and we hope that comes across, capturing the enthusiasm, passion and sense of fun prompted by discussing this thing we call music.

Jeux: A Conversation Over Lunch

JA: The thing about *Jeux* I don't understand is why, every time I listen to it, it almost sounds like a different piece of music, one I hadn't heard before. I can recall sounds from it, gestures, melodies, harmonies and so on, but each time I hear the whole piece from beginning to end, I remember something different, sometimes very different.

CD: I looked at *Jeux* with the students the other week. Before playing the first page or two at the piano, I told those with absolute pitch to shut up. I then pointed out that Debussy introduces this little meandering, chromatic theme, has a little bit of a flourish, and then he sticks it up the octave, a classic compositional gesture. Everyone said, 'Fine.' I then got them to look at the score and, even with that, it took a while before they realised he puts it up a major seventh, not an octave.

JA: That's the xylophone entry, yes.

CD: Yes, xylophone and strings. I find it remarkable the way Debussy can do something gracefully that would be so askew and distorting in pieces by other composers. The way he moves the harmony around is so fluid and plastic. I was flabbergasted when I first looked closely at the score to see just how saturated the chromatic space is. It is just as chromatic as Schoenberg, yet it sounds so full of light.

JA: It doesn't sound clogged, does it?

CD: No, and while it's not traditional diatonic harmony in the Mozartian sense, it doesn't sound atonal at all, even though it is just as chromatic as some atonal works. Nor does it sound like *Tristan* or that late-Romantic kind of chromatic saturation. It's astonishing to be able to do that and for it not to have the expressionist feel that you get from Schoenberg at the same time.

JA: Yes, it's mobile and free-floating, but it's not connected with that kind of strenuous chromaticism at all. As you say, it's not clear how that's been done. Even Debussy, one suspects, may not fully have understood what he'd done. There is another factor in *Jeux* that people occasionally neglect – they did in the '50s anyway – which is that he was following the plot. There's no doubt that many twists and turns in that music are plot-driven. The dancers are together, then the man runs off, then one of the women finds the ball, and so on. All of those things correspond to some change in the music. Any ballet can have a plot like that, so this does not entirely explain why the music has so many baffling discontinuities. But then, so did the piano etudes. There was certainly a massive change in Debussy's music at that time. I've always thought that Maurice Ohana must have been very keen on that period of Debussy because you find the same volatility in some of his music.

CD: *Jeux* is actually quite cubist.

JA: You get a bit of this, and then something else comes in, and you get another bit of something... It's all loose ends.

CD: What makes the mind boggle is what he would have done if the idea of having a plane crash had actually made it to the final scenario. [Laughter] What music would that have produced?

JA: The first ideas for the ballet were completely insane. They were risqué in other respects, as well. Debussy must have wondered what the hell he'd let himself in for, especially when the plane crash was mentioned. I've always assumed that idea was a sort of futurist touch – Diaghilev and Nijinsky wanted to have some technology on stage. After all, this was the first ballet in modern dress.

CD: And, of course, planes were only four years old at this point.

JA: It was very up-to-the-minute. At the same time *Jeux*, which has been analysed to death, remains slippery and out of reach. I first heard it in a concert with Dutilleux's *Tout un monde lointain*, which itself is pretty elusive, but it was the Debussy I didn't understand. The Dutilleux one could get some kind of hold on, but at the end of the Debussy, I thought, 'What happened?'. I didn't know what was going on in those 19 minutes. I couldn't follow it. It remains astonishing, each time you hear it.

CD: Yes. In an odd sort of way, the way I listen to *Jeux* is far closer to what some people mistakenly say about Messiaen, that it's not going anywhere. There are a few pieces of Messiaen that just are, without any direction, but not that many.

JA: We agree on that, yes: the cliché that Messiaen's music is static has little truth in it.

CD: Whereas with *Jeux*, it's not so much that it's not going anywhere, but I just have to let it happen, exist in it while it's playing and enjoy this wonderful noise that is going on. While I'm in it, I would quite happily have it go on forever, and yet, it lasts for what seems to be precisely the right amount of time.

JA: When I'm listening to it, more than any other music before about 1955, I'm not able to foresee a thing. Famously, that was a big problem for many people with pieces like Stockhausen's *Kontra-Punkte* or *Zeitmasse* or whatever. In the case of *Jeux*, the syntax seems perfectly straightforward, so the fact that we're not able to predict much is a tribute to Debussy's exceptional imagination. There are very few differentiated ideas. It's clear what those few ideas are, and they're not the world's most fascinating musical material to start with. Yet, even from what you just said, that octave leap that is not an octave leap, something completely unexpected is happening in every detail. Yet there is a certain logic of the unexpected.

CD: Yet this is where the non-parallel with Schoenberg is so pertinent, because that not knowing what's going on, the unexpectedness, that usually means some sort of Freudian dream, nightmarish kind of world.

JA: Quite, but *Jeux* isn't that world at all. It's also clearly a piece that continues to have a huge effect on contemporary composers. It seems to me that Unsuk Chin's music is very affected by it. I suspect that Simon Bainbridge's music, for example, might be. It's a piece I know Olly Knussen studied heavily. Messiaen wasn't that interested in it. Boulez famously was. I think I discern its influence on George Benjamin, and possibly also on Hans Abrahamsen, though that's just my idea. A lot of younger composers still look at this piece nowadays.

CD: The irony is that, structurally, *Jeux* with its fragmentation is closer than anything else in Debussy to mature Messiaen, yet it is not the Debussy that Messiaen loved. He probably first heard it when it was very fresh, when he was about 11 or 12 and, quite understandably, his first reaction to it was probably 'Huh?'.

JA: Indeed, as it would be! The other thing that still constitutes a bit of an obstacle for some people is the waltz aspect to the piece, because Debussy didn't really write waltzes. Ravel famously did, but somehow one does not associate the waltz with Debussy. So what's he doing? Except, of course, it's a sort of non-waltz – it's disrupted almost constantly. Perhaps the bravest thing about *Jeux* is the way it goes against so many of Debussy's stylistic traits. That is clearly deliberate. *Jeux* upsets everyone and everything.

Origins

In some respects, much of this conversation has most in common with a standard conversation book, covering the basics of Anderson's formative years and schooling. Even then, some might be disconcerted by swiftly encountering discussion of microbiology prompted by conveying some sense of his father's remarkable achievements. Discussion of instruments learnt is the catalyst for delving briefly into the world of playing percussion, while there is also some consideration given to potential alternative careers to music. The contributions of two early teachers, Oliver Knussen and John Baird, lead the conversation to key early works, notably *Light Music* (now classified as String Quartet No. 1), *Ring Dance*, *Diptych* and *Khorovod*. Finally, it is worth noting that part of Conversation Fifteen, Outsiders?, reflects on some aspects of Anderson's background that are given in straightforward terms here.

CD: Let's start at the very beginning with some sense of where you came from. Could you say something about your family background?

JA: It's not a musical one, in the sense that there are no professional musicians in the family now, and there never were that I know of, but there's a lot of good amateur music in the family. My father was a microbiologist, but he was very musical. He played the violin well enough to be able to play the Mendelssohn and the Bruch Concertos to a pretty good standard, so he was a talented violinist. I don't know if he ever could have been a pro, but he was a very gifted amateur. He was a literate music lover, whose tastes did not go beyond about *The Rite of Spring* and *The Young Person's Guide to the Orchestra*, but the standard repertoire he knew very well.

His microbiological activity interests me a lot. It's rather relevant now, because he discovered the mechanism by which bacteria spread resistance to antibiotics among themselves, a technique he termed 'transferable resistance'.[1] The important factor is that bacteria who have never encountered the antibiotic, with the help of this mechanism, can already be resistant to it. That's what they couldn't understand: how the bacterial resistance was spreading so quickly. This was a problem in farming originally, in the late '50s, early '60s, but it soon became a problem in the human use of such drugs. My father was very important in raising significant public awareness of the dangers of overusing antibiotics. He predicted the emergence of superbugs, which now, alas, are a fact of life – Sir Richard Rodney Bennett, for example, died of one. My dad was not very popular because of these views, which were totally against the accepted understanding. Antibiotics were only employed for the first time extensively towards the end of World War II and in a big way after 1945. The pharmaceuticals industries were not happy about this being challenged.

CD: It's also the whole *Star Trek* notion of eliminating disease in this glorious new age.

JA: Exactly. What's the advert about some detergent killing all known germs dead and all that? My father was one of the first to see what utter nonsense those aspirations were, and in fact that they could lead to the exact reverse of what they were saying. On the other hand, a sensible use of antibiotics, of course, is important to present-day existence; they have undoubtedly improved the quality of life in other ways. But their overuse concerned him greatly. The concerns he raised publicly effectively caused the Swann Committee to be convened, which eventually wrote the Swann Report.[2] He was excluded from it, basically because his views were already well known, and they feared that if he was on it, others such as the agricultural sector wouldn't cooperate. The report was not as severe as it should have been, but it was a major step in changing matters in Britain, and also internationally.[3]

---

[1] See E.S. Anderson, 'Origin of Transferable Drug-Resistance Factors in the Enterobacteriaceae', *British Medical Journal* 2 (27 November 1965), 1289–91.

[2] The Swann Committee was appointed jointly by Health and Agriculture Ministers in July 1968 and reported the following year. Cmnd 4190 was issued in November 1969: M.M. Swann, K.L. Baxter, H.I. Field et al., *Report of the Joint Committee on the Use of Antibiotics in Animal Husbandry and Veterinary Medicine* (Cmnd 4190) (London: HMSO, 1969).

[3] See Robert Budd, *Penicillin: Triumph and Tragedy* (Oxford: OUP, 2007) for a recent history of antibiotics. See pp. 176–83 of the same volume for a brief summary of E.S. Anderson's activities in connection with transferable drug-resistance to antibiotics.

CD: It's just been reported how it's part of the civil emergency planning that they reckon there could be 80,000 dead from a resistant bug gaining ground in the next 10–15 years.

JA: I hadn't read that.

CD: It was in the news yesterday.[4] Antibiotic resistance has been added to the National Risk Register of Civil Emergencies, along with terrorism, nuclear war and other types of things.

JA: I see such reports quite often, and when I do, I think of my father's achievement. When he died, there were a lot of obituaries in the papers – one was by a journalist who'd worked with him.[5] He was one of the first prominent medics to use medically trained journalists to help advocate his views. There was a very funny conference my father did, where a lot of leading pharmaceuticals companies were sat in the front row, presumably there to defend their use of antibiotics and drugs generally, their policies and so on. He put on the overhead projector an advert by one of them, I don't know who, which gave some ludicrous figure of how quickly bacteria of a disease could and would multiply unless antibiotics were used to prevent it or kill it, or whatever. He gleefully pointed out that if the figure in the advert were true, doctors and nurses would be fighting their way through a foaming mass of bacteria to even see the patient in the hospital bed. He painted an increasingly ludicrous picture of this situation, which of course caused great hilarity, but the pharmaceuticals companies sat with very grim faces.

He was also a pioneer in molecular photography. He was a very remarkable figure. When he died, I had to sort things out. I was very interested to discover more about him. He was friendly with a few musicians. I remember the violist Walter Trampler visiting the family more than once because he was a friend of my dad. My dad was an amateur musician, but he didn't like the sound of modern music at all. He never understood why Schoenberg didn't continue writing like *Gurrelieder*. Pop music, he simply abhorred. My mother was an amateur choral singer and things like that, but her speciality was modern languages. She is a very good linguist and wanted to be an interpreter at one point. Music is a great love of hers and she knows many lieder and opera libretti by heart; her first love is ballet, however.

My brothers brought the pop music into the family home. They were much older than me, and they brought in the then rock music of the early '70s, so that was progressive rock – now called prog rock. So the rock music I heard

4   6 April 2015.
5   See Anthony Tucker, 'E.S. Anderson', *The Guardian* (22 March 2006); available online at: https://www.theguardian.com/society/2006/mar/22/health.science.

was not The Beatles, which was long past, but Genesis, Yes, Pink Floyd, Focus and groups like that, who were using synthetic sounds that were very much connected with Stockhausen's sound world. In fact, they were using the same instruments, made in Putney by Peter Zinovieff, who was also the librettist for Birtwistle's *Mask of Orpheus*. Zinovieff was an electronics engineer, and he made these portable synthesisers called VCS3, which were very popular with the rock groups. This was really in order to fund his more experimental sound research. Anyway, I didn't know that, but when I heard those groups that my brothers were playing, I was effectively learning the sounds of avant-garde electronic music at that time as well.

I remember when I heard Ligeti's *Lontano*, thinking, 'Oh, but it's Tangerine Dream.' The diatonic clusters sounded very like that kind of progressive rock synthetic music. In fact, it was probably the other way round. Most of those groups knew their avant-garde music very well. Ligeti, of course, had been shot to fame by *2001: A Space Odyssey*. Stockhausen was hugely popular around then with rock groups, and still is. So, in effect, I was introduced to modern music sounds by the rock groups of that time.

CD: I had a similar experience with John Tavener, as the first time I heard one of the pieces with endless pedal notes, probably *The Protecting Veil*, my reaction was, 'But that's Pink Floyd.'

JA: The long drones in Tavener come from his knowledge of Byzantine chant, which often has the *ison* (or long held tone) against the melody. Tavener adopted that in many of his later pieces. My own experiences with the timbres of prog rock certainly eased my getting into modern music. But then, too, I heard a lot of modern music on Radio 3 and grew up with that.

My uncle on my father's side also occasionally wrote music. He was a doctor professionally, but also a very active self-taught musician who had known many professional musicians well, including Fanny Waterman. He wrote music in his spare time a bit, and had even been to an early Bryanston composition course, where the Dartington Summer School originally started. He was, I think, on it the first two years. He remembered seeing Hindemith and Nadia Boulanger there.

Basically, it's a very medical family on my father's side. The combination of medics and violins is very traditional among Jewish families, for some reason. My mother's family were also very cultured. My grandfather was a Thomas Beecham fan, and had seen the Diaghilev ballet in the '20s, but he was a businessman by profession. So there was culture in the family from several sides. I started piano lessons just before I was eight, but that was just normal family stuff. Long before that I'd begun to notice that I could run through music I knew from my parents' gramophone collection in my head when it wasn't being played. Eventually, at some time around the age of nine, I remember trying to make up pieces of my own in my head and that's how I started to write music.

When I started getting interested in modern music, however, my parents weren't keen. My stepfather – my mother remarried when I was about 10 – was a businessman who was also a keen amateur pianist, very much a music lover and also a ballet lover. He disliked the sound of modern music. His favourite composer was Mozart and, bless him, I was a little put off Mozart Piano Concertos for some years because he was always playing records of them. It was always Mozart, Mozart, Mozart for him, plus ballet.

The ballet factor did affect me positively because I went to see it from a young age. My stepfather worshipped Frederick Ashton and was advocating his getting a knighthood decades before he did. Quite early on I saw *The Rite of Spring* as a ballet [MacMillan's version for the Royal Ballet] before I heard it in concert. I'd heard it on record long before all that, and I knew it also from the Disney film *Fantasia*, but my first live experience of it was as a ballet. I must have known it quite well because I spotted that the version in *Fantasia* was all cut up and in the wrong order. I remember being kind of annoyed about that. So I'd known *The Rite of Spring* from records since I was about three, or as early as I can remember.

When I decided that I wanted to be a professional musician, to be honest, nobody in the family thought that was a good idea, which is kind of under-standable, because it's a very risky profession. I think they had aspirations that I would be either a lawyer or a civil servant. So I encountered a lot of resistance to being a musician, which is normal. I had to fight quite a lot during my teens to do what I wanted to do, and that may have helped sharpen my focus on it. Both my dads were very intellectual people. If you've got to sit down with them and argue through why you should be doing music professionally, you do have to marshal your arguments very thoroughly. I was left in absolutely no doubt that I had to think this through extremely carefully, and that it was a very drastic decision, and one I could regret for the rest of my life. I've seen enough profes-sional musicians who have regretted that decision. I've known composers give up. One has seen enough by now, of things, to know that the decision was much more drastic than I knew at the time, really.

CD: My response to my parents was, 'Well, I'll have to marry a rich accountant then.'

JA: Well, you *are* married to an accountant...

CD: Yes, but charity finance certainly doesn't make you rich!

JA: I gather that Stockhausen's first wife was the daughter of a rich industrialist and it seems that helped stabilise things for him. He did come from an extremely poor background. That said, it's clear they were absolutely devoted to each other, and remained so. I thought it quite likely that I'd end up doing composition teaching. Fortunately, I enjoy that very much.

CD: It is very hard to think of a truly professional composer, someone who purely earns a living from composing.

JA: It's very difficult, almost impossible. Well, Richard Rodney Bennett did so, through writing film scores. Perhaps Tippett is the last really major example I can recall of a composer who did more or less nothing except compose, and earned a living doing so...

CD: And even he, only later on.

JA: Yes, for the last roughly 30 years of his life. Most other composers do something else as well. The question is to try to manage it so that something else you do relates to what you compose, that the two activities are complementary, and one feeds the other beneficially. That's what I've always tried to do. Certainly, there was nothing in my background to predispose that I would write music at all, let alone modern music. I was lucky in having cultured parents, but that's it.

CD: You mentioned starting piano lessons round about seven or eight. Did you learn any other instruments?

JA: When I was nine I took up the flute for a while, but I kept hyperventilating so I had to stop. I tried two other instruments. When I was 13 I wanted to learn the cello, but the school didn't need more cellists, they needed a viola player. I found trying to support the viola under my chin very hard – it's heavy and I was terrified of dropping it. Alas, I used to drop it quite a lot. It was only a cheap hired viola, but I nearly broke it several times. I'm surprised it survived. I didn't like the tone of the instrument so near my left ear either – especially the way I played it. I learnt the viola unwillingly for about two years, got to Grade Four and stopped as soon as possible when I finished O Levels.

I realised I needed to diversify my instrumental skills a bit. I continued to play the piano, and also jazz piano a bit, by the way. Since the school still didn't need any cellists and it was getting a little late to learn another string instrument, I tried percussion, which I enjoyed a lot. Being a composer, I was very interested in percussion because it would involve me in contemporary music more. So I learnt percussion for about three years. My teacher at the school, Martin Allen, was a very good percussionist – he was a percussionist of Chachi [Odaline de la] Martinez's group, Lontano. He was a nice man, very kind, and he particularly taught me four-stick vibraphone and marimba technique, which I loved. He knew Bill Kraft, the famous percussionist and composer, who had played percussion for Stravinsky's later recordings on things like *L'Histoire du Soldat* and in the Monday Evening Concerts. So I heard a lot about all that from Martin, who had a copy of Bill Kraft's edition of the percussion part of *L'Histoire*, which he worked out with Stravinsky during the recording sessions he'd done with him.[6] That made it all very real and immediately you had a direct entry into twentieth-century and contemporary classics.

I was very interested in Boulez's music (as I still am), and there was a lot of tuned percussion writing in his work, particularly in *Pli selon pli*, which I adore. There was a thought of my doing that professionally since I was getting quite good at it, but when I entered the Royal College of Music, the standard of percussionists there, even at entry level, was phenomenally high. The other thing is, if you did first study composition at the Royal College, for practical reasons you had to do second study keyboard, piano. That was an absolute given and there were no exceptions. Since it was clear I wasn't really going to be more than a second study percussionist – even as that, God knows what level I would have reached in comparison to these incredible first study people – I gave it up. I continued to play percussion for friends, in a few concerts at college for other composers in their pieces and things like that. You are a percussionist, aren't you?

CD: Yes. I don't play as much as I used to by any stretch of the imagination.

JA: Did you ever play any of the Messiaen tuned percussion parts?

CD: I did the cowbells in *Et exspecto*. I also played the xylophone part in *Oiseaux exotiques* and *Un Sourire*, so yes, I've done a couple of them. I also did tam-tam in *Et exspecto* which is much more fun. At university, because we were always short of percussionists, if it needed more than, say, three players, the thing would be to get somebody from the back of the second violins to come and hit some cymbals. That really taught me quite a lot about the psychology of performance and of performing in a large ensemble. You could get somebody who would play a cymbal crash in exactly the right place, but it would look, and hence sound, wrong, because they were tentative about it. Whereas a percussionist will play a cymbal crash in completely the wrong place, and convince everyone that the entire rest of the orchestra has got it wrong. It's that kind of mindset that you get between different sections of orchestras. The timp part in Mahler 4, I remember being one of the most difficult things. Not difficult to play the notes, they're very easy to play, but in the slow movement you've got oodles of bars' rest and then

---

6   Stravinsky, *L'Histoire du Soldat (Suite)*, Israel Baker (violin), Roy D'Antonio (clarinet), Don Christlieb (bassoon), Charles Brady (cornet), Robert Marsteller (trombone), Richard Kelley (bass), William Kraft (percussion) – Igor Stravinsky (conductor), rec. American Legion Hall, Hollywood, CA, 10/13 February 1961, Columbia Masterworks MS 6272/ML5672 (LP); Sony SM3K 46291 (3 CD); 88875026162 (57 CD).

you have to come crashing in, double-sticking with little to confirm that you're in the right place until you're already committed.

JA: I did timps in the school orchestra for some years, which was a very useful experience, and also in some amateur orchestras for a good two or three years after I left school, now I think of it. I remember well the first timp part I ever played was in Schumann's Overture, Scherzo and Finale. I quite quickly realised the problem with playing with timps is counting bars' rest, especially if you don't have a score of the piece concerned, or don't happen to know it. There I was listening to this thing, and there was a very elaborate cued part in the middle movement. I was counting and counting, and then there was another cue, and then I counted more bars' rests and another cue and some more bars' rests, and then I realised we'd got to the end and I hadn't played. Sure enough, the timpani don't play in the Scherzo of Schumann's Overture, Scherzo and Finale, and they do play in the Finale. I thought this a rather comic instance of some copyist in the nineteenth century clearly earning themselves a little bit of extra dosh.

I remember one of the best gigs I ever did as an amateur timpanist was *Messiah* because you're paid a handsome fee for playing in two numbers at the end of the evening, more or less, and that's it.

CD: I had something similar with *Zadok the Priest* – a substantial full concert fee, which was a very nice pay day as a student for three minutes' work! One thing about percussion is that, more than any other instrument, there is an increasingly extreme disjunct between the exceptional virtuosity of what they do as soloists and the level of skill required for their day-to-day repertoire, namely playing in orchestras and ensembles. The latter is challenging, don't get me wrong, but it is mostly a challenge of musicality rather than also requiring hyper-advanced technique.

JA: The thing for me was being able to hear inside pieces. One thing that was a big revelation for me and influenced me a lot was the timp parts in Beethoven Symphonies. He wrote superbly for timpani, as I'm sure you know.

CD: Yes, they're brilliant, but very difficult even now.

JA: Very difficult, particularly the Eighth Symphony Finale. Murderously difficult. But very exciting, really vital timp parts, which are crucial. They're as important as the lead violin. You can determine the way that piece sounds with good timp playing. The other composers I know who did percussion were George Benjamin and Thomas Adès.

When I was at Cambridge as a postgraduate student I organised a new music festival in which we all pooled resources practically and I got the funding from PRS and other foundations. Looking back at it, these concerts were rather pioneering as regards repertoire. Thomas Adès conducted a memorable concert in which he premiered his *Chamber Symphony* – a fabulous piece which was a real revelation. I conducted another concert in which I gave the UK premiere of Scelsi's *Kya* and did Murail's *Treize Couleurs du Soleil Couchant*, and Nic Hodges played the piano in a third concert, as far as I can recall. It was about three or four concerts only, a little festival. In the concert I conducted the percussionist fell ill and we were doing a piece by Richard Emsley. I remembered Adès had told me that he played percussion and I knew what a fabulous reader he was, so I rang him up and said, 'Are you free? There's this very difficult multi-percussion part in Richard Emsley's ensemble piece.' He came to the first rehearsal and sight-read it marvellously. There's an incredibly complicated flourish early on, on the glockenspiel, and he played it at sight perfectly! So I know he was a very fluent percussionist. He was already brilliant at all he did, as he still is.

I was pretty good at percussion, but I increasingly felt, frankly, from my early 20s onwards, that if I was going to compose, it was taking such an amount of time to get it to the level I wanted to do it that I just couldn't do the other things. I thought, 'If I'm going to do this composing thing, I'm going to have to just do it.' I was hoping that I would develop enough other skills to earn a living, but after about 25 I gave up both percussion and also conducting, of which I'd done a certain amount.

CD: Were there ever any other potential paths at any point? I know that aged five I wanted to be a milkman.

JA: [Laughter] I wanted to make drains when I was about six. There was a careers day at school and my main memory of it is of people turning up in grey suits and trying to persuade us that, in spite of the fact that they'd all turned up in grey suits, these were not boring professions and that they weren't grey-suited people. I remember one set of accountants came in and said that. It wasn't the best PR job.

CD: We were the same. We had a 20-minute interview with a careers advisor. Mine only lasted about 30 seconds because she said, 'What is it you want to do?' I said, 'I'm looking for a career in music' and she just looked completely blankly at me. She had absolutely nothing at all that she could say about it because I wasn't saying I wanted to go for a career in the City, be a lawyer or a doctor.

JA: The head of my school wrote his autobiography and it had this list of statistics of what jobs the parents had. It listed company director, executive, medical and legal jobs, engineer, academic, journalism and writer, civil servant, diplomat, architect, banker, the theatre and cinema, accountant, politician, public relations, clergy and armed forces. Musicians were not mentioned at all, though several parents were indeed professional musicians; painters were airbrushed out too. A whole load of areas I cared about deeply, including mine, weren't even mentioned in that list. It confirmed that such activities as mine were of no importance to the school administration then. That was very much the official attitude at the school, and mostly in Britain at that time – music was fine as a hobby, nothing more. Perhaps it still is.[7]

I might have been some kind of modern linguist, but I'd done Classics A Level. I'd wanted to do modern languages, but my stepfather thought Classics were a better idea, which they were and they weren't, but I did as I was told. I don't think I could have done accounting because my maths was never that hot and you do have to be able to add up a bit.

CD: Well, I've known a few accountants [Laughter].

JA: Yes, creative adding... I thought a little bit about politics at one point because I was very disturbed by Thatcherism and its consequences. But I never thought I could do it. When I was at school, Parliament wasn't yet being televised; it was only on the radio so I only saw Parliament from the late 1980s, it was after I'd left school.[8] I'd heard enough Parliamentary debates, though, to know that Parliament of the 1980s was a very rough place, and that you had to be pretty tough to get any speech finished. And what party would I have joined? Not the Tories. I'd been interested in the Social Democrats but I hadn't liked the way they'd gone later. I was interested in the Labour Party but I disagreed with a number of key policies there too. So politics wasn't going to work out.

I never much fancied all the mechanical occupations that kids have fantasies about, like air pilot or whatever. I'd never really had that dream. I don't think there was much else. Some kind of academic I suppose, probably in English literature or, as I say, in modern languages. The fact that it's languages is also interesting because I'm very interested in communication as a problem, and that's why I think of music in linguistic terms. I'm very interested in etymology and the way that Messiaen used to be able to trace the etymology of a chord. He was probably right about those things. Words and musical figures behave similarly, in social terms. This is an area which is still too little researched, I believe.

Nonetheless, if I had done any of those other professions, I'd have spent much of the time not concentrating on what I was doing, but yearning for the next concert or the next musical thing. That was certainly how I felt at school when doing something that wasn't music. There were exceptions, but most of the time I was just longing to get back to the music. I didn't fancy a lifetime spent that

[7] See John Rae, *Delusions of Grandeur: A Headmaster's Life 1966–86* (London: HarperCollins, 1993), p. 150.
[8] The first televised speech from the House of Commons was on 21 November 1989.

way. In spite of the family feeling that this was not a good idea, I just didn't really see I had any alternative, so I thought I'd make a go of it somehow.

CD: Returning to music then, and moving on to teachers. You went to Westminster School.

JA: The students were quite a mixed bunch of people. I was bullied and beaten up quite a lot. It was quite a rough school below the age of 16. I was quite often bruised. One strong bully threw a table at me, I had billiard balls thrown at my head, and on another occasion I was slashed with an art knife – it cut right through my blazer and shirt, and it cut me too. No one paid much attention to bullying. I was just told this happens all the time. You had to be pretty tough to get through to the sixth form. Possibly because it was in central London, it wasn't as exclusive in its atmosphere as some public schools. Most people didn't cultivate posh accents or anything like that, so there were fewer of the superficial trappings of public schools than elsewhere. Someone else I know sent his son there a few years later as a boarder: he told me that after a while he and his wife had to insist their son become a day boy because he was so badly bullied day and night. So the problem that school had with bullying certainly did not end in my time.

Looking back on it now, I realise there was a distinction at Westminster, however covert. Some were children of wealthy or powerful parents, such as politicians, civil servants or landowners. Those people tended to mix with like people and less with the rest. An aspiring musician like me, with literary and artistic interests and all that, that wasn't the sort of company they kept and goodness they let one know it.

Some of the students certainly behaved as if they thought they would soon be running the country. That was where I first really encountered British snobbery. People who by the age of 16 had already decided who was who and what was what, and knew their place was at the top. Twenty years on, some of them had indeed risen to high places in the establishment, and good luck to them. I encountered anti-Semitism at Westminster also, among some staff and students – since I didn't have a Jewish name, people would assume I agreed with them on such prejudices. Only after I left did I learn that von Ribbentrop's son had been a pupil at the school in the 1930s. Nobody ever mentioned that to me while I was there. At least Westminster wasn't too obsessed with sport, and there was a more relaxed feeling to it socially by comparison with other such schools. After I turned 16 the bullying largely stopped, and despite being uncomfortable with many aspects of the set-up, I was very happy there on the whole from then on.

CD: So before John Lambert at the Royal College, were there any significant music or composition teachers either at Westminster or elsewhere?

JA: Yes, three. The first was Oliver Knussen, but he wasn't ever formally my teacher in the sense that I didn't take a course or study with him. I bumped into him at my first visit to the British Music Information Centre in Stratford Place, when Roger Wright ran it in early 1981.[9] Roger introduced us. Olly was very friendly and invited me round. I went to see him several times for very long sessions. He played me lots of music, looked at my scores a bit and offered advice. They were amazing afternoons – the whole of culture seemed to unfold before you, since Olly's enthusiasms ranged way beyond music into art, film, literature and almost anything else. It was he who advised me eventually to go and study with John Lambert, which I did.

At the same period I was taught composition by John Baird, who was Assistant Head of Music at Westminster. The Head of Music was the well-known counter-tenor Charles Brett, who could tell me about performing Pérotin with David Munrow's group (he's on the recordings) and who introduced me to Purcell's anthems. Baird knew quite a lot about modern music, but was really a Wagner man. He was head of the British Wagner Society for a while. I believe he also mounted what was said to be the first amateur performance in Britain of *Parsifal*, but he took an interest in new music. If there was a big concert by the London Sinfonietta with, say, Henze or Ligeti, or if Boulez was conducting a concert with the BBC Symphony, he'd take a few of us along. We were very lucky in having two teachers from the BBC Symphony Orchestra string section on the peripatetic staff. They would get us into BBC Symphony Orchestra rehearsals, which is how I started learning about musical rehearsal, and in that way I saw Boulez rehearsing *Pli selon pli*. And from Westminster it was easy to get to Maida Vale and it was also near the Festival Hall.

John Baird looked at my music. He wasn't about to pronounce himself the world authority on serialism, in which he wasn't interested. But he encouraged me to look things up, find out properly how something was done and then explain it to him, and if he felt it of more general interest, then to other students at school. In this way I did lectures at school on Boulez's *Pli selon pli*, on Lutosławski's Second Symphony, on Berg's *Wozzeck*, on all sorts of things. John spotted that I had a talent for that and he encouraged me to develop it and to teach myself in effect, which was very good. The other thing he taught me was harmony. Like a lot of people who taught me, he'd been taught by Bill [William] Lloyd Webber, who was the father of Andrew and Julian, and the best harmony and counterpoint teacher in Britain then. I benefited from having studied with

---

[9]   In addition to running the British Music Information Centre, Roger Wright (b. 1956) has, among other things, worked in senior positions at the Cleveland Orchestra, Deutsche Grammophon and the BBC, the latter including Head of Classical Music, Controller of Radio 3 and Director of the BBC Proms. He is currently Chief Executive of Aldeburgh Music.

a number of people who had worked with him. Lloyd Webber was a very strict teacher.

One thing that John Baird did do, which influenced me greatly, was to teach me Bach chorales. These, as anybody now knows, are little works of genius but use sometimes very abstruse and arcane harmonisations. They're very recherché, a rather hybrid exaggeration of Baroque harmony. They're not the most stereo-typically normal Baroque harmony in many cases, but they are extraordinary compositions. I knew damn all about Bach chorales before that. The first week I was there he said, 'Memorise this.' It was one of the harmonisations of *Ein feste Burg* and I had to come in the following week and write it out in four-part open score, but with normal clefs. Then the next week, he said the same thing with a different one. I don't know how many times that happened, but, sporadically, it would happen again and again, and that was a much better way of getting a student to understand what was going on in a Bach chorale than just laying down a lot of rules. As I was memorising he'd explain what the rules were held to be, but he made me understand that those were simply post-facto ration-alisations of a compositional practice which was highly developed. I therefore always regarded Bach chorales as real compositions, not as exercises. It may or may not be a commendation of this kind of teaching, but, on the one hand, it helped my harmonic sense very greatly in seeing chords not in isolation, but as ongoing voice-led progressions. On the other hand, I was never good at imitating Bach chorales because I found them so strange. I kept saying, 'But I've no idea what he'll do next. You say a leading note always has to be resolved, but it's not resolved. You say there are no consecutives, but here is a consecutive', etc. I wasn't very good at writing them, but I was pretty good at analysing them. That also got me into Schenker, which helped me a lot in composing because of the business of seeing and hearing through big structures – what held them together harmonically. Not the Forte–Gilbert textbook Schenker,[10] but much more an eclectic Salzer style of Schenkerism,[11] which has helped my music greatly in terms of large-scale harmonic aspects. My principal tutor and analysis teacher at the Royal College, the late Roderick Swanston, taught me all that.

The third person I encountered around this time was entirely on my own initiative. In August 1980 I heard a radio talk by someone about to have an orchestral piece premiered at the Proms, who was only 20 years old but seemed to have the most refreshing and direct relationship with sound and harmony. The following day I heard the work on the radio: it was *Ringed by the Flat Horizon* by George Benjamin, and I heard the repeat broadcast a few months later as well. The work impressed me hugely, and not only because of its superb harmonic colours,

---

[10] Allen Forte and Steve E. Gilbert, *An Introduction to Schenkerian Analysis* (New York: W.W. Norton, 1982).

[11] See Felix Salzer, *Structural Hearing: Tonal Coherence in Music* (New York: Boni, 1952).

but because of its flowing contrapuntal textures and memorable linear invention, all bound together with an uncanny sense of pacing. I decided to get in touch with this composer, which took several months, but by the end of 1981 I had done so and we met in November that year. George Benjamin looked at a somewhat involved piano piece I was composing (the style was somewhere between Berio and Carter, but very badly done) and went at once into the most extraordinary detail. He questioned every pitch, every harmonic area, every rhythm, everything. It was fascinating. We must have been at this for about three hours non-stop and I still have that marked-up manuscript somewhere. We became good friends from then on. From this experience, as well as from talking with Olly Knussen, it became clear I had to be far more selective about my choices in composing. It was a very important lesson that went in happily at an age where I could act on it quickly. Like Olly, George was very generous with his time. I owe them both a lot.

CD: The String Quartet is the earliest piece on the list I have of your works.[12]

JA: It's the earliest piece that's out, yes.[13]

CD: Ironically, it's one of the most recent to be heard.

JA: Yes. Finally I found a group who would play it, and play it well, 29 years later. In writing *Light Music* I was determined, just once, to see what would happen if I wrote an absolutely straight spectral piece with the techniques I'd been learning from the Paris spectral composers' music, partly from scores and recordings, partly from the article by Anne LeBaron and Denys le Bouliane.[14] Unsurprisingly, there are audible influences from Murail and Grisey in that piece, which I'm not bothered about. The reason I eventually released it was not because of that – although it's curious to see that a younger composer, aged 17 in 1984, was doing that in Britain, because not many people here were – but due to the fact that the piece has a dramatic trajectory, which I do regard as very personal. The material is pretty much party-line spectral stuff, but the way it's pushed about and the way the piece evolves from one end to the other makes a big dramatic curve. It's not just a continuous process, but a process that has many swerves and quite a lot of violence along the way. When I heard it, I thought, 'You can see I want to write operas', even though there's nothing of opera about the music in it. It's not lyrical in any way, but it's a very expressively overt piece, almost expressionist. Murail and Grisey's music avoids that sort of expressionist rhetoric.

---

[12] Published in 2013 as String Quartet No. 1 'Light Music'.
[13] Since this conversation, an earlier piece has been added to Anderson's catalogue, SING for chamber choir, 1981–82, revised 2019.
[14] Anne LeBaron and Denys Bouliane, 'Darmstadt 1980', *Perspectives of New Music* Vol. 29, No. 1/2 (Autumn 1980–Summer 1981), 420–41. This is discussed in Conversation Three, 'Training'.

CD: Did you try to get it played?

JA: I did hand the work in to the Society for the Promotion of New Music but the readers' reports were very sniffy and superior, dismissing it as incompetent and/or unplayable. I was uncertain what to do. I went to see Adrian Jack, who ran the *MusICA* series at the ICA.[15] We had a mutual friend in Sinan Savaskan, to whom *Light Music* is dedicated, and he knew Adrian well. Adrian suggested I send it to a well-known US string quartet, but I never received a reply, being 18 and completely unknown. Jonathan Harvey was interested in it – I showed it to him when he interviewed me for a place at Sussex University, in October 1985. His music, within three or four years of that, was to take a considerable swerve towards instrumental spectral composition, but it was not quite what he was writing at that time. The problem from my end was that I really did need to hear *Light Music* as soon as possible to learn from it. Not doing so caused a big hold-up. I didn't finish anything for the following two years. A lot of pieces were started but almost nothing was finished.

CD: And so the Quartet didn't get played until 2013.[16] Was it consciously put in a drawer or did it just fall by the wayside?

JA: When I auditioned at the Royal College I handed it in and they gave me a scholarship on the basis of that piece, which was very nice of them. When I got there, though, I couldn't find any students who could play it, so it wasn't played. Around that time, I began to make a string orchestra version of it, which I finished in short score. I have that somewhere. Making the string orchestra version of it, which added more layers of different strings and things, was one of the things that eventually catapulted me on to writing *Khorovod*, *Diptych* and *Stations of the Sun*. So it is a link between what I did as a student and my stuff from *Diptych* onwards. But every effort to get *Light Music* played failed, so after a couple of years I just put the piece away.

I suddenly looked at it again three or four years ago and thought, 'Well, I should like to hear that.' A mutual friend told Irvine Arditti about it, who saw it and said, 'We'll play it.' The Arditti Quartet then premiered *Light Music* at Aldeburgh in 2013 and since then the piece has been done from time to time. I'm very grateful for that. I do think that the trajectory of it is personal, even if the surface style is not. The moral I learnt from this experience is that you must hear your music as soon as possible. It's not complete, in my view, until you do. In that sense, I did not regard the work as finished until I heard it in Aldeburgh in 2013.

15 The Institute of Contemporary Arts.
16 Premiere: 15 June 2013, Aldeburgh Festival, Aldeburgh Parish Church, Suffolk, Arditti String Quartet.

CD: Did you revise or fiddle with it?

JA: Nothing beyond a couple of small notational clarifications, and a pause which was 30 seconds which I reduced to 15, but that I'd planned to do at the time if it was ever played. Other than that I changed nothing. I remained fascinated by string instruments. The only other early piece I've let out is a piece for two violins, which is also an experiment in bowing pressure and bowing position, but with much simpler material. Would you like to see that now?

CD: I would, yes.

JA: Okay. This is the manuscript. It is called *Ring Dance*. It was premiered by some students in Sweden in May 1988. It was written for an exchange concert between the Swedish Musikhögskolan and the Royal College of Music. They spent one week with us and we spent one week with them. These two players were handed this pretty odd score, which you can see. It is very slow. It's four pages long only and it lasts something like seven minutes. It's very slow, very loud and very sustained, and it doesn't have any silence in it, so it's a pretty extreme piece. As you can see, until halfway through bar 20, you've only got various combinations of the two lowest open strings, G and D. Well if you play this opening loudly enough, you'll hear a G an octave below the G string because it's a difference tone of those two open string pitches. If the open strings are tuned nicely that's what you hear. The piece is a study in difference tones and harmonics. The thing that was difficult for me about it was that I was using a very experimental string technique, with an extremely diatonic material. It is in a modal kind of style, but this really isn't Arvo Pärt either. Gradually the bowing position changes, and bowing pressure changes occur through. The piece is always loud and it only gets louder. It turns a very slow harmonic circle. *Ring Dance* is another term for *Khorovod*, which means dancing in a circle. Somewhere round the back of this *Khorovod* was going to appear – I started *Khorovod* a few months later. What I tried to work out in *Ring Dance* was a harmonic circuit that started on G and D, gradually moved away from it, and would very gradually cadence back into it at the end, eight minutes later. If you wanted to put it in a box, diatonic spectral music might be the label.

CD: Diatonic spectral music by someone who's heard Scelsi?

JA: Yes, but there's no pitch variation in *Ring Dance*, whereas in Scelsi there's lots of sliding. The transcriptions that Scelsi and Tosatti made of his finest music, such as the Fourth Quartet and *Anahit*, are incredibly good, but the harmony in *Ring Dance* is nothing like that. I felt that the harmony was beginning to be my kind of thing, simple as it is. Eventually we wind, very slowly, back round to the G and D at the end, and you then have them for a lot more time, with a huge scrunch on that at the end of it.

It was one of the first things I wrote after coming back from studying with Tristan Murail in Paris for a few months in 1987.[17] The very first thing I wrote when I came back was a set of four pieces for alto saxophone and percussion, one of which was a study in multiphonics and in spectral filtering of multiphonics. The material for that was what a French spectral composer might have done, but the other three pieces were just melodic studies, not spectral at all. It wasn't worth saving. *Ring Dance* was the next piece and is definitely not spectral. I have a certain affection for it. It's a tough piece. I like its sinuousness, and frankly, I got a thrill rehearsing it in Sweden. The rehearsal was superb, but the performance gradually became a bit uneasy and no wonder, because the audience was becoming restive as *Ring Dance* kept getting louder and I got one of those sort of boo-hiss reactions that you occasionally get. I'd never had that before. I guess the performers were a bit thrown by the audience atmosphere and they rushed the conclusion, which is the loudest bit of all. Of course, at that stage, I was a bit of an angry young man. When finally it stopped, the reaction was not good – as I recall a couple of people made paper aeroplanes out of their programmes and threw them. I was ashamed for the players, who were really crestfallen at having this reaction to their efforts, but otherwise I just didn't care. I showed the score to a British composer whom I knew slightly. He just said, 'There's no music in this, it's dreadful. Please take it away.' So I put that away in a drawer as well.

Ring Dance was the one serious follow-up that I was able to write at that time to *Light Music*. The fact that I eliminated quarter-tones and went for a kind of modal harmony pointed it towards *Khorovod*. Some of the harmonies in *Khorovod* you already find in *Ring Dance*. It really was an important piece for me. Anyway, when I got to Schott I showed them the piece and they thought it an exciting, abrasive piece, so it's being printed.

CD: Fantastic. I can't wait to hear it.

JA: I know that all sounds a bit lily-livered on my part, but after the quartet was turned down, like most composers who are young, I was very insecure. You have an exterior, a bit feisty and so on, but it's easy to be disconcerted by any discouragement, which is something I've borne in mind when teaching composition. Looking at *Ring Dance* now, I feel it's a study piece. Generally speaking, I do not write only one thing in my pieces. But *Ring Dance* is clearly only one thing pushed to the limit. That's one aspect of it that isn't typical of me. I like dialectic, contrasts, etc., and that's one of the reasons why I had to leave the spectral thing, because it wasn't dialectic enough for me. I always wanted to pit a musical idea against its opposite. Whereas, if you think about where they were in Paris in the spectral music of the '70s, they avoided that.

---

[17]   See Conversation Three, 'Training'.

CD: *Ring Dance* is your equivalent of 'L'Échange'[18] – the closest you'll get to writing a process piece.

JA: Totally, and I do like 'L'Échange'. I love that idea. Yes, absolutely.

CD: Until you looked again at these early pieces a few years ago, am I right that you were effectively saying that *Diptych* was your Opus 1?

JA: Yes, I felt that when I finished *Diptych* there was something in it, particularly its second half, that I hadn't done before. Everything you write is reliant on things you hear. The conscious pursuit for originality is very dangerous for a composer because if you're original, you'll be original anyway, and if you're not, you won't. There's no point in worrying about that – there's nothing you can do about it, so I just write music. Nonetheless, with *Diptych* I began to sort out something to do with the way modes and harmony and things work in my music, which, although I'd tried in the two-violin piece, hadn't gotten very far. With *Diptych*, I began to feel much more that I had some idea of the way I wanted a piece of music to work. It turned out that I couldn't look up in a textbook and find it there, or phone Tristan Murail and ask him how to do that, or anybody else. I was inventing this technique for myself, so I thought it was my Opus 1. It was laying out things. That and *Khorovod*, which were begun at the same time. At one point, one piece could have been the other, to complicate matters.

CD: Right, but *Khorovod* didn't appear until quite a bit later.

JA: Well, I started them both in 1988, after getting back from Darmstadt that year, which was very stimulating but which I didn't enjoy. The whole place seemed deranged, full of aggressive fanatics. Nevertheless, I met some wonderfully sane and exciting people there, and heard some great music in recordings such as Feldman's *Coptic Light* which was then new (the live concerts were largely dreadful, with some exceptions). I completed *Diptych* in 1990. I made some slight revisions before the premiere, but basically it was finished when I was 23. Whereas *Khorovod* dragged on and on. I gradually realised that it wasn't for orchestra, but was a large ensemble piece, which was going to be for 40 instruments. Then it was going to be 30, etc., until gradually I ended up with 16. The more I cut instruments out, the more I realised what I was trying to do was to make a massive, turbulent, hyperactive noise with as few instruments as I possibly could. Fortunately, just as I'd started drawing up the full score for 16 instruments the London Sinfonietta asked me for a piece. I said, 'Well, can I finish *Khorovod*?' That's how it was done. The world premiere was in December 1994.[19]

---

[18] The third movement of Messiaen's *Vingt Regards sur l'Enfant-Jésus*.
[19] 6 December 1994, Barbican, London Sinfonietta, Markus Stenz (cond.).

I made a substantial revision, even after that, to the final dance. I couldn't get the club rave section right. The original was too square and too close to the models of House that I'd been hearing. So I pulled it about rhythmically – making the rave rip itself apart rather more, recomposing the figurations to make them less strictly House and more like *Khorovod*. Then I transposed the whole section down a semitone into C-sharp to give the cadence back into the C tonic more shock force. I recall my dear friend Richard Causton and I sitting around a table in the summer of 1995, both of us frantically copying out the parts for the final version as I recomposed it. That final version of *Khorovod* was premiered, brilliantly, by the London Sinfonietta under Markus Stenz, in the Proms in August 1995.[20] The Sinfonietta then toured it to Hannover the following month – an excellent performance under Stefan Asbury. It was a relief finally to have nailed *Khorovod* down. Imagine, six years of obsessive work for a fifteen-minute piece – but I hope it was worth it.

[20] 16 August 1995, Royal Albert Hall, 10pm BBC Prom, London Sinfonietta, Markus Stenz (conductor).

Conversation Two

Enthusiasms

This conversation starts with a look at some of Anderson's musical heroes, before moving on to a discussion of creative misreadings and alternative views of figures such as Webern and Stravinsky, along with the partiality inherent in narratives of musical history, the construction of canons and attempts at providing the complete works of certain composers. Along the way, we encounter Anderson's inadvertently incomplete childhood knowledge of *The Rite of Spring*, the differences between versions of Boulez's Le visage nuptial and the interaction between Boulez and Cage in the early 1950s.

— ◆ —

CD: I wonder if you might tell me about who some of your musical heroes are?

JA: Just a short string of names would be Hildegard of Bingen, Dufay, Haydn. I'm pausing before saying Mozart because it's only specific areas of Mozart. Beethoven, Schubert, Mendelssohn, Schumann, Wagner. Then Debussy, Sibelius, Stravinsky, Janáček, Messiaen. Among Americans, Ives and Ruth Crawford Seeger. I'm assuming heroes are largely dead?

CD: Yes. It's probably politic for them to be dead.

JA: Well in that case, Carter and Boulez can now be added to the list.

CD: Hildegard was an extraordinary figure, and the music is really distinctive in relation to other things around then, judging by Christopher Page's pioneering recording with Gothic Voices.[1]

---

[1] Hildegard of Bingen, *A Feather on the Breath of God*, Gothic Voices with Emma Kirkby, directed by Christopher Page, recorded at Church of St Jude-on-the-Hill, Hampstead, London, 14 September 1981, Hyperion CDA66039 (CD).

JA: I heard the original BBC Radio 3 documentary broadcast by Chris Page in 1980. It made a deep impression on me. I knew some plainchant but I'd never heard anything remotely like these long, arching melodies in medieval music before. It struck me as very fresh, as did what was read out on the programme from her writings, her visions. I hadn't taped the programme so I worried that I'd never hear of either her or her music again. Then, to my surprise, a recording came out on Hyperion in 1982 with the same performers and the same title (*A Feather on the Breath of God*) as the radio programme, and it became a bestseller. I recalled the music very vividly – so much so that when I bought the recording I found I could remember some of the melodies note for note.

CD: Has this fed into your music?

JA: Not specifically. I've always wanted to write my music melodically – all my music's made from melody, really – but to date I've never quoted or paraphrased her melodies in any piece. Nor have I set any of her poetry, though I seriously considered it for *Heaven is Shy of Earth*. Both her visions and her music have the same quality of lightness, transparency and luminous precision which impressed me very much in Emily Dickinson's work. I have certainly tried to imbue my music with those qualities, but it was Dickinson I finally set in *Heaven*.

The long-breathing melodies of Hildegard, as well as their fundamental arch shapes, are perhaps most vividly reflected in the lengthy heterophonic central melody in *The Crazed Moon*. This is shaped as a single huge curve of melody which the whole orchestra sings for about five minutes – the idea was that the whole orchestra should sing a melody to commemorate the dedicatee. I still listen to Hildegard often, and I study her music both in scans from her manuscripts and the modern edition of her work published by Otto Müller Verlag. To me, her finest melodies such as 'Ave Generosa' and 'Columba Aspexit' are among the most beautiful ever created and I never cease to admire their wondrous clarity and economy of purpose.

CD: Dufay is certainly not a name that often crops up among lists of people's influences.

JA: Aside from the motet *Nuper rosarum flores*,[2] which has always been on my Desert Island, my real favourites would be his chansons, not the Masses, which I don't know so well. One of the blocks I have, by the way, with medieval and Renaissance repertoire is that music written for praying and worship is often not music that I can follow in the long run, because it doesn't seem to have a long run. It seems to get through the text and that, plus the cantus firmus, determines what it does. Of course, neither does it have directional harmony, in the sense

---

[2] Discussed in Conversation Three, 'Training'.

that one is used to hearing in a piece of Mozart or, for that matter, a piece of Messiaen. I do hear Messiaen that way, by the way, in spite of what one is told by so many. The prevailing view has generally been that he cannot do long-term directional harmony. It isn't true: he both can and does, even in later works like *La Transfiguration*.

CD: That's also how I hear Messiaen.

JA: That isn't found in Renaissance religious music, and it poses certain listening challenges for someone nowadays – unless you're happy just to have music wash over you indifferently, which I am not. Except for certain points, generally in Credo settings, the music seems just to be a formulaic way of getting through the text. An exception could be made for some repertoire in the Eton Choirbook, which has also influenced me quite a bit. Particularly John Browne's *Stabat Mater*, on which I did a dissertation as an undergraduate student, and is still probably the most famous piece in the book. That is quite a dramatic work, full of contrasts.

What interested me about Dufay, therefore, were the chansons, short pieces lasting about three or four minutes at most, in only two or three parts. The amount of invention going on within those parts, rhythmically, modally, and to use a word they wouldn't have had, expressively, strikes me very forcibly and gives me enormous pleasure. It's rather thrilling and that's affected a lot of what I do. Songs like *Navré je sui d'un dart penetratif*, *Vergene bella* or *Bon jour, bon mois* – I included a paraphrase of that in my ensemble piece *Tiramisù* – are some of my favourite music. I could pretty much write out those pieces by heart. I just adore them – the melodic and rhythmic elegance of them is very meaningful. It's harder to know how they're written than a Mass because a Mass usually has a cantus. In the songs, sometimes there is one and sometimes there isn't. There is an obscene song by Dufay which has a shrinking cantus firmus. I can't remember the medieval French for this, but the title is effectively 'I can no longer do what I used to do'. You have this cantus firmus, which is four notes long, that shrinks each time until it's very short indeed, which is rather obvious... In any case, I find the degree of invention in that repertoire very interesting and, for some reason, Dufay catches my ear more than Landini or Binchois. My view of Dufay is highly partial. It's focused specifically on certain issues that mean a lot to me as a listener and as a composer.

CD: And it's only certain aspects of Mozart too?

JA: Yes, my view of Mozart is also highly selective. I'm very interested in what could be termed his experimental aspects – the side of Mozart that could compose the ballroom scene in *Don Giovanni* having three different dances at the same time, or his use of wandering harmonic progressions and dissonances. I don't only mean in the 'Dissonance' Quartet (though that is an excellent example), but in many other works such as the Minuet K.355 and much of *Idomeneo* in particular. Likewise in *Don Giovanni*, as Messiaen pointed out, Mozart uses a highly colourful chromaticism that you just don't find in most of Beethoven. Mozart is often a very complex composer whose lines of thought are hard to follow, which intrigues me. Of course, anyone can learn from his melodic richness, but my melodic style comes as much from Romanian folk music or Gregorian chant as it does from Mozart, perhaps more so.

CD: Is Haydn equally partial?

JA: In terms of Haydn, it's some of the symphonies, but it's mainly the quartets. Pieces like the Op. 33 No. 1 Quartet, where in every movement the quartet almost changes its clothes stylistically and sonically so much that they sound like different instruments. That has affected me strongly. I was thinking of the Haydn Op. 33 No. 1 when I wrote my Second String Quartet,[3] where every movement is meant to sound like it's a different ensemble. The way Haydn does that fascinates me. For example, in the last movement of Op. 33 No. 1 he turns the whole group into a folk band. It sounds rather like the last movement of Bartók's Fourth Quartet. I always wondered if Bartók knew it. Haydn asks the first violin line to be played all on the fourth string, which gives a kind of folk feel to it, as does the accompaniment, so suddenly it's out in the open air.

I only got to know this quartet about 20 years ago but when I did I was astounded by the nagging theme used to close each part of the third movement, which is a minuet-come-waltz – as Hans Keller pointed out, it is the 'not so slow movement'.[4] I realised Brahms quoted this closing theme in the first movement of his Second Symphony, note for note, twice and at each of the transpositions Haydn uses it (a fact of which no Brahms specialist seems to be aware, to judge from the existing literature I've read). Also, the Quartet is meant to be in B minor, but it opens in D major more or less. The opening was regarded as disturbing enough by the nineteenth-century editors for them to add thirds to the second violin part, which makes it unambiguously in D major and much more stable. Haydn's opening is more chaotic than that. I gathered that it was the model for the opening of the Brahms Clarinet Quintet – and you can hear the similarity. My fascination with Haydn is partly because he continues to have such an impact on so many much later composers – when I listen to him I immediately start thinking about how I can compose my own music better – and partly because so often, in the quartets especially, he rethinks the ensemble in every movement, almost as radically as Stravinsky's Three Pieces

---

[3] String Quartet No. 2 '300 Weihnachtslieder'.
[4] See Hans Keller, *The Great Haydn Quartets: Their Interpretation* (London: Dent, 1993), p. 67.

for String Quartet, which I adore. Haydn's quartets are often wildly disparate, almost anti-symphonic on the surface. Very strange pieces. One of the Op. 54 quartets ends with a slow movement, which is interrupted by a sudden manic *presto* and then goes back to being a slow movement in C major – it's completely extreme. I love it when he does all that. I suppose, therefore, I'm attracted to what roughly speaking might be termed 'Sturm und Drang' Haydn. The symphonies also interest me a lot, not only the 'Sturm und Drang' repertoire, but so do the 'London' symphonies greatly, particularly the 'Drumroll', which I was terribly lucky to study for O Level and which I've more than once referred to in my work. Not by quoting, but I've used it as a formal model. So there are certain pieces of Haydn that have had a big effect on me, which are sort of epoch-making anyway in music history and which suggest far more than is there. Heroes, for me, are people who write music which really sets you thinking, except you're thinking notes, not necessarily concepts or music history. Great music switches your brain on in the most extraordinary, lively, playful way that leads directly into composing.

Getting nearer to our own time, Janáček and Sibelius are very crucial figures to me – and crucial these days, I'm happy to see, for many other composers too. They're different figures, but both had a slightly strange relationship to whatever mainstreams were around or, at least, Sibelius did after about 1911. Up until about then, he was writing more or less what was regarded as modern music and, certainly, with the Fourth Symphony he was writing pretty extreme music for the time. Once the modernist revolution hit, by the time he's writing the Fifth Symphony, he's most clearly, definitely and consciously not writing modernist music. Although the Fifth is very odd, the thematic material is plain, whereas the thematic material in the Fourth Symphony is itself very odd. Often in later Sibelius, the themes appear to be ordinary and I'm interested in that because you can follow what's done to them. It's a rather Beethoven-type thing, this, but Sibelius is even better at it. Take a banal idea like the opening horn call of the Fifth Symphony. Nobody in 1915 is going to think that that's interesting compositional material. It's not. The stamping chord in *The Rite of Spring* is interesting compositional material for that time, but, by 1915, nobody wants to write a large symphonic piece based on that opening horn call in the Sibelius Fifth. It seems completely against the whole Schoenberg aesthetic too, where the starting material is already sevenths and fourths in the First Chamber Symphony, a piece Sibelius knew and admired. Equally, nobody in 1926 is going to say that the opening tune of *Tapiola* is going to make an interesting starting point for a 25-minute symphonic poem. Most composition teachers, if brought such a starting point in 1926 would say, 'That's not going to go anywhere. Start with something else. Have you heard of *The Rite of Spring* or *Petrushka*? Don't work with this idea, it's boring.' Sibelius does something with that little material as avant-garde as anything that was going on anywhere else in 1926. It features in my article about Sibelius and contemporary composers,[5] because it's a piece that a lot of contemporary composers plugged into. I was criticised subsequently for that by a musicologist who, in true Boulez style, didn't name me. He complained that 'some' people were writing long articles about modern-sounding and contemporary-sounding certain textures and forms in Sibelius, but this was totally irrelevant because Sibelius was really extending the Liszt aesthetic. He feels that's the only valid way to look at it, but he misunderstood my article totally. My article wasn't principally about what Sibelius intended – although I did provide a lot of supporting evidence about his perception of nature and the way it affected his sense of musical time and timbre, which is very important to his music both sonically and formally. I then took those phenomena and looked at how they'd been understood or misunderstood by subsequent composers. There are some composers who are very fertile for misunderstanding.

CD: Of course, the post-war generation misunderstood what Webern was doing.

JA: Probably all of my enthusiasms are for composers who can be completely and thoroughly misread. I'm very interested in ambiguity and oddly, for somebody who was so definite about everything, the same was true of Messiaen, as we're now discovering. After all, Boulez understood him a very particular way and we know how important he was for Boulez, but that's not my understanding. It's not George Benjamin's understanding, nor that of Grisey or Betsy Jolas. Anyhow Messiaen, like Sibelius and Janáček, doesn't sit easily in music history books. Such composers are often referred to as 'maverick', which I find condescending. That's why three living composers who interest me a lot would be Michael Finnissy, Olly Knussen and Helmut Lachenmann, who have a pretty personal relationship to tradition and music and they don't seem to me to fit comfortably into any particular stream. Lachenmann has a very particular view on German music and music history in German society. I'm interested in people who tend to plough their own furrow a bit. Sibelius's letters and diaries clearly show after 1910 that he kept up with what was going on, but, at a certain point, stopped trying to keep his music in step with whatever was in fashion.

Some composers are more helpful to me creatively than others. Sibelius always has been very helpful, particularly in the composing crisis I had in 1990 which I partly solved through getting to know, thanks to Tony Payne, the first version of Sibelius's Fifth. That's still a piece I return to a lot.

CD: You mentioned Carter earlier, and he's really another composer that stands apart.

---

[5] 'Sibelius and Contemporary Music', in *The Cambridge Companion to Sibelius*, ed. Daniel M. Grimley (Cambridge: Cambridge University Press, 2004), pp. 196–216.

JA: He's one of the composers I most admire, in spite of not being particularly fond of the music's surface at times. If you think about it, it is very difficult after about 1950 to relate what Carter was doing to anything else. You can possibly hear analogous things in some of the denser bits in the Concerto for Orchestra or the Piano Concerto to some of the texture music of that period, to Ligeti and even perhaps some Penderecki, both of whose work he knew and said he admired at that time, but the resemblance is very much in passing. It is very hard to place Carter in terms of his era, except for the fact that when Neoclassicism was the dominant trend he was Neoclassical, and when it wasn't, he stopped being, but he didn't start being anything else that was a trend after that. He gave total serialism a very wide berth. The way musical trends come and go is very surprising. As you say, what about all those composers in the 1950s who completely misunderstood Anton Webern? They got something remarkable out of him, but it wasn't what he thought he was doing. This is just the way things go, you can't stop it.

CD: How different might the history of music have been if Webern hadn't been shot by that American soldier and had been around to explain his music himself?

JA: I have a view on that, based on Webern's correspondence. When he was writing to Schoenberg, he wrote what he thought would please Schoenberg. When he was writing to one of his fascist friends in the war – there were several of those Nazi friends, as we know – he would write something Nazi, alas. Then the following day he would write a letter to Schoenberg saying he despaired at his own race's anti-Semitism, et cetera. So, if you ask me, when confronted with the strong-minded young Pierre Boulez, who thought Webern was God's gift to music for a few years, Webern would not have said, 'Oh no you have got me entirely wrong. It was all from Schoenberg. I'm really writing very traditional pieces.' Of course he wouldn't, he would have gone entirely along with this and, indeed, there would probably have been some rather peculiar later Webern imitating Boulez a little. It could have been interesting... I don't think Webern would have behaved like Leibowitz, Max Deutsch and the other old Schoenbergians who survived – to say to Boulez and his kind that they were totally misunderstanding Webern. Webern would have gone along with Boulez, just as he went along with everyone stronger than him in his life – and that was quite a few people, as Webern was so shy. So I don't think if Webern had lived that the history of post-war music would have been substantially different. Look at what happened with Stravinsky who, if anyone, was meant to be a strong figure. He clearly was very influenced by Boulez, and benefited from that. I love late Stravinsky.

CD: I have my own theory about Stravinsky. It's key to me that he was a late starter.

JA: Yes, people tend to forget that.

CD: I have some understanding of that, in that I never did music O Level. So when I started A Level music, I perceived I had heaps of catching up to do.

JA: You were self-educated in that sense?

CD: Yes. I had done plenty of playing and I knew a fair amount, but I had this assumption, paranoia even, that there was all this repertoire and stuff that someone doing the O Level would know. I know now of course that is not how it actually works. It takes years to get to know the repertoire, whatever that is, and you can never know all of it. I was constantly trying to devour stuff to catch up. I still do that to a degree – education teaches you how little you know. The way I see it, as a late starter, Stravinsky had that compulsion to fill in the gaps. His entire life is basically spent doing the same thing wherever he is at. He is always Stravinsky and he is always exploring music, discovering things, trying to catch up. First of all, it is music that is closest to where he is, his own teacher and the Russian tradition. Then it is Western Europe and older styles. Once he has exhausted all of that and gotten back as far as Gesualdo, it made sense that he then goes more up to date with the biggest composers who are most recently dead, namely Schoenberg and Webern.

JA: Also he was very aware of the fact that everyone was suddenly talking about that music in a way that they had not before the war. So Stravinsky was catching up all the time.

CD: Yes, and/or this constant exploration of repertoire that he then turns into something for himself.

JA: This links up with something that Robert Craft pointed out – it seems very funny this – that in the '50s Stravinsky bought a book on how to write atonal counterpoint by Krenek.[6] Of course, he knew Krenek personally. In any case Craft was a bit surprised at that, but then realised that it was very typical of Stravinsky – he was always trying to educate himself. If there was a new book on Renaissance counterpoint or fugue technique or something, he would buy these things. He always wanted to learn. He wouldn't think that just because he was Stravinsky he couldn't learn. That is why he got Krenek involved, so that he could go to him and say, 'How do you deal with these things? Tell me.' That is the self-educator.

---

[6] Ernst Krenek, *Studies in Counterpoint Based on the Twelve-Tone Technique* (New York: G. Schirmer, 1940).

CD: To me *The Firebird*, of the big pieces, is the one where he has not yet worked out how to do this and be himself, so comes out almost as pastiche Rimsky-Korsakov.

JA: It isn't only Rimsky: there is certainly some Scriabin, some Balakirev (the middle section of the 'Infernal Dance' is straight out of *Islamey*), even bits of Glazunov and Tchaikovsky (who had both already affected the earlier Symphony in E flat). These things were recognised in *Firebird* much earlier than is realised. The near-quotes from Scriabin's *Poem of Ecstasy*, as well as the borrowings from Rimsky and elsewhere, were clearly well known by Russians of that time and were first written about in Paris in the early 1920s.[7]

CD: Once you get to *Petrushka*, with the combination of *ostinati* and jump cuts, etc., then it is Stravinsky all the way. I am curious whether Rimsky-Korsakov and Stravinsky ever had a conversation about imitation because Stravinsky is *so* Rimsky in the early years. Other things, too, but I wonder whether Rimsky expected his students to compose in something close to his style or discouraged it.

JA: There appears to be a Russian tradition in teaching composition of the pupil simply imitating the teacher, and learning by imitation. That is shown not only by Rimsky's students but also by those of Shostakovich. With the notable exception of Ustvolskaya, many Shostakovich pupils carried on reproducing his musical style for the rest of their lives. And it isn't only a Russian thing, either: we had in Britain a few students of Webern from the 1930s, who left Austria because of the *Anschluss* and settled around London, writing late-Webern style the rest of their lives. Leopold Spinner and Emil Spira were the main examples.

Nevertheless, *Firebird* so successfully outstripped all its models that I wonder what Rimsky's reaction to it would have been. In addition to the Russian influences, there's also some Ravel and other composers of whom we know Rimsky specifically disapproved. I saw a TV programme with Michael Tilson Thomas and the LSO[8] at the end of the 1980s, when he played the bit from Rimsky-Korsakov's *Mlada* where the evil Kashchéy appears, and you get just a very square version of the theme that Stravinsky later used for the Kachtcheï's dance. It turns out what Stravinsky did was to syncopate and derange a theme of Rimsky, as has been documented elsewhere.[9] You could argue that maybe

---

[7] See Boris de Schloezer, 'Igor Strawinsky', in *La Revue Musicale* 5/2 (1 December 1923), pp. 107–09.

[8] London Symphony Orchestra.

[9] For more on this, see Richard Taruskin, *Stravinsky and the Russian Traditions, Volume One: A Biography of the Works Through Mavra* (Berkeley: University of California Press, 1996), p. 629.

Stravinsky thought that one used folk music when you need the appropriate folk tune for spring or whatever, so when you have devil's music you use appropriate music about that particular devil. There's no question that Stravinsky's is the greater piece, but the borrowing is so literal that I think Rimsky might have felt profoundly ambivalent.

CD: Undoubtedly, and would he have been pleased or disappointed at the subsequent move away? Of course, *The Rite* is pretty much inescapable for any musician, never mind composer.

JA: Well, *The Rite* has been very important to me, basically because, as I said earlier, it is one of the pieces I recall hearing when I was only about three years old. Then much later there was this accident, which sounds silly to say in a way but anyhow: the Jewish side of my family come from Lithuania, so the fact that many of the folk tunes in *The Rite* are Lithuanian has a personal interest for me. A box set of Lithuanian folk melodies turned up at the Royal College library – it was some kind of donation. Stephen Pettitt showed it to me (he was then record librarian there),[10] and it influenced my music very much. I realised I was trying to discover the most basic musical material I could find and do something very elaborate with that. Many of the melodies in this box set only had two, three or four notes, but were instantly memorable. I wasn't just aping minimalism: it was an attempt at being very elaborate with something that was very simple, and in a way that's still what I'm up to today. Obviously, what I've just said about Sibelius would also help show me a way of doing that.

Paradoxically, I find the same thing in Boulez, just simply observing the different ways he reuses his material. I realised only in the last 15 years that much of Boulez's music, mostly between 1952 and about 1970, but also *Sur Incises* for example, is based on a single note row, which is the row of *Le Marteau*, and he'd already used it twice before that, it now turns out. For example, there's one sheet of sketches, of chord multiplications based on this row, which he used for two wildly different pieces: 'L'Artisanant furieux'[11] and the opening section of *cummings ist der Dichter*. It can be quite interesting in a class to show people this sheet and see how it was used compositionally. He has one way of using it for melodic polyphony in *Le marteau*, and he has almost the opposite way of using it for harmonic progressions in *cummings*. When you hear them you cannot hear any similarity at all. What that emphasises is Boulez's phenomenal levels of invention. The song's a duet, but *cummings* is purely chordal.

A lot of composers take very simple, even naive, premises, and do something completely unexpected with them. It's the same thing in some of Per Nørgård's

---

[10] Stephen Pettitt is a British music critic.
[11] Third song of *Le Marteau sans maître*.

music. There's a biologist, Professor Wartington, who's quoted by Nørgård a lot who said something to the effect that the most obvious facts will often be the most worth investigating.[12]

CD: I'm forever telling students not to forget the bleedin' obvious.

JA: A lot of Per's music is about that and a lot of mine is too. I like taking very obvious, normal, everyday musical facts and just seeing if they're perhaps nothing like so obvious. I find that rather magical because if you can do that with something people have heard many times before, and find a new use for it, it can be rather powerful. It can be more interesting than finding an unusual starting point and going from there. If the musical starting point is very boring, then you can apply all of your imagination to inventing with it. And because it is familiar material, there's a strong probability that listeners will be able to follow what you do with it much better perceptually.

CD: It strikes me that Sibelius and Janáček, and, if we're honest, Messiaen, if he hadn't had all his pupils, are all marginal figures in terms of the narrative view of twentieth-century history. I suspect Sibelius barely ever gets mentioned in most twentieth-century history classes. The only reason a lot of people mention Messiaen is *Mode de valeurs* [*et d'intensités*].

JA: That, or the Modes of Limited Transposition.

CD: Or they might mention the first movement of the *Quartet*.

JA: Because of the isorhythm.

CD: But anything that the music is doing more deeply tends to be overlooked.

JA: I fear that most people think it isn't doing anything else.

CD: It fascinates me the way that musical histories are constructed, as well, being at the Conservatoire and talking about these things, and being aware of the fact that you've got students with significant portions of repertoire that are overlooked by conventional narratives. It's obvious with singers, where nineteenth-century history, as it tends to be taught, entirely overlooks Italian opera. There may be mentions of Wagner, but that is going to be a very particular kind of singer and they're usually too young even to know if they're that kind of singer at that stage. Huge swathes of nineteenth-century opera is overlooked altogether. Yet, in 1825, who would anyone have said at the time was the most important composer or

[12] This remark is quoted near the start of Nørgård's own CD liner notes for the recording of three major organ works played by Jens Christiansen: Per Nørgård, *Unity Behind Trinity: Three Organ Works*, Jens Christiansen (organ), rec. 1990, Copenhagen, Kontrapunkt, 32081.

most famous composer in Europe? Certainly, it would have been Rossini, not Beethoven.

JA: You could equally well cite pianists and you get another very partial view, which often doesn't even include Haydn anymore. It will include Bach (they know they're not really meant to be playing it on a piano, but that is still accepted practice) but it basically goes Beethoven, Schumann, Brahms and it might go Rachmaninov, and then it just stops.

CD: They'll have some Chopin, Debussy and Ravel as well...

JA: Oh sorry, of course.

CD: It's what may be thought of as the 'petit Lang Langs'. He's really quite remarkable, but there are plenty of pale imitators. Moreover, we've mentioned singers and pianists, but this applies to pretty much any instrumentalist. Even if they play orchestral repertoire, there will be an entire history for their instrument that is really particular.

JA: And which the rest of us don't know about.

CD: No, though I've developed all sorts of bits of obscure knowledge about trombones or whatever it might be through our performance practice modules and I find it fascinating. All histories are simplifications, of course.

JA: You have to ask who wrote them, when and why. (In some cases, I wonder why they were asked to...)

CD: It intrigues me the nature of what simplification happens and how it changes from different perspectives. As we were talking about *The Rite of Spring*, it struck me that the bit where most readily I can see the direct line to some of the kinds of things you do is actually the opening part, just before the curtain comes up. We've got nature and it's this 'joyous kerfuffle' thing going on.

JA: Well, funnily enough, I've spent probably more time analysing, looking at and pulling apart that passage than anything else in the piece. You're absolutely right.

CD: Obviously, every single note of that piece has been picked apart.

JA: Oh, to death.

CD: Generally speaking, when it gets talked about, though, people mention the opening bassoon solo and then it tends to jump to the hammering strings and you'll get the sacrificial dance. In a way, even in a work which is as central as

The Rite of Spring, it seems that the bit that most pertains to what you're looking at is slightly on the outside.

JA: I agree. I learnt *The Rite of Spring* from a record that my father owned, the Doráti recording in Minneapolis, which is very fast and not now my favourite recording.[13] Incidentally, I now realise that he only used to play side one. So I thought the piece ended with the 'Dance of the earth'. I got to know Part Two a little bit later.

The 'Introduction' interests me probably more than anything else. That's one of the first passages of music I can remember being able to run through in my head, and really enjoying being able to do so. The 'Procession of the Sage' is the other passage in Part One that really fascinates me and has influenced me a lot, with the gradual superimposition of *ostinati* that do not make a random collage at all, using hybrid, non-repeating scales that make a huge resonant mode. That's the way I analyse the 'Procession of the Sage' and I also hear the 'Introduction', too, as a single big resonant mode. Even if that's not how it was written or conceived, in other words, even if historically I'm talking nonsense, aurally and creatively I think I've got a point. It seems to be palpable that the big tutti in the 'Introduction' of Part One doesn't sound random, that it has a very specific set of colours and sounds, like the bird passages in Messiaen's *Oiseaux exotiques*. This very much influenced the way I wrote *Khorovod*, using multi-register scales. What interests me is making polyphony where you can have the parts talking to each other rather than just random superimpositions.[14] So you're absolutely right, my view of *The Rite of Spring* is a composer's view. What's most important for me is two passages in Part One, but another composer will, and should, have a completely different view of it.

The idea that's got to go from music history is respect. If you really love a piece of music you must play about with it. It must really excite you and, if you're creative at all, you'll want to muck about with it, misunderstand it and hear it in all kinds of ways. That is also very valid for a listener, too. They should also be able to do that.

There's the old debate: should you be able to go through a university undergraduate music course without knowing your Beethoven or your Stravinsky (to name two key figures in music history)? The answer is probably no, you should know something about them, you should study them, they're great figures. The trouble is that's not a very creative way to teach those figures. If you just stand there telling people 'this is very important', the first thing they wish to do is

[13] Stravinsky, *The Rite of Spring*, Minneapolis Symphony Orchestra, Antal Doráti (conductor), rec. Northrop Auditorium, Minneapolis, 1953, Mercury MG 50030 (LP).
[14] See Conversation Seven, 'Understandings', for more on hybrid scales in *The Rite of Spring*, *Oiseaux exotiques* and *Khorovod*.

leave. I think that composers are more creative than that, and react to music in a more vivid way (but perhaps I'm biased!). That's why composers still make interesting teachers and musicologists. By the way, that's why I like your musicology, because you think like a composer. For all I know, you may be.

CD: I'm not.

JA: But you write as though you were. You write from an understanding of the creative point of view, an understanding of the intuition and the lateral thinking endemic to composing. Creative points of view are not necessarily historically accurate, but I don't know any composer – be it Beethoven's view of Mozart, Wagner's view of Beethoven, Lutosławski's view of John Cage, or anyone's view of Webern in 1950 – who respected what a previous composer intended. You get what you need from other composers.

CD: Composers, or anyone else for that matter, analysing the works of others reveal as much of themselves as the object of the analysis. This is why asserting a position of objectivity is absurd, it's a fallacy.

JA: Messiaen heard what he wished to hear in *The Rite of Spring* or in *Pelléas*. And using that, he awakened a lot of other composers to potentials in those pieces they wouldn't have seen. Take that footage of Messiaen teaching *Pelléas* in the Berio documentary.[15] He takes only one Interlude, the penultimate one in Act Two when they're about to go into the cave to find the wedding ring they know isn't there. That Interlude always caught my ear and I never thought much about why. The way Messiaen plays the piano and talks about it, it begins to sound like *musique concrète*. You begin to hear that the study of nature is a serious thing there. The way Debussy orchestrates and writes rhythmically, and so on, is all determined by this feeling of trying to get lost in this cave near the sea. The orchestra totally changes its colour and its rhythmic language in order to do that. Messiaen points that out, and I suddenly thought, 'Oh, I want to do that.' That became the third act of *Thebans*. It's about turning the orchestra into a forest, rather than having, as I was intending until then, concrete sounds of a real forest mixed with the orchestra. Just watching the film of Messiaen analysing that interlude at the piano directly affected the whole third act of my opera.

So looking creatively at a musical object, not respecting its historical context, not being completely intimidated by history, that is how many composers work – and why composers doing musicology is disturbing to a lot of musicologists. All these notions of contextuality can go out the window and it becomes

---

15 Luciano Berio, *Verso la scuola ideale*, TV programme in Italian from the series *C'è Musica e Musica* produced by Berio (RAI Radiotelevisione Italia, 1972).

deeply subjective, even random. Music history *is* productively random. I have no problem with that. I like the fact that you can drive completely contradictory paths through the same 300 or 400 years of music.

CD: Musicologists are merely trying to make sense of and simplify the randomness, but it does need the corrective of remembering that it is always more complex. Rather than lines, there is a more chaotic Brownian motion. Or perhaps chaos graphs would be more accurate. They can look at one level like a clear, very elegant pattern, then as you look more closely, there is a far more complex unpredictability about it, and as you get in further – or for that matter draw out further – the elegance returns, ad infinitum.

JA: We could make a list now of composers that form a certain pattern. There's the whole Sorabji-Alkan clan and their view of the history of music is basically some Mozart, certain Berlioz, Alkan himself of course, Godowsky a bit, certain Szymanowski pieces, the experimental Liszt, of course, is a big thing. The sort of satanic Liszt and the *Nuages Gris* Liszt. Then that goes into Sorabji and it slightly stops there. Busoni also features in that lineage, of course, the Piano Concerto and some of his Indian-inspired piano pieces. I don't agree with that view of that particular period of music, at all. A composer friend of mine has a very strange view of the history of the last 200 years, from what I know of him. It appears to be dominated by Satie and Ustvolskaya plus Stravinsky, Frank Martin, Ligeti and Claude Vivier, among others. Through talking to someone who has a completely different view of musical history, you can discern a lot of exciting viewpoints onto much other music that doesn't fit easily into musical history. Oblique angles. The trouble is that no history of music I know is based on oblique angles.

The thing about the heroes notion is that you're asking me to state my personal history of music. That's the way I interpret it. Things are so atomised now socially that maybe this is part of the problem of communication. Every single composer and possibly most musicians – and you've just hinted at this – have a completely slanted view and we can't get an overall consensus anymore.

CD: Or maybe it was an illusion in the first place?

JA: It probably was because now we revere a figure like Gesualdo who's become terribly important to so many composers and listeners, but who was not terribly important at the time.

CD: It's always been shifting grounds. When studying a Bach cantata with second-year students, I'll get them randomly to pick a number, between 1 and 199.

JA: I like that.

CD: For the cantata with the number they've picked, they have to find some basic information and then I get them to go to the bach-cantatas.com website to find out when the earliest recording was. When you've got enough people doing this, what it reveals is that you get one or two recordings in the '30s or '40s, usually just individual movements, then you start to get a big rash of them from the '50s onwards, but many are actually of radio broadcasts, they weren't commercial studio recordings. The students don't really know enough to parse the difference usually and I point it out in class rather than getting them to find the first commercial recording. Quite a few cantatas didn't receive their first commercial recordings until the 1970s, some even the '80s.

JA: Are you serious?

CD: The Harnoncourt and Leonhardt series, in fact.[16] Our view now of Bach is that the cantatas are not just the jewel of his output, but the kind of jewel-encrusted crown.

JA: Or its core.

CD: Yes. Going back to the 1950s, there were a few cantatas that were known, but they were not the centrality of what Bach was.

JA: So what was?

CD: The keyboard works, the orchestral works and the Passions. Very few people knew the cantatas beyond a relatively small number of famous ones. Richter changed that a bit, but the Harnoncourt/Leonhardt series was the first attempt at a complete recording of the cantatas. Or take someone else we've been talking about, Haydn. Doráti's series of the symphonies, which was made between 1969 and 1972, was essentially the first complete survey.[17] I read somewhere that there weren't sets of parts for some of the symphonies.

---

[16] Nikolaus Harnoncourt and Gustav Leonhardt started recording their series, on period instruments, in 1970 for the Telefunken label and completed it in 1990. In the meantime, Helmuth Rilling completed his modern instrument set in 1985. Both sets have been released in various formats, notably: J.S. Bach, *The Sacred Cantatas*, Leonhardt Consort and Concentus musicus Wien, Nikolaus Harnoncourt and Gustav Leonhardt (conductors), Warner 2564699437 (60 CDs); J.S. Bach, *The Complete Cantatas*, Helmuth Rilling, Hänssler HAEN98630 (71 CDs).

[17] Doráti's set has been released in various formats, notably as: Haydn, *The Complete Symphonies*, Philharmonia Hungarica, Antal Doráti (conductor), Decca 478 1221 (33 CDs). In fact, Ernst Märzendorfer completed a cycle shortly before Doráti's, but this was available in only a limited capacity on the Music Heritage Society label. It has recently been issued on CD: Haydn, *The Complete Symphonies*, Vienna Chamber Orchestra, Ernst Märzendorfer (conductor), Scribendum SC818 (33 CDs).

JA: Goodness!

CD: Robbins Landon's edition of the scores was only completed in 1968.

JA: So that was putting them in the repertoire?

CD: Yes. People knew quite a few of the symphonies, but nothing like all of them.

JA: This is fascinating because what you're saying is that the real discovery of Haydn, as we see him now, is happening simultaneously with, say, Boulez writing *Rituel in memoriam Bruno Maderna*.

CD: Yes.

JA: I find that very curious. In other words, Boulez's view of music history couldn't possibly have been informed by it before then.

CD: This is why it's entirely possible, when Boulez was asked about Mahler, he replied, 'We didn't know Mahler in France.'

JA: Yes, of course they didn't. Or Bruckner.

CD: People knew of Haydn and they knew a few key works but the idea of knowing the totality of a composer is a construct of the last 60 or 70 years with complete editions. It's a recording thing.

JA: Recordings and complete editions. It's what I called the Donaldson effect, because that's the complete editions room at the Royal College Library, where I studied.

CD: Yes, Bach would have been the first of those,[18] but listening to complete works is a really recent phenomenon.

JA: That's one of the reasons I bought the Deutsche Grammophon complete Messiaen boxset, because I realised that was a rather important staging post in Messiaen reception history. We have the whole output in a single box. Not always in performances I admire, but nevertheless a lot of them in one place in one time, from beginning to end.

CD: And yet, even with Messiaen, a composer whose output is relatively neat, the DG box is already incomplete as there are discoveries and new things to be heard.

---

[18]   The first volume of the Bach-Gesellschaft-Ausgabe appeared in 1851.

JA: Not least the Tui-Bird movement.[19] I really think that is a remarkable find. I was fascinated when you showed me Messiaen's short score. The final result, as premiered at the Proms, was a startlingly vivid piece of rather abrupt, almost Stravinskian cross-cutting between chords and ideas of balletic agility. In particular, the recurrent orchestral 'sneeze' chord, which opens the work and punctuates each verse of it, makes an astonishingly colourful impact, rather like one of those big punctuating chords in *Agon* or something. I recognise this sonority clearly from the real *Tui-Bird* recordings I've heard. And now I gather other things are turning up, like the first version of the opening 'Liturgie de Cristal' from *Quatuor pour la Fin du Temps*, originally toured in the army on a strange mixed ensemble including flutes, clarinet, piano, celesta and other instruments – like a miniature anticipation of the *Trois Petites Liturgies*.

CD: Yes, Yves Balmer's work on the *Quatuor* has turned up some remarkable things. That's a work that keeps on giving in that respect and these things underline that a composer's output is not a fixed thing even when they're dead.

JA: It certainly isn't. And now DG have done the same type of complete works boxset for Boulez as they did for Messiaen, and most recently they've done the same for Dutilleux as well. It's exciting, in a way, but it's all a little strange. Boulez's output is strewn with withdrawn and half-finished pieces. That's an output that's resisting exactly what DG did to it. It's an output made not to be anthologised and not to be issued complete.

CD: Yes, David Gable spoke at a conference in Cornell recently about both earlier versions of Boulez's *Le visage nuptial*, talking about what he felt had been lost, as well as gained, from the late-'50s version to the late-'80s version.

JA: Well, I had a funny experience with that work. I was present at the first rehearsals of the late-1980s revision, at Maida Vale, where it was done by the BBC Symphony Orchestra. All I had from my local library was the 1953 score. In the first movement, it was just about possible to follow, although there was a lot of extra figuration, but from the second movement onwards, following was almost impossible. Interestingly, a composer friend of mine asked him, in my

---

[19] Olivier Messiaen, *Un oiseau des arbres de Vie (Oiseau Tui)*, orchestration realised by Christopher Dingle. The work was originally intended for Messiaen's last completed orchestral work, *Éclairs sur l'Au-Delà....* The composer wrote the entire movement in short score, with indications of the intended orchestration. Christopher Dingle created a full score following Messiaen's indications and the world premiere of the work was given by the BBC Philharmonic conducted by Nicholas Collon at the Royal Albert Hall on 7 August 2015 as part of the BBC Proms.

presence, after that rehearsal, 'what have you done with the quarter-tones? Have you put them up or down because there aren't any in the final version?' Boulez laughed and said, 'No, no, no, it's much more complicated than that.' Well, when the final score became available I went through it and I can tell you it isn't. He put them either up or down. He changed the octave of some pitches as well, but he put the quarter-tones up or down. So there was an answer to that question. I've now heard the version from 1953, the one with all the quarter-tones – it exists in some archives and was performed and broadcast a few times. What was lost in 1988 is a certain generalised wildness. However, the 1953 version could not be played and sung exactly as written in a lot of places, so it had to go, exciting though it looks in the score.

CD: There's this wonderful anarchic spirit to it. It's that whiff of sulphur aspect.

JA: Nevertheless, the final version seems to me to be wilder than anything else Boulez did in the late 1980s. I like it very much, but I'm clear that I'm hearing something which has been heavily worked over, and probably it's been muted a bit in the process. Did you feel that?

CD: Certainly on hearing the bits of the earlier version, yes, though when I heard the final version in the '80s, I hadn't seen the earlier score.

JA: It's nevertheless an amazingly impressive piece.

CD: Oh yes, I loved it when I heard it.

JA: Well, we were both at the UK premiere. This DG boxset tendency: it's a sort of museum anthologising that we're talking about. I sense that increasingly this is going to be unviable. I don't think it's truly viable with Boulez. I don't think it's viable with Oliver Knussen's output. Composers' outputs are full of loose ends and paths not taken – all that kind of thing. I'm interested in those, rather than trying to sew everything up into a boxset and putting it in a sort of digital pile somewhere saying, 'That is the composer.'

CD: And it's not just problematic with Boulez and Knussen, it's a nonsense with Chopin as there are so many variants from all sorts of sources in his hand, where he wrote things on students' copies. It also means that an *Urtext* is especially difficult and, to an even greater degree than usual, risks acting as a set of concrete boots. Going back to the pedagogical aspect of it, though, some students may resist being taught it, but they do understand that it's a good thing to be able to put in order, say, Bach, Haydn, Mozart, Beethoven, Schubert, and also to be able to place a piece to within about ten years or so, which also becomes quite a fun game to play.

JA: Oh very important, useful, and an interesting one, yes.

CD: It's difficult to resist the temptation to put Rebel's *Les Élémens* in an exam. I remember my shock on first hearing that. I switched on the radio just as it opened. I'd missed the announcement and so I was there trying to work out what the hell it was. I completely failed the listening test, because I was convinced it must be post-*Rite of Spring* – Milhaud or someone like that.

JA: It's an amazing opening. It opens with this shocking material, but the imagination that thought that up also knew what to do with it. That's what's good about it. So often you get somebody who thinks up an unusual sound and that's all they can do, but his follow-through is marvellous. That really is a terrific piece. I like also very much, similarly, the Biber *Battalia*, which has a quodlibet that sounds a bit like Ives and so on.

CD: Oh yes, that's also an extraordinary piece.

JA: I'm interested in composers who can leapfrog like that. One of the funny things about Ligeti is one now sees how many ancestors he had, whereas, at the time, when that music emerged, he seemed like probably one of the most strikingly original and innovative composers of the period. He used to go on about the influence of Ockeghem, which was clearly true, but I'm really meaning just how Hungarian it is. It's very Bartók-like. Those micropolyphonic bits in *Atmosphères* sound very like Bartók, though there's just more of it – more parts, that is! It's not a contradiction of his tradition, it's an extension or an exaggeration of some things.

When an avant-garde movement arises that is iconoclastic, I'm slightly sceptical about it because usually it's a fib. I would say the Second Piano Sonata of Boulez and possibly the first Boulez *Structures* are the nearest to truly iconoclastic masterpieces, but, even then, there are two things you can still hear in those pieces. First of all, *Structures* sounds quite French – I mean, the sort of decorative side to it. You can also hear he's heard some Bartók, some Messiaen and some Jolivet. It doesn't sound like them, but clearly he couldn't have written that, even the Second Sonata, which is pretty extreme, without those composers. The other thing you can hear, contextually, is all the music he doesn't want it to sound like. So you hear this kind of negative. I hear the Second Sonata of Boulez as a sort of negative of Poulenc or Ibert or something. You hear it frantically fleeing those composers' worlds and, in a way, if they hadn't existed, it wouldn't be like it is. In that sense, even the most iconoclastic music is always altering or saying again, in a different way, something that's already been said, definitely. And in that sense I'm with Stravinsky, I suppose, because that's what he asserted so often.

45

CD: The other striking thing about this moment in the very early '50s is that you get Boulez with *Structures* and Cage with *Music of Changes*, and you've got absolute control from Boulez and freedom from Cage, not in how it's notated but in how it's created. The aural results...

JA: Astonishingly close.

CD: You play them to students and their view is, 'Well, it's exactly the same kind of music.' In fact, I would warrant that, if they didn't know the pieces particularly well beforehand, very few people would have the faintest idea which was which.

JA: No, that's absolutely right. There's a common search towards anonymity at that point.

CD: Yes, part of forgetting.

JA: Even then, the way I hear the Cage – this is maybe just me – is as a reaction to Boulez. Cage's music before *Music of Changes* was nothing like that. Technically it's got things in common, but the sound is quite different. What I hear in *Music of Changes* is that he's heard Boulez's Second Sonata, which we know he was crazy about. That clearly pushed him over to this much more disjunct piano writing, which was quite unlike his previous work. The Satie side temporarily vanishes in the *Music of Changes* – none of that neo-simplicity at all. You get only these extraordinarily varied isolated musical facts juggled about with an astonishing rapidity. But you know Cage said to Henry Cowell that it was Boulez's mobility that had influenced him, to make this much more jagged piano style, with changing register and discontinuity and stuff. He said that his influence on Boulez was the aggregate; that Boulez had taken on his concept of aggregate, and this became in fact the Boulez *blocs sonores*. It would seem, in some way, the randomness in Cage was Boulez-inspired, which was just what Boulez didn't like about Cage! And the harmonic consistency of Boulez, which one imagines is not what Cage ever enjoyed in Boulez, is what he got from Cage – it's very funny. There's a sort of simultaneous misunderstanding of each other, but there's an electricity about that period of their work that is extraordinary. As you say, it's something to do with trying to forget history. Even if that's an illusion, it's an interesting illusion.

CD: It's a very common one across music, and across the arts at the time.

JA: At that time, yes. One of the things that's difficult for me now to realise is that, when I was growing up, this was all only 20 years before. When you start hearing that music, you just think, 'This is very exciting stuff.' Through working as a musicologist, I suppose, I've had to come to terms with where things were by about 1981. That was a particular situation historically, of which, at the time when I was a kid, I had no idea. I don't think anyone did at the time. It was too close at hand to have had any perspective. It's much easier to put that music in the context that you just put it in, with the distance of 50 or 60 years.

By 60 years' distance, the music's also not an immediate threat, in the way that, for example, Donatoni apparently used to say about Cage, 'That bastard almost wrecked my life.'[20] In the '60s, Donatoni was so intimidated by the ideal of a random non-personalised music that he reached a dead end. Eventually he came back to being Donatoni, and in the case of his '80s music such as *Le ruisseau sur l'escalier*, quite superbly so. But my point is that you can't imagine a young or middle-aged composer now thinking that John Cage might be in danger of nearly wrecking their creative life, nor Boulez for that matter. It's there and you can enjoy it for what it is, with a perspective that even in, say, 1977 was very hard to have. The trouble for me is that I'm the notional ex-smoker, because I did believe for six months perhaps, as a kid, in the Boulez aesthetic. And then I swallowed the spectral thing too. There's a security about all that that I don't have or want to have anymore – I haven't since about 1988. When you're 21 it's very nice to have a security blanket and it's a little unnerving to throw it away. I remember, finally, that when I had to interview Boulez, for the BBC in 1999, I asked him, 'Where is music going?' he said, quite flatly, 'Where the next person takes it', and then said, 'If you'd have asked me, in 1955, I would have told you probably nonsense. I would have said "everything will be serialised and more organised and so on".' He commented, 'Well, it was not the case. At least experience makes you modest.' I said, 'Do you find it difficult that taboos, which you very strongly believed in and perhaps still do believe in, are not held by others?' He said, 'My generation needed those taboos. It's quite clear, whether I like it or not, that the next generation didn't need those taboos. So my view of music history when I was younger, as a straight line, was nonsense.' I said, 'Are you sad about that?' He said, 'No, I'm not sad about it at all. It made my life much more interesting.'

CD: There's another filter that could be put to music history, which is between composers who restrict or are closed, and composers who are more open.

JA: Oh, very interesting terms.

CD: By open, I mean composers who don't appear on the surface to have restrictions, even though there'll always be some kind of restrictions there. If you wanted to put it crudely, the difference between Brahms and Wagner. Certainly

20 See Andrew Ford, *Composer to Composer: conversations about contemporary music* (London: Quartet Books, 1993), p. 118.

between Sibelius and Mahler. Stravinsky is very much a restrictive composer, although arguably not in the very first period.

JA: In everything after that, yes.

CD: Yes. Messiaen certainly didn't like to restrict.

JA: There's a contradiction becoming apparent to me, thinking of myself. I don't really put myself into a category and I seem to be compositionally inclined, therefore, towards an unrestrictive attitude. However, it seems that many of the people I admire are more restrictive: Sibelius, Janáček or some Stravinsky, for example. Not Messiaen though. Perhaps that's the function Messiaen has in my life, teaching me how to be unrestrictive, but not incoherent.

CD: Finally, may I ask you about your admiration for Ives and Ruth Crawford Seeger, whom you mentioned at the start of this conversation? They aren't necessarily the first composers who come to mind when listening to your music...

JA: Indeed not. But under the surface, they've both had a huge effect on what I compose. In the case of Ives, it's the highly original way he combines many different things at once to form an overall vision. In the finale of his Fourth Symphony, this device is used with an overtone-type harmonic structure to overwhelming effect over the course of the entire movement. The other aspect of Ives I find very sympathetic is what might be termed his visionary side: the 'Thoreau' finale of the *Concord Sonata* or 'The Housatonic at Stockbridge' are the clearest examples of that. In those passages, the harmony is at once disarmingly simple and yearningly dissonant. He again uses overtone-type formations over very diatonic harmonies. That's a profoundly original aspect of Ives's work.

Ruth Crawford Seeger's output isn't large – for many tragic reasons – but it's clear that she was a composer of real genius with an exceptional imagination. Almost everything she wrote is phenomenally assured and radically new for its time. She too worked with the idea of combining layers – a very American thing in music, it seems – but without the Ives tendency towards quotation. She evolved a hugely expressive musical idiom, totally dissonant yet wonderfully varied, which is deployed to near-perfection quite differently in every work she wrote. For me, pieces like the *Three Songs*, the *Three Chants* (surely one of the greatest choral pieces of the last 100 years) and her magnificent String Quartet (1931) are key works and great music to which I return again and again. It's not merely that she uncannily anticipated later idioms like those of both Carter and Ligeti (though she did, to an astonishing degree), but there's far more to her music than that. Her solutions to each textural or formal issue are almost forensically precise yet always wonderfully surprising. She never gets it wrong, but exactly right – entirely so – at the very first attempt. I don't know of any real equivalent to that achievement. Certain passages in her work – notably the shifting accents of the Quartet's slow movement – are unforgettable and have made a deep impression on my music. I may add that if there's any composer of the last 100 years I deeply regret never having been able to meet, Ruth Crawford Seeger would be the top of that list.

Figure 1   Julian Anderson with Gérard Grisey, London 1996,
photograph by Christopher Wintle

Conversation Three

Training

This conversation essentially picks up the baton from Conversation One, 'Origins', looking at Anderson's training beyond school. It starts with considering John Lambert's characteristics as a teacher, from first meeting to his death in 1995, then the contrasting approach of Alexander Goehr. The conversation then moves on to contact with various key figures in Anderson's formation, from seeking out Tristan Murail for private lessons in order to understand spectral music, via summer courses with Olivier Messiaen and Per Nørgård to a robust encounter with Ligeti. Along the way there are fond reminiscences of the rich intellectual possibilities offered by Paris, the early perception of spectral music and the relationship to it of Nørgård and Rădulescu, as well as the quirks of the ondes Martenot.

CD: I wonder if we can talk about some of the remarkable people you have had as teachers in various settings. John Lambert was your first composition teacher beyond school. Why did you approach him?

JA: I went to John Lambert because both Olly Knussen and John Baird said I should. John Baird had been replaced by Olly Knussen when he left the Junior College to teach at Westminster School. They met once, because John had to show him the ropes of the new job, but independently from each other they both knew that John Lambert was a very good teacher. John Baird handed on about six or seven composers to John Lambert – one of the others was Richard Blackford. Since both arrows pointed towards Lambert, the choice was not accidental.

CD: Was this at the Royal College [of Music]?

JA: No, I studied with John Lambert for two years before College.

CD: Right, so what was your first meeting like?

JA: The first thing he looked at was my String Quartet No. 1 'Light Music' – the title being in the sense of light diffused in a prism, not in the other sense of that expression! He looked at that score, which I sent him in advance. I went down to his house in Brighton and he pored over it in enormous detail. He checked up on ring modulation and all of that, and he asked me a lot of details about the technical procedures behind the piece. The first half of the session was him saying, 'I see, and then what happens here technically? You did this this way?' He wanted to know precisely what he was reading. Once he'd got that done, he then said, 'Now let me look at it again.'

What John could hear of the piece in his head I don't know, because it was full of microtones and a very difficult score for anyone to read in their head, even now. I'd worked it out by using two little Casio keyboards tuned a quarter-tone out, sellotaping notes down and taping the result, splicing it and being able to hear chord progressions that way. That was pretty cumbersome, but it was a way of hearing it. Hearing it in one's head would have been very hard, and I wasn't going to fool myself I could do that. I brought that cassette down with me to the lesson with Lambert, but he wouldn't listen to it. He said, 'No, I want to just look at it', so he got as good an idea as one could get. And he was a very good score-reader – he was Boulanger-trained for God's sake![1] Very gradually, he pinpointed two or three weak passages in it, which I'd been very insecure about, and suggested the ending was too long. By the way, as I've pointed out elsewhere in these conversations, the only real change I made in that piece when I finally published it was to reduce that pause near the end of 30 seconds to a pause of 15, which I had always planned to do since that first lesson with Lambert.[2] Twenty-nine years later I'm thinking, 'John, you were so right, that ending is too long.' Then he wanted to know what on earth I was doing writing that piece. He said, 'Clearly, you didn't invent the idea of doing these techniques on instruments. You will have got it from somewhere. I want to know where.' I told him and he was a bit surprised, because he didn't like what he'd heard of Tristan Murail's music. Gérard Grisey he didn't know about, so, typically, he immediately asked to hear those pieces. He added that he would be happy to teach me 'if, that is, you find me worth studying with'. He was a very humorous man.

He tested my ear and found I could hear complicated chords and things like that. Some of the tests were tough – he really ransacked my ear for about 20 minutes at the start of the first lesson. As for the music, he said, 'It's good, but your shapes are a bit inept. There's always one bit that's a bit long or a bit short, it destabilises the work. It's not an interesting deviation, it's just wrong. For what

[1]   Lambert studied in Paris with Nadia Boulanger from 1953 to 1956.
[2]   See Conversation One, 'Origins'.

you're doing it's wrong, from what I can see.' He added, typically modestly, 'Until I hear this played, I don't know for certain. Have you had it played?' I said, 'No, I can't get anyone to play it, and the SPNM[3] have rejected it.' He just said, 'Oh typical.' He couldn't get it played either.

CD: What was his approach?

JA: He was trying to find out whether or not any piece you brought him was well written within the stylistic norms of the music. He was *not* trying to dictate your style. When he recommended Xenakis, he said, 'You won't find it's the best written music for the instruments, technically, but he's deeply inventive and knows a lot about pushing time and sound to extremes – you can learn from that.' But if I had come in, for example, with a piano part on ten staves, like Xenakis does, he probably wouldn't have tolerated it. He was sceptical of Xenakis's musicianship, despite admiring him considerably. So he taught me a good lesson in terms of trying to find out what you want to do, and doing it properly. If that's random then it should be very random, it should be consistently random, you don't just dip your toe in the water: you should be thorough about what you compose. I still believe that.

Openness was very important to John Lambert's teaching. Inevitably, at the age of 17, 18, 19, it wasn't quite every week a different style, but I was a young composer changing all the time. It didn't matter what I brought in, he could cope. Most of the time he knew exactly the thing you'd been inspired by and wanted to imitate. He didn't mind that. He knew that was a natural human activity at that age. What he did want was for me to sort it out properly, and he knew that that was going to take some time, as it does with most composers.

He discouraged me, very helpfully, from comparing myself too much with others. I was worried about whether I'd get known early enough. John Lambert said this was totally unimportant. He'd also taught Olly Knussen who'd, of course, been freakily gifted as a young composer and had a symphony played when he was 15. John encouraged me to just forget about that problem altogether. George Benjamin and Olly both said the same thing to me and they were right. It was good to drop that anxiety. As it turned out, I made my debut at around 23, which is quite early enough. John was fantastically generous and patient with me, for five years.

Difficulties arose because he had trouble getting his own music played. He changed style dramatically midway. He'd been a rather Hindemithian, [Peter] Fricker-type composer until the mid-'60s, then suddenly, in about '65 or so, he went modern, as it were. When he did that some colleagues, like Anthony Milner, distanced themselves from him, thinking him too trendy. The younger

---

[3]   Society for the Promotion of New Music.

modernists didn't know what to make of this middle-aged gentleman – he was nearly ten years older than the Manchester School composers – who'd suddenly tried to join their ranks, and he was a misfit. (I also think it possible that John's openness about his homosexuality, still illegal until 1967, may have damaged his career to some extent, but I may be mistaken.)

CD: I guess Stravinsky's turn to serialism posed quite a challenge for composers of Lambert's generation, especially the ones taught by Boulanger and following the exemplar of both Hindemith and Stravinsky. If they felt the same imperative as Stravinsky to explore the post-war developments, it is easy to see how both sides viewed it as jumping on the bandwagon.

JA: That was John Lambert's problem, yes. The best of his music was much more than just trendy, particularly the Second String Quartet, which John wrote around the time I was studying with him, coincidentally. It's a fine piece. In fact, that was partly his reaction to a cello piece of Rădulescu, *Das Andere* (1984), which I showed him and played him – but typically for John his quartet doesn't sound anything like Rădulescu.

His isolation from the music establishment was something that was very painful to him, and occasionally that made him difficult. In later years of my study with him, he'd always want to pile me up with an envelope of his scores and I was meant to somehow promote his music to others, which I had no experience of doing. When you're 21, you can't do that. That's the only criticism I have of John, but we didn't fall out. On the contrary, he was a wonderful man and a great teacher.

He was reserved in his judgements on my music. He was never a man to throw his hat up in the air and say anyone was a genius. He thought it didn't do anyone a lot of good, and he was right. He'd be nice, encouraging, but not generally more. When the second part of *Diptych*, 'Pavillons en l'Air', was premiered at Dartington, he didn't like the first tape I brought of it. Then it was played again and he said, 'Well, I like it a bit more the second time.' It wasn't a ringing endorsement. I thought that piece had sort of slightly got somewhere and he wasn't entirely discouraging, but he said, 'Well, it's not bad.' That slightly began to change when he heard Olly [Knussen] do *Tiramisù*. He thought that was much more along the lines of what I *should* be doing. I like to think, therefore, that he would have enjoyed *Khorovod*, and he was still alive when *Khorovod* was premiered. But he was ill already in December 1994[4] and couldn't come up to London to hear it. By the time it was broadcast he had died, so he never did.

He died in March '95. He was only 66 or 67. I think he was worried that his whole life had just been wasted because, like any other composer, he wanted his

[4] The premiere was 6 December.

music to be esteemed and it wasn't. It was only just towards the last few months of his life that a CD was finally being issued of his work on NMC. I wrote the programme notes for it.[5] I was very glad I was at the recording sessions too, but John died just before it was in the shops. Still, he knew it was happening, and that gave him enormous satisfaction, plus some confidence that things had not been entirely in vain.

CD: Then you moved onto Sandy [Alexander] Goehr.

JA: Which was, by the way, exactly what John Lambert didn't want me to do, which is partly why I did it. After five years – I'd been with him two years privately and three at the Royal College – there was one place John didn't want me to go anywhere near, which was Cambridge. He didn't like the music either of Robin Holloway or Alexander Goehr. He didn't respect either of them as teachers and he was very insistent that I shouldn't go anywhere near them. By that stage, having been with John for five years, I slightly took that as a cue to do it. I felt I really needed to get away from John Lambert's world.

I applied to study with Robin, but before I was interviewed Robin phoned me and said that he was going on sabbatical to write an opera, in consequence of which I'd have to be interviewed by Alexander Goehr. I'm amazed at my chutzpah now, but I said I wouldn't. I didn't know Sandy Goehr's music very well and I didn't like what I thought he stood for. Quite rightly, Robin told me to stop talking nonsense.

I went for an interview with Goehr and found a delightfully genial and fascinating personality who looked at my scores carefully and said, 'Well, you've been very well trained, like any John Lambert pupil.' Now that was a contrast already with John, because John had been pretty negative about Sandy, whereas Sandy was very respectful and an admirer of John's qualities as a teacher.

We had a very interesting conversation, which touched on all sorts of different areas. For one part of the MPhil in Composition you had to write on a special topic. I had put down Ligeti. Goehr said, 'Oh everyone does Ligeti. Can't you think of something else?' I said, 'I didn't really want to do Ligeti, but I thought it would be more acceptable to you than what I really what to do, which is Scelsi.' Sandy said, 'That's much more interesting. I don't know anything about him.' Sandy mentioned that he'd heard, from various British aristocrats, about this strange Italian Count who composed. Also, his former publisher Howard Hartog had known Scelsi a bit, and that's all he knew. Well, after a conversation like that, where somebody had done exactly the opposite of what you thought they'd do, in all respects, and proved jolly interesting and very open to many different stylistic

---

5   John Lambert, *The Music of John Lambert, 1926–1995: Solos and Ensembles*, Anthony Aarons (trumpet), Charles Ramirez (guitar), Albion Guitar Quartet, Sounds Positive, Bingham String Quartet, David Sutton-Anderson (conductor), NMC NMC D026.

areas, you really want to study with them. So I did study with Goehr. It was one of the best decisions I ever made.

CD: When I first came in this room I like to think that if I hadn't known that you're a Goehr student, and a kind of grand-student of Messiaen, via Goehr, I'd have spotted that you were by the *Liber Usualis* on your shelf.[6]

JA: Funnily enough, there's another one there. I always brought a backup copy because I'm always lending them and was frightened of losing them as it was out of print for 30 years. Later an American company reprinted it and I bought one. Then another was in a sale in the Roman Catholic shop next to Westminster Cathedral so I bought it again to make sure I had a spare copy. Sandy put me onto plainchant. How did you realise Goehr was interested in that?

CD: He told me that Messiaen said to him, 'You're not a Catholic, but this is the cheapest pattern book you'll ever find.' He spent his however many francs it was on it, and he said Messiaen was absolutely right. He tells his own students exactly the same thing.

JA: Yes, he told me that too. By the way, when I mentioned that to John Lambert, he was thrilled because John loved line. He loved long inventive lines. He was so glad to see me studying plainchant. That's something I show my own students too and usually the result is, 'Oh my God, why didn't I see this before? It's wonderful.' Whether one likes plainsong as such or not is not the point. In fact, I do and often they end up doing so, too.

The other thing is, for example, I became quite obsessed, at one point, with *Nuper Rosarum Flores* by Dufay, the piece that was written to open Florence Cathedral. It has a double cantus firmus based on the plainsong 'Terribilis est locus iste', which, of course, was used by Messiaen in the *Transfiguration* and is the title of a movement in that work.[7] In *Nuper Rosarum Flores*, Dufay uses two transpositions of the plainsong simultaneously in a kind of slightly hocketed cantus firmus. Although I've never really used cantus firmus technique as such in any piece, most of the pieces are written as though I might have done, if that makes any sense. There's a sense in which things are being held together by a long thread, over which I improvise musically, but the thread is still there somewhere. I wrote *Khorovod* originally on one single sheet of paper as a single long line of melodic ideas: that was my long thread, which I then spent five years doing all kinds of funny things to and even erasing. It was a way of getting the

---

[6] The *Liber Usualis* is a large collection of the most commonly used plainchants in the Catholic liturgy for the Mass, Divine Office and feasts of the Church year. Depending on the edition, it comprises around 2,000 pages.

[7] 'Terribilis est locus iste' is the twelfth movement of Messiaen's oratorio *La Transfiguration de Notre-Seigneur, Jésus-Christ* (1965–69). The text is from Genesis 28:17.

whole concept of the piece, its moods and tensions, onto paper in one single sitting. I got that way of working from studying plainsong.

In addition, at Cambridge I was able to visit Robin Holloway a few times when he wasn't busy with his opera or away. I didn't show him my music, but he played me what he was composing (this was the first time a composer had been willing to show me how they composed in such detail, and it was a thrill), plus we'd play each other CDs or tapes of the latest music we'd heard. He was wonderful company and that was the start of a long friendship.

CD: Did you study with Tristan Murail privately?

JA: Yes: he wasn't teaching anywhere officially at that time. I first heard the name on Radio France in early 1981, but although I heard Grisey on Radio France then I don't recall any Murail. The London Sinfonietta did an excellent piece, *Mémoire/ Erosion*, in autumn 1981. The piece is quite simple: it's really based on pulse, or the gradual distortion of periodicity. It doesn't use many microtones or the techniques which made him famous, but with simple means he creates a very distinctive atmosphere. The harmony and instrumentation are acutely heard and imagined. I made a point of trying to seek out further stuff and eventually, after about a year, I came across an orchestral piece called *Gondwana*, which is still one of his most famous works. That was played to me by George Benjamin, whom I'd since met. I'd heard something else in between on French radio – I discovered I could receive French radio over FM, because our house was on a hill. I remember hearing *Gondwana* and being very impressed and slightly puzzled that there wasn't more fuss about him here.

CD: Even in 1989, which was when I got the CD of *Gondwana*, I remember not understanding why he didn't appear to be part of the conversation except as a footnote to Messiaen.

JA: I wrote the programme notes for that CD by the way... Around the early '80s, too, I used to read *Perspectives of New Music* in the Central Music Library near Victoria Street. They had Denys Bouliane's huge report on Murail and Grisey doing big sessions at Darmstadt in 1980.[8] That report is still one of the best introductions to spectral theory in English. The fact that it was so very early is pretty amazing. It was a very thorough account of Grisey's treatise on time and various theoretical precepts that Murail and he had set out that year over about two weeks. Clearly it had made a huge impact in Darmstadt, the irony being that Darmstadt was, of course, the home of serialism and that spectral music got its international launching pad between 1978 and 1984 really at Darmstadt also. That's a fact that's often forgotten.

---

[8]   LeBaron and Bouliane, 'Darmstadt 1980'.

The Paris music scene after Boulez's departure in 1966 became a little bit closed, in the sense that what was going on there didn't travel abroad so much. This is true internationally – there was suddenly less communication. It was a very interesting period musically in Paris, and I've written about that in articles, but it didn't communicate that well with the outside world. It rather expected the outside world to show an interest in it.

CD: Perhaps Paris hadn't adjusted to no longer being the cultural capital of the world after World War II.

JA: This was true of painting as well as music. Anyhow, a schism developed which still obtains. There was a sort of Anglo-American axis, which could sometimes connect up with Holland and Scandinavia, but a sort of schism developed between that area of contemporary music and France, Germany and Italy, who operate on a quite different circuit. To this day, there are not many people interested in both circuits. I was always interested in both, simply because it didn't seem very sensible not to be, given that they were nearby geographically. Above all, I liked the sounds of what I heard on both circuits.

Having enjoyed things on record, I visited Amsterdam in 1986 and heard some Hague composers live on that visit – I heard a concert with an early performance of Andriessen's *De Stijl*, also some music by de Bondt and others. When I went to Darmstadt in 1988, there were very few young British composers there. I later discovered from the clarinettist Roger Heaton, who had been as a player to Darmstadt in 1980, that the only British composer he encountered there was James MacMillan. I don't know what MacMillan ever made of that visit. He would have encountered both [Brian] Ferneyhough and Gérard Grisey at length in Darmstadt – both were teaching for a whole week there. As far as one can tell, it didn't affect MacMillan's music in any direct way, but I should like to ask him about that. It is historically interesting that he was present.

One knew that there was this other kind of music developing in Paris. It didn't have a name then because the article by Hugues Dufourt that gave it the name 'spectral music' was not widely distributed.[9] (Finally, in the mid-'90s, people started using that term.) Anyhow, the long and short of it was that, except for that article by Bouliane – where the term 'spectral' is never mentioned – there was no other way of my finding out how this music was being composed, or even hearing very much of it. Murail was played here a certain amount through George Benjamin's advocacy. Grisey was not, nor was Dufourt, nor Lévinas, nor Rădulescu, nor Vivier.

---

[9] Hugues Dufourt, 'Musique spectrale: pour une pratique des formes de l'énergie', *Bicéphale*, No. 3 (1981), 85–89.

So I went to Paris in 1987 for some time, not only to hear that music, but really to study it. I studied privately with Murail, briefly – a little over three months. I'd saved up money doing odd jobs after I left school in order to fund this and I got some assistance from home as well. It wasn't like the lessons I had with John Lambert or, later, Sandy Goehr. I specifically said to Murail, 'I want to study your and Grisey's techniques.' I just wanted an A to Z of that as it then existed and that's what I got. We met roughly three times every two weeks for about two hours a session. I was there some of March, then back in April, May, June. I was able to learn most of what had happened in the previous eight or ten years. It was still all relatively new and I've still got the notes I made on all that.

One thing that concerned me was that, although I'd already been studying nearly two years with John Lambert then, and I'd been guzzling scores of various sorts since I was about 10 or 11 and had written orchestral pieces, I'd never had any conventional training in orchestration. One thing I realised very early on in examining scores like *Gondwana* or Grisey's *Partiels* very closely was that I needed to study orchestration more thoroughly by itself. I felt I didn't even really know enough about it in terms of Debussy or Ravel, although I knew their music well. So I was spending most of my spare time of those months, when I wasn't composing or digesting what Murail was teaching me and going to other events at IRCAM[10] or wherever, in the library of the Pompidou Centre and the CDMC[11] – the French music information centre which is still a marvellous place – going over the minutest details in orchestral scores, either traditional or contemporary, teaching myself how to orchestrate.

Murail would say, 'If you've studied the orchestration of Debussy and then Messiaen, you can understand how we orchestrate.' But I hadn't studied those things properly. I had studied serial technique very thoroughly, I even knew a bit about chord multiplication, and rotation, tropes, etc. I'd studied other techniques, and I'd done traditional harmony and counterpoint, and some analysis. I'd also investigated chance operations and stuff, but clearly traditional orchestration skills needed further serious study and that was when I did it.

CD: A reflection perhaps of the Germanic basis of our training in the UK, emphasising pitch and being sniffy about the French interest in the sound and colour of the music. Anyway, did Murail teach you orchestration?

JA: Not as such, but he helpfully recommended Charles Koechlin's *Treatise on Orchestration*,[12] which he admired strongly. I knew Koechlin's *Les Bandar-Log*, but had no idea he'd written this huge treatise. I bought a second-hand copy and

---

[10]   Institut de Recherche et Coordination Acoustique/Musique, the Paris-based institute for scientific and artistic research into music and sound.
[11]   Centre de Documentation de la Musique Contemporaine.
[12]   Charles Koechlin, *Traité de l'orchestration*, 4 vols (Paris: Max Eschig, 1954–59).

devoured it: an amazing, inventive book, extraordinarily wide-ranging. It already quoted from Bartók's *Music for Strings, Percussion and Celesta* and Schoenberg's *Erwartung* in loving detail – surely the first time they were cited in such a book. It's still full of remarkable orchestration ideas, many from Koechlin's own works, and I'm astonished it's never been translated into English. It's one of the very best of its kind.

The trouble with spectral music for me was the melodic aspect, which was almost nil. The only way of creating melody was to sort of shine a torch up and down a chord, a spectrum, and that didn't strike me as an entirely satisfactory way of creating melodic ideas – though to be fair one should add that precisely that type of arpeggiation is often used in traditional Western melodies, but not usually on its own. That left me with a problem, as I was realising melody was very important to my music. I'd grown up listening to Schubert, for goodness' sake!

The complication here is that by the age of 16, under the influence of a number of pieces including Messiaen's *La Transfiguration* – a wonderfully rich score which is still my favourite of all his works – Olly Knussen's Third Symphony, Murail's *Gondwana*, some Michael Finnissy, some Vivier and a whole load of other things, I had reacted very strongly against serialism. That attitude was encouraged when I went to Paris and mixed with the spectral crowd. They were incredibly dismissive of serialism. It was another example of the younger lot wanting to overthrow the older lot. By the way, I didn't then enjoy the later melodic pieces of Stockhausen, which could have helped me. I later came to them through Vivier's work, and now I like them very much, especially *Trans* and *Inori*, but then they were a closed book to me.

When I got back to Britain and studied at the Royal College of Music, I began to realise that there was a lot about the previous era, the serial music of the '50s and '60s, that I hadn't really understood. I'd spend quite a lot of time studying and listening to *Kontra-Punkte* or *Pli selon pli* and learnt a lot more from them, but I felt odd doing it. I'd been told that that era was finished and that that technique was over, and that we had to sort of chuck it really. That was another one of those useful complications that meant what I was learning in Paris was not as myopic as it might have been. I remember at one point saying to a spectralist that I'd been very struck by hearing *Kontra-Punkte* of Stockhausen. He just shrugged his shoulders. It wasn't in their world.

I didn't at that time know Hugues Dufourt, which I wish I had done, because Hugues, whom I now know quite well, was trained serially. He studied with Jacques Guyonnet, who was in Boulez's Basel composition classes. Guyonnet's a Swiss composer and as far as I understand it, he taught Dufourt the Boulezian techniques. Dufourt made this interesting fusion between that and something which became spectral theory and aesthetic. If I had got to know him in the late '80s, I might have been able to make more sense of my ambivalence about the aesthetics and techniques of serial and spectral music. On the other hand, Hugues Dufourt's music is almost entirely harmonic, which is fine for his work, but perhaps not for me. I still like reading his writings because he had a double training in philosophy and music. He's a very thoughtful and stimulating writer. His article about spectral music, the defining article, doesn't name anyone. It's not a history of that music.

CD: Oh, I hadn't thought of that.

JA: It doesn't even name Ligeti. I think it mentions Monet or something. That's quite typical of him. It talks about certain problems to do with the way that music was evolving, but it does not name any names at all. Which, by the way, is more or less in the tradition of Boulez articles as well, after a certain date anyway – they never named anybody he was criticising. At the same time as studying with Murail I was attending Boulez's lectures at the Collège de France. It was pretty incredible that you could go and hear Boulez for three hours twice a week – at the Collège de France and there was a Saturday afternoon session at IRCAM. I met a lot of young composers there. Also, IRCAM offered free seminars by some pretty distinguished people. I remember on a previous visit I had heard Messiaen analyse *Chronochromie*. Well, you know, you just walk in off the street and hear Messiaen analysing *Chronochromie* – that's pretty amazing! I heard Kaija Saariaho, who analysed her new IRCAM commission *Io*. Lachenmann gave a seminar, Berio, and Marco Stroppa. I had a big argument with Stroppa about music notation, which was great fun. It started up a firm friendship. It was a lovely range of composers. If you could sit there and ask intelligent questions they were perfectly happy for you to be there – it was open to anyone. It was also relatively open aesthetically. Later I heard Steve Reich do a talk there and stuff, but nobody from Britain, except George Benjamin and Jonathan Harvey. When I came back to Britain, I really missed all that, hugely.

There was also an IRCAM analysis course run by Robert Piencikowski, who is now a Boulez expert in Basel. He analysed [Lachenmann's] *Mouvement (-vor der Erstarrung)* for about eight weeks, twice a week in May and June 1987. Also Berio's *Coro*, both of which were in the repertoire of the music season. The point was that those analysis courses, which again were absolutely free, were always calibrated to the repertoire of the EIC[13] or IRCAM. It really was the icing on the cake after eight or ten weeks spent trying to understand *Mouvement (-vor der Erstarrung)* when you went and heard a performance at the concerts of the EIC, for whom it was written, conducted by Peter Eötvös to whom it is dedicated. Then the following day Lachenmann gave a three-hour seminar and you could ask him questions.

---

[13] Ensemble InterContemporain, a new-music ensemble founded by Boulez.

This was pretty heady stuff. I was just 20. It was a great way of getting past the tinkly surfaces, rolling up your sleeves and finding out what's going on in a score. I learnt a huge amount from that. I also went to IRCAM's seminars on computer music, which I couldn't entirely understand, but at least one could see some of the demonstrations of what the computers were doing and what was possible at the time. I suppose I spent the next 10 years digesting all that. Plus digesting the other problems that I've said I'd encountered before I left, like what to do about all the Boulez, Stockhausen repertoire between '50 and '75 roughly. In parallel, I investigated what was going on in British music, which led me to a very detailed study of Oliver Knussen's music, to which I felt especially close. I wanted to know how things were made, and the many years spent studying Knussen were hugely educative for observing how a marvellous composer puts music together very intricately.

CD: You also attended summer courses taught by Messiaen and by Nørgård?

JA: Messiaen was the same year as the Paris visit – it was just after that in July 1987. I went back to Britain for two weeks and then went straight over to Avignon. The Messiaen course was really ending the whole Paris experience, which was a very nice way to end it. I had, as you know, met him already through George Benjamin so I could go up and ask the odd question. In any case he'd always stay behind and was not remote, he was very friendly to everyone.

I remember us discussing George Benjamin's *Antara*, which premiered during my Paris period earlier that year, and Messiaen kept saying, 'I don't understand how he writes so many microtones.' That's the only piece in which Benjamin has ever done this, and it's done with great flair. Finally, I said to Messiaen, 'He's got two electronic keyboards tuned a quarter-tone apart, and he tests everything on them.' I'm certain George Benjamin had already told him that, but apparently he'd not understood. Then he said, 'Oh, perhaps I should do that if I ever want to use quarter-tones.' Then he reminisced a bit about the Russian microtonalist Wyschnegradsky, whom he'd known well. Little comments like that were fascinating to hear.

CD: Of course, that's the time he was emerging from his post-*Saint François* slump and was looking for new ways forward, so it's possible he really was contemplating using microtones. After all, he'd briefly dabbled in them in the late '30s.

JA: I believe he had just finished *Un Vitrail et des oiseaux*. It's possible he might have tried to use microtones for his birdsongs... In any case it quickly became ·clear that Messiaen was well aware of what Murail was doing, in particular – he followed his work closely.

I remember in Avignon, Messiaen analysed *Chronochromie* again, and I have to say it was more or less the same, except it was about three times as long. What we were being given was his treatise on rhythm.[14] He was basically reading it out, but then he embellished. The embellishments were the real thing because he'd head off somewhere else and start talking about whether or not one needed to organise music so carefully and what the pros and cons of it were. That's where you really got into something interesting. Then discussions and questions would go across the floor and that was great.

In the skylark sections in the 'Antistrophe' of *Chronochromie*, I never understood what the keyboard glockenspiel was doing, because there's a counterpoint on keyboard glockenspiel above the 'Skylark' passages. Messiaen never said anything about that. I said to him, 'What's that? Is that another bird?' He said, 'It's just decoration. It pleases me to have this decoration there. I thought just having the three xylos was getting a bit boring so I put some decoration on top.' I was very struck by that because I was used to Messiaen saying, and you know it from the scores, 'This is that.' Everything has a little arrow saying what it is, how it was written. It was obviously the bits that didn't have arrows that I wanted to know something about. That little moment I thought, 'Oh, in other words he's composing, he's using his creative imagination.' He didn't have much to say about it, it was just something he liked to put against it and thought it needed that. The fact that he bothered to put it there I thought was interesting because almost every other occasion when Messiaen uses the trinity of xylos, he doesn't do that, and isn't that also the first time he used the trinity of xylos? It's as if the first time he invented that sound he didn't think it could carry enough musically, so he had to have something else going over it, a nice little bit of counterpoint. Little things like that. The fact you could just walk up to Messiaen and ask such things was wonderful. I could have spent several years wondering why that was there. Messiaen was as free with his material as anybody else would be, but he never gives that impression in his treatises.

CD: No, nor in the conversations. He gives the impression that the music appeared in pre-destined form on tablets of stone.

JA: Exactly. So the Messiaen course was about two weeks in Avignon, and I was able to sit in on Loriod's piano class a little bit as a listener. I also attended Jeanne Loriod's ondes Martenot class a bit and was able to have a little half-hour lesson with her on the ondes, which was amusing because I got the hang of it quite quickly and she said I should consider studying it. I had the rather grim vision of myself spending 40 years wailing away in front of an orchestra with

---

[14] Olivier Messiaen, *Traité de rythme, de couleur et d'ornithologie*, 8 vols (Paris: Alphonse Leduc, 1994–2002).

this Art Deco monster and thought, 'I *can't!*' I quite liked the instrument, but it's a period piece. It's in a rather curious situation because it has to be used for those Messiaen pieces and Honegger's *Joan of Arc at the Stake*. As far as I know, internationally those are the only pieces that are regular rep, along with the Jolivet Concerto.[15] There's a lot of other French pieces that are not played outside France, like that whole repertoire for ondes sextet such as Roger Tessier's fine piece *Hexade*. As *Hexade* vividly shows, the trouble with the ondes is that no synthesiser or synthetic mechanism has managed to do what it does. We're stuck with this thing. Theoretically we should all be writing for it, because it's clearly going to be around and it's very versatile, but I don't want to write for it for the simple reason that, although there's a lot of other things it does that Messiaen never uses, just finding somebody to play it adds so much to the costs. As I said before, you do like people to hear pieces. One could write a companion piece to *Turangalîla*, but I'm not sure *Turangalîla* needs one.

CD: The [*Trois petites*] *Liturgies* maybe.

JA: Yes, possibly.

CD: *Saint François*, well probably not!

JA: No!

CD: A little five-minute prelude to the opera!

[Laughter]

JA: When I was a postgrad student at Cambridge, Thomas Adès wanted to do the Messiaen *Liturgies*, which I don't think had ever been played in Cambridge. From the Messiaen course I knew Jacques Tchamkerten[16] and I got him to come over. We managed to find some money to get him. I wrote an ondes Martenot solo piece for him, which he may still have. I wrote it in two days and gave him the manuscript so there is an ondes Martenot monody by me somewhere, which would be a little like some of the melodic writing in *Khorovod*, on which I was then working.

CD: Funnily enough, the ondes started getting an afterlife in the last few years through the pop side of things, with Jonny Greenwood.

---

[15] Since this conversation took place, Thomas Adès has used ondes Martenot in his opera *The Exterminating Angel*.

[16] Ondes Martenot player and author of 'From *Fête des Belles Eaux* to *Saint François d'Assise*: the evolution of the writing for ondes Martenot in the music of Olivier Messiaen', in Christopher Dingle and Nigel Simeone, *Olivier Messiaen: Music, Art and Literature* (Aldershot: Ashgate, 2007), pp. 63–78.

JA: It's true, he has given it a considerable boost.

CD: In Canada they are producing a new instrument, L'Ondea, which apparently will certainly be cheaper than an ondes.

JA: The ondes are now being made again in Paris, because the patent lapsed, but they are terribly expensive.

CD: They are doing something similar in Canada. There's a fascinating film, *Le Chant des Ondes*,[17] where it becomes clear that one of the difficult things is the *touche*, which has this leather bag full of material, but it was a secret formula.

JA: I know, because Monsieur Manière wouldn't tell anyone what this substance inside the *touche* was.

CD: The film shows it being reconstructed by one of the old workers from the ondes workshop.

JA: Have they discovered what's in the sack or not?

CD: Yes, they've got the formula, but what's great about it is that it's unpredictable, it's never the same twice.

JA: Interesting. Perhaps that would account for why, whenever I've heard Tristan [Murail] play the ondes, it always sounds quite different from Jeanne Loriod playing it. You know Tristan Murail is one of the reasons I got interested in the ondes Martenot, because he and his wife, Françoise Pellié, are both ondes Martenot players. I think that's how they met, because they were playing keyboards in the electronic sub-group of Ensemble L'Itinéraire. They played many other synthesisers as well, but ondes were included. For instance, Hugues Dufourt's *Saturne*, which is a classic of the '70s L'Itinéraire repertoire, has two ondes Martenots but the players of the ondes Martenots in *Saturne* play about 10 other synthesisers each.

CD: Aside from the Messiaen, which other summer courses left a mark?

JA: I applied to study with Per Nørgård at Dartington in 1990 because he was a great composer and teacher. There had been a kind of spree of Danish contemporary music on BBC Radio in about '86, with all sorts of Danish composers introducing their and other people's work, like Hans Abrahamsen and Karl Aage Rasmussen. I'd also heard a long interview with Nørgård on the radio around then and I found him a very interesting and sympathetic character. In 1988, by

---

[17]   Caroline Martel (director), *Le Chant des Ondes* (Les Films du Paradoxe, 2012), DVD EDV 311. NB: Shown in anglophone countries under the title *Wavemakers*.

accident when I was in Sweden, I came across the recording of his pioneering work *Voyage into the Golden Screen*, which didn't feature in the BBC's Danish series. I'd never even heard of it. The second movement is his infinity series piece which eventually led to his Second Symphony. I was not at that stage that interested in the infinity series. What gripped me was the first movement of *Voyage of the Golden Screen*, which is two superimposed Justly tuned overtone spectra a quarter-tone apart with retuned strings, which is sort of like harmonic Scelsi in a way. It was written just after some of those Scelsi pieces – such as *Anahit* or the Fourth String Quartet – which of course Nørgård didn't know because no one knew Scelsi then. It's astonishingly prescient – very beautiful and an amazing sound. I thought anyone who'd written that must be a fascinating guy, so I applied.

Meanwhile, in early '89 I had written two articles for a French musical journal called *Entretemps*.[18] One was a history of spectral music, which was the first really historical article, because as I said, the Dufourt article didn't do that. I tried to give a historical genealogy through to the late twentieth century. The other article was on Murail's style, some technical things to do with ring modulation, harmony and acceleration patterns and so on. I worked very hard at those with the help of a couple of computer friends, because the acceleration and deceleration curves are logarithmic. It's quite a complicated maths so I needed help with that. In the historical article, I tried to draw attention to the Romanian spectralists like Rădulescu and Niculescu, parallel figures like Eötvös, Barlow, Maiguashca, Vivier, Grosskopf, etc. Above all, I made a big claim for the Per Nørgård *Voyage into the Golden Screen*, which dates from 1968–69, as being the first piece of spectral music. One of the main things about spectral music was about applying electronic-type techniques and effects and aesthetics to purely instrumental music. The year before *Voyage into the Golden Screen*, Per Nørgård had done an electronic piece called *The Enchanted Forest*, which does exactly the same thing – the synthetic piling up of spectra – but with sine-tones. You get beats all the time and he thought this might be more interesting on instruments. Then he composed the first movement of *Voyage into the Golden Screen*, which I think was done as early as 1968. The second movement, the infinite row one, was done in 1969 and the piece was premiered that year. I think that Horațiu Rădulescu would have been very angry with me because he always made the claim that he was the first ever spectral composer. Apropos of that, by the way, the first Romanian piece of spectral music that I've come across – there may be an earlier one – was by Octavian Nemescu and dates from 1967. It was a piece for chorus and orchestra called *Four Dimensions of Time*,[19] which lasts

[18] 'Dans le contexte', *Entretemps* 8 (1989), 13–23; 'De Sables à Vues aériennes: Le développement d'un style', *Entretemps* 8 (1989), 123–37.

[19] *Four Dimensions in Time – IV*, 'Illuminations', for mixed chorus, orchestra and tape.

about 15 minutes. It is simply an overtone series on C, up to about the 45th harmonic or so, in normal tuning, no microtones, but with a lot of filtering, *glissandi* of harmonics, mutes, harmon mutes filtering the sound in the trumpets and trombones, plus changing vowel shapes in the chorus. The chorus part is interesting because that piece must have been written in ignorance of *Stimmung*, which was premiered the following year.[20] So Nemescu's is also quite a prescient piece. But the matter of historical priority is of no importance: they're all good composers and that's what matters. Nemescu's best piece of this sort is a tape work called *Natural* from 1973, which is a powerful study in gradual growth and change. (You can hear it nowadays on YouTube.)

In any case, I felt that the Nørgård *Voyage* was really the first piece that could be said to be applying acoustic research on instrumental music in a deliberate way to make you change your perception of timbre, which is one way of summing up what the spectral thing was about.

So I went to study with Nørgård at Dartington for a fortnight, and I wasn't disappointed. He was a wonderful lecturer on both his music and traditional repertoire: he gave fascinating, quirkily perceptive analyses of Bach, Schubert and Chopin, as well as brilliant seminars on his own work and that of Abrahamsen. I brought along the French book [*Entretemps*] to Dartington in 1990 and showed him my article mentioning *Voyage*. We got on personally very well. He was quite critical of my music in a rather similar way to John Lambert. He always felt that it didn't reach the point – that it sort of always drew back when it was just getting somewhere. I was writing both *Khorovod* and the *Diptych* at that time and that particularly helped me finish the *Diptych*, which I did shortly after.

CD: He was encouraging you to be fully yourself.

JA: In effect, yes, to be more strongly defined and clear. That really helped. Usefully, and generously, Nørgård got Dartington to commission me to write an orchestral piece for the following year. I was about to compose the second movement of the *Diptych*, 'Pavillons en l'Air', so I made it first in a chamber orchestra version for them, because I really needed to hear that. Diego Masson conducted it, and then I reworked it for full orchestra.

Nørgård and I stayed in touch after and he got me to Denmark in early 1991 to do lectures on spectral music, because he hadn't really known about the spectral movement at all and thought the Danish students would find this useful. He was intrigued by meeting this guy who had put a piece of his that was very important in his output into a context of a European music stream that he hadn't known or had anything to do with. He was fascinated to see that there was a link.

[20]   9 December 1968, Paris.

When I played Murail the *Voyage* he absolutely agreed with me and said immediately that this is the start of it all, but they didn't know it. He was quite astonished, so was Grisey. They sort of adopted the piece. I don't think to this day that the spectral composers are that interested in much else of Per Nørgård's music, which I regret, but I've noticed among younger spectralists, and younger composers generally, that the first movement of *Voyage* is something of a reference point now. If I had any role in putting it there I'm proud, because it's a very good piece. It sometimes helps Nørgård become better known in mainland Europe than he would otherwise have been. Ultimately his output will break through, but it still hasn't done the way it deserves.

CD: And how about meeting Ligeti?

JA: The Ligeti encounter was due to an unusual circumstance at the Bartók seminar in Szombathely, Hungary, in summer 1990. They announced that Ligeti would teach composition. I'd heard terrifying stories about what Ligeti was like. I didn't think he'd take me for his class in Hamburg. I'd done harmony and counterpoint, but he expected people to have done eight-part invertible counterpoint for years and years. The standard of technical traditional training that he expected was way beyond anything that I'd ever done. I'd done sixteenth-century counterpoint up to four or five parts, with cantus firmus or not, and I had done two- and three-part invention and fugue. Not very well, but I did it. But Ligeti required far more than that – like Boulanger, incredibly old style. So I didn't even bother ever applying to Hamburg because I just thought he'd say no.

I went to the Szombathely course in 1990, came into the teaching room and found that there were 100 other young composers in the room also. I thought, 'What is going to happen?' We waited. Then Ligeti came and said, 'I'm looking for the composition class', and we said, 'That's us', and he said, 'What, all of you?' 'Yes.' 'Oh my God, I was told I'd have 10 people! What am I going to do?' So, for the first session he simply gave an impromptu, and I must say fascinating, seminar on the aesthetics of composing – he was very playful, very lively. He talked about the difference between, as he put it, 'emotive composing' which he said was Schoenberg, and 'un-emotive composing' which was Stravinsky – objective composing versus subjective, that kind of thing. This was nothing very unusual as a concept, but the way he elaborated it was very fascinating, witty and unusual. I thought, 'Oh good, this is going to be fun' – I was learning a great deal.

CD: And, as with any composer talking about their fellow composers, it presumably revealed much about him alongside the insights into Schoenberg and Stravinsky.

JA: I felt he was really describing himself all the time, yes. The Ensemble Modern was in residence with Peter Eötvös, and they were meant to be playing pieces of ours which we'd sent in advance. It became clear that there were far more pieces to play than could be played in the workshops with them. I was about to have a piece of mine played in front of Ligeti by the Ensemble Modern with Eötvös, to the extent that Eötvös had already called out how he was going to subdivide each bar and everything and he had marked up the score. Then Ligeti suddenly said, 'This schedule is totally impossible. If anyone has a cassette of their piece, please can you withdraw it from the workshops.' I put my hand up because this piece had been played at the Royal College. He said, 'Right, tomorrow morning we'll listen to it.' A practical workshop on the piece would have been very useful, but I was not sure a consultation with Ligeti on my music was a good idea.

I was soon proved right. It became very clear – because he kept turning pages well ahead of the tape – that he didn't like it at all. At the end he just shut the score and said, 'I have nothing to say.' He turned to his assistant on the course who was Manfred Stahnke, and said, 'Do you have anything to say?' Stahnke, in a very awkward position, just said, 'No.' Ligeti said to me, 'Do you have anything to say?' And I said, 'Look, I've come here at considerable inconvenience and you certainly do have something to say about this, even if it's something unpleasant. I think I'd better hear it.' Ligeti said, 'Alright. You have a very good technique and you hear what you write and all that, but it's totally boring.' The piece I played him was more or less a derivative mixture of second-hand Murail, Boulez and George Benjamin.

He continued, 'There's something funny going on because as a person you've got a lot of character and I like your impertinence very much. But I don't like your music. You're obviously a quirky person, but the music is not.' He just kept saying, 'I think you need to ask yourself why you are doing this.' I realised this, finally, was just what I needed to hear. I thought he was being a bit blanket condemnatory of most young composers, because we'd seen enough by then to know that's what he did. Nevertheless, I was very impressed by what he told me. After that, I spent some months going over both the *Diptych* and what I'd written of *Khorovod*, and I shaved them of extraneous stuff that didn't really belong there. It helped me hone my music. He said 'be ruthless' and I was. And I still am. I got the message. What he was really saying, which Sandy Goehr also subsequently said, was, in effect, 'You're on your own. You can compose but it's up to you to find out what to do now and I can't tell you.' Sandy's attitude was, and I think still is, that if a young composer doesn't know what music to compose, he was certainly not going to tell them. I believe that too. So from then, yes, I was on my own.

Figure 2   Dancers from the Rambert Dance Company in *The Comedy of Change*,
2009, choreography by Mark Baldwin, photograph by Tristram Kenton

Conversation Four

Dance

Dance is of fundamental importance to Anderson, and should not be overlooked as a factor in any of his pieces. After briefly noting the importance of ballet in his formative years, this conversation explores Anderson's early collaborations with choreographers, from being paired with Adam Cooper on his first day at the Royal College of Music to the first project with Mark Baldwin, *Towards Poetry*, which featured Darcey Bussell as soloist. The status of music in the dance world, the openness of dance audiences to new music and the potential value of dance for composers are discussed before moving on to works by Nijinsky (along with the negative attitudes of Debussy and Stravinsky), Ashton and MacMillan, as well as ballets to key modernist classics, such as *Le Marteau sans maître*. Anderson's work with Mark Baldwin is explored at some length, with detailed information on *The Comedy of Change* in particular, revealing along the way the extent of Anderson's love of birdsong.

CD: Ballet has been very important for you. At what point did you first work with dance in mind, which isn't necessarily the same as your first piece written for dancing?

JA: In fact in my case it's very much not the same thing. That comes from two things, both of them background issues. One is that my dad had a record of *The Rite of Spring* and also used to play things like *Polovtsian Dances* and *Scheherazade*, which, though it wasn't originally a ballet, was made into one.

CD: The wonderful Ballets Russes version.

JA: Yes. There was a lot of that Russian music, and also the great Tchaikovsky ballets and so on. This was the first music I heard, so it comes partly from that.

It comes also from the fact that my mother and stepfather were very keen ballet fans. They used to go to ballet and modern dance a lot and took me and the rest of the family along sometimes. From the age of about 10 onwards I saw lots of modern dance and ballet. I was very lucky. I became very aware, even as a kid, that I was thinking of music in terms of movement, that I needed sometimes even to move when I was composing, to dance to what I was doing, physically, although I'm not a dancer. There are two ways I hear music. One is physically, in that sense – I don't want to use the word rhythmically, because as I say, it's a very physical thing, in terms of dance – and the other is in terms of line, or melody, if you prefer.

John Drummond spotted the dance elements in my music when he heard *Khorovod* and put me together with the choreographer Mark Baldwin, so clearly it struck Drummond as a typical feature of my music.[1] A lot of contemporary composers don't seem to go to ballet and don't show any interest in it. The other day I mentioned to a composer friend that I'd been looking at a DVD of Ashton's *Symphonic Variations*. I was disappointed to find the composer with whom I was talking didn't know who Ashton was or that he'd made a ballet of Franck's *Symphonic Variations*. In dance terms, that's a bit like saying, 'I didn't know there was a composer called Beethoven who'd written a Fifth Symphony.' *Symphonic Variations* is absolutely right up there with Beethoven's Fifth, as is Balanchine's *Agon*, which I saw at the age of 12 for the first time and had a devastating impact. I'd never heard the piece before, so you can imagine the impact of both Stravinsky's music and Balanchine's dance together, both of them new to me. I was just in a daze for weeks after. This extraordinary clarity and brightness, matched with this set of sounds I never knew an orchestra could make – 'What was that twanging?' and so on. Things I now know were flute harmonics combined with three cellos and the bass, all kind of weird things – wonderful.

CD: So which was your first dance work?

JA: I didn't realise when I went to study with John Lambert he was very involved in dance. For the first two years I studied with him privately the subject did not come up. All that changed on the first day of my studies at the Royal College which was unbelievable, a day I will never forget. I think there was an aural class at the start, then harmony and counterpoint, history and so on. I had a composition lesson with Lambert, then a piano class, then my initiation into the electronics studio. All in one day, it was just amazing. Then, at the end of the day, we had to go to Talgarth Road to the Royal Ballet School to start working with a whole load of choreographers who were about to take A Level dance and

[1]   John Drummond (1934–2006) spent much of his career at the BBC, including as Controller of Radio 3 and Director of the Proms. He also spent a period as Director of the Edinburgh International Festival.

go into the profession. We had to provide music for their dances. That was the first dance piece I ever composed. The choreographer was Adam Cooper, who became famous later as the Swan in Matthew Bourne's *Swan Lake*, and I think he still does some choreography. Anyway, we were originally going to do a piece on Graham Greene's story, *May We Borrow Your Husband?* which is about bisexuality, with two gay men seducing a married man – his idea, not mine. That didn't really work and we did a purely abstract ballet with an electronic score, so I combined the electronic course with the dance problem. That meant that every week I could bring along the piece, as far as I'd got, and his dancers could dance to it. Occasionally he'd say, 'Look, I just cannot work with that sound. I've tried. I've taken the tape home and I don't know what to do.' Then I'd show him something else and he'd say, 'I can work with that', so there was some give and take. That piece lasted about seven or eight minutes. It all took about nine months and was a very interesting experience. It was a violent electronic score called *Saison en enfer* after the Rimbaud, and it was a pretty violent dance, as I recall. It didn't work without dance so I left it where it was.

CD: That was in your first year at the RCM. Did you do any other dance pieces as a student?

JA: No, I didn't do any more dance until 1994–95, when I did a ballet, which was withdrawn, called *Three Parts Off the Ground* with a dancer called Sarah Matthews. Our collaboration, through neither of our fault, didn't quite work. The dance was performed just once, it was not a success and I withdrew the score, but it was another useful experience. It was good working with her, nevertheless. Then, virtually the month after that, John Drummond put me together with Mark Baldwin, with whom I've worked on and off ever since, though there have been other choreographers with whom I've also collaborated very happily.

CD: So how many ballets have you done with Mark Baldwin?

JA: The first was an extension of *Poetry Nearing Silence* in a longer version for tour by the Royal Ballet, and it was called *Towards Poetry*.[2] The original idea behind that was that there were, at that time, two amazing principals of the Royal Ballet. One was Darcey Bussell and the other was Deborah Bull. They're very different dancers, but they were also being portrayed a little bit as rivals, so Mark's idea was that we should have a little fight between them. I wrote music for all that, and then it turned out that the tour of the Royal Ballet was splitting into two parts and going simultaneously around the country – Deborah Bull was on one team and Darcey Bussell was on the other. So it was finally staged differently. And who could complain – I got Darcey Bussell! Once I knew Darcey was in the

---

[2]   See Conversation Six for discussion of *Poetry Nearing Silence*.

cast I wrote her a violin solo concertante movement, which I added in just before I submitted the score and we had a very brilliant solo by her. What a fabulous dancer to work with. That was wonderful because the piece was played about 20 times, with really good audiences. Richard Bernas, who I'd always admired for his ensemble Music Projects, was conducting and we got on very well. The Royal Ballet liked it enough to bring it to the main stage the following year. So it was done again in London for about seven performances.

At the rehearsals for one of those, Mark said, 'Alright, what's our next one?' I'd had the idea for years of doing something based on the phrases of the radio in Cocteau's film *Orphée*, so I said, 'Well, I'd like to do a piece called *The Bird Sings With its Fingers*.' I didn't need to explain anything to him. He immediately said, 'Done.' The next one after that, some years later, was *The Comedy of Change*, and he also choreographed my viola solo piece *Prayer*. There was one other one he did as well. Anyway, it was about five collaborations.

CD: How about *Khorovod*, given that's very much to do with dance?

JA: Mark Baldwin's never done it, but *Khorovod*'s been done by several other choreographers and that was a very interesting experience because I originally had hoped it would be a dance piece. I like seeing it choreographed, but the problem is it's already about dance explicitly.

CD: So it's the problem Diaghilev had with Ravel's *La Valse*, saying that it's a portrait of dance, but it's not a dance piece.

JA: *Khorovod* is so berserk that it's a problem getting any live dance to compete with that. One of the best versions I saw was one where the choreographer later told me she had problems choreographing the penultimate section, the 'Rave'. She had them all suddenly run off at this huge explosion, and the stage was just left with this gyrating orchestra. Gradually they came on again towards the end of it and the dance took over again. I thought that was very striking dramatically, but there are many ways of doing it.

CD: Are there other pieces you'd like to see danced?

JA: *Stations of the Sun* is one. When Andrea Quinn was chief conductor of the Royal Ballet, she was planning to try and introduce them to it. It didn't happen for various reasons, not least because she left the Royal Ballet quite soon afterwards. That piece is very much dance-imbued, but it's difficult for me to single out a piece of mine that isn't.

CD: You said before that very few composers seem in tune with dance. I wonder whether part of that is to do with a perceived disconnect between the role of the music and that of the dance, a lower status for the music. If you're working in an opera then it's essentially the composer's opera. If you're working in ballet or dance, quite often it's difficult even to find out who the composer is.

JA: Yes, looking at dance reviews and the whole publicity side of it, I know what you mean. Having said that, personally I've always been treated very generously by the dance critics. They've always reviewed my music as well as the dance, they've never just reviewed the movement. I can think of several instances where dance critics show very great astuteness, more astuteness sometimes than music critics, about the qualities of the sound of the music. In particular, Clement Crisp is *very* good at that, and has never taken music for granted.

It's a two-way street. If you're not careful, choreographers tend to just use bits and pieces, and make a little potpourri, something that John Drummond was very insistent on discouraging. But composers, in their turn, must take an interest in dance. We're very lucky at the Guildhall that we have a long history of collaboration between the composition department and the London Contemporary Dance School, at The Place. Every year our postgrads do a ballet with them, so I've seen lots of those. I set up a similar project once at the Royal College when I was Head of Department there. I was so lucky that I was working with a choreographer on my very first day at the Royal College. It would be good if most undergraduate courses had this. I appreciate not every composer is going to want it, but the earlier you introduce composers to what movement can do, the more likely they will show a cultured interest in it.

CD: Part of the role of educating undergraduates, whether in conservatoires or universities, is introducing them to experiences they've not yet encountered, broadening their horizons in the hope that various things create sparks for them.

JA: Exactly. People might also bear in mind two other factors. The audience for contemporary dance in this country is consistent and big. It just turns up. There was never an audience problem for contemporary dance in this country the way that there has been one, intermittently, for contemporary music concerts. The other thing is you get grand rights and it's often much more money than you'll get from any concert performance for the same music.

CD: And dance tends to be done in batches of performances, as tours or seasons, rather than just a premiere and that's it.

JA: Oh yes, absolutely. That said, I accept that the dance area, including the critics, have sometimes been bad at recognising the composer as an important factor in dance works. I also feel very strongly, though, that the contemporary music arena has seen opera as its summit. Ballet is often seen by composers as a specialist area and not more than that.

CD: I wonder whether it's also been undermined by both Debussy and Stravinsky.

JA: Oh, sure. Ironically.

CD: Particularly the way they spoke about Nijinsky. If ever there is a clear example of where, just because somebody is progressive in one art form it doesn't mean they're progressive in another, this is it. Neither Debussy nor Stravinsky could understand what Nijinsky was doing, but when you see the choreography, it fits the music like a glove. There are some bits of *The Rite of Spring* choreography, the 'Dance of the Earth', there are about 30 seconds in that where there is no corps de ballet, everyone is doing something different. You don't get anything like that in music until the '50s and '60s, with Xenakis's *Metastasis*, Ligeti's *Atmosphères* or the 'Epode' from Messiaen's *Chronochromie*.

JA: Well that bit of the *Rite* is a sort of mass phenomenon in movement. There are accounts of people rehearsing that passage at the time of the premiere, running around madly with little pieces of paper, losing their way. They found it very hard. Just to qualify that a little bit, Stravinsky is a complicated case because his on-the-spot verdict on *The Rite* as a ballet was very positive at the time of the premiere.

CD: Oh yes. He later tried to rewrite history. It's this bizarre situation where he wants to claim absolute credit for the scenario and concept of *The Rite of Spring* and at the same time make it seem as if it's an entirely abstract musical work that has nothing to do with dance.

JA: Which is ridiculous. I have a few reservations about Nijinsky's *L'Après-midi d'un faune*. We know now, because the choreographic score of Nijinsky has been deciphered, that there are two forms of that ballet. One version was gradually handed down by people who were in the original production, and the other is the notated form that Nijinsky wrote a few years later, which is slightly different. I do not have reservations, though, in what I've seen of the Millicent Hodson reconstruction of the ballet for *Jeux*. It's an amazing idea for choreography – most of the time the dancers are nearly immobile. I do feel that Debussy didn't realise how very lucky he was to have this extraordinarily musical and sympathetic choreographer. After all, let's face it, even when the ballet of *Afternoon of the Faun* was done, the music wasn't that old.

CD: It would have been just under 20 years – it was premiered in 1894, and the ballet was 1912.

JA: It was modern music at that time and it's rhythmically very complicated. Right from the opening flute solo, you can't hear the beat half the time, and at the reprise of the tune in the second half there are two metres going on simultaneously to the ear. I respect Nijinsky's very orderly treatment of it. What I don't like is Nijinsky's portrayal of the fawn. It's too explicit and in the spirit neither of the Mallarmé nor the Debussy. That includes the famous orgasm at the end. I think what Debussy saw in that was a certain tendency towards vulgarity that he couldn't tolerate. Having said which, his treatment of and behaviour towards Nijinsky over *Jeux* was not good.

CD: It's not even just the letters and the attitude. Even before the premiere he was slamming Nijinsky.

JA: Publicly?

CD: Yes. He was completely derisory in an article on the morning of the premiere.[3]

JA: Oh I didn't know that, that's mad.

CD: Now, having said that, I can see why there is slightly more disconnect between the spirit of what was going on and the dance for *Jeux* than there is in *The Rite of Spring*.

JA: Well there clearly is a massive disconnect between music and dance in *Jeux* – everyone noticed it.

CD: But what tends to be forgotten there is that he would have had the piano score. Now, the piano score for *The Rite of Spring* is pretty close to the music.

JA: As close as you can be, yes.

CD: Whereas the piano score for *Jeux* gives no idea of what the orchestra is going to do.

JA: That's very true. The colour and depth, acoustically, of the score of *Jeux* is astonishing. You're quite right. Nijinsky and the dancers would have had a bit of a shock hearing *Jeux* on the full orchestra. Having said that, it is known that the dancers, when they first heard the full orchestra for *The Rite of Spring*, had an enormous shock just simply because they'd never heard anything so loud in their lives – but that's not quite the same thing. It was not a secret beforehand, with everyone pounding away, from Stravinsky's first play through with Diaghilev, that this was going to be a very loud, violent piece. That was obvious and Nijinsky's choreography duly reflects it.

You've touched on another interesting thing. Remember Nijinsky worked on both ballets at the same time, but the choreographic approaches are diametrically

---

[3]   An article printed in *Le Matin* on 15 May 1913, the day of the premiere, is reproduced in Edward Lockspeiser, *Debussy: His Life and Mind – Volume II 1902–1918* (London: Cassell, 1965), pp. 266–67.

opposite. In his approach to *The Rite of Spring*, he was clearly intent, and Marie Rambert confirmed this, to render every accent in the music. Every accent in the music had to be on the stage. This is what is now known, somewhat dismissively, in the choreographic profession, as Mickey-Mousing, but, from what Millicent Hodson's reconstruction shows, the way Nijinsky did this was extraordinary and the impact of it must have been tremendous. Marie Rambert says that it practically doubled the force of the piece. Quite clearly in *Jeux* that is not the approach at all. There are many moments when they stand still. In fact, Debussy complains about this in a letter, saying he doesn't understand what Nijinsky's doing. In that sense, both ballets mark the beginning of modern dance, but perhaps *Jeux* especially so, because of the counterpoint of action with inaction in the choreography. Nijinsky has a huge orchestra yet there are just three characters and sometimes they're not doing anything, at others they run around, all kinds of things. You realise Nijinsky was highly alert culturally to what dance or what movement with sound could be like. I admire Millicent Hodson's reconstructions of both those ballets. In her *Rite of Spring* you realise how much the orchestration is analogous to Roerich's colours and circles for the sets and costumes. Stravinsky knew Roerich well – they'd consulted long before Nijinsky was involved. They were closely in touch and Stravinsky relied a lot on Roerich for many details of ethnic research. The result is so astonishing: even if it can't be exactly what we had in 1913, it's as close as anyone is ever going to get. The most successful ballet version before Hodson's came along, which is still in the repertoire, was Kenneth MacMillan's at the Royal Ballet, with costumes and scenery by Sidney Nolan.[4] It refers to elements of aboriginal art and costume and is clearly not a Russian version at all. It's very effective. The first time I saw the MacMillan, I recall thinking how odd it was that *The Rite of Spring* was being danced to, because one heard it all the time in the concert hall, never as a dance. Now, if you look at the world's ballet seasons, everywhere somebody is doing either the Hodson or the MacMillan or new ones. The MacMillan is a masterpiece, but the Hodson reconstruction is the one that jump-started everyone's awareness of this as a theatre piece again. That culturally changed *The Rite of Spring*, so that by the time the centenary hit, it was no longer seen just as an orchestral showpiece.

CD: I find it astonishing how many of these classic ballets have never been filmed. When I wanted to play people dancing to *The Rite of Spring* to the students in the 2000s, the only way of getting it was through that American bootleg company, House of Opera. They had the Maurice Béjart, in a Belgian TV broadcast from 1970. Now there's the DVD of the Hodson.[5]

[4] First performed 3 May 1962, Covent Garden.
[5] It is available in a performance from 2008 of the Mariinsky Ballet and Orchestra under Valery Gergiev, released in 2009 on BelAir Classiques, BAC041 (DVD); BAC441 (Blu-ray).

JA: I also have the Hodson on a BBC film from autumn 1989, which is better than the commercial DVD. It was very important to my work on *Khorovod*. I started it the year before, but the BBC broadcast really kicked me into action. That's the first time I saw it, and there was a half-hour documentary before it. The following month, virtually, the Berlin Wall came down and there was a lot of attention on Poland and Eastern Europe generally. Somehow *Khorovod* got caught up with all that, but it was also very much bound up with having seen *The Rite of Spring* as the original ballet for the first time. *Khorovod* would not have had that soundworld without having seen the Nijinksy for the first time, and also getting very into Roerich around then, seeing the wonderful costumes and scenery.

CD: And *Jeux* is only available on YouTube, or in a completely different chore-ography, which is okay, but it doesn't convey at all what was radical or important about the Nijinsky. And why has nobody done *Parade* on DVD?

JA: Have you ever seen that? *Parade* is amazing, with those cubist costumes. The BBC has an archive film of it from the '70s – I don't know why they don't release that.

CD: Another one is *Daphnis et Chloé*.

JA: The Ashton ballet to that is not on DVD as far as I know, and the original Fokine is long since lost. It's surprisingly easy for ballet still to get lost if you don't have a Benesh or Laban notation person in the room and you don't very carefully document it. Dancers' memory for movement is astonishing and can last even half a century, but it's very vulnerable, and there are some very important ballets lost, Balanchine's, Ashton's, a lot of Fokine lost, and also some MacMillan as well. Commercial DVDs of dance are not very numerous, they never were. It's been very underdone as an art form and some musicians are still dismissive of it, as I say.

CD: It's extraordinary, though, that those core Ballets Russes ones, which both dancers and musicians will agree on and they both need to be able to see, they're so important and nobody has done them, even in another choreography. Other than a handful, mostly Stravinsky, they are not available. You just cannot see *Daphnis* danced. You mentioned MacMillan. Have you ever seen his *Agon*?[6]

JA: I've seen, I think, one photo of it, which looked quite interesting but I haven't. Was it filmed?

---

[6] MacMillan's *Agon* was performed three times by the Royal Ballet on 20, 22 August and 3 September 1958.

CD: No. It's from 1958, so very early, and what's fascinating about it is that, for the vast majority of people in this country, it provided their introduction to the ballet, including the music, of course. Balanchine didn't come over with New York City Ballet until the mid-'60s.

JA: And what was the reaction?

CD: Well, you get it reviewed by both the dance and the music critics, but the dance critics in particular are very sniffy about the music in the MacMillan version, and then, when they've seen the New York ballet with Balanchine's choreography, suddenly the view of the music changes.

JA: Interesting...

CD: So it shows that it really was a kind of unified conception of sound and movement from Stravinsky and Balanchine.

JA: And that it helped them appreciate the piece.

CD: Yes. With the MacMillan they're saying he's doing his best with what they clearly think is awful music.

JA: Well, I have seen MacMillan's first Stravinsky ballet, which was *Danses Concertantes* and is extraordinarily fine and inventive.[7] I'm intrigued by the *Agon* simply because the photographic still I have seen looks kind of along the lines of the follow-up to his *Danses Concertantes*, which really launched his career and got everyone talking about him. In *Danses Concertantes* his use of the stage was so inventive. He had people half in, half out of the wings, even just fingers pointing from the wings – that's what I mean by inventive. It used classical dance vocabulary in a very ironic and distorted way, much in parallel with Stravinsky's Neoclassical music – very elegant and witty.

I've seen so often that contemporary dance audiences will listen to, say, Xenakis perfectly happily and get the point of it entirely with a good piece of choreography, but if you played them Xenakis in a concert hall perhaps they would not know what to do, if they hadn't already heard it. We are a very visual culture, in the West, and the visual component can help people listen better. That being the case, if it's a really creative response rather than just a cartoon illustration, dance can do wonderful things for heightening the audience's perception of contemporary music.

I never saw the Béjart ballet to *Le Marteau sans maître*. To judge from the number of performances it got, it was a success, and that will have made that piece much better known to a lot of people. I would be equally interested to see

---

[7]   First performed on 15 January 1955 by Sadler's Wells Theatre Ballet.

his ballet to Stockhausen's *Stimmung*. I know that Roland Petit's choreography to Xenakis's *Kraanerg* was not judged a success choreographically, although all the dance critics remarked on the excellent score. One of them, I think it's Clive Barnes, said it may be one of the great dance scores of the century, but went on to say that the choreography didn't match it. I think Petit didn't know what to do with the huge masses of *glissandi* and so on – he'd not dealt with music like that before, so he just cut the music up, arbitrarily, into duets, trios, pas de deux and so on, and did quite classical ballet moves.

CD: No, it needed something far more plastic.

JA: Yes, and as a result of that, Xenakis took against his own piece. The other curious case, which you'll know about, is Roland Petit's choreography to *Turangalîla*, which by all accounts was incredibly good. Messiaen thought it was good too and the photographs are amazing. I would love to see that, and now that Hubert Devillez is dead, I'm hoping that one day we might get that back.[8]

CD: Yes. I wonder whether it was filmed. I'd be surprised if it wasn't.

JA: Somebody should try and find out. By all accounts, Petit's choreography was not a Mickey-Mousing of the Messiaen, it was something much more subtle. In particular what interested me was the slid choreography. When you look at those pictures, they're sliding and using the floor as an element in the dance.

CD: Have you had contact with dance outside of the specific pieces of yours that have been danced to?

JA: I was on a dance jury once at the Royal Ballet School with Peter Wright and Lynn Seymour. We were judging final-year choreographic work and had to give an award. About three or four weeks later Lynn Seymour and I were asked to come back and comment in more detail to the choreographers (Peter Wright wasn't free), Lynn from the choreographic point of view, I from the musical point of view. I learnt a lot from Lynn Seymour that day, because she told them they weren't using the stage space creatively. She gave the example of people coming on stage. I had to help her with this. We came on from opposite sides, and she told me to hop or slouch and come on in a straight line and she came on diagonally in a different way to see what happens. Then we went off. She led me off and led me back on again in a different way. It was to do with how to get on and off stage, how to reverse the stage and how to use the stage as a space

---

[8]   Hubert Devillez wanted to turn Messiaen's *Turangalîla-Symphonie* into a ballet. When Roland Petit choreographed the work, Devillez issued a lawsuit against Messiaen (and, extraordinarily, won).

creatively, imaginatively. This was wonderful and has to be something that us composers can learn from in terms of how we deal with our musical material, our sound material. I'm not saying space has an equivalent, physically, in music. What I mean is, the actual physical stuff of dance was being examined there; the bodies, and the ways they can traverse an area, in an inventive, meaningful way. Then the students had a go at trying to invent their own ways of coming in and out, and entrances; does everyone come on at once, or not? Why not?

CD: So what musical parallel might you have in mind for that sort of exploration?

JA: Take, for example, *Dérive* of Boulez, which is based on a six-note row, and all the chords are six-note rotations of that row. It's a very six-y piece, it's for six instruments too. Since all the chords are six notes, you'd expect that he would introduce all the six instruments in one go, but he doesn't. The first chord is just piano solo. The second chord is piano and flute. The third chord is piano, flute and violin, and so on. Then he begins to accelerate and introduces them all. That's an equivalent of what Lynn Seymour was teaching us that day about how dancers can use entrances and exits as an inventive factor in the spacing of a ballet, and in the presentation of a ballet. That two-hour session taught me a huge amount about how to compose. The best choreographers are more inventive than your average composer in how they use the stuff they're given. People say about working with Nijinsky that he couldn't really verbally tell you what he wanted to do, but he'd show you. Similarly, somebody who worked with Nijinska on *Les Noces*, in the '60s with the Royal Ballet was David Drew.[9] He's given an interview on DVD where he says it was the same thing with her – she could not explain verbally, but she could show you physically.

CD: That's the one on the marvellous Royal Ballet DVD of *Les Noces* and *The Firebird*. He's brilliant as Ivan in *The Firebird*.[10]

JA: Yes, that's it. Hans Keller got this absolutely right, that verbal communication and musical communication are very different. Musical sound is not verbal. One of the examples that Keller used to give is the idea of canon, with one voice entering and another voice entering in imitation of it. If you do that verbally, as soon as the second voice enters over the first you'll just get nonsense. You probably know Glenn Gould's *Idea of North*, a radio piece where the opening was structured after a Bach fugue, but with overlaid interview fragments. It's interesting, he cross-fades and various things, but you get gibberish whenever people talking are simultaneously at the same level of loudness. In music, you can do

9   David Drew MBE (1938–2015) was a member of the Royal Ballet from 1955 to 2003. Not to be confused with the music critic of the same name.
10   Stravinsky, *The Firebird* and *Les Noces*, The Royal Ballet, Opus Arte OA0833D.

that. It's normal. You do it all the time. It's one of the great privileges music has. You can't do it in a film. You can try splitting the screen and so on, but it doesn't really work. You can't do it in a play. You can't do it in any other field, except in dance. You can have more than one choreographic level going on, as Nijinsky does in *The Rite of Spring*, and we can do it in music. I'm interested in that – it's something that you cannot do in words.

CD: So is this part of what stimulates you creatively with dance?

JA: Yes. We're back again, to the physical substance of what we're working with. Just thinking about that. Don't take it for granted. Don't just say, 'Well I've got a clarinet, so I'll just write clarinettish stuff.' Yes, you could do that, but examining what a clarinet is, and why it is as it is, and thinking about what the clarinet really is – I'm not being very articulate here – and composing with that, rather than just taking it for granted, is deeply stimulating. It's really mostly thanks to dance that I feel that way. I've learnt so much from Balanchine, or Ashton, or Merce Cunningham. You know I am interested in Cage, but I find Merce Cunningham's attitude towards dancing, if anything, even more intellectually stimulating than Cage's attitude towards sound. Cage's attitude is very interesting, but Cunningham is even more inventive. There is, occasionally, with Cage, a little bit of a sense of routine. He'd decided to do chance operations, and he just did more of them. When you look at the way Cunningham choreographed a piece like *Rainforest*, and compare it to the way he choreographed *Roaratorio* by Cage, it's quite different. Or, if you look at the rehearsals of him choreographing the piece that Bob Lockyer commissioned for BBC2 called *Points in Space*, which was a wonderful ballet, you see he's being very rigorous in a quite different way. Maybe it's simply because it's not my area, but I find the quality of inventiveness in dance more interesting and it causes me to write music more readily sometimes than listening to another composer would.

CD: You have presumably experienced this ingenuity in the dance pieces done to your music. Mark Baldwin's choreography for the solo viola piece *Prayer* is one of the more recent ones.

JA: What's nice is that Mark Baldwin turned it into a ballet which has many dancers. I'd suggested making it an intense solo and he smiled and said he'd think about that. Well he turned it into a dance with duets and trios, then they'd climb up the walls and all kinds of things were going on. The violist is onstage, like another character. When that was done at The Place a few evenings in a row, the violist was the brilliant Stephen Upshaw, who played marvellously. I was very happy that the dancing was in counterpoint to the music, as Mark's stuff usually is.

CD: How would you describe the partnership with Baldwin?

JA: The collaboration between me and Mark is not based on the dance imitating what I sound like, or me imitating his dance movements. So it raises the question, to which I still don't know the answer fully, of what is going on in this collaboration. The procedure is still a mystery to me because he doesn't tell me a lot. In the case of *Comedy of Change,* the one thing that was in his mind was something that I was deliberately not told. He wanted me to write a faster music than I'd written in *The Bird Sings.* This time he wanted more rhythmic pulsation in the music, but he didn't want to tell me that at all and he never did. Rather, as was the case with *The Bird Sings,* Mark spoke in terms of colours, because he was a visual artist originally. We also discussed the biological aspect of it, as it was for the bicentennial of the birth of Darwin and the 150th anniversary of the publication of *On the Origin of Species* in 2009.

CD: Wasn't it co-commissioned by the Asko Ensemble in Amsterdam?

JA: Yes. I got a request for a piece from the Asko Ensemble and virtually the same week Mark Baldwin emailed me about doing a ballet inspired by *On the Origin of Species.* The answer to both was a very positive yes, but they were both aiming for 2009 and I could not provide two such pieces, and they both agreed that I could combine the commission. It was always going to be a concert piece as well as a dance piece, and, in fact, all my ballets have been both. Mark had me meet Professor Nicky Clayton, a neuroscientist from Clare College, Cambridge. She advised us on the scientific angle of animal communication. She's a specialist in the behavioural patterns of animals, particularly members of the crow family, or corvids. The crow family are some of the most intelligent and musically adaptable birds, and she's done astonishing work on this, seeing how she can communicate with them, how they interact with each other and with people: changes of behaviour that are meant to be evolutionary and take millions of years, can take a week in the case of a crow. That's not unknown in birds, generally, in spite of the small size of some of them. That gives you pause for thought.

I've always liked nature: over there is a pile of birdsong CDs. This started with my feeling that I knew about folk music, but I didn't know about natural music. I thought that was odd, especially given my interest in Messiaen. When I listened to birdsong in the garden and stuff, I never could distinguish one bird from another. This changed via a specific incident. In my teens I subscribed to Westminster Libraries and their branch near Charing Cross Road had a recording by Jean-Claude Roché.

CD: Oh, yes, I've got some of those.

JA: There was a listing for a record called *Oiseaux Méditerranéens*.[11] I thought, 'That's interesting.' It was only when I was travelling back home on the Tube that I looked at the back of this and I thought, 'Oh, my God. It's all Messiaen's birds.' The birdsong opening side two was La Bouscarle. There was Alouette Calandre from *Et Exspecto*. There were so many of these birds that I knew from his music, so I thought that if anything was going to get me interested in birdsong, this album might be it, if only because I'd be interested in comparing them with Messiaen's usage.

I put the record on but I completely forgot about Messiaen as soon as I started listening. It was like a door opening onto a whole world of music that I hadn't thought of or been able to hear before. Probably, I was in the right state psychologically, because of the Messiaen connection, but I knew that I would never want to imitate Messiaen's birds – that's fatal. Anyhow, the birds didn't sound like Messiaen. They sounded like themselves, and that was very interesting. I did not begin transcribing. I just listened and listened. I taped it so I could listen again and again. I was astonished by the colour, the variety of rhythm, the variety of pacing, and the variety of tuning. For many years, it was a treat for me, after a term at work as a teacher at the music college or at the end of finishing a piece, to go off to HMV and buy another Roché record (or a CD later). This way, I became well acquainted with birdsong from around the world. I also read books about it. There was a book about animal communication published by Yale, which I read very thoroughly, and I also acquired a love of whale song from George Benjamin. He played me the famous Roger Payne vinyl record of whale song, which fascinated me.[12] I bought those and other recordings of any animals that made interesting noises. Deer are very interesting, and I've got recordings of them. Now, all this, rather like the ethnomusicology side of me, is done from the armchair. I don't make a very good field recording ethnologist. I don't go out into the field. I do it entirely from pre-recorded stuff by other people, always. I've just never had the time, really. It's a hobby, but it's a hobby that's quite obsessive.

CD: So what do you get musically from this hobby?

JA: In each case, it's about expanding the range of what sound and music can be in your life. That's helped my music a great deal. What I've learnt to do with birdsong is to input it into the music metaphorically, influenced by the way birds interact. As you may know, there are some birds that sing duets or even trios. These are very co-ordinated in the most remarkably fast hocketing. Incredible. Like a song which sounds absolutely continuous, but when you listen carefully, you realise a bird is singing one note, another bird another note, and then back

---

11 Jean-Claude Roché, *Oiseaux Méditerranéens*, n.d., SRL J.-C. Roché et Cie LPL 2409 1Y (LP).
12 Roger Payne, *Songs of the Humpback Whale*, released 1970, CRM Records SWR 11 (LP).

to the first, very quickly, or there will be a part of a phrase which is started by one bird and then completed by its mate, which may be on another tree or in another bush. It does seem to function as a bonding social mechanism.

CD: How about the melodic aspect of birdsong?

JA: The contours of birdsong are so interesting. The shapes, as Messiaen points out, are often very close to the basic melodic shapes you find in plainchant neumes. Those have always been important in my music, because I write a lot in line, and I've studied plainchant a lot, so that was a natural way into it. There may be a connection with Messiaen's attitude towards birdsong in terms of trying to find neumes and things like that. However, I am not trying to be scientific, although I do read scientific books about these things, especially Donald Kroodsma's wonderful books on American birdsong, which is one of my particular favourite areas. Australian birdsong is another. Nicky Clayton showed us bits of film of the lyrebird of Australia. Well, I'd been a fan of lyrebird song long before Messiaen's *Éclairs*. There's a cassette of it just up there. When *Éclairs* came out, I was very interested to see how he treated it. As you point out in your book, it brought a new music out of him: suddenly a whole orchestra is playing birdsong in very fast rhythmic unison, changing tempi, timbres and colours. He never wrote music like that before. I learnt a lot from birdsong about tuning, polyphony, melody, structure, and also a lot about timbre. A lot of birdsong is very interesting in terms of timbre, and I've dissected hundreds of birdsongs using AudioSculpt – the spectrogram software from IRCAM – or SPEAR – the spectral software from Columbia University. I could spend a morning doing that and get a hundred ideas for new pieces, but not based on transcribing the actual sound, although the sonority, the shape, the rhythm and the way it proceeds may influence what I do.

CD: Can you give a specific example of where birdsong has underpinned some of what you have done in a piece?

JA: Yes, the opening passage of *The Stations of the Sun* was to do with birdsong, not in terms of the sound, but the way it constantly veered between very fast heterophony and actual polyphony or polyrhythm was inspired by analysing dawn choruses. It doesn't sound like it, but that was the source of inspiration behind it. Birdsong can be very supple in going from completely metre-less rubato passages to very strongly metred ones and back again.

CD: So is this kind of rapid change of sensibility partly behind *The Comedy of Change?*

JA: Yes, I put all of that into *The Comedy of Change*. The other thing was the physicality, because Nicky Clayton talked to us about courtship displays, in both vocal and physical terms. The two species that influenced *The Comedy of Change* a lot were the bowerbirds in Australia, which are birds which collect objects in little homes they build called bowers. They are like museum collections, with a particular kind of object. They might collect a particular shade of moss, it could be lichens, it could be pebbles, or it could just be anything of a particular shade of blue. There's one bird – I think it's the Satin Bowerbird – that loves blue, so it just collects blue. There's a marvellous David Attenborough documentary where they were filming in Australia. The bird is not shy of people. Attenborough moves an object away. The bird turns around, sees that, comes back, puts it straight back, and then leaves again.

CD: So there's the movement and, to anthropomorphise it, the character of the bird.

JA: Yes, it's all to do with display. In fact, the whole of *The Comedy of Change* is to do with the idea of display as a means of survival. The term that Nicky Clayton taught us was 'conceal/reveal' – the idea that the bird hides in the courtship ritual, and then suddenly emerges and vividly displays something, such as a birdsong, some plumage or a dance. I looked at a lot of film of birds doing this, watching what movement they made and how fast they did it. You can make rhythms of colour that way, by shifting your wing – 'open, closed, open, closed, open, closed' – and you dance around at a different speed from the wing. Or maybe you dance around in one direction and the wing opens the other way, so it seems to be opening the wrong way relative to the circular pattern. I thought a lot about how the visual rhythms could go into music.

The fourth movement of *The Comedy of Change* is about the 'conceal/reveal' principle. There is a melodic pattern of which I made hundreds of different variants. Each starts slow, then gets very fast just at the end. This keeps happening. I made graphs of it, and using OpenMusic I transcribed those drawings into an object called the break-point function. OpenMusic is IRCAM's pre-compositional software – you can sketch musical techniques. The break-point function is effectively a thing that you draw with the mouse or a line pen. You draw a shape and it analyses it into as many parts as you want. You can break it up into a sample, listening to 100 little bits, 10 or whatever, or you can determine where the samples are if you don't want them regularly. Depending on how many samples you take of it, you'll get different kinds of information, different kinds of continuity. That programme allows you to apply it to any parameter you want. It's great fun to play with.

CD: How about the 'comedy' aspect of the piece? Certainly that Attenborough documentary is comedic in the modern sense.

JA: The 'comic' side of it is because, quite often, the courtship displays seem to us very strange and the behaviour very odd, grotesque and comic. The lyrebird, famously, of course, incorporates what could almost be recordings of sounds that they've heard, of people talking.

CD: Yes, car alarms and all sorts.

JA: People sawing down wood, even.

CD: The trouble with the lyrebird is, what is its own song?

JA: It's a rather fluty but loud song full of leaps and things, which is more or less what we get in the movement in Messiaen's *Éclairs*.[13] I know enough Australian birdsong to be able to identify some of the imitations, since the birds are so accurate. In fact I'm not sure what is going on there, because it sounds basically as if the lyrebird has some type of recording device inside – its imitations sound more like recordings of the sounds or animals concerned.

CD: I have wondered whether the rapid xylophone bit in the Messiaen movement is something the lyrebird in question was mimicking, some other bird or a car alarm or who knows what.

JA: It could be. That's a passage which is such a different sound from the rest of the piece. With *The Comedy of Change* I ended up writing a lot of fast music, you see. The only movement that isn't really fast is the penultimate movement. Mark had said something about some point or other having more, well, he used the word 'soul'. There was one biologist who said to him that the apparent difference between an animal and a human being was this question of something like 'conscience'. Mark wanted a piece that somehow reflected that. He said I could chuck that idea if I wanted, but I didn't mind it at all. The penultimate movement's a long melodic line – there aren't that many long lines in the other movements, they keep being disrupted. But this penultimate movement is a very human kind of line, and indeed it gets quite bluesy, in a way. One of the hardest tasks in music today is to write a good lyrical line that isn't a cliché.

CD: And how does the last movement fit in?

JA: It's the most polyphonic movement of the piece, with about five layers at once, and it is bounded by a virtual clock within the music. There's a stroke on the Japanese rin (a temple bell) every 15 seconds, which happens without fail right the way across the movement as a marker. Other kinds of much more spontaneous and irregular time and rhythm are heard in relation to that. It's all about layers of time.

---

[13] 'L'Oiseau-Lyre et la ville-fiancée', the third movement of Messiaen's *Éclairs sur l'Au-Delà...* (1987–91).

I was thinking of a sequence in the first programme of *Life on Earth* – David Attenborough again – where he goes down the Grand Canyon to illustrate the top soil and then the first geological layer, the second, the third and the fourth.[14] You go further back in time as you go down further. I thought about the possibility of having simultaneously different speeds of evolution and different speeds of change. I decided that these would not be stuck in a particular register, except the rin. I wanted to have very long, sustained notes that changed very slowly. They start the piece, the synthesiser and the violins, and they're like the Japanese mouth organ known as the shō. About two minutes into the piece, they suddenly go down into the bass, and they stay there for quite a while. There's one bit where they're in the middle as well. Also, the longer the notes are, the less rhythm and metre they generally seem to have. I worked a lot with the question of how duration affects our perception of metre and speed, and that piece is very much about that. It's the most complicated piece in the set, and that seemed a good place to put it, at the end. Eventually everything is wound up into a very aggressive texture of two voices in a very fast, rhythmic counterpoint in the middle register. Then there's a final spectrum at the end with the last stroke on the rin.

CD: There is this polyphonic exploration of time and line at different speeds, so where does that leave harmony?

JA: The only harmonies in *The Comedy of Change*, which generally avoids chords, are either a few accompanying chords or they're interruptions of the music. That happens at the end of the fifth movement. There's this very clear chord that stops the music and freezes everything, and that happens at the end of the whole piece as well.

CD: Can you give any examples of how the dance aspect interacted with the music?

JA: We were working with Kader Attia, who's a conceptual artist of considerable inventiveness. He's an Iranian living in Paris, and he has a wonderful sense of turning ordinary objects into something magical. He wraps people. Christo, as you probably know, wraps bridges, buildings and things, but Kader Attia likes wrapping people – well, he does a lot of other beautiful things as well.[15] In the penultimate movement, somebody is being wrapped in tin foil. There was a

---

[14]   David Attenborough, 'The Infinite Variety', episode one of *Life on Earth*, BBC TV, first broadcast 16 January 1979.

[15]   Married couple Christo (Vladimirov Javacheff) and Jeanne-Claude (both born 13 June 1935) jointly produced artworks for many years credited initially to 'Christo', though their large-scale outdoor works were retrospectively credited to both in 1994. Jeanne-Claude died in 2009.

problem with this as the penultimate movement's the quietest of all. The first two minutes of it are just one line, with no harmony at all and very fragile instrumentation. Mark liked the counterpoint of this very thin line with this strange, mysterious activity of wrapping a person, which you would expect to be accompanied by much active music. Again, he was thinking in counterpoint to the music, so he insisted it had to be there. Mark and I usually get on like a house on fire, but, this time there was a lot of discussion between Mark, myself and the conductor Paul Hoskins about how this passage would work. As I recall, both Paul and I feared it could be very disruptive for the musicians and the audience to have such a loud noise of tin foil being wrapped during the quietest music in the work. Then a Board Member of the Rambert Dance Company who was at the rehearsal said that what we needed was industrial tin foil, rather than commercial kitchen tin foil. Industrial tin foil's used in large quantities and is designed to make very little noise.

CD: How on earth does somebody in that kind of position know that sort of thing? What a bizarre thing to know.

JA: How she knew it, I have no idea – but I'm jolly glad she did! She brought in some industrial tin foil and, sure enough, it was much quieter. Now, of course, Mark knew that the idea behind the slow movement was the idea of the human soul, so he wanted somebody being wrapped, but I believe the wrapping was actually Kader Attia's idea. I'm not sure, to be honest.

It happens right at the back of the stage in half-light. Against that there's lots of other dance going on in different groups at different speeds, often fast when the music is slow, and vice versa – that's Mark Baldwin's trademark, and it worked brilliantly. What you don't realise at the end of the movement is that the wrapping is now an empty shell – the person inside has left: it remains there in this perfect image of a person right the way through the whole of the finale as well. Just after my music finishes with the final rin stroke, dancers are hovering next to the person in foil – we still don't know that it's hollow – and they squash it! That's the last thing that happens in the ballet. It's not clear what that means, but it's to do with the impermanence of things. Kader Attia said his whole design in the ballet was to do with impermanence and change. I didn't really need an explanation for that concluding gesture in the dance. I can only say it's exactly right for the mood of the end of the piece, which is quite aggressive. A two-part polyphony is suddenly cut into by this very big chord that just stares at you and doesn't seem to resolve the music. (I've noticed that many of my endings don't resolve. If the music is about to resolve in some way, I untie it again, as also happens at the end of Stations of the Sun.)

CD: So this was a three-way collaboration then?

JA: Yes. I didn't see very much of Kader, but whenever we did speak, he was very poetic and elegant about what he was doing, and it seemed to be along the lines that we were all thinking. Mark and I don't speak much. We just work, and the result just happens. Nicky Clayton spoke to all of us, and we were all thinking about the same things because we were all reading the Darwin book. It was a very happy collaboration, which produced a concert work I would never have written that way otherwise. It's very good to write a concert work by not writing a concert work. It takes your mind in different directions. It was written quite fast because I'd just finished *Fantasias*, and probably I was feeling the release of two and a half years of struggling with the problems of polyphony in that work. *Fantasias* is very polyphonic, and so is *The Comedy of Change*. Having discovered those techniques of how to combine lines in *Fantasias*, I had a lot of fun with them in *The Comedy of Change*.

CD: You wrote *Transferable Resistance* shortly after *The Comedy of Change* and that presumably also has a relationship with science.

JA: Yes, it's another piece about biology. In this case it's to do with my father and his pioneering work discovering how bacteria outside the stomach of a cow can develop a mutation that is resistant to antibiotics without being in contact with the bacteria inside the stomach. This is very difficult to understand and my dad was the person who cracked it, and named it Transferable Resistance.[16] The Royal Society, who hadn't yet twigged that my dad had been a Fellow, asked me to write a fanfare for their 350th anniversary to be played by the LPO[17] brass. I decided to split the brass into four groups around the hall to write a spatial piece to last about four minutes. It again builds on techniques of polyphony that I developed in *Fantasias*, but it's to do with integrating that with more static, harmonic material, which pulses and goes in spatial directions. The polyphony often goes in one direction and the chords move in another, despite which it's not too hard to play. Then, it turned out that Nicky Clayton, who'd been advising us all for *The Comedy of Change*, was getting her Fellowship at the Royal Society at that very ceremony. I'd no idea until I saw her come on stage and receive it! I'd like to do more pieces about biology or microbiology in different ways. Meanwhile, dance remains a vital source of continuing inspiration in my music, and I hope to work more with it.

---

[16] See Conversation One, 'Origins', for more on the work of JA's father.
[17] London Philharmonic Orchestra

Conversation Five

Folk

Folk naturally follows on from Dance, being similarly fundamental to Anderson's creativity. The link between dance and folk prompts reflection on the nature of community and society, as well as the loss of a common musical language. Questions of authorship are raised, before Anderson speaks of the seminal importance of Barrie Gavin's Bartók documentary *The Miraculous Circumstance*. The importance, or otherwise, of other folk traditions is explored along with the role of folk music in the works of Stravinsky and Bartók, and the extent to which the use of folk material resonates with audiences. The unfixed nature of folk music is the catalyst for a discussion on the revision of works.

— ◆ —

CD: We've already spoken about how your love of dance came very early on. Folk music is also very important to you and, though not exclusively, a substantive amount of folk music and the associated traditions are also about dance.

JA: Yes. A lot of folk music is prompted by dance. In a lot of cases they happen simultaneously as a matter of course.

CD: Obviously it's a continuum, but the dance side of things in its physical manifestation is very much late-twentieth- and twenty-first-century modern contemporary Western dance, whereas folk explores much older traditions. That being the case, to what extent is there an overlap of dance and folk for you? I'm not thinking so much musically, but in terms of how you think of dance and folk together?

JA: I've never thought of it that way. It's very interesting you mention that because you're quite right, of course, that in many cultures if you sing, you dance. I'd never thought of there being any relationship in my music as such, though there must be some because so many of my first published pieces were about dance, as we've said, and were about folk-dancing at that. *Khorovod* is an obvious case, *The Stations of the Sun* also, so clearly I'm aware of there being such a link, but I never thought of that consciously at all until you raised the question.

I suppose a lot of this though is to do with two related feelings of loss, which I'm aware of now. I wasn't aware of it that way when I got interested. One is the loss of community. I think that's widely felt. There are many very desperate attempts, often right-wing I'm sorry to say, at recapturing the sense of community. A TV show from my youth, called *The Waltons*, was based on that – though it wasn't right-wing of course.

CD: [Hums the theme tune]. 'Goodnight Johnboy' and all that.

JA: Exactly. This was made around the time that Vietnam was ending badly and Nixon was being ousted. You can see why America wanted to latch onto community in a big way then. In my case, there are two things. First of all, in spite of the title Hampstead Village, there wasn't much sense of community where I grew up. We knew the neighbours and so on, but everyone seemed to be living in their own world. My first encounter with anything like a community was at school and it wasn't a very happy one. When I began to realise that there had been communities that were, in some sense, unified and to some extent 'peaceable kingdoms', as Blake would have put it, naturally I was very struck by that. Also very sad because I couldn't participate in that, I'd never known it. It struck me as a thing to aspire to, but with certain reservations attached. You can idealise it too much and in the wrong way.

The other loss is of a common musical language, which perhaps relates to the other anyway. I began to realise that only gradually. I guess I thought that everyone might at least potentially enjoy the same range of music I did, but that was not at all the case. Some part of me probably does fantasise that there are more people out there that listen to, say, a Boulez setting of Mallarmé, Count Basie's version of *Li'l Darlin'* and Honegger's *Horace Victorieux* very happily of a morning. But it seems there aren't that many people who do, which doesn't make me in any way special, but it does mean that when you get enthusiastic about something, there's not necessarily anyone you can share it with immediately. Whereas, if you're listening to the latest pop hit and everyone around you knows it, that gives a sense of belonging and community. There, too, I found at school also that I was isolated because I wasn't constantly wanting to sing the latest film tune hit or whatever the pop hits were of the day. It's not that I didn't know them, I just didn't like them very much, with the possible exception of ABBA (which dates me!).

I'm psychologising after the event here. These things are deeply instinctive. So the taste and attraction for folk music, or any other music, is like Marmite, which I happen to be on the liking side of. It's as instinctive as that. I heard some folk music in a particular TV programme and was absolutely gobsmacked. Because of that, I realised I had something to learn from traditional music of various sorts. I never stopped myself and wondered why I was doing this, or asked what I was hoping to achieve by exploring this. It was just a feeling of need.

CD: Is it the loss of a common language or is it actually the growing awareness of the reality of language as the world shrinks?

JA: It's both. I was never a fan of Esperanto, which is an absurd language because it's an artificial digest of several different languages. It has no flavour. A real language that evolves, even a sub-dialect like, say, Valley Talk, that's genuine. It just happened between people, it grew, whereas Esperanto didn't grow. It was one person who said, 'Right. I'm going to make a universal language.' Of course that's a creative act of some interest in itself, but it's not the same as a language that just grows up from a community's needs.

CD: That's the charge put against serialism really.

JA: Not without some reason. The lack of communal language and my realisation of just how much that lack is a problem relates to my strong interest in but very ambivalent relation to serialism. It also relates to an event when I was nine: the death of Benjamin Britten. We were a cultured family so I remember discussion of pieces like *A Midsummer Night's Dream* or the *War Requiem* at the dinner table when I was a kid and we had the records of those pieces. Then one day in my prep school, the music teacher suddenly said, 'I want to tell you a story.' He began telling us this long story about a very gifted boy called Ben and how this boy had been noticed by his parents to have a special musical talent. How he'd done this, that and the other and grown up into a very distinguished man who played the piano, conducted and had written music. The teacher spun out the story for about 10 minutes. Then he suddenly said, 'The story I've been telling you is a true story and the man who it's about died yesterday. He was a real person and he was called Benjamin Britten.' We all looked at each other and said, 'Did you hear that? Benjamin Britten is dead.' Now, my point is that wasn't a musical school. It had music in it, but that's rather like the exchange in *Fawlty Towers* where two guests come to the desk and ask if their room is airy, and Fawlty remarks irritably that there's air in it. No insult to Mr Burton-Nickson, the only music teacher there, who was a lovely man, a good organist and a sweet piano teacher, but it wasn't a musical school. And yet, in between beating each other up, throwing compasses at each other, smearing each other with ink and kicking footballs, we knew who Benjamin Britten was. There is no present-day equivalent of that kind of common knowledge when it comes to any living composer I can think of.

When I was about 13, the only composer to occupy remotely that kind of position was Peter Maxwell Davies. Everyone knew that he lived in Orkney. When I mean everyone, I mean if you were remotely cultured, you'd have heard that. You heard about this guy who did screaming nuns and mad king pieces or something. Some vague idea. What strikes me about Britten was the ability to make very simple common material sound fresh and personal. The only other person who had it around the same time was Copland. I can think of two other composers to have had the potential for this since: Michael Finnissy and Olly Knussen. This can only be done properly if it's done with what I'm going to have to call integrity. In other words, it's got to be somebody who writes complex quarter-tone quartets one day and then writes beginner piano pieces and takes each of them as seriously as the other. Whenever I've done beginner pieces, they've been related to bigger pieces, even been sketches for them, simply with fewer layers because they're for people who can't play many things at once. When I saw the commonality that Britten managed to achieve to some degree, naturally I'm sorry that that isn't possible now because it's a very potent means of communication. Perhaps it was a rather middle-class kind of commonality, though to be fair to him, it wasn't just middle class at the time – I think a lot of different people in this country and others were affected by what he wrote.

The voice of folk song is very important to me because authorship is so confused in that situation. There is somebody singing to you, but they would not necessarily regard it as their song or even their version of the song. It's simply something they know that they are singing now, for whatever reason; it's part of their culture. It's produced by the culture, something they've inherited. That doesn't necessarily imply authorship.

CD: The caveat I'd put on that is that you get situations where such and such a song is the song that Harry sings or that's a song that Helen sings.

JA: Exactly.

CD: So if someone else came and sang it there'd be an awkwardness, like sitting in someone's usual seat. An awkwardness that would be regarded as rudeness if the person singing knew that Harry or Helen sang that song and hadn't squared it with them first.

JA: Or it could be, sometimes, over there they sing this song, but they don't sing it the way we do. We sing it this way. This is our version. That also can be a collective thing. Yes, you're quite right. When Bartók was going round folk song collecting he'd often be told, 'She knows all sorts of songs I don't know.' So there are all kinds of ways of looking at this. Some kind of feeling that this was a community experience was confirmed when I saw Barrie Gavin's film *The Miraculous Circumstance*, the film he made for the Bartók centenary in 1981 with Bert Lloyd, which broadcast on BBC TV in March that year.[1] I watched because I was very keen on Bartók. I didn't realise that these folk traditions, at that time, were still alive. They recorded old people who'd sung for Bartók as young people. One of them was interviewed in the programme saying that Mr Bartók had a large horn and asked me to sing into it, then my voice came out of the horn. Of course, some countries in the Eastern Bloc were better at preserving their folk traditions than others, certainly better than Britain has been at preserving its indigenous folk singing. There's had to be a folk revival in Britain. We have the records that Grainger and other people made in the first two decades of the twentieth century, but mostly it's a re-created tradition. Well, that's better than not having one, but it's not the same thing as something that's actually living.

The shock of the film was to see these extraordinary sounds and all these alphorns and God knows what were being played by living people actually doing this as part of their daily life. I couldn't believe that. I had no idea. Then instinct took over: I liked very much what I was hearing, the music spoke to me in a very immediate way and was something I just needed. Every item in that programme excited me deeply, and it was certainly mixed up with some sense of what we've lost. There was also a feeling that it was not tarted up for us. In other words, that it was sung the way that they wished to sing it, not the way that they thought would sell more records.

CD: Can you give some sense of just how profound an influence the Gavin film *The Miraculous Circumstance* was on your music?

JA: Quite apart from the fact that it informed a lot of music I was trying to write as a teenager (but failed to complete, mostly), it went into *Khorovod*, to some extent *Tiramisù*, certainly bits of *Diptych* and *Stations of the Sun*, *Imagin'd Corners* because of the alphorns, and it also went a bit into *Book of Hours*, which is dedicated to Barrie Gavin. It may yet pop up again.

CD: Beyond that documentary, what other folk traditions have inspired you?

JA: The Swiss Cottage Library had a very rich collection of traditional musical records, which they bought just as assiduously as pop or classical music. What struck me first, unsurprisingly, were things which I knew had interested twentieth-century composers. The main one would have been gamelan. I encountered Indian classical music both that way and also because a lot of Indian classical music was broadcast on Radio 3. The BBC broadcast quite a lot of Thai

---

[1]   Barrie Gavin (director), *The Miraculous Circumstance*, broadcast on BBC Two, 21 March 1981.

music as well, on television, at the Proms and on Radio 3, thanks to Donald Mitchell, who was an authority on Thai music when he wasn't publishing Mahler and Britten and founding Faber Music... What an astonishing polymath! So I fell in love with Thai classical music.

The real discovery from the Swiss Cottage Library collection was music from what is now the former Yugoslavia, specifically Croatian two-part polyphony, which is in very close intervals. Something like what we call semitones and tones. When you hear it now it sounds a bit like middle-period Bartók. Not coincidentally: Bartók knew that music very well. It's also known as 'Istrian polyphony'. The idea that you could have linear counterpoint in such a narrow pitch space really fascinated me. The beats and the graininess of it also attracted me very much, and the timbre of the instruments; the sopile, which is a Croatian shawm that makes an extraordinary strident sound, or the dobra, which is a kind of lute-type instrument, and the gaida, which is the bagpipe of that region. I was instinctively attracted to Slovenian, Croatian, Bulgarian and also Macedonian folk music, that whole region, and also a bit of Greek folk music. When I was in Corfu as a kid in 1977, if I remember rightly, I had no idea that in the middle of the island there were still villages with traditional musicians singing and playing. The Smithsonian even issued a record of that recently and I was very excited by it. The music uses metrical and modal patterns quite close to some Macedonian and Bulgarian folk music.

CD: How about Polish folk music?

JA: That cropped up by accident. There were records at the library, but I was very into listening to short-wave and long-wave radio. I have on tape a Polish folk dance by a trio of violins and double bass which I recorded off air in summer '81. I know now that it's an *oberek*. It has very strange tuning and odd accentuations, in an uneven triple metre with the accent very often on the last beat and with wonderful semitone clashes. I found that very attractive indeed. That might come in somewhere – I meant to do something inspired by it in one of my quartets, but as yet I never did.

For some reason, possibly just to do with the concert music that I like, the main folk music I love has been from Eastern Europe from Russia right the way through to the former Yugoslavia and also the Baltic States, especially Lithuania. That all attracted me greatly, more at first than any English folk song singing that I heard. It was only much later that I heard Grainger's recordings of Joseph Taylor[2] and then other acetate recordings from the period that began to interest

---

[2]   Joseph Taylor, who lived in Lincolnshire, was considered by Grainger to be the finest folk singer he encountered. Grainger's recordings of Taylor and others can be heard on the British Library website: https://sounds.bl.uk/World-and-traditional-music/Percy-Grainger -Collection (last accessed 31 July 2019).

me quite a bit, but not as instinctively. I found the modal language less sympathetic and less exciting, frankly. It's not a criticism, it's just instinctive taste.

CD: But stuff from the Celtic countries is another matter, isn't it?

JA: Yes, I got into Irish and Scottish folk fiddling very much, especially from Shetland, and that informed some of the string writing in *Khorovod*, *Tiramisù* and perhaps *The Stations of the Sun* a bit. But the big fascination has always been Eastern Europe, along with my obsession with *gagaku*, and a strong interest in Indian music and, to a lesser extent, Indonesian gamelan.

CD: How about music from Latin America?

JA: Not so much. I was never excited by salsa and Caribbean folk music hasn't meant much to me – it's wonderful but somehow not my thing. In the '90s I heard some remarkable folk music from Papua New Guinea – UNESCO Records issued several field recordings from there which I found quite revelatory. I don't know whether that will ever be reflected in something I write. The point is a piece doesn't usually arise directly because of any of these things as such, but studying and listening to that music affects what you do. Then maybe in a piece you suddenly find a moment where you know you are going to refer to one of these things. I don't write a piece called *18 Lithuanian Folk Songs*! I never know how these things are going to come out in my music, or if they are.

CD: Well, your Second String Quartet is called '300 Christmas Carols',[3] but that makes your point as it's not a setting of the carols in any kind of obvious, surface way.

JA: Exactly, and this brings up the question of appropriation, which is a very fashionable word among musicologists at the moment. In this, of all ages, at the flick of a switch on the Internet you can now travel the world virtually and dip into this and dip into that. We're all tourists now. You can't legislate for how profound somebody's knowledge must be before they reflect in their own creative work something that they love. I hope that my music is free of any sense of patronising, imperialist attitude, like Marie Antoinette putting shepherdess's clothes on. It's not meant to sound fake 'traditional'. But I deplore the fact that so few musically interested people, whether in pop music or Western classical music, want to know anything beyond their wonderful but very limited areas. They are so lacking in curiosity to find out what the rest of the world has made of sound and has done with music in social and cultural contexts. And if you misunderstand that music, that's a creative act too.

---

[3]   String Quartet No. 2 '300 Weihnachtslieder' (2014).

CD: When people say Messiaen misunderstood what the Indian rhythms were about, who cares? He wasn't writing Indian music.

JA: Nor did he think he was. I think us composers are very transgressive in that sense. I don't think we easily fit into these rules and regulations. Certainly, I am the sort of composer who if somebody says, 'You can't do this', or, 'You shouldn't do that', the first thing I immediately wish to do is that. I don't like people who legislate for our cultural world and try to fence it around with dos and don'ts. I hope that stage of cultural legislation is passing, because it's rather immature. Here am I, having grown up in London or Fleetwood or wherever, so I'm not about to dance around the village green, am I? [Laughter] As long as I'm not pretending to do that then I'm okay about all this.

CD: There are, of course, numerous groups of Morris and other traditional dancers keeping those things going, rejuvenating them even, and it's worth noting that, at the same time as you were discovering all this in the '70s and '80s, the folk revival in this country, which went back at least to the '60s, was thriving.

JA: Very much so, yes, and this relates back again to *The Miraculous Circumstance*, as Bert Lloyd was a key figure in the UK folk revival. He was also a friend of Bob Dylan and was much involved with Dylan's controversial change from acoustic to electric guitar. He was at the crucial Newport concerts where that happened. Bert Lloyd was a fine singer himself, with a very particular vocal style, to some extent modelled on the recordings Grainger made of people like Joseph Taylor, with a narrow, selective vibrato and a tendency of the voice to crack in certain places for expressive purposes. Slight droops up or down at the ends of phrases. A beautiful, mildly ornamental, dulcet way of singing, which benefits from amplification because it's quiet.

There's also a two-fold connection between Lloyd and the avant-garde. First of all because Bert Lloyd was very good friends with Roberto Gerhard.[4] Lloyd made a translation of Lorca's *Lament for the Death of a Bullfighter*, for which Gerhard did an electronic score for the BBC Third Programme.[5] Lloyd also introduced Gerhard to various other folk traditions. One of those turned up in two late pieces of Gerhard called *Libra* and *Leo*, both for ensemble. There's a tune in *Libra* which, it turns out, is music from a village at the mouth of the Orinoco River. It was a field recording Lloyd had made there, which he played to Gerhard, who couldn't get this out of his mind. It formed one of the generative materials for *Libra*.

---

[4] A Catalan-Spanish composer and scholar, Roberto Gerhard (1896–1970) fled Spain after the Civil War, settling in Cambridge, with the consequence that, during his lifetime, his music was better known in the UK than Spain, where it was shunned by Franco's regime.
[5] Gerhard's piece of the same name was composed in 1959.

Libra was his wife's star sign, Leo was his, so it was a bit of a personal piece. He brought the tune back at the end of *Leo*, like a little personal signature.

Now those pieces were some of the first really modern music that I heard. So, though I didn't realise what was going on, one of the first pieces of modern music I loved had pentatonic folk fragments in it all the way. It only struck me much more recently when I came back to that music how odd that is. Also not something that Gerhard had done for the previous 15 years, as he'd avoided folk music like the plague. He'd done a lot of Spanish- and Catalan-inflected pieces, then he'd got interested in Darmstadt- and Donaueschingen-inspired modernism and he avoided the folk stuff for 15 years, from 1953 right the way until 1968. Then suddenly it comes back in his later pieces. In his Fourth Symphony, among all the concatenations and eruptions of sound, a Catalan folk song will pop up from time to time.

That must have resonated within me. When I look occasionally at my early attempts to write that kind of music, when I was 13 or 14, you find that there are all kinds of sevenths, ninths and regulation dissonant tritones, and all that stuff. However, there are also funny pentatonic-type things as well, which are quite odd in that context and suggest that I was trying to find some way of integrating these interests. The first time I became aware of this affecting me was a piece for choir called *SING*, which was based on four notes of a pentatonic scale: E, F sharp, A and B, but in any octave. There were no other notes at all. The reason for that was I was trying to find something the school choir could sing.

CD: And could they?

JA: No, but that's another story [laughter]. In the middle of all this chromatic stuff I was trying to write, at the age of 14 I wrote this piece that just has a pentatonic mode all the way through. I was trying to see how I could integrate what I was learning. I certainly always felt there was no disjunction between my modern music enthusiasms and folk music. In 1979, Lawrence Morton published his article about the folk tunes and *The Rite of Spring* and people suddenly realised just how much of it is actually folk tunes.[6]

CD: I was going to say, you'd grown up listening to *The Rite of Spring* completely unaware of how folk-inspired it was.

JA: Exactly. The instinctive attraction to what I was hearing in folk music was probably because of that.

---

[6]   Lawrence Morton, 'Footnote to Stravinsky Studies: *Le Sacre du Printemps*', *Tempo* 128 (March 1979), 9–16.

CD: To this day people are not really aware how much of what we would now call folk music there is in stuff like Haydn and Brahms.

JA: There are researchers who know, of course, or who are getting to grips with just how much of it there is. One of the most pernicious lies ever told about composition is the idea that you must invent everything from scratch. I never understood where this myth came from because I don't think any sensible composer has ever thought this. Even Boulez didn't, in the sense that when he was doing his most tabula rasa piece, he took someone else's row deliberately.[7] (Cannibalism, as Feldman points out somewhere, exists in contemporary music as well!) People get surprised at how many of the tunes in *Petrushka* and *The Rite of Spring* are not by Stravinsky, but they should not be. That would be contrary to the whole enterprise. You don't make things like that up. You look them up and you work with them.

CD: It's sampling.

JA: Thank you. Of course, in a sense, both Messiaen and Stravinsky sampled their whole lives anyway, in different ways. I'm quite convinced Stravinsky used more folk tunes in *Les Noces* than have been recognised, probably in *Pribaoutki*, the Three Pieces for String Quartet and other pieces as well. They may not be, because, as Bartók said, either these are folk tunes in Stravinsky or they're the most excellent imitations of them. As Bartók also said elsewhere, the point is that you absorb the stuff so you ultimately don't know whether you're using it, or not. In *Shir Hashirim*, I was trying to find a very simple setting for the line, 'Ana dodi v(e)-amar li: Kumi lach ra yati yafati, Ulchilach!',[8] which means, 'My beloved spake and said unto me, arise my beloved and come away'. A melody came into my head which I was worried about, because I knew it was a tune I'd heard and liked in the first movement of Lutosławski's Concerto for Orchestra. I got my Steven Stucky book out and he'd looked at the article by Zofia Lissa, which explains that they're all traditional tunes from a certain region of Poland.[9] So I'd quoted a traditional Polish tune, not Lutosławski, and my use of it was quite different from his. I'm not Polish after all, but that tune was in my long-term memory by then and it popped up there. I thought, 'Great, I didn't invent it.' I like those things to flow through my music, rather than being a conscious attempt to put on folk dress, which I would really loathe and would be a sham.

---

[7]   Boulez's *Structures Ia* uses the mode of Messiaen's *Modes de valeurs et d'intensités*.

[8]   Song of Songs, 2:10:

יְעָנָה דוֹדִי וְאָמַר לִי קוּמִי לָךְ רַעְיָתִי יָפָתִי

וּלְכִי־לָךְ:

[9]   Steven Stucky, *Lutosławski and his Music* (Cambridge: Cambridge University Press, 2009), pp. 48–58.

CD: On the one hand, there is using this material just as material, and there may be some thought of it being folk-derived, but it's not necessarily there to be recognised by the listener.

JA: No.

CD: That's simply what it is. On the other hand, you then have folk stuff which very much does have a reference, is meant to be recognised as such and then has a clear cultural currency with a particular audience. You're saying you are not so interested in the latter approach.

JA: That's right. I certainly did not intend that anyone in Lithuania or anywhere else should recognise the tune on which the opening of *Khorovod* is based. It's completely re-done, diffused into the music. It was just a sequence of notes I enjoyed, was good to use and made the sound I wanted. It wouldn't be possible to reconstruct the tune from that score because it's stated heterophonically, so nobody's playing the original tune – it's all decorated in different parts.

This is an interesting point. Did Stravinsky, for example, want anyone to recognise and know the folk tune at the opening of *The Rite of Spring*? I think he simply wanted to give it the feeling of something starting, the beginning of *a* world, of things sprouting and growing, as he said later. The important thing was that it had a certain modal quality that gives it a slightly timeless feel, that would stand out in Paris 1913. It's rather lost in time. And that sense of timelessness interests me a lot. But I wasn't trying to do that when I was doing *Khorovod*. The sections were determined by a sequence of the times of day. The few folk tunes that I did use were appropriate to that time of day. The opening one is about the sun rising over a farm, so it was appropriate, but I'd have used it even if the text had been wrong, because I like the tune. I'm not interested in saying to the listener, 'Here is this thing for this reason.' In a symphonic work that would be a little like what Shostakovich did in the Eleventh Symphony, where quite specific traditional or well-known Russian tunes are used because of their cultural association or their texts. Am I going to suddenly have the whole orchestra quote 'You'll Never Walk Alone'? Maybe I would, I don't know. I rather like it...

The reason I mention that is because my first-ever conscious experience of heterophony, not that I knew the word, was hearing football crowds singing 'You'll Never Walk Alone'. I didn't know the tune at the time, but I remember hearing especially the final bit getting very out of phase, in octaves with no harmony, just this huge crowd. I was very touched by that. I've always liked it and I don't believe the tune is copyright, so you never know, it might pop up.

CD: It's more recent than you think. It's from *Carousel*.

JA: Well that's out!... I had no idea. Tunes that are immediately recognisable are very few indeed in our present culture – hits come and go, but very few last. That said, I don't know if they sing 'You'll Never Walk Alone' in Germany, so if I were to allude to it in a work commissioned by a German orchestra, what significance would that melody have in there?

CD: Yes, and then you've got Bartók or Grainger or whoever collecting folk tunes and very explicitly saying it's a particular folk tune and they're putting it out there because they think it's valuable and should be heard, but it's presented to a whole bunch of people for whom it meant nothing at all.

JA: The tension you outline there is where something that had a collective meaning at one point from a certain society is yanked from that society, with all the best will in the world of course, and placed into a totally different context where it doesn't have any meaning. This is where personality comes in. If such material corresponds to the composer's personal needs, it's going to be meaningful because the composer will invest it with a meaning, it will resonate with them and they'll compose accordingly. For example, if the composer has been, even temporarily, a visitor to the community where the musical material meant a lot, that knowledge will inform the way that composer treats the melody when they come to composing with it themselves, because they will have witnessed that intensity and emotion. That is certainly true of Bartók.

CD: I find it a real shame when you get people being sniffy about the way Bartók or Grainger or Vaughan Williams used folk tunes, saying that that's how people did it then, but that it's not best practice now, with the implication it lacks validity or worth.

JA: Well some people have become very legislative, but I don't think they proposed anything much better in its place. Bartók's rather Ferneyhough-like transcriptions of the details of a folk song are a little odd. Although they honestly reflect what he found precisely, in as much detail as he could find it on the recordings, it's not clear whether he was correct or not in his theory that these micro articulations contained, as it were, the dialect of folk music.

CD: When you get those sorts of transcriptions and people talk about the rhythmic complexity of it, that doesn't mean it's anything other than a four-square song. It may be, even within the fluidity of folk practices, that this person simply has an idiosyncratic sense of the rhythm and pulse. That doesn't mean the performance is necessarily anything other than excellent, but it simply reflects the way this one person performs it.

JA: One of the problems here is the definition of 'the song' or 'the melody'. There is quite a lot of evidence that Cecil Sharp, Vaughan Williams, Lucy Broadwood and a number of other people in the first 20 years of the twentieth century were trying in their publications to make the songs commercially viable and approachable.[10] Anyone who could read sheet music could sing this 'authentic' English ballad and whatever. The whole problem is: what is the song? And that's where Grainger comes in, because Grainger wasn't in favour of boiling it down to a single version of the song, which is effectively what the Sharp and others were doing. In other words, getting rid of the ornaments, getting rid of the *glisses*, getting rid of the irregular metres, getting rid of the irregular intonations, and just trying to distil from what's left a very simple tune which could be published by Booseys and sent around the world. Grainger wouldn't do this, because he wasn't sure that such 'original versions' of the tunes really existed.

CD: Yes. The complicating factor of it though is that, if you then try and take a particular rendition of it, you end up privileging that and placing it on a pedestal, just as reproducing one performer's approach to ornamenting Bach, Couperin, Mozart, even Chopin, can be misleading, yet playing this music without putting that in does not really reflect the practice of the time.

JA: Grainger provided alternatives for different ways the singers sang the same melody in different verses. So you can see quite readily that there isn't any one preferential version.

CD: The broader point is that, when these people went round with their phonographs, or cassette recorders later on, and they've got the last known exponent of some song or fiddle tune, that's invaluable to a collector. However, the question that doesn't seem to be asked is whether this was someone who even their peers regarded as being good at performing this.

JA: That's true. If you read the preface to Grainger's *Lincolnshire Posy* he goes into some detail about the circumstances in which he met the singers concerned, how old or infirm they were or whatever. When any composer is writing a piece where there are no alternatives, then they are privileging a particular version of everything. I think about this quite often because of the 1960s attempts at mobile form in music. These were done for several different reasons: some were doing it for linguistic, cultural reasons – by analogy with the later work of Mallarmé (that's Boulez's source for open form); or else due to an interest in noise and statistical phenomena, in the case of Stockhausen; and in Xenakis's case to do with mass events, standard deviation, normal distribution, and for different reasons, perhaps philosophical or even mystical, in John Cage's case.

---

[10]   Lucy Broadwood (1858–1929) and Cecil Sharp (1859–1924) were pioneers in studying British folk song, joined later by Vaughan Williams. In addition to collecting thousands of tunes, they founded what became the English Folk Dance and Song Society.

I would like to be able to compose a piece rather like the *100 Million Million Sonnets* of Raymond Queneau.[11] There are 10 sonnets and each of the 14 lines in all 10 has the same rhyme scheme, scansion and even sound, so there are 10 possibilities for each line. You can combine any part of any of them and end up with a new sonnet. There are 10^{14} possibilities for making sonnets from this material, hence the title. The results are impressive and colourful. I've always wanted to produce a piece of music like that, so that it would be possible to have many variants of different sections combined with many other variants of other sections and for a different work to come out. It will still be the same piece as far as I'm concerned, in the sense that a folk singer sings the same tune in different ways and it's still the same tune. I don't know how I'd do this – it would be quite different in both aim and result from the 1960s open-form attempts. Perhaps there could be 14 versions of the piccolo line or whatever. With computer software now it would probably be possible to do all this on an iPod and just flick a switch and you get different parts set up! The publisher's nightmare...

I'm fed up of the myth, which is not entirely wrong, however, that there is only one right way for things to go. When you look at sketches, often you can see quite well why the composer rejected the 10 first versions of something or why the version that they published is the most viable one. There are instances, though, where that is not entirely the case, such as in *The Rite of Spring* sketches. I often look at the sketches for 'The Games of the Rival Tribes' in class and I've made a version to play on piano of how that section would originally have gone. One student commented that it doesn't appear to work as well as the final version, it's got certain awkwardnesses, repetitions and excessive amounts of stopping, etc., but who knows? – we might have gotten used to it and it might be just as good. I thought that was true. What I like also about folk music is precisely that, as far as I'm concerned, when I'm hearing the recording I know it's just that recording of that singer or player at that time doing that. That's all it is. It isn't 'the' piece. Perhaps there the concept of 'the piece' does not exist. I can learn a lot as a composer from that. In a sense it eased up my composing, because I became easier about saying, 'I have to decide this today. This is my best working solution to the musical situation. I'll go with that.' There is a feeling of playfulness, rather than feeling you're committing yourself irrevocably, even though actually I am. [Laughter]

CD: Have you ever been tempted to make major revisions to earlier works?

JA: No. Only in the case of *Khorovod*, where despite having spent five years on and off working at the music, I finished the first performing version in quite a

---

[11]   Raymond Queneau, *Cent mille milliards de poèmes* (Paris: Éditions Gallimard, 1961).

rush, so in a sense I was still composing it after that. It was only in summer 1995 that the work was completed to my satisfaction.

CD: But are you thinking of going back and re-doing bits of, say, *Khorovod* or *Heaven is Shy of Earth* or *Thebans*?

JA: No, not at all. I'm not tempted. I'm not the same composer I was then, so I can't. When I was editing the recording of *The Comedy of Change*, I was thinking, 'I wouldn't do that now. I wouldn't even begin a section that way now.' The music felt completely remote from me, which is fine.

CD: Do you find yourself looking at your earlier pieces as if somebody else composed them.

JA: Yes. Sometimes I'm pleased by what I find, at other times very much not. And sometimes I think, 'Why did I do that?' Have you had analogous experiences?

CD: Oh yes. I have had the experience of reading something and forgetting that it was my own article or whatever and thinking, 'That's a good point, why didn't I think of that?' That's nice, except I then tend to wish I was that clever now.

JA: Exactly.

CD: I had a PhD student doing stuff on Gaspar Cassadó.[12] She wrote in one place how the Casals recording of the Bach Cello Suites was effectively an ur-recording of it, an ur-performance of it, because Casals essentially created the performing tradition of the Cello Suites and that recording basically introduced the work to the world.[13] I asked whose term 'ur-recording' was, and she told me I'd used it in a supervision a couple of months earlier. [Laughter]

JA: It's interesting, isn't it? Occasionally I've looked back at an earlier piece and wished I could do that now. And that in turn has sometimes prompted new pieces.

So it can be helpful, though it's very dangerous to look back too much. I'm not the sort of composer who won't ever look back at my work or listen to it, as some say. But when you ask a lot of composers what their favourite piece of theirs is, they say that it's the last thing they finished or the next piece. I agree with that. I don't mean to imply that I'm not interested in my music. If I didn't mean it, I wouldn't have written it. I'm not trying to pretend that it doesn't matter

[12] Gaspar Cassadó (1897–1966) was a Catalan cellist and composer.
[13] J.S. Bach, *Cello Suites*, Pablo Casals (cello), recorded at Abbey Road Studios, London, 23 and 25 November 1936, and in Paris, 2–3 June 1938 and 13–16 June 1939, HMV DB 3671/3; DB 3399/401; DB 3402/4; DB 6538/40; DB 6541/4; DB 3674/7 (78s). There are numerous reissues of these landmark recordings.

to me at all or any nonsense like that. Of course it matters to me, very much so. But I couldn't do what Boulez did, returning to a piano piece he wrote 40 years earlier and make new orchestral music. Boulez is a strange mind in many ways, a wonderful mind, but odd. That somebody who was so obsessed with the future as an aesthetic notion should be so preoccupied with his own past is very strange indeed.

CD: Yes, and the fact that everything really comes out of a very narrow, limited period.

JA: I think he was fighting against that from another angle, with all this talk about the future and cutting oneself off from the past and so on. So no, I don't revise. I do the revision during the composing. I think people appreciate it if you did mean the piece that you hand them to play. After all, my music can be tricky to play. Why should they spend all those hours on stuff I didn't really mean? So there is a bit of a moral responsibility. Publishing, printing, copying, performing all take money and time. The start of that chain is the composer. If you didn't mean what you're doing, then you've no right to expect other people to spend all that time and money with your product. You've got to earn that respect. Just vamping at the piano in a self-indulgent state of hyper-excitement, then writing it down and calling it a composition isn't good enough. In that sense I'm very tough on myself while composing. The revision goes on during the composing. Every passage is worked over, and entire pieces of music get rewritten. That's what it's all about. It's so that I don't have to do it in 20 years' time. [Laughter]

Conversation Six

Composing (or Not)

This conversation starts off with Anderson reflecting on his broad approach to composition, before the discussion turns to different types of commission and different ways that he starts work on a piece, leading to a discussion of *Poetry Nearing Silence* and an early sketch for what would become *Incantesimi*. The importance of musical syntax is explored, as is the choice of language for verbal jottings, from which emerge discussions of rhythm and notation. The conversation then turns to the extent that any material can create associations for diverse audiences and Anderson's views on writing for amateurs or beginners, as well as the use of extended techniques and electronics. The conversation then looks at times when composing has been more difficult, with times of compositional crisis and works that are rejected, notably with writing what would become *Fantasias*. In the midst of this, the value of creative misunderstandings is also noted.

CD: You've composed in numerous genres, with everything from solo instrument via chamber music to large orchestra with soloists and chorus, and ranging from a small-scale piano etude lasting under a minute to an opera lasting around about 100 minutes. Your range is clear, but do you feel drawn to any particular vehicle for your expression?

JA: Yes. The sound of the orchestra inspired me to be a composer. My parents used to play radio broadcasts of orchestral music, or recordings on vinyl of orchestral music, or we'd hear it on the TV – there was a huge amount of classical music on mainstream TV until about 1995. When I first started to try to compose in my head, as a 9 or 10 year-old, it was orchestral music that I imagined. Having said that, I always wanted to assemble a balanced output without specialising in anything. I love writing opera and plan to write a second one, but I don't want to specialise in this or that or the other. Recently I've composed a lot of chamber music. I like to change the palette. But if there is a core focus, it's probably the orchestra. At the same time, I had a marvellous time last year writing my second quartet, so I hope to write more quartets. I want to be somebody who can do the range. I admire Mompou very much – he only wrote piano pieces lasting between one and four minutes his whole life – but that's clearly not what I'm at.

CD: Would you say that the orchestral attraction means that if you wrote an oratorio with voices and orchestra, that it's essentially an orchestral work that happens to have a bigger range of palettes?

JA: No. I've had a lot of experience with voices, for example, and am a choral singer myself. So in a work for solo voice, chorus and orchestra like *Heaven is Shy of Earth*, the chorus or soloist is clearly the focus in any movement which isn't purely instrumental. And in my concertos the soloist is more often than not the focal point – I don't like concertos which don't balance. No, in those situations I've been careful not to write surrogate orchestral music with a soloist or chorus just added on. It's quite different from writing a purely orchestral work.

CD: I realise that, for a composer, each individual work is a unique manifestation, like a child or a baby, but do you perceive relationships, strands, themes or ebbs and flows in your music?

JA: From the age of about 16 the central concern has been a very linguistic one, really, to do with the actual syntax of music. Musicology has long since decided that music is not a language, but my interest in perception tells me otherwise. I'm very concerned with how the music sounds physically and how people might be able to perceive not only individual sounds but their succession in time. Also I hope that people from any kind of background can hear what I do and get into it somehow – it's not intended for only one kind of audience at all. Therefore, it seemed to me that the only thing one could go on was how the brain works, really – how the brain chunks sounds and sonic experience. For example, visually a large number of coins is something you cannot count. Similarly, as we know, aurally a large number of sounds in a small space of time and register is something you cannot perceive in detail, but you can perceive the overall shape. It's a statistical thing and a composer must take that into consideration. As I say, such criteria of perception seem to me almost the only tool to work with because anything more specific cannot be generalised. So, a serial approach was too specific. Even at that age of 16 I was beginning to feel that the spectral approach, although it aimed at something much more general and universal, was too culturally and technically specific. Hence the problem many spectral composers have had in writing vocal music, because spectral material doesn't naturally lend itself to the voice in so many ways. I agreed with the approach of the spectralists to look at perception as a starting point, but I didn't agree with them beyond that. I felt any kind of sound and any kind of material, including the most familiar, could be grist to the composer's mill. The fact that it could be familiar material didn't bother me. I became concerned with not excluding from my music sounds that could be familiar to listeners.

It seems to me that if, before the piece starts, you and the listener might have shared some of the sounds that they were going to hear in the piece before, then that could be creatively powerful. I don't only mean the sound of a trombone, but the actual harmony, or the rhythmic language or whatever. That can be a powerful means of communication, almost like a Baroque series of affects.[1]

Through archive recordings that have now been reissued, I have heard something of traditional music from around the world from about 100 years ago, before those parts of the world had been constantly exposed via technology to Western harmony. They teach you a great deal about what music can be, and what musical activity can be. The way things are now – with everyone everywhere having radios, the Internet, etc., and with the commercial mass marketing that's gone on certainly since 1960 – that's both good and bad. It's bad because many things get evened out and destroyed, which is awful. What's advantageous as a composer is that you can send out signals and be more sure that different people might understand them in a similar way. That's scary, but also interesting.

CD: What sort of thing do you mean?

JA: Though nobody will be able to spot this in my music, I once made a large catalogue of phrases, of melodic gestures, quite a long time ago. I still think about that, though I don't use it consciously when I compose. I spent nine months solidly examining melodic gestures from everything I could find, plainsong, every kind of musical tradition you can think of: pop music, Hildegard, Mozart, Messiaen, Boulez, Xenakis, whoever and wherever. It was very interesting to do that. I found similarities, for example, in certain melodic gestures used in Xenakis and Boulez and The Beatles. Well, they were all active in the 1960s. That's possibly not a coincidence.

CD: Well, The Beatles, certainly Paul McCartney, went to various avant-garde concerts, so something may have filtered through.

JA: Yes. I don't know much comparative musicological work of this sort that's been done widely. Melodic gestures from pop songs certainly do feature in my work. Occasionally I can spot them. These are just very common melodic gestures. When people do not have a formal Western art music training and they

---

[1]   The aesthetic theory that passions could be represented by specific types of gesture.

use Western musical materials, when you find someone like Paul McCartney or John Lennon working with certain kinds of melodic formula from blues and jazz and so on, and turning them into, say, 'Yesterday', for example, or 'Eleanor Rigby', it's very refreshing because they are not jaded in their uses of these things. You get a more interesting degree of invention with those materials than you'd get from an academically trained composer from the same period trying to write straight tonal music. So that's one factor.

I did the same thing with harmony. I never thought of harmony as just one chord in isolation. This comes from my training during which, as I said, I had to memorise Bach chorales. I've always thought of harmony as a trajectory of chords. In that sense I'm a very Western composer because it's always about going somewhere and landing somewhere, or evading that landing. Although I was very excited with contemporary art music in the West, including the high period of serialism, I did become concerned, as a listener as well as a composer, that the bottom seemed to have dropped out of whole areas of music. I was very struck, for example, by the fact that Michael Finnissy was able to write settings of Australian sea shanties just as much as he was able to write a dense passage like the first few pages of *English Country Tunes*, or even modulate from one to the other. There are sections in that piece that are amazingly transparent, like 'My Bonnie Boy', which is just a monody and starts as only on the black notes – a device I nicked, by the way, for my second piano Etude. Thank you, Michael. [Laughter] So, although I do not want my music to be eclectic, and I hope it isn't, the musical origins for my work could be termed eclectic. I was very conscious of the fact that I made a break when I was about 20. I'd been trying to write various things, serial things mainly, and then I'd had a go at spectral music a little after that. But there was a break where I just stopped composing and thought a lot for around six months about what music is. Every 15 years or so, I do that again. Basically, there is nothing else I can go on but the sheer physical stuff music is made of and the way the brain can chunk it. That's the way I work.

CD: That's the broad approach, but how about the specifics. For instance, if you have a commission, with certain parameters, does that make it easier or harder to begin composing a work?

JA: Commissions tend to come in two types in my life. One is a phone call from somebody like, to give a specific instance, Nicholas Daniel: 'Would you write a piece for oboe and piano?' Well, I'd never dreamt of doing such a thing, but the idea appealed and it was a nice surprise. A couple of years ago, I got a letter from Julian Bream asking if I'd write a guitar piece. I'd vaguely thought of writing a guitar piece, but it wasn't on my agenda at that time. I decided to accept as the idea appealed musically. That's what I'm writing now. The other type of commission is the sort which, if I'm lucky, chimes in with something that I've long wanted to do. I have a long list of stuff that I feel I really need to write, that I've wanted to write for eons. If a request comes in that chimes in with one of those things, I'll do it. For example, when the BBC requested I write a big piece for the 2006 Proms, I offered two ideas, of which one was a plan for the oratorio *Heaven is Shy of Earth* and that's the one the BBC wanted. That was very lucky. *Thebans* is another such case – it had been around in my mind since 1984 but was commissioned only in 2009, when I started composing it.

The problem with a commission, whether you've cherished it for a long time or not, is not to go stale. The starting point for my music is very general – as already explained, it's based on auditory perception in a very basic way. That can apply to any kind of music and any kind of thing that I might write. This might cause me to approach everything from the same angle and write very self-similar results, and I really don't want to do that. I don't mind the fact that from some pieces to the next there may be consistencies. You can't help that. It's like walking – it will come out in your personality without thinking. The trouble with my type of approach is that, because of its generality, it can hamper the imagination as much as stimulate it, and I became aware of that quite early on as a danger.

CD: You talked about your starting point there, so here comes the dumb question. How do you begin a work? Or, what are some of the ways that you have begun?

JA: Well, since it happens to be around, here is the score of *Poetry Nearing Silence*. I decided to write the piece very fast to see what happened if I set myself the seemingly impossible task of writing a 15-minute piece in about a week. I wrote a movement a day. Each morning I wrote a short score of the movement concerned and then in the afternoon and evening I revised it and copied it out into full score. I use the word 'copy' more than 'orchestrated', because the piece is for few instruments, so the final score was more like a fair copy. Then I slept and next day I did the next one. The actual starting point is over there, Tom Phillips's little book *The Heart of A Humument*.[2] I found that in a bookshop, loved it, and each day I opened the book at random. That was very important with *Poetry Nearing Silence*: the arbitrariness was quite deliberate. I'd see a picture and if I liked it and thought I could write a piece about it, I composed it right away. Then the next day, without any premeditation, I'd open the book again. Sometimes I came up with ones that I didn't want to do. I made one other rule: one of the pieces should use one of the pages I didn't want to do, just to see what happened. That was fun. So the starting point was the combination of image and word in that book, and whatever associations the book stimulated musically. The subject of the piece in that sense is music and the image. It was a disquisition on what programme

---

[2]   Tom Phillips, *The Heart of A Humument* (Stuttgart and London: Hansjörg Mayer and Talfourd, 1985).

music is because, although I give the phrases as titles in the programme, I don't really explain what they mean and it's not clear in the book what they mean.

The associations they happen to have with me are not necessarily what anyone else would have. I just let that flow through. For example, the phrase 'In Bohemia screwing' I took to be about Janáček (I got the country wrong – he was Moravian). Anyway, Janáček was a highly over-excited man who was constantly having affairs in Bohemia and in Prague, among other places, where he shouldn't have been, so I wrote a manic Janáček parody. For 'Lashing in Italy' I thought of Hans Keller's complaints about the sadistic character of Bartók's dissonant quadruple stops in his Fourth String Quartet. I've always loved the Fourth Quartet, so I wrote an homage to that. There were various private jokes going on in each movement. *Poetry Nearing Silence* was an exercise in irrationality, in highly subjective responses to random stimuli with an artificial deadline of a week to see what happened. I was interested in the Oulipo writers' group, especially by their notion of writing under artificial constraints.[3] I'd got to the end of movement eight, which is now the last movement, and I stopped there because that was the end of the deadline. So that's one instance.

CD: So that's a deliberate set of extra-musical inputs and fairly extreme restrictions. Presumably there are also works where you start with musical ideas.

JA: An instance would be this sheet of paper here, which is a sketch for the piece I'm going to write for Rattle and the Berlin Phil (see Figure 3). It's not quite the first sketch – there is one previous one, but here there are four musical lines. There should be five. The idea of the piece is to have five kinds of music, which are heard in either solo or duet form. Each music could involve many parts of the orchestra. Then, eventually, they're going to be heard in combination, all five at once.[4] What I'm doing here is trying to sketch these and seeing how they look when they're on top of each other. That's the sketch for very high violin music, which was also in my previous sketch. These other things are not in my previous sketch. They're little emblems of what the music might be. The funny thing about it is that the music is phrased. Quite often articulation is present from the first sketch, whereas many will leave that until much later. For me, how it is going to be played, and on what instrument it's going to be played, is so crucial to the initial idea that I have to put a lot of that in. These lines can have any dynamic. They should be at variable dynamics, that's going to change through the piece. The piece is modelled on the finale of Mozart's 'Jupiter' Symphony, which has five musical ideas in counterpoint, but it won't sound anything like that.

---

[3] Founded by Raymond Queneau and François Le Lionnais, Oulipo (Ouvroir de littérature potentielle) was a loose group of French writers and mathematicians who used constraint as a governing factor in their works.

[4] See Conversation Eighteen, 'Partnerships', for discussion of the finished piece, *Incantesimi*.

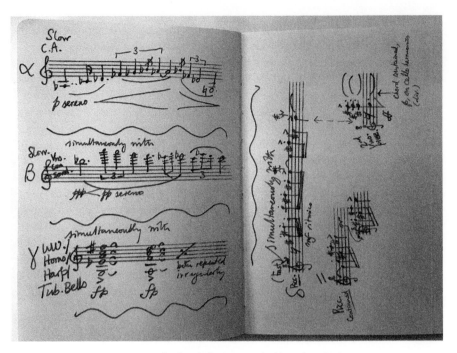

Figure 3   An early sketch for *Incantesimi* by Julian Anderson,
subsequently published by Schott Music Ltd

CD: So these ideas were the starting point.

JA: Well, as it happens, the starting point isn't only that, but also a photograph of the roof of Milan Cathedral. The sight of those wonderful towers on top of Milan Cathedral with twilight at the back and this light beaming over the roof prompted me to want to do something with height, light and space. The piece is going to be quite high in register. So the physical starting point is sketches of the sort I've just shown you. Sometimes they're verbal, usually in French, funnily enough.

CD: What's the reason for that?

JA: You know this French expression, '*à l'infinitif*'? It doesn't mean you'll do it, it means it is something to do, and you might do it, or you might not. There is no equivalent of using the tense that way in English. In other words, you're not ordering yourself to do it, you're saying, 'I could do it. This is something good to do. What about doing it?' It's quite close to a subjunctive-type feeling, but it's not that either. I don't know of another language that can do that. I was delighted when, two or three years after I'd switched to French verbal sketching because of this, I found, through the French edition of Peter Hill and Nigel Simeone's book, that Messiaen uses it.[5] In the original diary entries, where he said 'write a piece for this or that' or 'write an oratorio on the transfiguration', what he would say is 'écrire'. That could mean 'I will do it', or it could mean 'that's something which would be interesting to do'. I got it not from Messiaen but from Marcel Duchamp. There was a big break in his work after *Nude Descending a Staircase*.[6] He reconsidered what he was going to do with his art and he kept a very interesting notebook. It was full of things to do. One was buy a dictionary and mark in it words to be marked. There is an American interview with him from about 1967 where he was asked, 'Did you ever do these things?' and he said, 'No, no, no. It was *à l'infinitif.*' It was exploring the possibility of things to do. For me, the verbal part of sketching is always that. It's not an imperative and I became concerned that in English I was telling myself to do things, whereas in French it was more like, 'You can do it, or you can't'.

CD: I suppose the closest you'd get in English is saying, 'How about such and such?'

JA: Perhaps, but that's asking a question, whereas the French *infinitif* isn't.

CD: Or writing it maybe with a question mark in brackets.

JA: Well I kept using lots of question marks when I was jotting to myself in English and I became fed up with them. [Laughter] I wanted a language which could do that without asking a question all the time. I know this sounds highly pretentious, but it did make a difference. I've never done much verbal sketching, but there was something about the French language that helped. I became very sensitive to this question of language when I was studying Classics. There's a very early piece of mine for six percussionists called *The King of Persia* (1981) that's long since in the drawer, as it were. It was inspired by the fact that in Ancient Greek, if you say, 'The King', with the definite article, it just means any king, oddly, whereas if you say 'King', without the definite article, it meant the King of Persia. They had a lot of trouble with the King of Persia. They had many wars with Persia and they knew that just 'King' was that guy over there who's always causing trouble. In Greek they also have a verb, 'to rhythm', and we don't have that in any Western language that I know.

CD: Some people more recently have used constructions like 'rhythmicing'. I find it's a bit ugly.

JA: Yes. In Greek you could talk, for example, of 'rhythming' music, or 'rhythming' words. Funnily enough, that resulted in another percussion piece

---

[5]   Peter Hill and Nigel Simeone, *Messiaen*, trans. Lucie Kayas (Paris: Fayard, 2008).
[6]   1912.

of the same period, also withdrawn, called *Rhythming Music*, a study for two side drums. I became very aware – and this is a Wittgenstein-type thing – that what you think is very much determined by the language you use. Being interested in different languages, I became very interested also in the musical equivalent of that problem.

CD: How different Western art music might have been if we had rhythm as a verb...

JA: I really wonder about that. One person who would have leapt at it, obviously, would have been Messiaen. He had to invent a word for himself, 'rhythmatician'. Yes, the history of Western music in terms of rhythm is a very peculiar problem and it would have been very different conceptually if they'd have had the word as a verb. Rhythmic music is not the same as music that itself is rhythming. When you say rhythmic music you mean music that has a strong sense of rhythm, but it doesn't tell you what the music is doing. Whereas rhythming music tells you the music is 'doing rhythm', it's making itself with rhythm, it's forming rhythm, and that's not the same as just rhythmic music. I also wonder if Stravinsky ever knew that linguistic fact. I'm sure Xenakis did.

CD: Oh, undoubtedly. Whether Stravinsky did is perhaps more debatable. I can't imagine that his knowledge of Greek was any better than his knowledge of Latin, given what he did to that in *Oedipus Rex*. [Laughter]

JA: Quite.

CD: Having had Stravinsky, Messiaen, Xenakis and others, is there a better sense today of rhythm as more than just a noun or, for that matter, just an afterthought or by-product?

JA: One criticism I have of some contemporary music is that it seems to work with durations, but not to face the question of metre. Metre is much more embarrassing for a contemporary composer who's abstract in inclination, because metre has associations with dance. And possibly with dancing, and even with rock music and all kinds of other associations. As soon as you deal with metric patterns you are not stylistically pure any more. Immediately, if you have a siciliano rhythm, that has a history. If you just deal with the set of durations which happen to be three to one to two, which is what a siciliano is, you could do a Messiaen-like rhythmic set of operations on that, which would be totally ahistorical. Or rather, would be historical to Messiaen and Stravinsky, or Messiaen's view of Stravinsky's *Sacre* and things like 'personnages rythmiques'. If you don't regard it that way but regard it as a siciliano, then there's a whole overtone of history. Grisey and the spectralists didn't deal with metre, Boulez definitely didn't, and Messiaen, not really. When I heard *Tanzsuite mit*

Deutschlandlied by Lachenmann, which is a dance suite and all about metre, I was really interested in how he dealt with those dance patterns. He has dances and tarantellas in other things. *Mouvement (-vor der Erstarrung)* has a big tarantella in its final section (which I believe is modelled on the riotous overture to *Donna Dianna* by Reznicek). The siciliano in the *Tanzsuite mit Deutschlandlied* is, bar for bar, modelled on the 'Pastorale' in Bach's *Christmas Oratorio*. You can't hear that directly in the piece, but it's in there. Somebody like that, who's very experimental in sound, but also tying his music, all the time, into history, showed me how one could use these very basic, common materials of metre and consonance and so on, and form links with history without being overtly nostalgic. I felt it was fresh material for me. I didn't want to compose neo-Bach or neo-Schumann, or rewrite Bruckner. It wasn't like that. It was to do with phenomena that are around that have had a history. But I also like the fact that I can look at such phenomena from just a purely ahistorical acoustic point of view as well, so you have both.

CD: So what has this meant for your thinking on metre?

JA: I reduced it to the basic question of upbeats and downbeats. In essence, it seemed to me that if you have a set of durations, whether they're regular or irregular, if they're all evenly accented and have equal value in the music, there's no stress and hence no sense of metre. As soon as one of them is more stressed than the others, and predictably so, if there's a repeating pattern, then you have the feeling of metre. Usually you would be also leading up to the stress – that's the upbeat. However, the upbeat and stress could happen on any beat of the bar if I chose. And in my music these things sometimes happen at many speeds at once. That led to *Khorovod*, which is all about those upbeats and downbeats happening in different parts, at different speeds, simultaneously. Then the question was how to notate them in one conducted metre, which might have nothing to do with the metres that you think you're hearing.

I gradually became suspicious of Messiaen's marvellous achievement of separating pitch and rhythm. I began to feel that this was not something I could do anymore. You can see from my sketches that they're not just pitch sets, they've already got rhythm and, often, metre. I don't often plan pitches without rhythms because the whole way pitches sound in music depends on what rhythm they have. I can't personally separate pitch very easily from rhythm. I know that it's perfectly possible to do so conceptually, but what interests me is the link between pitch, rhythm and stress. For example, if you're working with consonances, are you consonant on the downbeat, or what sounds like the downbeat? The obvious link to make is a consonance on a downbeat. That's the tonal norm. If you pull that about, as I do a lot, there are all kinds of other possibilities.

CD: In other words, far from being nostalgic, you are confounding those historical associations, turning them every which way.

JA: Absolutely. And studying folk music of different traditions has taught me that all kinds of things like that can happen. One big influence on all of this, also, is the Indian classical tradition because their notion of *tal* and how the *tal* relates to the mode and the *raag* interests me very much.[7] In the later stages of a traditional Indian *raag*, after the *alap*, the *tal* comes in and, once it's well established, there are increasing variations on the *tal* which both the sitar player and the tabla player – if it's a sitar and tabla – are making. They do these wonderful elaborate cross-rhythms across the whole duration of the *tal*, even across three or four *tals*. They only land on the downbeat together at the end of that. You might have a hugely slow polyrhythm going. Then the whole thing lands together again. You feel those things pulling together, and then you'll get a consonance when they land together. That interests me a lot.

CD: Of course, the sense or otherwise of metre and stress are intimately entwined not just with durations, but also bar lines and the whole business of notation.

JA: And in particular the size of note values chosen. For example, in *Book of Hours*, very fast sections are usually in quavers, not in 16th notes, and because they're in 8th notes, they're much easier to play. I'd already tried that once with *Alhambra Fantasy*, which is largely very fast and in large note values, and it seemed to work. I got hints on this from seeing the way Boulez re-notated his music over the years. For instance, the last toccata in *Éclat* was originally in 32nd notes, then it was re-notated in 16th notes, and in the now-published score it's in 8th notes. He did the same thing with *Le Marteau sans maître* and a number of other pieces. As he conducted more and more he used larger and larger note values. I began to realise that the size of note value, and therefore the metronome mark chosen, could have a huge impact on the playing style. It is no accident that Brian Ferneyhough chooses to write in units of the quaver, of the 8th note, slow 8th notes, generally, with multiple, very dense subdivisions of that. Of course, the scores have multiple beams for every note. If it's going to be fast, they have four, five or six beams, even. Now, for what he's doing, aesthetically, that lends a very particular kind of look to the score. I once notated the opening of Ferneyhough's *Lemma-Icon-Epigram*, the first page of it, at four times the published note values, and when you do that, it looks a bit like Elliott Carter or Wuorinen, somebody like that. But that's not at all appropriate for Ferneyhough, and would not result in a suitable performance of his work.

CD: This psychological impact of the notation for the performer is critical to how a piece sounds.

JA: It's a question of finding the notational style that best conveys the essence of the piece. I'm quite open about what that might be. It could include graphics

---

[7]   The *tal*, also known as *tala*, is the equivalent of metre in Indian classical music.

and all sorts of things, if needed. One of the cleverest notated scores is the last paragraph of Cardew's *The Great Learning*, which, on the Deutsche Grammophon recording, sounds a bit like Ligeti, with clusters that gradually thin out into consonances.[8] What he's done is to say in words that you all start singing together on any note and then you change to a note you can hear someone else singing. If you do that, the texture will thin out and become consonant – triadic, interestingly. That process happens several times in waves. For what he was trying to do, which was a piece that anyone can get up and sing immediately, that notation is absolutely right. It would not work for Ligeti's *Lux Aeterna* or many other things.

CD: It's remarkable how precise in effect such scores can be so long as the people performing them are doing so in earnest.

JA: When I do classes on notation, I play recordings of various pieces by different composers and ask the students to guess how each of these sound extracts is notated. One of them is a Stockhausen extract, a very orderly sounding passage from *Aus den sieben Tagen*. When they see that the score is just words, and rather simple instructions at that, that obviously produces a shock. Then they want to know, 'Well, who was playing? Did Stockhausen know them well? Was he in the recording? Did he supervise the recording? Did they know his music well?' You quickly realise that Stockhausen's improvised recordings worked because they were by collaborators of his who were playing his notated music all the time.

CD: Going back to Cardew, he's an exemplar, if you like, of the angst that there was among a lot of left-leaning composers, certainly Marxist composers, about how they could be aesthetically true to themselves and compose music that was in keeping for the masses, for the proletariat. And yet, Bach was doing this a couple of hundred years before, because everybody went to the church, from the lowest of the low to the highest of the high. The music was for, and had to be for, everybody. The chorale tunes were recognisable by absolutely everybody as much as Christmas carols and things like that.

JA: Yes. There are two twentieth-century composers, it seems to me, who managed to do this in a creative and valuable way. One is Vaughan Williams and the other is Copland. What I'm puzzled about with Bach is the way he treated those well-known tunes, which was often incredibly contorted and harmonically elaborate.

CD: You only have to think of 'Jesu, Joy'. The notion that with this chorale tune as his basic material, he starts in this completely random other place, with the chorale only coming in part way through these apparently unrelated musings.

---

8   Cornelius Cardew, *The Great Learning*, The Scratch Orchestra, recorded at Chappell Recording Studios, London, 15 and 16 February 1971, Deutsche Grammophon 2538 216 (LP).

JA: Yes, and they've had to listen to three or four minutes before it appears, as often happens in the cantatas, exactly. They were listening to very modern sounds for those times. Some of those chorales for the *Orgelbüchlein*, the more chromatic ones, as Messiaen used to point out, sound like Debussy or Schoenberg. I don't understand how Bach got away with it. And a twentieth-century example is Messiaen, because he did have conflicts with his parishioners at some points. We know that when he got the job at La Trinité, he had to promise not to use too much anarchic harmony – and promised he wouldn't. But of course he did. I know, from people who were studying with Messiaen in the '50s, that they used to go to hear his services, and that he'd improvise a bit of what was becoming *Messe de la Pentecôte* or something, and the congregation would be pretty disconcerted, but nobody ever thought of getting rid of Messiaen. They put up with it, because they knew he was famous, I suppose, and ultimately, they began to find that the sounds did illustrate some of the more extraordinary things in the Bible. I know, for example, that late on in life he did a big improvisation about the Creation, and one can imagine what that might have sounded like. You didn't have to be too broad-minded a music lover to get what he was at, particularly if you had commentary from the priest beforehand, as you did on those occasions. So Messiaen, maybe, in terms of his relationship with his parish, is the nearest equivalent to Bach's situation, but I don't think Messiaen used well-known tunes in his music – except plainsong, which he used all the time.

CD: Yes, but very few plainsong melodies would have the same recognition factor. The kind of thing Bach was doing would be as if you suddenly had 'Silent Night' being played on a trumpet in the middle of a piece, or something like that. The piece might be about something completely different, and, depending on the context, it would set up not just recognition, but a whole raft of cultural references that put a different dimension on to what is being heard.

JA: Funnily enough, 'Silent Night' does feature in my Second Quartet, which is subtitled '300 Christmas Carols'. Partly because of my five years singing in the London Philharmonic Choir, where we used to do things like the Vaughan Williams *Christmas Carol Fantasia*, what interests me is that, at the time when Vaughan Williams started writing in his mature style, it was something more or less modern. It wasn't by the time he died, but at the time he started his representative composing, it was more or less contemporary music of that time. It is a mishmash of various things, particularly Ravel – some harmonies from *Valses nobles sentimentales*, plus *Daphnis*-type progressions, plus bits from Debussy's *Pelléas*, but all done in a very personal, original way. It's interesting to me that he could use that style and adapt it only very slightly to write a piece like the *Carol Fantasia*, which can still be sung by anybody. I've written some simple choral music, but I've always tried to keep it entirely in my own style and idiom. I don't know whether or not the time has passed where such things are possible, because what one knows of easier choral music written recently is often pastiche, more or less. Quite often it's pastiche Vaughan Williams, funnily enough, plus various light musics in a more or less pleasant way. But there's little link between that and, say, what I would normally write as a concert composer. Socially, that is an interesting problem.

CD: I wonder whether that's a slightly false perception, because pop music as a mass culture thing is a relatively recent phenomenon, but there always was pop music. The vast majority of people would have been getting their music from the music halls and the penny sheet music, broadside ballads and that kind of thing, so I wonder the extent to which this connection really existed.

JA: Well, maybe I'm idealising. But I think there is a connection, for example, between – to be specific – 'Jens the [Road]mender', which is one of the most popular songs written by Carl Nielsen, and the melody in the violins about three minutes into his Fifth Symphony, which is quite a simple melody, but with a very strange, uncertain harmonic context. Now, the Fifth Symphony is, by any standards, one of Nielsen's most complicated pieces. It's also one of his most dissonant in places. I'm not aware that he felt there was any difference between writing the song 'Jens the [Road]mender' and writing that tune in the Symphony. And what about the second subject of Brahms's Second Symphony, which sounds to me like one of his *Liebeslieder-Walzer*. So does, for that matter, 'Wie lieblich sind deine Wohnungen' in the *German Requiem*, which sounds like one of his more popular piano duet waltzes that you could sell for penny sheet music. In the 1950s, I think it was Aldous Huxley who said that he was becoming concerned that the gap between Boulez and *My Fair Lady*, as he put it, was much wider than the gap between *My Fair Lady* and '30s Stravinsky.

CD: As you say, you've written for amateurs, so what has been your approach to straddling this potential gap?

JA: Since I use a harmonic or modal vocabulary which goes from the most consonant to the most dissonant, it's obvious that the most consonant end of it can be played or sung by people who are used to singing consonant diatonic pop songs. When I've written, for example, a simple piano piece, I have written it in a vocabulary which, physically, a beginner pianist can manage, but I've always done that in a way that links with my serious music. For example, there's a piano piece called *Somewhere Near Cluj*.

CD: My son played it.

JA: Oh, thanks, that's nice to know. It is still used by the Associated Board and when Thalia Myers[9] asked me to write it I immediately said yes. The reason I said yes was because, when I was studying piano as a beginner pianist, no one ever gave me the *Five Easy Pieces* of Stravinsky, Bartók's *Mikrokosmos*, or Mompou, or Satie. I discovered these pieces in my local library and realised that I could play them, but what they gave me for lessons was beginner piano pieces with condescending little titles that were blatantly insincere, presumably by composers thinking all a beginner pianist can cope with is little childish titles, and little childish pieces. Well, thank you, but at the age of eight I loved *The Rite of Spring*, and I didn't want to play junk. What eight-year-old does? The attitude behind the pieces I was given as a beginner pianist was deeply condescending and uncreative. It was enough to put anyone off music altogether.

CD: And many kids knew the *Rite* from *Fantasia*. Also these days, the best children's programmes and films don't patronise them. In fact, they are often pretty sophisticated. I'm thinking of something like *Charlie and Lola*, which has an episode where the characters enter into works of art. Even films like *Inside Out* or *Up* – they're fun, but they also deal with some pretty meaty things.

JA: I didn't know as a kid that just after writing *The Rite of Spring* Stravinsky had written music I could have been playing, like *Les Cinq Doigts*. As I say, I was never given those pieces to learn. By the time I discovered them, I was using them as sight-reading practice. *Mikrokosmos* is very useful for that. I love those pieces, and some of the best are the simplest. Bartók did have that wonderful knack of having just five notes in one hand and three notes in another and giving you a real piece of Bartók. Amazing. Because I love that period of Bartók, that period of Stravinsky, and because of the fact that I started using diatonic modes myself, I said yes to Thalia and wrote *Somewhere Near Cluj* as a sketch for *Stations of the Sun*. The first few notes of *Somewhere Near Cluj* and the first few notes of *Stations of the Sun* are the same. Everything was to do with the bigger orchestral piece. I literally took every problem to do with mode, to do with melody, to do with modal modulation and worked it into the piano piece. There's an unstable note in *Somewhere Near Cluj*, which is F. It's never clear if the F is going to be natural or sharp. It ends the piece in the natural position and, amusingly, somebody at Faber Music, Martin Kingsbury, of whom I'm very fond, said, 'I think that's a wrong note at the end: it should be a D.' It was interesting that for once, because it is a very simple piece that anyone can play, somebody in the publisher could start saying that they think there's a wrong note. I disagreed with Martin and it stayed in the score, but I warmly appreciated his thoughts. It was an interesting exchange.

---

[9] British pianist Thalia Myers (b. 1945) was the instigator of the Associated Board of the Royal School of Music's *Spectrum* series of piano anthologies, in which contemporary composers were invited to write short pieces ranging in difficulty from grades one to eight.

I found the same experience when I wrote choral music. Sometimes editors would start saying, 'Is that note really necessary?' I'm perfectly happy to say why a note's there and try to show that it does make musical sense.

I got that unstable F from the first piece in Janáček's *On an Overgrown Path*, where it is never clear if the third is going to be major or minor, it keeps oscillating, even at the end. Again, nobody ever handed me the *Overgrown Path* pieces as a kid, which are like little sketches for Janáček opera scenes. You can relate them directly to bits in *Kát'a* or *The Cunning Little Vixen* or whatever, with these suggestive little titles. I could have played the easier ones. Socially, my feeling is that, if I have an idea that can be distilled onto what you might call a postage stamp, and stripped of a lot of ornamentation, and just stated very clearly, then I'm very happy to make that into a piece that a beginner pianist or an amateur trumpeter can play. That's fun and it's brought me some very nice experiences in the sense that, like you just said to me, 'My son played that.' It's nice that as a composer your name can come up with people, just in daily life.

CD: For Wilf, he was excited to do a piece by a composer that I knew, of course, but it was also the idea that composers are people who might ring on the phone at some point. It's an ordinary thing, not something fundamentally removed.

JA: There is something very unusual about what has happened to musical sound in the last 100 years that makes it very exciting. The more unusual sounds – noises, new tunings, etc. – have seemed not to go into much commercial music. That does mean that concert composers occupy a particular place in society, which is not that of mass production. Although, even then, you're going to have to be careful saying that, because you can look at quite a bit of rock music and find those sounds, or sounds quite close to them, so it's all a matter of context.

CD: Yes, you'll find a lot of extended techniques all over the place.

JA: Jimmy Hendrix.

CD: And also in jazz as well.

JA: Coltrane pioneered many of them. A friend of mine found a record from the late '20s called *Sax O Phun* by Rudy Wiedoeft.[10] He's the saxophonist, and the pianist is Oscar Levant, who was later a pupil of Schoenberg. It involves the fastest and most precise slap tongue, very fast *glissandi*, microtones and so on, all of it ornamenting, frankly, a rather banal little tune, but making something rather magical and funny out of it. Jazz particularly has been a pioneer in the field of extended instrumental techniques. I'm always struck by the fact that very

---

[10]   This can now be found on YouTube by searching for 'Rudy Wiedoeft Sax O Phun'.

few composers who use extended techniques acknowledge jazz. That's a little bit wrong, frankly. Coltrane was before Lachenmann, really, and the most extreme Coltrane is really out there.

CD: Very much so. The other area of extension is electronics, of course, which also happens to be used extensively in some aspects of popular music, sometimes inventively, other times not. However, in terms of concert music, speaking as an outsider to both composer and music tech things, it strikes me as being terribly difficult to make electronics a musical necessity.

JA: Generally, yes, absolutely true.

CD: It is hard to avoid the sense of it simply being effects applied to the music. Having listened to an awful lot of student composers fiddling around with MaxMSP,[11] an awful lot of that now sounds quite clichéd and/or predictable and/or simply uninteresting to my ears.

JA: Just dealing with strictly the acoustic problem that you've raised, the integration question is a very serious issue. This goes right back to Varèse's *Déserts*. It's not merely the fact tape and orchestra are never played together in that work. Varèse did use sample percussion sounds and things that are typical of his work in the tape part. There's not a total discontinuity. Nevertheless, the gap is rather acutely felt between the two sound sources. I know that Chou Wen-Chung, who was working on copying the score for him, still feels that the electronic interludes just don't work, that they are of lower technical quality than the actual orchestration of Varèse, which is so magnificent. He saw Varèse working with his Ampex tape recorders and wondered how Varèse was going to make electronics anything like as sophisticated, as incredibly perceptive and razor sharp as his orchestral sound, which is so absolutely ruthlessly brilliant. I agree on the whole with Wen-Chung – he wittily described Varèse's primitive electronic equipment as the equivalent in sound of a Model T Ford! Though *Déserts* should nevertheless be played with the tapes because they're there and Varèse wanted them. It's exciting to hear 70-year-old Varèse trying these things out. Every piece that combines live instruments with any kind of electronic or electro-acoustic sound has to face the problem of how the two are integrated. The Roberto Gerhard Third Symphony manages this integration of tape with orchestra much better, by the way, especially in its opening and closing sections.[12] The other day, I was playing somebody the third region of *Hymnen* with orchestra and was amazed by how well Stockhausen combines the tape with the orchestral

---

[11] A widely used visual programming language developed by IRCAM and the basis of much interaction between performers and electronics in live situations.

[12] Roberto Gerhard, Symphony No. 3 ('Collages') for orchestra and two-track tape (1963).

sound in that piece. On the other hand, I'm not convinced the electronics are needed in Boulez's *Répons*. It's a lovely piece, but the electronics seem like icicles on top of a completely normal Boulez instrumental piece. There's a much closer connection in *Anthèmes II*, in which the solo violin and electronics really bind together to form something unique. But I hear no connection in *Répons* between the modulated electronic sounds and the orchestra at all except that they're based on the soloists' flourishes. Beyond that they sound like another world entirely to me, and not productively so.

CD: So how did you approach that in *Book of Hours*?

JA: The harmonic structure of that piece determined a lot of the electronic sound, using, for example, frequency modulation spectra, which I used in the ensemble harmonies as well. So, the tape sound has a relationship to the instrumental sound. I made a scale from 1 to 10 of relationships between the instrumental and the electronic sound, from as similar as possible to as different as possible. There were sketches for all the electronic sounds as I was writing because I had to know technically what was possible and was doing constant experiments. Whether it has the effect I intended or not I don't know, but I gave the matter careful thought, since by 2005 it was 15 years since I'd had a public performance of an electro-acoustic work. I was aware that by 2005 I could seem like someone dipping their toe in the water without really knowing what the water was. So I worked very hard at the whole problem.

CD: In a sense, because you've not carried on using electronics, would you say that microtones are what provide that different world of colours for you in a more classic kind of way for you as a composer?

JA: Yes, you're absolutely right. It's surely not an accident that it was in the month after I came back from IRCAM that I started writing the first microtones that I'd written since I was a student. I'd never thought of this link. It's also connected with another bit of software that I started while at IRCAM called OpenMusic, which is pre-compositional software. It allows one to hear microtonal tunings very easily. I hadn't had any software before except Sibelius itself that did that. It must be something that my music was already pointing towards because I came back from IRCAM at the beginning of July and by the middle of August I was writing the passage six minutes into the *Symphony* where the microtones first appear. There's a clear correlation. They continued in my music until the Violin Concerto, when they suddenly vanished. I'm not entirely clear why, and they've returned since anyway.

CD: Your use of electronics and microtones can be seen as opening up new creative possibilities. Can we talk a little about times when creativity was more difficult? You mentioned in another conversation about the crisis you had at the end of your student years, essentially finding your path, and you said it was your 'first crisis', which suggests there have been others.

JA: Yes, I had another crisis in 1999. I spent a year writing *Alhambra Fantasy*, which is a bit different from my previous music. Every so often I go through these crises, which always remind me of 1990, where I just stop what I'm doing and take a good look at everything. I call it house-cleaning. I try to go back to square one and scrutinise what I am doing – otherwise one's style can become a collection of bad habits or ticks that you just regurgitate in every piece. So it is useful to have such house-cleaning. Composers who have been through crises of being unable to compose for a year or two are better composers for it, if they come through. Ligeti certainly went through it. Boulez clearly has been through it more than once. I believe even Stockhausen did. There is a use in being able to stand back from the whole mêlée.

CD: How does that fit into a schedule that is, by necessity, planned years ahead?

JA: I'm quite careful how I schedule things anyway – when I was doing *Fantasias* I didn't take on much other composing work for that period. After I'd nearly finished the short score of a previous orchestral piece for the same commission and discarded it, it became clear that I needed to stop and rethink things. Especially because I'd already been asked for the opera. I don't think I could have written the opera without the experience of writing *Fantasias*, though they're very different pieces. You know what operas are like. You put everything into them so there was no way I was going to be able to sustain that without really taking a good look at my music.

CD: Forgive me here because I'm going to bring sport into things, but we are used to the idea of a cricketer or whatever being in or out of form. Certainly with writing, there are times when everything clicks and flows naturally, whereas other times I just feel out of form. Last summer was one such occasion and I talked quite openly about it with my criticism class. The difference between now and, say, 20 years ago is that I know the various tricks and things to be able to get something written even when I'm not feeling that it's particularly good. I can do the job. Nonetheless, I suspect that if those reviews were randomly put in front of me in 10 years' time, I could probably pick out the ones where I was coasting rather than actually writing, but there's no way I could do what I think of as proper writing. Is that the sense of what you're saying?

JA: Yes it is. The phrase 'coasting' is absolutely perfect. Why I threw out that previous piece, just before *Fantasias*, was because it was coasting. I'd written a fair amount of orchestral music by then and I remember waking up one morning in a cold sweat, realising that every passage in the new piece was a bad rewrite of a passage in a previous piece of mine.

CD: Was the discarded orchestral piece similar in any way to *Fantasias?*

JA: No. It was called *Isfahan* and was originally conceived as part of a projected trilogy of pieces dealing with Islamic culture and architecture. *Alhambra Fantasy* would have been the first. The second would have been a chamber piece called *Lorca in Granada*, which I never wrote, and *Isfahan* would have been the third piece. It also relates to Vivier, because he wrote a number of pieces inspired by cities on what's now called the Silk Route: *Samarkand* and *Bouchara*, pieces like that. He never did Isfahan even though it has one of the most famous and spectacular mosques. My ideal, in terms of wanting to write about Islamic culture, is the supposed period in Granada when three religions – Christianity, Judaism and Islam – coexisted peaceably, although there's dispute now about how peaceable it really was. Part of me felt that perhaps that could be held up as an ideal. Anyway, I did write *Isfahan* for orchestra, but badly. I finished it in short score, realised it wouldn't do, and had to chuck it. So I took stock and re-examined every facet of my technical and aesthetic premises. Everything was up for grabs, which is also exciting.

CD: When you talk about chucking a piece, does it literally go in the bin or on the fire? Or does it go in a drawer somewhere?

JA: It varies. There are times when nothing but the bin will do. I've still got the first version of Act I of *Thebans*, which was never played. I've still got the orchestral piece *Isfahan* that was chucked in favour of writing *Fantasias*. I do want to write *Isfahan* properly one day. Some pieces get recycled because if you change the place and context you're putting something in, it can suddenly be much better than it was in its original place. My philosophy is, if possible, not to throw it in the bin, but there are times when that is irresistible. There are also times, I'm sorry to say, when I have lost one or two pieces, but not that many. There is a piece called *Infinite Round*, which was intended for *The Bird Sings with its Fingers*. I ended up with a version that I liked, but it just didn't fit into *The Bird Sings* at all. I chucked that from there, and then I lost it for about five years. I found it in December 2006, completely by accident, just as I was beginning to think about writing *Alleluia*, which I wrote in the beginning of 2007. So I used that for the middle part of *Alleluia*.[13] Because of an incident like that, I try not to chuck things out.

CD: Where it is an actual rejection of a piece that has failed your creative quality control, it takes remarkable ruthlessness to throw away months of work, even metaphorically.

---

[13]   The incorporation of *Infinite Round* into *Alleluia* is discussed in Conversation Ten, 'Singing'.

JA: Yes. As I say, I've still got *Isfahan*, but whenever I look at it, I'm glad I rejected it. Sad, but you have to face facts. When I got to know Gérard Grisey he told me about such a crisis, which eventually resulted in *Dérives*, his Op. 1. He was on the scholarship in the Villa Medici in Rome and he had nothing to do but work. He wrote down a note and he immediately wrote a major seventh above it and he thought, 'Why did I just do that?' So he wrote down another note, and then wrote a tritone and thought, 'Why did I just do that?' He tried to rid himself of all these post-serial habits that he'd accumulated over the previous decade, to find out what music really was for him. The result was his first spectral piece. In my case, I had no idea what the outcome would be.

CD: Presumably, that's what happened with Sibelius. I didn't write anything for quite some time after I completed both *Messiaen Perspective* books and my *Messiaen's Final Works* book all in the same autumn. I needed to re-gather my forces a bit, but there was part of me wondering whether I would write something else again. Could I still write?

JA: I'm not at all surprised to hear that that applies to writing. Since I write words only more sporadically than you I've never had a crisis about the writing. Since writing is just a holiday from composing for me, it forms a very different part of my life, but your situation is very parallel to mine.

CD: The kind of research I do is not simply just generating lots of material and then putting it out there. I tend to spend a long time reflecting and thinking about what it means.

JA: Yes, and the writing reads that way because it's about what it means. It's not just data. What's great about your writing is that it always reaches beyond the mere assemblage of facts. Also, it's not just spewing out pre-existent categories made by Derrida or Foucault or, for that matter, Mr Rosen or Mr Kerman or whoever. You are not doing what you do to fill out forms already established by other people, as it were. It's always specific to the piece of music that you're dealing with, and it seems to be prompted only by that, not by fixed methodology.

CD: The idea that you start with a pre-existing theory and apply that to what you are doing is prevalent in some areas of musicology. Sometimes that can be helpful, but I've preferred developing the theory from looking at the material.

JA: My stepdad trained me essentially in the scientific method, empiricism. The empirical attitude is you don't start with a theory. You take the evidence of what you see, you then deduce a theory from the evidence, and then you test that theory against the evidence. In science, a theory is only as good as its last test. It is not assumed to be absolute at any point because you may well find evidence the following year or whatever that contradicts or alters the theory, the hypothesis that you've set up. You have to test it against the evidence and you don't set up the hypothesis before you've examined the evidence. I believe that should also apply to at least some musicology.

CD: Of course, there's a value in seeing what happens if, for instance, you apply a particular analytical approach to something as a filter.

JA: Indeed, but that's another matter. That's also speculative: seeing what happens if you use a method on something to which it doesn't appear to apply. That's experiment – garnering evidence by seeing what happens, but not trying to force the evidence that you come across into a pre-existent theory.

CD: It's completely pointless with a composer like Messiaen, who I've done much of my writing on, because the music is just so eclectic, in the best sense. No particular analytical method works for him or, at least, none works for everything all the time.

JA: No, and I don't think one method will ever turn up that does, for anyone. Messiaen wrote so much about his own technique, and yet we are only now really being able to discover what he was up to. Messiaen research is at a very interesting stage right now because until really the mid-'90s, everybody just believed everything Messiaen said. It's not that I don't believe anything Messiaen says. He just had a very personal view.

I find this interesting as a composer. It teaches me. It helps me compose. Your view on your own music is only the first view chronologically. Since you are writing the music yourself and creating it, you're its first listener. That's not the ultimate purpose of the piece and you have a totally subjective, biased viewpoint.

One of the things about musicology that interests me is contextuality, which has turned up some very interesting insights. There's an assumption with people who do contextuality that if they've discovered what, say, Sibelius intended by this or that passage in the Fifth Symphony, that just discovering what he intended is enough, but it isn't. What's interesting is seeing how that passage can be misunderstood.

CD: Which can be very useful.

JA: It's the history of music. Did Wagner misunderstand Beethoven's Ninth? Beethoven didn't have a clue he was doing what Wagner said he was doing in composing that work.

CD: I encountered a creative confusion in an entirely different sphere just this last week. I sent my mother a card for Easter. I picked it up in Wells in Norfolk, a nice picture of some beach huts, put it in the post and she rang me and said, 'Oh thanks for the card, it was very clever.' I had no idea what she meant and she said, 'Well, it's like Da Vinci's last supper the way that they are lined up and you've got the sand in front of them, there are 12 of them and there's even one which seems like the disciple leaning over and so on...'

JA: Was that deliberate?

CD: No, it wasn't an Easter card at all. It was just a picture of some beach huts!

JA: She was Easter-ising it. Fascinating.

CD: I just thought it was a nice picture of some beach huts where we were visiting, but it doesn't make her reading of it any less true.

JA: No, on the contrary I think it makes it very true and is a perfect instance of a creative reading of something which circumstances turn into something else. The way she misread that card is exactly how most composers hear other music, because they have to be involved creatively in what they hear. Whatever anybody says about originality, anything you write reflects something you've heard. That incident with your mother reminds me, for example, of Lutosławski's mishearing of Cage's Concert for Piano and Orchestra, which is what produced his aleatoric style. Certainly it reminds me of Stockhausen's statistical analysis of the middle movement of Webern's String Quartet, which is fascinating and ludicrous. Who is to say it's not there, since he found it was. If Webern didn't intend that, that doesn't mean that it can't be seen that way, even productively. If it's going to help Stockhausen write *Gruppen* that's fine as far as I'm concerned.

CD: Returning to the difficult birth of *Fantasias*, how did you find your way out of the creative impasse after you ditched *Isfahan*?

JA: Very much like what Grisey told me, I just wrote down something and thought, 'Why did you just do that? Why didn't you do something else? What exactly is going on here?' Then I went for a long walk one afternoon and I heard the piece that I wanted to write, *Fantasias*, very clearly in as much detail as I've ever heard anything in my head. I thought, 'Well, I can write that quickly now.' It actually took two more years. [Laughter] The piece that I was imagining was very fast music. It needed elaboration and it turned out to need a lot of notes. Also the order of the movements kept changing.

CD: But that was presumably a more everyday compositional challenge, as it were, rather than the more fundamental one of being able to write anything at all.

JA: What is now the finale, which was originally the second movement, took nine months on its own. When you look at the score you can see why that would be.

CD: Or even just listening to it you can.

JA: Yes. It's scary stuff for me! I try to listen to it objectively because I don't like to remember what it was like to write it. [Laughter] Eventually, all I could find was these two notes, E-flat and B-flat. They had to be E-flat and B-flat, no other notes. That led me to wondering what they were and how they could resonate on which instruments and so on. So I started with that. You have to start somewhere, and that grabbed my attention. So that was where I began.

One of the other problems was to create a more contrapuntal approach. Counterpoint is a very difficult word to define. So indeed is polyphony. I'll just say that for me in *Fantasias*, the music was about combining lines. Not that I wouldn't write chords, but equally that the basis would not be just a single line, like in *Khorovod*, but combined lines, sometimes lines of very different character. That pulled me out of what would have been a rut otherwise.

CD: So how long was the eventual genesis of *Fantasias*?

JA: I started it in January 2008 and I finished in about August 2009, but if you include the previous work on *Isfahan* as part of the same period, which I would do, writing the wrong piece, then it's nearly two and a half years on a 25-minute orchestral piece. That's not excessively long but it's certainly not fast and it was longer than I expected by at least twice as much. The Cleveland Orchestra were very patient and gave it a stunning premiere with Jonathan Nott.[14] Then the following year the National Youth Orchestra played it at The Proms under Semyon Bychkov and they did a fantastic job. Since then the LPO found it easier. The piece seems to be settling down the way the *Khorovod* did, because when *Khorovod* was first rehearsed, everyone said it was at the limits of being playable. The Cleveland Orchestra never said that about *Fantasias*, but it was a real workout. I knew that, of course.

CD: You said Cleveland were patient...

JA: Oh very! I'm very grateful to the administration of Cleveland for waiting and to Daniel Lewis who had commissioned it. He was a very friendly commissioner, a really lovely person, and so is his wife. Great people, and a great set-up there. They were happy for me to take as long as I needed over what was clearly a difficult and big piece to write. What more could a composer want?

---

[14]   19 November 2009, Severance Hall, Cleveland, Ohio, conducted by Jonathan Nott. Repeated on 21 November.

Figure 4   Julian Anderson with Christopher Dingle,
London 2019, photograph by Wilfred Dingle

Conversation Seven

Understandings

This conversation broadly is an attempt to understand what is going on now in much of composition. Inevitably, there are no firm conclusions, for it is like trying to hold smoke, but it raises various issues with our perception of any music. A key thread from the start is whether there is a broad term for what a significant tranche of composers has been doing since the latter part of the twentieth century. The importance of Messiaen's example is outlined and Anderson discusses how his understanding of that, along with parts of *The Rite of Spring*, led to his use of multi-register scales in *Khorovod*, and how it is also how he hears a range of other music. After noting the aesthetic of free improvisation and performances of musical graphics, and the restrictive approaches of some in the latter part of the twentieth century, the possibility of a non-technical term to encapsulate the more open musical approach prompts discussion of the term 'decorative'. Negative perceptions in Britain of French culture lead to noting the not entirely positive impact of the progressive canon promulgated by Messiaen and the restricted range of influences deemed acceptable by the following generations, after which the conversation returns to terminology with terms such as Impressionist and Classical and composers talking about their own music.

JA: We had German reviews for *Thebans* last week, which, as usual, I haven't read myself, but Schott told me about them. One of the phrases that apparently came up was, 'It's not avant-garde music. It's not traditional music. What is it?' That amuses me. I've been trying to answer that question ever since I started. That reviewer seems to me to have put their finger on something. Perhaps it's just music, and people have a lot of trouble with that.

CD: There are various people, starting with some of the bigger late-twentieth-century names – Messiaen being an obvious case – where what they're doing is not tonal, it's certainly not serial, it's certainly not atonal. It really ranges between aspects of all of those things and other things as well and it raises the question of how should we refer to it?

JA: That's why Messiaen started talking about colours in his music so much, surely.

CD: Well, yes. It's no accident he starts talking about colours in a big way towards the end of the '50s because it sidesteps the entire issue and puts everything on the same footing. It could just as easily have been food or smell, or something like that. The twentieth century saw the rise of composers actively defining themselves in terms of 'isms', rather than people afterwards saying the music fits into this or that 'ism', which may or may not fit with the composer's own perceptions. This happened in Monteverdi's time to a degree, but the extent of self-definition in the twentieth century is unusual in musical history. Whether named by composers or others, while all such terms and 'isms' are hopelessly imperfect, they tend to be a close enough fit for people to know that they're talking about a particular kind of music. Do you think we've maybe got past the era of composers themselves trying to define what it is they do?

JA: No, I don't. I wish we had. Composers, when they arrive and put themselves forward, generally do so with a very specific focus, a very specific aim, and they announce that. One composer writes only loud music for wind, brass and percussion. Another composer mostly writes short, quiet piano pieces. Another composer specialises in writing for the harp. Another composer uses very gradual glides of pitch in every piece, so their music sounds like slow-motion Doppler effects. You know that whenever you go to a piece by them that's all you're going to hear.

This is common in the visual arts. Series paintings, and Christo who used to wrap bridges or buildings, or whatever. He was the wrapper. Obviously, there's a blue period in Picasso. I also think of Sam Francis, whose use of acrylics is very distinctive. He varied the constituents of the style, but what you see in a Sam Francis canvas between about 1965 and the end of his life does not change hugely. Nancarrow would be another example. Scarlatti perhaps is an example, but Scarlatti has a pretty odd output for a Baroque composer, with about 550 keyboard sonatas that focus on rather restricted but fantastically imaginative solutions to compositional and sonic problems, all within binary sonata form. Is there anybody else who wrote that number of pieces like that at that time? I don't think so.

CD: Not that I know of.

JA: But now what's happened is that the Scarlattis of the world have become the dominant way of proceeding. The Hague School has, to some extent, been influential on a lot of young composers in saying, 'Find something and then, whatever it is, just do that.' Ligeti's whole output is focused studies of a certain kind of problem and that's what he does. Essentially, his whole output is of etudes – on an incredibly high level of invention.

George Lewis is an example of how an unrestrictive attitude towards composition can prove very creatively fertile. A few years ago I was knocked sideways by hearing Lewis's marvellously vivid *Will to Adorn*, and was delighted to get the LPO to give the UK premiere of that work in 2014. It's one of the finest examples of extended techniques being deployed with expressive force and real necessity in recent music. Since then I've got to know George well and been enriched by the tremendous wealth of culture and insight he brings to everything he does. I've learnt such a lot from that.

I feel very sympathetic for Stockhausen. I see him as a synthesiser – sorry, I don't mean any pun – somebody who puts together very different techniques, very different aesthetics even, different kinds of music sometimes within the bounds of the same piece. I feel sympathetic to that, not from an eclectic point of view. I'm fascinated by the range of what music can be, and just being monomaniac doesn't seem to me to answer an expressive need, or, at least, not mine while composing.

CD: I wonder whether eclectic is a word that tends to get used when, in fact, we are talking about the difference between composers who are – and again, these can sound more loaded than I intend them – open or closed. Open as in the Mahler approach – you can have the whole world in there – as opposed to closed, and the Sibelius approach of, 'No, it needs to be very tightly controlled.' Now, of course, they're not necessarily mutually exclusive and it can be open in one area and closed in another. So I'm wondering why being eclectic would necessarily be a bad thing? Isn't it just another word for being open and inclusive? Is it maybe a term that needs rescuing, in the way that, say, 'liberal' needs rescuing from being used as an insult by the political right in the US and, to an extent, the UK?

JA: The trouble with the term 'eclectic' is that it implies a casual approach of 'pick 'n' mix' to creative activity – a bit of this, then a dollop of that, and so forth. And there certainly is too much of that going on now as well, if you'll forgive me saying so. That's not what I'm up to.

CD: More recently, it seems to me that there is a significant body of composers with a synchronicity of sorts, towards a way of thinking that has gone beyond the more constricted sensibilities of the mid- to late twentieth century, but it is a trend for which, as yet, we have no collective term or label that makes any sense.

JA: Messiaen is a crucial figure here. If you look at the reception history of his music, from about *Oiseaux exotiques* onwards, people could not begin to deny that this was a hugely exciting and accomplished piece of music, very distinctive, no one else would have done it, and clearly it was modern music. Yet it had a lot of features that modern music was not meant to have. Firstly, it was grossly illustrative and modern music wasn't meant to be; abstraction was at its height then. Secondly, it's all got very strong pulsation, another taboo of that time. That's thanks to the bird calls and the Greek metres in the percussion, so it's dance-like and vigorous, which almost nobody else was in the '50s, except Tippett, and he's quite apart from this musical arena. And at the end of *Oiseaux exotiques* Messiaen announces the birth of minimalism! I sometimes think that if you took the 11/4 bar of *The Rite of Spring* and added the last page of *Oiseaux exotiques* to it, you'd get the Hague School... So Messiaen works with extremes of repetition, which were also frowned upon at the time he was composing it. Imagine the impact in that tiny little Marigny theatre – you can hear that on the recording of the first performance.[1] You can't ignore it. It will not go away. Fascinating.

The pitch vocabulary of *Oiseaux exotiques* is quite troublesome. There aren't any ready tools to describe it. If you look at Peter Hill and Nigel Simeone's book on *Oiseaux exotiques*, they make an interesting attempt to chart the harmonic synthesis in the music, but they can't come up with a technical term to describe the whole harmonic policy of the piece. They do recognise that there are certain key areas, focal points that bestride the polyphony and make it coherent: so it sounds both individualised and yet unified. It's very cleverly done, but there's no technical term in existence to cover it.

I relate it to the 'Procession of the Sage' in *The Rite of Spring*. The way I hear that is not only as a set of superimposed *ostinati*, but also as one big multi-level mode comprising many independent layers, whose constituent parts cross-relate in numerous ways. In such passages and also the Messiaen birdsong passages as well, I hear a very big scale or mode, like a huge resonance, which can have different areas or filtering, but which is still a whole thing. It is palpable to me that it can be heard coherently as a whole, with different areas coming back and forth to your attention. The same thing happens in *Oiseaux exotiques*. I also hear other birdsong polyphonies, for example the 'Epode' in *Chronochromie*, that way. In fact, this relates to how I wrote *Khorovod*, because I had such scales going on in much of the piece, which are what I call multi-register. They're not necessarily based on the octave at all, but are multiple-register scales, hybrid scales that do not regularly repeat. These result in lots of different modal sub-areas and sub-categories, and also lots of false relations between them. In one octave the pattern might be F, G, A-flat, B-flat, C, which in the next register, down or up, you

---

[1]   The recording of the first performance of *Oiseaux exotiques* is discussed in Conversation Fourteen, 'Practices'.

might have D, C, B natural, A natural, G, F sharp. So they share certain notes. Then, if parts wander in and out at different speeds, you hear a total harmony or a total modality between them, which is not just montage. You hear each individual area, but you also hear it as a whole. The Introduction to part one of *The Rite of Spring* is the origin of this type of polyphony. It emerged as early as that, as a direct consequence of tonality disappearing.

I also think some of the Ives pile-ups may have been done instinctively this way. I'm thinking particularly of the final movement of the Fourth Symphony, where everything eventually melts into a big harmonic spectrum on D, going right up the series. It keeps hovering around there, and it seems to me that the denser parts in that movement are not collaged, but are a way of filtering out different resonances of what will eventually become this single and fundamental resonance area.

I relate it all to resonance. In that sense, I relate a lot of contemporary music to the use of a total acoustic resonance, which is characterised in different pieces by different kinds of interval, different kinds of accidentals, different speeds, different ways of working. This may sound very general, but I think I could demonstrate it clearly if I had the time. This is one of the big innovations in modern music that hasn't really been dealt with properly. The music could be described as modal, and Messiaen's music can be described that way if you have to have a word for it, but it's not modal in the sense of mode as a static object. It's a view of mode as a polyvalent thing that can change and have quite distinct registers, including extremes of dissonance and consonance, as well as triads and even clusters.

CD: As you know, the term I used for Messiaen was 'omnitonality', but I wonder whether 'omnimodality' would be better.

JA: The trouble is, 'tonal' and 'tonality' have such, forgive the pun, overtones, associations. On the other hand, modal always implies either folk music or plainsong or something, and that's not necessarily involved in any of this.

CD: No.

JA: I hear some passages of Boulez like this. I'd relate it also to Webern. For many years people were puzzled that, in some later works, he keeps using the same pitches at the same octaves all the time – there's all this pitch repetition in a 12-note piece, so it doesn't sound 12-note. Gradually, people looked at passages like the opening of the Symphony, or large amounts of the Cantatas and the Piano Variations, and found that he's fixed the pitches, they're frozen in certain kinds of registers. In a sense you can consider the first part of the Webern Symphony as being one big chord, a fixed-pitch chord, or I would say a mode. It's one of these modes which also includes a lot of consonance. There are triads all over the place in the first movement of the Symphony Op. 21. He doesn't hide that away, and in the Cantatas he even emphasises it. So in Webern there is already a continuity between consonance and dissonance in the same vocabulary, because the music's got past that question as a stylistic choice, and it's showing there is a bigger modal world that can include all of these things. To just call it 12-note seems inadequate.

Late Webern is, therefore, very similar to the multi-register modes in Stravinsky and Messiaen. I think of a lot of modern and contemporary music as being involved with this kind of question, bypassing – not ignoring – but bypassing the stylistic taboo associated with things like triads, octaves or, for that matter, ninths or sevenths. In the Ligeti summer course I attended, he would flinch if he saw too many ninths or tritones, because he associated that with the '50s when he arrived in Cologne and everybody was writing those intervals. He said, 'That's become boring now', and he wanted to get rid of them. He virtually forbade composers to write them. I was suspicious of that too. I understood where Ligeti was coming from. For somebody of his generation, Cologne in the '50s must have been like totalitarianism: you had to conceal any octave or consonance you wrote. But he was already openly having octaves since *Lux Aeterna* in 1966. Was all this really still an issue for him in 1990? Ligeti had to forbid the dissonant intervals now, because they'd become worn out for him by all that post-Webern music. I never wanted to have that taboo, or the other taboo, really.

CD: This makes me think of the sounds you get with musical graphics. So many of the performances that you hear of graphic scores, or other things using musical graphics, tend to conform to a predictable aesthetic.

JA: It's a very good point.

CD: The same goes for much free improvisation. It often fits into that 1950s aesthetic, Boulez's anarchic intervals, and trying not to sound like a style improvisation of anything tonal or modal or jazz. That may have been useful, even essential at that time, but now it is really a pastiche of that soundworld. It's a soundworld I love, but it raises a lot of questions for me. Why shouldn't graphics be played, for instance, just using all the white notes on the piano?

JA: No reason.

CD: But they conform to the '50s and '60s performance style and aesthetic.

JA: Even among young players.

CD: Yes, they think that's how they're supposed to sound. It is not truly free improvisation, or liberation from the tyranny of Western stave notation in the case of musical graphics, but a style improvisation of a predictable aesthetic. It reminds me of goths – they do not wish to conform to the norms of society, of prevailing fashion, and they don't conform to that by conforming to a very clear set of conventions that is much stricter than those they are reacting against. Their dress code has become a kind of uniform, and the soundworld of much free improvisation has also become a uniform that shows you belong to the club. It's very nice, but just as restrictive as only listening to Mozart-era tonality.

JA: There are a lot of assumptions. I was re-reading the Boulez–Cage correspondence recently. Cage sent one of Feldman's early graph pieces and Boulez reacts badly to it, fairly predictably. He points out that if Feldman writes a box in high register, and it says, 'Any three notes', you could play a cluster, or a chord with a fourth, or even a triad. Boulez is right: you could play a purely triadic or consonant or diatonic version of Feldman's *Projections* and you would not be playing the piece wrong, according to the instructions on the score. Yet we all know that what Feldman wanted to hear, and what David Tudor played at that time, were dissonances of a particular post-Webern, post-Cage aesthetic. As you say, there is no reason that that need be so. I'm not quite clear what Cornelius Cardew's views on this were. He wrote the biggest graphic score ever, to my knowledge: *Treatise*. It's certainly very suggestive musically. When you look at it you can imagine all kinds of sounds, but for me they're not necessarily the sounds that players make in the '60s aesthetic. They all try to sound like AMM.[2]

CD: Cardew's views on it may have changed radically, given that his views on everything changed radically.

JA: The trouble is that Cardew died before he'd really come to terms with all the things that he'd done. It's a short life, but it's a very busy one. What's wrong with playing, say, 10 pages of *Treatise* with only using the white notes, or maybe only using the dorian mode, or Bartók's acoustic mode? Since there are no instructions of any sort, it's hard to argue that you're wrong. I did free improvisation for several years, because John Lambert ran a group at college. Now I think of it, the majority of the noises and sounds that we made were in that same aesthetic you mentioned – we played dissonances and extended techniques. And when I went back to doing a bit of free improv a few years ago, with groups like the Mercury Quartet, it was using that same sonic vocabulary. The Mercury were great, because we didn't discuss at all, we just did it. One night at Dartington we were improvising in the Great Hall at 3am, just by ourselves, and we really let go. Another night we improvised in the woods around the Tiltyard, with the owls and that wonderful view through the moonlight. It was lovely. This sort of

---

[2]   A British free-improvisation group founded in 1965.

thing is really healthy for musicians, and from time to time I do it again because ideas crop up which would never arise in other circumstances. But it is true that the sonic aesthetic of such free improvisation tends towards some sounds and not others.

CD: And there is the sense you'd not last long in such a group if you tried to play in a different aesthetic, just as much as some composers have been closed to all sorts of areas.

JA: The omnimodal approach, if we're going to call it that, does not depend on exclusion. The composer may want to focus each individual piece in a particular area, but it's not obligatory. Composers of my generation were too often encouraged to be myopic in our vocabulary. I've spent a lot of time in the last 25 years assembling a large range of vocabulary which I find exciting to work with, and which I hope is in some way characteristic. I can't say if it is or not, but I really like using it. I don't want to write music that only does one thing. There are composers who maybe need to, but I don't. It's like trying to compose with hands tied behind your back. It can be interesting, like watching one of Houdini's escapes. Ultimately, for me, though, it becomes very limiting, except in the hands of a great composer who has got supreme imagination, like the best Xenakis and Feldman, to name two composers who worked with very limited materials in wildly different ways. In their finest works they succeed phenomenally well in pushing the imagination through this grid of restriction, so that it seems incredibly fresh. But there are a lot of lesser Xenakises and lesser Feldmans. It's very easy to ape the mannerism of a tiny thing just being done to death. That's why I mentioned the Hague School, because, although I admire Andriessen, Wagenaar and others, I have big problems with the Hague School as a whole. I hate schools in music because they produce music that's interchangeable.

CD: We've been talking in technical terms, but when we use words such as Impressionism, or Symbolism, or Romanticism and so on, they have nothing to do with technique in one sense. Each is an encapsulation of something broader, usually across multiple art forms, which, whatever the composers felt, somehow seems to fit. It has struck me over the last few years that there are quite a few composers – you are one of them, we get it in George Benjamin's music, and, say, Saariaho – with an ability to make the music shimmer from within, in a luminescent way. It very much comes from the Messiaen side of things, through the spectralists, but has gone far beyond that. Other than a few premonitions – moments of *Parsifal* and some bits of Debussy – it strikes me as being a more recent development, one that, in effect rather than technique, is shared in some way by a lot of the music I admire. Different people are producing it in different ways, and I'm certainly not suggesting there is no darkness, far from it, but there is a more diaphanous quality.

JA: That's true, but in British culture there is one word you must never get saddled with, and that is decorative. You haven't used that word, but it could be implied by what you're saying. There is a long history in the UK of that word being used to dismiss artists who are regarded as insubstantial. The classic case of this is Patrick Heron, the abstract artist who was active in Cornwall from about 1956. Heron had big influences from Matisse and Braque – most of his early influences were very French. His dad ran a company called Cresta Silks, which designed tablecloths, scarves and pillowcases. Many well-known artists at that time created fabric designs for commercial use. Matisse did some, and Henry Moore did quite a few, including a bizarre fabric design for a woman's dress based on barbed wire. When Heron exhibited his first canvases the critics said, 'Mr Heron is effortlessly decorative (he designs for Cresta Silks).' As Heron comments, 'That's how they got rid of me.' There is this English prejudice against French art, that it's decorative and this supposedly makes it superficial. I've had to argue a lot with that view of French culture, and it still is a gendered kind of language.

CD: You still get it in popular culture with the effeminate French dandy and so on.

JA: I agree with Heron that decoration in its highest sense is one of the greatest values in art. To be able to decorate an object or a basic shape melodically, harmonically, physically, whatever it may be, like a medieval manuscript or something, is one of the greatest achievements. Islamic art is highly decorative. You must come across this prejudice against decoration because you're a French music man, among many other things.

CD: It's something that can be traced very clearly. Laura Hamer has pointed out that the kinds of words in the late nineteenth century that were being used to describe French music are the same words that were used to describe female musicians and female composers, and they are all intended to denote weakness. I would add that what so often tends to get overlooked is that this country had a Germanic cultural bias in-built from literally the very highest level.

JA: Well, from the Royal Family.

CD: Which was reinforced enormously by Prince Albert.

JA: Massively.

CD: And at that point, Britain was still German-loving and French-hating.

JA: And that continued until World War I.

CD: Yes. The French were regarded with deep suspicion, culturally, and so everything French was light and superficial.

JA: That prejudice lasted. I heard something similar from people who were in Maxwell Davies's classes at Dartington in the '70s, when Max was really at the height of his influence on younger composers. He was referring to Debussy and most French music as superficial. It somehow wasn't the real thing. Hans Keller had this prejudice too. Conversely, when Roy Howat and others discovered Debussy's use of golden sections, Max decided he was ok because Max liked that kind of proportional working. So that made Debussy acceptable, apparently. With due respect, I think that's nonsense. The British attitude towards French culture is very problematic.

CD: Unless you go way back to the seventeenth century or something, it's hard to think of a British book on French music before that Martin Cooper book.[3]

JA: I don't think there is one.

CD: And it's then a couple of decades before you get another one, the Rollo Myers.[4] The lack of interest is extraordinary.

JA: This is one of the reasons, by the way, that Boulez succeeded here in a way that Dutilleux didn't initially. Obviously, Dutilleux is a very different kind of figure, and he's not an international cultural reformer the way Boulez became. But the other thing is that Boulez's route to Britain was through Germany. It was not through Paris. He was played in Germany, and that's where Glock and everyone heard it, at Donaueschingen or at the ISCM.[5] It was Germany that first gave the really big international break to Boulez, and he went then to Britain, and from Britain to America.

CD: Which, incidentally, is similar to the path that Berlioz had as well, except rather than America he went to Russia.

JA: Boulez said there is no French tradition in his eyes, because what he sees is Rameau, then nothing, then Berlioz, then nothing, then Debussy, and then, presumably, him. I don't quite see things in that way.

CD: Incidentally, I did a study day on French chamber music last year. It was based on *BBC Music Magazine*'s public poll of people's favourite chamber music, which was fascinating in a way as there is nothing French on the list until you get to the latter half of the nineteenth century. When you think about it, before

---

[3]   Martin Cooper, *French Music: From the Death of Berlioz to the Death of Fauré* (London: Oxford University Press, 1951).
[4]   Rollo H. Myers, *Modern French Music: From Fauré to Boulez* (New York: Praeger, 1971).
[5]   International Society for Contemporary Music

Fauré, Saint-Saëns and Franck emerge, how many French chamber works can you name? Unless you go back to the Baroque.

JA: I can't think of any.

CD: But, from the point that you start getting Fauré, the Germans drop out from the list entirely.

JA: So what you've got is Haydn, Mozart, Beethoven, Schubert, Schumann, Brahms...

CD: Yes, a little bit of Brahms, but then Fauré, Franck, Debussy, Ravel and Messiaen take over.

JA: If you think about it, a lot of people do follow that. It's the music lovers' path through chamber music.

CD: I started with the Franco-Prussian War, and went up to World War II, because the final piece was Messiaen's *Quartet*, but I wanted to mention Boulez, as I thought it was important to go beyond the scope of the pieces people had voted for. I played them a bit of *Sur Incises*, and said that one of the things that you periodically get in Boulez is a *moto perpetuo* quality. One of the first things I'd played them was the first Saint-Saëns Violin Sonata, with its driving final movement. My conclusion was that, while Boulez would probably hate the idea, he is the inheritor of that Saint-Saëns tradition of the real hell-for-leather *moto perpetuo*.

JA: That is interesting; I've never made that link myself. There is one figure, by the way, in this cultural problem, who is deeply interesting, because he goes across boundaries – more than Berlioz does, though he influenced Berlioz – and that's Mendelssohn. You've got a very strong influence from Mendelssohn in Britain, France, Russia, many different areas, and of course Germany as well. Different aspects of Mendelssohn get appreciated by those different musical traditions. For example, the oratorios obviously went into the British tradition, but what doesn't come up here in composers at that time is his wonderful light, fantastically fast orchestral writing. You get a bit of that later in Elgar, but by that stage it's via Strauss and all sorts of other people. By contrast, in Berlioz you get the immediate follow-up to that side of Mendelssohn, and in Russian music you get a fusion of the two with a lot of Balakirev, a lot of Rimsky-Korsakov. Tchaikovsky's scherzos are still very indebted to Mendelssohn. A late example is the scherzo of Balakirev's First Symphony, which is pure Mendelssohn, and a very late example is Stravinsky's *Scherzo Fantastique*, which was blatantly modelled on the Balakirev. I'm interested that Mendelssohn was somehow able to cross all these boundaries and be understood, or misunderstood, in so many different ways.

Getting back to the difficulty for French-influenced culture in this country, it's interesting that, with certain UK composition teachers, the Boulez that's recommendable and that has always been recommendable, is roughly between 1946 and '55. The Boulez after that, especially from 1965 onwards, is regarded as much more suspect. Again, the word often used is 'decorative', which is uttered with a kind of moral disapproval. The other prejudice is that some music is just too well-made, that this is somehow a sin.

CD: The same thing is levelled against Ravel.

JA: The other side of this coin, which is also part of the problem, is that in Messiaen's later years his own prejudices had become a little bit problematic, culturally. Even in the 1950s, when Sandy Goehr mentioned Brahms to him he said, 'Ça non. Du moins Schumann' [Not that. Schumann, at least.] Boulez has the same prejudice. In the '70s he was interviewed by some American newspaper and, asked why he didn't like Brahms, he said something to the effect that Brahms is old-fashioned, going back to Classical models, whereas Schumann was much fresher. It's as if in French minds, some part of French culture, Brahms is somehow not acceptable.

CD: Schumann was the very first thing that Boulez heard Messiaen analyse in the harmony class.

JA: Loriod of course was a marvellous Schumann player and Messiaen loved him, whereas you can't imagine him analysing Brahms's Fourth Symphony or Bruckner. Now, by the end of his life, I'm sorry to have to say – and you know what a hero he is for me – Messiaen was prejudiced against whole swathes of music. Schoenberg was a major bugbear. He thought Schoenberg's music wasn't heard. For Messiaen, this business of 'pas entendu' was the most serious criticism.[6] If music was 'pas entendu' then it was almost not music at all, or certainly not properly composed, and you couldn't respect it. There were quite a few contemporary composers who got that criticism. He said about Maurice Ohana, 'Il n'entend rien du tout' [He hears nothing at all]. I thought, 'But I know Ohana's music, and it has a very distinctive sound, what do you mean "pas entendu?" Do you mean, you don't like the sound it makes? That it's palpably not a pretty French sound, but it's something else?' I have challenged one or two other French people who use that criticism. Does it mean the composer didn't know anything about how their music was going to sound? Or that they hadn't considered the sonic aspect properly? Or that it doesn't sound like they meant it to sound? Because it seems to me that Schoenberg did know how his music

---

[6] Literally 'not heard', that is, the composer does not know how the music sounds.

would sound and meant it to sound that way. You may love it or hate it, but that's how it's meant to be.

I feel now that Messiaen was expressing personal distaste, which he had every right to feel. However, bringing this into a class is more questionable, and by saying 'pas entendu' he's devaluing the music by saying it's incompetent. You have influence on your students as a composition teacher, and you must be careful not to prejudice them. If you say the composer cannot hear what they are writing, you really mean they are no composer at all. Messiaen's list of proscribed composers had become too absolute by the 1970s.

CD: But I would challenge that it started in that period. Going back to the '40s and the whole Stravinsky thing, it was Russian Stravinsky, good, Neoclassical Stravinsky, bad. What you get in Messiaen is this very specific, French-aligned progressive canon. It's hugely influential through his students and all sorts of other people as to what music is regarded as progressive throughout the latter part of the twentieth century.

JA: And in shaping, for example, the repertoire canon of the EIC in Paris, and IRCAM concerts and so on. You can play Varèse's *Ionisation* or the *Serenade* of Schoenberg, but you can't play Stravinsky's *Danses Concertantes* or the Hindemith *Kammermusik*. I never saw Kurt Weill played by the EIC, whereas the London Sinfonietta did play Kurt Weill, David Atherton being quite a specialist of that.

CD: Yes, there are some wonderful recordings. Going through the repertoire studied in the Messiaen class, you get Monteverdi, a bit of Bach and Beethoven because you have to, but only on very specific things. You get Mozart because he is God, Berlioz, Wagner and Schumann, but you don't get Mendelssohn and you definitely don't get Brahms. Then there's the Russians, and people like that. But the Brahms strand of post-German musical thought, certainly the abstract strand, is entirely absent. This can also be seen with Stravinsky and twentieth-century composers.

JA: Again, there is a prejudice against abstraction.

CD: With Stravinsky especially, I think it's a very personal sense of betrayal.

JA: Also, it's political, because I think Messiaen felt the salon set-up in Paris before World War II was pretty much tilted against him, or the kinds of things he was interested in. I think Messiaen associated Neoclassicism with a chic circle, notably Chanel, who was very closely aligned with Stravinsky. That kind of money, or the Singer-Polignac salon, were a very chic new music set that had a certain kind of image with fashion, and a certain kind of literary fashion as well, with Cocteau. Poulenc was heavily involved in this circuit, and alas a bit of a snob as you can see from a few of his letters. That's what Jeune France were really reacting against. They wanted something more naïve and forceful, even unsophisticated. Messiaen just despised all that Neoclassical circuit, and I think the social aspect of it – not without overtones of homosexuality at times – scared him. In a way, a reaction was inevitable, but the long-term consequences were very serious for contemporary music. Feldman provocatively said when he went to Darmstadt in 1984 that the trouble with the students there was they didn't know Neoclassical Stravinsky, so they didn't have any love of instruments.[7] The list of ins and outs in Darmstadt was then and still is far too much determined by the old Messiaen–Boulez kind of agenda.

Of course, different countries and circles have their prejudices. The problem is that now a whole region of contemporary music, or maybe several, has grown up in total ignorance of some key culture, and I find that very disturbing. This type of cultural blanking out of important areas has bad overtones. It's alarmingly similar to what happened to Germany between '33 and '45. Of course, Stalin did the same thing, and, to some extent, he succeeded, alas.

CD: He did. So, if you're a post-war composer, post-war artist, and you look at the kind of music that was liked by the dictators, then you're going to want to avoid that, as it becomes guilt by association.

JA: You know Jésus Aguila's book about the Domaine musical. He quotes Boulez as saying that Souvtchinski's attitude towards Stravinsky towards the end of the war was quite heavily coloured, both by Stravinsky's political affiliations before the war, and what had happened with some of those people who had remained in Paris during the war, including Stravinsky's son, Soulima, who Souvtchinski thought had become a collaborator.[8] Boulez said that Souvtchinski certainly made it clear he disapproved of that. Somehow Boulez brings it up as an aspect of why Neoclassicism had to go. It seems to me that the Boulez set thought of Neoclassical Stravinsky as right-wing, as of course do more recent critics. Then there's Stravinsky's very unfortunate admiration of Mussolini at the time. Those things were major factors in the music being blanked out with some disgust. But if you were to eliminate all music by composers whose politics you disliked, you'd not have much music left, in classical or pop music!

CD: For Messiaen, I say it's really personal for him with Stravinsky more than the French Neoclassical people, who he doesn't slam in quite the same way, because it's a real sense of betrayal for him. Messiaen discovered *The Rite of Spring* and

[7] A transcription of Feldman's 1984 lecture can be found in (among others): Chris Villars (ed.), *Morton Feldman says: selected interviews and lectures 1964–1987* (London: Hyphen Press, 2006).
[8] Jésus Aguila, *Le Domaine musical: Pierre Boulez et vingt ans de création contemporaine* (Paris: Fayard, 1992), p. 45.

The Firebird and *Petrushka* and *Les Noces* in his youth and was absolutely blown away by them. Then, just at the point where he is finding his own approach to music making, which is fundamentally to do with portrayal, with expressing stuff, that is exactly the moment that Stravinsky starts saying, 'No, music is nothing more than notes.'

JA: Which would have been profoundly repellent to him.

CD: It's the anathema of his entire compositional approach.

JA: What's problematic is the consequence of that. It even goes into the spectral generation. Only Grisey ever spoke to me about Stravinsky's Neoclassical and 12-note music, for which he had some affection, but few others did. I wrote an article recently about the influence of Dutilleux on younger French composers,[9] and in it I was describing the French situation as I perceived it between 1970 and about 1990. There was a very specific list of acceptable influences. Japanese *gagaku* and Ligeti were high on that list. You could have very dense orchestral textures with multi-divided strings and all that. You could have microtones, titles which were either Japanese, or else, if they were European words, then abstract words in the plural like, say, Jean-Claude Éloy's ensemble piece *Faisceaux-Diffractions* – a good piece, by the way.

The tendency towards stasis – long sustained sounds with slow evolution, etc. – didn't start with spectral music, it was already going on a lot in French music in the late 1960s and before that in Boulez's *Pli selon pli*. There was also a tendency towards exotic timbres that were hard to fit into normal tuning (the fourth movement of the Boulez is all about such timbres). That was all absolutely ok. But it seemed to me, if you look at the successful orchestral and instrumental music of that period in French culture, there's a total blanking out of whole areas of other things that music can do. This, perhaps, was one of the reasons that spectral music was slow to spread outside of France. Another was that German new music was dealing with very political questions, which French music was sometimes ignoring altogether. There were a few people who stick out, for example, some Aperghis does deal with political problems as does Vinko Globokar, both of them Paris émigrés, but, basically, French art music didn't do that. It was very decorative music, it was very timbre-based music, and that goes for *Pli selon pli* and even *Notations*. It covers a large area, and I regard this as the Messiaen influence. It's not that the music sounds like Messiaen, but that's where his influence ended up. One of the big things that it did often exclude, whatever Messiaen himself thought about this, was melodic line.

---

9   Julian Anderson, 'Timbre, Process and *accords fixes*: Dutilleux and his Younger French Contemporaries', *Contemporary Music Review* 29/5 (2010), 447–61.

CD: Ironically, given that Messiaen claimed supremacy for melody in *Technique*,[10] though of course that's quite a bit earlier.

JA: Indeed, but apart from Boulez's vocal writing, with all of those French composers from the '70s onwards, the focus is on timbre and texture. There was a certain conformity and the first pieces at IRCAM were very acceptable in that kind of way. They were an electronic realisation of the same things. I hear the same priorities in *Répons*, for example – and not to its advantage. In the worst cases, the result is so specific and almost immediately dated culturally that it just didn't export at all. Fortunately, in the long run, the best spectral music proved durable and culturally richer than that list of proscriptions would imply. But it's interesting that in Grisey's earlier spectral pieces, metre is nowhere in there, it doesn't exist. It's only with *Vortex Temporum* that, quite late on, he suddenly really attacks that problem in a very lively and interesting way. Even then, he was apologetic about that to me. When he was working on *Vortex Temporum*, he said to me, 'You'll be very surprised by the opening of my new piece, it sounds like Steve Reich.' Now, if you listen to *Vortex Temporum*, the opening is not inspired by Steve Reich, it's inspired by a phrase from *Daphnis and Chloé*. Nevertheless, it's both metric and repetitive, and Grisey felt a little awkward about it. The soundworld from the Groupe de Recherches Musicales is not metric. There is no reason why tape music couldn't be metric, but it never was at that time. The electronic interludes Birtwistle and Barry Anderson made for *The Mask of Orpheus* are, by contrast, strongly rhythmic – but that is very unusual for IRCAM music in the 1980s, or even now.

CD: The thing is that, more recently, despite often trenchant views and prejudices about this or that music, a term that encapsulates what's been happening more recently remains elusive, regardless of whether people are for or against whatever it is.

JA: What you're searching for is a word, like Impressionist, or Expressionist, or whatever, to describe the kind of recent music we're talking about, which goes across quite a lot of countries.

CD: Yes. Sonorous ought to be a contender. Some people think that sonorous is a bad thing when we're talking about music. But, after all, what does 'sonorous' literally mean? Full of sound. Well, that's music, isn't it?

---

[10] See the openings of chapters 1 and 8 of Olivier Messiaen, *Technique de mon langage musical*, 2 vols (Paris: Alphonse Leduc, 1944; single-volume edition, 1999); published in English as *The Technique of My Musical Language*, 2 vols, trans. John Satterfield (Paris: Alphonse Leduc, 1956; single-volume edition, 2001).

JA: Yes, that's all it is.

CD: Another slant is that there is a kind of fizzing quality to a lot of this music. There is an energy there, even when it is not rich-scored or fast-moving.

JA: A sort of latent energy, yes.

CD: And it isn't an abrasive energy, but an invigorating energy.

JA: It's difficult, though, because I can think of many exceptions to all this, and I'm sure you can too.

CD: As with any such term. Neoclassicism, in architectural terms, is the eighteenth century, and that's when we've first got classicism in music. As for Romanticism, Mozart, and Haydn were called Romantic in their own lifetime. Their music appeared to align with the early Romantic literature, which is much earlier than we tend to place musical Romanticism.[11]

JA: I had no idea. Now you say it, I can see why that might be. I'd just say, good, because the thing about much of the rest of the music of that period, that was presumably not regarded as Romantic, is it's stiflingly unimaginative. Mozart and Haydn are very personal, which makes it Romanticism, in a way.

CD: There's a wonderful review from about 1794 talking about Dittersdorf, Mozart and Martini. It basically says that the trouble with Mozart is that it's far too chromatic, far too difficult for people to play, it's not easily remembered and is just far too complex.[12]

JA: It reminds me a bit of Charles Burney's descriptions of C.P.E. Bach. That famous sentence about when he was playing, I think it was a Fantasia – which was later fitted to the words, 'To be or not to be' – and he says that beads of sweat from the emotion of it were visible on his forehead, as he played the clavichord and *bebunged* his way through it. Of course, *bebung* itself is an expressive device, it's rather like an ondes Martenot wobble on each note.

---

[11] For instance, in 1805 the *Berlinische musikalische Zeitung* observed that 'The instrumental works of the Bachs, Grauns and Bendas changed little by little and finally entirely in the genial, Romantic works of Haydn, Mozart and their successors.' Cited in Cliff Eisen, 'Mozart, Wolfgang Amadeus', in Christopher John Murray (ed.), *Encyclopedia of the Romantic Era, 1760–1850, Volume 2* (New York: Fitzroy Dearborn, 2004), p. 762.

[12] '[Mozart's] melodic writing is overburdened with too frequent changes in harmony, with accompaniments and ungrateful intervals that are often very difficult for the singer to remember and produce.' Unsigned, 'Ueber die Mode in der Musik', *Journal des Luxus und der Moden* 8 (July 1793), 401, reproduced in Henry Haskell (ed.), *The Attentive Listener: Three Centuries of Music Criticism* (Princeton, New Jersey: Princeton University Press, 1996).

CD: A form of vibrato created by key pressure. Getting back to Impressionism, leaving aside the whole fact that for painters themselves it was originally an insult.

JA: Oh, like atonality was? Interesting.

CD: Yes, one of the critics, Leroy, mocked one of the early exhibitions, in about 1874, as being of 'Impressionists'. But we're talking about a term that has stuck, and aligning the art with the music, a specific kind of art with a specific kind of music. We can sense the kinship there, but as soon as you get down to the technicalities of it, they are poles apart in key respects. One thing that made the visual art distinctive was the speed with which it could be painted, thanks to the advent of pre-mixed paints. So they could do things very quickly in the rapid brushstrokes. Music has an equivalent of that, but, ironically, to get these sweeps of sound requires incredible detail, and far more finely nuanced musical writing than anybody had achieved before. So in fact, technically it's the exact opposite.

JA: Although it seems aesthetically akin. Yes, that's true.

CD: We could even, in terms of talking about labels that you put on things, debate the extent to which there was a disconnect between contemporary music and broader public in the later twentieth century, or mid- to later twentieth century or not, but it is there to a certain degree.

JA: Yes.

CD: And it occurs to me that part of this is the fact that composers, the artists – because it's not just music – are self-defining their own 'isms' through matters of technique, rather than the 'isms' being defined by the actual aesthetic responses of people.

JA: Well, sometimes it's difficult to get any!

CD: There is that.

JA: Perhaps I've gone about writing music in a curious way, because on the one hand I'm very technically conscious, and on the other hand I often write music very spontaneously. I like the combination of having a very precise set of technical areas, and then just being able to surprise myself, and include things that I hadn't previously thought of as being relevant.

CD: Essentially jumping in technical puddles with your wellies on.

JA: Yes, and it is a very physical process. It's playing with sound, and I like that aspect of composing enormously. It is very liberating. But it does mean I find talking about my own music tricky. I've given some seminars on my own music, but I spend much of my life talking about other music. When I did those two articles about Olly Knussen's music,[13] and to some extent this is true of my article about Michael Finnissy's orchestral music too,[14] I picked pieces that were very knowable in terms of how they were done. I'm interested in knowing how things were done, and I could show that in those articles, because I knew there was a definite answer. When I talk about my music I give some technical information, but at a certain point I can't go on about the technique because the music is not the same as the technique.

CD: Presumably, when you're composing, you're thinking about technique no more than an instrumentalist is thinking about scales and arpeggios, or whatever.

JA: Yes, and I can give a precise example. I had to give a seminar recently on my Second String Quartet. Having spent 15 years thinking about it and trying to write it, I finally wrote it very quickly in about six weeks. I knew that it was using this macrotonal tuning system, or aspects of it, in a way that I hadn't done before, and I was aware of other technical things. But most of the time, when I was writing the final score, I was just writing. And listening, I should add: that was the most important thing, the sound. There were certain specific things to do with the 300 Christmas carol tunes that I had as a reservoir and things like that, but I was just improvising with that material. Only when I looked at the piece after I'd finished and had to do a seminar on it did I then begin to realise some of what I'd actually been doing. It was quite straightforward, some of it, and some of it wasn't. But in places where I'd just been improvising with that source material, I didn't know what I was doing with it when I wrote that score. And maybe I don't want to.

13 Julian Anderson, 'Harmonic Practices in Oliver Knussen's Music since 1988: Part I', *Tempo* 221 (2002), 2–13; 'Harmonic Practices in Oliver Knussen's Music since 1988: Part II', *Tempo* 223 (2003), 16–41.
14 Julian Anderson, 'The Orchestral Music', in Henrietta Brougham, Christopher Fox and Ian Pace (eds), *Uncommon Ground: The Music of Michael Finnissy* (Aldershot: Ashgate, 1997), pp. 169–210.

Figure 5   Julian Anderson with Martin Suckling,
London 2019, photograph by Wilfred Dingle

Conversation Eight

Beginnings (and Endings)

This conversation explores Anderson's orchestral music from the tragic impetus for *The Crazed Moon* to *Eden*. The harmonic nature of *The Crazed Moon* and the avoidance of the pitch C in *Stations of the Sun* are noted before discussing the brief gap in composing before *Alhambra Fantasy* and the way that work's examination of form led to it occupying a pivotal place in Anderson's output. The importance of Pierre Schaeffer's *Solfège de l'objet Sonore* to the musical approach in *The Bird Sings with its Fingers* is explained, while a picture of a Finnish lake and Sibelius are revealed to be key factors in *Symphony*. The use of what Anderson calls 'macrotones' is explored, leading to a more general dialogue about non-tempered tunings in performances of Schubert, Haydn and Handel, before returning to their use in Anderson's *Eden* and the influence of Brâncuși's sculptures on that work. The conversation concludes, appropriately, with a reflection on how pieces end.

CD: You said in another conversation that you started to compose because you love the sound of the orchestra, so I wonder if we can look at some of your orchestral music, starting with *The Crazed Moon*.

JA: That was the only slow piece I wrote at the time. Except for the second part of *Diptych*, most of my music between '88 and '98 was very fast. It was because of that list of adjectives I assembled describing my previous music.[1] My teacher, John Lambert, said, 'I do get bored of seeing music always at crotchet equals 40.' Then, when I started writing the opposite, he said, 'Hey, what happened?' [Laughter]

---

[1]   See Conversation Fifteen, 'Outsiders?'.

CD: So what prompted the return to slow music?

JA: A friend of mine had died, a young composer called Graeme Smith, who was a lovely guy. He just dropped dead of a brain haemorrhage one evening on a railway platform. He was working as a freelance for a few years, and had decided to go back to study composition at postgraduate level. He was about to come study at the Royal College – not with me, but we knew each other well. He worked in Tower Records in Piccadilly. I remember, he found me the Reinbert de Leeuw recording of [Messiaen's] *La Transfiguration*, which had just come out.[2] I went to collect it and thank him, and that was the last conversation we ever had. Then I suddenly heard from our mutual friend Richard Whitehouse that Graeme had dropped dead. Neither of us could believe it at first. A few months later I saw a lunar eclipse and the two events became connected in my mind with Yeats's poem *The Crazed Moon*. I liked the poem and it matched the mood for this memorial piece.

I felt it was about time I tried to see if a change to a slower speed were possible without any loss of personality. I rewrote the piece a lot while composing – it took over a year. The first sketch was very fast, more obviously crazy. It was all about rhythmic displacement. That turned up, much altered, as the opening page of *Stations of the Sun*, which was the next piece I wrote. That shows you the extent to which projects can get mixed up.

CD: The right music, but for the wrong piece.

JA: That happens quite often. So yes, *The Crazed Moon* is a one-off. I don't think I've written another piece like that. I wrote a very long harmonic progression which is strewn across the structure of the entire work. The progression is only completed just before the end. At the start, after the offstage trumpet intro-duction, the orchestra comes in on A. You get a chord, and many others, of course, and then all kinds of other things happen. But chords from the slowly unfolding harmonic progression continue to appear from time to time, and the progression comes to a cadence near the end, also over a low A. Then the offstage trumpets come back. Whether it can really be heard that way or not, I don't know, but the whole form was to do with long-range harmonic progression.

CD: The vertical was to the fore more than in previous pieces?

---

[2] Messiaen, *La Transfiguration de Notre-Seigneur Jésus-Christ*, Yvonne Loriod (piano), Arturo Muruzabal (cello), Martine van der Loo (flute), Harmen de Boer (clarinet), Peter Prommel (marimba), Ruud Stotÿn (vibraphone), Henk de Vlieger (xylorimba), Koor van de BRT Bruxelles, Groot Omroepkoor and Radio Symfonie Orkest Hilversum, Reinbert de Leeuw (conductor), recorded at Concertgebouw, Amsterdam, 29 June 1991, Auvidi Montaigne MO 782040 (2 CDs).

JA: Yes, it's full of chords, and they are stated vertically, which my music had generally avoided for the previous nine years. Nonetheless, the verticals are not just static, they're moving, always part of a progression.

In the middle there's the most elaborate heterophony I ever wrote: a long central lyrical section in which the same melody is sung by the orchestra in numerous ways at once. I wanted the sense of a huge crowd of people singing. I'm fond of recordings of Gaelic psalm singing, so that comes into it. That would seem to be apart from the harmonic progression, but it's not, because the notes it starts on are G and E-flat, which are the key notes of the piece – they spell the initials of the dedicatee (G.S.). Gradually the heterophony ascends one octave higher and splits into three parts, each with their own heterophony. Eventually the parts fold back into a unison and there's a big chordal climax at that point, which is the next bit of the chord progression that we haven't heard for a few minutes. So even when it goes off somewhere else, the main steps of the harmony are still being borne in mind, and, I hope, could be heard. It's difficult to know to what extent the listener would hear it the way I hear it. It's a very subjective piece.

I was aware that *The Crazed Moon* has a relatively conventional shape, but I wasn't bothered by that. It seemed to me that *Khorovod* and other pieces were such an odd shape that this piece could evolve in a conventional form. If you look at somebody like Michael Finnissy, he can write the straightest ternary form you ever heard in one piece, and in the next the most way-out 40-minute shape. I like that range. In *The Crazed Moon* I allowed the form to be very simple.

CD: We then move from the moon to *Stations of the Sun*, which was a Proms piece.

JA: That was one of my first larger commissions. Just as it came in, I came across the book entitled *The Stations of the Sun* by the historian Ronald Hutton.[3] It was about the way the seasons are characterised by folk customs, like giving eggs at Easter or winter wassailers, and so forth. I wanted to do a piece that would reflect the passing of the seasons. I didn't want the seasons to unfold in order: spring, summer, autumn, winter. The order of events in the final work is completely unseasonal.

CD: But folk and seasons fits in, at the broadest level, with the sensibility of things like *Khorovod* and even *Ring Dance*, doesn't it?

JA: In a way, yes. Certainly the idea of combining change and circularity was important to the piece. Obsessively so in the last three minutes. By the way, I

---

[3] Ronald Hutton, *The Stations of the Sun: A History of the Ritual Year in Britain* (Oxford: Oxford University Press, 1996).

didn't use the pitch C in *The Stations*. I tried to get away from it – I'd had so much C and C octaves in my stuff. So there's no C.

CD: Not-*In C*!

JA: Exactly! In *Stations of the Sun*, the basic mode has a lot of perfect fourths. I hadn't used fourths prominently for years, so that was also something fresh for me. The mode uses harmonics of C-sharp, F-sharp, B, E and A, with D as a sort of resultant bass fundamental. That bass D is deliberately withheld until the last three minutes. I keep D out of it otherwise. That mode was like a magnet for the piece. The other factor, which is related, was the pentatonic scale – and by that I mean the intervals of the black notes on the piano, not just any five-note mode. One way of analysing that is to reduce it to a three-note cell – a minor third and a major second – which is transposed onto itself, producing all five tones. The music starts with that three-note cell on the notes E, D, B. Gradually as that's developed it turns into part of that mode of fourths I mentioned – so that turns out to be pentatonic as well. I sketched all of this first in my beginner piano piece *Somewhere Near Cluj*, which was a study for *The Stations*.

The challenge was to find areas that move away from the home mode. I was composing sharply contrasted sections, so it was essential that the music really would have a feeling of different harmonic areas, contrasting registers and characters – that relates to the idea of different seasons, the changing positions of the sun, and so on. Then an echo of the main mode might occur – just a tincture of it – but each time a different one, a different aspect of it. In an abstract musical sense the piece was to do with polarity, and also, therefore, very sharp contrasts of speed. It has much more contrast than *Khorovod*, which is largely fast. *The Stations of the Sun* has a wider variety of tempo. I don't know whether the last section is very fast or very slow because it's so fast it's hovering.

CD: Did it strike you at the time that you'd gone from a piece about the moon and eclipse, so the complete absence of sun, to one about the sun?

JA: No, not at all. That finally hit me when we put them on the same record for Ondine, and I feared there were rather too many of those kinds of titles on the disc! I don't call pieces 'Dustbin III' or whatever. There are clearly topics that I don't address in my music, very much the way that Patrick Heron does not paint naked bodies ripping each other apart, but his contemporary Francis Bacon did. That says a lot about each of them. I've always been slightly concerned that I might get a reputation for wishy-washy, poetic titles that mean everything and nothing all at once and so on.

CD: Transcendent would be the adjective I'd use, which I don't think has negative connotations.

JA: I just try to find the right title. Curiously, once I find it, I cannot get rid of it. *Khorovod* was always going to be called *Khorovod*. It is the right title for the piece. Titles are difficult and I spend time with composition students debating this topic – the title can make a big difference to the success or failure of a work. So no, I wasn't aware of the moon/sun title sequence between these two orchestral pieces, but it's clear that I'm interested in cycles: the moon and the sun are both cyclical and both of those pieces have harmonic circuits, appropriately enough.

CD: Around the time of *Alhambra Fantasy*, which feels orchestral despite only having 16 players, there is a bit of a gap.

JA: There was a break after *Stations of the Sun*, which was basically due to my dad's illness, which required my immediate attention. Just a little later, I became Head of Composition at the Royal College of Music and that required a lot of my time. It's not so surprising that I didn't do much composing that year. I did the extended version of *Poetry Nearing Silence* for Mark Baldwin's ballet.

CD: So this was a time that might be called a crisis, though maybe not quite as dramatic as that might imply.

JA: I wouldn't call it a crisis, but I did change direction around then. A feeling of uncertainty is almost palpable when you hear the opening of the *Alhambra Fantasy*: it's full of silences and fragments of sound. It's not clear what's going on and neither was I when I wrote it. That was interesting for me, more interesting than writing another piece in the comfort zone. Having said that, though, I've just remembered that the first two notes of the *Alhambra Fantasy* are B-flat and C – both of which I'd used a lot in *Khorovod*. [Laughter]

CD: This orbit of B-flat, C or D kept cropping up in your works from the '90s.

JA: But in *Alhambra* it's very different – it's not octave tripled as it was in those previous pieces. With *Alhambra Fantasy* I asked myself what would it be like if I wrote a piece where I didn't know, when I started it, what the shape would be. I deliberately had no idea. The piece was written bar by bar in full score. It was a very odd experience.

The opening section lasts, roughly, three and a half minutes, and I was planning to dedicate the work to Gérard Grisey. But at that point Grisey suddenly died. I stopped working on *Alhambra Fantasy* for a long time. I just couldn't continue; I was frankly in a state of shock – Grisey was only 52. Everyone who knew him was horrified.

When I began again, it was clear I would dedicate *Alhambra Fantasy* to his memory. That's why, right after that three-minute opening section, there are a lot of allusions to – not quotes from – Grisey's music. For example, there's a sequence of pulsating polyrhythms on drums, which refers to several pieces of

Grisey. At the end of the piece, there's a massive crescendo which climaxes in a very short cymbal crash, which is a reference to the end of 'Modulations'. But in 'Modulations' the cymbal crash ends the work. In *Alhambra Fantasy* the cymbal crash is not the end: the harmony continues for a long time after it – an obvious symbolic gesture. There were other little allusions to Grisey which I've probably forgotten. I was devastated by his death. Grisey was a civilised, amusing and highly cultivated man with a real streak of idealism. I miss him still. Even now whenever I complete a piece part of me cannot help thinking, 'What would he have made of it?'

Writing *Alhambra Fantasy* I wanted to compose a lively piece which, paradoxically, he might have disliked. Grisey was totally the sort of person for whom you did not do the expected. He never did either. *Alhambra Fantasy* has some very diatonic elements, yet Grisey didn't like diatonicism at all. Therefore, I emphasised this aspect because I felt it was in the spirit of a tribute to him that it be dialectically in contradiction to Grisey's taste. I took my cue from Stravinsky's *Symphonies of Winds*, in which Stravinsky deliberately wrote music as far as possible from Debussy.[4] Similarly, *Alhambra Fantasy* was about as un-Griseyesque as possible, despite containing shadowy allusions to his work.

CD: Like a photographic negative.

JA: In a way. All of this is what I call a contrapuntal composition, a pretentious term I know, but it says what I mean. I usually have at least four different concepts and ideas running around the piece simultaneously that act in counterpoint to each other, and may even be contradictory. That really began with *Alhambra Fantasy*. Since then, I've usually worked with three or four concepts behind a piece, not just one – concepts that are not mutually compatible. I find that very stimulating. It also makes the composing process more exciting. It's much harder to pre-plan. Hence the fact that I didn't know the form of *Alhambra Fantasy* in advance. As I say, I think it sounds like that. You get a section of three and a half minutes. Then suddenly you get a very different section which probably lasts 12 – it's completely lopsided. In reality it is more complicated than that, because the long second part divides into many smaller parts and as it progresses, new sections start up with increasing frequency so that in the final section, every phrase starts with a bang, which I consider to be the start of a new 'section'. The final 'section' lasts only a few seconds.

CD: This was a pivotal piece, then.

---

[4] Stravinsky's *Symphonies of Wind Instruments* (1920) is dedicated to Debussy, who had died two years before. The final chorale originally appeared as a piano piece written for the 'tombeau' issue of *La Revue musicale* published in tribute to Debussy.

JA: Yes, in a sense my output is basically divided around *Alhambra Fantasy*. Until then, I was following more or less a pre-set plan that I'd laid out in 1984 or '85. Since *Alhambra Fantasy*, I've never followed any such plan. I don't know whether anybody else listening to the music would hear it, but that's when I began to feel that I was living more dangerously as a composer. If I hadn't done that, the excitement I'd had in the latter part of the '80s in setting out on that journey would not have been maintained. This was my way of doing so.

CD: Your chamber orchestra piece *The Bird Sings with its Fingers* followed soon after *Alhambra Fantasy*.

JA: Yes. Somehow, these pieces are all concerned with moving through life because there were a lot of deaths in my life around then: my stepdad died as I was writing *The Bird Sings with its Fingers*, and then, in 2006, my dad died. Those things happen in anybody's life, and somehow it will filter into the work. The pieces are not about death, but somewhere or other, there's something about loss going on.

CD: We spoke elsewhere about the dance aspect of *The Bird Sings with its Fingers* and the influence of the Cocteau *Orpheus* film. What was the musical starting point for the ballet?

JA: There was a new interest, which fed into more recent things too: the *Solfège de l'objet sonore* by Pierre Schaeffer.[5] It arose out of my doing historical research on the origins of spectral music. Everyone said Messiaen used to play those Schaeffer records in his class in the '60s. Then in the '90s they were issued on CD with the commentary printed in French and English. I bought them in Paris, listened and found them very interesting – Schaeffer had a very different mode of thought from anyone else in music at that time. I wonder whether Lachenmann heard them, because Schaeffer was trying to establish a syntax for sound. It could have influenced Lachenmann – certainly it has things in common with his approach. When any sound is possible, what do you do? Schaeffer tried to establish some order to sounds, and the CD examples give vivid instances of how he did it. *The Bird Sings* was the first product of that research in my output.

CD: Can you given an example of how this manifested itself?

JA: In the third movement I started with the sound of a side drum, swishing from side to side with a jazz brush. The piece starts from that, orchestrating it

---

5 Pierre Schaeffer, *Solfège de l'objet sonore: Trois microsillons d'exemples sonores illustrant le: Traité des objets musicaux* (Paris: Editions du Seuil, 1966). It has been reissued more recently by the Institute national de l'audiovisuel (France).

on the rest of the group, transforming it, elongating it, stretching it in various ways. It's dealing with sound, but not from the spectral aesthetic at all. I thought I'd try to make *musique concrète instrumentale* – that's Lachenmann's phrase, but I mean it quite literally. I thought I would follow those criteria in that piece a little bit: smooth sounds, unstable sounds, degrees of graininess, variable density, and so forth. You can see that a lot of these things probably also influenced Xenakis. Schaeffer-type thoughts about sound and structure have been very stimulating in a number of other more recent pieces too.

CD: As mentioned before, the pieces we have discussed so far all have decidedly poetic titles, as do many of your works. In the midst of all these wonderfully evocative titles, *Symphony* sticks out as being boldly abstract. How did it end up being called *Symphony* and is it as abstract as that suggests?

JA: No. It was triggered by a painting, *Lake Keitele*, by Akseli Gallen-Kallela, who was a close friend of Sibelius. It's of a lake unfreezing in early springtime in Finland. I've been in Finland at that time of year, more than once, and it's very beautiful. I saw and heard lakes unfreezing – you can hear the ice grinding away. Rather thrilling. I'd wanted ever since to do a piece somehow related to that. I'd already seen a version of the Gallen-Kallela painting in Finland in 1999 – he made at least four versions in total. Shortly after that another version was purchased by the National Gallery in London, where it still is.[6] It's curious, because he's not a well-known painter here, but I've noticed that when people go into that gallery they get drawn to *Lake Keitele*. It's become so popular they put it on giant posters in Trafalgar Square, on coffee mugs, T-shirts, everything. Something about the use of colour and light on that canvas is strikingly original – though initially it seems quite austere. I bought a big book about Gallen-Kallela in Finland, so I had some idea of his cultural context. Then I saw the painting in the National Gallery and started work on the *Symphony* the same day.

I knew immediately that it was to be a piece for orchestra which would have precisely the sound and the opening that it had, and that it would be something to do with latent energy. I struggled for months with the title of the piece. The working title was 'Unfreezing', but that sounds totally prosaic. I tried to think of Latin, German or Finnish versions of it, to no avail. I went on writing the piece and suddenly it struck me that it was in part a homage to Sibelius, which was not the original intention.

CD: I was going to say that the starting point of a lake is very much a Sibelius trope. As we know, his symphonies are not as abstract as first meets the eye.

---

[6] It was acquired by the National Gallery in 1999.

JA: Indeed, but I was not thinking of Sibelius at first. I say that because it later emerged that the opening three notes are quite close to a musical idea in Sibelius's Fifth Symphony, which I didn't intend at all.

CD: Consciously, at least.

JA: I was fine about that when I realised it. I was wrestling with this title and finally took the manuscript into Faber's office with the title *Symphony* because I thought it was vaguely looking that way. But it was a stopgap title, so I thought. However, the title just stuck – as so often happens. At the opening, almost nobody is playing the right way.

CD: Confounding the sense of tradition that the title *Symphony* implies.

JA: Yes, there's what I call vertical bowing (otherwise known as brushed bowing). Although many have used that, I don't know of an orchestral piece that starts with it and nothing else, as this piece does. One by one, the string players start playing with this noisy, vertical bowing. I like the sound of that: I wanted the opening to emerge so quietly from the concert hall that you wouldn't hear it had started. At the premiere in Symphony Hall, Birmingham – which is on the CD – I myself couldn't tell it had begun.

I tried that once before with the opening of *Tiramisù*, where the lead violinist starts playing a very high trill while the conductor's applause is happening. So the violinist is already playing when the audience applause stops, and it emerges out of it. That high trill is very close to the frequency of clapping. That was one attempt – and this was another – to bridge the gap between the concert and the piece, and make the two seamless. I've never yet found a way of making the end of a piece do this, which I would love to do – so that you didn't know it was over.

CD: So that the piece blurs its own frame.

JA: Yes. Howard Hodgkin paints over his frames so why shouldn't a composer do the same in sound? Anyway, the piece is called *Symphony*, yet the piano is being bowed with string, the flutes and clarinets play breath tones, the strings are scrubbing their instruments vertically – nothing is as it should be, culturally. It doesn't shriek extended techniques at you, but in fact almost everyone is playing some kind of non-normal technique. Bit by bit, they introduce the pitch content of the basic cell of the piece, which grows and changes continually. Finally that's why it's called *Symphony* – it's about growth and change, which is central to symphonic writing.

Then the Sibelius parallel came in and I eventually realised how that would affect the piece. I like the one-movement Seventh Symphony, and I wanted to have a continuous one movement of about the same length, with a four-movements-in-one plan. I didn't want to model the piece otherwise on Sibelius's Seventh Symphony. So I superimposed the temporal model of that onto the form model of the first movement of Sibelius's Fifth Symphony. In other words, the piece is a one-movement work, or four-in-one movement work like the Seventh Symphony, yet it accelerates and transforms continuously like the first movement of Sibelius's Fifth. It combines various aspects of what might be, in the background, some kind of sonata-type form, but very distantly – which by the way you also find in Sibelius's Seventh.

CD: Did you have hybrid forms by any other composers in mind?

JA: I hugely admire the Chamber Symphony Op. 9 of Schoenberg, which is obviously a four-in-one as well, though I don't think it relates to my piece so much. This all relates really to the nineteenth-century fantasia. I'm thinking particularly of Schubert's 'Wanderer' Fantasy, which is four movements in one, while also being a large sonata form. The same is true of his F-minor Fantasy for piano duet, one of his very greatest and most complex works. So there are all kinds of ways of looking at those things. The symphonic fantasia was an obsession of Sibelius, and the Seventh Symphony was called *Fantasia Sinfonica* at its first performance. At one point, just before finishing the Fifth Symphony, he thought of lopping off movements two and three altogether and just having that composite first movement, calling it *Fantasia Sinfonica No. 1*. Calling a piece 'Fantasia' may raise associations in my mind, but it doesn't in anybody else's nowadays. It's a sufficiently general term to mean almost anything could happen. In the case of *Symphony* you're dealing with something very specific, with very specific overtones, which are treated interrogatively in the work.

CD: The piece is critiquing the genre of its title.

JA: Yes, every convention of symphonic writing that I thought I could handle questioning, I questioned. Something grows. There is a basic cell, which is presented in the opening, it grows and changes shape, but things are not as they should be, in the sense that the instruments are not playing normally. There are recapitulations, but they don't function as that properly. In fact there are two recaps, one in timbre, the other in pitch. The recap of the opening timbre of brushed bowing happens in the wrong place, about 12 minutes in on different notes. It's the start of a very fast scherzo, so in fact it's not a recap – more like a transition. The opening pitch cell does not recur at the original pitch until towards the end of what seems to be the slow movement of the work, on an oboe. The pitch recapitulation is in totally the wrong place with regard to the timbre, and a fairly odd place in formal terms. That's what I mean by 'interrogating' sonata form and all those conventions.

CD: It poses all sorts of questions about what musically is being remembered as the piece progresses.

JA: Yes, things are not where they should be, even if the standard thematic and formal constituents are there somewhere. But they're in funny relationship to each other.

CD: In addition to the extended techniques, you also go beyond traditional tuning.

JA: It was the first piece since I was a student where I used non-tempered tunings. While working on the first section, I discovered a new way – new for me, anyway – of using microtones. As you know, I don't them call microtones, which are intervals smaller than a semitone. I call my system macrotonality, because it only uses intervals larger than a semitone. I wanted to find a way of using notes that are not in equal temperament, but which are not adjacent and don't sound ultra-chromatic. These macrotones were already implied in the horn parts of *Imagin'd Corners*. There is also a bell-like section in the middle of *Stations of the Sun* where I use a very few such tunings, about 10. Other than that they'd been absolutely banned in my music for years. That was a big change resulting in a period of many years up to the present in which I used them in varying degrees, so the piece was a bit of a breakthrough for me.

CD: What prompted the return of non-tempered tunings?

JA: I remember very distinctly the point where I suddenly realised that I needed this. At the end of the big evolution at the start of the first part of the piece, it ends up on two chords and the music just got stuck. It needed to break out of this area completely. It's another process of unfreezing, if you will, and it needed to change nature totally in some fundamental way and I couldn't work out what. I tried everything – nothing worked. Suddenly, I realised I needed to break out of equal temperament. The idea for what I would do with that came, as very often with me, at absolutely the same moment as having the idea of doing it at all. I immediately set up this pitch system of macrotonality, using harmonics 5 to 16 of a harmonic series on different fundamentals. To paraphrase: I approximate the 7th, 11th and the 13th harmonics to the nearest quarter-tone. The 7th harmonic on many instruments, including the strings, is pretty near a quarter-tone flat in practice – in theory it should be less. So the ear accepts that as a good approximation of the 7th harmonic, much better than the normally tempered tuning would be, and it changes the timbre totally. The 11th harmonic is an exact quarter-tone in theory so it's no approximation in practice. This means the 7th harmonic of one harmonic series can become the 11th harmonic on another one, without changing its pitch. The other strange thing about all this is that I did it with the aim of writing fast music. Spectral music was usually slower in tempo. That was the other premise: could I write fast non-tempered music, where you can really hear the unusual intervals clearly? I thought that if I did that, there can only be a very few non-tempered pitches at any one time, and it's got to be precise, not smudged. That led to me tuning a clarinet and flute down a quarter-tone, and also having a synthesiser tuned a quarter-tone flat, though playing piano sounds.

CD: Just a practical question, how is that done at the beginning of the piece? You get your normal tuning to A...

JA: And then the synthesiser plays tuning A pitched a quarter-tone flat for the instruments that are meant to be tuned a quarter-tone flat. There are practical issues. The clarinet tuned a quarter-tone flat must use the same mouthpiece as the normally tuned clarinet, otherwise there's one mouthpiece that's not been wetted – the reed has got to be wet to play the instrument.

CD: Should they tune first, before the rest of the orchestra?

JA: Perhaps. The advantage is this: if you ask for a non-tempered note it will always be exactly a quarter-tone flat, precisely. The disadvantage is that if you want a melody that has certain normal notes and certain notes tuned flat, you have to hocket between a normally tuned player and a player tuned flat. That led to the whole of *Eden*, which is a giant hocket for orchestra. I decided to make a virtue out of a vice, as it were, and make big melodies on the orchestra that would go perpetually between tuned notes on the tempered scale and ones that aren't. They hocket very fast. That was a lot of fun to do, but I have had to resort to a number of other tricks to deal with this – I don't want to write hockets for the rest of my life.

CD: When I listen to any of these pieces that have this macrotonal tuning, in a funny sense, I don't hear it. What I mean is that there are pieces that use microtonal tunings and they just scream microtones at you, but this seems entirely natural.

JA: Funnily enough, other people have also said this to me. For me, at any rate, it's a new colour. There was a wonderful exchange between Bernstein and Copland about 12-note technique – Bernstein was asking Copland in the 1960s why he was using serialism. Bernstein had very mixed feelings about that technique although he did use it – but almost always to write jazz, which is interesting. That's a very American thing to write jazz with 12-note technique – Gunther Schuller made a big thing of that, also Milton Babbitt and other people.

CD: We have a brilliant US saxophonist, John O'Gallagher, at the Conservatoire whose improvisational technique is a development of that, using Webern-esque pitch cells. He's shown that that's what Coltrane was doing in his later years.

JA: Somehow that fits in, because a lot of American jazz is quite chromatic. Anyway, Copland's answer to Bernstein was that he'd run out of chords. [Laughter] He felt he needed more chords, and via 12-note technique he found them. Copland always said this was the real reason: it made him hear a harmony that wouldn't otherwise have occurred to him. That's the same reason that I use this tuning. It gives me more colours. It gives me more modal colours and I need more colours. It was at that point in the *Symphony* when this first became clear me. The music was straining at the leash. This provided the way out of that impasse in the work, and suddenly there were a whole load of extra colours to use. It just really appealed to me, physically, as a sound. I could immediately think of many other uses for it. Every few years I've said to myself I can't think of any further use for macrotonality. Each time that happens, I start a piece and it comes up again, I find another use for it. The funniest instance of this was the opera, which I never expected to have any special tuning, but tuning is a very useful dramatic device: when something abnormal or something outside normal time is happening, macrotonality signifies that quite clearly to the audience, because the difference in colour due to the tuning is very audible.

CD: It is similar to Stravinsky's use of the octatonic scale in *The Firebird* signifying the magical and fantastical.

JA: Perhaps... Arnold Whittall did an article about me called 'The Macrotonal Music of Julian Anderson'.[7] It's a good article, but I don't want to be seen as a specialist in that type of tuning. It's only a factor in what I do, and it's not the dominant factor. It's never used throughout the whole piece, except in the case of *Eden*, which is a study in that and nothing else. In *Symphony*, there are sections that use it and sections that don't. That became part of the shape of the symphonic argument, too. You can stretch or compress the basic thematic cell to make it macrotonal. So in the first scherzo, which uses the macrotonality technique for the first time, you hear the cell in its normal form, then stretching, compressing, in different tunings and so on. I liked that as another form of symphonic development. It seemed entirely normal to me that, if you had this resource and were writing symphonically, you would put the basic cell through those non-tempered modes as well. That would also be a form of changing its movement and its colour. So it's a colour thing, really.

CD: It also reminds me of hearing a performance in the early '90s of some Schubert, using one of the fortepianos from the Finchcocks Collection. Something that you never get through listening to the recordings of these things is that the piano persistently lost its tuning in the performance.

---

[7] Arnold Whittall, 'Measure of Authenticity: The Macrotonal Music of Julian Anderson', *The Musical Quarterly* 156/1930 (Spring 2015), 7–22.

JA: Really? During a piece?

CD: Yes, they retuned three or four times during the concert, but even still, it would go out.

JA: So this must have happened a lot at that time.

CD: Well that's the thing. Some people were complaining that it was horribly out of tune, but for me it was revelatory. What I was hearing made so much more sense. I found the music incredibly affecting with this whole other range of colours. In one of the Impromptus in particular it added to the emotional content hugely compared to the stripped, precise, tempered tunings that we have now. That's aside from the whole question of which temperament Schubert would have known.

JA: Do you think that music was composed with that factor in mind, in some way?

CD: Well, it would have been the sounds that he was used to. It's not a matter of him consciously thinking, 'I'm going to write it like this because the instrument will be out of tune by this point', it's just the fact that he would have had a fortepiano in his room and he's not going to be re-tuning it every five minutes as he's playing at it.

JA: Nor would a performer on something like the 'Wanderer' Fantasy. A large continuous movement doesn't allow for re-tuning like that, nor do the longer movements of the *Hammerklavier*, for example. This must have been a factor.

CD: Yes, and subsequently I've heard all sorts of things, generally earlier music, done in non-tempered tunings. The most remarkable for me is a wonderful set called *The Virtual Haydn* from Tom Beghin, who's at McGill University. The set deserved to win armfuls of awards. It came out in 2010 from Naxos on audio-only Blu-ray.[8] They've now released it on CD, but it's best to listen to it in surround if possible. It's all of the keyboard music done on seven instruments, ranging from clavichord to fortepiano, with various different types of harpsichord and a couple of different pianos. It includes a short-octave harpsichord, which was actually far more common in Vienna than the layout we have on everything now, which was known as the French keyboard at that point. The short-octave makes it possible to play various chords that are unplayable on a conventional keyboard as it has notes that are split into two or three. So it's got that for a start,

---

[8]   Haydn, *The Virtual Haydn: complete works for solo keyboard*, Tom Beghin (keyboards), recorded April 2007 to March 2009, McGill University. Naxos NBD0001–04 (4 Blu-ray discs)/8.501203 (12 CDs + DVD).

which is interesting in itself. Then you've got the acoustic aspect. They went into nine acoustics. Not just the hall at Esterházy, but also Haydn's study, the Lobkowicz Palace, Holywell Music Room in Oxford and so on. A whole range of places where Haydn would have gone, and then also a contemporaneous room in Canada as well. They acoustically sampled these rooms in great detail. Then, in real time as he was playing, he was surrounded by this whole bank of speakers and the acoustic would be re-created. So it's not the acoustic being applied to the recording afterwards, the acoustic could be heard by him in the studio.

JA: And that's what's recorded.

CD: In surround sound. There was a huge screen with a picture of the relevant room while he was playing, and Beghin says in the accompanying documentary that he became far more aware of the acoustic space. On top of all this, there are about half a dozen different tunings as well, including a meantone tuning for one of the pieces.

JA: Meantone tuning interests me very much, as it relates to the harmonic series better than equal temperament.

CD: There is a piece, a *Capriccio* that for a long time people thought was just that. Then it was discovered it was based on a song about pig castration, a sort of 'Ten Green Bottles' song, but to do with pig castration.

JA: That's a bit recherché...

CD: Well, it reminds us this was an agricultural community. What you hear is that, as it gets closer to the castration happening, Haydn goes into more and more remote keys, with increasingly strange tunings until you reach what's normally called the wolf's howl, though here it's the pig's squeal. He is using that tuning as a factor. The set also has these other tunings, and the way it's put together is a series of 10 concerts, with various different permutations.

JA: I've got to hear this!

CD: It is absolutely fantastic. The nice thing that it also has is the little piece for musical clock played in every single acoustic on every single instrument.

JA: So you can really sample what the different instruments and acoustics sound like.

CD: Yes, the clavichord sounds fine in Haydn's study, but put it into the middle of the Lobkowicz Hall and it's lost, whereas the big French harpsichord sounds fine in the Hall and is overpowering in the study. They've even thought about the recording perspective in terms of where the listener is placed. So even in the same acoustic, in one concert it is a conventional audience perspective, but, for another, it is as if the Prince is sitting next to the harpsichord.

JA: Glenn Gould did something like that while recording Scriabin. Gould had several different positions of microphone and kept splicing and editing between them, but what you're describing is a much more developed and historically informed version of that.

CD: Yes, it's fascinating, and great playing as well. The slow movement of the E-minor Sonata sounds gorgeous.

JA: I was similarly fascinated by the recording by Hervé Niquet and Le Concert Spirituel of Handel's *Fireworks* and *Water Music*, which they did in meantone tuning.[9] The meantone tuning is, in a sense, what I was trying to do with the macrotonality, to create a mobile and easily useable form of meantone. It's very close to that. The Niquet record came out just before I worked on *Heaven is Shy of Earth*. Niquet had got funding to build oboes and other instruments in meantone tuning. I'm not clear from the CD liner notes whether they have found historical oboes that were tuned that way, but I presume they have. They imply that you could have a Just Intonation 7th and a normal 7th, plus a Just 11th and a normal 11th. In any case, they go between the two. I'm not quite clear what their historical authority is for this, but the result when they are in meantone tuning is an astonishing beauty of timbre and colour. Hearing a good 80-piece band play absolutely precise meantone tuning is a remarkable sound, just breathtaking. I heard that in the middle of my period of using the macrotonality tuning a lot. The thirds, the sevenths, elevenths and even the thirteenths are tuned Justly, and it sounded so ravishing and so right. I'd like to think that's how Handel experienced it.

CD: And *Eden* is exuberantly steeped in these wonderfully elemental colours. It came as the last work of your CBSO[10] residency.

JA: It was also a very optimistic one and I wanted to give them a nice send-off. A composer colleague said they felt the work 'smiled' and I'd like to think it might be true. Following *Book of Hours*, I wanted to write an orchestral piece which had a very different kind of colour from the *Symphony*. I wanted to do a whole piece on macrotonality just to have that world to play with for 10 minutes. I had always loved the Brâncuși sculpture *The Kiss*. He did several versions of it. In his big Romanian project around his largest sculpture *The Infinite Column*, the gate

---

9   George Friedrich Haendel [sic], *Water Music & Fireworks*, Le Concert Spirituel, Hervé Niquet (conductor), recorded at l'Arsenal de Metz, France, September 2002, Glossa, GCDSA 921616 (SACD).
10   City of Birmingham Symphony Orchestra

leading towards it in that park is called *The Gate of the Kiss*, which has *The Kiss* image from his sculpture of that name reproduced on it many times. I know Brâncuși's work well, including all the versions of *The Kiss*. His workshop is kept just outside the Pompidou Centre, and you can see several versions of *The Kiss* and *The Infinite Column* there too. It's a very special place.

The reason *The Kiss* inspired *Eden* is not only the very optimistic spirit of that sculpture, but because the couple are completely locked into each other in an embrace. That reflects what I said before about writing hockets: making a melody by alternating instruments tuned normally and those tuned a quarter-tone flat. That coupling device in the sculpture is mirrored in the music. In *Eden*, only solo string instruments play melodies mixing normal tuning with macrotonality.

The other connection with the Brâncuși *Kiss* was that I wanted to see whether it was possible to write an orchestral piece that was 'prelapsarian' in a certain sense. *Eden* is trying to deal with the origins of music, in some way. It can be interesting sometimes to think about the basis of your art. Dealing with the overtone series, and a style of string playing that's largely non-vibrato, rather like viols, gives a feeling of a kind of plainness, in some way. It's something stripped of any but the most basic elements I could work with musically. So *Eden* starts with this white-note melody on the viola.

CD: Hence *Eden*, in other words. And this neatly picks up from *Book of Hours*, combining the spirit of *Old Bells*, one of its starting points, and the viola, the instrument that jigs away at the end.

JA: I wanted *Eden* to be the most colourful piece I'd ever written, with the tuning and the orchestration giving an expanded range of colours. As I've already explained, the whole piece became a set of giant hockets for orchestra, which was very enjoyable to compose. Somewhere or other I read an ethnologist pointing out that hocketing is more common in traditional musics around the world than polyphony. If you all share a melody and everyone contributes one note of it, it's an effective way to bond a group together. Sharing is expressed by every person articulating that melody in a locking pattern – everyone has their place and is of equal importance.

CD: So *Eden* is very much the orchestra as a collective.

JA: It's not a hierarchic world, *Eden*, not at all. Every member of the orchestra is as important as every other, and contributing something central to the music in this long daisy chain of melodic patterns. It's a very particular kind of world. The instruments tuned down a quarter-tone include flute, piccolo, cor anglais, clarinet, bassoon and a trumpet as well as a sampled piano tuned down a quarter-tone. Some harp strings are also tuned down a quarter-tone. There's a set of steel drums, which, although they're tuned normally, sound as though they might not be, because when you strike a steel drum it makes a little glide. You also get octaves in the resonance of steel drums, which fits very well with the resonance of the piece. I thought of the piece as having a burnished kind of sound.

CD: The irony is that it now takes a lot of sophistication to create the impression of naivety.

JA: *Eden* is very simple and very complicated at the same time. It represents an extreme of both at once.

CD: And with the Brâncuși, it is another piece with Romanian connections.

JA: I've felt a strong affinity for certain aspects of Romanian culture for a long time. I thought of *Eden* as a little homage to some aspects of Romanian culture that interested me, and Brâncuși stood for that. Then, when I was writing it, I thought that, because it's only 10 minutes and the piece it is nearest to in duration is *Imagin'd Corners*, *Eden* would work well if it was played before *Imagin'd Corners*. Sometimes they are done as a pair, which I like, but each may be played on its own. They seem to belong together in some ways. They both deal with intonation problems prompted by the harmonic series.

In these pieces I was taking the most bare and simple elements and discovering they weren't simple at all. I've quoted to you before the phrase of that biologist to whom Per Nørgård drew my attention: the most obvious facts are often most worth investigating. *Eden* is very much about that too, as was *Book of Hours*. That is not what I'm up to now.

Eden was a nice way, from my point of view, to end the Birmingham collaboration, which was such a positive event in my composing life. The orchestra were quite sympathetic about the new tunings and we collaborated well over it. They played it very beautifully. It meant that I didn't end my residency with a safe piece, but something a little more quizzical and unexpected than that.

This is paralleled in my preference for ending pieces with something a bit unexpected. The final thing you hear in many of my pieces is something new starting to form, but it breaks off before you can get to grips with it.

CD: It's one of the Messiaen paradigms as well. There are also quite a few pieces where the piece ends and then just does a little bit more, to make you think it's going to go round the whole cycle again. I'm thinking to a degree of *Vingt Regards* where there's the big chord sequence and then he just takes it a little bit further than most people would have done. You get it in quite a few of the *Catalogue d'oiseaux* pieces as well.

JA: 'La Rousserolle effarvatte' has a most interesting ending – we're back round to three in the morning, the piece has already looped around to its start and is some way into that before it simply stops. Also 'Le Courlis cendré' has a very strange conclusion.

CD: That has a kind of Gallic shrug at the end.

JA: The 'Tui' also is definitely an end like that.[11] I've always heard the ending of *Oiseaux exotiques* as pretty strange. I'm not quite sure what it's doing. I don't hear it as final. Of course, Messiaen said that there was no end to *Couleurs de la Cité céleste*. The end of *Et exspecto* is another matter. That is the end.

CD: It is the end, except that it's an end that feigns to go on forever, and in a way that's how I hear *Oiseaux exotiques*.

JA: Oh, I suppose that's right. In that case, then, *Des Canyons aux étoiles...* ends that way as well. One of the greatest endings he ever did was the end of *Éclairs*. It is a chord he had virtually never used before, the added second, or ninth if you prefer. It's quite unlike any other ending he did.

CD: It's a very sophisticated game that he is playing there. A major is continually present through the whole of that last movement, either in the melody or in the harmony. If one of the melody notes is A, C-sharp or E then the harmony isn't, and if the harmony contains the notes of the A-major triad, the melody avoids those notes. So there's this ever-present A major, but then there's basically an interrupted cadence just before the end and the final chord sounds both fresh, yet inevitable.

JA: What is extraordinary is that, again, the movement gets everywhere and nowhere at the same time. It's full of progression, and yet it stays exactly where it started in some way. That is a very difficult thing to do. The feeling of time in Messiaen is much more complicated than many people think. The theorists tell us it's just static, but it's not just as simple as that. A piece by Rădulescu, say, such as *Thirteen Dreams Ago* for 33 strings, really is as near to being static as you can get while having any change at all. Just having a single sound going nowhere like La Monte Young is the ultimate stasis. But that isn't Messiaen. Messiaen is extraordinarily virtuosic and complicated in his handling of time and expectation: he plays with those things. That last movement of *Éclairs* is most ingenious of all in this respect. As you say, it's imbued with A, and yet at the same time the cadence at the end is somehow a surprise. I can't understand how he does it. It shows there was no lessening of his invention. There were new things cropping up at the end of his life. That movement is more interesting, in some ways, than the last movement of *Des Canyons*, which could be compared to

---

[11] Olivier Messiaen, *Un oiseau des arbres de Vie (Oiseau Tui)*, orchestration realised by Christopher Dingle.

it in some ways. The last movement of *Éclairs* is more inventive in its handling of time, and tonality, and modality, for the reasons you've just said.

CD: Yes. In some ways it's a more classically perfect movement, though the last movement of *Canyons* is more extraordinary, just in terms of the otherness of texture that you get in there. Closer in spirit, if I might say, to *Eden*, and I suppose the subject matter is not unrelated, essentially being a vision of a new Eden in the form of the celestial city.

JA: Yes, there's an affinity there. Well, in terms of endings, Enescu was also very much in my mind when I was writing *Eden*. His Second Piano Quartet does something bizarre. The first movement has a beautiful coda dominated by a repeated bell figure in the piano as it fades out. That's the end of the first movement. Yet at the start of the second movement, the piano starts up with exactly the same figure, at the same speed. Although the music then goes off somewhere else, that bell figure keeps recurring until nearly halfway through that second movement. It's a stroke of genius, because it implies that everything has changed while nothing has changed. There's a sense of time rotating or revolving.

There's also a remarkable piano piece Enescu wrote in 1916 called 'Carillon Nocturne'.[12] When you hear it now, it sounds like a mixture of *Catalogue d'oiseaux* and Stockhausen's *Mantra*. It's an amazingly imaginative piece, quite unlike any other piano music of the time: it's full of what are termed non-harmonic spectra simulated on the piano – Enescu was trying to imitate the bells at his local monastery in Sinaia. The piece gets nowhere, yet has a huge amount of internal activity. It's an ecstatic journey that doesn't move, lasting about seven minutes. I'm much more attracted to that ecstatic vision than I am towards neo-medievalism. I respect Tavener and Pärt for what they do, but for me it denies too much of what music has got up to over the last 100 years, things that I would like to have in my baggage. There's no need to deny all that.

I'm closer to the position of Mompou, who said '*recommencer avec tous les moyens de notre époque*' [start again with all the means of our epoch] and I agree absolutely with that. The idea of seeing if you can somehow start again, but not denying the technical changes that have enriched music today. I don't want to dream of another world, an older world. What I want to do is to bring about a bit of magic while you're listening to the music and then you go out into the street. Michael Finnissy once said to me that pieces shouldn't end because life doesn't – you go out into the street. I agree with that too.

CD: So you have no one way of ending.

[12] From the Suite No. 3, Op. 18.

JA: That's right. My endings are usually quite different from each other, but in many cases they end just as they are about to open out to somewhere else. That feature seems common to the ends of *Stations of the Sun*, *Book of Hours* and *In lieblicher Bläue*, among others. On the other hand, *Eden*, *Sensation*, *Imagin'd Corners*, *Tiramisù*, *Khorovod* and *Van Gogh Blue* have endings which are definitely cadential and conclusive. In any case, what you do at the end of a piece is very important: it will determine much about how people remember the work.

Conversation Nine

Puzzles

The first pages of this conversation explore the differing ways in which Messiaen and Boulez communicated and mis-communicated how they composed. It then moves to an exchange about Messiaen's opera, *Saint François d'Assise*, exploring its poor initial reception, other notable productions, frustration at the lack of a full staging in Britain and the innovative nature of the use of aleatoricism in 'The Sermon to the Birds' scene. In the midst of this, the conversation also explores the use of the vernacular in Janáček, Schoenberg and Bach, and it finishes with some brief observations about how minimalism was viewed in its early years.

CD: You have been refreshingly honest in these conversations not just about how you have composed, but also the things that are not clear even to you. This strikes me as being an important corrective to the apparently incontrovertible statements made by various composers, including ones whose music we both love, such as Messiaen and Boulez.

JA: One of the things that makes Messiaen continually so fascinating is the unexplained gap between how he made the music and what the music is. We can all think of ways of combining his techniques. After all, he was very open about them from *Technique* onwards.[1] Anyone has a recipe there that they could use to make pieces of music, quite easily. I once did a pastiche Messiaen piece of some size. At the Royal College of Music, for our second-year portfolio, we had to do a set of stylistic pastiches. It was a sort of stylistic/technical exercise. I asked permission to do one of my items in the style of Olivier Messiaen. They

[1]   Messiaen, *Technique de mon langage musical*.

174

said, 'Well, not later Messiaen', meaning not *Livre d'orgue* or something, but they added, 'You can, if it is the tonal/modal period of Messiaen.' So I wrote three songs, which were as if Messiaen had composed a song cycle between *Chants de terre et de ciel* and *Harawi* – just after *Quartet for the End of Time*, roughly speaking. It was a very interesting experience because one can assemble his techniques, but to make a musically convincing piece is not easy. I set poems which were either from *Poèmes pour Mi* or *Chants de terre et de ciel*. It was a useful exercise to see just how much the recipes don't make Messiaen. I wished after a while that I had opted for almost any other composer than Messiaen. The difference – the gaping gap between the razor-sharp precision of all that *Technique* equipment and making an interesting piece of music – is vast. You switch on the radio and you hear any piece. Within five seconds, no matter what period of Messiaen, you can identify the composer. I could pick only one, the second 'Pièce en Trio' from the *Livre d'orgue*, as an exception. If you switched the middle of that on and didn't know that Messiaen had written the *Livre d'orgue*, you might have no idea it was Messiaen. That is the nearest to absolute anonymity I can think of in his output. Even *Mode de valeurs* does not have anything like that degree of anonymity as far as I am concerned.

The question is: how did somebody who was as eclectic a composer as Messiaen – dangerously so by any normal standard – maintain such a strong musical identity? I would guess that if you have such an idiosyncratic view of music, it doesn't matter what you are listening to or what art you are being influenced by, it will come out as sounding like yourself whether you intend that or not. Messiaen's sources and techniques are eclectic; but the stylistic personality is immediately distinctive.

CD: It's the exact opposite of the emperor's new clothes. Messiaen borrowed from all over the place, clothing himself in material from all sorts of other people and other places in order to end up completely naked.

JA: The more he borrows the more personal he gets. That's why he's so confident in doing it. Another composer would feel intimidated by such a welter of invading models and materials. Messiaen only heard Messiaen in everyone else. That's why I ended my article on this topic by saying that the people he borrowed from had, in effect, borrowed from him in advance.[2] I think also of Tōru Takemitsu, who is a bit underrated these days. When you think of what went into the making of Takemitsu's output, it's a very strange mix of things that should not have

2 Julian Anderson, 'Messiaen and the Notion of Influence', *Tempo* 63/247 (January 2009), 2–18. This article was one of the major prompts for the research of Yves Balmer, Thomas Lacôte and Christopher Brent Murray that culminated in the landmark book *Le modèle et l'invention: Olivier Messiaen et la technique de l'emprunt* (Lyon: Symétrie, 2017).

meshed together at all and would not do so in anyone else's head. Yet, as with Messiaen, a few bars of almost any Takemitsu will tell you who the composer is.

Perhaps we're addressing here the essence of what's termed originality. Alexander Goehr asked Messiaen how he made *Oiseaux exotiques*. Messiaen just said, 'Well there is this bird and there is that bird, there is this Greek rhythm and there is that Greek rhythm.' Goehr asked how he put them all together into the music. And Messiaen couldn't say, because basically that is where the composing is going on.

CD: When I spoke to Goehr, he recalled that Messiaen shrugged and didn't say anything at all, that his expression was, 'How could it be any different?'

JA: Which is also very meaningful.

CD: At the time when I was told that by Goehr, the impression we had, from Messiaen himself and everything then written about him, was that the music was formed in blocks of granite from the outset. Now we know that whole movements moved around, sections moved and stuff like that.

JA: As you've pointed out elsewhere, most of the major pieces were not even composed in order.

CD: It is this analogy of inspiration being like seeing a hilltop in a lightning flash and then it is seeking to find that. He clearly had such a clear vision of how things should be and sometimes it took him a while to get it into place, but he had a very clear sense of when it was right.

JA: And then you get 'très bien' on the end of the manuscript...

CD: If asked, though, why the final order was right, the only answer he could or was prepared to give was to list the ingredients.

JA: The comparison here between Messiaen and Boulez is very interesting, because Boulez got very reluctant to say how he was composing with chord multiplications. He went through the peculiar stage of publishing books that purported to tell all, but wouldn't do so. *Penser la musique aujourd'hui* is the main one of those, where very few of the music examples are properly explained.[3] He gives the results, but he does not explain them properly. There is an article written by Heinemann in the late '90s which goes quite a bit further.[4] Finally, in

---

[3] *Penser la musique aujourd'hui* (Paris: Gonthier, 1963); published in English as *Boulez on Music Today*, trans. Susan Bradshaw and Richard Rodney Bennett (London: Faber, 1971).
[4] Stephen Heinemann, 'Pitch-Class Set Multiplication in Theory and Practice', *Music Theory Spectrum* Vol. 20, No. 1 (1998), 72–96.

2005, the sketches for *Le Marteau* re-emerged.[5] If you know those sketches, you can then reconstruct all the tables for the major pieces. Interestingly, it turns out that the majority of Boulez's output is derived from those same tables of rows and chords.

The reason I'm telling you this is that there was a letter from Sir William Walton to Robert Ponsonby in 1976 saying he's been reading *Boulez on Music Today* and he really wanted to understand, but couldn't.[6] Richard Rodney Bennett told me about a phone call he got from Dudley Moore, who'd bought the book when it came out and had rung Richard because he was one of the translators, saying, 'Alright, this chord multiplication thing, what is going on?' They spent about two hours on the phone trying to work it out again because, although Boulez had finally explained the music examples in that book to Richard, he couldn't recall much of what Boulez had said in detail. And in the last interview with Stefan Wolpe, in the *New York Times* just about two months before he finally died of Parkinson's,[7] he'd been reading *Boulez on Music Today* and said something to the effect that everything in the book was 'too climactic', adding that the reader must feel very stupid as a result. Now let's examine what's happening culturally here: it's the mid-'70s and you've got Stefan Wolpe, Dudley Moore and Sir William Walton all reading the same musical book. That book is clearly going places. In cultural terms, Boulez was a very hot ticket in the early '70s with all his conducting and so on. A lot of musicians were asking how Boulez put his music together, but his book was not telling them. These days it's only the interest of people like you and me. The wider musical public is really not interested. Maybe they will be again, but the hot moment, when everyone was talking about Boulez, was that time. I'm sorry, but he messed that up. Whatever the reasoning behind it, it's a very sad story. That range of people were buying his book, plus a whole load of musicologists and music students, yet there it was refusing to tell us what was going on. I can't see the sense of that. If he didn't want to publish about his musical technique, why publish the book? You can always not publish. If you do publish and present music examples which you refuse to explain properly, there's something funny about that.

CD: The trouble is that it feeds into the sense of composers in the middle of the century simply saying 'stuff you' to their audience.

[5] Pascal Decroupet (ed.), *Pierre Boulez, Le Marteau sans maître: Facsimile of the Draft Score and the First Fair Copy of the Full Score*. A Publication of the Paul Sacher Foundation (Mainz: Schott, 2005).

[6] Robert Ponsonby, *Musical Heroes: A Personal View of Music and the Musical World over Sixty Years* (London: Giles de la Mare, 2009), p. 50. Among numerous roles, Ponsonby (1926–2019) was Controller of Music at BBC Radio 3 from 1972 to 1985, also becoming Director of the Proms from 1973.

[7] Joan Peyser, 'Wolpe: A Thoroughly Modern Maverick; About Stefan Wolpe', *New York Times*, 6 February 1972, D17. Wolpe died on 4 April 1972.

JA: The ultimate example of what you're saying, presumably, is the Babbitt article, despite the fact that the title was not by him.[8] Nevertheless, the sense of the article, if not quite the title, is not one I agree with at all. Just withdrawing music into a protected academic environment is not the answer. These days Boulez says that the reason he refused to explain himself was because he wanted people to be stimulated by his reflections, but not end up with the same results. I wonder about that. I think he was just being secretive. Anyway, whatever the reason, you get on the one hand Messiaen who puts in his scores, 'This is this interversion, this birdsong, this Greek metre' and whatever, telling you exactly how he has done it. On the other hand, you have Boulez who won't tell you a thing. Perhaps Boulez acted that way partly as a reaction against Messiaen, and it is also a reaction against the Darmstadt drawing-board mentality. We know that Boulez always had slightly mixed feelings about Darmstadt and especially about Stockhausen's obsession, as Boulez saw it, with exact methodology. After a certain point, Boulez thought that was just foolish, unmusical and not how you planned a piece. The technique is not the music. Boulez also rightly thought that a lot of what was going on at Darmstadt was just superficial – 'cashier's mentality', as he put it. Now we are in the very fortunate situation of being able to see how Boulez's wonderful music was made, but that also suddenly catapults you back into the score and the music as it is heard, which is what composition is really made of in my view.

CD: The ingredients are not the finished dish.

JA: Yes. Studying the sources of a composer like Messiaen only goes to show just how profoundly personal and original this figure was and why not one bar of his is mistakable for anyone else. The diversity of Messiaen is deeply superficial.

CD: People call Messiaen 'naïve' in a condescending negative sense, as a polite way of saying it's all rather obvious. The mistake they make with something like *Saint François* is that because they can hear the Saint François theme and that comes back at the surface, they assume the composition is only held together at the surface. They have not bothered at all to dig a little bit deeper to see what else is actually holding this stuff together.

JA: Which is a great deal.

CD: The themes are his solution to giving the audience something to grasp on to across this vast time span, but the Saint François theme in that respect has nothing to do with the unity of the musical material at all. Or, rather, if it does, it is where it is transformed in various ways.

---

[8]   Milton Babbitt, 'Who Cares if You Listen?', *High Fidelity* 8 (February 1958), 38–40, 126–27.

JA: Like at the beginning of the death scene. The way he transforms the theme at the opening of the last scene is extraordinary, very powerful and strange. People haven't paid attention to that. Most commentators just say it's a transformation, which explains nothing more about it. There are all kinds of things pulling that piece together in terms of tonal unity.

CD: I have noted some things in *Éclairs*, but it becomes, if anything, even more of a mystery because I don't for a minute think that I have done more than scratch the surface.

JA: I think you have done a bit more than that. What I would like to know is why that piece is so much better than any other Messiaen after *Saint François*? Not that I underestimate *Livre du Saint Sacrement*, which has many qualities, but it seems to me the invention in *Éclairs* is superior. How he found the freshness of that piece at such a stage in his life – I don't understand how that was managed.

CD: The only partial explanation I have is just that Messiaen got a real shot in the arm from all the concerts worldwide for his eightieth birthday.

JA: Do you think he finally felt accepted?

CD: Partly that, but also he was burnt out after *Saint François*. My hunch, and it could be no more than that, is that it was the experience of going around the globe for all these concerts. It is less the adulation, which would have been a bit bittersweet for him, and more that hearing so much of his music in such a concentrated timescale, hearing some things that he wouldn't have heard for a while, stoked the embers of his creativity.

JA: That could be a very disturbing experience for a composer but, looking at the time frame in Messiaen's later life, it does seem to make sense.

CD: Especially culminating with the success of *Saint François* at the Festival Hall. Compare that to the reviews of the original 1983 production, some of which were just so patronising.

JA: I have a lot of those in my scrapbook. Yes, the tone of the British ones was pretty patronising. Peter Heyworth dismissed it as an oratorio on wheels.[9] The feeling one got from reading Peter Heyworth's review was that Birtwistle was the real thing, but this was old-fashioned nonsense and really we don't need that. Birtwistle or IRCAM – meaning Boulez's *Répons*, of which he was a big champion – was what mattered to him. I remember Roger Nichols reviewing

---

[9]   See Peter Heyworth, 'Messiaen's St Francis', *The Observer*, 4 December 1983, 34.

it positively, but I don't remember anyone else in Britain doing so. Almost none of the reviewers had any conception of their luck and privilege that they'd been able to witness the world premiere of that work, even in France. I made quite serious efforts to get to the last performance, but failed to do so. I was only 16.

CD: Well, it was before I'd even heard a note of Messiaen.

JA: When the BBC and Ozawa decided to put on the three scenes in March 1986, the lead up to it was nothing. Then it was a huge success and the initial reaction to that was for the BBC to get the broadcast premiere, which was Nagano's Hilversum performance in 1987.[10] I did a 15-minute talk on the piece for *Music Weekly*, as it then was, and that was my debut on Radio 3. Then the Southbank decided to really go to town on Messiaen's eightieth birthday and that the opera would be the centrepiece. Michael Rennison's semi-staging was very honourable and the third act was televised.

CD: It still ranks as one of the supreme musical experiences of my life. It took a good two weeks for my feet to touch the ground after that. [Laughter]

JA: I was knocked for six, definitely. I'll never forget the effect of 'The stigmata' scene in that performance. I couldn't believe music could have that impact on me or anybody.

CD: It's a scandal really that well over 30 years after the premiere, there's still been no full staging of *Saint François* in this country.

JA: There have been stagings in Spain, which has had terrible economic difficulties...

CD: Those two things aren't necessarily connected.

JA: Well, one didn't *necessarily* cause the other – though with seven flutes, seven clarinets, a chorus of 150 and three ondes Martenot, that opera is definitely a budget-buster! [Laughter] There is almost no major opera house in mainland Europe that hasn't staged this, some of them more than once. It's gone to America, Japan even, and still no British opera house has done it. Whether you love or hate Messiaen, nobody can deny, some 30 or 35 productions on, that this is a major item in contemporary musical theatre, and is here to stay.

---

[10] Philippe Rouillon (Saint François), Maria Orán (L'Ange), Groot Omroepkoor, Nederlands Kamerkoor, Radio Symfonie Orkest, Radio Kamer Orkest, Kent Nagano (conductor), concert performance at the Muziekcentrum Vredenburg, Utrecht, 28 September 1986. It was later released on CD: KRO KK 8802 (4 CDs).

CD: It's the sort of thing Birmingham Opera Company would do, though ENO is the most likely place to do it, or was until austerity hit, but it would have to be in English.

JA: The Coliseum is the size of place you need for that opera. People do *Pelléas* in English, after all.

CD: Yes, and they do Janáček in English as well. Back in 2007, I was on the jury for the *BBC Music Magazine* Awards. Jan Smaczny was also there and something he said made me sit up. One of the recordings was a production in English of *Kát'a Kabanová*.[11] We were going round the table and someone said, 'But, Jan, what do you think about it being in English? I imagine you hate it because the language is so specific.' He said, 'No, actually I love it. I think it's really helpful with this music because Czech is so far removed from most listeners in this country that this means people can get to grips with it.' He said, 'It's a whole different experience if you're hearing it in your mother tongue and can actually experience the language of it.'

JA: That's a very interesting remark because I had expected you to say the obverse. One piece where I'm strongly in favour of the local language being used is *Pierrot*. As soon as you don't have to make an effort to understand, your reception of it is transformed. This is one of the reasons why I like Cleo Laine's recording of *Pierrot* very much, though it's approximate pitch-wise while very accurate rhythmically.[12] Also, Cleo Laine was a great vocal artist: she really knows how to use a microphone and she knows how to deal with words very well. For once, you just sit back and understand every single word, with somebody colouring them and pacing them. You don't have to make any effort of comprehension, not for the slightest moment. Schoenberg in later years was in favour of it being done in English to English-speaking audiences. The Monday Evening Concerts in LA had a tradition of doing it in English, because they were founded by Peter Yates, who knew Schoenberg well. They invited Boulez to do *Pierrot* in one of their concerts, but he then discovered they did it in English and he insisted it be done in German, so they did something else instead. That seems misguidedly absolute on Boulez's part.

CD: It's an irony given that he's so set against period performance and stuff like that, [Laughter] because the language thing is one of the areas where things have gone completely the opposite in the last 70 years from what they used to

[11] Janáček, *Katya Kabanova*, Cheryl Barker (Katya), Jane Henschel (Kabanicha), Robert Brubaker (Boris Grigoryevich), Welsh National Opera, Carlo Rizzi (conductor), recorded at Brangwyn Hall, Swansea, 11–15 December 2006, Chandos CHAN 3145(2) (2 CDs).
[12] Schoenberg, *Pierrot Lunaire*, Cleo Laine (sprechtstimme), Nash Ensemble, Elgar Howarth (conductor), rec. ?1974, RCA Red Seal LRL1 5058 (LP).

be. What astonishes me, given that we've now had five or six complete cycles of Bach cantatas, is that nobody has done one in English.

JA: I never thought of that. What an interesting point.

CD: Were he around today, and once he got over the shock that people were still playing his music, Bach would have been apoplectic at the idea of people listening to cantatas without understanding the words.

JA: He was a good Lutheran. Surely he would have been appalled.

CD: Yes. There have been a couple of *St Matthew Passion* recordings. Jeffrey Skidmore did a very good live recording with Ex Cathedra in 2009,[13] but, other than a few reissues of cantatas in English from the '50s, that's about it. The thing is, there would be a market.

JA: It's a question of getting the best possible translation. I say that because I have not-so-distant memories of singing a terrible English translation of the *St John*. The last chorus has been permanently wrecked for me in one way, because the translation read 'Lie still, lie still'. You don't say 'Lie still' to a corpse – it's still already! [Laughter] Going back to *Saint François*, I am fairly sure that Messiaen would not have liked the Peter Sellars production, but, at the same time, he would have recognised that it had jump-started the opera back into people's imagination. After that production, it became the piece to do.

CD: There are things that I think he would have liked in the Peter Sellars, such as the birds on the TV screens, and the exuberant strip-light colours. He would have liked the fact that it was vibrant and colourful, unlike some of the productions there have been of it, including that horrendous one in Paris in 2004.[14]

JA: That was just a nightmare – more than four hours in complete blackness. It was like sitting in a mausoleum.

CD: At the end of Act I we emerged and the sun was coming across the Place de la Bastille and the audience were like the prisoners in *Fidelio* coming out of their cells.

JA: It was a denigration of the piece. I nearly left early. Finally I just listened for two hours with my eyes shut. Yvonne Loriod was furious.

13 J.S. Bach, *St Matthew Passion*, Ex Cathedra Choir & Baroque Orchestra, Jeffrey Skidmore (conductor), Orchid Classics ORC100007 (2 CDs).
14 6 October to 5 November 2004, Opéra Bastille.

CD: By contrast, I think Messiaen would have appreciated that in 1992 Sellars got the essence of the piece. This is where Messiaen's question is telling – the one Loriod told Peter Hill about. When Sellars wanted to do it, Messiaen asked, 'Is he a believer?' That was actually shrewd, because he wanted to know whether it was someone who, on a fundamental level, got what the piece was about. Even though there were things about it he wouldn't have liked, I think he would have respected the fact that it was an earnest and enthusiastic response to the opera.

JA: Well even Yvonne Loriod admitted that Sellars did love the work. Also, Messiaen might well have realised that stagecraft is a much more complicated thing than he knew, that there are many ways in which this opera can be staged – like any great opera. I thought the use of light and lighting in the Sellars was extraordinarily vivid. One had seen Sellars put TV screens onstage before, but for once he had an opera which needed them. When you had all these birds and all kinds of stuff popping up on the TV screens, at all the different speeds, it became a sort of cornucopia. I think Messiaen would have loved that. There were hundreds of birds in that production, very much in the spirit of the music. As Messiaen said, his opera is a spectacle, and Sellars made it just that.

CD: Compared to that 2004 one, coming out of the Sellars, which I also saw at the Bastille, Paris at Christmas time seemed rather pale by comparison and that is really what you should feel coming out of that piece. The thing that Messiaen would have really fought tooth and nail about was the visual anonymity of the Angel, not necessarily the big stripy wings, but he would have had a real problem with a visually drab Angel.

JA: Yes, I found that curious. Obviously Sellars is making a statement there, saying anyone can be an angel. That is a nice idea, but it didn't correspond to the music.

CD: There are other things that he could have done which would have gone against the iconography of an angel.

JA: But it should be somebody spectacular, special and remarkable.

CD: It is a complete 'other'.

JA: I had no sense of that at all. The Angel sings, 'I come from afar and am going a long way.'

CD: An echo of Mélisande, of course, who is also from far away.

JA: Messiaen, like any opera composer, found in writing the opera that he took himself to some extraordinary places he'd not gone before, as in the bird choruses for the 'Sermon to the birds'. These sound, as he proudly said, literally like nothing else. I have been searching for a follow-up to that ever since I first heard it. I don't think anybody has quite realised how that combination of freedom and strictness works so extraordinarily well. Particularly the opening written ritornello and also the big central bird chorus. Somehow this all hangs together harmonically, but how is that achieved, when he is not even co-ordinating most of the lines? It sounds like no other orchestral music composed by him or anybody. The combination of stability and instability in the bird choruses is one of the great compositional lessons of our day. I've tried to learn from that. There are passages in my piece *Fantasias* that I couldn't have written without it. Some of the superimpositions in the fourth and fifth movements, for example, were certainly prompted by that, even though there is nothing aleatoric in my score. In a sense, Messiaen is more radical because he is free.

The 'Sermon to the birds' is one of the very few new ideas anyone has had in the past 35 years for writing aleatorically. I know Messiaen didn't like that word, but it is rhythmically aleatoric in a new way. So much of what happened in the 1960s in that field was chucked in about 1980 and avoided by most composers since then. For example, you don't find any aleatorics in Lachenmann. It's all in conventional metre. There are probably a lot of things that went wrong in the 1960s – the full implications weren't understood then either. That part of Messiaen's 'Sermon to the birds' is one of the great signals that randomly super-imposed or partly aleatoric music still has fresh possibilities.

CD: As it happens, we've had a couple of very talented doctoral researchers at the Conservatoire whose compositions are explicitly building on some of the conceptual approaches from the '60s. In their words, they are grandchildren of experimental music, as both of them feel there is much more foraging to be done in this area.

JA: Well, that's certainly true of open form. Even though I did not realise it this way, at one point I was going to have the movements of *Fantasias* playable in any order. The idea was to leave it up to the conductor and orchestra to decide which would suit them best. Once I finished the piece I decided against that – the movements sort of ran to their places.

All of this is a way of saying that straight lines in the history of music don't work. I think of musical history more as concentric circles. Certain things come round again and again. Did you ever see that book of conversations with Honegger called *I Am a Composer* published in the early '50s? At one point he says he's frightened by the exclusivity and extremism of the Boulez generation – whom he nevertheless supported in many ways. He points out that the concentration of the serialists on total dissonance will produce an unfortunate reaction in the musical public. He predicts that after all those undiluted sevenths, ninths and tritones, the public will turn desperately towards the most banal music imaginable to get some relief from the relentless complexity of modern music. It's an extraordinary passage. In effect he predicts a complete reaction against modernism which will send music into a kind of primitive state. It's quite amazing. Of course, it's common sense in another way.

CD: And ironic for someone who'd been part of the whole 1920s thing, which can be seen as reacting similarly against *The Rite of Spring* and Debussy.

JA: Certainly as thinning out by comparison. That's perhaps what gave him the insight. I don't see it as swings of a pendulum because, when things swing back, usually they aren't the same. I see music history as either circling or spiralling, not directional. It may seem strange now, but until the mid-'80s, minimalism seemed to be a part of modernism. One heard Pärt, Reich and Riley at modern music festivals, not elsewhere.

It was a very tabula rasa movement, after all (perhaps not coincidentally, *Tabula Rasa* is the title of Pärt's most famous piece). Minimalism seemed like another example of modern music's tendency to push to extremes, like Ligeti's *Lontano* or whatever. *Music for 18 Musicians* or *Drumming* was the same kind of thing in a way, just with a strong and persistent pulse.

CD: Certainly my first experience of minimalism, which would have been '84, '85-ish, probably through percussion stuff, was very much that this was these composers' experiments, exploring different ways of listening.

JA: Exactly, which seemed totally part of the modernist aesthetic. What I didn't anticipate was the prominent rise in the '80s and '90s of neo-Romanticism, from which I feel very remote anyhow – but oddly, there have been those who thought my stuff connected with that. I don't know whether to be more flattered or baffled...

Both: [Laughter]

Conversation Ten

Singing

Unsurprisingly, this is a conversation about Anderson's writing for the human voice. It charts his experience as a member of the London Philharmonic Choir, which he joined when he was starting work on *Heaven is Shy of Earth*. Some of the influences on that oratorio are noted, before discussion of *Four American Choruses* prompts consideration of the combination of unpredictability and control in 'Beautiful Valley of Eden'. *Heaven is Shy of Earth* is explored at some length, including some thoughts on the text of the Mass, while a discarded sketch is revealed as the source for part of *Alleluia*. The *Bell Mass*, written for Westminster Abbey, causes the conversation to take an unexpected turn, with observations on Pope John Paul II's visit to Britain in 1982 and the impact of Vatican II on music, before exploring the work itself.

CD: We spoke elsewhere about you being primarily an orchestral composer, and aside from ensemble pieces, anyone looking at your output at the start of the new millennium would have placed you clearly as an orchestral composer. However, the 2000s saw the voice come to the fore, notably choral voices. This is presumably related to you joining the London Philharmonic Choir.

JA: Yes. As I said before,[1] I was asked to write a piece for the 2006 Proms on a large scale. I had two ideas. One was for a sort of masque – it was another version of the idea I'd had since 1999 to set *The Tempest*. This would have been done in the round using the whole of the Royal Albert Hall space, with singers and instruments everywhere in the building, lasting about an hour. The other idea was for an oratorio, which would use Emily Dickinson and parts of the Latin

---

[1] See Conversation Six, 'Composing (or not)'.

Mass and other related texts. The BBC chose the oratorio, which became *Heaven is Shy of Earth*.

I'd already made a setting of Dickinson in a work for the Cheltenham Festival in 1995 for baritone, violin and piano, a slightly odd combination, called *I'm nobody, who are you?* I'd been keen on her poetry since reading a fascinating article on her by Robert Craft.[2] What I find intriguing about people like Dickinson and Hölderlin is their status of being outside or very marginalised by the society of their time. Van Gogh is another such. Then they drop dead and virtually the next year they're world-famous cultural figures. It's extraordinary. The only music equivalent I can think of is Bizet, oddly. He did not know by the time he died, quite suddenly, that *Carmen* was the hit it became only weeks later.

CD: I feel sorry for Berlioz, though it took slightly longer for full recognition of his own music to come. In his last few years, quite aside from the personal tragedies like his son dying, the Gounod *Romeo and Juliet* must have felt like a stab through the heart in terms of everything he'd striven for. If Berlioz had lived another couple of years, he would have seen signs that the Gounod opera was the end of an era not the beginning of one, with the younger generation of composers essentially vindicating much of his own approach.

JA: Yes, Berlioz is a very tragic case. The output may be somewhat uneven, but the best of what he achieved – especially in terms of orchestral timbres – was staggering, and it was never properly recognised during his lifetime except, oddly enough, in Germany and particularly Russia. You get echoes from it all over Russian music.

Starting the oratorio, I was frightened by writing a big piece for chorus and orchestra. Around the same time, the South Bank Centre asked if I'd be able to write a chorus and orchestra piece to re-open the Royal Festival Hall after elaborate refurbishment. Would I write the first music, officially, to be heard there? I accepted this idea but at that point I thought I didn't really know how pieces for chorus and orchestra work in any detail. So I looked at a lot of pieces that used it, Messiaen's *Transfiguration* being one of the first, which I already knew well. There were a lot of nineteenth-century pieces, some contemporary chorus-and-orchestra pieces like Vinko Globokar's *Voie, Sometime Voices* by George Benjamin, *Transit* of Ferneyhough, *World* by Michael Finnissy and also the Ligeti Requiem. I came to the conclusion that I didn't know enough about this medium from the inside. I had an ex-student, Richard FitzHugh who had joined the London Philharmonic Choir, through whom I'd met some people singing with it. They suggested I audition. I did, as a second bass, and I sang

2   Robert Craft, 'Amorous in Amherst', *The New York Review of Books* (23 April 1987), reproduced in Robert Craft, *Down a Path of Wonder: Memoirs of Stravinsky, Schoenberg and other Cultural Figures* (Norfolk: Naxos Books, 2006), pp. 399–413.

in that choir on and off for seven years until the end of 2012. I couldn't do their tours, because of time, but I could sing in rehearsals for those tours. So I was able to learn, for example, the two Ligeti unaccompanied choruses from the early '50s, some Tavener pieces (being a second bass, I was saddled with singing the drone in *Song for Athene*, which is very tiring!), the Howells Requiem and a lot of unaccompanied choral music too.

CD: So how long did you sing with the choir?

JA: From early 2005 until 2012. The first gig I did with them was *The Dream of Gerontius*. Although it's a very fine piece, there are some weaker passages in the second part (some of 'Praise to the Holiest' sounds like bad Sullivan to me). On the other hand, the instrumental Prelude to Part II where Gerontius is floating through space is extraordinary. It doesn't have any centre of gravity, nor any real direction, yet it's completely tonal. That's remarkable.

But I hadn't realised how difficult the piece is to sing. We were doing it with Sir Mark Elder who said, rightly, that we had to sing off copy. We were allowed to have our copies with us, but we had to look at the conductor the whole time. Elder, I have to say, was astonishing. We'd been rehearsing this thing for weeks, nothing else, but when he came in at the piano rehearsal he knew our parts far better than we did. Also he's very able at telling you visually how to sing, with what tone quality. He gives you everything a chorus singer could possibly want, which, given that he's also got to give everything the orchestra needs and the soloists, is quite a task. He'd given advance instructions to the trainer, Neville Creed, about where he wanted us to breathe, place consonants and all that: he had all that by memory too. With mostly his eyes and hands and just a few words, I knew immediately what to do, I knew what sound to produce. What I'm about to say sounds absurd, but I don't think I fully appreciated what great conducting technically is until that experience, at least not in what's called standard rep. I thought those pieces must, basically, run themselves, how difficult can it be and so on. Utter nonsense. Seeing Elder guide us through *Gerontius* was a revelation.

CD: I presume the Elgar was not the most demanding thing you did with the choir?

JA: *Gerontius* is indeed tough in many places, but we did all kinds of repertoire. We did *A Relic of Memory* by Mark-Anthony Turnage, which is one of his most powerful works, also a complex one. I've got decent relative pitch and I'm used to contemporary pitches and so on, but it was a real challenge. I'm glad we sang it. In the second half we had to do Rachmaninov's *The Bells* in Russian, which is 40 minutes of very chromatic music with a Russian text at top speed. I admit

I was sort of having nightmares about the Rachmaninov before that concert.[3] It was a really tough concert, but we brought it off. That was one of the most exciting things we ever did.

I'd been attending orchestral rehearsals as much as I could since I was at school, but when you're actually involved and you've got to deliver, you really learn about the practice of music making. The artist Tom Phillips was in the Philharmonia Chorus for a while, in the 1950s I think, and he commented that he had a great deal of the pleasure and not much of the responsibility for the performances of *Missa Solemnis* under Klemperer or whatever – which is a very good way of putting it. I know what he means, but the truth is if you go wrong, people will hear you. (In my years with the LPC I became a little notorious for swearing loudly in rehearsals when I made a crass error.) In *Gerontius* I was extremely nervous that I was going to get out during the Devil's chorus in Part II, which is very chromatic, very fast and very polyphonic. You would hear it if a lone singer were in the wrong place. The texture is exposed. I found this very demanding and a very good way of reassessing my whole musical technique in a curious way. I hadn't expected that.

CD: How about the social aspect of being in a choir?

JA: I loved it. I was singing with people who were, by and large, not professional musicians. They were in various trades, architects, bankers, accountants, IT people, whatever, but with a very lively, almost devotional attitude towards the music. They really wanted to be there. They'd paid to be there: they have an annual subscription. They were really committed to music. In a funny way I felt I learnt again, through singing in a choir, why I'd entered the profession in the first place. They had a direct, undimmed love of music (Boulez points out somewhere that 'amateur' really means someone who loves what they do). Naturally there were areas of the repertoire I didn't care for personally, but that wasn't the point. And it was a really big repertoire. I've got a list somewhere. It's something like 200 pieces of varying sizes from little choruses like the Vaughan Williams *Three Shakespeare Songs* to the Ligeti, quite a bit of contemporary music, plus the block-busters. Then, of course, I ended up writing for them, [Laughter] which was an interesting experience in itself. I always ensure I'm able to sing at pitch any note I write. If you're writing a choral piece, you're soon found out if you can't because the chorus ask you to sing through tricky bits over a drink in the bar or whatever. It's not bad for a composer to have to do that.

---

[3]   23 August 2006, BBC Proms, Royal Albert Hall: Turnage *A Relic of Memory* (UK premiere), Prokofiev Piano Concerto No. 2, Rachmaninov *The Bells*. London Philharmonic Choir & Orchestra and Philharmonia Chorus, Vladimir Jurowski (conductor).

CD: So in what ways did this choral repertoire inform your approach to *Heaven is Shy of Earth*?

JA: I'm going to follow Tippett a little bit and say that when you're writing an oratorio for the Proms or wherever, it is a public statement. I agree with Tippett's somewhat Jungian term 'collective' for such pieces, in the sense that they address some bigger topics. In the case of *Heaven is Shy of Earth*, the Janáček *Glagolitic Mass* was a major factor – I tend to dialogue with other pieces in the same genre when I write. I suppose this may come from Sandy Goehr, who was always talking about composing with models, but I don't entirely know whether he meant what I'm meaning by it. I've told you that *Khorovod* was modelled on the first part of *The Rite of Spring*, but in such a way that I don't think that's too evident. The only Stravinsky allusion you can hear vaguely is the last chord, it sounds a bit like *Les Noces*, which is not a model for the piece at all. That was a deliberate red herring on my part. [Laughter] With models, I chew on them like a dog chews on a bone until I've got what I need out of them. Then I forget them. You have to be able to do that and then kick out on your own. In the case of *Heaven is Shy of Earth*, the two models are the *Glagolitic Mass*, which I did not want to emulate in style, but in spirit, yes, and the Brahms *German Requiem*.

CD: Those are not pieces I would naturally pair, but, now you say it, I can see the resonances with both, though it's not so much to do with sounds they make.

JA: As you know, one of the movements of the Brahms *German Requiem* does not set the traditional Requiem text. The fourth movement, the waltz, sets 'Wie lieblich sind Deine Wohnungen' – the same text that I was setting in the mezzo solo movement (movement IV) in *Heaven is Shy of Earth*. I set it in Latin, and that has another precedent, which you know and love, the fifth movement of Messiaen's *Transfiguration*.[4] So there were threads going in several directions. Principally in the direction of the Janáček and the Brahms, but the Messiaen is somewhere in there too. Janáček said his *Glagolitic Mass* was a Mass of the forests, and the idea of an outdoor Mass appealed to me very much. At that time I was looking at a lot of photography by Josef Sudek, a Czech photographer who died in 1976. He was an early surrealist in Czechoslovakia. He did a very fine book called *Janáček Hukvaldy*, which is a photograph sequence of the places in Hukvaldy that Janáček knew, the forests around there and their wells.[5] If you remember, Janáček wrote articles for his local daily newspaper – there's one

---

[4] 'Quam dilecta tabernacula tua': the text is from Psalm 84.
[5] Josef Sudek, *Janáček Hukvaldy* (Prague: Supraphon, 1971). Movement 2 (entitled 'Janacek's Wells') of JA's piano concerto *The Imaginary Museum* (2017) was prompted by a photo in the same volume.

article called 'Wells' which just deals with the noises and gurgles that he heard in wells in his local forests.[6] That all seemed to me to be relevant to this piece.

I was thinking very much of that Sudek book when I wrote the piece, and also of John Cage's statement when he was making his tape collage piece based on *Finnegans Wake* called *Roaratorio*. He was asked to explain the title, which is from *Finnegans Wake*. He commented that it's like the whole world has become a church in which we roar. That describes the Janáček Mass very well. I had that image in mind, the idea of seeing everything in nature as somehow sacred. It's certainly the message of the Dickinson poems that I set and perhaps of *Heaven is Shy of Earth* as a whole. It was the first piece on a large scale where I'd addressed spiritual questions in a big public way. The *Four American Choruses* were an attempt to deal with that, too, but this was a much bigger canvas. I thought very hard before I did it, because it was putting my head on the block in a way.

CD: Making such statements requires making yourself vulnerable, and it is something that will cause some to think they know what you're about in a much more simplistic sense than is actually the case.

JA: That's right.

CD: You mentioned the *Four American Choruses*. Those were from your Birmingham residency, and pre-dated you joining the London Philharmonic Choir, interweaving the orchestral pieces.

JA: Yes, the *American Choruses* were composed over about two years. The first of them was written just after the *Symphony*, and the last of them just before *Book of Hours*. I wrote one early on, the very simple first one. Most amateur choirs could do that piece. The second one, where the chorus parts aren't co-ordinated, is a bit different. That took me a long time because I was interested in that problem of how to control, or not, what is going on vertically. I wanted to ensure that whichever vertical coincidence between the four parts happened, it would make a good and interesting result.

CD: So it's about not knowing precisely what will happen, but you want to be sure of the boundaries of the chance?

JA: Yes, I'm interested in the idea of chance. The '50s, '60s and '70s exploitation of that was one set of ways of doing it. There are many further possibilities in chance, but not necessarily in the ways that people used it at that time. For example, Cage is not interested in selecting from chance operations (with some notable exceptions). For him and his followers, if you commit yourself to the

---

[6]   Leoš Janáček, 'Wells and fountains', reproduced in *Janáček: Leaves from His Life*, ed. and trans. Vilem and Margaret Tausky (London: Kahn and Averill, 1982).

process you just obey the chance results. That, as you know, is not the way that I work, so there is a big difference between me and the Cage philosophy. At the same time, the Cage thing has affected me deeply, because it opens so many doors: if you let things happen you can discover a lot. It's not totally random, because Cage is very insistent that you should obey the instructions he gives you for putting those pieces together – but he cannot entirely predict what the result will be. I'm broadly sympathetic to that, but since I keep selecting things, obviously I'm subjective in my way of employing it.

CD: So how did you go about reconciling control and unpredictability?

JA: With the second of the *Four American Choruses*, 'Beautiful Valley of Eden', which is the one that had the biggest impact on my music in the long term, each chorus section is co-ordinated only among themselves. The sopranos sing together with themselves, the altos similarly, and so on, and each section has its own conductor. There is no co-ordination between the sopranos and the tenors, or the sopranos and the altos, or between the basses and the sopranos, or anyone. It took me about a year to write that piece, on and off. I had several goes at it. I give cues so that one part has to have reached a certain point before the next part is cued. Plus I usually give a bar for nothing before a group comes in. I got that from Stockhausen's *Gruppen*. If you look, whenever a new orchestra comes in, there is a conducted bar for nothing and then the orchestra starts. I've heard from conductors of *Gruppen* that this works brilliantly. In my case, I didn't only do it to be practical, but also because I would then have even less control over when the next group comes in. Originally I didn't give metronome marks – although eventually we had to put them in as choruses wanted some more guidance about speeds. Nevertheless they are all marked as approximate, so what with that and the extra bars for nothing at the start of each entry, I really don't know when the next part is going to come in.

CD: That's the unpredictability. Where does the control come in?

JA: I just tried out, at the piano again and again, every single vertical that could possibly happen between the parts. So you can imagine what kind of work that is.

CD: That's thousands and thousands of permutations and combinations.

JA: It meant hours and hours of checking. I wanted to write parts that were independent and identifiable as parts in themselves, with a rhythmic or melodic interest of their own, and also know that any vertical coincidence between them would be acceptable, as far as I was concerned. I also wanted to know that there would be a progression of vertical coincidences that would make harmony that would go through the piece, even though I wouldn't ever know exactly what that harmony would be. So it was a bit of a tongue-twister really. Finally, though, it does sound as I meant it to sound, so I can't be a true chance composer, because I did have a precise idea of what I wanted it to sound like.

The ideal performance is for the four chorus parts to be in different areas of the hall. They sing together only for the last bar. I wanted to show very definitely that the last bar is together. The words are, 'Thy sweet rest.' So I thought, 'Thy. Sweet. Rest. Stop.', then you see it's all together. That never happens anywhere else in the piece, or at least not intentionally.

CD: Isn't it difficult sustaining a metrical disjunction, though?

JA: People are influenced in the sense that, if one group starts at one speed, the next group may be affected by the speeds they hear elsewhere, despite the tempo indications. Sometimes the fast tempo ends up being slightly like double the slow one, or something like that. I always try to encourage conductors not to use easy ratios like that, but just take their cue where they're meant to start conducting and then not think about the speed of any other group. That's why I'd like them to be as separated as possible physically.

CD: To avoid them falling into rhythmic alignment with each other.

JA: Yes. The other piece that was an influence on this one was the Cardew *Great Learning*, specifically the seventh paragraph. As I mentioned in another conversation, this is the one with the ingenious instruction that everyone enters together on any note at all, but when you move to a new note you take a pitch you can hear someone else singing. What then happens is that this mass of microtonal mush at the start gradually focuses, as more and more octaves and then other constants like fifths and thirds turn up, and it becomes quite pentatonic. You can hear this effect if you listen to the Deutsche Grammophon recording that Cardew did – it's got quite a starry cast: Brian Eno, Gavin Bryars, Tom Phillips, Howard Skempton, of course – all that lot singing, or chanting or whatever. After about 10 minutes, rather Ligeti-like, this thing has gone gradually from a microtonal sludge to a pentatonic chord in the most magical way. Whenever I've participated in an organised performance of that piece – once when I was a student at college, and once elsewhere – this is what always happens. You can even try it with, say, a group of eight singers only. It doesn't matter whether it's eight or 40, this is what happens. Cardew must have known this. I thought a bit about that when I was making my 'Beautiful Valley' piece, which is perhaps also a nod in the direction of Cardew. It's also a nice piece because of the idea of different people singing at different speeds and all that – sharing a text, but singing in their own way. Perhaps that also links up to the heterophony thing in Gaelic psalm singing, because the idea there is a communal praise but everyone is unsynchronised, so they bear witness to God in their own way. 'Beautiful Valley' is a homage to that ideal, too.

The relations between the parts vary. The opening is deliberately a cop-out. It's more rhythmic than melodic, with lots of superimposed fifths. So I have very simple rhythms at very different speeds, always in fifths, and you hear a very simple kind of harmony. I didn't have to work hard on that passage in terms of vertical coincidence because it's obvious you'll get a chord of fifths, but with very different pulses. I repeat that for a certain amount of time. I remember the first time that the soprano part moves just one note away from it, I thought, 'Right, you're off. That part is going to move and then you've got to really take the risk.' It was a lot of fun, but that fifth chord gives a certain simplicity and cleanness to the thing, which recurs near the end. In a sense it's a reverse of the Cardew seventh paragraph. What you've got is a simple start, which gradually becomes more and more complicated.

In the last big section, all the parts enter on D, and spread out from there. They enter at different times and are kind of heterophonic to each other at that point, deliberately. Then they gradually move away from each other and become more polyphonic. That was a lot of fun to compose. It modulates from an out-of-phase texture of similar parts, not canonic though, to a real polyphonic difference between the parts, until eventually they end up freezing on yet another chord of fifths, but done very gradually over about three minutes. I learnt a huge amount doing it, and I've always wanted to do an orchestra piece that was written out that way. I haven't yet done it. Maybe I will. It would be very difficult to do that with 90 players.

CD: And a less homogenous set of sounds, unless you stuck to just strings or brass.

JA: Yes, the point about the chorus is it's easily divisible into four. Those four parts are always there. There isn't any such division in the orchestra that's so simple. So I don't know how I'd do it. I did think of doing that in *Eden*, but *Eden* is all written out in bars. I do want to do more music where the parts are not synchronised, and which follow up what I found in that piece. Certainly it affected all the harmony I wrote afterwards. It was a different use of consonance from my normal stuff because of the chance element.

Four American Choruses is curious because it's not a particularly crazy-sounding set of choruses, but they had a big effect on what I was doing. I like being able to write music which amateurs can sing or play, but which is not different from the music I usually write – we've touched on this already when I talked about writing beginner piano pieces and all that. The *American Choruses* was another example of that, and yes, another example of social involvement. That was a real involvement with the people in Birmingham who love music, coming in to sing in those halls. I wanted to participate in that, so it was another interaction with that area, which was lovely.

CD: There's a sense, then, with those pieces of broader society, and, in the various sacred pieces, there is a more explicit social function. Have you ever written for a professional chamber choir along the lines of Polyphony or Sinfonietta Voices?

JA: I haven't. All the smaller choral pieces I've written, except for the *Four American Choruses*, have been for cathedral choirs. The *Bell Mass* that I wrote in 2010 for the Westminster Abbey Choir has been done by the BBC Singers and could be done by a contemporary music choir as it involves some microtones and things so that would work, but no, I haven't. I've had various ideas for writing for that kind of set-up, like the Neue Vocalsolisten Stuttgart and, of course, James Weeks' group Exaudi in this country, but I've not written anything like that.

CD: Of course, cathedral choirs are also professional choirs, though their particular tradition makes it necessary to parse a difference between them and those secular professional choirs. In terms of composing, there is presumably a much bigger difference between them and large choruses. To what extent with something like *Heaven is Shy of Earth* did you find yourself bumping against or being aware of this difference in potential capability, not least the simple fact that a large body of voices is a less agile thing than say 12 voices?

JA: I wrote *Heaven is Shy of Earth* for the BBC Symphony Chorus, who do a lot of contemporary music. More than the London Philharmonic Choir, who already do quite a bit of modern music. I'd heard the BBC Symphony Chorus sing all kinds of repertoire – Henze's *Raft of the Medusa* or Tippett's *Vision of Saint Augustine*, which is a very complicated piece – so there was a lot I could ask for. *Heaven* is not the world's most demanding choral music, but it's more demanding than it might have been for a different body of singers. I knew that Sir Andrew Davis, who was conducting the premiere, knew all about choruses and choral music. I could push the boat out somewhat. At the same time, with *Heaven is Shy of Earth* I began finding a slightly more transparent orchestral style, which reappeared again in *Thebans* and in my Violin Concerto. In all cases the starting point for this was the question of balance – making the voices audible. Also, the Albert Hall acoustic responds in a very particular way so that a single note on, say, the violins can just hover there. There's no need to put another note in if you don't need one. I was quite surprised by how transparent the opening movement of *Heaven* is.

CD: Where do you think that came from?

JA: There again, we have a story like *Book of Hours*. *Heaven is Shy of Earth* is not written for the London Philharmonic Choir to sing, but it's dedicated to two people who are very good friends of mine who sing in that choir, who met in that choir and, as a result of meeting, married: Ian and Laetitia Frost. They got married in South Africa the previous year (2004) and they asked me to write a piece for their wedding, which I agreed to do. They said, 'There will be a trumpeter and an organist. We don't know the level of either.' So I wrote a very simple trumpet piece called *Solemn Melody,* which was played as they were signing the register. As I was writing it, I realised there was something funny about the way the few notes were moving around. They were never quite doing what I expected them to do and I wanted to explore the implications of that much more once I'd finished the trumpet piece. So I gave it to Ian to take to South Africa and said, 'This is going to be the basis of an oratorio I'm going to write and I'd like you and Laetitia to accept the dedication of that oratorio, if you will.' Then they came back from South Africa and it turned out that the trumpeter was the ex-principal of the Berlin Radio Symphony Orchestra! [Laughter] So I could have written something way more complicated. Moreover, having looked at the piece, that trumpeter said, 'I think this would sound best on flugelhorn.' They brought back a recording of it in this quite resonant church played on the flugelhorn. I thought that sounded wonderful. I'd always loved the flugelhorn, particularly since Tippett's Third Symphony. I thought, 'Fine. I'll have a flugelhorn.' And that's how it begins.

Like *Old Bells* in *Book of Hours*,[7] that trumpet piece is orchestrated into the first movement of the work and it gives you much of the harmony of the work. There's a chord that recurs several times in the piece which puts the whole of the first two phrases into a single vertical.[8] I made chords for the rest of the piece compressing pairs of phrases into big chords of seven or eight notes and that gives you the progression in the last movement, which begins with a set of just such chords. It's literally the trumpet tune you hear at the start verticalised. It's a kind of serialism I suppose, but I hope the serialism is audible here... With this very simple flugelhorn melody, the problem in the first movement of *Heaven is Shy of Earth* was how to colour it in such a way that the harmonic implications of the modality were emphasised, and that's where my macrotonality tuning system came in again. Such tuning comes in very early and remains a feature of certain movements of the work. Obviously, not on the chorus, but done in such a way that when the chorus is singing, sometimes it sounds as though they might be singing non-tempered pitches, because non-tempered tunings are embedded in and around their polyphony.

CD: So the trumpet piece was your musical starting point; it forms a prologue, and there are the Dickinson poems, but you've also got the structure of the Mass.

---

[7] See Conversation Twelve, 'Memory'.
[8] See CD of *Heaven is Shy of Earth*, track 9, at 2' 55".

JA: The plan was not to use the Credo. Stravinsky's setting of the Credo in his Mass was so perfect, and also Janáček's setting is so marvellous, I just felt I couldn't compete with those. In place of the Credo I put Psalm 84 and I had thought out which Dickinson to use when and where. The first entry of the mezzo, which is in the Christe part of the Kyrie movement, was originally going to be part of a Dickinson poem, 'Behind me–dips eternity–Before me– immortality'. The two phrases were going to be that, but it didn't really fit into the movement. So the mezzo sings the Latin 'Christe' while the chorus sings the 'Kyries' and Dickinson got postponed to later in the piece. The Gloria movement is called 'Gloria (with Bird)' – the bird is the Dickinson poem about a bird – and the mezzo sings the Dickinson, with a little bit of the Latin, but the chorus do the Gloria. In the next movement, she sings Psalm 84 on her own with the orchestra. Then in the middle of the Sanctus she sings the poem which gives the piece its title, *Heaven is Shy of Earth*, and the chorus takes this up also. For the last movement everyone is singing the Latin text.

CD: So Dickinson features in two movements, and Psalm 84 essentially provides another poetic element.

JA: Yes, but the Dickinson element in the premiere was somewhat reduced, because I wasn't satisfied with the Gloria so it was not sung. The piece came out at about 35 minutes at that point. Four years later I wrote the Gloria a second time, revising as I went along. Most, however, was as originally written in 2006, but I also added some new bits into that movement. The new version was premiered in November 2010 at the Barbican with the same orchestra and chorus, but conducted by Olly Knussen.[9] Although the piece won a BASCA award in its shorter version,[10] the longer version has a better formal balance. I felt there should be at least two Dickinson texts balancing out the shape of this piece and explaining who the mezzo-soprano is. To some extent I identify her with Emily Dickinson and that was made clearer by her added intervention in the Gloria.

CD: Why combine the Dickinson with a Mass setting?

JA: Why not? As it happens, I never asked myself that question. I like the framework of the Latin Mass because it's very traditional. When you're working with a tradition you can kick it, you can pull it about, and you can be very insolent with it, as Janáček was. The *Glagolitic Mass* is not a normal Mass setting and he knew it. That's why he wrote off this card to somebody who said, 'What a pious

---

[9]   26 November 2010, Barbican, Susan Bickley (mezzo-soprano), BBC Symphony Orchestra & Chorus, Oliver Knussen (conductor). This performance has since been released on Ondine ODE1313–2.
[10]   2007 BASCA (British Academy of Songwriters, Composers and Authors) award for Choral Composition.

piece and what a pious old man.' He said, 'I'm neither pious nor old!' I enjoy engaging with the Mass. I'd also sung the *Missa Solemnis* with the LPC – which is a nightmare. It's murderous. It's very high. There are many leaps. It's also wonderful music, but it's an absolute killer, particularly the Gloria, which is huge and is unbelievably demanding. I learnt a certain amount about how to pull the Mass text about from that piece. So I was trying to encapsulate the six movements of the Mass and go against the traditions of setting them, or with them, according to how I felt. I thought the piece through that way really, just dialoguing with what I knew people had done with this fascinating text. It's interesting setting a text that's been set hundreds and hundreds of times before. There aren't that many texts that have. The Lord's Prayer is another one, the Kaddish would be another one. There are only a few such texts in the world. Some Shakespeare sonnets would also do it, but there is another factor about setting the Mass text: it sounds wonderful. The phonetics of the Latin Mass text are composed by a supreme orchestrator of words, somebody who had a fine ear for verbal sonority; so it's a very good text to set. I also sang the B-Minor Mass with the choir. It all went in. It was all useful experience.

CD: The Mass is an iconic text – it's one that musicians can't avoid regardless of whether or not they are religious, or religious in that specific tradition. It's an intrinsic part of being a musician, like knowing your scales, as it crops up so often, yet it's depressing how many students have no idea what the Mass text is.

JA: Yes, isn't it?

CD: As a text to set outside of the liturgical context, isn't it also very challenging in terms of the arc of it. Depending on how you are as a composer, it strikes me that the Agnus Dei is a hard thing to end on.

JA: I didn't find it so myself, because, apart from anything, the last line ('Dona nobis pacem') is a good ending.

CD: Well, let me put that another way. Part of the problem with an awful lot of pre-twentieth-century ones, certainly, is that the composers want a nice bang, a strong sign-off, at the end of the Mass. Even Beethoven does it.

JA: That's true.

CD: Which is as at odds with that text.

JA: In fact, as you know, the ending of the Beethoven has been a source of some controversy because it's sudden; although it works, it's a strange ending all the same. The period over which I was working on *Heaven is Shy of Earth* covers the

Iraq War and I was working in America at that time (at Harvard), so there was plenty of reason to be thinking about peace. There always is, but there certainly was then. I felt a connection between certain issues in world events and that piece. I didn't shout this out from the rooftops – it's a purely personal matter, but the reason I didn't include a Credo is because the whole piece is a Credo really. There are conservation connections, too. If the piece is to do with the beauties of nature it's partly because those are under threat, so that's another message. Again, I leave people to make their own mind up about these things. I didn't make it an eco-Mass or a peace Mass or whatever. I don't shout these things out because to do so can seem trite.

The sequence of moods in the Mass texts is evocative. I've set it twice now, because the *Bell Mass* also sets it. I like the progression from a sort of formalised address to whoever makes this world happen at the start, then a celebratory but very long text with many moods and changes of direction, the Gloria, which is a big shout for joy in a way, but it's much more than that. There are many other aspects to it and qualifications to that joy. And then I didn't set the Credo in the *Bell Mass* either.

CD: Was that your decision? It was for Westminster Abbey, wasn't it?

JA: It wasn't required for the service concerned. In any case, Psalm 84 in *Heaven is Shy of Earth* read to me by that stage as if Emily Dickinson had written it, but in Latin, if you see what I mean. It read very similarly to her nature poetry. The funny thing is the German translation of Psalm 84, which Brahms used, 'Wie lieblich sind deine Wohnungen', could literally mean 'Nice apartments, Lord.' [Laughter] 'Tabernacula' does not carry that overtone in Latin. No estate agents here!

CD: No, although of course literally tabernacle is a tent.

JA: Indeed. So no estate agents there either... 'Nice tents'! The Brahms and the Messiaen have this utter serenity in common, though not much else, and, as you know, other movements of the *German Requiem* do not have that.

CD: No. There's not so much resting in peace.

JA: Far from it. The Brahms setting of Psalm 84 is very touching because it's a waltz, a surprising genre for a sacred piece. It's a celestial waltz. I found that very interesting, so I thought, 'What am I going to do with it?' I chose to set mine in a different tradition, which is the incantatory manner, the *style incantatoire* found in modern French music. So it was a piece modelled after certain French twentieth-century vocal pieces, like the opening number of [Messiaen's] *Cinq Rechants*, certain pieces by Ohana, Jolivet's *Épithalame* and that kind of thing.

Certain pieces of Jehan Alain, another a composer I value very much, also go into the mix.

CD: Not that it could be described as uniformly *style incantatoire*, or, at least, that's not a uniform approach.

JA: No. In the last part of the setting of Psalm 84, there is one line that is set twice in a row. It's a line that you also find in the Latin Requiem Mass: 'Domine, exaudi orationem meam'.[11] The first time I set it, the soprano sings almost like a priest. She cries it out in a very declamatory way and she's accompanied by ceremonial bell sounds in the orchestra with some macrotones giving different tuning, with wood chimes and tubular bells and bell attacks in the woodwind. They are resounding like that around her voice, annunciating this in a public way, as if she were officiating at a service. The second setting of the same line is completely contradictory of the first. It's a very intimate, personal setting of the line with a sudden change in the harmony. It's closely associated with my dad's death. He died just before I had written that passage and I was thinking of him very much when I wrote that second setting. That was, as it were, from me to you, rather than the soprano talking to a collective assembly. I liked the fact of having these two contradictory settings of the same texts one after the other in the same movement. Then at the start of the Sanctus she goes straight back to being a priest again.

There are so many different ways of playing with these texts, putting them across differently without being polystylistic. I realised as I ended the psalm movement that the way I did those two contrasts was quite operatic. The mezzo was becoming a character, so then, in the Sanctus, she announces the word 'Sanctus' and there's a huge outpouring of heterophony from the chorus each time. That movement, also, has one of the most prominent uses of macrotones in the piece. Halfway through it, the mezzo crops up again as Emily Dickinson with this text 'Heaven is Shy of Earth'. The chorus takes that up and sets it a second time, and then they go straight back to singing just the word 'Sanctus' for the final section. At that point, the tuning goes off into macrotonality again – a Just intonation type of tuning. I'm suggesting by that a connection between the tuning and an idea of something sacred. The overtone series is a natural phenomenon found in our ear even and in nature, so using that tuning here seems to me to suggest something fundamental about the world and the nature of sound.

CD: A harmonic window onto an extraordinary other world, which is actually our world. A holiness in all things. But then you have the Agnus Dei, which is a very different text.

---

[11]   O Lord, hear my prayer.

JA: I set the start of the Agnus Dei more or less as a motet for unaccompanied chorus with orchestral interludes, which then get more interwoven as it goes on. As I mentioned earlier, it begins with the trumpet tune converted into chords in the orchestra; then you get a motet on the unaccompanied chorus setting of the first 'Agnus'. There's another sequence of chords from the orchestra, with some macrotones in them, a second polyphonic 'Agnus', and then the chorus and orchestra come together. The third 'Agnus' is more polyphonic, with chorus and orchestra united; it also features macrotones. At the climax of the Agnus, there is a confrontation between two chords, each with the same non-tempered interval (a C flattened by a quarter-tone), until eventually they combine into a single chord. The end of the piece just breathes very slowly between three spectra until finally it puts them together, and it cadences in several keys at once in a way. That very slow breathing rhythm was partly modelled on the end of Stockhausen's *Hymnen*, which features Stockhausen himself breathing. I didn't include breathing noises at that point of my piece, but it seems to have a very gradual respiration trying to balance between these three different harmonic areas, finally just landing in all of them at once.

CD: It was the biggest thing you'd done at that point, wasn't it?

JA: By some way: it's about 43 minutes. I was a bit shattered. Then the phone rang and it was ENO wanting to see me and you know what that led to, because they'd heard the oratorio at the Proms. What I'd been thinking about increasingly was, 'How am I ever going to write an opera?' because I was thinking more about an operatic work. *Heaven is Shy of Earth* was leading towards that. ENO were right to wait until I'd had a piece of that size for voices and soloists and orchestra performed to see if I could sustain a full-evening opera. I'm glad nobody asked me any earlier, frankly. Well, they did ask for a chamber opera, but I didn't feel I was ready.

CD: But first there was *Alleluia*, which is a very different kind of piece.

JA: Yes, it was originally going to be 10 minutes but it came to 18 – something I don't usually do. I let it do that because I wanted it to be a concert piece that could be sung on other occasions.

CD: Why Alleluia?

JA: My original idea was only to set the word 'alleluia' again and again; indeed, the last section does just that. Then Bayan Northcott showed me a Latin poem called the Alleluiatic sequence, which, rather like the Benedicite, depicts all creation singing 'alleluia'. So I set that for the first part of the piece. It also arose out of a rather strange conversation I had with Kurt Masur, who was originally going to conduct the piece. He'd heard *Shir Hashirim* and emphasised my setting of the word 'alleluia' which comes several times at the end of the work. I've always liked that word and wanted to write a piece about it. There's a very different piece I very much enjoy called *Hallelujah*, written in the 1960s for unaccompanied choir by Kagel, which deals with the word in a very dissecting, structuralist way. I wanted to do something dealing with that set of syllables and the Latin verses gave me a context for it, so that I could spend the last third of the piece only on that word. I'm now glad I didn't use the whole piece just for one word. That wouldn't have worked.

CD: How does the choral writing differ from *Heaven is Shy of Earth*?

JA: It was an easier piece to sing, partly because I knew the chorus I was writing for personally.

CD: And they'd come and hit you if it was too difficult...

JA: Don't joke about that! [Laughter] It's more like a concerto for chorus and orchestra. There's this very big *ad libitum* passage in the middle, which is, to some extent, modelled on Ethiopian Jewish psalm singing, where everyone is singing the same tune out of phase with each other. I liked the sound of that so I modelled that section of the work on such singing. The other thing is that the whole final section, dealing with just the word 'alleluia', is based on a four-part sketch that I'd written for a much earlier piece, *Infinite Round*, but never used (see Figure 6). I found this way of writing in four parts, usually two plus two, so that each pair of parts moves at the same time, but there are four parts moving. I was trying to write a passage of music which was entirely on white notes of the keyboard. The idea is that you can change any of the accidentals to any of the pitches and it would work harmonically (including double sharps and double flats). Literally any spelling that you could make of accidentals in front of those notes was meant to work.

I got this procedure out of doing a piece for Stephen Gutman, my fourth piano Etude called *Misreading Rameau*, where I changed the clefs of a Rameau piece called 'Le Lardon' at random in order to create harmony that I found more enjoyable than the Rameau – excuse me for putting it that way, but that's not one of Rameau's most exciting pieces. The idea of modal redefinition of the same music is a Bartók thing and it goes back a long way. I'd always wanted to work more with that. I'd been working with that, to some extent, also in *Khorovod*. In *Alleluia*, from about 11 minutes in, there's this four-part writing which in the first statement is entirely on the white notes. When it loops back around you get one sharp, then two sharps, and then I gradually add more and all kinds of things happen, but the shape of it remains the same. Except for the last two minutes, that's the whole last section of the piece, roughly speaking. Sometimes

Figure 6   The original sketch for *Infinite Round* – annotations
show sketches for its use in a score. © Julian Anderson

that chaconne is on the orchestra, sometimes on the chorus, sometimes on the wind with the chorus singing a melody through it.

Alleluia is a slightly unusual case, because many of the things I've composed have worked with or against some kind of genre. *Alleluia* doesn't. It's just itself.

CD: With the *Bell Mass*, by contrast, you were dealing directly with a vast tradition and a particular type of music making.

JA: That was the one time in writing large-scale choral music where I didn't have to be cautious about the voices at all, because it was written for one of the top British cathedral choirs. In that tradition, whether the singers are male, female, or adults or not, they are all highly trained and can sight-read almost anything, so I could do all kinds of things.

CD: And it's a second setting of the Mass text.

JA: Yes. Having set much of it in *Heaven is Shy of Earth*, I wanted to set it again, but completely differently. I'd like to do other Masses too. I really love the Bruckner Masses, and I've sung them.

CD: Oh, they're gorgeous, yes.

JA: And they're all so different from each other. It was also fun to work with bits of the Mass text, by the way, that I didn't set in *Heaven*.

CD: It was for Westminster Abbey, and isn't it also mixed up with your memories of hearing the bells there ringing when you were at school?

JA: Yes, those are bells in D, and I've known them since I was 13. You'd hear the bell-ringers practising around midday in the middle of each week. It was a magnificent sound. James O'Donnell, who commissioned the piece, was a part-time teacher of that school. In those days he was an assistant at Westminster Cathedral; then he was Master of Music, in succession to David Hill. Then he was appointed to Westminster Abbey. He was the first Catholic to be the Head of Music at Westminster Abbey.

CD: In modern times, that is.

JA: Oh yes, of course!

CD: As a Catholic, he became the first person to take them to sing at the Sistine Chapel.

JA: Yes. He's an amazing musician, and he's also been very good at the ecumenical side of things. Incidentally, when I was a kid at Westminster School, the Pope visited Britain for the first time.

CD: That would have been 1982.

JA: Spring 1982.

CD: It was around the same time as the Falklands.

JA: The news was breaking exactly around the same time.

CD: The whole trip nearly collapsed because of the Falklands.

JA: Now, there was a funny story about that visit. For the first two terms I was at Westminster School, the headmaster, John Rae, taught us English. He told us that there was a debate going on as to whether or not the Pope would land in Vincent Square in a helicopter and then be taken from Vincent Square to Westminster Cathedral. The Pope was going to visit Britain in just under a year's time – that was how I first heard the news long before it was public knowledge. I should explain that Westminster School's playing fields are in Vincent Square. So the debate was not about whether a helicopter landing on those fields would spoil the fields. No, they were very concerned about a Catholic Pope landing on Protestant playing fields. I'm not making this up, you know!

CD: No, I can believe it.

JA: There was a serious debate about whether the future of the Church of England could be compromised by the Pope landing on the Westminster Abbey School playing fields...

CD: [Laughter] It does beggar belief, except it's all too common. Tim Day gave a paper noting the clear anti-Catholic sentiment in letters to the *Times* about the Westminster Cathedral Choir in the 1940s and 1950s, with their dangerous 'continental' way of singing, for which read Catholic, saying that this was corrupting the English cathedral tradition.

JA: This business about the playing field was pure anti-Catholic prejudice. Vatican II was only about 15 years before this. Until then, in Catholic churches everything was in Latin.

CD: Now, it's mostly Anglican churches singing in Latin. [Laughter]

JA: I know. Well, High Anglican ones. The irony is that Vatican II, although it had many commendable things, had a destructive effect on Catholic musical culture, because, once the Mass was in the vernacular, the existing rich liturgical music was largely sidelined. You've shown the differing responses of Catholic musicians of that period, meaning particularly the contrasting reactions of

Messiaen and Langlais. You've argued very convincingly that the *Transfiguration* is actually a positive anti-reaction, as it were, to Vatican II.[12]

CD: The distinction I make is that it's Messiaen's reaction *to* the developments of Vatican II. It's not a reaction against.

JA: Yes, because Langlais reacted against and got into trouble.

CD: When I first started talking about this, I had people say to me, 'Oh, why would this be particularly important?', basically saying, 'Oh, no, it's not going to be a reaction to Vatican II just because he's writing in Latin.' Still, people were buying into this whole idea that Messiaen's head was completely in the clouds and completely unaffected by anything going on around him. My point was, 'Well, no, you're just looking in the wrong places for what he's being affected by.' The thing that had been the completely unchangeable facet of his life, namely the Church, was having an earthquake.

JA: There was no precedent in his lifetime for that.

CD: In anybody's lifetime. For many generations. Arguably, not since the Council of Trent.

JA: You have to understand that I didn't really know about it. I wasn't involved in the Catholic church. When your articles first came out suggesting it, I was very surprised. It took me some time to understand what the situation really meant.

CD: It completely revolutionised everything. To anyone who was a Catholic, it would have affected them. What that effect was is a whole other question, but there was not a single Catholic on the planet who was left unaffected by that.

JA: An equivalent of an earthquake, as you say. Well, the thing is that with the *Bell Mass*, I was asked to write a piece for the anniversary of Westminster Abbey.

CD: The 450th anniversary of the Abbey's Collegiate Charter, granted by Elizabeth I in 1560 according to my notes.

JA: It was going to be a Mass – that was James O'Donnell's idea. I then said, 'I'd rather set it in Latin.' That was fine, because it was the Anglican church, ironically. This discussion is very apropos, because, of course, *Heaven is Shy of Earth* is not liturgical at all. The *Bell Mass* had to be dual-function – singable liturgically or in concert. That attracted me in the same way that the ballet/concert

---

12 Christopher Dingle, 'La statue reste sur son piédestal: Messiaen's *La Transfiguration* and Vatican II', *Tempo* 212 (April 2000), 8–11.

dual-function thing attracted me in *Comedy of Change*. The first performance was in a service. It was not a concert premiere. That was quite important to know.

They would be speaking the Creed. Knowing that there was no Creed cleared out the problem of setting that. The reason that I have a problem with the Creed is the laundry-list element of it. In the phrase of Stravinsky, 'There is much to believe': well, he sets it that way. He sets it almost like a monotone chant, if you remember.

CD: It's almost an anti-setting, less florid than most plainchant versions.

JA: It's very rapidly gone through by Stravinsky. Bach cuts it up into many little numbers and so does Beethoven.

CD: Liturgically, in both Anglican and Catholic traditions, it's perfectly fine to have the Apostles' Creed rather than the Nicene Creed. I'm just thinking whether I can recall any setting of the Apostles' Creed, which musically and structurally makes far more sense. It would balance the Gloria and so you'd have a much more satisfying arch.

JA: Like you, I don't know of any setting of it, so I didn't consider that option, though it would be much easier to do. Anyway, they were speaking the Creed, so I was let off that question. The next question then was whether or not to have an organ. I wanted an organ to make sure that I could fly a bit freer on the pitch front. One movement, the Benedictus, features non-tempered pitches for the soloists with drones from the choir. I've always found the text of the Benedictus very touching. As a kid I was very moved by the setting in Beethoven's *Missa Solemnis*, which is just fantastic, it's so simple. I wanted to do something a bit like that – very still and serene. I also love the Stravinsky setting, but mine is very different from that. Perhaps I learnt from the Stravinsky in terms of clarity and polyphony. Many of my models were medieval – the *Messe de Tournai*, which I've loved since I was 13, was a major influence – and Stravinsky's models for his Mass, we now know, were Landini, Dufay and, to some extent, Machaut. He was reading a lot of literature about medieval music, and being advised by various people, including Nadia Boulanger, about medieval music. That piece does have an imaginary medieval quality to it, as well as a Byzantine element, and I wanted to have both of those in my *Bell Mass* as well. The Byzantine element is due to the use of the *ison*, which is what the drone is called in Byzantine tradition. With the Benedictus, I hoped to make a movement that sounded like a very old rite. I tried to create an imaginary ritual that was not like any I'd heard.

CD: How did you go about that?

JA: The first thing was to devise the macrotonal modes, which were based on superimposed overtone series. Those are what the soloists sing. Then I had the *ison* in the choir. Sometimes it's single-octave drone, sometimes a unison drone, or a fifth doubled at the octave – it keeps changing. Then, at the end of it, for the 'hosannas', which I set only once, unlike in the Stravinsky, I made a canon in a mode that changes in each octave and has a lot of false relations. It's a multi-register mode again. It has a lot of parallel sixths, so it sounds very bell-like.

CD: Hence *Bell Mass*?

JA: Well, everywhere in the piece I was trying to derive the modes from the resonance of bells all the time. Because I know the pitch of the Abbey bells is in D, the ideal would have been to have the bells ringing during the piece, but they cannot be heard in the Abbey. It's to do with where they are. You have to go outside to hear them. They're in a pair of tall towers at the top of the north-west entrance.

So I made bells in the music instead. I've got one of those UNESCO volumes, of Romanesque and Gothic Czechoslovakian manuscripts. There was a particular page which very much inspired some passages in the *Bell Mass*.[13] It's a combination of music notation with illustration. In the *Bell Mass* at certain points there's a fixed chord and then polyphony emerges out of that as if the chords are unfreezing and melting. The chant in the manuscript in question interacts with and seems to melt out of the drawing, as if almost dropping off the page. I set the Hosannah in the Sanctus as an ad-lib passage the first time. The second time is metric and, as it develops, you get a big chord with polyphony melting out of that and descending. That was very much inspired by the old Czech manuscript.

A lot of the piece is really about the interaction of line, harmony and mode, and changing the mode as you go. The mode, as always in my music, is a developing rather than a static phenomenon. I was also portioning out areas of complexity and density, and contrasting areas of simplicity. One of the most complex bits is the 'Amen' of the Gloria, which is a sudden free-for-all. That was meant to be like a bell being struck and then reverberating, but here the bell is actually an *ad libitum* polyphony. Nevertheless, the end result is a perfect-fifth resolution, but it's arrived at randomly.

CD: As it happens, we had a doctoral student at the Conservatoire who explored aleatoricism in choral contexts. It's not a composition PhD, though he's involving plenty of composers, but a combination of practice and theory from the perspective of choral conducting.

---

[13]   *Czechoslovakia: Romanesque and Gothic Illuminated Manuscripts* (Paris, UNESCO 1959), plate 16.

JA: And choirs need that kind of notation to achieve the kind of rhythmic fluidity that I sometimes want. They adapt to it quickly in practice. There are two ad-lib passages in the *Bell Mass*. Both of them were inspired not only by bell resonance, but also a form of ceremonial religious music as I mentioned, Ethiopian Jewish synagogue ritual. I've got a CD by Simha Arom, who is an authority on African music generally (and who had trained Berio and Ligeti in African polyphony). This is a heterophonic texture, and very remarkable. That influenced the *Bell Mass* a lot. It's partly a homage to that. Also, Jean-Louis Florentz's recordings of Ethiopian Christian ceremonies, which Ocora issued on the Radio France label.[14] Florentz's field recordings of Ethiopian music are excellent and also influenced the ceremonial aspect of *Bell Mass*, but it doesn't imitate any of those traditions. It's made up in my head, if you will, plus the resonances of the bells.

CD: You've mentioned how a cathedral choir is a highly trained professional choir. How did that affect the writing?

JA: I knew that, within reasonable limits, I could write almost any chord I wanted. Cathedral choirs don't use much vibrato, so you hear the notes incredibly clearly. That was lovely to be able to do. Whenever James O'Donnell's choir did it or any others that I've heard – All Saints, Margaret Street have done it, St Margaret's, Westminster, Gonville and Caius, Cambridge, and other choirs – I've always had that same absolute clarity of pitch that I love so much in cathedral choirs.

CD: Do you have any preference for boys' voices or women's voices?

JA: It's been done by each. You get a different sound, but either is possible. It doesn't bother me.

CD: One or two have got mixed choirs now. Wells has one of each, so you'd think that they'd have the facility to be able to mix and match a bit.

JA: What's interesting is the Stravinsky Mass is usually now done with women, but if you hear Westminster Abbey do it with boys, it sounds quite different. By the way, do you know there is a piece by Rădulescu called *Do Emerge Ultimate Silence*, for 34 children? They are spectrally tuned, of course, it being Rădulescu! Each of the voices has little monochords[15] which I gather they have to pluck to get their pitch. He gave me a recording and it does sound most extraordinary. I like the idea that music can be contemporary and spiritual without being sentimental.

---

[14] *Liturgies Juives d'Ethiopie*, recorded by Simha Arom and Avi Nahmias, Jerusalem, 1986, Maison des Cultures du Monde W 260013; *L'Assomption à Däbrä Gännät: L'Église Orthodoxe Éthiopienne de Jérusalem*, recorded by Jean-Louis Florentz, Jerusalem, July–September 1987, Radio France Ocora 560027/28 (2 CDs).

[15] A monochord is a simple instrument with a single tuneable string.

CD: Not what the Parisians call Saint Sulpice style.

JA: Precisely. Now, the other thing, which is a factor in a lot of my music, is the painted churches in Romania and Moldavia. The art in cathedrals in the West is usually kept indoors. What's lovely in Romania is that the building becomes the art, and you have a double shape. You have the shape of the church, but the painting is on the outside walls. It is often not in the same shape at all, and is going in its own structure. It's rather like the illustrations on some of the Assyrian sculptures in the British Museum, where you have a horse or something. Then you have writing or an illustration going across it that doesn't obey the horse shape at all. The Romanian painted churches are more colourful. There are places on the outside walls where the weather has done its worst and the paint gets blown off. That, too, was an inspiration for me in terms of the polyphony getting smudged. In the *Bell Mass* that happens, and I felt it was analogous to the paint partly erased on these Romanian churches. I admire the way these churches interact with their landscape and the colours around them.

We're back, a little bit, to *Heaven is Shy of Earth* – the idea of nature and spiritual things interacting, and the spiritual thing becoming part of the natural world by being inside it, in that case. That's in the *Bell Mass*, too. I suppose that's why I resorted to what you might call natural tuning in terms of the macrotonal modes in the Benedictus – so that they sound like natural horns or something.

Bell Mass is not an outdoor Mass, in the sense that I'm working with the acoustic of a church or a cathedral, but it's got an outdoor flavour in both tuning and mood. That's really because of the Romanian painted churches. It would be nice to paint the outside of Westminster Abbey, but I didn't suggest that! [Laughter] It would look better than it does, because when I was a kid, it was full of pollution.

CD: Everything in London was black when we were kids. We all thought the Albert Memorial was a very dour, grim thing, but it was pollution and the statue being painted black so it wouldn't act as a beacon for the Zeppelins in World War I. Now we can see it was Victorian bling. But Westminster, St Paul's, were all black.

JA: They sanded all the stones so it looks incredibly pukka and far too clean now. I'm used to cathedrals looking muckier than that... So let's paint the thing. Nobody likes painting churches. They like everything to be stone. You know, in medieval times, churches were painted indoors.

CD: Yes. In what's left of Binham Abbey in Norfolk they have an artist's impression of what it would have looked like and it's spectacularly colourful. For that matter, the Parthenon was very brightly coloured.

JA: The Parthenon was painted. The Elgin Marbles were painted. You know they thought it was dirt? When they came here, they rubbed some of it, and 'cleaned' it away.

CD: Well, that was a reasonable assumption given what our buildings looked like at the time, thanks to the grime you're now wishing they still had!

JA: Well, I suppose so.

Figure 7   Julian Anderson with Benet Casablancas, Olly Knussen and orchestral
manager, March 2009, photographer unknown, from the collection of John Fallas

Conversation Eleven

Olly

What follows is, in essence, Anderson's tribute to his close friend, Oliver Knussen. After my initial prompt, it required no input from me.

OLIVER KNUSSEN, 12 JUNE 1952–8 JULY 2018

CD: This is 9 July 2018. We've just had the news today that Olly Knussen has died. Obviously he's a very close and important figure for you. Would you like to share your thoughts on Olly and what he means to you in all sorts of respects?

JA: I've noticed that when famous people die, most people talk about themselves. This is probably because they don't want to think about death. They immediately think about themselves in relation to the deceased – talking about themselves is, in a way, some kind of comfort. So, inevitably, some of what I say is going to involve myself here.

Olly Knussen was such a huge part of musical life internationally that it's very hard for somebody my age to imagine it without his presence. Given that we met in early 1981, we knew each other 37 years. So quite apart from his international prominence, I've known him far longer than I've known any other musician. I am, naturally, very shocked by his death. Although his health had been worrying for some years, it does come as a surprise. It's hard to be objective about the death of someone who was part of your life for that long.

The funny thing about Olly Knussen is that, although I was becoming aware of contemporary music in the late '70s, I discovered his music later than that of many other recent composers. I missed the broadcast premiere of his Third Symphony at the Proms in 1979. I'd never heard the name then – it's fair to say that until the Third Symphony premiere Olly was not so prominent here, and he'd only returned from the US three years before that. More recently, while doing research on other things, I accidentally saw an archive copy of the *Radio Times* for the week of that premiere and it rang a bell. The blurb about his music was rather misleading, making it appear vaguely eclectic, and I have a distant memory of reading that and deciding not to bother listening as a result. Which shows promoters how attempts to second-guess the audience can be very misguided.

Some months later I found a score in my local library of his First Symphony. I did not recall his name. The preface to the score mentioned this bizarre circumstance that the guy was only 15 and conducted the world premiere at no notice. I borrowed the score and found an alarmingly assured piece roughly in the style of 12-note British symphonists like Richard Rodney Bennett or Racine Fricker. It looked like the work of a mature composer, albeit a fairly conventional one. (I noticed the percussion listing was incomplete and wrote in the missing instruments myself. Lately a friend of mine came across this score in a second-hand shop and copied me that page, which was amusing.) It showed me that my own attempts at orchestral composing were, as I was beginning to suspect, woefully inadequate, and I started trying to do something about that right away.

The BBC broadcast the Third Symphony and also his suite from the *Wild Things* opera in early 1981 and I was very struck by those. Two months later, by chance, I met him at the British Music Information Centre. We were introduced by the centre's then Director, Roger Wright, and we hit it off. We discovered we were living in the same area of London, and every few months I'd go over to see him. He'd pile me up with scores and records, play me all kinds of things – I recall Boulez's *Pli selon pli*, Xenakis's *Pithoprakta*, some Finnissy, some recent Americans and Scandinavians, and of course his own music too. He offered advice on what I was composing and was generally very forthcoming. But from 1983 his conducting career took off suddenly and I saw him very infrequently until the early '90s. Then we met up again and I was incredibly fortunate to work closely with him.

The culture that went with Olly was enormous, as I've found with other composers: it amazes me we composers have such a reputation for being isolated. In my experience any good composer is fascinated by lots of other music and many areas of culture. It's part of what makes composers good, and good company too. But even by those standards, Olly's width and depth of knowledge and enthusiasms was awesome. There was a huge range of film, literature and visual art. As with Michael Finnissy or George Benjamin, when you asked a question about any music, the reply led to the other arts straight away. For example, I asked him in the '90s about *Flourish with Fireworks* and he referred me to *The Fairy Feller's Master-Stroke*, a canvas by an insane Victorian fairy painter called Dadd (there was a whole school of such painters, which I'd known nothing about till then). It's a tiny, manically detailed painting, in the middle of which there's this little fairy with an axe who has just broken open an acorn, which clearly is going to have another little world inside it. There's an implication of worlds within worlds, a sort of fractal idea, and that's what influenced the music, which is made of one little idea constantly changing size and shape. Shortly after that, by coincidence, there was an exhibition of precisely that art at the Royal Academy so I got to see that painting live.

Olly was obsessed with films, so I learnt much about world cinema. He was also crazy about soap and TV comedy and so on – *Curb Your Enthusiasm* was a major obsession. The only TV thing I managed to introduce Olly to was *Frasier*, which at first he didn't quite get. Then, suddenly, he became fascinated by David Hyde Pierce's miming ability. Olly clocked onto the vaudeville-like character of Niles, the movements, the miming, the eyes and so on – it's almost balletic. One elaborate mimed sequence to a Mozart symphony was what really got Olly into *Frasier*. He loved that.

So the reason the friendship flourished from my point of view was that he was just one of the most interesting people you could ever meet. It's astonishing to think he was 29 when I met him, but he was already quite long in the tooth in terms of the music profession, as he'd been in it nearly 15 years.

At this point I guess we have to get into his background and how that impacted upon things. A friend of my father's family in the Jewish quarter of Newcastle was the composer Wilfred Josephs, who wrote mainly for film and TV while also doing concert music. Because he was the only composer that anybody in the family knew, when I started writing music I was taken round to see him, which was rather terrifying (I must have been about 15). One thing that shocked me greatly was that he asked early on, 'Which contemporary composers do you like?' and when I mentioned Olly Knussen I got a terrible reaction. He almost shouted that I shouldn't take Olly seriously, and suddenly all this business about the premiere of Olly's First Symphony came up. I was told how he was pushed by his father, who was principal double bass in the LSO, and made into some kind of ridiculous wunderkind figure. Until then I'd not appreciated the extent of the music profession's distaste for that whole episode. Many years later, I was in Albemarle Street in 1999 at the Royal Institution with Olly and another friend of his. We were going to hear a lecture by Robert Craft for the Royal Philharmonic Society. We entered the entrance foyer to the hall and Olly simply froze. He blanched, and we both asked if he was ok. The foyer was full of old men in their '80s, most of whom I'd never met. Olly said, 'Those are all the people who used to run the British musical profession and who told me I couldn't have a career in it.' That is what the early exposure of his music had done to Olly Knussen. I had already realised this was a difficult memory for him but that was when I really saw what a terrible trauma it was in his life. I realised that this had nearly ruined him, cut him up, and just what a terrible business that had been.

Later on, in one of the last interviews he gave, for Andrew Palmer's book of conversations,[1] his advice to young composers was to try and get as much as you can written and enjoy doing it while you're young and out of the limelight, before things get difficult later – he emphasised that they would certainly do so. Many years previously when Olly gave me the same advice, that's just what I did. I had my student years to muck about with experimental music and spectral music, to write my bad Lachenmann pieces, my bad Olly pieces and my bad everyone else pieces for a few years that were very valuable – and you don't get that back. It was very good advice. John Lambert, who taught us both, told me about that whole business with Olly's First Symphony and he said, 'There wasn't any stopping it. Once it emerged that Olly at the age of 14 could write symphonic music fluently, they commissioned him and there was nothing I could do except protect him as much as I could from the reaction.' So he did what he could, but there was an unpleasant backlash which took years to dissipate, and my opinion is that this permanently scarred Olly.

I'm mentioning this because basically, if I think of Olly now, I also think, even though he was eventually played a great deal, he was a very tough man who had had to come through some really dreadful times. He was a wonderful but complicated personality and yet there were times when he managed to get that amazing music out and also do some astonishing conducting. As regards the repertoire of the conducting, it started very broad. He conducted all kinds of things as a young conductor. Very gradually it focused on what he most wanted to conduct in the time he had available. From the late '90s, Olly's health was becoming dicey. He had terrible pains in his knees, legs and back, and there were health scares. He never talked about it this way, but I guess he began gradually to concentrate on conducting the music to which he felt the closest. After the many years he'd done helping vast numbers of other composers, there was no reason that somebody who was pretty pushed for time should continue to conduct music they didn't feel any sympathy with, because he'd really done the galley slave years doing all kinds of things.

When he was 50 and 60 there were lavish international celebrations, I'm happy to recall. Yet in a curious way he was, if not exactly underestimated – but there was still some attitude of reserve towards him in many quarters. I can't understand where that came from given that, more than most composers, he did a lot for his colleagues. He didn't found a record company for them like Colin Matthews did, but think of what he did for Elliott Carter alone. When Olly started conducting Carter in '82 with *In Sleep, In Thunder*, it wasn't played that much and it was often played badly. Olly changed all that. His performances of what remain very difficult works were crystalline, lively, even humorous. His recording of Carter's Concerto for Orchestra, made under very special conditions

---

[1]   Andrew Palmer, *Encounters with British Composers* (Woodbridge: Boydell, 2015).

with expert players, wasn't just the best recording the piece has ever had (or is ever likely to have) but powerfully, vitally expressive: it got you into the whole world of that music.[2] I first understood that when I first flew into New York. The opening of that piece is like flying into New York and suddenly 'zing', you're in this teeming world. You sense that the piece is not only about America, as Carter admitted, but specifically about New York. It was written for the New York Philharmonic and Carter lived in New York all his life. It's Carter's celebration of that city, its portrait. The piece overwhelms you. There are moments of poise, like a sort of oasis, and then another thunderstorm looms in and engulfs you. Olly got all that across almost instinctively. Of course, he knew America very well, and what he did for Carter was to bring him out of the ghetto and into the bigger world because the performances were both big in mentality, and also big-time exposure. Then Barenboim and others all caught on – not forgetting the considerable championship of Carter by Boulez over many decades. But Olly's persistence with Carter's music was unique.

I think Olly's conducting turned Carter's composing around in some ways. That late *Symphonia* wouldn't have existed without Olly, nor would *Three Occasions*. Carter wrote the first of the *Three Occasions*, the 'Celebration' (John Adams wrote *Short Ride* for the same Texas commission, by the way). Then Olly said to Carter, 'Why don't you write two companion pieces?' and, as Carter admitted, the other *Occasions* came about as a result. The *Symphonia*, in the '90s, was more or less the same. That again went back to an old idea of Olly's: a big triptych à la Debussy's *Images*. He suggested to Carter doing something like that. Olly himself had thought of doing that sort of piece. Alas, Olly never wrote his, but we did get Carter's *Symphonia*, and we also got Olly's fantastic recording and performances of that. (That recording was a remarkable piece of work in itself: the editing took Olly over a year – I'm not joking, he really micro-managed every detail.)[3] I remember when he did *The Rite of Spring* at the Proms. One felt at that concert that the Prommers had sort of taken Olly to their hearts. It was very nice to see that, taking to him the way that they'd previously taken to someone like Boulez.

Turning to his own music, it is remarkably evocative. Olly was rather uniquely able to refer consciously in his music to other music without being polystylistic. There's one piece that dabbles in that and he later got quite critical of that aspect of it, which was *Higglety Pigglety Pop!* – though in many other respects that work was very close to his heart. But there are only very small passages of that piece

2   Carter, Concerto for Orchestra, London Sinfonietta, Oliver Knussen (conductor), recorded at Henry Wood Hall, London, 15–16 February 1991, Virgin Classics 0777 7592712 2 (CD).
3   Carter, *Symphonia: Sum Fluxae Pretium Spei*, BBC Symphony Orchestra, Oliver Knussen (conductor), recorded at Henry Wood Hall, London, August 1998, Deutsche Grammophon 459 660–2 (CD).

that deal with polystylism, and of course they're done way better than most other people. What I love about the music is that, if I may be honest, when listening I don't give a damn how well made it is – it just totally convinces me musically. I sit there getting very involved and excited by the whole sound world, and that for me is the mark of great music. In a very different way I feel the same about a piece like *Red Earth* by Michael Finnissy; I don't sit there thinking about the proportions that I know underline that piece, though I've done an analysis of it. This applies to any piece which convinces me as a musical statement without any regard for how it's made – Feldman's *Coptic Light* comes to mind. I enjoy music that embodies a whole world, no matter how long or short pieces are. Some of Olly's music is longer, some shorter, but what I like is the fact that immediately you're plunged into a very distinctive world. There are few other recent composers of whom that's true to such an extent.

What I learnt most from him was professionalism in terms of notation. Olly grew up with the LSO and saw what worked in rehearsal and what didn't. Because he conducted orchestras for much of his life, you can rely on Olly's notation. If he writes something in a score, it'll work. He didn't allow something into a printed score that doesn't work. From the technical point of view, there's naturally lots the public doesn't need to know about how an orchestral piece is put together – the aural result is what counts. But for students and the profession, a score of his will show you how it's done properly. Olly's scores show you this magnificently, and he remains a gold standard in that respect.

We were not writing the same music. There are just a few passages in my music influenced by his work directly, but after due consideration I've let them stand because they're fairly early and one must be honest about one's origins. But many aspects of my music were very far away from his home territory, and he was enthusiastic about that. For example, he had no interest in microtones – nor even what I term macrotones. We had a running joke about this because of course I wrote several pieces that he conducted that used non-tempered pitches a lot, particularly *Book of Hours*. I think he thought of it as a slightly Frenchified side of my music, that the French do these sort of microtonal spectral things. On the other hand, he was intrigued to see the way I dealt with it. He was particularly keen on my Second Quartet, which slightly surprised me as it could not be further from his own area. But he made it clear he was very excited. I was writing my Third Quartet a few months ago and he really wanted to hear that – I'd found some new types of non-tempered harmony and he wanted to hear what that was. Alas he never did. The other running joke between us was that I would say after finishing a piece that I was never going to use non-tempered pitches again. The next piece would come out and I'd have found another way of composing with them. Olly would giggle, 'I see that you broke your promise again!' In any case, more generally it was fantastic the way that Olly could sympathise with stuff that was very far away from his own palate; that I admired very much.

Writing a piece with electronics and microtones for Olly Knussen is like writing a piece for Boulez that uses C-major triads – I knew when I wrote *Book of Hours* that it was not home territory for him. All I did was to make sure that he didn't have to worry about the tuning because everyone who's playing microtones is detuned, so it just happens. With the electronics he said, 'That's fine as long as you and the technicians look after it and I don't have to worry about it because I don't know anything about electronics, so it has to run itself.' I had that aspiration anyway – you have to, with electronics. I wanted the piece to be playable generally, not just at IRCAM but anywhere, so that was a very useful tip from him. Some funny things happened in rehearsals. In the second part of the piece, at one point the synthesiser comes in a quarter-tone flat with a harp sound, in rhythmic unison with the normally tuned harp. Olly looked at the harpist as if the player were mad. You see, the score is transposed so there are no microtones written, just played – everyone playing microtones is detuned so there's just a reverse flat before the staff and the pitches are written out normally. He was just conducting and suddenly he heard the most bizarre tuning from the harp. Olly was very tickled because he really had been fooled. The synth sound was convincing and it was placed right next to the harp. It had him creased up for hours.

Olly's breadth of mind influenced me a lot when teaching composition. I keep in mind that people come from completely different angles and you should respect that, enjoy it and relish it. Our mutual teacher John Lambert had this also. Above a certain level of technical accomplishment and musicality, what makes composers interesting is the difference between them. A teacher should encourage that.

Olly's personality was very unshowy. Perhaps, because he could do anything and seemed to know everything, he could unintentionally be a little intimidating. Olly reading a score was awesome. I never worked with Boulez, but I gather it was quite like that in the sense that it was just like reading a book for him, and there's not many people like that. With Olly this was a bit scary.

A conversation with him was very exciting, but I'd struggle to keep up sometimes because of the amount of culture and knowledge that he loved sharing. I didn't know about half of these things. One thing that we did both get into together was a Finnish painting, *Lake Keitele*, which eventually fed into the *Symphony*. I'd encountered it when he was conducting *Stations of the Sun* in Helsinki, and he introduced me to the art of Akseli Gallen-Kallela. We both loved to visit the Academic Bookshop. It's a huge, fantastic cathedral of books with architecture by Alvar Aalto. Olly recommended a book about Gallen-Kallela in the Finnish art section, and that's where I first saw the painting that became the source of my *Symphony*, which I then saw in an art gallery the following day. Things like that would happen all the time.

I would sometimes try it the other way round, but that didn't always work. Olly was quite particular in his tastes, and preferred to discover things himself, not be shown them by others. By the way, I remember his attitude towards Messiaen was curiously ambivalent. Messiaen and he had encountered each other directly at Tanglewood in 1975. Messiaen had heard the tape of the first part of the Third Symphony, which the Boston Symphony had premiered the previous year. Messiaen was very struck by the music, and also by the Shakespeare connection – that piece is a kind of portrait of Shakespeare's Ophelia. When Olly was packing his archive to go to the Sacher Foundation last year, he found the card on which Messiaen wrote with great affection about Olly's music and their mutual love of Shakespeare. But I believe Olly sometimes found the slightly sanctimonious atmosphere around Messiaen a little bit much to take. The cult of *L'Itinéraire* around Messiaen wasn't his world and he felt a little bit left out of it. He heard about those people long before anyone else in the UK because Suzanne Cheetham, a pianist friend of his and Sue Knussen's, studied with Loriod and Messiaen in the '70s, came back with tapes and things of early Lévinas and Murail and so on, so he knew all about that. It was Olly who first said to me, because I'd heard some Murail, 'Yes, but the really interesting composer of that group is Gérard Grisey'. Olly had come back that week from hearing a recording in Stephen Plaistow's office in the BBC of *Modulations* and had been deeply impressed: 'hunt that out, you won't regret it.' Then shortly after, as you know, I heard some Grisey on French radio. I ended up liking both composers!

Basically, if anyone was doing anything musically, he made it his business to know. Even if he didn't like it, he made sure he knew. If you take something like *Wild Things* or his other opera, *Higglety*, which seem quite outside modernism – they're perhaps not the sort of music you turn up to hear at IRCAM, Darmstadt or Donaueschingen or whatever – yet they are deeply informed by modernist music. The whole way they're constructed, the cut-up way time works in those pieces, which is very odd, all kinds of things, taught me how to absorb lessons from modernism without imitating modernism. In other words, like learning from Mozart or Josquin des Prez or whoever, that you don't just go for the stylistic surface, though that can be fun too. So that was also a very good lesson, transmuting the musical surface into a cultural phenomenon that could mean a great deal to you without you wanting to write music like that.

A few years ago, Lachenmann's *Tanzsuite mit Deutschlandlied* had its British premiere at the Proms. The following morning I had a fascinating discussion about it with Olly, who sensed its roots in Kagel (to whom he was very close). He had a very different perspective on it to anyone I'd ever heard talking about it in Germany, who usually would reproduce what Lachenmann says. This was a different view on it. He had said somewhere in an interview before then that he thought that kind of extended-technique instrumentation worked best on ensemble, not on the orchestra. But *Tanzsuite* changed his mind about that – he saw it did work brilliantly on orchestra and, typically, became very excited about this.

Then there were his crazes. Suddenly he'd get keen on Castiglioni or Myaskovsky's symphonies, or Honegger or Milhaud, and you'd get CDs through the post. At one point it was Machaut, then Scarlatti, then Rubbra symphonies, then José Maceda's invented instruments. Cardew was another enthusiasm. I always looked forward to seeing what would crop up next. I think one of the last ones was the music of the Japanese pianist and composer Yuji Takahashi, and a CD duly dropped into my letter box. It was no good putting them aside if you were busy or something, because not infrequently he'd phone and ask you what you'd made of it!

One morning while talking to him I was getting very annoyed about Ligeti's *Le Grand Macabre*, which I'd just seen again after many years at the ENO (I was at the UK premiere back in 1982). I criticised it severely. There was a pause and he said, 'I think you're prejudiced against it.' He patiently pointed out all kinds of good things I'd either missed or not mentioned – for a good 15 minutes. Now, when you think of Olly Knussen, you don't think of *Le Grand Macabre*. It has nothing in common with his work, is no kind of influence on it, but he knew it inside out. Inevitably, I eventually listened again, and found of course there's a lot of truth in what he'd said. He had that gentle way of getting rid of pretensions and pre-fab opinions.

There were musical disagreements, of course – I couldn't follow him in all his crazes, and he certainly did not approve of some things I enjoyed, and was not shy in saying so, which was fine. In any case, he had always thought things through carefully. In other words, I thought he was often very right even when he was wrong. It's rather what John Cage's dad said to him about his mum when they were having an argument: 'John, your mother's always right even when she's wrong!' That's how I felt about Olly's opinions... When I disagreed they were still very well-founded opinions, so it was always worth discussing.

I said to him once, teasingly, 'So are we ever going to see a microtonal piece from you?' I was joking, of course. He said, 'I've got more interesting ways of spending my time', and indeed he did. But in the next breath, he mentioned a microtonal electronic work by Jean-Claude Éloy that he'd recently come across and thought very striking. He never wrote electronic music, but he knew all about it and was very interested in technology. He was a lifelong Stockhausen fan, and couldn't have been more delighted than when he worked with Stockhausen on performances of *Gruppen* and other pieces. Interestingly, Olly preferred to hear *Kontakte* without the piano and percussion: he felt the electronic tape was sufficiently absorbing and beautiful on its own, which is true. It's forgotten a bit now how close he was to Stockhausen later – I mean, who else but Olly could have been simultaneously a fan of and close colleague with Stockhausen, Henze and Kagel? By the '90s I doubt they were speaking to each other, but they all liked working with Olly. No wonder, given the performances he gave of their music! He was a champion of women composers; he was delighted at having discovered or promoted Minna Keal, Betty Oliviero, Augusta Read Thomas, Helen Grime, Charlotte Bray, Arlene Sierra and many others; he was a big fan of Thea Musgrave and Kaija Saariaho. He never preached about this, he just did it, wonderfully.

Recording technology was another long-term obsession. Firstly in terms of his expertise in editing recordings, and things like that, but also as a listener. For the last three decades he had recordings in and players for all formats: 78s, 33s, CDs, iPods, streaming. When I got the second model of iPod, with many more gigabytes of memory and other new features, he looked it over quietly for about 10 minutes. 'I'm going to have to get that.' A lot of the friendship was based on mundane things like that... Going to a record shop was unbelievable fun, but the real treat was going around an art gallery. He once took me around the Cleveland Art Institute, showing me the pictures that meant most to him and encouraging me to roam and discover. That visit has a particular poignancy now, since his death. Olly was working for years on a large orchestral piece, *Cleveland Pictures*, based on some of the same paintings he showed me in that gallery. I know he finished some movements, but he withdrew them before they were played. It was a work very much bound up with his long friendship with the then Manager of the Cleveland Orchestra Tom Morris, who shared Olly's enthusiasms and his sense of humour, too. But there, Olly's surprising lack of self-confidence got the better of him. He was very vulnerable.

I prefer composers who see the world from an extraordinarily personal, imaginative point of view. Disagreeing with that is as instructive as agreeing with it. You'll always learn from such people. Even when Olly was talking about some piece of Milhaud that I couldn't see the point of, I'd learn a lot. It was a continual education. He read many languages even though he left school at the age of 15. Olly read books in French, German, Italian, Dutch and Spanish a bit as well. He even read Russian. All that went into his music and his conversation.

I guess one thing in common between us was to do with harmony. My harmonic sense is very different from his and his is a very particular kind of ear for harmony, but I relish that in his music and we both agreed that this aspect of music was hugely important. I don't want to write those chords, because he wrote them – I don't need to do that for him. But it was a sensibility which meant a lot to me. I'm pleased to learn from his music about how a harmonic progression can still be something fresh, enjoyable and new, because some people still think that's old hat. And we talked about it sometimes, because harmony was something about which we both cared a great deal.

I fear now that when I tell people about him, they won't believe me because it is a little bit incredible that all that was in one place and in one mind. And it's very good music, amazing music, and it will last. I'm hoping that in the next 30 years it will become part of mainstream musical life and stop being a cause that you have to champion. Because if anyone made modern music more part of life, it would be Olly Knussen.

Figure 8   Julian Anderson with Jonathan Finn, London 2019, photograph by Wilfred Dingle

Conversation Twelve

Memory

The first part of this conversation explores recording, starting with its fixed nature as an artefact and single recorded performances becoming synonymous with the work. The changing status of recordings, their use for discovering the music of other traditions and the relationship with the record in the fields of jazz and pop are all explored. The second part of the conversation is an extended exploration of *Book of Hours*, starting with how the sound of a needle on an LP has various connotations relating to the past, sparking some observations on change and redundancy in technology. The medieval sources of inspiration for *Book of Hours* are explored, followed by explanation of the opening material's roots in the beginner piano piece *Old Bells*, the surprise of the viola jig at the end and the influence of Flanders and Swann.

CD: When composers such as Stravinsky and Messiaen had their formative experiences, performance was completely ephemeral. By our generation, recordings had changed that relationship with music and performance. There has been plenty of evidence in our conversations of the profound benefits of recordings for discovering repertoire, but are there any dangers or frustrations for you as a composer, or simply as a lover of music?

JA: The trouble remains that recording still implies rigidity, whether it's a download, the physical object, or whatever. You press Play and hear that recording at the same speed, the same articulation and everything as it was before, and that is very misleading. Even with someone as precise as Boulez, I'm sure on a different day he might change his mind. I've been very fortunate to work with a number of really wonderful conductors, but I always want them to be free to do the music as they feel it. If I think something is wildly out of tempo, and they don't show any sign of changing, then the most I might say, and then only if asked, is that I was wondering about it. Most of the time, though, I'm very happy to let them take over and interpret the music accordingly. They're called interpreters, after all – well please go ahead and interpret. I don't write a score to be played the same way every time. Stockhausen is one of the composers whose recorded legacy was meant to establish exactly how the music should go in every respect, no argument. He clearly saw it that way. He wanted exactly those speeds and exactly the style of interpretation and everything. So the recordings are incredibly careful. But when I've heard his specialist interpreters like Kathinka Pasveer, Suzee Stevens, Ellen Corver the pianist, and Marco Blaauw the trumpeter, playing his music live, there is something they do in the live performance that is not quite there in their, nevertheless, very fine recordings made under his supervision. There is some sort of spontaneous music making that just lights up and dances. The studio accounts, correct as they are, sometimes do not quite possess this.

CD: Paul Hillier spoke about that in terms of his recording of *Stimmung*.

JA: Oh really?

CD: The more recent one from a few years ago.[1] It is in surround sound as well, a Hybrid SACD, so it's absolutely glorious. When it came out, he spoke about involving Stockhausen, saying, 'I felt a controlling hand taking over.'[2] Stockhausen is a very particular case. In general, there is a danger that when a recording of a new work comes out it is, for a while, *the* recording of it.

JA: That's a very interesting topic, because that's affected how many contemporary pieces are learnt by other composers, let alone performers. There's a problem with *Gondwana* (1980) by Murail, which is, in many people's opinion, one of his best pieces and is a crucial piece of that period. Murail was very satisfied with the French premiere given by his colleague from Ensemble L'Itinéraire, Yves Prin, conducting the Orchestre national de France at what is now the Grand Auditorium, after nine hours of rehearsal. For that time, it was a huge amount of rehearsal on a piece lasting 15 minutes. Nevertheless, there are certain discrepancies between the recording and score. There's at least one passage which is significantly quieter in the recording than the score would

---

[1] Theatre of Voices, Paul Hillier, recorded September 2006, Stavnsholtkirken, Copenhagen, Harmonia Mundi HMU80 7408 (SACD).
[2] Paul Hillier, 'I felt a controlling hand taking over', *The Guardian* (28 September 2007), available at http://www.theguardian.com [accessed 13 February 2017].

imply. In any live performance I've ever heard it's been absolutely deafening, but isn't in that recording.

Most composers who have ever heard the piece have never heard it live. They've learnt it from Yves Prin's 1980 recording, which was issued on CD in 1989 – I wrote the programme notes – then reissued, etc. and is now on YouTube or wherever else.[3] If the piece had two or three recordings, then you'd at least have an alternative. I'm lucky to have heard several live performances and I've got tapes too, under one or two other conductors, so I'm aware of the range of noises that piece can make, which is significantly wider than the recording implies. For most composers, though, that recording has become *Gondwana* in a sense. That is a misleading situation which applies to quite a lot of contemporary orchestral music.

CD: And has been since recording came about. It took a long time for anyone really to see the point in anyone other than Britten recording any of his operas.

JA: I hadn't thought of that. Yes, in fact the second recordings of the Britten operas sometimes followed, I was surprised to see, many decades later. That's true. That meant, also, that tenors singing the Peter Pears parts tended to imitate Pears. I hadn't thought of Britten, of all people, as exemplifying this, but I see exactly what you mean.

CD: I may be wrong, but I suspect that Rattle's recording of the *War Requiem* was the second recording of it. That's the early '80s.[4]

JA: That's 20 years later!

CD: Yes. Almost exactly.

---

[3] Tristan Murail, *Gondwana*, Orchestre national de France, Yves Prin (conductor), live recording 20 December 1980, Radio-France, Adda/Salabert Trajectoires SCD8902 (CD).

[4] Elisabeth Söderström, Robert Tear, Thomas Allen, Boys of Christ Church Cathedral, Oxford, CBSO Chorus, City of Birmingham Symphony Orchestra, Simon Rattle (conductor), recorded 1983, location unknown, EMI CDS 7 47034 8 (2 CDs). Britten's recording was released in 1963 (Decca) and Rattle's in 1983 (EMI). A performance under William D. Hill was released in 1975 in the US by the Klavier label (though only briefly available on import in the UK), and some live broadcasts from the intervening years have been issued much more recently (the broadcast of the 1962 premiere in Coventry Cathedral was released by Testament in 2013, a 1966 performance conducted by Karel Ančerl was released by Supraphon in 2013, Cascavelle released a 1967 performance by Ernest Ansermet in 2010, and a 1969 Albert Hall performance under Giulini was released by BBC Legends in 2000). Nonetheless, until Rattle's recording was released, Britten's was the only recording that could generally be heard. It is only relatively recently that live performances of repertoire from radio broadcasts have been routinely issued commercially, a fact that can distort perceptions of the recorded history of a work.

JA: Now I think of it, a lot of performances, even these days, of the *War Requiem* sound like they're imitating the first recording.[5]

CD: Yes, and it's a wonderful recording, so why not? But it's a big work and one that clearly has a lot in it.

JA: It's a very good point. The *War Requiem* is a very widely played piece and yet we have the same problem as with the Murail of the first recording almost becoming the piece.

CD: Almost to the extent that you half expect to hear the tape hiss from the recording.

JA: I realise that whenever I think of that piece, any bit of it, in my head I'm always hearing that first recording with, as you say, the tape hiss on top, the whole tone of it. That never occurred to me. But the Rattle recording did strike out into a different interpretative strategy.

CD: Going back to recordings more generally, I think we're undergoing a change at the moment. I may be completely wrong about this, and it's a gross simplification, but I see it like this. You've got the first era of recording where everything was, in essence, live, in that it is single takes. It can't be edited.

JA: So it's something like a performance, in a way?

CD: Yes. It's going to be four minutes of something, otherwise you have to go back and do the whole four minutes again. You can't just drop it in. Then editing comes in. Even before that, really from the early electric era, you started to get the record companies producing their version of Beethoven's symphonies and you start getting a sense of music as competition, of there being winners, a best version and stuff like that. The music as artefact. The recording as artefact. We've now got to a point where there are many versions of works that, even in the 1980s, we would have thought of as being relatively obscure repertoire for a recording. There are umpteen versions of most things. You'll never entirely get rid of the sense of recording as artefact, but recordings have been around long enough now that, for most core repertoire, there are too many recordings to do a sensible 'Building a Library' [on BBC Radio 3's *Record Review*]. In the 1980s, for 'Building a Library' they could actually cover every recording of a particular

---

[5]   Galina Vishnevskaya, Peter Pears, Dietrich Fischer-Dieskau, The Bach Choir, London Symphony Orchestra Chorus, Highgate School Choir, Melos Ensemble, London Symphony Orchestra, Benjamin Britten (conductor), recorded January 1963, Kingsway Hall, London, Decca SET 252/3 (2 LPs); 478 5433 (2 CDs + Blu-ray).

piece with most repertoire quite comfortably. Now they have to be very selective for most of the repertoire that they do.

JA: They might just be able to manage that for Stravinsky's *Agon*, but not for *Turangalîla* anymore.

CD: No, and certainly not for the Messiaen *Quartet*. It's leading to a healthier situation. We're going back to the ephemerality of music. The sense that a recording is not going to be *the* version of something.

JA: No, it's information. Very useful information, but no more than that.

CD: The generation below us are far more used to the idea that they'll download something, listen to that recording and then delete it off their computer.

JA: I do see this. It's very unlike my childhood – that sensation one had, having grown up with one recording of a piece, of going to a concert and finding it was all very different. Cage was very amused when he saw Stravinsky conduct in the 1960s. A kid in the audience was with his parents sitting in the row in front of him. He'd heard a recording of the work being performed and kept saying loudly, 'That's not how it goes.' It's interesting that the two most virulent opponents of recording as a medium among composers were Benjamin Britten and John Cage. Cage said repeatedly that records have brought about an unmusical society, that they're not music and that if you destroyed all records people will have to make music for themselves again. Which is a very interesting point.

CD: This was also being said in the 1910s. There's an article as early as that in *The Times* that says recordings are turning people into passive listeners and threatening creativity.[6]

JA: Of course, the other person who said this repeatedly was Britten himself.[7]

CD: Yes, though it has to be said, I wouldn't know even a quarter of the music I now know, or different interpretations of music, without recordings, even if I do strongly advocate live performance. In 1989 the most bizarre thing happened. In retrospect, it can only be down to the fact that I'd gone to 30 or 40 concerts in a row, but then I heard the *Missa Solemnis* for the first time. I loved Beethoven, especially late Beethoven, but I stood there at the *Missa Solemnis* and the entire thing passed me by.

[6] Unsigned, 'Mechanical Amusement', *The Times* (7 September 1910), 9.
[7] Notably in the Aspen speech: Benjamin Britten, 'On Receiving the First Aspen Award', speech given on 31 July 1964 at Aspen Music Festival, Colorado. The speech is reproduced in full on the festival website: http://www.aspenmusicfestival.com/benjamin-britten [accessed 30 September 2017].

JA: How bizarre.

CD: Not a single note seemed to permeate me at all. Not dislike – just complete indifference to the whole thing.

JA: You must have been musicked out or something.

CD: That's the only explanation, because then the following year at Sheffield in late autumn Gardiner's recording came out.[8] There were various glowing reviews and I thought, 'Well, I'll give this another go.' I ordered the CD, put it on and sat absolutely transfixed and gobsmacked, as one should be with the *Missa Solemnis*. [Laughter] So much so that I then played the entire thing again straightaway and missed a class with Peter Hill as a consequence.

JA: I'm sure Peter understood!

CD: I went up to him afterwards and said, 'I'm terribly sorry I missed the class, Peter. I've just discovered *Missa Solemnis*.' He said, 'Oh well, that's far more important.' [Laughter]

JA: Wonderful. I've got that Gardiner recording and love it, but then I tend to eat *Missa Solemnis* recordings for breakfast.

CD: It's an odd thing because I'm normally such a believer in hearing the music live and that is always the best way to experience something first, but I'd certainly have missed out on *Missa Solemnis* for a long time without the recording.

JA: There are two or three areas where recordings are invaluable. New music is clearly one, despite the fact that many pieces only receive one recording for far too long. Nevertheless it's at least good information as to how the piece can sound. Now radio companies throughout the world are on the net and often keeping broadcasts available for months at a time, so that you can often pick up the same piece as it goes round different places, before the commercial recording happens, and you can build up a picture. Another vital area of use in recording is musics of other traditions which you simply record in situ, effectively field recordings. That, of course, is invaluable. I've noticed that one listens to those recordings with a totally different mentality from the way you'd listen to the *War Requiem* recording. Somehow, to identify the piece as that recording, in the case of a repertoire work of Balinese gamelan seems by definition absurd. You know it's simply how that recording on that day, at that particular temple, sounded

8   Beethoven, *Missa Solemnis*, Charlotte Margiono (soprano), Catherine Robbin (mezzo-soprano), William Kendall (tenor), Alastair Miles (bass), Monteverdi Choir, Orchestre Revolutionnaire et Romantique, John Eliot Gardiner (conductor), recorded All Saints' Church, Tooting, London, November 1989, Archiv Produktion 429 779–2 (CD).

then. You know it's not the only way that piece can go. You know that from the start, somehow, just because of the genre of music it is.

For example, one of my favourite recordings at the moment is by Hariprasad Chaurasia, the Indian Bansuri flautist, of *Raga Jait*.[9] Nobody would even begin to think of that as the only way that *Raga Jait* can go, even though the amount of variation from one Indian classical musical performance of the same raag to the next is not as big as people tend to think – the rules being fairly strict as to how a raag can be played. Nevertheless, the Chaurasia recording is how that raag was played in June 1990, and as it happens I was present at that performance. I know it's simply what I heard that evening. I didn't even know it was being recorded. Recording does perform a very valuable function in preserving things like that, or making them available if the tradition is, as it were, non-transportable.

CD: This gets curious with jazz. You get it in other things as well, but it seems to be particularly endemic in jazz, which we think of as being very much more improvisation-based. There is that self-same knowledge that a particular take will be the way it happened to be at that time. Of the moment. And yet, you will get the jazz buff saying, 'Do you know Miles Davis's take 7 of this.' They've got the different takes and each ephemeral thing has become an artefact.

JA: Like a work of art, really. Yes. It's been treasured almost excessively in that context. Yes.

CD: I find the relationship between jazzers and recordings really quite intriguing.

JA: Here's an example of the same thing, in the same area, but by somebody who was not a jazzman, Henri Dutilleux. He loved a boxset called *Sassy Swings the Tivoli* – Sarah Vaughan doing a series of concerts in 1959, I think, at the Tivoli Gardens in Denmark, in Copenhagen.[10] He particularly recommended her recording of 'Lover Man'. He was crazy about it. He said, for him, that particular performance by her of 'Lover Man' made the piece into one of the greatest pieces of the century. What effectively he was saying was that that interpretation is one of the great pieces of the century. The interpretation had become a piece. Like *Gesang der Jünglinge*, it's a tape that you play.

CD: Yes. It's like the pop situation where someone will produce an album and then they'll perform it live. For them, the album was just capturing stuff as they went along. David Bowie, when he was touring, was notorious. You'd get

---

9   Pandit Hari Prasad Chaurasia: *Raga Jait*, Pandit Hari Prasad Chaurasia (flute), Fazal Qureshi (tabla), live recording Kufa Gallery, London, 28 June 1990, Navras Records NRCD 0007 (CD).

10 1963, actually. Sarah Vaughan, *Sassie Swings the Tivoli*, live recording in Copenhagen, 18 July 1963, produced by Quincy Jones, Mercury 20011 SMCL (LP).

some people getting frustrated that the guitar riff in 'Ziggy Stardust' or the arrangement of it was slightly different from this thing they got that's absolutely fixed, I was going to say in aspic, but it was actually in vinyl in those days.

JA: I wonder, for example, about *Sgt. Pepper* – which is most definitely a studio product. Could there be another version of 'A Day in the Life'? I just can't imagine it any other way.

CD: Some people have done cover versions of it.

JA: I didn't think they had of 'A Day in the Life'...

CD: Yes, there's a Bee Gees film called *Sgt. Pepper* built around Beatles songs and they did 'A Day in the Life' as part of that.[11]

JA: I mention it because, as you know, it's two songs literally cross-cut with another. It seems to be almost the ultimate studio product as a piece because of the sharply different acoustics and the songs being totally unrelated.

CD: 'Strawberry Fields Forever' is another one. Funnily enough, relatively recently McCartney has done 'Strawberry Fields' live. Of course, it's one of Lennon's songs and he was doing it as a tribute.[12] But these more complex songs are all bound up with them stopping touring. Firstly, touring was just so horrible for them by 1966, but also they were doing increasingly experimental stuff and it was becoming very difficult to do that on stage. Those Beatles albums from *Revolver* onwards were intended to be artefacts, as electro-acoustic music really, and our experience of them, as of so much music, was not of performance, but of a record player and a piece of vinyl.

That, of course, is something you play with in *Book of Hours*. To me that's a work about time and memory, here and now against things remembered, misremembered, part-decayed, part-idealised, part-all sorts of other stuff as well. We'll get on to the *Book of Hours* element of it, but Part II starts with the sound of a stylus that's being placed.

JA: Yes, and everyone warned me that in a short time nobody would understand that sound because it's redundant technology. In fact, last year records outstripped CDs in sales and they're enjoying quite a vogue at the moment.

---

[11]   *Sgt. Pepper's Lonely Hearts Club Band* (1978) starring the Bee Gees. The soundtrack, released as a double LP on A&M Records (AMLZ 66600), featured covers of numerous Beatles songs by a variety of artists, including 'A Day in the Life' performed by the Bee Gees.

[12]   'Relatively recently' turns out to be 1990, when McCartney included it in his setlist for concerts in the US and UK as a sequence given in tribute to John Lennon in what would have been his fiftieth-birthday year.

CD: They do, although that sound of the stylus slipping into the groove is one that, for our generation, was the necessary prelude to so many formative musical experiences.

JA: It's just like a gate opening or something. You can't pretend that the latest generation playing records will have that feeling though.

CD: No, their relationship with LPs or vinyl is a very different kind of thing. For me, aside from it being brilliant music, that one sound in *Book of Hours* signified to me that this was music that is of my generation.

JA: That's true. When you say it's about memory and so on, it's very specific in my case. Like you, that was how I grew up. That was one of the gateways to music, the sound of the needle going onto the record. It has a certain warmth and a certain roughness which appeals to me, even if CDs have many other virtues.

CD: Were you aware incidentally that some pop groups, such as Portishead, were also cultivating deliberately low-fi memories and resonances of the pre-CD age?

JA: I was aware of that, yes. Of course, the abuse of record players became a very important factor in DJ-ing because of the scratching of the needles, which is a sound I find very difficult, because the worst thing you could do when I was a kid was scratch a record. It was really destroying the needle and the record and the source of all this magic. I've always found it a little bit setting my teeth on edge whenever I hear that kind of DJ-ing. But you're right that that moment in *Book of Hours* is a reflection of a moment in history, perhaps especially for people our age.

CD: Ironically, it's hearing that nostalgic evocation of past listening that's brought home to me that this was a piece of my present, whereas current students, certainly my children, will hear it very differently. In that respect, it's similar to the cultural references in, say, Haydn. We can read that they're there, but we don't hear the piece in that way.

JA: Yes, what I wanted was a sound that would make it clear that the opening of Part I had got decayed in some way and was acoustically damaged. That was the initial idea, the idea of a manuscript that has been damaged. There's a book that meant a lot to me in my 20s, published in 1988, called *Dictionary of the Khazars* by Milorad Pavić, a Serbian writer.[13] Two of his novels appealed a lot to me – the other was a novel in the shape of a crossword puzzle, called *Landscape Painted*

13 Milorad Pavić, *Dictionary of the Khazars: A Lexicon Novel*, trans. Christina Pribicevic-Zoric (New York: Alfred A. Knopf, 1988).

with Tea.[14] The *Dictionary of the Khazars* is a novel in the shape of a three-part dictionary. The Khazars are a nation that disappeared in medieval times. The people were absorbed into different cultures and eventually the Khazars' state ceased to exist. That is factually true. The book is a collation of all the Hebrew sources on the Khazars, all the Islamic sources on the Khazars, and all the Christian sources on the Khazars. Since it's in the form of a dictionary, you can read it in any order. Of course, the total picture builds up if you read all of the entries. You don't know in the book whether Pavić has made up some of the scholarship or whether it's genuine. Our family used to own something called the *Encyclopaedia Judaica.* I did look up Khazars in that and found there was a great deal in Pavić that was true. A lot of it corresponded to what I'd read in this strange novel, but of course a lot didn't because it's magical realist fantasy. The deliberate blurring of fact and reality is also a factor in my piece *Book of Hours.* Now, what Pavić does at one point is to say he's quoting from a medieval manuscript. He quotes from this source, which is fictional, then at a certain point he stops, inserts square brackets and just says, 'Here the manuscript is damaged.' That's the end of the quotation. I thought that was a marvellously inventive way of handling this juggling act blurring fact and fiction – to make up a document and then make up the damage of it! That is what Part II in *Book of Hours* was saying. It's like the first part has been damaged. That links up with these pop groups that you're mentioning and so on. Then the question was how to get that across.

I'll never forget the time when I went to see a friend who lives in Notting Hill. The Notting Hill Classical Record Exchange was nearby. If I visited him I'd always pop round there first to see if there was anything interesting. That day I bought a very rare Romanian Electrocord state record from the '80s that I'd been searching for many years to get. I bought it, then went to see my friend. I was having trouble beginning Part II of *Book of Hours,* but, just as I walked to his home I thought, 'Wouldn't it be fun if I played this Romanian record at home, but what came out was *Book of Hours.*' Then I thought, 'You've got it! That's how you begin Part II. Imagine that this record does contain *Book of Hours* Part I and that will be your starting point for Part II.' At IRCAM, electronics meant synthesis or filtering concrete sounds, or all kinds of gizmos like that, but it did *not* mean playing with cultural memory. At least, that's not what they advocated using a recording for when I was on their course in 2002. So that was exactly what I did.

CD: Part of the attraction of it presumably is that you've got something which is now an old form of what was, as we were growing up, the most advanced aural experience, put alongside what, in 2003 or 2004, was then the most advanced.

---

[14] Milorad Pavić, *Landscape Painted with Tea,* trans. Christina Pribicevic-Zoric (New York: Alfred A. Knopf, 1990).

JA: Which then also itself grows old.

CD: Yes, and it underlines the speed at which things date and become part of history in a way that having electronics alongside instruments with a history of 200, 300, 400 years curiously doesn't in quite the same way.

JA: Not quite the same way, no. Electronics brings up questions of period authenticity somehow more vividly because redundancy is much quicker. I still own a Yamaha DX7 Mark I, which is now a period instrument from the '80s. Sometimes I hire it out to people performing Murail pieces of that period, which is amusing. We were all told in the '80s that this was going to be a new standard instrument that every orchestra would have. It didn't work out that way. Electronics is a very interesting medium in music, because it's a peculiarly vivid reflection of technological changes and that in turn reflects society very directly.

CD: I suppose an analogous period is the development in keyboard instruments say from the beginning to the end of Haydn's career, when they were changing all the time, with different keyboard layouts, different ways of making sounds, different tunings and stuff like that. Then you eventually end up with first the fortepiano and then the pianoforte, which, in its essence, didn't change that much.

JA: That's right, but except for MIDI I don't see any stabilisation ahead yet in the technology field. For example, I used to record on MiniDisc and that's now a period piece of technology. *Book of Hours* is certainly partly about that phenomenon in my life. I was nearly 16 when the first CDs came on the market in Britain in January 1983. I've still got the *Gramophone* issue announcing it. There it is, this big, new, shiny round image of it on the front cover. It was very much part of my growing up, the arrival of digital sound, though, in fact, the first experiment was made in Britain in the 1960s by Peter Zinovieff. He'd experimented with computerising the recording process, with very limited memory banks. According to David Cockerell, his technician, Zinovieff invented the first digital sound sampler.

CD: It relates to the Post Office, with the digitisation of sound for telephones.

JA: Oh in that sense, yes. That's a very interesting story because, apart from any connections with intelligence and all that military stuff, the telephone system has a curious technological history. The idea that you can convey the vibration of a voice so that the person receiving the sound will recognise not merely the words, but the identity of the person who is speaking is a very interesting task. The vocoder is the key to it.

There are various, little talked-about, electronic pieces made in Cologne in the 1950s using what we would now call the phase vocoder or vocoding. This was not a preoccupation of Stockhausen at that time, curiously. You'd have thought with *Gesang der Jünglinge* that he would have wanted to use it, but he didn't. The person who explored it a lot was Herbert Eimert, who did a number of pieces, of which the best known is *Epitaph für Aikichi Kuboyama*. He was a fisherman who was killed by the H-bomb exploded by the Americans at Bikini Atoll.[15] The piece takes a poem in German which an actor narrates. It is gradually more and more distorted by means of filtering with the vocoder, dislodging the different frequency regions of the person's voice. Another thing I also heard around the same time, which was in my mind a bit with *Book of Hours*, was a little piece about two minutes long by Eimert called *Zu Ehren von Igor Strawinsky*. It's a piece where the text means literally to honour Igor Stravinsky (for his seventy-fifth birthday). They spoke that into a tape and then they got it vocoded. They separated out the frequency ranges with the vocoder and then dislocated them in time. You get all kinds of magical chords and things. It starts very dislocated, gradually accumulating and then being resonated across various kinds of spectra. You hear the words more and more. It's a little process piece. I often wonder if Steve Reich had heard that because it sounds a little like his tape pieces with speech from the '60s.

CD: There's that Alvin Lucier piece as well, *I Am Sitting in a Room.*

JA: Which I also like very much indeed. I used none of these sounds in *Book of Hours* but they were in the background. The extent to which the electronics does or doesn't mimic real sounds is used as a compositional factor throughout.

CD: The memory aspects of this – back to the Middle Ages, as it were – where did that connection come from in *Book of Hours?*

JA: When I was studying at IRCAM for the first time, which was April 2002, I went to FNAC round the corner, which is still one of the best-stocked stores in Paris for culture and anything actually – I owe it almost as much in musical education as I owe the Swiss Cottage Library! They had this marvellous very affordable paperback of the *Très Riches Heures du Duc de Berry*, published by the Bibliothèque national de France. I had seen reproductions of this all my life on table mats or whatever, but I'd never had a copy of it. I looked through and was absolutely amazed. It's an interesting period of drawing because perspective is not quite there yet. They're trying to get it, but it's not properly implemented. Sometimes things seem to be on top of each other that are meant to be in perspective relationship. It's nicely on that cusp. I found that transition interesting. I loved the intense colours, especially the magnificent blues. I also

---

[15] See M.J. Grant, *Serial Music, Serial Aesthetics: Compositional Theory in Post-War Europe* (Cambridge: Cambridge University Press, 2001), p. 194.

liked the combination of the times of the year with the seasons and the astrological clocks and all that. I brought it back to the IRCAM studio where we were studying – the Salle Luigi Nono – and that was really the start of the piece. At that point I thought I would set some texts in the *Très Riches Heures du Duc de Berry* for countertenor, electronics and ensemble. It seemed to me that the purity of countertenor voice would interface well with electronic sound. I made some experiments using recordings of things like the countertenor solo in the Agnus Dei of Bach's B-Minor Mass, cross-phasing that, trying to filter the voice out, and distorting it in various ways. I got somewhere but, as the piece progressed, I realised that I just didn't want text. Text would make it too literal, so the countertenor wouldn't have enough to do. I chucked the voice at that point.

I grew up with David Munrow's recordings of early music which are very much behind *Book of Hours*, particularly the recordings of the boxset called *The Art of Courtly Love*,[16] which deals with really late Machaut, but goes up to Dufay. The middle album of it deals with the so-called *ars subtilior*, which Munrow and others have called the fourteenth-century avant-garde movement, and it comes very much into the second movement of *Book of Hours*. I was interested socially in the rival Papacies at Avignon and Rome, that period which is very much associated with the *ars subtilior* movement and with wildly experimental movements in poetry and other things.

The other thing that I was doing a lot, when I was revisiting IRCAM for the main course in June 2002, was going to the museum of medieval art in Paris, which is called Cluny because it's the site of some former Roman baths with that name. The Musée de Cluny collection is exceptionally rich. One of the central pieces in it is the *Lady and the Unicorn* sextet of tapestries. It's roughly contemporaneous with the *Très Riches Heures* and it has the same problems of perspective. Little bits of local perspective of the lady's cape are correct, but the perspective of the whole is not right. Also, in the decorative space surrounding the main platform where the lady and the unicorn and other objects are, you have objects flying or hovering, which can't fly and can't hover, like rabbits on a chain, or birds that are not flying but that are on a twig and the twig is suspended in mid-air. There's a wonderful combination of irreality and reality. The first five tapestries are about the senses, but in the sixth one, 'À mon seul désir', it's not really clear what's going on. Nobody knows what that last tapestry means. The unicorn may also, in part, be a sexual symbol. There are all kinds of implications in those tapestries. I opted not to call my work 'The Lady and the Unicorn' because it sounded too programmatic. *Book of Hours* is more general as a title. In fact, *The Lady and the Unicorn* is quite as important to the piece as any Book of Hours.

---

[16] *The Art of Courtly Love*, The Early Music Consort of London, director David Munrow, recorded 1971 and 1973, EMI/His Master's Voice, SLS 863 (3 LPs).

CD: So do the electronics help that sense of irreality?

JA: Yes, in that the electronics was to take the ensemble music just a bit beyond what it can do, particularly via the percussion. Non-harmonic percussion sounds, like gongs and bells and so on, are not tempered. They make a link therefore with the non-tempered electronic sound. Sometimes the electronic sounds are like an extra percussion instrument that isn't there. There might be a colour or a punctuating sound on the orchestra, which is taking it just a bit beyond. It's closest to percussion in terms of its inharmonicity and its lack of tempered frequencies and so on. That's only one function of it.

The medieval aspect to the music came in really with Part II, in a set of what could be called two-part inventions; I didn't know what to call them when I was writing them. They are contrapuntal duets or trios, or even 12 parts at one point, which are influenced by *ars subtilior*. They take certain rules to do with cadence patterns and the rhythmic language of that music and stretch them. This was very evident to Olly Knussen when he was conducting the first rehearsals of the piece. He knew *ars subtilior* from the same recordings that I grew up on. He turned to me at one particular point, where there was a very *ars subtilior*-type canonic duet, and he joked, 'You're a bit of an *ars subtilior* queen...' I was amused but pleased, because I'd hoped it would be obvious without being blatant. I didn't base any of it on literal passages, but returned to Willi Apel's edition of that repertoire, which I'd studied as a teenager. He did a volume of late fourteenth-century French secular music in 1950 with a preface by Hindemith, which is still one of the good sources for that.[17] It's very well edited, no tempi, no dynamics, just literally what's in the manuscript in modern notation. Later I was able to find a copy of that book through Travis & Emery and later editions also. CMM published volumes by Gilbert Reaney of Italian and French late fourteenth-century secular music which has most of the *ars subtilior* pieces that Apel didn't have.[18] There's a very wild piece by somebody called Zachara [de Teramo] called *Sumite karissimi* [sic],[19] of which Reaney says rather amusingly in the notes, 'I don't think this can be played even today without the aid of electronic equipment.' Indeed, in his transcription it looks just like a passage from Elliott Carter's Second String Quartet, it really does.

CD: This is why it is so important for students to hear and study medieval music, especially composers, as so much of it sounds so contemporary.

---

[17] Willi Apel (ed.), *French Secular Music of the Late Fourteenth Century*, foreword by Paul Hindemith (Cambridge, Massachusetts: The Mediaeval Academy of America, 1950).

[18] There are seven volumes in this part of CMM. Gilbert Reaney (ed.), *Corpus Mensurabilis Musicæ 11: Early Fifteenth-Century Music*, 7 vols (The American Institute of Musicology, 1955–83). Full details of contents are available at http://www.corpusmusicae.com/cmm.htm.

[19] This is in Vol. 6.

JA: The connection between that fourteenth-century avant-garde and modern music is an old fad and it certainly didn't start with me. Ursula Günther had done some work on this too, but my digest of this is entirely personal, non-scholastic and creative, let me emphasise that. The *ars subtilior* composers worked with numbers in a strange way. You took a number, a large number like let's say 27, and one part would divide it into three 9s, another part would divide it into nine 3s, and a third part into perhaps 10 plus 10 plus 7. Now, in between, of course, they will have certain coincidences but they won't all completely line up again until the 27 beats are completed. I use that device a lot, and not only in *Book of Hours* either.

In 1998, just after finishing *Stations of the Sun*, I set up a whole system for producing this with a computer. I have some printouts of it here. I got my good friend Jonathan Finn, who founded Sibelius software, to set up a plug-in programme in Sibelius where you could input the numbers at the start and say how many beats and what metre you wanted it, and it would then write it for you, just rhythmically I mean. I wrote some passages of music using that, which were going to go towards an orchestral piece I didn't write (or rather did, but withdrew) called *Isfahan*, which was to do with Islamic architecture.[20] The preoccupation with that type of rhythmic architecture was an old one, and some of that comes into Part II of *Book of Hours*. There's a particular passage where I accumulate more and more of these two-part *ars subtilior* inventions in different metres and tempi, with different stresses, using medieval metric theory as the basis of the rhythmic language. It is then distorted by different mensurations going into different speeds. That eventually gets out of control and also goes into different tunings. But eventually all the numbers line up and the parts land together on a big consonance.

CD: So how about this sense of time, or different ideas of time passing?

JA: In Part I there's a section which is almost entirely in regular quavers, though many different accents of them, a kind of additive metre with quavers. That was to do with the idea of counting time in regular clock-like fashion. Each of the illustrations of the Book of Hours has a clock at the top showing which period of the year we are in and therefore which star sign we're in and so on. It was to do with that idea of clock time versus musical time.

CD: So there are the aspects of time and memory, and the medieval influences, but there are also explorations at different levels of relationships between simple and complex gestures and textures. The beginning could barely be more simple, in one sense – just four notes of a major scale.

---

[20] See Conversation Six, 'Composing (or not)'.

JA: That arose out of a bet with, funnily enough, the same person I just mentioned, Jonathan Finn. We're good friends, and we were on holiday in Holland to hear the world premiere of my *Four American Choruses*, by Simon Halsey with Groot Omroepkoor (before he brought it to Birmingham). All I remember is Jonathan and I were playing chess (I lost as usual) and he suddenly wondered if I could write a piece of music which had no complications at all, almost no accidentals, only crotchets and minims, but was still like me. I liked this idea and said that I thought I could write a piece for a beginner pianist that would still be me. He was more doubtful, having heard a lot of my music. I said, 'I bet you I can, and the bet is this: if I write that piece, I will incorporate it into the piece I'm writing for Birmingham Contemporary Music Group with IRCAM electronics. I will transcribe it quite literally and that will show you that it was a piece by me because I wouldn't put such a piece into a work for electronics partly done at IRCAM and all that stuff, unless I actually meant it.'

The following day, I took the train to Paris from Amsterdam, which in those days was about four hours, and I wrote the piece on the train. A friend – an ex-student, the gifted American composer Chris Trapani – met me off the train. I played the piece to him. It's called *Old Bells*. I didn't mention the bet, but I asked him, 'Can you just tell me whether or not you think this sounds like my music?' He said, 'Well I would never have believed this, but it does sound like your music, although the restrictions in writing that must have been quite hard to work with. How long did it take?' and I said, 'I just wrote it on the train.' I did make a couple of little changes later that day, but that piece was published more or less as I wrote it. It has very few accidentals. There are one or two but very few, and no triplets or anything like that. It's largely crotchets.

What happens is an ascending scale, starting C–D–E–F. Then it's imitated a fourth lower. The question is: when will the left hand enter relative to the right hand? In other words, what will the time distance of the canon be? Depending on that and when the right hand comes back in, again with another scale, you can give the illusion of two parts, or one part that keeps going up as the right hand goes further up and the left hand comes in with the new one.

This has a link with the so-called Shepard illusion or Shepard scale, which is a scale that infinitely self-renews.[21] My piece is like an elementary version of the Shepard scale, and it's also just crotchets and minims and so on. It's obviously based on the resounding of bells. The last sound in the piece, which is a compound fourth D and G, is based on the most common kind of bell resonance that you can get, which is a minor third with an added fourth. On D, that would be D, F and G. You can hear that in *Mortuos Plango* by Jonathan Harvey, which is based on the great tenor bell of Winchester Cathedral. You can hear it in many bells, particularly church bells, which is what my piece was

---

[21] Named after American cognitive scientist Roger Shepard (b. 1929).

evoking. The church bells aspect of it linked it with medieval culture. I also wanted to begin the IRCAM piece with the most fundamental bit of musical material I could think of. That seemed to be the right way, so my mind was already heading that way when I made the bet with Jonathan Finn.

CD: So what changes did you make to *Old Bells* in *Book of Hours*?

JA: I had to make two adaptations in *Book of Hours*. The first was that I did not want to have the piece open C, D, E, F because *Khorovod* and several pieces around the time of *Khorovod* had opened with C. I'd made myself a promise after several C pieces that I would not have C at the beginning or end of a piece for a long time. There are many other reasons not to, because for example if you're working on a mode that starts on C and has D in it and G and so on, you will get open strings, so on an ensemble you'll hear that. If you're working in C sharp, you won't get open strings. That became quite important to the sound of *Book of Hours*, not to have open strings on the string parts. You'll notice that at the end, the coda with the viola tune, it's on C sharp all the time, it's not on C. It would sound very different if it was on C. It would have been easier to play, but it would also have a lot of ringing open strings.

In *Book of Hours* I wanted the resonance to be given not by the string instruments but the electronics. Therefore I didn't want open strings to occur much. This determined a lot about the sound of the work. As soon as I'd transposed *Old Bells* up a semitone, I realised that I also had to do a little bit of elaboration. Although you can follow it quite clearly and every bar of *Old Bells* is there in *Book of Hours*, there are some small changes or additions. First of all, there are inserts. Every time that we get to the end of a phrase of *Old Bells*, there's an electronic little moment which freezes the harmony at that point and does some filtering of it. Secondly, I began to add other, faster scales that transposed more and more until, when it came to the big carillon at the end of *Old Bells*, it became a gigantic carillon that *Book of Hours* has about five minutes in. I have real church bells, which I recorded and filtered and so on. At that point, the transcription of *Old Bells* has really run out. So it is transcribed note for note, but I allowed myself some latitude in elaborating it and making it more suitable as ensemble music.

CD: And that superficially simple opening strikes me as being one of those things performers curse composers about, as they are quite a challenge, yet the difficulty only shows if it goes wrong.

JA: It remains one of the most tricky-to-play openings I've ever written, the first four notes of the major scale in crotchets at a very slow speed together and perfectly in tune on tubular bells, celesta, piano, harp, low E-flat clarinet, which is difficult to tune, and strings, and all that. The irony is that everyone looks and thinks, 'Oh, very simple,' and then they start rehearsing it and realise that this isn't easy at all. Many conductors have sworn at me having rehearsed that opening. It's very exposed... But perhaps it's useful for new-music groups that have to play so much music with so many polyrhythms and so many different notes, to have to play just the four notes of the major scale in crotchets.

CD: With that simplicity of the crotchets, it strikes me there's a pre-echo there of Creon's music in *Thebans*.[22]

JA: Absolutely. When I got to writing Act II, I thought *Book of Hours* had been a very good preparation for it.

CD: Might Creon's music be viewed as a sort of dark music equivalent to *Book of Hours* too?

JA: Absolutely true too, yes. Creon's music in *Thebans* would be the 'Book of Horrors' or something... This is the oldest thing in the world: to see whether you can take the most familiar object and make something fresh of it. Well, at least my delusion was I could. I don't know whether I could, but I tried to do it because I found the material interesting. What are these first four notes of the major scale? Well, they became absolutely everything. I looked at them interval-lically, like a serial composer would, as an ordered set or an unordered collection, permutated and all that kind of thing. I also looked at them in terms of frequency relationships, the major second, the major third, the perfect fourth, the minor second, etc., and ring-modulated them, frequency-modulated them. That gave me the whole middle section of the first movement, which is based on frequency modulations of those intervals. As I say, everything in the piece could be derived from those first four notes. Ultimately, to my surprise, even a jig on the viola at the end. Having repeated the opening of Part I at the opening of Part II, I didn't want the opening to come back at the end. I did want some kind of scalic music and the viola solo was what cropped up at that point.

CD: Which is something of a gear change.

JA: There was a certain amount of comment on the viola jig in the first perfor-mances. People asked, 'What on earth is that about?' Now the structural reason is it's the return of C sharp and it's also based on the scalic material, that's quite clear. But you can do those things without necessarily making a gesture like that viola solo, which seems to evoke dance, or possibly medieval music, or possibly a jig. This is contextually to do with the electronic interlude before it. Eventually in the interlude I isolate one frequency, C sharp, which gradually emerges out

[22] See Conversation Thirteen, 'Opera'.

of it. There's then a page of very plain sustained notes on the ensemble, which doesn't go anywhere, although C sharp is always there with various chords that phase in and out of each other. It's a sort of desert, musically speaking, absolutely nothing. After the incredibly full sound of the interlude, one needs this total emptiness – it's a musical void. Then, of course, I had to fill the void somehow, so I wrote this viola jig, which as soon as I happened upon it, I felt was absolutely what was needed. The electronic interlude is pretty abstract, if violent, and I needed something more directly evocative than that. I've written jigs before on string instruments, in *Khorovod* and other pieces, but I did not really think about this one, I simply did it. I've explained the structural justifications for it and, if you like, thematic justification. To be honest, I didn't understand it, so I used it. If I had been able to understand it, I would have felt very disappointed, but it was very surprising to me. It combined very strangely with the remnant shards of electronic sound. You get a few little reminiscences of earlier bits of the piece as well in that coda. The climax of Part I comes back briefly, and so on, but the viola dance just goes on. Each time a reminiscence occurs, the viola continues as if nothing has happened.

Now the other worry was how to conclude *Book of Hours*. For that, I went back to the first sketch of *Khorovod*, which ended with the last falling melodic scale that you hear at the end of *Book of Hours*. I never used this in *Khorovod*, so it needed using up. It has nothing to do with *Book of Hours*, except of course it's almost an inversion of the scale the piece opens with, but that's not why I put it in. I wrote the final bar because it sounds as though the piece is trailing off somewhere else entirely, modulating in pitch to somewhere quite different and then just shrugs its shoulders and stops. Right before that it does seem to cadence more or less on to C sharp very clearly and I had to get it away from that. So it goes D, C sharp, B, A, G. G has played very little role in the piece – and it's an open string, too. That's the last note you hear, and in a sense it's a total irrelevance.

CD: As a tritone, it is arguably as far from C sharp as possible, equidistant in terms of the octave.

JA: Yes, indeed. I liked that and I also liked the fact that it was coming from the sketch for a different piece from 11 or so years before. It was found material from somewhere else in my output that I hadn't used. Since the end of *Book of Hours* was deliberately oblique to the rest of the piece in some ways, tacking a melodic figure which came from an irrelevant sketch on to the end of it seemed in the spirit of this slightly collaged conclusion, a bit like a Chinese box into which you put different objects and see what happens.

The other thing relating to this ending is the song about the ostrich by Michael Flanders and Donald Swann, whose stuff I knew a lot as a kid. It's in their album called *The Bestiary*.[23] The ostrich is burying its head in the sand. *The Bestiary* was not recorded live, it's a purely studio product by George Martin. As a kid, I always used to find that slightly unnerving. There's no applause. Their other two albums, *At the Drop of a Hat* and *At the Drop of Another Hat*, were both recorded with live audiences.[24] I particularly found this song about the ostrich upsetting because it ends with an atomic bomb exploding. The ostrich is constantly burying its head in the sand, ignoring what's going on. Then, in the middle of a phrase, the song ends with this gigantic explosion. I associate the last part of *Book of Hours* with that because the mood of it is almost in denial of the cataclysmically loud and aggressive electronic music before it. I thought briefly of having the viola line trail off and then having an explosion at the end on the electronics, but I decided that I'd leave that to Flanders and Swann. I'm not saying that it's about anybody burying their head in the sand, or that it's about nuclear war, although of course I did grow up with that as a very imminent prospect. (It's still an imminent prospect and people are in denial about it. The weapons are still there, probably not being looked after.)

There was something not right about the viola solo being there. It seemed a very abnormal way to behave musically at the end of that piece. For that reason, I stuck to it. You put in the middle of a landscape an object that simply does not belong there, although it's not totally irrelevant and somehow does mesh into the landscape – yet it still shouldn't be there. Obviously Dalí, Magritte do that all the time. And that is what Bernd Alois Zimmermann does in *Stille und Umkehr* (1970), one of his last pieces, in which an orchestra is inflecting the note D above middle C in all kinds of different ways, very abstract and pure. Then across this whole piece about timbre and texture, he puts a side drummer playing a blues rhythm! That struck me very much.

The coda also relates to the opera. It's as if the viola is like a character suddenly at that point in an opera, dramatically. That's where the piece becomes more like a dramatic scenario, or a film perhaps. I remember thinking at the end of it that I'd like to do an opera soon.

CD: Is there a certain element in it being jig-like that, at the end of the day, all of your music is about dance?

JA: Yes, I felt it was very connected with that factor. There are two other parts of the piece that dance. One is the fast quaver passage in Part I, which is also the clock passage, but it is quite dancey because of the additive accents and so on.

---

[23] Michael Flanders and Donald Swann, *The Bestiary of Flanders and Swann*, recorded London 1963, Parlophone PMC 1164 (LP).

[24] Michael Flanders and Donald Swann, *At the Drop of a Hat*, live recording, Fortune Theatre, London, 21 February 1957, Parlophone PMC 1033 (LP); *At the Drop of Another Hat*, live recording, Haymarket Theatre, London, 2 October 1963, Parlophone PMC 1216 (LP).

The medieval motets bit [in Part II] also has a certain dancey rhythm to it, but since they keep being superimposed, you get several dance rhythms at once. This viola coda was, let's say, more straightforwardly dance-like.

Perhaps I also felt that in *Book of Hours* as a whole, dance had perhaps slightly underplayed itself and that I could put a bit more in at the end. I would love to see the piece choreographed. By the way, there is a jig earlier in the piece but it's a bit hidden. Inside the big carillon about five minutes into the work, there's a piccolo going berserk at the top of that texture doing a slightly microtonal jig, again slightly medieval too, but in very funny tuning on top of all these bells. It's the highest partials of the bell spectrum that I used there. So the seed for the viola jig is, in a way, planted earlier. Again, it's somehow typical of me that when using a bell spectrum, I had to have a jig on it...

Figure 9   *Thebans*, Act 2, English National Opera,
London 2014, photograph by Hugo Glendinning

Conversation Thirteen

Opera

Our conversations began in the weeks before the premiere of Anderson's opera, *Thebans*. Unsurprisingly, the opera was a recurrent topic in those early sessions and this, the longest conversation of this book, is an amalgamation of exchanges from before and after that important event. It starts with Anderson reflecting on the status of opera during his formative years and revealing that the idea for the plot dated back to having to translate Sophocles at school. Thoughts on the suitability or otherwise of potential plots for opera, and a preference for those that leave some things unsaid, lead on to the way that *Thebans* took Anderson's music into new territory. The difficulty of undertaking chamber opera or comic opera is also noted. There are insights on Anderson's manner of working with his librettist, Frank McGuinness, and he also explains the unusual approach to dissonance used in the opera. After a dialogue on the staging of the first production, and staging of opera in general, the conversation concludes with some observations about characters, the characterisation of the different acts, and the variety of musical approaches the opera elicited from Anderson.

— ◆ —

CD: *Thebans* is your first completed opera, but didn't you previously work on something to do with *The Tempest*?

JA: I did, that's right, in 2000. That still exists as a short-score sketch, of about 30 or 40 pages, which is quite a lot of music in short score. I had seen a fine open-air staging and planned to do it as a sort of masque, with voices and instruments everywhere, not just on stage. But I told nobody about this except two friends not directly involved – Jonathan Finn and Shinichiro Okabe. I didn't mention it to anyone at Faber, or to any composer colleagues. Why I didn't I've no idea, but

247

it wasn't a formal commission and I knew this project would be something for much later. So I just left it in a drawer, where it still is.

CD: Has composing opera always been something that you thought you would do at some point?

JA: Yes, but I've had rather mixed feelings about opera, and especially contemporary opera, for a long time. When I was a kid it was just at the start of the revival in opera composition. Of course, Hans Werner Henze never stopped composing operas, but there was, on the whole, a gap when many concert composers were not really interested in music theatre to that degree. Obviously Maxwell Davies was a particular case, but that was more making the concert hall a theatrical event, which was the way *Eight Songs for a Mad King* was often done, or *Vesalii Icones* with dancing, etc. Maxwell Davies's only full-scale opera, *Taverner*, wasn't heard much after its first run, which was before my time. Birtwistle had written this opera called *Punch and Judy* that nobody ever played; it existed as a kind of myth. As Stephen Pruslin, the librettist, put it, it had imploded after the first production in Aldeburgh. Although people spoke of it as an important work in his oeuvre, I couldn't assess that as there wasn't a recording until much later. One also heard that apparently there was a much bigger new opera by him that would involve electronics and dance, but it hadn't been finished. The other imponderable was [Stockhausen's] *Licht*. *Licht* is now complete and we can look at it and see what we think it is, but at that time even the first opera hadn't been premiered, so Stockhausen was a very mysterious figure in terms of music theatre. He'd written no operas, which is quite a strange background for someone embarking upon a week-long cycle of seven! One had no idea what that would be at all. Of course, *Donnerstag* wasn't premiered fully until 1981 and we didn't see it in Britain until 1985. (I didn't understand it then, either: it took a long time to get the point of Stockhausen's *Licht* pieces – they're so completely unlike any other music theatre.)

Opera was a strange thing. I never particularly subscribed to any theory that it was alive or dead, but it was clear that something funny had happened to that genre and I wasn't clear what it was doing. My background family-wise is more balletic. The family were ballet fans and as a kid I went to a lot of modern dance as well as classical ballet. I also listened to a lot of opera and increasingly I saw some opera on television. Yes, I always had the ambition to do it, but I didn't want to do television opera.

CD: Why not?

JA: There were two examples that I had seen on the BBC, which had both seemed awkward. I saw a repeat of the first televised version of Britten's *Owen Wingrave*, which felt very unconvincing both musically and visually.[1] The BBC also commissioned a television opera from Alun Hoddinott for his fiftieth birthday called *The Rajah's Diamond*, which starred Geraint Evans.[2] That seemed more or less like Sherlock Holmes – a detective story with music. The music seemed to work and it was well-paced, but I still wasn't convinced about television opera as a genre. Then, when *Licht* started coming out, one saw what an odd piece that was going to be.

CD: It was Edward Gardner, wasn't it, who asked you to write *Thebans?*

JA: Yes, it was his idea. It was soon after the premiere of *Heaven is Shy of Earth* at the Proms and I can't ever thank him enough for this.[3] I started writing *Thebans* just after the *Bell Mass*.[4] I wrote Act I between about June 2010 and April 2011. For the remainder of 2011 I wrote *The Discovery of Heaven*. Then I chucked the existing Act I, except for Jocasta's aria, and started again. I wrote the new version of Act I and the rest of the opera between late 2011 and early 2014.

CD: How quickly did you settle upon Sophocles and the Thebans plays?

JA: Very quickly. *The Tempest* project I'd started clearly was not suitable for a first opera. Also, Thomas Adès had by then tackled *The Tempest* very successfully in 2003. It's a famous play, and I'm perfectly happy to do my own version of it at some point, but it wasn't sensible to do that soon after a very successful version, in the same country with the same publisher. So that wasn't a viable proposition then, but I'll come back to it some day. It's clear that my ideas on this are very different from the Adès version, which, however, I admire very much. I think there'd be room for another version in a decade or so.

The other idea I had was the Sophocles idea, which I had gotten many years before when I was doing Classics A Level with music – a very strange combination. I don't know of anybody else who did that. Without going into the rationale of how that came about, I was not particularly crazy at having to do Classics A Level. I'd wanted to do modern languages, which for a musician is obviously extremely useful. When studying the classics, we had to translate *Oedipus the King* from Greek into English, because it was one of the set plays. So I had to spend a whole term and a vacation translating every word of it with

---

[1]   *Owen Wingrave* was first broadcast on 16 May 1971 on BBC2. It was repeated in October 1972 and in 1993. Excerpts were broadcast as part of a special for Britten's sixtieth birthday in 1973.

[2]   The first broadcast was 24 November 1979 on BBC2.

[3]   6 August 2006, Angelika Kirchschlager, BBC Symphony Orchestra & Chorus conducted by Andrew Davis, Royal Albert Hall.

[4]   First performance 29 June 2010, Westminster Abbey, Choir of Westminster Abbey, James O'Donnell.

a dictionary, line by line. When you are 16, that's quite a task, and I was getting nowhere on it for weeks and weeks. I knew the plot anyway and I thought, 'I know this is 2,500 years old, but I'm getting bored.'

That changed when I reached the nadir point. I thought I'd translated yet another line wrongly. It was in the debate between Tiresias and Oedipus. Tiresias has been brought on stage to tell Oedipus the King how to cure the city of its plague. He won't say a thing, because he knows the truth of the situation. He says, 'I'll go, there's no point in saying anything.' Oedipus says, 'But there are these people around you who are all dying, you have to help them.' Tiresias keeps saying, 'This is pointless, you will get nothing from me at all, I just want to go.' At one point I translated the following line from Oedipus to Tiresias, 'You would provoke anger in stone.' I thought, 'Obviously I've got that wrong.' I looked up the words ten times more and it kept coming out as, 'You would anger a stone' or, 'You would provoke anger in a stone' or, 'You would provoke a stone into anger.' Finally I realised that this was precisely what Sophocles meant. Two thoughts followed. First, I was absolutely thrilled by translating a line which could have been said this morning, but was in fact written 2,500 years before and with such a modern mode of speech. The other thought I had was, 'This character needs to sing.' Then I thought, 'Wouldn't this make the most marvellous opera?' The Stravinsky is a strange one-off thing that isn't really an opera at all. It's called opera-oratorio and it has a speaker in it anyway, constantly breaking everything up. So I thought, 'Why isn't there a proper opera on this?' I discovered there is one by Carl Orff, which I didn't like. I didn't at that point know of the Enescu, which is a quite different thing anyway (and marvellous – it sets the entire life of Oedipus from birth to death).

I got the idea of doing the Sophocles Theban trilogy as a single opera, but not in chronological order. When I went to the ENO meeting and suggested this, I prefaced it by saying that I'd thought about this idea for a long time, but I'd never written an opera so they should tell me if the idea was rubbish. To my surprise, they thought it a good idea and said yes. That meeting was with Edward Gardner, then Music Director at ENO, and John Berry, then its Artistic Director.

CD: With the notion of combining all three Sophocles plays, *Thebans* was hardly going to be a small-scale opera.

JA: The theory nowadays (everyone has theories) is that you start with a chamber opera and you learn your craft that way. If you look at Benjamin Britten, though, he'd never written a chamber opera before he wrote *Peter Grimes*. *Paul Bunyan* is not a chamber opera, it's an operetta and quite a substantial piece of work, requiring far more than chamber forces. Chamber opera is harder to do than full-scale opera in several very important ways. It is very exposed. The instrumen-tation – the balance with the voices – is a real a problem. There are all kinds of very serious issues that if you haven't already tackled a big opera can prove very difficult. Of course, a chamber opera is cheaper. A big opera is a riskier proposition for everyone involved, I see that. Britten's chamber operas were able to do something that wouldn't have worked on a large scale. *Curlew River*, for me, is the most brilliant example. On the other hand, I can imagine a re-orchestration of *The Turn of the Screw* for a larger orchestra (for example, the solo strings don't quite balance against the timpani at certain points). I can imagine it working. Whereas *Curlew River* is so spare, bare and so empty, and needs that church resonance around each sound. It's an astonishing achievement and I respect it a lot.

CD: I mentioned on the phone the other day that there had recently been an opera done on *Under Milk Wood*.[5] You said that you were frustrated, because that had been one of the things that had occurred to you as a possible topic for an opera. I have to confess, *Under Milk Wood* strikes me as a very difficult thing to do as an opera, because it is so bound up with not just the poetry, but also those particular recordings, specific radio artefacts of Richard Burton doing it.

JA: You're right. I've got two recordings of it, the classic Richard Burton one that Douglas Cleverdon produced for the Third Programme[6] and the first performance, which was some time before, in New York, with Thomas himself doing the narration.[7]

CD: Oh, yes. That was a frantic event, wasn't it?

JA: There are contradictory accounts of this, but if some are to be believed, he completed *Under Milk Wood* just before the performance, so it appears it was all very much last-minute.[8] Of course, like a musical score, other people have to

---

5   John Metcalf, *Under Milk Wood: An Opera*, first performance 3 April 2014, Taliesin Arts Centre, Swansea, Wales. Keith Turnbull (director), Wyn Davies (music director).
6   Recorded 24 January 1954, London, Argo RG 21/22 (2 LPs); Naxos AudioBooks NA288712 (CD).
7   Recorded 14 May 1953, Poetry Center, New York, Caedmon TC 2005 (2 LPs); reissued on CD as CDs 9 and 10 of Dylan Thomas, *The Caedmon Collection*, Caedmon UACD 95(11) (11 CDs). Thomas was First Voice and also Revd Eli Jenkins.
8   This account corresponds to the detailed narration concerning this 1953 New York performance by the writer Billy Collins, in his recorded introduction to the Caedmon CD reissue of that performance cited in the previous footnote. It is found on track 1 of CD 10 of that edition. A somewhat different account of the work's genesis, including an account of the history of *Under Milk Wood*'s manuscript, is found in Humphrey Carpenter, *The Envy of the World: Fifty Years of the BBC Third Programme* (London: Weidenfeld & Nicolson, 1996), pp. 139–44. According to those Carpenter interviewed, including Douglas Cleverdon's widow Nest, Thomas only completed *Under Milk Wood* in London a few months later. The famous BBC Radio production, starring Richard Burton, was first heard a few months after Thomas's death, on 25 January 1954. The commercial recordings of that broadcast have never been out of print since.

have the parts for a radio play or a spoken play. There was no photocopier in the building so everyone was frantically copying out by hand what he was writing. It is an extraordinary story.

What I like about *Under Milk Wood* is its formality, the presence of the narrator, the fact that, rather like the Stravinsky–Cocteau *Oedipus*, it explains itself as it goes along. At the same time, it's very mysterious, even mystical. As intended, it does for the Welsh town of Llareggub partly what *Ulysses* did for Dublin (a world experienced through 24 hours), except that Llareggub is famously just 'bugger all' backwards. I like the humour of it, the poetry of it, and above all Thomas's almost orchestral sense of verbal sonority and rhythm. It could make a marvellous opera – whether on stage or on radio. But perhaps that's just what Douglas Cleverdon made of it.

CD: Even beyond that, take something like [Ginsberg's] *Howl*. It's a wonderful poem, but to my mind I could not see the point of a musical setting of it, because it's a very performative type of poetry, there's such musicality in the words. There are some texts where I think, 'How could they be set?' Then again, you get the Britten *Donne Sonnets*, and he does manage it.

JA: Exactly. There are cases like that. To be honest, I still find it very difficult to imagine any setting of [Wilfred Owens's] *Anthem for Doomed Youth* and yet Britten did so successfully in the *War Requiem*. You have to be very confident that your music can bring something else to the text.

CD: That being the case, what do you look for in an opera plot?

JA: I'm looking for something that can be universally misunderstood! What I mean by that is something that can grab people from any background, but at the same time can be ambiguous enough to mean different things to different people. That was certainly what attracted me about the *Thebans* plot. Why these people are doing what they do is very difficult to understand. Even from the Sophocles it's not really explained properly, yet the actions are compelling. I'm looking for something which can offer some, but not all, of the answers. I don't want something that gives them all the answers in one go. And I don't want to preach to the audience, or lecture them. I tend to look at topics that have holes in them, where somebody's reason for doing what they do is not explained – which is not quite the same thing as having deliberate aporias, as in Proust, where you can feel the author is trying to confuse at times. What I enjoy is a plot where you can suppose various things, but you're not given the full answer.

CD: Which is how real life works.

JA: Yes, but people tend to want to know facts whereas, if something is a myth, weird things happen, and there's never any explanation – that's what myths are expected to be like.

The difficulty in doing *Thebans* was to make it seem believable. That's not the aim of all operas, but with this opera it was. That it should be believable that the characters would, in any one of these situations, act the way they do. That was tricky because so much is not explained and there are discontinuities in the myth, and many problems, dramatically, especially in *Oedipus the King*. That play stretches credulity well past breaking point, frankly.

I'm also looking for a plot which, even if it's not a myth, is well known enough to be mythic. That's one of the reasons, for example, that Rasputin as a topic was hovering around my mind for the second opera, though it's now discarded. He's somebody on whom everybody has a view, but nobody really understands who he was. He's a very interesting figure – he's the outsider who doesn't belong, who invades a household, rather like the outsider in Pasolini's *Teorema*, and who changes everyone he meets.

CD: A little bit like Dostoevsky's *Idiot*.

JA: Almost to the point where one wonders if Rasputin had read it or something, and was consciously acting out that. There's another role in Russian society of that time, which you may know of because people say Shostakovich later adopted it – the *Yurodivy*, meaning the holy fool, the simpleton. The Fool in *Boris Godunov* is one such, who tells the truth that nobody else dares say, in very plain, almost banal, terms. Whether or not Shostakovich ever filled that role for Stalin, certainly some other people did.

CD: So in *Thebans* you have got this set of three plays that everybody knows, certainly *Oedipus the King* at least.

JA: That is an advantage, to start an opera with such a well-known story.

CD: The counter to the universality is that someone might think that there is surely no dramatic tension because we know what is going to happen. That is not a problem in music because there are any number of pieces where we know them exceptionally well, yet still find them full of tension. Dramatically, because we know the what, does that mean you are able to concentrate more on the why?

JA: There are a number of advantages to it. It is much easier for a new opera if people already have some idea who the characters are. If you make up a story you have to tell people who everyone is. That wastes time. There are various ways of handling this. Obviously *Pelléas* is about withholding that information, and that is a viable way of proceeding. There is only one contemporary opera that I can think of which follows up *Pelléas* in this respect: *L'Amour de loin* by Saariaho.

CD: Which is a wonderful piece.

JA: It is quite *Pelléas*-like in many ways, though I understand it was partly seeing *Saint François d'Assise* in the Sellars staging that inspired Saariaho to do it. Other than that, there are few modern operas which withhold much. The tendency is to splurge. I have a theory that if you did the withholding thing now to the equivalent degree that Debussy did it in 1902, you'd get terrible reviews and probably nobody would want to stage it anyway. They would just say it is too obscure, it doesn't relate to life nowadays and all that stuff. People like clear answers.

It's rather like the mentality of Orson Welles when he was filming *The Trial* by Kafka. Anthony Perkins, the actor from *Psycho*, was Josef K. and Orson Welles kept saying to him, 'A little more guilty please, just a little more guilty there, Anthony.' Perkins had read the Kafka like everybody else on the set; this guilt isn't in the Kafka. Finally Perkins said to Welles, 'I've the impression that you think that Josef K. has committed a crime and is guilty, because you keep asking me to look guiltily at the camera and act guilty all over the place. But that's not in Kafka. It's kept very ambiguous.' Apparently Orson Welles then shouted, 'He's as guilty as hell, otherwise how the hell is all this happening? Of course he's guilty!' Well if you go and see the Orson Welles film, that's exactly what is happening. It's a particular view and, of course, Welles being a brilliant filmmaker, it has its qualities, but I don't think that is really very faithful to the Kafka.

Already in the rehearsals for *Thebans* I have had quite a lot of questions from singers and other people as to what the characters are thinking and feeling, but I don't want to give all the answers in the music, nor to them personally. I think they now understand why. In that sense I have been influenced by *Pelléas*. Nevertheless, I felt if everybody knows the plot then you could be more ambiguous – precisely because the plot is well known.

CD: There is not so much need to spell out *what* is going on.

JA: Exactly, it's not the question of what, but why. Not how, because Birtwistle's *The Mask of Orpheus* is about how you tell a story, which is retold many times in loops and flashbacks, variants, premonitions and all kinds of things. It goes around and keeps retracing its steps. I don't do that. Ritual opera of that sort has been coined by Birtwistle and he does it very well, so he doesn't need me to do it.

I didn't want it to be abstract, but I didn't want it to be so crashingly obvious, because otherwise why tell this plot yet again? So ambiguity is what I hope makes the project pointful, but I can only do that with a well-known plot. Even *Antigone* is relatively well known, and though *Oedipus at Colonus*, which is my last act, is much less known, it *is* known. It is a very difficult play to understand, but that is even better for the ending of an opera. It ends in a bit of mystery. For the first two acts the plot is very clear – not the motives, but the plot – so I thought a bit of mystery for Act III was just the right way to end.

CD: I suppose part of the reason why Sophocles has endured is that there are age-old themes, both in terms of personal relationships and also the political level. There are things that are taken to extremes, but which are always going to find parallels throughout history. In your head, is it in a timeless *Pelléas*-style world where there are nevertheless resonances for you in terms of where we are culturally or politically today?

JA: Yes there certainly are, but I didn't want to ram them home. If you say it was 2,500 years ago, it becomes something fake antique and I didn't want that either. So when you say timeless that is exactly right. What does Frank McGuinness's libretto say at the start? It says Thebes. Full stop. It doesn't say anything about what that looks like, or when it is, or where it is, or where it was, or anything like that. In other words, somewhere. Thebes is anywhere.

CD: Just as Maeterlinck's Allemonde is anywhere and everywhere.

JA: Yes, and the ENO staging has got this right. It's unclear what era this production might be in. The suits and dresses Christof Hetzer has brilliantly designed for it are a perfect mix: those of some of the people give the impression that it could be nineteenth century or mid-twentieth. Yet Tiresias' costume refers to a specific twentieth-century figure – the legendary Egyptian singer Umm Kulthum – while those of Antigone, or Jocasta who has a blue flowing robe that you would never find in twentieth-century society, look much more ancient. This means that whatever parallels I see with present-day politics and society – and I see a number of very strong parallels – are implied, but again I don't have to emphasise them too strongly. I've left the director and designer to make their own decisions on this.

While composing I thought a lot about the contemporary or earlier twentieth-century political parallels in some characters. With regard to the situation in Act I, there's an epidemic and everyone is trying to find the scapegoat for it. It turns out that the family ruling the city is in an absolutely catastrophic state and this propels the action forward. The scapegoat is sought when society is in disorder and frightened that its whole fabric is collapsing, as it is in Thebes in Act I. In that situation, people always seek blame and this is why fascism always gets the upper hand in that sort of situation. So that's absolutely traditional and it has every contemporary parallel. There is a lot of violence in this opera – most of it enacted off stage – but that doesn't make it particularly modern as far as I am concerned because all that violence is in the ancient Greek plays anyway. What makes it modern is the fact that motives don't change, that societies are curiously self-similar – and therefore this plot remains hugely pertinent.

I often thought about Elias Canetti's book *Crowds and Power* when I was writing the choral music for the opera and about the role of society's pressures on the characters.[9] The Canetti book is very articulate about the ways people will behave in a crowd, doing things that as individuals they wouldn't tolerate; it's about the group mentality. Canetti draws parallels with nature, rather like Xenakis did with mass events. Of course, Canetti had fled fascism. It's a warning about fascistic tendencies – the way demagogues control crowds. (One of the demagogues he singles out is the orchestral conductor!) So I thought a lot about that book's views on how power can be abused and how crowds behave. For individual characters, individual situations, I sometimes found exact equivalents in present-day politics.

CD: It has often struck me that the things in a piece like Stockhausen's *Momente* that would have seemed most contemporary at the time are the ones that most date them now.

JA: Yes, it's true. I am very fond of the piece, but I think I know the passages that you mean.

CD: It's the Hammond organ, all the stuff that would have been very *Star Trek* at the time, that now makes it seem quaintly '60s.

JA: Indeed, but all that has become a brand now. You can go to the Conran shop and see 1960s furniture being a brand. It's kind of cute.

CD: It's not a criticism of *Momente*, just that the things that seemed most progressive in the mid-'60s were the ones that made it seem least contemporary when I heard it at Huddersfield in 1994. I guess it's anything that situates something in a particular age, so it's the same with the typewriter in Satie's *Parade*.

JA: Although I admire Tippett's operas hugely, there is one that does fall foul of that. *The Ice Break* was set perhaps rather too literally in what can only really be late-1960s America. There is some very good music in that opera, but there are a lot of issues that make it very difficult to stage it convincingly now, whereas with *King Priam* there is no problem at all. One of the surprises for me was *Nixon in China*. I didn't think that that would succeed long term. I got that wrong, it has been very successful. Maybe what I am saying is, it wasn't the kind of opera I wanted to do. But it's a fine piece all the same.

---

[9]   Elias Canetti, *Crowds and Power*, trans. Carol Stewart (London: Victor Gollancz, 1962). First published as *Masse und Macht* (Munich: C. Hanser, 1960).

CD: *Greek* is another one. One of my students was talking about what they called the shocking aspects of it. I had to say to them, 'Well, frankly I never ever found it shocking.'

JA: What is very funny about this is that I have noticed that some younger people do. Whereas people our age wouldn't find anything remotely shocking in the plot of *Greek*, because of the way we grew up, when we grew up. I like *Greek* a lot, it's one of the most powerful operas of that period.

CD: I had to tell the students that the TV version of that was essentially what the world was like, that is what pubs were like. Of course, there is no smoking in pubs now, which is a good thing, and also society has moved on substantially in terms of the petty racism that was around in the early '80s and also some of the other deep divisions. Current students are quite shocked to see what the world, what Britain was like.[10]

JA: When younger people see news footage from that time, of things like the miners' struggles, all those things, it is a shock to them.

CD: The subject matter of the Oedipus plays – not so much *Oedipus at Colonus* but the other two – is violent, it is dark. Now if someone was asking me for adjectives to try to encapsulate your music – and of course that is an impossible thing to do in a few words – I would reply that it has an affirmative aspect to it. Not that it shies away from dark things, but that there is often an exuberance and also a kind of luminosity, an inner glow. Your music sometimes strikes me as being like those strange creatures you get at the bottom of oceans that light themselves from within. You think, 'How on earth does it do that?' That musical bioluminescence is still there with *Thebans*, but the opera has also taken you into completely different territory. Such things aren't mutually exclusive, because there's scope for an awful lot in an opera, but did you have any trepidation about the subject matter?

JA: One of the things that always attracted me to opera was the scope that you could have for different kinds of music. Thank you for what you say about my music because, although I never sit down and think, 'Here's another oppor- tunity to write luminously', I'm ok about that aspect of it. In fact, years ago Colin Matthews said to me that he thought that if I wrote an opera it should be a comic opera – he'd just heard *Tiramisù*, which does indeed have a kind of humour about it, from the title on. However, I did not want to do a comedy as my first opera, because it's so hard. That's the toughest task of the lot. One day maybe,

[10] This passage of conversation was held in 2014. Sadly there have been worrying signs more recently of portions of society overtly tolerating racism.

but that really is difficult. When I started work on *Thebans*, I wondered momentarily if the plot was going to be unsuited to my music, but I forgot about that as soon as I started writing properly because it just seemed to produce music from me. I just went with the music it was producing. Not that that was an entirely straightforward matter because I wrote the whole of Act I twice; the first version didn't work. Maybe this was part of that, I don't know. In any case, a number of colleagues also said things like, 'That's a rather dark plot, is that really what you want for your music?' The fact is that I never really paused to think about what kind of music it was that I was producing before this opera. I simply composed, that's all.

The question this really begs is the relationship in opera between the character of the music and the plot. That was very much up for grabs in *Thebans* because of my love of *Pelléas*, where some very intense things provoke almost no reaction from the orchestra at all. Famously, the love scene provokes complete silence from the orchestra. I've always thought that ever since *Pelléas*, at the latest, the relationship between music and stage can be re-examined, and that a purely illustrative approach would be one facet only of what I might want to do.

I liked cartoons a lot as a kid, and more recently John Zorn and composers like that have studied the music Scott Bradley and Carl Stalling wrote for the *Tom & Jerry* or *Bugs Bunny* cartoons, and even issued it on CD without the visuals, so you don't see the visual justification for what you hear. What you hear is something vivid and very virtuosic, but it changes character and pace every five or seven bars or something, and you can't hear why. That interested me and I thought a lot about what that implied in an operatic context.

CD: So you are saying that *Thebans* sounds like a *Tom & Jerry* cartoon? [Laughter]

JA: I will give you one example where that went in. There is a very brief hysterical interlude on the orchestra towards the end of Act II. It's just marked, 'As fast as possible'. Act II is the Antigone drama. This plot was musically very difficult to put on stage. Creon has proved a total nightmare of a ruler, a sort of Stalin-plus-Mussolini, who has let power go straight to his head and is manipulative, lying, lacking in any pity. He's decreed that he will kill his son's bride, Antigone, because she wanted to bury her own brother – her own brother having attacked the state and waged civil war on Thebes, as Creon explains at the opening of the act. He therefore decrees that the body must be left to rot and for crows to eat. At a certain point in Act II he has to change his mind. He encounters Tiresias, who says in effect, 'You're fucked mate. Everything has gone completely wrong.' But when Tiresias is asked, 'What should I do?', typically, being Tiresias, he replies, 'Let me go home.' Creon decides the decree to immure Antigone is to be undone. Too late, there is panic. They find she's hanged herself, and her bridegroom, Creon's son Haemon, reacts by committing suicide in front of his father.

The problem for me was trying to deal with that turnaround in Creon's mind. I could set the text musically, and I did that, but there had to be some kind of frantic orchestral gobbledygook that was like the whole first part of the act sped up to a ridiculous extent, like a mind in total turmoil and confusion, that could somehow render this sudden turnabout – would embody it in some way. So I wrote a very short, intensely fast and furious interlude that ends with the dead bodies of Antigone and Haemon being dumped on stage. Now there, it seemed to me, I learnt something from the *Tom & Jerry* mentality, from the hyper-fast, exaggerated portrayal of something in a sort of exaggerated manner. Also, the music for the dead bodies to be brought on and dumped on stage is vulgar, shrill and unpleasantly vivid. That is almost the only time in the entire opera that you hear music remotely illustrative to that degree. Even then, there is some ambiguity about the interlude. Is that just simply the turmoil of the crowd trying to rush off and find these bodies, or the turmoil in Creon's own mind – or the hysteria accompanying the suicide, or whatever? It could be any of these things or a mixture of all of them.

CD: What would be an example of the other end of the scale, with indifferent music?

JA: The classic case of that is in Act I, when Oedipus is confronted with the truth about his origins. This was a problem for me, because the most famous bit of Stravinsky's *Oedipus Rex* is when Oedipus is told the truth and the music is very cold and strange. He announces very calmly that he understands everything, that it is all made clear. That speech is a famous part of the Sophocles original, and I couldn't set it that way because I couldn't compete with that. I tried to set it in an hysterical way and that didn't add anything, because it is already pretty dreadful in itself and seemed tautologous.

So I finally didn't set it at all. Oedipus has a silent aria at that point – he doesn't react. That's the Debussy solution, perhaps. The music has deliquesced into a woodland twittering, which by the way looks forward to the woodland music for Act III. It is not really facing reality at all. I tried to make a very beautiful woodland music in the chorus and the orchestra as Oedipus is being told all this horrible stuff – it's the only spoken passage in *Thebans*, by the way. And he doesn't react at all, he just leaves the stage without any show of emotion, after a pause. There are several abrupt pauses in the middle of that. Then there is the longest pause and he just goes.

CD: He's in shock. It's too much to take in, to comprehend.

JA: Yes. We know what he is going to do. I felt, also, that by not having the hot emotion there I could catapult that emotion into the aria he sings when he comes back on stage, self-blinded. That made it more of a set piece, and that is why when I came to writing that blinded aria, it became almost a blues, which I hadn't expected. I wanted a clear genre where you could sing out your sorrow, but I didn't want to write a genre piece exactly. It is not like the blues in Tippett's Third Symphony. It has blues elements, let's say. I felt I could project all the emotion into that because we had not had it earlier. In Stravinsky's *Oedipus Rex*, it is the chorus who narrates when Oedipus comes back on stage. He doesn't sing anything, he doesn't have a chance, whereas, in Sophocles, he has a big speech. I didn't want to avoid that; I could really develop his vocal character at that point. So I wrote this semi-bluesy thing with a very clear double form of two verses and a refrain.

It is curious that we are not conservative theatrically in this country. I recently went to see *Happy Days*, which was selling out at the Young Vic with Juliet Stevenson. This is a pretty strange play, with the main character encased in a mound, first up to her waist and then her neck. Nothing happens at all. There are very strange on- and off-stage noises that you can't really follow. There is no plot. Now if I did a large opera like that, I think in the UK there could be a reluctance to stage it. The grand-opera world still wants a linear plot – not so much the chamber-opera world, which has different norms. Everybody has said to me through this project, 'You are going to make it clear musically aren't you, that the plot of Act II happens after the plot of Act III? Otherwise nobody will know what is happening.' What we're doing is announcing at the start – by projecting the words on the gauze screen – 'Past' for Act I, 'Future' for Act II and 'Present' for Act III, which gives you the time frame. I'm happy about that. The reason that Act III represents the present is because Act III is really in a perpetual present. It is about eternity, timelessness and death.

That explains why, if you have to have a why, Antigone's dead body is seen in Act II and she comes back on stage alive at the start of Act III. But this is an opera house, it is not real life, and such things happen in films all the time. This shows you that at least some in the opera world are jolly scared of even the slightest detour from normal plot, unless you are going to do a Birtwistle cubist thing, which, as I've already said, I don't do. If you are going to be completely blowing the plot apart and having some loops and all kinds of time tricks all the time, then ok that is another animal.

Anybody who has read Sophocles' Theban plays must have noticed that if you do the plays in the order of the plot, even in the theatre you end up with a play – *Antigone* – that doesn't work well as a conclusion to the evening. Whereas *Oedipus at Colonus*, which we know was one of Sophocles' last plays, is all about endings. It is about somebody finding an ending to their life and that person was Sophocles quite as much as Oedipus. Sophocles was looking back at the characters of his two biggest previous successes, *Antigone* and *Oedipus*. There are even near quotes from those earlier plays. He's trying to tie up loose ends, but in such a strange way that you have a mystical conclusion, which is very unexpected. That is so clearly the end of an opera and not the middle. It wouldn't make even surrealist, cubist time sense to put that in the middle of an opera. If it is going to be anywhere, it has to be at the end, which means reversing the plot of Acts II and III. Well, I thought that was more fun to do. If you have to have an explanation for these things, Act III explains what you saw in Act II and even to some extent what you saw in Act I. It provides all kinds of reverse clues and solutions as to why those dramas had to play out the way they did. For me, that is perfectly natural.

CD: And 'Past', 'Future', 'Present' neatly orientates without needlessly pinning everything down with simplistic answers.

JA: I am reminded of something Jean Barraqué said, that he didn't understand music and he never understood it, he didn't want to understand it.[11] I think I know what he meant by that. What that means is simply that the more you think you know about a piece of music – and this is a Boulez saying too, by the way – the less you really understand it. The more you investigate, the more you find out the reasons why a piece of music is as it is, whether contextually or technically or whatever, the more you realise that it remains very mysterious, even increasingly so. This is not some vague poeticisation, it's a practical reality of experiencing, studying and loving music on a daily basis.

CD: I was thinking about this last week listening to [Messiaen's] *Éclairs* at the Barbican. As you know, I have done quite a lot of work on that piece and I found it very pleasing that, despite all I'd done, I still came away thinking, 'That's a bloody good piece of music.' And that's the end of it.

JA: But the research you have done on that piece is nevertheless valid and important. If the piece remains as you just said it does, and it's such a masterpiece, then one wants to know about how on earth it happened. Yet finally one faces the truth that finally you can't explain it.

CD: No. In one sense I can explain every single note of the fifth movement of *Éclairs*. On the other hand, it is craft and inspiration combined.[12] Even though I know all of the techniques and everything, I certainly couldn't even begin to sit down and write that or, for that matter, 'Par Lui tout a été fait'.[13] There are some pieces where I can see how it would come about, but I just cannot imagine how anyone can have the conception in the first place for something like 'Par Lui tout

[11] 'Je l'ai toujours dit, je le dis encore à mon âge, je n'ai jamais *compris* la musique, et je n'y *comprends* encore jamais rien.' See Jean Barraqué, 'Propos Impromtu', in Laurent Feneyrou (ed.), *Jean Barraqué: Écrits* (Paris: Publications de la Sorbonne, 2001), p. 178.
[12] See chapter 16 of Christopher Dingle, *Messiaen's Final Works* (Farnham: Ashgate, 2013).
[13] Movement 6 of Messiaen's piano cycle *Vingt Regards sur l'Enfant-Jésus*.

a été fait'. Returning to opera, you said that you would quite like to do a comic opera at some point.

JA: Yes, I would, but not for the moment. One of my favourite operas is Verdi's *Falstaff*, and I was intrigued to discover recently that that was one of John Cage's favourite operas.

CD: Really? I'd never have guessed that, though now that you say it, it makes sense.

JA: What he liked, apart from the humour of it, was the complexity of the writing. He liked the layered-ness of it, having fugues in an opera, and all that stuff. He found the ensembles very exciting.[14] He really loved *Falstaff*. He heard it when he was working on the *Europeras* project in Frankfurt. I like *Falstaff* very much indeed. I also like some Gilbert and Sullivan. I especially admire the speed with which words are clearly delivered. I don't think there is a great modern comic opera. That would be an interesting and unusual task, but the fact that there is no great modern comic opera is itself a warning. I need to be more operatically experienced to do it. It could only be from a third opera onwards that I could do a comic opera, but I've thought of various things along those lines. Peter Shaffer's *Black Comedy* could make a comic opera. It would be about the same pacing, funnily enough, as the play, which isn't that wordy, but I'm not sure that the music would really add anything that the play doesn't already have, so I don't know if it's needed. The 'Head' episode from the second series of *Blackadder*, when Blackadder is made Lord High Executioner, could make a comic opera. There are resonances of Gilbert and Sullivan there, obviously, with the Lord High Executioner from *The Mikado*, but comic timing and musical timing are two very different things, and there's the question of the rights. I wasn't sure that there was anything that my music could add to the very good version that we know from TV. I have the complete *Blackadder* scripts, and I have studied that script closely. There are certain lines that I would love to set, but that doesn't neces-sarily make an opera. Music is going to impose its own sense of timing and you really need to be very secure in your sense of musical stage to do that. I still think comic opera is the hardest.

I've been quite influenced by the scripts of *Fawlty Towers*, and not only when I did *Thebans*. They're remarkably well-constructed and thought through. You can learn a lot about how to plan a piece of music through studying those scripts. I know that Cleese and Booth planned them almost as geometric diagrams of how many plots they could have in action at the same time, and how to make them maximally coincide as near the end as possible. The best example is an episode

---

[14] See Joan Retallack (ed.), *Musiccage: Cage Muses on Words, Art, Music* (Hanover and London: Wesleyan University Press/University Press of New England, 1996), p. 223.

called 'Communication Problems', which is about betting, or partly. A vase has been lost, which was owned by a nightmare guest, who is partly deaf, or might be playing at being partly deaf, called Mrs Richards, who is also trying to sell her house. There are also a whole load of misunderstandings involving the Major figure. All of those things come together in the last line in a most extraordinary way. I've learnt a lot about how to write pieces of music from studying that script, but I don't feel any need to set that script to music. The *Fawlty Towers* scripts are so tight, music would slow them down.

I pay a lot of attention to audibility of words in opera. You can learn a lot from Sondheim about the audibility of words in fast-tempo music. *Sunday in the Park with George* particularly has a lot of words, and the first part of *Into the Woods* is interesting because there are so many different famous nursery rhymes or myths woven together. You do understand who everyone is, and what they're doing, even though it's about 10 different stories to do with the woods all wrapped up, one after the other. (Olly Knussen recommended *Into the Woods* to me, by the way.) That's clever. But it is also helped by miking in that type of theatre.

CD: You have done things for other theatrical settings, notably ballet. Now there is the obvious difference of having an explicit plot and voices, etc., but musically what did you find were the biggest differences or challenges for you in writing opera as opposed to dance?

JA: Perhaps I find it easier to envisage a stage picture of a ballet. I was very concerned with the opera not to do what Messiaen did with *Saint François*, to impose a particular stage vision, feeling that I had neither the expertise nor the experience to do so. There are certain composers who have a lot to do with the staging and it's not usually the best result. Possibly because I grew up going to so much more ballet than opera, I've had a very good experience every time I have done a major ballet and it has always looked like I thought it would, even when the choreographer has not specifically told me in advance.

Now with an opera there are far more people involved. There is the factor of the librettist. We saw each other maybe 15 or so times in three years. Frank McGuinness lives in Dublin, I live in London. We weren't physically able to meet very often. So we would meet and discuss every time he started an act libretto, what was going to happen, what to cut out and so on. Then he made a version which he then would cut further for me, because his versions were always play length, and a libretto has to be shorter – but meaningfully shorter, not just a strip cartoon. There must be enough depth in the words to give you something to work with, dramatically and musically.

Then once he'd done that, Frank would come to London and read it out loud to me. He had a wonderfully resonant, dramatic speaking voice, which I always found inspiring to hear. Eventually he said to me with each act, 'I've done as

much as I can, now you compose it and you will know where to cut further.'
The agreement was that I would not do more than cuts or tiny rewrites. I could
change 'that' to 'which' or add a 'but' here or an 'if' there, I could change the
order of lines and I could cut out lines, but real rewriting beyond that was his job.
As it turned out, I didn't need that because he'd done a very fine job.

CD: Were there any significant disagreements?

JA: Perhaps only concerning the end of Act III. We had agreed that we
wanted to have Oedipus' death there, but that we also wanted something else.
The Sophocles play has several different possibilities. With my encouragement,
Frank had entirely cut Ismene, Antigone's sister, out of Act II. That was partly
to shorten it and also because in consequence Act II comprised all these men
persecuting one woman. And one's seen enough of that in real life, alas, so it
seemed to emphasise the horror of Act II. There is a sexist element to Creon.
Even in the original play he is not nice about women, and Frank brought that
out. Antigone is also isolated in tessitura in Act II: there is no one anywhere near
her register. That's very useful dramatically. Each of her entrances is a shock in
vocal register because only she is up there, the rest aren't. So that was a terrific
decision. However, Frank wanted to include Ismene in Act III. I said that we
couldn't have her in Act III – if she is omitted from one she must be omitted
from both. Eventually he agreed with that, but he gave two versions of the end
of Act III, one ending with Oedipus' death, the other with a lament by Antigone,
and it would be up to me which to use. I decided to combine them into a single,
I hope clear, conclusion. They are his words, but I made that version from them
both. I had never expected to be granted that amount of liberty by a librettist. It
was very surprising and wonderfully generous.

CD: Can you recall any specific changes to lines that were made?

JA: There was the messenger rushing on singing 'The Queen is dead.' Well, you
can't have a countertenor singing that. [Laughter] I knew that was a potential
giggle cue, so I changed it to 'Jocasta is dead.' Somehow lines that might sound
quite rhetorically impressive when declaimed don't necessarily work when sung.
People think that opera is very rhetorical but it's not. The music might be, but
the words of an opera are pretty simple most of the time.

When I'd finally assembled the libretto as set, which of course was much
more cut than what he sent me, I phoned Frank in great nervousness and said
it was so much cut that I was scared what he was going to think. Modest as
ever, Frank reminded me that we'd agreed it was my job to do just that. I also
added a few stage instructions, mainly in Acts II and III. Those are in square
brackets, to distinguish them from ones he originally wrote. It also means that
they are in the nature of suggestions from me as to how this could be staged,

but I realise there are other things that you can do. Then it is up to the producer and designer.

When Frank finally saw the libretto that had resulted from this, he was not only fine about it, he approved of my few added stage directions, particularly my idea that there should be violence between Oedipus and his son Polynices in Act III. Now there is already verbal violence in the Sophocles: Oedipus curses his son in shocking terms. It is truly vile. So we see that Oedipus is himself a bad father. One also senses that this isn't the first time this has happened. I was faced with the decision as to what to do musically with it. The music was getting much more active, until I was impelled to write the stage instruction that although blind and infirm, Oedipus physically attacks his son, and he has to be hauled off him. Frank absolutely approved of that. He thought it was utterly in keeping with the spirit of the play and the character of Oedipus. He has to be seen to have a very serious flaw. After that, you see his transcendent exit towards a sort of mystical death. However, you see it differently, because you've seen this guy, warts and all, and that is exactly the point.

CD: The 'Oedipus complex' concentrates on the relationship with the mother, but the character who has inadvertently killed his own father is unsurprisingly not a model father himself.

JA: Father is a very important word in this opera. Father is the final word of the opera. That was my decision – I picked that out from Frank's libretto. It is all very well Oedipus having unintentionally killed his father off stage long before Act I and then narrating about it, but, in order to see how bad a father/son relationship can get, it had to be more explicit on stage than that. Polynices is asking for his father's support and approval for an attack on Thebes. He wants to win it back for him, and his father won't have anything to do with this disgusting project. In Act I Oedipus already went way over the top when he was cursing the killer of Laius. His music goes way over the top at that point too (it's a slight parody of a well-known composer, but I'll not say who!). Then, in Act III, I thought that we could have a parallel with that hubris, and that's the encounter with his son.

So Oedipus' physical attack of Polynices in Act III is of crucial dramatic importance. You see this terrible incident and sense this has happened many times before. What we now see in Act I with all the characters being brought on stage right away – this is Pierre Audi's brilliant idea[15] – is that at one point Polynices approaches Oedipus for help, but Oedipus shoves him violently away. That is a pre-echo of what you will see in Act III. It explains a lot about the relationship between Antigone and Oedipus too. Also about why she is obsessed

[15] Director of the first production of *Thebans*.

with burying her other brother whom, presumably, she has seen hit by her father more than once – there is a history of physical abuse. So that all tied up.

I never thought I would have to write music for a scene like that confrontation in Act III between father and son. When I took on this opera, it wasn't part of the project. As now composed, the climax of the fight between Oedipus and Polynices is on the major chord. This is significant, because of the particular role the major triad has had all through *Thebans*.

CD: And unexpected.

JA: There is a social thing behind this, which is going to sound stupid and probably it's just me being a little silly, but it is something that I needed to have when I wrote this opera. I've worked with consonances all my mature composing life; it has been one of the basic things I always wanted to do. I felt very strongly attracted by that. This goes back to answering your question about why I chose this plot. One of the main things to decide, theatrically, was what role the major triad was going to have in *Thebans*. I decided, very early on, that every time Creon sings the word 'poison' or 'death' or 'murder' or whatever, I would land on C major. There's a parallel with the sudden C major chord in the middle of Act II of Berg's *Wozzeck*. After a very distressing domestic scene, Wozzeck hands his weekly wages to Marie to a C-major chord on the strings, which in that context is the most ghastly and terrible shock. So I based a whole vocabulary for Creon first of all on the C major triad, and then other triads. What happens with Creon is that every time his music tries to resolve, it goes onto a dissonance, on a strong beat. So it was a very simple inversion of tonal laws in which all the strong beats are consonant; here, every time there is a strong beat it's always a quite sharp dissonance like a ninth or a tritone. That goes all the way through Creon's music. Creon's vocal style is also rather ornate, much more than Oedipus'. It is oily and gives a feeling of somebody who is very good at self-presentation, but who has also something to hide.

When it came to Act III, the culmination of Oedipus' attack on Polynices is a C sharp major triad shrieked out by the brass and wind (C sharp is very important in that act as a whole), and shattered fragments of that remain in the aftermath. I suppose I'm trying to make the major triad sound dissonant and even unpleasant. It is too easy to associate the major triad or, in acoustic terms, consonances with nice big arrival points like Grisey did in *Les Espaces*. I love that, but it has become a bit of a cliché now. I wanted to use consonance as something more fluid or ambiguous. Similarly in Act I, there's a big, sustained, very loud triple octave when Jocasta starts her final speech to Oedipus, 'May you never know who you are.' So the most consonant things always crop up at the tensest points dramatically.

I am also saying something socially about the major triad. One of the things that surely attracted me towards modern music is that it used all the sounds that

I couldn't hear in other music. The major triad has been used and abused excessively in so many genres of music. So the major triad does need re-examining. It is a material I want to use, but it can be dangerous material used without any awareness of what it is. So with this big use of the major triad in the very ugly climax of Act III, I try to make it sound as harsh as, say, a very dissonant piece like *Sun-Treader* by Ruggles or something. [Laughter] I have tried to use it in an almost expressionist way, but I agree it is exactly not the sound you would expect at that point.

CD: The notion of hunting out the 'poison' of C major would have been very appealing to some people 50 or 60 years ago as a concept – they would have found it absolutely horrifying to be using C major.

[Laughter]

JA: Yes, but I thought I would go ahead and actually do it. The idea of it as poison is absolutely a '50s attitude towards consonance, no question. This is very strange for me because it has not been my attitude towards consonance, but I can see that there are many sides to that phenomenon. So *Thebans* brought something out of me that otherwise would not have had to come out, and I hope it's musically valid.

CD: How does this relate to the opening of the opera? In a way, that's neither consonant nor dissonant, though it's clear there's something poisonous permeating this world.

JA: When I rewrote Act I, that was one of the first decisions I had to make. It was a mistake with the first version of Act I. At the start the chorus originally sounded jolly healthy, despite their awful lines about the plague and so on. I thought I should really make the chorus sound sick at the start, so they are not even singing – they just use breath. Then gradually they learn to sing, but it's fairly harsh singing, as suits the words.

The overall form of *Thebans* is this: it starts with a collective sound of a group of people, and ends with the voice of a single individual. It's going directly from that chorus sound at the start through to Antigone's solo voice at the other end. If you were to speed up those illness sounds in the chorus and orchestra at the start, transposing them up several octaves, you'd get something quite like the opening of Act III. Act III opens as a variant on the opening of the opera, but much brighter and more furtive. It's as if everything has become part of nature and it relates immediately towards the sound of crows and rooks – real sounds in the natural world – whereas the opening of the opera does not. The naturalism of the opening of the opera is of a more human sort.

CD: In the same way that, broadly, the third act is more transcendent, its music is a more transcendent noise than the opening?

JA: Yes, that's right. At the same time, I felt that the first act is about the danger of collectives, and gradually the opera homes in more on individuals. In Act III the chorus is off stage. It is not clear what the chorus is in Act III. It could be the voice of the wood. This is a Janáček-like thing, as in the choral voice of the river in the final act of *Kát'a*. At some points in *Thebans* Act III the chorus gives Oedipus orders and says, 'Back away from here – move on. None should touch that ground.' Is he imagining that? Who are these people? You don't know. The audience will hear this, see the surtitles and see Oedipus stop when the chorus says, 'Stop.' The word is shouted at him at one point but there's no visible source. So the chorus can then disappear into being a wordless chorus of the wood, or a part of the orchestra. The fact that there is no visible chorus in Act III is one of the major changes. We must not see them, so they become just part of nature or even a part of Oedipus' mind. Pierre Audi considered that Act III is almost entirely in Oedipus' head. So that even Antigone is just a figment of his imagination; he certainly treats her as though she is. Like his son, he doesn't appear to realise that these people have any independent existence from him.

CD: So you are presumably a different composer for having written *Thebans*.

JA: Yes, I have changed far more as a composer in writing the opera than during any previous composing project. The main difference is time. This has taken over three years. The terrifying thing is whether the earliest music that you have written is still going to fit by the time you have finished the darned thing. I am not the first composer to face that issue! [Laughter]

CD: About 20 years in Wagner's case, though he managed another opera or two in between.[16] Of course, Stravinsky's *Le Rossignol* had a break with the small matter of *The Firebird*, *Petrushka* and *The Rite*, and with that you can really hear he's made big changes as a composer.

JA: I decided that the form of *Thebans* would emerge through composing it. That, by the way, is how Pierre Audi approached it. He listened to a passage, and quite often asked me, 'What were you thinking of there?' If I had any answer, he often did something quite different. Great! I don't want somebody imitating the music, but he gets into a dialogue with it and does something much more inventive. I love that. It is much more contrapuntal and a lot of fun – and makes for a terrific staging.

---

[16] Wagner started writing the libretto for *Der Ring des Nibelungen* in 1848, began *Das Rheingold* in 1853 and finished *Götterdämmerung* in 1874, having paused from 1857 to 1869, during which time he wrote *Tristan und Isolde* and *Die Meistersinger von Nürnberg*. The first performance of the entire cycle was in 1876.

CD: In watching the opera I thought the staging worked very well. The one thing that jarred slightly was that I expected the staging in Act III to be more 'other', perhaps verdantly so. Maybe that's too literalist, but it seemed quite barren and I felt it ought to be verdant.

JA: I was quite shocked by that too at first, but now I think this staging is perfect for Act III, though there are doubtless other possibilities. I was asked to draw up a little plan of the whole opera in stage terms, very loosely, as something for everyone to bounce off. It had times of day for each act. I also put in colours and seasons, just as guides for mood. The order was Act I = Autumn, Act II = Winter, Act III = Spring. The dominant colour for Act III therefore was green. The time of day was dawn and morning.

CD: That's exactly what I expected from it.

JA: It's what I expected, too, and it's not what either Pierre Audi or Tom Pye, the wonderful designer for this production, provided. I now totally see what they're doing, and I fully support it. I asked a friend of mine to make a MIDI mock-up of each act as I finished it. I remember Pierre Audi listened to Act III one Saturday morning. He had already begun to stage it and wasn't happy with it. He listened all the way through, following it with the vocal score, and he said, 'We have to rethink this completely.' He then began to see Act III as a Beckett-like staging, very barren, very surreal. I didn't mind the surreal, but the barren surprised me. I wanted more green. When the set was shown, I said to Tom Pye, 'Can you at least project more green?' He said he could. He didn't say he would, because that was something that he and Pierre were going to talk about, and Pierre clearly decided to have mist but not green. As you saw, there wasn't much green, whereas, when I heard the music, I was thinking very much of... verdant is exactly the word. Pierre rightly pointed out that this was not David Attenborough naturalism. Indeed not! [Laughter] I'm very happy with the resultant staging – it's much better than my original idea.

The art of staging operas is complicated. Of course there is more than one point of view. I made a policy of not intervening. I thought about it, and in fact at one point I rang Frank McGuinness, the librettist, and said, 'This new staging of Act III is puzzling me. Would you come over when you're next going to be in London?' Frank, bless him, took the next plane virtually, because he also cared a lot about the mood of Act III. He was extremely enthusiastic: he saw what the staging was, and said, 'It's Beckett. It's *Endgame*, really. Everyone is in rags. Everyone is almost buried in the landscape. It's got echoes of *Happy Days* and of several Beckett plays.' Suddenly I saw the whole point of it. Oedipus is pretty loathsome at certain points in that act, and so are several others: this staging somehow brought out the ugliness of several of the characters involved. But it was also capable of luminosity when needed – as at the end, with Oedipus' transfiguration and Antigone's lament. At the start of Act III, the stage looked like the devastation after World War I, or perhaps a nuclear holocaust.

CD: It looked like those Passchendaele pictures.

JA: I think it was meant to. When you open the curtain at the beginning of the act you can't really work out what all these lumps are, and they turn out to be people. It was magical. I thought it brought the whole act across very effectively. The crowd that got it first was the theatre crowd. Theatrical people came up to me and said they really liked the staging of Act III particularly. Operatic people came up to me and said that they had expected Act III, from the music, to be more colourful. I was very happy overall. What I liked about the staging at ENO was that it wasn't literal: it was imaginative and strong.

CD: The other thing it made me think of, though, was that, increasingly, many opera directors seem to be allergic to colour.

JA: Well I think Audi and his team got my staging exactly right. But more generally you're onto something there. There's a real problem with colour. I suspect we're both thinking of that awful production of *Saint François* at the Bastille in 2004.

CD: Yes, but countless others as well, from productions of Monteverdi to Poulenc's *Dialogue des Carmélites*. Black as the fundamental colour can work well, but it has gotten so predictable. I'm bored of productions that are basically a black space with occasional bits of colour added. I have a theory that a lot of opera directors and designers, because they sit in darkened theatres all the time and an unmade stage is completely black, with black drapes behind, they think that if there's just the smallest slither of colour that that's really colourful.

JA: No, it's not.

CD: They really do need to get out more.

JA: I'm surprised designers swallow this nonsense. I was very lucky with Tom Pye. He didn't behave that way. We were also very lucky to have Jean Kalman, who is one of the great lighting experts in opera and theatre today. I was very happy with him and with everything else. I was extremely lucky. I'm deeply grateful to Pierre Audi for giving *Thebans* such a splendid and convincingly sympathetic first production.

I saw it in two opera houses, because in 2015 it was revived in Bonn Opera, and on a smaller stage it seemed to work. The most memorable stage picture in a sense was the set for Act II, particularly when Antigone walks down, with the light behind the rocks, which I thought was very beautiful. I do think we got an absolutely top-class designer in Tom Pye. He did a terrific job for everything and it was easy to work with him.

CD: You've touched on this a little, but how does *Thebans* relate to your other music?

JA: Well, there is more nature in this piece than the others. Nature has been coming in more and more anyway, but I was able to let it in completely in Act III. The challenge for the opening of that act was to create forest music. Originally I was going to do a recording, going with a technical assistant into forests and do some *musique concrète* and so on. That didn't get beyond the planning stage. I suddenly thought it would be much more metaphorically rich and interesting to do a forest on the orchestra. What that eventually became, curiously, was a passage that is more lacking in pitch and has more extended instrumental techniques than anything else I've composed. They are there to evoke a natural sound, and this recurs periodically throughout Act III. The first thing that you hear in Act III is a whole load of woodblocks doing a rattling sound, which effectively could be viewed as woodpeckers. Could be. A lot of breathing from the brass, bowing on the bridge of the strings with the strings damped, things like that.

CD: So we've got these forest sounds which may or may not be actual forest sounds, and, as you do in different ways elsewhere, there's coherence through timbral associations and sonic relationships rather than straight themes. It feels like you're in the same landscape, but it's not the same music.

JA: That's exactly it. Now, in the one piece where I did go towards themes more, *Symphony*, I also used some sounds such as vertical bowing at the opening.[17] In a way, the opening of Act III is doing the same thing for the forest that the opening of my *Symphony* did for a lake, where I tried metaphorically to render lake sounds in the orchestra, in such a way that you wouldn't necessarily think, 'Ah yes, a lake.' I hope it is similarly ambiguous at the opening of Act III. You hear these noises and you're not sure what it means, but it could be forest noises. It is a kind of basic musical sound on top of which all the act is heard. Whenever there is silence, it is not silence, but more of that noise. It replaces the silence. That is something I would never previously have done. So that's also new for me. I don't have any particular view of where that might next go in my music.

The other thing I'm doing is commenting, in some way, on the relationship between nature and culture. This is an old Shakespearean thing. Having Act III in the forest reminded me very much of *As You Like It*, where the whole court goes off to the forest. I also liked the idea of Oedipus finding his life's goal in

---

17   See Conversation Eight, 'Beginnings (and endings)'.

nature. My use here of extended techniques is nothing to do with Lachenmann or Sciarrino at all, who in their very different ways are clearly the masters of using extended techniques as a total structural principle.

CD: There are resonances and relationships between Acts I and III, and the opera ultimately ends up immersed in nature, but Act II has a very different feel to it, a very long way from nature and culture. Is that deliberate?

JA: Act II, dominated by Creon, is the creation of his fascist state. That state is rigid, inflexible and oversimplified, so I stripped the music down to very primitive rhythmic levels. There is page after page of just crotchets, which is something I've never done before, and was specifically meant to suggest something which is working too regularly, which is too rigidly enmeshed in itself. It's at the opposite end from the natural sounds of Act III. Obviously Act II's rigid music, with its very heavy, repeated tramping, is like an army on the march. The tramping crotchets are deliberately contrasted with Antigone's music, which is rubato, fluid, passionate, harmonic, resonant and all the things that Creon's state is definitely not. These contrasts take the place of themes for me and, I hope, for the listener.

CD: Are there other particular sounds associated with any characters?

JA: When Antigone is around, there tends to be a cor anglais. That's Antigone's instrument, but it's not always there. I didn't want it to be too blatant. With her first big entry, where she sings that she did bury her brother's body, there's a cor anglais solo followed by a huge, resonant orchestral chord. The cor anglais and Antigone continue as a duet after that. Oedipus doesn't have an instrument, though. He has different types of music depending on what he's doing. So I varied it. Creon has his crotchets for Act II and for Act I he has his over-florid vocal style, which comes back also in his very brief appearance in Act III. This suggests to the audience that we haven't gotten anywhere, which is true. Part of the reason for having Act III happen before the plot of Act II, is to avoid any sense of goal. What I'm suggesting is that, although Oedipus finds his heart in death, to borrow that wonderful line from Messiaen's *Cinq rechants*, the whole way that Act III is presented suggests that we're never going to change, that we all know these people are doomed, because we've seen what happens to them later in Act II. I deliberately wanted to deprive the opera of a neat moral. If there is a moral, it is that people do not learn.

CD: Even when I first flicked through the pages of Act II, I felt there were bits there which do not look like any of your other scores.

JA: I think that's true.

CD: Would it be too strong to say that what we might call the fascist Creon music is the antithesis of what you would normally regard as decent musical writing?

JA: That's partly the case, not entirely, because it's very easy to write music you think's bad music and that wasn't my aim at all. I hoped to write music that is a very ruthless, accurate portrayal of a particular situation. The reason Creon is put into power – you see why in Act I – is because he seems plausible. He's got a solution for everything. He's amiable and practical. This changes just at the end of Act I where abruptly he orders Oedipus off stage, interrupting his blues by saying, 'Right, that's enough of that, go inside.' Then you see there's a very ruthless character underneath. What I was trying to do with the endless crotchets in Act II was to find a way of writing sonorously and effectively, but to portray this machine that works too well is too absolute. If you look at the writing, a lot of it's canonic. That won't necessarily be evident from the vocal score, but at the opening of Act II when the orchestra enters, that's all canons, on the brass mainly. I wanted to make the part-writing sonorous, so it still has the kinds of harmonies that I find exciting. I tried to make the harmonic progressions and the cross-phrasings of the canons as good as I could make them, with the very strict restriction of having only crotchets as a note value.

CD: Let me clarify. I'm not saying you were trying to write bad music, but that it's music which is against your usual sensibilities.

JA: That's the marvellous thing about opera. It forces you out of your habits. It's rather like writing a novel. In Joyce, the whole nature of the physical language changes according to the situation. That's why *Finnegans Wake* is so amazing. I was trying to do that somewhat in *Thebans* – to make my music change according to the circumstance and allow the opera to enlarge my musical vocabulary. That was a very positive thing, because working with a restriction like writing using crotchets is pretty daunting at first. It took me a while to find the right notes for that, and yes, it was going against my nature. I mentally made a list of things I don't do, and tried doing them. [Laughter]

My feeling is that *Thebans* is quite direct when you hear it, but it might pose a challenge for some people because it has the widest vocabulary of sound of any piece I've written. It has everything from sheer noise to mechanical canons all in crotchets. It has microtones, diatonic modes, 12-note harmony and many things in between. Basically, I've applied very strict control mechanisms to modulate between these things so that I don't think the result sounds like a hodgepodge, but it was quite a task to control them, and to pull them together. In some way I've always wanted to do a piece that had this range and maybe that's why I picked this plot.

CD: The richness of emotion and characters?

273

JA: Yes. So it's at the opposite end of something monolithic like *Neither* by Feldman, which is a very fine piece and I certainly learnt things from that, but it's clearly not what I'm doing here. I do admire composers like Messiaen or Stockhausen who have a wide range of technical and, therefore, emotional devices at their hands, and yet can remain characteristically themselves. Feldman did the few things he could do superbly. The same is true of Varèse, but Stockhausen or Messiaen are much more all-embracing kinds of composers and I feel more in tune with that kind of mentality, in terms of having a broad sonic vocabulary.

CD: That very small-C 'catholic' approach.

JA: It's very exciting for me to see how I can modulate, for example, from a passage that's entirely diatonic, perhaps, to a passage that then is very chromatic, and from that to microchromatic, then to noise. That could be one way of doing it. In fact, it's more often less schematic than that. Indeed, there are passages in this opera that are simpler than anything I've ever written. What you might call 'Creon's crotchets'. [Laughter]

CD: That sounds like a follow-up piece in itself.

JA: Perhaps... In any case, there are a lot of passages in *Thebans* where there's just one line on the orchestra (perhaps the violins) plus the voice. Or even, like the opening of Act II, just the voice for two minutes without any instruments. It's so exciting in opera: the variety of textures, harmonies, melodies and compositional strategies you need. Opera brings that out of a composer like no other medium I know. It really stretches you.

So I learnt a massive amount both through composing *Thebans* and through seeing it staged. At ENO I went to every performance. It was the greatest experience of my life, no question. Edward Gardner conducted fantastically, with such total commitment. Pierre Audi, Tom Pye, Christof Hetzer and Jean Kalman were amazingly inventive. We had a first-class cast, really all stars; the chorus were wonderful. Everyone pulled together to make this thing happen. I don't know what I've done to deserve such treatment, but I am deeply and lastingly grateful. Now I've got the opera bug: I'll be doing another one in a few years.

Practices

The composer's relationship with time is the catalyst here for a wide-ranging conversation. The initial pages explore the distance between the length of time required to write and the duration of the resulting music. The significance of first rehearsals, the value of seeing other composers' sketches and preliminary versions of works, and the importance of thinking about sketching strategies are all considered (along with the choice of pencil). Anderson's uneasy relationship with the metronome is explored, prompting discussion about composers' tendency to change their minds and not having exclusive insight into their music. An exchange on historically informed performance ensues that, after debate about general trends, looks specifically at changing fashion in the performance of Mahler and the tempi in some of Messiaen's slow movements. Metronome issues then return centre-stage, notably in Anderson's *Khorovod* and the music of Carter, before the myth of the all-knowing composer is debunked. The conversation concludes with further examination of tempo in Messiaen and Boulez.

— ◆ —

CD: Composers manipulate time – that's a given part of what they do – but the relationship with time in the process of composing is problematic. The music that goes fastest will have many more notes and will presumably take longer to write out. The music that is the slowest has fewest notes. There's an inverse relationship with the time of the musical material. How aware are you of these things?

JA: It came up the very first day I remember composing on paper. I had started composing in my head, not on paper, just making the sounds up – it was all orchestral music. After about a year or so I decided it was time to try and write some of this out. That's when I realised what the problem with composing was, because up till then it had seemed so easy. You just walk around in circles, avoiding the football on the field – I started composing in my head to relieve boredom while playing football at preparatory school – and you make up your piece, whatever it is, in real time, as if you were hearing it on the radio.

Then you try to write it out in full score: suddenly you realise it's very difficult to do that. You need an incredibly good ear to know what you're hearing, what instruments are playing it, and then write it out literally – even if you were hearing it quite precisely. In Stephen Fry's first volume of autobiography, he says that with no effort he can hear orchestral music he likes in his head (Mozart and Richard Strauss are mentioned), perfectly by memory, but he cannot play it or write it out or sing it.[1] Obviously some part of his brain does know the integral relationships within the music and can shunt those very precisely, including harmonies, melodies, rhythms, timbres and all that. Composers have to write all that down.

CD: And every detail must be there for every single instrument.

JA: Exactly. I could hear these orchestral pieces in my head, but I couldn't write them out. Writing the music out is so remote from the speed at which it's played. Even for the slowest, simplest music it's very remote. With the fastest music the difference between how fast it sounds and how long it takes to write down becomes terrifying. Without wishing to melodramatise matters, I would describe this as the composer's nightmare. It's a daily nightmare and it doesn't go away.

CD: Presumably the amount of time it takes varies quite a bit.

JA: Yes, I have never found out why it takes me less time to write some passages than others. In theory you're perfectly right that just physically, a very fast passage with a lot of notes going by very quickly should take longer to write out. For reasons I don't understand, sometimes such passages can arrive very quickly and can be written out physically much more willingly than a slow passage. I remember that particularly from when I was working on *Khorovod* – the slow part took far longer to write out than the majority of the piece, which is extremely fast. It was most odd. I was trying to write the piece for nearly five years, and that probably complicated matters. Similarly, recently my String Quartet No. 2 (and a lot of that is fast) was composed in about six weeks. I know too that one of Tippett's densest pieces, the *Corelli Fantasia*, with that incredible fugue and stretto, was written in just six weeks, which is truly extraordinary. This from a composer who was not known as fluent, and did not think of himself as such.

I'm deeply aware all the time of the fact that the physical act of writing music is so non-real time. A lot of composers have found this very challenging. For

---

[1]   Stephen Fry, *Moab is my Washpot* (London: Hutchinson, 1997), p. 86.

instance, that's one of the reasons why, in later years, Vaughan Williams used to have his symphonies arranged for two pianos and play them through in private to a group of friends before they were scored. He needed reassurance in private from friends that it would work in real time. As his biographer Michael Kennedy commented, RVW needed a committee of composers to vet his symphonies.[2]

Then there's Giacinto Scelsi, who wrote almost none of his mature music down without elaborate assistance. Recently the Scelsi estate has been very open about making available some of the tapes that Scelsi made of improvisations that led to the pieces that he and his assistant Vieri Tosatti notated in full score. Clearly Scelsi had a very strong intuition, which was real-time intuition, of what could happen next at any moment. He simply couldn't control it sufficiently to put it down on paper. Scelsi made these electronic tapes, which are very detailed and made with great care – he multi-tracked and everything. Then he needed assistance because the kind of sound he heard in his head was very complicated and a professionally trained musician had to advise him on how to achieve that sound in full score. Tosatti was incredibly good at drawing out of Scelsi's tapes what he meant. The only parallel I can think of is Eric Fenby's work with the blind and paralysed Delius. It's clear from what Tosatti and others have said that Scelsi could be fussy (though Tosatti's accounts of this were somewhat confused and contradictory). He was not just letting them do anything. Clearly, the problem in Scelsi's case was time. When you hear a good score of Scelsi that was notated really well by Tosatti and himself, it feels as though it just flows on naturally. *Anahit* or the Fourth String Quartet would be two examples of that, and very beautiful they are too.

CD: Absolutely, I adore *Anahit*, it really deserves to be much better known.

JA: I'm very concerned to compose every detail correctly. It's part of my job, so I would never use anyone else to decide the slightest musical detail for me. However, Scelsi's unique case proves that other methods can work at least some of the time. There was a price to pay, however. Much later, when Scelsi became very famous as a composer, Tosatti became frustrated and denounced him as a fraud. It was very sad, not least as Tosatti's widow Valeria Ravot has attested that Tosatti adored working with Scelsi, cared deeply about realising his music properly and was extremely exacting in rehearsing it. So I cannot recommend Scelsi's weird working methods to others.

The music I compose cannot be improvised in Scelsi's manner, but I do improvise at the piano. I tried taping it, and it's like a rabbit in a snake's gaze. When I switch the recorder on I feel self-conscious and freeze up, so recording

---

[2]   Mentioned at various points in Kennedy's classic *The Works of Ralph Vaughan Williams* (London: Oxford University Press, 1964). See, especially, pp. 287–88.

it doesn't work. In any case, most of what I improvise is rubbish. There will be a kernel somewhere of something, and my philosophy is that if I can't remember it the following day, it wasn't any good.

CD: There is the story, probably apocryphal, of the writer who had a recurrent dream with the most brilliant idea for a novel, but he could never remember any of it when he woke up. After some time, he kept pen and paper by the bed. The next time he had the dream he wrote it down as soon as he woke. In the morning he looked at what he had written and it was 'Once upon a time, in a land far, far away...' and so on. It was just a stream of the worst possible clichés.

JA: Winston Churchill recalled that one night he had the most vivid dream about the structure of the universe – suddenly, in a flash, the whole meaning of life and the physical behaviour of all matter became clear to him. He woke up in the middle of the night, got up, and frantically scribbled page after page of detailed notes on this revelation. Or so he thought. When he woke the following morning, he looked at what he had written. It was one single, shaky sentence which read, 'The entire universe is permeated with a strong smell of turpentine.' So one can overestimate intuition!

Almost all the changes I make during the period of composing a work are to do with timing. I focus on each piece individually. You come up with orchestration issues, polyphonic challenges or whatever that you haven't faced before, and I like that. The real problem isn't that, it's getting the music to flow time-wise. MIDI doesn't really help you because the instrumental differences of articulation accumulate so much in a performance – even in a piano piece – and MIDI knows nothing about that. If you ask it to play so-called rubato, it does so very clumsily.

For passages using non-tempered pitches – the system I call 'macrotonality' – I usually use an extra keyboard (an electronic one) tuned a quarter-tone flat. Oddly, for the first section I wrote using that system, the first scherzo in my *Symphony*, I didn't need any kind of keyboard. I suddenly found I could hear the quarter-tone pitches in my head. Elsewhere in the work, though, I was playing them at the two keyboards. That can help a lot in complicated passages.

CD: What about using workshops on pieces in progress, as some people do?

JA: Aside from one workshop on the opening six minutes of my *Symphony* – which I workshopped in Birmingham just to check all the extended techniques worked – I never had any workshops of any piece of mine – unless the read-through of a couple of horn sketches with the horns of the CBSO counts. But other than that, never. I grew up in the school of hard knocks. If you got it wrong, either you had to revise the piece or chuck it. You only found out if it was wrong by the time it was too late to do anything about it.

CD: Everyone concentrates on the premieres of works, but what all this presumably means is that, particularly with a large orchestral work, the first rehearsal, which is when you hear it for the first time, is one hell of an event.

JA: Yes. It's much more important than the premiere for the composer, in terms of deciding whether you have written what you meant to. I remember very acutely the first rehearsal of *Diptych* with Olly Knussen and the BBC Symphony Orchestra. He had come in and they'd tuned. I had never heard a full orchestra play my music before. The piece was to be premiered at the Barbican three days later. I was scared stiff. I knew that if this didn't work, that was it, really – period. It was part of a big weekend of new music at the Barbican, and there were a few of my pieces being played alongside well-known and much-older colleagues. The premiere of *Diptych* was at the end of the first day's concerts, so it was in the most exposed possible position. Anyway, there I was in the BBC Maida Vale Studio 1, sitting right at the back of the room with my score. Olly said, 'Right, let's go from the top', and I discreetly left the building. I was terrified. I just thought it was going to sound rubbish. Finally, I screwed up the courage to return. I went back in at the loudest point of the first movement. It was deafening! But it sounded as I'd meant it to: it was the piece I'd meant to write. Ever since I'd started composing at the age of 11, I'd been dreading that day. I can't describe the intensity of my relief that it all sounded as I'd imagined. I don't think Olly or the orchestra ever knew I'd been out of the room.

CD: And you are surely not the only young composer to have felt nervous about whether the pacing of the music would work once it was actually played.

JA: A very great deal of what I do as a teacher is trying to help students with this question of time. I have learnt a lot about it through studying other composers' sketches. There is still far too little written about how composers sketch. It's a much under-studied area, though I know there are a few books touching on it. For example, it's only very recently that a scholar has published a book about Berg's *Wozzeck*, trying to show how scenes were sketched.[3] They have put up online all the surviving sketches so you can see them in the rather horrible handwriting Berg used.

CD: It's hard to imagine a great work going any other way, but sketches can counter the sense of the music being carved in tablets of stone.

JA: I was helped enormously while I was writing both *Khorovod* and *Diptych* by Anthony Payne, who gave me a tape of the private first performance in modern

---

[3] Patricia Hall, *Berg's Wozzeck*. Studies in Musical Genesis, Structure, and Interpretation (New York: Oxford University Press, 2011).

times of the original version of the Sibelius Fifth Symphony. (This tape has a curious history. Tony copied it from Robert Simpson, who copied it from Robert Layton, who copied it from Erik Tavastjerna, who was at the rehearsal in Helsinki!) It turned out that what Sibelius had gotten wrong was largely the symphony's timing and proportions. It's the same music, essentially, but the order of things was quite wrong in places, notably at the opening, to my great surprise. Occasionally the transposition of things is wrong too. The mistakes in timing, form and in pitch seemed to be related. When I say mistakes, I mean vis-à-vis the final version of the Fifth Symphony, which clearly is the best by the way. There is no question of that. I listened to that tape many times. This was long before the commercial recording on BIS.[4] It taught me a lot about how pieces are assembled by great composers. The Sibelius Fifth first movement in its final form sounds wonderfully organic. It starts from a little primary figure in the horn and bit by bit it grows and changes before your ears, gradually taking shape, but this was faked: the music did not come to Sibelius that way. He really had to stitch pieces of it together to give the appearance of gradual growth. This was a revelation.

Looking at the score of Mahler's Tenth, in the published version where they put the *particell* at the bottom from the third movement onwards,[5] then seeing the sketches of Mahler's Ninth and Seventh and then some sketches for Wagner's *Ring*, confirmed what people had said: that Mahler or Wagner or whoever could sketch very large stretches of music in two or three days, because they were basically just frameworks of tune and harmony, on two or three staves only. That is to say, they were capturing the time flow of the piece as quickly as they could. All sorts of other details followed only once the timing had been gotten down more or less accurately.

CD: So how do you sketch?

JA: I've thought a lot about the best way for me to write music down, in each piece and in each part of each piece. How you first get down a musical idea can tell the composer a lot about what the nature of the piece is. For example, in the opening section of *Stations of the Sun*, I wrote down a short score that began with the first three notes, which are E, then D and then E. I tried to sketch the bar after that and wrote another part, and another and yet another. I realised that I was just writing the full score. At that point I started again and wrote it straight into full score paper very slowly, because there was no way of paraphrasing what I needed to do there. Anything that any part did could suggest to me something that could happen on another part. That was very slow-motion improvising on the material

4   Sibelius, Symphony No. 5 in E flat major (original version), Lahti Symphony Orchestra, Osmo Vänskä (conductor), recorded in the Church of the Cross (Ristinkirkko), Lahti, Finland, 11–12 May 1995, BIS, BIS-CD-800 (CD).
5   The *particell* is the short score.

I could hear in my head with the three notes, E, B, D, on which the whole work is based. It was a very slow dialogue between me, a full score and a piano. A bit of a sketch pad to one side, just for checking various things. I write music in pencil, but the pencil is 2B, which is thick enough that, even if you pencil it lightly, it will photocopy as black, but you can erase it and it doesn't leave a trace. The 2B pencil is very useful to composers, even if you fair copy onto computer.

CD: I was told firmly, first of all by my music teacher, Ian Gorman, then by the conductor of the first youth orchestra I played in that, as a musician, I should always have a supply of 2B pencils.

JA: I know it sounds silly, but it really is important, because it means I can write straight into full score if I need to, make mistakes and erase as I go. I don't have to keep redrawing the full score. That's how I wrote the first section of *Stations* and also, by the way, how I wrote the final section of *Stations* for which, again, I could not devise any paraphrase in short score. On the other hand, the second section of *Stations of the Sun* is just a violin melody with a bass drum so I could certainly write that in short score! Oddly, the most complicated section in the work – the multiple melodies with carillons[6] – was first drafted in short score, and then scored up very slowly. Looking at it now, I would have thought that a full score would have been needed right away for that section, but that proved impossible. It was one of the hardest sections to compose.

For the rest of the work I varied my sketching methods freely to suit the needs of the music, and I continue to work that way. When a composer tells me that they have a regular method of sketching all their music, I become a bit suspicious. One shoe size does not fit all, and if you force yourself to sketch every work the same way you're in real danger of shutting your imagination to many musical possibilities. You may even spoil the musical invention altogether.

I emphasise this because how you first get it down on paper can affect your relationship to your music and to time very drastically. If you can capture a large span of music on paper within two or three hours of writing a sketch, then you're much nearer the real time. If the music lasts five minutes and the first sketch took three hours to write down, that is at least, I don't know what that ratio is...

CD: That's going to be 1 to 36.

JA: Well, that's better than some things because you can be sure that when you write the full score of that passage out that it will take much longer than that. If the best I can do is 1 to 36, and that feels pretty fast, then that tells the general public the truth about composing: look, folks, 1 to 36 is *very* fast composing! I think that's why a lot of people give up, because the discrepancy between what

---

6   Bars 220–59, from 09' 33" to 11' 35" on the Ondine CD.

they can hear and how long it takes to write out is so bad that they just can't face a whole lifetime of this.

CD: Yes. It's hugely time-consuming.

JA: You've said it in your question. It's very remote to the feel of the live performance. The way I go about this now is to read through passages again and again until I'm convinced that they do speak at the right speed, but even then there is guesswork. Let's take, for example, the first act of *Thebans*, which is the longest uninterrupted span of continuous music I have composed to date, 55 minutes. I remember being very scared until the first dress rehearsal. It was terribly hard in the middle of composing that long act to get any sense of relationship with where I had come from musically or dramatically, and how it was going to hang together in real time. I remember phoning composer friends up who had written operas and saying, 'How do you do that?' They all said, 'Well, we don't really know.'

CD: And this is, presumably, the attraction of supplementing performance indications with metronome markings.

JA: I would like to stop using metronome marks because I don't have an absolute sense of metronome like Stockhausen and others. The metronome is one of the great problems with music. Every time I write a metronome mark, no matter how hard I try to get it right, I find that it is the wrong speed in performance. Quite often I write metronome marks that are considerably faster than those that are going to work in practice, but it has been the other way around too. Even if I give only one metronome mark for a whole movement, that doesn't necessarily mean that I want the whole movement taken at that one speed, or at any one speed. Quite apart from anything else, I change my mind on what speed I want from performance to performance and from hall to hall. I certainly change it from the time I finish the score until the first rehearsal. At the first rehearsal I'll know very quickly if a passage should or shouldn't go at the metronome mark I have written. It's got to a point where, for example, with *Thebans*, there's now a note saying, 'The metronome marks are all approximate and you should adapt them to the performance venue.'

Now, as I say, I wanted at a certain point to stop writing metronome marks and to just write allegro or 'very fast', 'slow', etc., and just leave it to the performers to work it out. However, given the diversity of idioms around nowadays, I don't think anyone could be expected to know any one style as well as that. We live in a very shattered culture, so you can't assume anything. I continue to put metronome marks into my scores, and I continue, despite my best intentions, to get them wrong, I'm afraid. If you look at the score of *Fantasias*, the tempo for the fifth movement is now slower than the fourth. Originally when I wrote the movements it was the other way round. Then I thought that the fourth movement's point was in being very short (it lasts a little over one minute) and I would like it to be extremely fast. If you listen to the recording, however, that is not quite what we did, partly because of the Festival Hall acoustic. We did something else again with the National Youth Orchestra in 2010 and the next time we will do something else as well, probably. There is definitely a challenge to the conductor there. You have two fast movements, one after the other. One of them lasts barely a minute and the other lasts over eight minutes, and you have to differentiate between these in such a way that the sequence makes sense. I now know it can work in several ways, so what use is a metronome mark in these circumstances?

That's just one instance. With the opera I found that in the first act particularly, the tempi are faster on the whole than they should be, so we slowed them down a little, partly for verbal comprehension and partly just letting the harmony speak at the speed it needs. Mind you, just as we were assembling outside here, Edward Gardner rang me about the Messenger aria in Act I, which is one of the big set pieces. The Messenger comes on saying that Oedipus has blinded himself and Jocasta has hanged herself and all that. When I heard it last week I said, 'Take it much slower than that, my tempo is far too fast.' What they realised today – and Edward Gardner can be totally relied upon – is that the opening two phrases, about the first quarter of the aria, should go at the speed I have marked. Then it should change to the new, slower tempo I gave them at the end of last week. That's this time. When it is done in Bonn next year with another conductor I may change my mind on this. Why not?

CD: These are things that get overlooked so much with performance studies. First of all, composers change their minds.

JA: All the time. I cannot emphasise that strongly enough. There's nothing unusual in that. It's better to remain open to the sonic reality of your music when it is played. But one tries to get things within the correct range of the speeds needed. There's one composer who published an orchestral work which starts with music in 3/4 time, with a metronome mark saying that one bar is equal to 144 beats per minute – it's impossibly fast. There are two recordings, one of which is at about 92 to the bar, and the other, with the composer conducting, is barely 88 to the bar. Clearly the published tempo is nowhere near reality. Much as I admire that composer in other ways, I would like to avoid that kind of confusion.

CD: Then also, composers don't have the sole exclusive insight into everything that might happen with their piece.

JA: No, they are the first people to hear it inside their head, but they are not the last people to hear it. At least that is what we all hope!

CD: Then you can even take it a step further, which is taking a Bach three-part invention and doing that on xylophone, vibraphone and marimba – it still works. Bach is pretty indestructible, but you get huge debates with the cantatas, say, about whether it should be one voice per part, three voices per part, or a chorus of a hundred. Now, I find the scholarship fascinating for one voice per part, and I love the musical results, but I also enjoy the music done in all the other ways. Ok, Bach never had it with a chorus of a hundred, but if a large chorus wants to perform it, is someone going to come and throw these people in prison?

JA: The mentality of some is such that they would quite willingly throw people in prison for this, which is absurd. I don't have a hotline to J.S. Bach, and I haven't done the research some of those other people have done, but I wonder just one thing. The final form of the B Minor Mass – the full version – is far longer than anything else of that period in that genre. It cannot have been intended for existing performance circumstances of the period. It had no tradition of performance, little hope of performance and it is difficult to know why Bach finally assembled it that way. Well, that at least shows that the composer had an eye for things other than his immediate circumstances, as any composer quite often does anyhow. The Puritan attitude behind what you are talking about is what annoys me. I don't have a purified view of my music and if I hear it one way, that does not mean I cannot hear it any other way. Yet this is the way the public are encouraged to think in some period performance – we are meant to sit there in awe, no matter how it sounds, thinking, 'Oh so *that's* what the composer meant.' Anyhow, now you don't find a symphony orchestra that will play the Bach concertos or suites.

CD: Yes, it's very rare, which is sad.

JA: Well they don't play Haydn much either nowadays, and I guess this is at least partly why. Orchestras could play this repertoire perfectly well – whether or not they imitate what is now thought to be period practices is not the point. Frankly they could play it the way they used to in 1928 or 1930: that style of performance has, as you well know, a tradition of its own behind it. Whether you like it or not, that tradition exists and you can't suddenly airbrush it out of history.

CD: Things have moved away from the most Puritanical approaches in recent years. Research into historically informed performance approaches is now looking at producing possible *ways* of playing rather than *the* 'one true way' of playing things. People are starting to do things like using portamenti again and stuff like that. Except, that is the one thing that the period instrument brigade, much of whose stuff I adore, barely use, slides in string playing and also in singing.

JA: Correct me if I am wrong, but I have seen a lot of chin rests in Baroque orchestras and things like that – but there were no chin rests then (the chin rest was devised by Louis Spohr). The whole thing is a hybrid and, as such, it is a fresh sound. There is only one period recording that I know of where portamenti are used extensively. Norrington did a disc of Wagner overtures, where he used no vibrato but he used portamenti everywhere in the strings.[7] As far as I know, that experiment was not repeated.

CD: I wonder whether the reception of the Wagner disc was, in part, because both audiences and performers have lost the ear for it. A few people have done things in chamber music, but not so much in orchestras. Of course, there is evidence from historical recordings, such as Elgar's. It's a real shock when you first hear him conduct 'Nimrod', but, once you get used to it, you realise that the lines take on a much more living quality. I simply do not buy the idea that orchestras only started doing portamenti around the time that recording began.

JA: No, there's no evidence of that.

CD: They would have been using it in Beethoven and in Bach. They would have been using it all over the place.

JA: The other thing is the question of vibrato, of course, which is a parallel issue. I have heard very early solo recordings of violinists, all of which have quite a bit of vibrato. What you are told by those who don't wish for vibrato, is that that was only for certain specific solo performances and would never have been used in an orchestral context. I would like to see the evidence for that assertion, because certainly the earliest violin recordings I have heard have quite a lot of vibrato, except for that curious set of late ones by Joachim. Another problem is that the first recordings of orchestras were made in very abnormal circumstances, with peculiar seating arrangements and abnormal numbers of players, due to the inadequacy of the recording equipment, so it is hard to know what to think of them. Some give evidence of vibrato in string sound, some don't. Leopold Mozart said that vibrato should not be used all the time: but that is not the same thing as saying it should not be used at all.[8]

CD: Well, again, most historically informed practitioners *do* use vibrato now, but it is not in the same way as mid-twentieth-century perma-vibrato. Rather it is varied as an effect. The bigger point, though, is that practice varied from place to place. These are tastes and sometimes local fashions, so it is very difficult to generalise. The Franco-Belgian approach was significantly different from the Germanic approach, and there's plenty of evidence of that both from early

[7] Wagner, *Orchestral Works*, Jane Eaglen (soprano), London Classical Players, Roger Norrington (conductor), recorded 1994, EMI CDC 5 55479–2 (CD).
[8] See Leopold Mozart, *A Treatise on the Fundamental Principles of Violin Playing*, trans. E. Knocker (Oxford: Oxford University Press, 1948), pp. 203–04.

recordings and treatises. Someone who is very good on all of this is the violinist David Milsom, playing concerts where he changes approach depending on the repertoire. The cellist George Kennaway is another.

JA: That is a much more honest approach. Then there are Elgar's recordings. There are two recordings as far as I remember of *Cockaigne* Overture.

CD: There are actually three, but I *think* you are probably referring to the two electrical recordings. There's also an acoustic one from nearly 10 years earlier.[9]

JA: I've never heard the acoustic recording. In the first of the electrical recordings the orchestra is on the whole using a very restrained, fast sort of vibrato, but quite a lot of *portamento*. With the second one, which is well into the '30s, the string sound is definitely with much more modern vibrato-type sound on every note. Both are conducted by Elgar and he apparently was satisfied with them both. So where exactly are we?

The dogmatism of this has got absurd. I suspect it is to do with money and advertising, alas. Once some realised that there was money to be had in stealing the thunder from the symphony orchestras, there was a move by some to subvert the orchestral culture by saying, 'This is the only way to play it.' At times a quasi-moral superiority was attempted, and it became a product that you could sell using the hackneyed adjectives 'authentic', 'period' or whatever. It was very heavily marketed. Many of these performances are wonderful. I am just saying that what was going on was a very shrewd marketing tool, in my view, to establish a territory and get it away from another area, which they put out of business to some extent, or at least some tried to. What you now find is symphony orchestras try to imitate the sounds that you hear on OAE[10] and orchestras like that and adopt those on modern instruments, which is a fascinating sound, and may result in some interesting textures. I enjoy it – but it can't be called 'authentic' or even 'period' really.

I don't mind any of this. It is all very lively, and it has helped freshen up the performance of the so-called standard repertoire considerably. What I don't like is the way that such revivalist practices try to destroy what was actually a continuous, if distorted, and certainly changing performing tradition. In other words, what had become the noise of, say, Furtwängler in the 1940s, or Karajan and the Berlin Phil in 1960. Whether you love or hate that noise, you can show that it has a very distinguished lineage that goes right back, continuously, to Classical times. It was surely changing and there were habits that were being

9   The Symphony Orchestra, recorded (?)Hayes, 28 February 1917, HMV 2–0728 [HO2498af] (78s); Royal Albert Hall Orchestra, recorded Queen's Hall, London, 27 April 1926, HMV D 1110–11 [CR 332–5] (78s); BBC Symphony Orchestra, recorded No. 1 Studio, Abbey Road, London, 11 April 1933, HMV 2b 4174–6/DB 1935–6 (78s).
10   Orchestra of the Age of Enlightenment: a period-instrument ensemble founded in 1986.

exaggerated, possibly bad ones, all kinds of things that probably Beethoven or whoever else didn't know about, and might not have expected – but you can trace the lineage, which is something, after all. About 30 years ago I heard the Polish composer and conductor Andrzej Panufnik conduct a beautiful performance of a Mozart symphony on Radio 3. It was a fascinating performance not only in its own right, but because Panufnik had studied conducting with Felix Weingartner, who in turn studied with Liszt, who both studied with Czerny and knew Beethoven and Schubert both personally and through Czerny as well as his father, who also knew Haydn well. It would be absurd to exaggerate such lineages, but there you do have a direct and not very long chain of high-level musical training leading from 1989 back to the 1790s. So that is a direct tradition, and one should pay attention to it, however distorted and changed.

I regard period performance as a new performance practice. It is fresh, it is lively, it is interesting, often exciting, but it means basically establishing a completely new performance style partly based on things read, rather than heard. It is also based on things that they have decided now, like having chin rests, or having a conductor where there wasn't one, or not playing Beethoven's Ninth or the *Missa Solemnis* with a piano continuo, even though we know that there was a piano continuo in the first performances of Beethoven's Ninth Symphony and the score of the *Missa* has that part written out. In other words, they pick and choose what they like and what would sound convincing for today's audience; and what they don't like, they drop. They have every right to do that, but it doesn't make it more true to any period save our own. And as I say, some have cast aspersions on what were the mainstream traditions of orchestral playing which go back a long way. I don't see anything wrong with having both. Of course, the finest musicians involved in period performance practice – Robert Levin, Mackerras, Vladimir Jurowski, Simon Rattle or François-Xavier Roth, for example – have done brilliant things, truly revelatory performances which I cherish. Perhaps some others have not.

When I was in Birmingham in about 2002 there was a performance of the 'Pastoral' Symphony by a distinguished conductor of the old school. This conductor used to lead the Vienna Philharmonic and also ran his own string quartet for a while, and had studied, way back before the Second War, with a number of very distinguished teachers who went back even to the Wagner era. He did a very elegant performance of Beethoven's 'Pastoral' that, as the person sitting next to me pointed out, was very much Deutsche Grammophon 1960 style. But it was a beautiful performance in that tradition. It had an authenticity of its own and what frightens me is the attempted destruction of that tradition, even wilful destruction of that performance knowledge and expertise by others, who are very expert at doing a very different kind of performance. That is the dilemma for performance now.

By the way, this affects contemporary music too. I mounted a conference here [at the Guildhall] two or three years ago on the topic: Is there such a thing as the authentic performance of contemporary music? For example, are we to go back to playing *Le Marteau sans maître*, those fiendishly difficult vibraphone and xylorimba parts, with just two sticks? Which was how they were played at the time.

CD: That is Boulez's point, he's said it at various times, including when he was at Royal Birmingham Conservatoire, but it stems from Boulez's antipathy to period instruments.

JA: Well he was a bit narrow-minded about that.

CD: Although I would say that there is an exact parallel between the performance styles that you are getting out of Domaine musical and in contemporary music circles, on the one hand, and, on the other, what was going on in the period instrument movement in the '50s and '60s. In both cases, there's a rejection of the pre-war Romantic style. In both cases also, there is a characteristic dryness of acoustic in a lot of the recordings that they seem to favour. It is all about a *Texttreue* approach that the score is king and that nothing should interfere with the score.

JA: That parallel is fascinating to me. I hadn't thought of that.

CD: The irony of that is something that has completely passed Boulez by. I have heard Boulez say that same thing about *Le Marteau sans maître* and it is his trump card as to why you shouldn't do it. However, it's a poor example. A bassoon from 1830 or a French bassoon from 1913 sounds significantly different from a modern German model, whereas (and I speak as a percussionist of sorts), using two sticks or four on vibraphone makes a difference to the effort involved, but not so much to that actual sound, not as much as the choice of beaters, for instance, and they have changed quite a bit since the 1950s.

JA: By the way, I don't necessarily agree with Boulez that you shouldn't. It might be interesting to do, because he did write it for that technique.

CD: Regardless, I think you're ascribing too much motive where it doesn't exist.

JA: I may be being cynical.

CD: Well, I think you are perhaps mixing up what the record companies wanted from period performance, particularly the multi-national record companies in the '70s and '80s – and there be as cynical as you like – as opposed to people who had realised how different all aspects of performance were in previous eras. They were just wanting to see what happens when you try some of these approaches, which are often radically different and for which there is oodles of evidence. Yes, they probably became zealous about it at times, and some were more zealous than others in fighting their corner, but that's because that first generation had such a fight to be heard at all.

JA: That is true.

CD: So they had that kind of converse mentality in an oppressive world. From their perspective, they were a relatively small number of enthusiasts trying to take on the might of the musical establishment, the record companies, initially, but also the Berlin Phil under Karajan, which nobody would say then, or now, needed much defending. In an attempt simply to be heard, they were saying, vehemently at times, 'But we think you've got this wrong. What the composer's written makes more sense this way.' That very easily, naturally even, becomes from some, 'It's wrong to play it your way.'

JA: Yes, that is a pretty accurate summary of the process. But I do think some performers have been somewhat, shall we say, opportunistic in exploiting the advertising strategies of recording companies.

CD: Or was it the record companies exploiting and exaggerating the claims of the performers? Regardless, there have been changes in mindset in the last 15 to 20 years that come from feeling more accepted. Some of what René Jacobs did with Mozart, for instance, is wonderfully fresh and inventive, and clearly not prescriptive or preaching. You get the feeling it could be significantly different from performance to performance.

JA: He is a fantastic, inventive musician. I always find his performances very stimulating.

CD: Then there's having Villazón sing Monteverdi's *Il Combattimento* – his recording from about a decade ago.[11] If that had happened 15 years before, then the knives would have been out, but it is absolutely fantastic hearing that kind of singer doing it. It is not the way you would always want to hear it, but it is truly thrilling. There is now a more nuanced approach to historically informed performance, it has moved away from finding *the* answer to exploring possible answers. 'Authenticity' is a word that we'd happily ban at the Conservatoire when talking about performance practice, make it an absolutely *verboten* word, because it's an impossibility, as Taruskin pointed out 25 or more years ago.[12] Historically informed performance is now the preferred label, inferring that scholarship and the past is part of it, but acknowledging that we are in the twenty-first century.

---

[11] Monteverdi, *Combattimento di Tancredi e Clorinda*, Rolando Villazón (tenor), Patrizia Ciofi (soprano), Topi Lehtipuu (tenor), Le Concert d'Astrée, Emmanuelle Haïm (direction), recorded in Paris, November 2005, Virgin Classics, 0946 363350 2 5 (CD).

[12] See, among others, Richard Taruskin, *Text and Act: Essays on Music and Performance* (Oxford: Oxford University Press, 1995).

JA: I've read Taruskin's robust views on this and I partly agree with him. However, what I am really trying to say is that there are many forms of history and many forms of tradition, and that I don't think that the rather superb-sounding orchestral performance practices of, let's say DG 1960, should be thrown out. After all, since that is the orchestral noise I grew up with, I guess that is the orchestral noise I am writing for. The sound of the modern symphony orchestras as I first experienced them in concerts on the radio from 1973 or something onwards is the noise that I have in my head. It is those orchestras playing anything from Bach to Xenakis. That is the range of noises that I presume I am writing for in my orchestral music. For any other sound, I have to write specific instructions in the score to make sure that certain things are not being done, like vibrato for example.

CD: The big point is that fashions change and they change remarkably quickly. The way that string players played changed within a generation. The way that people play certain pieces can change within a generation. The Mahler Five 'Adagietto' is the classic case of that in recordings from 16 years apart by the same orchestra. There's the 1947 Bruno Walter recording...

JA: I don't know that.

CD: Well the earliest recording I know (other than Mahler's piano roll) is Mengelberg from 1926,[13] but Walter's recording with what was then the Philharmonic Society Orchestra of New York in 1947 was his own favourite recording.[14] He even gets the New Yorkers to use some *portamento.*

JA: Which they wouldn't do by then, yes.

CD: They didn't really do before the war either, not as a rule.

JA: Oh I didn't know that, fascinating.

CD: This is the other thing: practice varies from place to place, you can't have blanket assumptions. Well, between Walter and Bernstein you get a huge change. Bernstein was remarkably consistent at around 11 minutes 20 seconds in each of his recordings,[15] while Bruno Walter takes 7 minutes 38 seconds.

13 Concertgebouw Orchestra of Amsterdam, Willem Mengelberg (conductor); recorded May 1926, Concertgebouw, Amsterdam; Matrices WAX 1548 and 1549; Columbia L1798 (78s); Naxos 8.110855 (CD).

14 Philharmonic-Symphony Orchestra of New York, Bruno Walter (conductor); recorded 20 February 1947, Carnegie Hall, New York; Matrices XCO-37365–373880; Columbia 12666-D – 12637-D (M-718) (78s); Naxos 8.110896 (CD).

15 New York Philharmonic Orchestra, Leonard Bernstein (conductor); recorded 7 January 1963, Philharmonic Hall (now Avery Fisher Hall), Lincoln Center, New York; Columbia M2S

JA: I take your point on that and I am thinking of what has happened since. You get Abravanel, for instance, later in the 1960s also doing a Walter-type speed; then there is a whole splurge of '70s recordings which are much slower. More recently it has sped up again.

CD: It has sped up, but it is still more like nine or 10 minutes. The Abravanel was just over eight minutes.

JA: There was this big fuss in the *Musical Times*, with a number of articles in the 1990s which I am sure you know.[16]

CD: Well Kaplan did it. He was the one that did it much closer to the Bruno Walter or the Mengelberg recording, which is only 7 minutes 9 seconds.

JA: Colin Matthews, who is a Mahler expert of course, wrote in at the time when all of this was going on. He wrote something to the effect that making it last seven or eight minutes *is* doing it very slowly.

CD: The point is that it is Adagietto and not Adagio – it is a love song.

JA: Exactly, so it should be singable. And that speed also brings it closer to its rather obvious model, the Adagietto (same key) from Bizet's *L'Arlésienne*.

CD: It has a lilting quality to it at that speed, but I also love the Bernstein '87 recording with the Vienna Phil, which sounds fantastic and is utterly wonderful.

JA: That does sound wonderful but I'm sorry, I can't really face listening to it.

CD: It is a completely different conception of what the piece is, but it still works and that is the thing. Both conceptions work, but the change in performance fashion happened in a very short period of time. Incidentally, Bernstein is at the higher end of the slow speeds. Haitink clocks in around 14 minutes. Of course, the piece became associated not with a love song, but with funerals even before *Death in Venice*.

JA: Funerals?

698 (LPs); Sony Classical SX12K 89499 (12 CDs). Members of the New York Philharmonic, Leonard Bernstein (conductor); live recording 8 June 1968, at the Mass on the day of burial of Robert Francis Kennedy, St Patrick's Cathedral, New York City; Sony Classical SX12K 89499 (12 CDs). Wiener Philharmoniker, Leonard Bernstein (conductor); live recording September 1987, Alte Oper, Frankfurt am Main; Deutsche Grammophon 423 608-2 (CD).
16   Gilbert E. Kaplan, 'Mahler and Tradition: Is There or Isn't There? Gilbert E. Kaplan and Peter Franklin in Search of One', *Musical Times* Vol. 133, No. 1797 (November 1992), 559–63.

CD: Yes. Bobby Kennedy's, and, for that matter, Boulez played it after Eisenhower's death in 1969. The Bobby Kennedy funeral performance was recorded.[17] Then it is used in the film *Death in Venice*, so all this culturally increases the sense of it being a dirge before you get your resurrection in the next movement. It is a conception that works, but it is one that, so far as we can tell, never even remotely crossed Mahler's mind.

JA: I am sure not. Again the question as to whether or not he would have gone along with it is one that intrigues me. He would have realised its extraordinary force in that elongated slow speed, even if it is probably miles away from what he dreamt he was writing when he wrote it. Now we come to the first movement of Messiaen's *Vingt Regards*, because there you have a tempo marking that is extraordinarily slow in the first edition. Did Loriod ever issue a second edition?

CD: No. She threatened to.

JA: Well you know what tempo she generally took for that?

CD: Yes, I saw her do it relatively late on and have got three recordings of her playing it.[18]

JA: Loriod's take on that first movement was always fairly fast, but the performance I heard at the Bath Festival (1986) was quite surprisingly fast. As you know, originally it says that the triplet semiquaver equals an extraordinarily slow pulse.

CD: It's supposed to be 60 bpm – and has symbolic proportionate relationships with tempi in other movements.

JA: Peter Hill's recording is at that speed, but another thing about Peter Hill's recording is the miking, the particular kind of piano he is using, which is a very special model of piano.[19]

CD: Yes, a Fazioli.

JA: Right, and Peter's own particular way of dealing with slow movements, and his sense of piano colours, responds well with spacious tempi. For example,

[17] *Robert Francis Kennedy – A Memorial*, various artists, Columbia D2S 792 (2 LPs).
[18] Recorded 13 March 1956, Paris, Véga C 30 A 60/61/62 (3 LPs); Universal/Decca 4817069 (13 CDs). Recorded October 1973, Paris, Église Notre-Dame du Liban, Erato OME 1; Warner 2564 69986–5 (2 CDs). Live recording 27 October 1985, Radio Bremen, Schwann AMS 5201 (2 LPs).
[19] Recorded at St Paul's New Southgate, 16–20 September 1991, Unicorn Kanchana DKP(CD)9122/23 (2 CDs).

Peter's recording of 'Cloches d'Angoisse', the sixth Prélude, makes that into Messiaen's first great slow movement, for which there is a very good case.[20] He plays it in a very intimate manner. Peter clearly is very at home with rendering that side of Messiaen in a very daring way that few pianists attempt now. It's much more common in the organ world, because of the sustain of the instrument, and cathedral acoustics, etc. I liked it when Peter asked Loriod, 'Where do you stand on that first movement of *Vingt Regards* and on those tempo questions generally?' and ultimately she said, 'Well, it is partly a matter of personal taste', which that first movement of the *Regards* particularly highlights.

CD: Yes, even with someone as clear-cut, superficially, as Messiaen, with clear metronome marks and all sorts of *Texttreue*-like statements about fidelity to the score, tempi and, especially, metronome markings are vexed issues.

JA: They are with every composer. My only advice to all players of my music is, particularly in any music before about 2005, for God's sake take the metronome marks with a pinch of salt. Except for one piece, *Khorovod*, where they are absolutely what I mean. I emphasise that because *Khorovod* is a very fast virtuosic work. Early on it was regarded as a very difficult piece to play – in the first three or four years of its existence. Thank God Markus Stenz, doing the premiere, did not take any of the tempi slower at all. It was a very good performance. I triple-checked those metronome marks, and they are the right speeds. I'm never going to change them for that piece because if it goes any slower the character of the work is lost. That's a particular factor with *Khorovod*. For the rest of my music there's considerable latitude about speed, provided the character of the music is not lost.

CD: With *Khorovod*, obviously, an orchestra ideally hits all the notes and plays it all at speed, but are you saying that if an orchestra is struggling, they maintain the speed because the tempo has the spirit of it? If there is the odd misplaced bit, that's no disaster?

JA: Exactly. There is a kinship here, bizarrely – I say bizarrely because on paper it doesn't look anything like it – between that piece and certain facets of Ferneyhough. As I said earlier, I studied percussion for a while. There is a passage in *Khorovod* with marimba scales which are very fast and go rapidly from low to fairly high on the instrument. I know how big a marimba is physically. I knew the distance between the top note at the end of one scale and the bottom note of the next scale was a bit idealistic at that speed, but I wanted the piece to have that sense of just being on edge, I didn't want it to sound safe. I absolutely

---

[20] *The Piano Music of Olivier Messiaen*, recorded at Rosslyn Hill Unitarian Chapel, 21–22 February and 25–26 September 1985, Unicorn Kanchana DKP(CD)9078 (CD).

agree with you, though, I would want a performance to be up to speed and if certain notes fly off or are missed, it doesn't bother me so much in that particular case in some passages. It's a very wild piece. As the years go by the piece gets, I suppose, more comfortable because people are just used to it.

CD: It reminds me of Stravinsky's tongue-in-cheek comment about needing to transpose the bassoon solo at the start of *The Rite of Spring* up a tone every 20 years or so. There's also Strauss who, if I recall correctly, bemoaned towards the end of his life the fact that textures in his early orchestral works where he hadn't expected the players to get all the notes – he just expected and wanted a wash of sound – were being played too precisely, too well after several decades in the repertoire. That suggests that an historically informed performance might be done better by a non-professional orchestra.

JA: When you're a very young composer and you write a very difficult piece, people tend to be critical. As the piece becomes known they tend to say, 'Well, it's very hard but we'll almost make it', and then go for it. When Vladimir Jurowski first did *Khorovod* with the LPO in 2003, he had very little rehearsal time. It was two hours plus the day. Jurowski knows a lot about contemporary music, but the LPO are not a specialist new-music group, even though they have long experience of working with composers and are excellent players. I was astounded. They played it in the Festival Hall at top speed, brilliantly. I couldn't believe that in nine years since the premiere, the piece had settled down to the degree that it was possible for a non-specialist group to do it on just two hours of rehearsal. In fact, we didn't need all of those two hours.

So I have a very funny relationship to the metronome. I sort of hate it. I would love to get to the stage where I don't have to use metronome marks and where the conductors will just feel what's right.

CD: Is the metronome mark just a tool that then needs to be forgotten?

JA: I would like that. If you compare different recordings Stravinsky made of the same work, there are wild discrepancies. It's not just age. It's many things. A different example is Elliott Carter. There are a few passages in works of the 1960s where how it sounds at the speed he's marked, and how he thought it would sound, may not entirely be the same thing. At that time he was writing each piece for many years, working over each passage in great detail until he really was satisfied. The downside is that occasionally perhaps he lost perspective on how a particular set of details would sound when played fully up to speed. There are a couple of passages like that in the Double Concerto, which I nevertheless admire hugely – it's one of the most inventive pieces he ever composed – a couple in the Piano Concerto, and even in the Concerto for Orchestra, which is maybe my favourite of the three. The climax of the Concerto for Orchestra is terrific

– all deafening multi-layer craziness, a wonderful moment – but just a couple of bars after that, as it's dissolving, there's a chord progression in the strings that is just never going to sound with all the other stuff that's going on at that speed. I played it through at the piano and realised that it's very important. There are now three fantastic recordings available and you don't hear this chord progression in any of them. It's a masterpiece, but perhaps that's a slight miscalculation on his part. Perhaps it doesn't matter because the piece has a tremendous impact at that point anyway, but it's a slight shame.

CD: When Stravinsky wrote *The Rite of Spring*, Monteux said at the first rehearsals with the orchestra, 'These bits of orchestration need changing and these tempi need changing.' Monteux was the person standing in front of an orchestra all of the time and he understood how these would go, and Stravinsky did it.

JA: Without question – even though he himself had never heard it at that point.

CD: Increasingly during the twentieth century, the myth has grown that composers will necessarily always know precisely what's going to happen, or that they ought to know precisely exactly how everything is going to sound in every respect.

JA: There's not one composer I know of whom that's true. Some composers go on making changes long after the first performance. Until now I've largely resisted making anything other than minor changes after a premiere. I'd rather do revisions during the composition process itself and then feel that the piece is right, so generally I don't revise, not significantly. But it's a big myth that composers know everything. They can't. If they're writing in a new idiom which is personal to them, it may well involve things that they've never heard before, which means that it's very difficult to know how to do it.

CD: It's also related, though, isn't it, to the whole notion of *Texttreue* that began to dominate in the middle of the twentieth century?

JA: And is still with us.

CD: Yes. Once something is on the score, it is set in blocks of concrete.

JA: For example, the notorious fanfares in the finale of Debussy's *La Mer*. Clearly he didn't know whether they were meant to be there or not. He couldn't make his mind up. So, of course, the answer is, if you want, put them in and if you don't, don't. It depends on whether you are convincing with it. One thing that shocked me is that I've heard a conductor in the last 10 years or so, who has been doing some Messiaen exactly as they claimed the metronome marks in the score to be. They sound all wrong to me.

CD: The thing is, for me, that I don't think it's necessarily the actual tempo itself. It's Schnabel's thing that music can be fast or slow at the same tempo.

JA: That's like the finale of Beethoven Op. 111, by the way.

CD: Yes, that's precisely what it is. That absolute tempo is a different thing from a sense of speed and flow. I know who you mean and, for me, the trouble is that it's rigid.

JA: I remember in *Saint François* with this conductor, the Angel's music was unbelievably slow, remorselessly so. I felt very sorry for the singer who was clearly having trouble even beginning to phrase this thing at those glacial speeds. I then went home and checked in the score and it's actually not far off from what the conductor did, but what Messiaen clearly meant was, make it sound like that. Not do it literally, rigidly, at that speed.

CD: The Messiaen *Quartet*[21] is one piece where it can work both ways, as long as you go with it. Messiaen's own recording of the *Quartet* is so illuminating. The tempi in the slow movements are actually there or thereabouts to start off with, but there is such an ebb and flow to what's going on, the music breathes, it has an arc to it. Of course, once the violinist hits the final note and can do nothing about it, he does then slow down. It's a particularly mean trick to do to somebody.

JA: Poor Jean Pasquier...[22]

CD: Nonetheless, in the *Quartet*, those movements can also work with a kind of metronomic relentless approach. What frustrated me for a long time was that was the only approach taken. I can understand why people did it: they looked at the score and it looks like it should be relentless and absolutely metronomic so people did that in an unthinking way. Now, performers need to be absolutely clear whether they're doing that or whether they're following Messiaen, who frankly plays it like Rachmaninov or Chopin, just much slower than most Rachmaninov or Chopin.

JA: May I raise another problem? Boulez's interpretations of *Chronochromie*. I'm thinking of the last block of music in the first movement and also the last movement, which is the same music more or less – it's the eagle from Sweden,

---

[21] *Quatuor pour la fin du Temps* [Quartet for the end of Time].
[22] The violinist on Messiaen's recording: *Quatuor pour le fin du Temps*, Olivier Messiaen (piano), Jean Pasquier (violin), André Vacellier (clarinet), Étienne Pasquier (cello), recorded at Schola Cantorum, 1956; Club Français du Disque – Musicdisc 30 RC 719 (LP); Accord 461 744–2 (CD); Accord 480 1045 (CD).

isn't it? The tempi in the score are those of Doráti's recording.[23] It's not brisk, it's monumental and sounds quite Varèse-like, but it's on the move. It sounds more or less like some giant terrifying bird. Boulez always takes that coda much slower than marked and draws each chord out hugely, especially in his last recording.[24] I heard him do that live several times with the BBC Symphony Orchestra, the same way, in Messiaen's presence. Messiaen never stopped him. Probably Messiaen also found it convincing.

CD: I'm fascinated by Boulez's performances of *Oiseaux exotiques*, especially the Himalayan bird pounding away at the end, the White-crested Laughing Thrush on the final page. Funnily enough, it's a work he's never done a studio recording of, which is really quite surprising. There are at least three live recordings,[25] but the difference, particularly between the first one in 1964 and Messiaen's eightieth birthday concert in '88, is that Boulez takes that final page at about half the speed. It absolutely is half the speed of the premiere.

JA: There's a second edition of the score and I know some of the tempi are different. I also know some of the dynamics are different. Does the second edition of the score correspond in any way to the changes you mention?

CD: Yes, absolutely. Messiaen puts in an additional much slower metronome marking for that bird. I'm curious, and I've no idea whether I'll ever find any evidence one way or the other for this, about the relationship between Boulez's performances and Messiaen's revisions to the score. Did the revisions prompt the change in performance approach, or did Boulez start doing it more slowly, prompting the revisions? Or, for that matter, did this really drastic change come out of conversation between them?

JA: It would be good to know. I know one thing, the tam-tam crescendos before the Prairie Chicken were vastly inflated from the first edition to the second, in terms of the amount of crescendo.

---

[23] Messiaen, *Chronochromie*, BBC Symphony Orchestra, Antal Doráti (conductor); recorded at No. 1 Studio, Abbey Road, London, 27 September and 11–16 October 1964, HMV ASD 369 (LP).

[24] Messiaen, *Chronochromie*, Cleveland Orchestra, Pierre Boulez (conductor); recorded at Masonic Auditorium, Cleveland, March 1993, Deutsche Grammophon 445 827–2 (CD).

[25] Yvonne Loriod (piano), Symphonieorchester des Bayerischen Rundfunks, Pierre Boulez (conductor), live recording 17 April 1964, Herkulessaal der Residenz, Munich, Col Legno WWE 2 CD 20084–2 (CD); Philippe Entremont (piano), Cleveland Orchestra, Pierre Boulez (conductor), live recording 19 and 21 November 1970, Severance Hall, Cleveland, OH, Musical Arts Association, TCO 093–75 (CD); Yvonne Loriod (piano), Ensemble InterContemporain, Pierre Boulez (conductor), live recording 26 November 1988, Théâtre des Champs-Élysées, Paris, Disques Montaignes XXIIII (CD).

CD: Yes. They become far more like *Et exspecto*-type things. The recording of the premiere performance of *Oiseaux exotiques* really is miraculous.[26]

JA: Amazing. It must be one of the best performances ever of the work. It is astonishing. It's on a par, perhaps even better than what survives of the Adrian Boult *Wozzeck* from 1934 which is extraordinarily good for those times in terms of Second Viennese School performances.[27] What Rudolf Albert did for the Domaine was remarkable. Also it says a lot for Boulez's abilities as a fixer. He was able to get players who could cope with that really tricky piece. What we're also talking about implicitly, since you've raised Boulez, is the problem of *Le Marteau sans maître*, where notoriously the metronome marks in each successive edition of the score have gotten slower and slower. His last recording is extremely good, and particularly wonderful singing by the way, but I fear he's rather lost the spirit of some of the fast movements.[28] In Bob Craft's recording the fourth movement, which is extremely fast in the original score, is madly quick: he really gets it up to the original speeds. The musicians can actually play it. If you try and neaten it up so that you hear every single note, it doesn't have the right character. Boulez and speeds is a very interesting matter, because there are very strange things in many recordings by Boulez of all kinds of music. At times there's a tendency to slow down very fast movements and speed up very slow ones. I think it's to do with his notions of performance practicality. The good side of all this is that he's much more fluid and spontaneous as a performer than he used to be.

CD: His recordings have become more flexible in some respects, almost more Romantic. He was never going to be conducting like Furtwängler would, but, in a more limited way than you might mean with other people, he became more interventionist.

JA: There is more breadth and more suppleness. What it all shows is that there are no absolutes in performance. Every composer and performer should remember that.

---

[26] Yvonne Loriod (piano), Orchestre du Domaine Musical, Rudolf Albert (conductor), live recording 10 March 1956 (world premiere), Petit Théâtre Marigny, Paris, Véga C 30 A 65 (LP), Accord 4769209 (4 CDs), Accord 480 1045 (7 CDs).

[27] Concert performance broadcast from the Queen's Hall, London on 14 March 1934 by the BBC. The surviving excerpts are available as a bonus on a recording of *Wozzeck* in Italian with Tito Gobbi in the title role, Ponto PO-1053 (2 CDs).

[28] The commercial recordings with Boulez as conductor are: Marie-Thérèse Cahn (chant), live recording Petit Théâtre Marigny, Paris, 21 March 1956, Véga C35 A67 (10" vinyl); Jeanne Deroubaix (chant), recording date and location unknown, released 1964, Adès 14.008 (LP), Accord 4769209 (4 CDs); Yvonne Minton (chant), recorded ?1973, CBS 73213 (LP); Hilary Summers (chant), recorded September 2002, IRCAM, Paris, DG 00289 477 5327 (CD). Robert Craft's recording, with Margery Mackay as singer, was first released in 1958 on Columbia Masterworks ML 5275 (LP).

Conversation Fifteen

Outsiders?

This conversation starts by looking at some of the outsider figures who have inspired Anderson, prompting an extended discussion of the violin concerto, *In lieblicher Bläue*. After that, Anderson reflects on his own position, leading to an exchange about composition as a communicative rather than isolating activity. In the last part, Anderson reveals how the open attitudes of his teachers, Lambert and Goehr, helped negotiate some of the more partisan approaches of others.

CD: Some of your works have been inspired by or even included material by figures who worked outside the circle of their contemporaries or even society as a whole, notably Hölderlin with your recent violin concerto, *In lieblicher Bläue*.

JA: In the last few years I've become aware that most of the writers to whom I seem attracted have a slightly oblique relationship to their period. Now they're subsumed into the canon, as Hölderlin or Emily Dickinson have been. But during their lives they had distinctly odd relationships with their society.

CD: Do you find that people try to pigeonhole you in ways that are uncomfortable, or simply, at best are only partial and are restrictive?

JA: I don't know, I've never consciously thought that. I've been treated generously, for which I'm very grateful; I'm not in any way complaining. Perhaps in some circles in mainland Europe I may be seen in a different way. On the one hand, I'm known as somebody who has advocated spectral music quite a lot. After all, my first articles were published in French, not English, and were on that topic. They know of me in that connection, but they are also aware that my music doesn't fit into that category.

CD: In terms of the spectral influence, would you say it's less a strict technique and more a certain sensibility in terms of approaching sound? That it's opened up sound worlds for you, but there's no compulsion at all to follow any of the technical aspects of it?

JA: Yes, that's a brilliant way of putting it. In the case of my Violin Concerto, if you listen to certain sonorities, you would hear that I had been affected by discoveries in spectral music, but there's not a microtone in it. The Violin Concerto sketches had lots of microtones and they gradually just dropped out. I realised that microtones played on a solo violin don't tell as well as they might and the world of the piece didn't seem to need them. Up to the last bar I was still open to writing some, but there aren't any.

CD: So how did you get to know the Hölderlin poem *In lieblicher Bläue*?

JA: I came across it thanks to Richard Stokes, who taught me German at school and who is now well known in the music profession as a writer on and coach of French chanson and German lied. He was an extraordinary teacher: he used to have a class of 13-year-olds groaning 'Ich grolle nicht' to Fischer-Dieskau's recording on a cassette, realising that for 13-year-olds 'Ich grolle nicht' is probably a perfect text – frustrated love and all that. He taught very strict grammar in a conventional way, absolute old-style, but he also mixed it with getting us to sing in German, and not only Schubert either. I recall we had to sing to Marlene Dietrich recordings. I don't know the English words for, was it 'Where Have All the Flowers gone?' I only know 'Sag mir, wo die Blumen sind'. I never learnt it in the Bob Dylan version.

My knowledge of Hölderlin goes back to those lessons. Richard Stokes recommended Michael Hamburger's Hölderlin volume, which is basically the complete poetry, as much as was then known, translated in parallel. I took the Hamburger book out of the library, and it fell open at a page with a long passage of prose headed *In lieblicher Bläue*, 'in lovely blueness'. I started reading it very fast in German and English simultaneously. I became incredibly excited by its imagery. I remember feeling, 'Oh, so I'm not the only person, somebody else also feels this way.' It's difficult to tell you what the poem's about, because, as Anna Russell used to say in describing the Rheinmaidens' song in her *Ring* lecture, 'I won't translate it because it doesn't mean anything', a line I cherish. It's not that *In lieblicher Bläue* doesn't mean anything, but it doesn't mean quite what you think. There are various ideas to do with the colour blue, with church windows, with a church steeple and the bells ringing in the church. Then a whole load of other things comes in to do with the seasons and to do with Oedipus.

I love the poem very much. The poem turns out not to be entirely by Hölderlin, which is a complication I hadn't entirely understood when I first read it. It was published by somebody called Waiblinger, in his novel *Phaeton*, about a mad architect who leaves random jottings behind, and this is supposedly one of them. Waiblinger was a close friend and the first published biographer of Hölderlin. He knew him well in his so-called years of madness, meaning all the years he spent in the carpenter's tower in Tübingen. He certainly had access to what Hölderlin was writing then. He may well have nicked papers at that time. There's a strong resemblance between a lot of this poem and things that we know Hölderlin did write at that time. So the provenance of it is a little bit uncertain, and he may have 'stranged it up' a bit, in order to make sure it appeared as mad as he wanted his hero to be. Personally, I don't care who wrote it. I care about *it*. What really excites me is that poetry and that language.

CD: That's the same with any work with disputed provenance. Why should it make a difference whose name is on it? Whether Shakespeare plays are by Shakespeare, or certain pieces attributed to Bach are actually by Bach. If it's good literature or music, who cares?

JA: Exactly. Society loves the idea of the mad artist, but I've never really believed that half the artists who are classified that way really are mad. There are rare cases where they are, but in the case of Hölderlin, there's substantial evidence that he wasn't. Basically he was tortured in a mental asylum. It was a terrible place. Hamburger relates it with such vividness it would make you cry. Dreadful treatment, absolute torture. After three years of that, he was discharged as an incurable case, meaning there was nothing further that they could do to him. We'd all be a gibbering wreck after that.

So the Hölderlin case arouses a lot of strong feelings. I never felt tempted, like Heinz Holliger, to set all those little poems that he wrote in those last years on the seasons. Holliger's cycle *Die Jahreszeiten* for chorus, from the mid-'70s, is based upon those. That later became absorbed into his much larger project for ensemble and chorus called the *Scardanelli Cycle*, which lasts nearly three hours. These poems are full of the most banal clichés about the seasons – this, by the way, directly relates to the final part of my concerto. As I understand from German readers and speakers, these poems are somewhere near a level of absolute poetic commonplaces. They were little presents for people, just to cheer them up.

Towards the end of his life, Hölderlin had become a tourist attraction: people in the literary world would turn up to see him – the mad poet in the tower, as it were. The trouble is that people said that sort of thing so much that he started playing the part, signing himself by another name, Scardanelli. He also misdated the poems in a deliberate attempt to distance himself from the whole thing. It may have been ironic: people forget that poets do have a sense of humour. One of them is dated 9 March 1940; another is dated 3 March 1648. That whole thing interested me, and I thought I'd like to see if I could do something about that, towards the end of *In lieblicher Bläue*.

The main part of the concerto is a personal reflection on images that came to me musically as a result of reading the prose poem. In particular, this business about blue, about which I subsequently wrote two more pieces: one of them the guitar piece, *Catalan Peasant with Guitar*, based on a blue painting by Miró; the other is *Van Gogh Blue*. I've always loved the colour blue.

CD: And you're wearing blue now.

JA: Yes! One of the reasons that there's a natural attraction to blue on the part of many painters, many poets and many creative people is, obviously, because it's the first colour you see in a clear sky. There's also the idea of the heavens being above, as it were, which is of course nonsense, but that's a basic human instinct. It also colours one's feelings. People get Seasonal Affective Disorder if they don't see a blue sky and enough sunlight. Sunlight and blue sky feature in a big way in the Hölderlin poem. It describes a bright-blue sky with sunlight shining on a church steeple. I let the image of the steeple, of the church bells, of the blueness, etc., all filter into the music.

CD: What do you mean by that?

JA: There's no such thing as a blue chord, technically, though there are such things as blue notes and they do feature in some of the melodic lines. There are one or two passages where the melodic line flirts towards a sort of blues-ish feeling. That comes back in the final melody of *Van Gogh Blue*, which is more specifically akin to a blues. That was one way I reflected the colour in the music. Another way is the purely subjective, attempting to make a sonority that to me evoked that kind of image, of a very bright-blue sky shining on a church steeple. There's a particular sound that comes back twice in the piece. It's sustained very quietly in the wind with a vibraphone tremolo in the middle and very mixed wind spacing. At the first performance, someone said this sounded almost electronic and thought that it must be a microtonal chord. That is not derived from spectral analysis of anything as such. It was derived, basically, by trying to work out a mid-register image of height, of space, of the sky. You instinctively don't associate that with the bass register. I also thought that it should be non-harmonic, because of the church steeple, meaning the bells. That sonority was arrived at purely empirically. That, for me, is a very blue, colourful moment in the piece.

The form of the Hölderlin poem is difficult to discern and I wanted my piece to be similarly in a rather odd shape. I didn't know the shape of the piece before I wrote it. As with *Alhambra Fantasy*, though for very different reasons, it was composed bar by bar, which made it exceptionally difficult to write. I didn't know that the end would be where it was. I knew that the relationship between the violin and the orchestra would keep changing, from simple melody on the violin with an orchestral backdrop, through dialogue with the orchestra, to open antagonism. In the middle of the piece, a point of maximum antagonism is reached. The second half is a long set of cantilenas for violin with the orchestra in a supportive role. They're simply collaborating. That remains the case until the final section where the violin soloist turns their back on the audience and from that point on only plays the most banal four-note phrases without vibrato. That's obviously a parallel with the Hölderlin banal poems about the seasons. The last thing you hear is an extremely high note on the violin. I thought of the soloist as being on a very high tightrope. The piece just fades on that.

People don't seem to understand that if you write something that is very beautiful – and I'm not saying that anything I have written is – you might not be doing it in ignorance of the world and its troubles, but in full awareness of it. Do you remember what Messiaen said to Paul Crossley in a TV interview? He said: 'Nous avons une monde qui est terrible, plein de choses horribles. Ma musique a un message d'espoir, ... d'espérance et de lumière.'[1] I'm not religious in that way, but I'm very concerned with spiritual matters. People don't seem to see that if you create something which deals with a kind of spiritual beauty, that you might be doing that because you think society does need that. If you make a stained glass, it's not necessarily because you don't know that outside the cathedral there is somebody who is starving from hunger. You can't perhaps solve the problems of the hungry starving person outside, but you may be able to illuminate, in every sense of the word, the spiritual life and psychological state of people who see your stained glass. That doesn't seem to me to be a bad activity. You might even be able to do both.

CD: I've just been reading a book of Terry Pratchett's non-novel writings. One of the themes that comes through is that he takes issue with being described as science fiction, with people saying it is just a form of escape. The point he makes is that you can escape to something, not just from something. And for him it's very much escaping to – to explore somewhere and not escaping from somewhere.

JA: That's fascinating. When people tend to get militant about the social function of art, there is this assumption that if it doesn't directly address the worst possible problems in society head-on, it is just escapism, socially irrelevant or elitist. I don't think that's true. Imagine Messiaen's situation in the war in the camp, or after the war with his first wife's terrible illness. It takes an act of considerable courage in those circumstances to go on to create beautiful, joyous pieces like

---

[1]   We have a terrible world, full of horrible things. My music has a message of hope... hope and light.

he did. Consider the mental and physical stamina needed – very tough. He was very determined.

CD: Getting back to the Violin Concerto, you said that you first tried to write some of this music, or you were reaching towards it, as a teenager. Presumably that wasn't as a violin concerto?

JA: It was.

CD: Oh really. It was a violin concerto in your teenage head?

JA: I can't explain why this was, but I always had the idea of this as a piece for violin and orchestra, based on the Hölderlin poem. No idea why.

CD: Curious.

JA: Specifically a very high violin, which it is a lot of the time in the final piece. If there had been such a thing as coloratura violin, in register, I would have said it was for that. It does use the G string much more in one or two passages, but a lot of it is very high. I did not know at that time (when I was 13) the Szymanowski First Concerto. Much later I heard Carolin Widmann play it before I wrote the work for her, so I knew she could do all those high things very well.

I suppose I thought of the violin as being, to some extent, the poet narrating, as it were, to the orchestra and the audience, but there was no idea of the violin turning their back on the audience at that stage. In the summer of 2014 I had the idea of sending the violin off stage for the start of the work. By that point, the equivalence of the solo violin to Hölderlin was clearer, and I wanted to have the violin not playing in the normal soloist's position on stage for a lot of the piece. The turning of their back on the audience only happened when I wrote that final passage. In performance it is quite unsettling.

CD: Hölderlin was an outsider and we've discussed several other outsiders. I can think of several ways in which you also might have felt yourself to be an outsider, such as not wanting to play football at school, that you had divorced parents at a time when that still carried a stigma, that you have a part-Jewish heritage, that you were in a school where some people's parents were not just well-off, but exceptionally wealthy and/or powerful. Then there's being gay as well. Either then or now, did you or do you ever consider yourself to be an outsider?

JA: The trouble with that is that it has a sort of romantic or novel-ish image or connotation, which I don't think is what you mean.

CD: Well, there is the notion that every life can be told as a series of successes or failures. Someone might look at you and see a figure who's had tremendous success, won various prizes, went to Westminster School, would appear to have had all sorts of advantages, appears to know everyone, etc., etc. Yet I can still see reasons why you might regard yourself, nonetheless, as an outsider.

JA: In fact, like most people I suspect, I did at times feel what you're saying – and some of my family also did.

My father felt he was an outsider because his medical research had put him on the outside of the accepted part of science, as regards commercial pressures. He was offered very substantial bribes by large companies to shut up. This left him with a permanent distrust of the pharmaceuticals industry and of commercial behaviour in connection with medical matters. The fact that he was, as I said before, excluded from the Swann Report Committee was something he felt very keenly.[2] A good friend of his was Élie Wollman, a very eminent microbiologist active in Paris after 1945, who'd been part of a research team which had eventually been awarded the Nobel Prize, but Élie Wollman hadn't – he'd been away in the US for a while.[3] His exclusion from that was something which both he and my father felt was wrong. I was around people who were very distinguished and very high-achieving, but were somehow at odds with what society expected them to be.

Now, when I discovered I was gay I already felt as though I was an outsider. I'd been made to feel that since I first went to boarding school really when I was eight, which was pretty tough. Although I had some good times there I certainly felt out on a limb for long periods. One result is my accent is sort of mixed up. Accents count for a lot in Britain, and in different ways. My parents were both from the north, my father from Newcastle, my mother from Lancashire. But both had a sort of RP-type accent. People tried to speak that way then, it was how you got on. That was the only accent I knew from my home in London.

CD: I was aware of such things myself. There were various points when I was a student where my perception, rightly or wrongly, was that people were presuming I went to public school. For some, this was their comfort zone, for others, there was an inverted snobbery. The point, though, was that it was all based on the fact that I had a reasonably well-spoken southern accent without much hint of the fact that I came from a working-class, east of London background.

JA: When I went to this tough northern prep school, everyone had a different accent from me and I was bullied for that. Within days I was out on a limb. That feeling didn't stop until well into my twenties, possibly even later, because as soon as I was recovering from all that school business, AIDS hit. There was a lot of sinister anti-gay talk in the 1980s by Tory politicians; it was the Thatcher

[2] See Conversation One, 'Origins'.
[3] The 1965 Nobel Prize in Medicine was jointly awarded to François Jacob, André Lwoff and Jacques Monod.

era and one recalls the whole tension of that. Tory politicians were talking about re-criminalising homosexuality, which had only been decriminalised the year I was born, so it wasn't even 20 years earlier. I don't know how close this ever got to being even motioned in the House of Commons, but there was other anti-gay legislation around then.

There was a lot of deep prejudice. I was intermittently politically active. I was on a few gay marches and protests. I felt very early on a big identification with many people who seemed to have been thrust out, for whatever reason – artists, poets, painters, conscientious objectors, Quakers, whoever. Not generally in my experience composers, funnily enough. Whenever I came across it in a composer I wasn't so convinced. For example, I once explored the music of Havergal Brian, who is regarded as an outsider. (His status as outside is itself questionable: his published writings show he was more personally in touch with the latest musical developments than many.) But I didn't find his music convincing.

CD: I know what you mean. He's full of interesting ideas, but I find myself wishing someone else was working with them.

JA: Quite. Ives is another outsider case of course, but if you look at his life, he was also an insider. He was terribly successful at business and was a Yale club man, he was in every society at Yale. He wasn't outside really. Musically, he was very individual, but pretty quickly, after he gave up the insurance and devoted himself full time to music, he found a way of getting himself well known. It took a long time for the full stature of the music to be recognised, that's true, but you couldn't really describe Ives as a true outsider. He was more successful during his lifetime than that.

I felt too that contemporary music was addressing me in an exciting way that a lot of other art wasn't. It turned out that this music was also outside the mainstream of society, to a large extent. That wasn't why I liked it. I just liked the sound it made and I enjoyed the music, but when you discover it's not what society expects music to be, you begin to wonder about that society.

In addition, being interested in spectral music, Sciarrino or Lachenmann in the early 1980s, at a time when very few people here were, to some extent put me out on a limb. The funny thing is I went to Darmstadt in 1988, where such things were in fashion, but I found the coteries there distasteful. When I went to study briefly with Murail in Paris for four months, I enjoyed his teaching but again I found the spectral clique generally somewhat concerning. I was much drawn to Gérard Grisey because he seemed personal and idiosyncratic. I also looked out Horațiu Rădulescu because almost every other composer warned me not to bother with him. He proved to be an interesting and cultivated person.

I've tried to retain an open attitude. Because I was gay, and it was illegal to be gay before the age of 21 in the 1980s, I was scared. At that age, that's a lot of years. They're very long years and I was very frightened. Then the AIDS thing came along. The months I spent in Paris in 1987 were much more liberating, but when I came back I was absolutely slam back in Thatcher's third term.

CD: And every sign at that point that she'd just go on and on!

JA: I didn't enjoy being in Britain at that time. I try not to pursue this line of thought too far because you can drive yourself very easily into a corner where you see yourself as the loner fighting against all the odds. 'Nobody understands me', and all that. I am certainly not saying that.

I've tried to remain generous to my colleagues. I don't always think it's a very generous profession at the moment because everyone is so desperate. Nevertheless, if I've put on concerts of other composers it's not in order to get my back scratched in return, but because I think their music is good. I put on a concert of Steve Martland, whose music is very different from mine, in the Philharmonia series. As soon as the next possible post, a postcard came saying, 'Thank you. I didn't expect this. Thanks for doing it. You're an exception in a profession that isn't always very generous.' So I wrote back to him saying, 'So are you.' Not all composers are so scrupulous in saying 'Thank you'.

CD: Did you feel a sense of isolation early on?

JA: Well, in the late 1980s one of the problems for me was I didn't like a lot of music that was being pushed in the UK. For example, the new Soviet music which was promoted very heavily then here, wasn't my cup of tea. I was sympathetic humanly, but I didn't like it. Schnittke and Gubaidulina just didn't appeal to me. I tried again and again and didn't get it. Whereas much of the new music that I did like was not being played here.

[Pause]

I do feel there is a class system in this country, and I dislike it. One sometimes sees decisions in the arts being made which reflect these unthinking habits and prejudices, and I'm strongly opposed to that. So I went about life in my own way and I worked very hard, and I continue to.

I do like teaching very much and the nice thing about teaching is I can forget all about myself, which is quite pleasant. It's very useful for a composer to be able to forget about themselves. I always take my model for this as Messiaen, when he said the joy of his class was that he left himself outside. I can't remember the exact phrase.

CD: He could take his coat off and put on that of the student.

JA: Well, as a teacher your job is to help. When I'm teaching, I'm just interested in helping that student do what they do better because that's what I'm being paid to do and I like doing it. My job is to see what the students need to know musically and to make sure they know the full range of what music can be, so that they can make choices. Otherwise you can't choose. But it's not my job to make the decision for them as to what they do next. My job, if I'm experienced enough, is to be able to guide them as to how to do it better, to help give them some sense of culture and of what musical techniques they need to know. As regards to what style they write in or what they try to do with it and so on – that's not my business.

In fact, it's very interesting for me precisely because they don't write the music I would write and I don't want them to. As I said a moment ago, I'm very proud of all my students, and have learnt a huge amount from them. Between teaching, where you can forget yourself for a long period, and then composing, which whatever anybody says has to be at least partly about yourself – though John Cage said it wasn't, yet even his music exudes a very strong sense of personality – between those two things, you can sort of assemble a life that's viable. The motor that drives the whole thing is the composing and if I can do that the way I want to do it, everything else seems to fall into place. When I can compose, I'm perhaps at my happiest.

CD: Is composing in itself inherently an isolationist activity?

JA: I don't think so. If you're writing music other people have to play it, or you have to play it to other people, so I would say the contrary. Inherently it's a communicative activity, even if it's very difficult to say what's being communicated or what the activity of communication is because it's non-verbal. If a person notates a musical score for orchestra, there are rather a lot of decisions that person has to make. It isn't really possible for that person to make those decisions with a lot of other people around. In that sense, what you're saying can be true – one has to be alone and focus on the music. It's very hard work.

Now, of course, for somebody like Scelsi, because he used collaborators, it was not an isolated activity – and maybe this is why he worked this way. He needed another brain to filter what he did and to help him tell himself what he'd done. He wrote some rather remarkable music in that peculiar way. Delius also, of course, used a collaborator because he was physically unable to write music any other way towards the end of his life. He managed, by sheer chance, to find somebody [Eric Fenby] who was able to sympathise with his mind to a remarkable degree.

In my case, there is no question that working alone for long hours helps focus the brain. I find that every note I write, every decision I take in the score, requires so many before and after and 'What ifs', and has so many consequences that, if

I'm not alone, I can't quieten the brain enough to make those decisions. I can't even really listen to what I'm doing. I would say composing is isolating only in the sense that to make the decisions that composing needs, if you're doing it in a Western notated form, involves a huge degree of concentration and therefore one has to be on one's own. But the activity is one of sharing with other people sounds or sequences of sounds that interest and excite you. That is communicative, not anti-social, as such. Even if the language in which you address them may not be one with which they're entirely familiar. May not be, I don't say 'isn't'. I don't wish to prejudge people.

CD: What I'm suggesting is it's a form of communication that involves being very solitary, or being solitary for long periods.

JA: Yes, it can do. That's also a very personal thing because some composers will not see people for weeks on end while they're doing it. As it happens, I'm not quite like that. For example, I'll spend a whole day composing if I can, but I'll then take the evening off and see friends. I need to do that in order to refresh my mind. There was a rather funny observation Robert Craft relates. W.H. Auden said of the composer and impresario Nicolas Nabokov that he'll never be a great composer because he cannot bear to be on his own enough. I think I can.

On the other hand, I'm quite sociable. I don't exist within a plastic bubble of isolation. I like to make sure that there's some part of each week where I do see friends and I'm not feeling hived off from the rest of life.

When I'm writing music, I'd hope people will enjoy it since I find it exciting myself. If I don't find the music exciting, I shouldn't let it out. It follows that even if when you hear the work you're not fully satisfied – and what sane composer would be? – you must nevertheless hope each time you're writing music that the piece will be good. Otherwise why bother? Inevitably, when pieces are played you then realise that you haven't done what you'd hoped. If you've any sanity you realise that and you try to learn from your mistakes.

Xenakis and Françoise Xenakis were very close to Varèse in the 1950s. When the first performance of *Déserts* happened in 1954, there was a famous riot: it's been released on CD, you can hear it all.[4] Xenakis was at home recording the broadcast live, which, by the way, was the first stereo broadcast of the ORTF. Varèse came round the following day: Xenakis and Françoise Xenakis were very shocked by what then happened. Varèse asked to hear the tape of the broadcast and he broke down in tears. Varèse, of all people, who was always talking about roughing the audience up a bit and startling people. But Varèse hadn't been able to finish music for 15 years before *Déserts*. Françoise Xenakis, who's a novelist, said the final refusal of the public to accept what he'd passionately created for

---

[4] On *Archives Hermann Scherchen (de Purcell a Varèse)*, Tahra TAH 599–600.

them broke him. One more big refusal like that – because he was no longer 31 or 28, he was 71 – after a lifetime of that, he couldn't face it again.

In other words, whatever the composer says, they do give a damn what people think. If it could break Edgar Varèse it can certainly break lesser people. A friend of mine had a piece played abroad a few years ago and it caused a real uproar – and this composer has no history of causing such uproars. I took the line of saying 'Oh, you should be flattered. That's marvellous, you've got your first riot. Terrific.' The composer kind of giggled, but it had clearly been a shock. Being yelled at by a whole hall of people is not funny. We know that Stravinsky was still so angry about *The Rite of Spring* riot in his 80s that he wrote a little inscription at the end of the manuscript saying basically, 'I hope nobody ever has to experience what I had to experience that evening ever again.'[5] Now, why at the age of 86 would it even bother him, the world's most famous composer? But it still did.

So I stick to my thesis that a composer writing music is basically trying to be generous. You're trying to get people interested, to give them something worthwhile. You are sending a message out of some sort. If people refuse to hear it, that's very hurtful and that's why some composers give up.

CD: Whenever I've been involved in organising events or concert series, I never try to second-guess what the audience would like. I put on things I'd be interested in and then I'm guaranteed of at least one person in the audience.

JA: I feel the same way about my music. If I don't like it there's no chance anyone else will. I agree also that you have to believe when you put on a concert that you would like to sit down and hear it. A concert should be a bit like a dinner in the sense that you have to experience it in time, from beginning to end. You should believe, as the person organising it, that something positive and worth experiencing will come out of your chosen sequence of pieces. I relate that to composing. You have to believe that somebody else is going to want to hear what you're writing, so I don't fundamentally feel composing's an isolated act. It requires isolation to get it physically done, but it is not an isolationist activity. It's essentially a generous act. I'm quite sure that Messiaen must have wondered, later on in life, whether or not the eight or nine years he spent bent over the full score of *Saint François* had or hadn't been worthwhile. They definitely had!

CD: Yes. There was a danger of him ending up a bit like Berlioz towards the end of his life, worried about *Trojans* and quite despondent. We would have liked him to live as long as Carter, but it's fortunate that Messiaen lived just long enough

---

[5] A facsimile of the final page is reproduced in Vera Stravinsky and Robert Craft, *Stravinsky in Pictures and Documents* (New York: Simon & Schuster, 1978), p. 76.

to see *Saint François* at the Festival Hall and also to get his confidence back and be in full flight again. Also, to see that the opera was getting a full production at Salzburg.

JA: On the one hand, one thinks of Messiaen's incredibly successful life, but you've scratched below the surface, as have Peter Hill and other people, and there's quite a substantial portion of that life that I would not have wanted to experience at all. In comparison, mine seems pretty innocent. For a start, I've never had to live through a World War.

CD: Yes, touch wood.

JA: Good point!

CD: When I asked Alexander Goehr about his time in Paris, he spoke about how he went to Messiaen and he also tried to go to Max Deutsch, and Max Deutsch said, 'If you're with Messiaen, you can't be with me. You have to choose, it's one or the other.' I wonder whether Goehr's open-mindedness was partly a result of that experience. He was aware of just how damaging shutting off avenues could be.

JA: You're right. He was and is. Not only because of that, but because when he'd studied with Messiaen he'd also taken informal lessons with Pierre Boulez. In the first years after he left Paris he was still writing in an idiom that was more or less acceptable to the Domaine musical and Boulez played the music quite regularly. Then Sandy wrote the *Little Symphony*, which is in quite a different style, much more like what we now think of as mature Alexander Goehr, but very much not on the agenda stylistically of the Domaine musical. He found himself dropped by Boulez and others. (To be fair, in the 1970s Boulez conducted Goehr again at the BBC and elsewhere.) I think that experience also made him alert to such embargoes and to what exclusion could be like, in practice, for a young composer. I always found Goehr very sympathetic on that score. When I was telling him that I'd found it very difficult to know how to respond to the strict techniques of the spectral school – which he asked me to tell him about – he used his own life experience in Paris in the late 1950s and the early '60s to help me. I understood that I might end up writing music that wouldn't be acceptable to the Paris crowd, and that I should be perfectly happy about that. He knew about Parisian musical politics.

I'd run into later forms of Parisian musical politics. In my case, it was the spectralists versus the serialists, and both of them versus the minimalists, and everyone hated Cage. And that was about it, really. This isn't just a casual fight. In practice, it's often about funding. One of the first things the spectral ensemble L'Itinéraire had to do when Boulez arrived back from America to found IRCAM was to fight it. Boulez had apparently convinced the Ministry of Culture that if they founded the Ensemble InterContemporain for him, there wasn't a need for any other new-music group in Paris. This was going to make life very difficult for Itinéraire, for Musique Vivante, for Musique Plus, Ars Nova – there was a lot of other new music in Paris, but Boulez didn't really count all of that, because he'd been away for a decade. So the struggle is often a very practical one in musical politics, it's not just theory. Nevertheless, the sides were very clearly drawn in Paris and you couldn't belong to the Boulez clique while belonging to the spectral clique. Since I was clearly interested in spectralism I used to feel guilty about the fact that I regularly went to the lectures of Boulez at the Collège de France, which I followed assiduously during the same period, but I didn't tell most spectral composers that. I remember once I mentioned to a young spectralist that I was attending the Boulez lectures. He said, 'What do you want to attend that for?' That was the attitude.

Sandy Goehr would listen to what I told him about these factions and he helped me understand that this was just nonsense. A really musical person does not proceed according to such agendas, but uses their ears, their instinct, their technique and culture, and follows those. This helped me put what I experienced in Darmstadt and Paris into perspective.

I was terribly lucky that my two principal composition teachers, Lambert and Goehr, were idiosyncratic figures who were independent, open, remote from stylistic prejudices and lively: really the best people to study with. They both encouraged me to discover, and to bring discoveries to them. They wanted to know what I'd found out. That's remained a very big inspiration. When I'm teaching, I encourage my students to do the same thing, because I want to know what's going on and I try and keep myself well informed. They're often interested in music I know nothing about, so that helps me understand them better, but it also helps me understand more of what's going around in the music world. Goehr and Lambert were fabulous teachers.

Since I was being taught at a very high level by people who weren't dogmatic, this may explain why one of my pieces is riddled with quarter-tones but the next piece I wrote has none at all – and yet they're the same music [Second String Quartet and Violin Concerto]. I don't regard the surface of the piece as being the only medium to define what the piece is or what you're saying in it, whereas there are other composers who cannot exclude writing microtones ever, because it's almost like a political belief for them.

CD: And there are composers who would never dream of writing microtones.

JA: There is no 'have' or 'have not'. It's like a filter – or a change of aperture, if you will. Some pieces will need a certain kind of filter to express what they've got to say and others will need a different one. That can mean, in some cases, using no extended techniques and no microtones or whatever. In another case, it can mean using a lot of both possibly, but not for reasons of being in step with this or that fashion.

CD: Would you say that centring works like *Khorovod* and *Diptych* on the pitch C and the pitches a tone either side was a deliberate embrace of something that is so fundamental yet had been loudly shunned by quite a few people?

JA: Yes. It was very refreshing to deal with it. There was a symposium on tonality at the Darmstadt summer school in 1984, for three or four days – I didn't attend it, but I saw the reports on it – but it was the fact that Darmstadt mounted a symposium on tonality and people were like, 'What? Why would you discuss that there?'

The Darmstadt I went to was already a bit more closed than that. These days, you wouldn't even have such a symposium. It's interesting, the way these swings go. But in the 1980s, Friedrich Hommel, who ran Darmstadt, kept it more open. For instance, they had Clarence Barlow talking about the use of probability. I bought his treatise on his piano piece *Çoğluotobüsişletmesi*, which includes examples of what happened when he tried to get a computer to write tonally. He tried to reconstruct the rules of tonality via probability and things. He would take a pitch and say, 'What happens if I want maximum predictability?' Well, the computer will say, 'Just repeat the pitch', you see.

To some extent, that's like the opening of *Khorovod*. If I want everyone to hear the C, I'd better repeat it a long time. [Laughter] Then, the next notes are B-flat and D. I'm measuring the rate at which I introduce those. The other paradox, though, being that that whole opening is also based on a Lithuanian folk tune... But the idea of getting a computer, of all things, to simulate tonality intrigued me. That's taking tonality as if it had just landed from Mars, and seeing what we can make of it. Or rather, taking the basis of tonality, the questions of consonance and stress and predictability, and re-examining those afresh. Those are perfectly interesting things to work with and I don't see any reason why Western tonality has to be the only way to use them, and why we shouldn't use them.

CD: My Conservatoire colleague, Michael Wolters, writes music which is conceptually out there, but tonally is often very straightforward, in some respects.

JA: Those two things often go together. It's the same thing with Chris Newman – very strange conceptually, but with almost Satie-like material.

CD: Often based upon found musical materials in Michael's case.

JA: Kurt Schwertsik caused a big scandal in Darmstadt in '62 by cutting up bits of Liszt's *Liebesträume*, à la William Burroughs, and putting them together into a new piece. There was a huge riot. By the late 1980s, tonality – or at least consonance – was being used, but I didn't feel that what the minimalists were doing with it was what I was trying to do. Many other people weren't using it, so yes, it felt fresh at the time. Whether it really was as fresh as I thought it was I've no idea, but it felt as though I was using material that I had been told not to and that was fun, no question. I still occasionally feel that frisson.

CD: And people now may not realise now that those early pieces of yours were provocative in their use of musical materials that others rejected or sneered at.

JA: All the pieces that came out in about 1993–95 were all being worked on from about 1988. I was trying to sort out my technique. Therefore, the pieces were not immediately completed, or if they were, they were then immediately revised in the light of other things. And as we've said before, they were centred around C. There's something basic about C.

CD: I can still remember my first piano piece from *Jibbidy F*: 'I am C, middle C, left hand, right hand, middle C.'

JA: Well, it's right in the middle of the keyboard. All these pieces were to do with centring the harmony, centring the modality, finding a centre to everything from which you can fly off in many different directions. It was this centrifugal technique I was trying to find. Therefore, I needed to know where home was, musically. There had to be a home, even if it didn't occur at the start of the piece. *Khorovod* is quite blatant. The note C starts the piece, it occurs many times, and it ends the piece too. But the *Diptych* does not start with octave Cs. They occur about three minutes in for the first time, and they're quite a surprise when they do occur. They're not implied, they appear out of the blue. Then they gradually gain prominence until the end of the whole piece.

Each piece approached this material very differently, but the material was essentially based on just the simple low overtones of B-flat, C and D, in equal temperament. Another change in the late 1980s was getting rid of the quarter-tones, which was a very difficult decision to take, because I felt that that was one of the freshest things about the spectralists. But I just began to feel I was stuck in a kind of spectral jelly. I couldn't move freely in that, so the first thing I did was to get rid of all the quarter-tones, so I could move about freely. The next thing I did, which I've already mentioned elsewhere, was to write a list of all the adjectives to describe my music of the last few years.

CD: A similar thing to what you later did with *Thebans*,[6] though that was listing what you didn't do.

6   Discussed in Conversation Thirteen, 'Opera'.

JA: On this occasion, the list consisted of things such as slow change, rich harmonies, long sustained tones, etc. Then I wrote down a list of all the opposites. I thought it would be interesting to try to write that type of music, just to see what would happen if I threw the whole thing away and started without that spectral security blanket. That was the opening of *Diptych*, which is all short notes and all very fast, and all high, and doesn't have any bass, and no sustain at all, and has no chords. Anyhow, when I did all that, I suddenly realised that I couldn't show this to my Paris friends because they wouldn't understand. So I worked it out for myself, which is more fun and is what composing is all about.

Quartets

Even a few years ago, nobody would have associated Anderson with the string quartet. With the youthful *Light Music* finally being performed in 2013 and two further string quartets under his belt, the genre is now a firm part of his catalogue. This conversation provides a detailed look at the Second and Third Quartets and, reflecting the nature of the genre, some of what follows gets quite technical, though there is also much that isn't. It starts with Anderson's treatment of his source material in the Second Quartet, before moving on to the treatment of pitch and rhythm, and the way the genre puts a lens on technique. The Third Quartet prompts reflection on how pieces open, before giving specific observations on each movement. Among myriad other things, Anderson reveals the harmonic framework of the Quartet, enthuses about an important new harmony for his music and explains how the extraordinary conclusion to the work is created.

— ◆ —

CD: Having spent several years on *Thebans*, which was your largest work in every respect, you turned immediately to the intimacy of writing a string quartet, a medium you hadn't touched since your teenage years. Why did you make that move?

JA: I was going from 40 staves per page to four, which was enormous fun. My first quartet, *Light Music*, had been premiered finally in 2013, at the Aldeburgh Festival by the Arditti.[1] Because of that, I really felt the string quartet, as a medium, had suddenly begun to unfreeze for me, psychologically. As soon as I heard the Arditti rehearsing *Light Music*, I knew what I wanted to write. The project of working with

---

[1] 15 June 2013, Aldeburgh Church.

the large collections of Renaissance German Christmas carols, *Weihnachtslieder*, went back a long time. I didn't know it would be a quartet, I just wanted to do something with all this. Some of them are still sung as carols here. 'Wie schön leuchtet der Morgenstern', 'In dulci jubilo' and things like that are well known in Britain and America, everywhere. I came across many others that are equally lovely. I studied a lot of them and made a big pitch reservoir from them. I wanted to do a piece that would explore some kind of intonation issues. Having heard that the First Quartet did actually work, I thought it was time to follow some of that up. This was not going to be a string quartet belonging to the 'great quartet tradition', and I had to signal that somehow or other. If you call a piece *Light Music* that signals it, so I needed to have some way of signalling it for the Second, because I didn't want to have that baggage hanging over me. Then, somebody asked me, what the piece was going to be called and I said, because I'd been looking at them, 'Oh, it's called Three Hundred Christmas Carols.' And I said it had better be in German, because they're German Christmas Carols: *Dreihundert Weihnachtslieder*. They said that was a very strange title for a quartet: 'What on earth can a quartet with that title be like?' That was exactly the reaction I needed. [Laughter] I knew then I was outside the tradition and I could get on with it.

CD: Nonetheless, did you have any earlier string quartets in mind, alongside the material from the carols?

JA: Apart from the German carols, Haydn's Op. 33 No. 1 (one of his strangest pieces), Stravinsky's *Three Pieces for String Quartet* – each of which not only sounds like it's not for string quartet, but for a different combination than the previous piece, and almost by a different composer – and the Ruth Crawford Seeger Quartet, which is an incredible masterpiece. That was it, really.

CD: So what did you do with the carols?

JA: It was related to the psycho-acoustic thing that I'd been exploring for a long time. Do we perceive melody as notes, intervals that is, or as a contour? It could be either. Psycho-acousticians say there are these two ways you can perceive melodically. Contour is the one I was using in this case, and it's the one I've used a lot.

CD: Why is that?

JA: Because that's like dealing with the plainchant neumes. Contours don't say what the intervals are, they just say to go up or down. They're archetypal shapes, melodic codes if you will, but they can be stretched or compressed to any size. 'Go up one' could be up one octave or any other interval. If your mode has an octave gap at that point, that's what it would be. You can still write a two-note neume, the same shape, whether it's going up one small interval or a very large one. In plainchant it looks like the same neume, it's just stretched. I've loved working with that for many years.

317

CD: So how do you apply that to the carols?

JA: I wrote lots of these Christmas carols out. I took the rhythm out straight away and I reduced them to contours. Then I took the clefs away and just saw whether it was going up, down, how far, etc., then applied those to all kinds of modes, which are mainly modes from my macrotonal tuning system. It's superimposed bits of overtone series from harmonic 6 to harmonic 16, approximated to the nearest quarter-tone. That's what I was working with for that piece, so that I could have the tunes in their original modes that they come in, or they could go into one of these hybrid macrotonal modes, which involve very irregular intervals and non-tempered pitches. The tunes change size and shape all kinds of ways, intervals, tuning, everything.

That didn't quite provide enough variety, so I got recordings of German bells from the right period. There aren't a huge number of church bells in Germany surviving from that period. In fact, Cologne Cathedral did survive and I used the great tenor bell, called Dicker Pitter. That had already featured as one of the bigger chords, just momentarily, in the first movement of *The Discovery of Heaven* and I wanted to use it again (I used it for the last time in *In lieblicher Bläue*). I made modes out of those spectra, sampling them at different points of their resonance and then making pitch collections out of those to the nearest quarter-tone, and I filtered my carols through some of those as well.

Then with regards to the rhythm, the thing that interested me in the original collections printed in the Renaissance is that the rhythm isn't anything like when you get 'Wie schön leuchtet der Morgenstern' in Bach. It's quite irregular. The same thing is true of many of them, they don't have a regular metre at all. They're in additive rhythm, free combinations of ones, and twos, and threes. Lovely. More like a dance, or even Messiaen-type rhythm. That's the kind of rhythm I based mine on.

CD: So what exactly did you do?

JA: I'd apply the rhythm of one to the tune of the other and that kind of thing, so they'd end up bouncing about. I decided to write a suite with many movements so it couldn't be mistaken for a normal quartet. Having said that, I ended up with seven movements, and we all know there is a famous Beethoven quartet in seven movements, but that's a very different kind of thing, and I wasn't thinking of that.

CD: Can I just stop you there? In one of our earlier conversations, you were talking about Messiaen's separation of rhythm, and you said you didn't do that, that you'd become suspicious of it.[2]

---

[2]   See Conversation Six, 'Composing (or not)'.

JA: Yes, and I did in this piece. When did we have that conversation?

CD: It was one of the earliest.

JA: It was just before I wrote the Second Quartet, you see? I was very influenced by an interview I read with the painter Patrick Heron, some of whose work I like very much. He gave an interview sometime in the '60s in which he said, 'I never draw on my canvases.' Then he immediately began to do just that. I'm a bit like that. If I say to somebody, 'I don't do this, I would never do that', at some point soon after I'll think, 'Why don't I? Let's see what happens.' The separation of pitch and rhythm in the Second Quartet was almost certainly, now I think of it, because I told you I didn't do that, so I thought this time I would. If you hadn't reminded me, I wouldn't have remembered that. The reason not to separate pitch from rhythm is because if you're interested in forms that progress and transform through time – and goal orientation interests me a lot – you can easily end up with no goal if you separate pitch and rhythm from each other. You're going to end up with circularity, de-phased *ostinati* and all kinds of patterns that are fascinating, but they're non-directional. I previously felt I couldn't use that. But then suddenly in this piece, I found I could.

CD: Which, again, is yet another way in which it's remarkable how the hell Messiaen manages to make it work.

JA: He does. The fourth movement of *Turangalîla* does go somewhere, the fifth movement also and that's full of that kind of malarkey, even more so. It's remarkable. How does a non-teleological technique lead to such a strong sense, to my ear and yours I suspect too, of real goal direction?

CD: Yes, there are some pieces, like the first movement of the Quartet, which just stop – *Chronochromie* or the sixth movement of *La Transfiguration*, where he just opens and closes a door on another world.

JA: Whereas the chorale movement of *La Transfiguration*, the very next one, is a progression from the first chord to the last, no question, and long-term, not just chord by chord either. It's magnificently done. I like the idea of having your cake and eating it, and Messiaen's a classic case of that. People say it's not consistent. So what? My Second Quartet is also about having your cake and eating it. It should theoretically be static, but every movement does usually go somewhere, or there's a dialogue between directional and non-directional. The opening of the third movement, which has fast whirly-gig *ostinati*, would appear just to be going round and round, but I made the *ostinati* progress, change and so on. The other thing was to try to find extended techniques that were not borrowed from Helmut Lachenmann, whose music I like far too much to want to imitate. I discovered by accident, though I know I'm not the first person to use it, that you can bow a string instrument with a pencil. I was looking for a sound world that could be very fragile. The pencil provided the key for me as it can stroke, bounce or have a rhythmic tap, and you hear the pitch much better than you do with *col legno*. With *col legno* you hear a tap with very little pitch, but with a pencil you hear mostly pitch yet with a tapping sound. And if you do a bouncing pencil, it can sound like cicadas, or crickets, or something.

The third movement was also inspired by a wonderful device they used to have on Renaissance and Baroque organs, the Zimbelstern.

CD: Is that the rotating star thing with little bells?

JA: Exactly. It looks very pretty. I took recordings off the net of Zimbelstern, slowed them down, analysed them, and came up with some of the rhythms of the third movement. That's basically a Zimbelstern on string quartet. [Laughter] In mainland Europe, when you ring bells, you don't change-ring, generally, you just ring the bells in any order.

CD: Yes, the bells are constructed differently to British bells.

JA: I listened to some of those and that gave me some rhythmic patterns which are periodic, but irregularly so and in different phases. That was very suggestive for the rhythmic language of the whole Quartet. That was the mix of it. Basically, the piece goes through something like 10 tunes per movement, but it's very free.

CD: So is it actually closer to about 70 Christmas carols?

JA: Yes, something like 70 to 80 Christmas carols. I get through more of them in some of the faster passages, and with some I just strung lots of pitches together and put them on any mode I wanted. Frankly, if you're working that way somebody, cynically, will say that the source material could be anything. Of course, the answer is that it could be, but it wasn't. [Laughter] The fact that I used these old Christmas carols did influence my composing, simply that.

CD: In other words, you're not expecting the listener to hear the carols, like a sophisticated game of *Name that Tune*...

JA: I don't believe that the listener would hear anything, unless they were really trying, more than the faintest fragment of Christmas carol tune. You might notice that the viola at one point quite early on plays 'Wie schön leuchtet der Morgenstern', but there are other things going on at the same time and it's in spectral tuning with a quarter-tone and so on. Eventually, the same tune comes back just about 10 seconds into the last movement, but it's played in a hocket as a mixture of cello harmonics and viola bouncing a pencil. Again, the timbres are not exactly going to encourage you to hear it as a tune, even though it is in the original rhythm and mostly the original pitch. But there are plenty of other things going on, brush-bowing and so forth. The moods of the movements were influenced by the texts also. The overall title is a clue-giving device, a little bit like a murder mystery: this is clearly not a normal quartet.

CD: Do not adjust your sets!

JA: Also, the players keep retuning their instruments. The viola retunes quite radically and the cello retunes by a major second for the last five movements. There are all kinds of quarter-tone retunings. So it's full of colour contrasts, mood contrasts, and it has melodic shapes that might ring the odd bell, literally, as it happens. You're offered this little labyrinth to play with as a listener.

I never thought there was any point – and here I differ with the spectralists and certainly with early minimalism, even though I enjoy that music – in wanting people to hear how I wrote a piece of music when they listen to it. What could be more boring than to hear, when you're listening to a piece of music, the composer telling you, 'You see, I did this, now I did that, now I did it this way'? It's so tedious. It's my job to write the piece the way I want to write it, and if it doesn't sound good, I've not done my job right, simple as that. In some of the early, more demonstrative, minimalist and spectralist pieces, you can hear quite a lot of how they were composed, but that's only good for a certain period. You sometimes need to refresh art, like Bridget Riley did in the visual domain, where if you look at a shape overlaid in a moiré pattern, it makes your eyes flicker. It can be exciting, but you know it's only going to go so far.

CD: The technique is not the endpoint for you.

JA: Not at all. The Quartet is meant to be aurally as diverse and varied as possible, as the Stravinsky *Three Pieces* are. I was trying to ape the Stravinsky in terms of variety of sound, so that each movement would sound like a different ensemble. At the same time, I tried to make the piece cadence at the end. I have a proper end for once. It is one of my few endings that does actually cadence. It tries to cadence into a kind of B-flat major, except they're brush-bowing the wrong way, so there's a lot of bow noise.

CD: It seems that with a string quartet you feel you can give the players a real workout in terms of techniques.

JA: There's certainly scope for that. There's something called 'decoupling', which has become very much the done thing among young composers of a certain sort. This means that you notate on separate musical staves the bowing action, the right-hand and left-hand actions, and pitch as well. This type of notation occurs in the sixth movement.

CD: The equivalent of what Berio did with the recorder piece *Gesti*.

JA: Did he? I never saw that score, but you find it in pieces by James Dillon, and many younger composers also. Funnily enough, the only movement that's entirely in normal tuning is this same sixth movement, which is hyperactive and mostly based on bell resonances. It's entirely in normal tuning, but it's rhythmically very jagged. I was using those clashing bell rhythms from German and Swiss bell-ringing. Eventually, the notes started getting longer and longer, and at the end of the movement everything gets very stretched out. As that happens, there's more chance to experiment with changing bow position, and changing intonation, and changing bow pressure. I began having to write three or four lines of instructions above the normal stave, and so, for the next two pages, you have pitch on one line, bowing pressure on one line, bowing position on another line. It was the easiest way of writing out what I was trying to hear.

By the way, on the last page of the sixth movement there's one of the few instances in my music of a real microtone producing acoustic beats. I usually avoid beats but there, on the viola, for a bar-and-a-half, you have a very loud A and A quarter sharp at the same octave, beating away, gradually going into unison. When it reaches unison, that was a nice way of cadencing. The piece ends with a very long, sustained version of the chord that began the same movement. Then it was just a question of winding the whole Quartet down in a final movement with all these little bits of Christmas carols again, and brush-bowing.

In several places there are allusions to the Ruth Crawford Seeger Quartet. It has this third movement made of sustained notes with pulses, crescendos that go in and out of phase. It's an unbelievable sound for 1930 – it sounds like dephased tape loops. I alluded to that sound in a few places as a little homage to that composer. I really love Ruth Crawford Seeger's music. She was a great composer, and it's tragic she didn't write more. I'm happy to say that my Second Quartet has now been played in the same concert as the Crawford Seeger, but for the premiere it was the Scelsi Fourth Quartet, of which I'm also very fond.

CD: You wrote the Second Quartet very fast, and it sounds like you were enjoying yourself.

JA: It was enormous fun to write, one of the happiest composing times of my life. It was very complicated and intricate to plan, but somehow it just fell into place. After three and a half years of opera, to write a piece lasting about 26 minutes in six weeks was a big surprise. I've never known anything like that. All the time I was thinking of having fun with the Arditti over this, and the rehearsals have always been a lot of fun. After all, I'd been trying to write a new quartet for the Arditti since 1995. That's nearly 20 years. Also, every composer warned me to watch myself when I finished the opera as, after three or four years' work, everyone has a massive depression. So I scheduled the quartet for the few weeks right after I finished the opera. The Arditti, bless them, premiered it bloody well, and did it many times since.

CD: Moving on to the Third String Quartet, on first hearing it struck me as having a certain kinship in sensibility, rather than the minutiae of technique, with Act III of *Thebans*. I'm simply talking about it having something of the same acoustic arc, starting from little noises almost, what could be scrabbling critters, to an end in what seemed to me to be a blazing, not necessarily comfortable, radiant brightness.

JA: There may be some kind of archetypal shape that this in some way enshrines. I certainly wasn't aware of consciously relating it to *Thebans*. That's completely new to me as an idea. I tend to feel, which doesn't mean I'm right, that my music's changed a huge amount since *Thebans* and, in a way, polarised into apparently opposite directions, though in truth they're the same direction with different manifestations of technical problems.

CD: Let me just clarify. I'm not suggesting it's directly related to *Thebans*, but perhaps *Thebans* opened the door to some of it.

JA: You may well be correct, but I hadn't considered that. What you may have touched on is an archetypal musical shape. Openings of pieces are very important. Grisey said to me that when he started sitting on composition juries, he'd quite often find a striking opening, but that by seven pages or 10 pages in, it wasn't anything like so interesting. The level of maintenance, let's say, through the piece was often very uneven. One of the distinguishing features that I look for in a new score is to see invention on a consistent level throughout the work rather than just an arresting initial sound, because really anyone can think of an arresting initial sound. It takes a certain amount of imagination and musicality, obviously, but if you don't have any notion of the continuity an opening could give rise to, it seems to me that the piece will fail.

CD: Do you have any strategies for avoiding a piece simply drooping in interest after its opening?

JA: The problem of opening a work nowadays is that people want to strike the listener right away with something very startling. If you do that, the likelihood is that you won't be able to follow it up: you don't give yourself much room for manoeuvre. When one thinks of openings of the past, two really superb ones that occur to me are 'The Drumroll' Symphony of Haydn and the Tchaikovsky Fourth. In the case of the Tchaikovsky, it introduces ideas that go through much of the work. In the case of Haydn, the introduction recurs through the movement and turns up much faster as a link theme at the end of the exposition. Both introductions are like little keys to the music, but one's not sure what their meaning really is when they first occur. They're both, in different ways, somewhat oblique ways of opening the symphonies concerned. The opening of *The Rite of Spring* is equally odd. It doesn't set the tone of most of the piece, if you think about it. Whereas the opening of *L'Après-midi*, on which it is rather obviously modelled, does set the tone for that piece. That's a surprising opening in itself, but if you consider the piece as a whole, it's the way you'd open that piece. Whereas if you consider *The Rite of Spring* as a whole, the last thing you'd do is open that piece that way.

So I think a lot about this kind of problem, and I've noticed over the years that my openings tend not to be assertive. The opening of the Third Quartet is definitely an example of that. Now in opposition to that, there are certain kinds of opening which are deliberately without any preamble at all – *Khorovod* opens with all cylinders blasting. With the opening of the Third Quartet, I was intent on not revealing everything.

CD: Once the movement builds up, it becomes apparent you've got these various irrational rhythms all playing against each other. Now I'm not suggesting it's mechanical in this way or any sonic resemblance, but it's a little bit like one of the Steve Reich pieces in that we gradually get a sense of the rhythm of the whole, whereas you could not get it from the opening.

JA: That's right. One of the sketches of the opening says 'As if blown in the wind'. What I was trying to do was to create a musical wind chime, as if the wind were blowing on those notes and they shake, and then it blows them some more. When I was in America in the late 1990s with the cellist Fred Sherry, he had a marvellous wind-chime set which was tuned in the overtones of the harmonic series from something like 6 to 12, in Just intonation. Really beautiful. With this opening movement of the Third Quartet I felt it would be nice to have a set of wind chimes that kept changing pitch.

CD: You could suspend the quartet by ropes from the ceiling, on little platforms, gently swaying while they play. [Laughter]

JA: I don't think even the infinitely patient JACK Quartet, for whom this piece was written, would tolerate that!

The degree to which metre is perceived in the whole work, or not, was thought through very carefully. In the first movement, the silences accentuate the lack of co-ordinated pulse to the ear. It would have been possible to write this movement out rather like Lutosławski notation, so that each of what Lutosławski would call a 'bundle of notes' could have been written without bar lines, with cues as to where you start, a scatter effect, which he does in his String Quartet. I've always had slight unease about this, although he's a very great composer and I adore his music. At the time when he first thought of it, it was very fresh for him and released all kinds of creative possibilities. The problem is that it is not possible in those circumstances for the composer to create in detail within such an *ad libitum* 'bundle'. A composer can compose, that's to say, what anyone is playing, but they can't control the details of what happens in a part relative to any other, since everyone's playing *ad libitum*. In my experience, there is usually one precise sequence of pitches that's creatively better than others. It's my job to find it.

CD: There's also a danger with that kind of aleatoric notation that you get the 'wobbly bridge' problem, which is that people may start walking separately but quite rapidly get pushed into step with each other.

JA: I think of that as the 'metronome experiment', but we're talking about the same thing.[3]

CD: I'm talking about the Millennium Bridge, which started wobbling because they hadn't realised that as soon as it wobbled slightly, everyone would start to fall into step with each other and it amplifies. When that happened with the Millennium Bridge, various people pointed out that what they used to do when a bridge was built was get the military to walk over it to test it.

JA: It's interesting that these old techniques are very soundly based. I didn't know that. There is a very good moment which does this in *Pithoprakta* by Xenakis, a piece I've always adored. It's the densest passage of the piece, around two-thirds of the way through. It deliberately combines the different playing techniques used in the piece all at once. Two trombones suddenly enter to produce very low *glissandi*. At that point, the entire orchestra suddenly goes first onto *col legno* technique, and then gradually to pizzicato. When they go over to pizzicato, Xenakis has many different speeds of pizzicato so that you get clouds of sound. He gradually eliminates anyone who isn't playing a quintuplet quaver: the texture goes from being the most chaotic in the piece to being the most ordered – everyone at the end is playing the same pulse. It's a brilliant moment.

In the case of the opening movement of my Third Quartet, it traces a path from hesitation to continuity. It is a little like what Steve Sondheim said he was trying to say at the start of *Sweeney Todd*, which was, 'I'll tell you a story.' In other words, gradually you're led into the piece. Such pieces, incidentally, are dangerous because there are many people in the trade of new music who have a very short patience span. Many people like to know immediately that they've heard something and what that is. But without in any way trying to sacrifice a quality of distinctiveness, an opening needn't always put all the cards on the table.

---

[3] This involves a large number of metronomes sat on a wobbly surface, all set to the same speed but started completely out of synch. Over time, they automatically synchronise. Search for 'Metronome Experiment' in YouTube to see this.

CD: So, you don't reveal your hand too early, but is there a particular game that you're playing?

JA: The whole Quartet was to do with tonality. I wanted to focus on exploring whether or not there is a way of establishing clarity of key centre, or pitch centre, in a piece that isn't just a reproduction of standard tonality. In other words, can that be a model without being literally mimicked? Can the benefits of what tonality can do for a musical syntax be discovered in other ways? That seems to me a very interesting problem and in a sense it's what I've worked on all my life. For this particular piece, it became a complete obsession.

CD: Can you give some indication of what you mean by that?

JA: In the first movement, the pitch B-flat is meant to be very important, but, even though the first pitch you hear is B-flat, there's no way at the opening to know that it's any more important than any of the other two or three pitches that are floating around. That's deliberate. I want to drop a hint that it might be important, but not immediately declare it. Gradually as the movement progresses, there are more hints, until we get to the last bars where, very clearly it seems to me, B-flat is the tonic of the final chord. I wanted the tonic not to be stated right away, but to emerge. That's one of the things about tonality, and not only in its standard forms, but in its developed forms, that I began to find slightly tiresome at the hands of the less-than-great: composers tended to declare their harmonic aims rather too quickly for my taste. Obvious exceptions would be the opening of *Tristan* or of Beethoven Nine, but the opening of Bruckner's Ninth, which is obviously modelled (like so many of his openings) on the Beethoven, has no ambiguity at all. It's quite clear that it's in D minor right away. I began to feel that tonality didn't have as many options, or perhaps the composers using it didn't explore as many options for oblique openings as I would have liked.

CD: In that respect, Debussy's *Jeux* is a piece that manages to move on from the ambiguity of *Tristan* without aping it at all.

JA: *Jeux* is very interesting because you think, 'What does that octave signify?' and you get many different possible implications for it. *Jeux* is a very good example of what I am trying to do in that way. Not in its perpetual changing every few bars, but that opening is extraordinarily exciting, and very suggestive indeed. Yes.

CD: And you don't get full confirmation that what you suspect is the key until the last bar. Returning to the Quartet, you're playing with notions of tonality. How about the classic string-quartet paradigm of dialogue?

Figure 10   The final version of the harmonic clock used for String Quartet No. 3
'*hana no hanataba*' by Julian Anderson, subsequently published by Schott Music Ltd

JA: Well, in the first movement, because they're all playing the same kind of music, there is no real dialogue. There's no thematic working, no melodic working at all. It's just a texture, or a texture that gradually transforms, so that it deprives me of the ability to make dialogue between the players. That's something else I have got saved up for later in the work.

CD: Yes, it's some kind of polymetric *moto perpetuo* that starts fragmented. There's a nice set of contradictions. Having established that, there is a marked contrast with the second movement, which still has the irrational rhythms, but turns them into a kind of wonky dance.

JA: That's right. The second movement is thematic in the way that the first movement deliberately avoids, that's the first thing. The second thing is that it states its tonics. There are two of them, E-flat and A, and it states them very clearly, one after the other (see Figure 10 for the 'harmonic clock' for the Quartet). While composing I was thinking a lot about how consonant or dissonant, relative to the tonic, other things are. I'm making it sound as though the piece had no extra-musical inspiration, which is true. This was a problem as I was worrying about what to say in the programme note. I couldn't say it was based on my granny's birthday or a mountain I once saw or the stained glass of Chartres or anything else. It's about the music itself. And that's slightly unusual for me, except that it's probably true of all my music from another angle.

Anyhow, probably for those reasons, any discussion of this piece is going to get very technical, much more so than on any other piece of mine, so I apologise in advance for that.

CD: Where does the subtitle fit in? What does it mean?

JA: I wanted to call it 'Bouquet of Flowers'. It is a collection of movements which are independent yet belong together, and that subtitle seemed a good way of indicating this. There's a nice word for it in Czech, 'kytice', but nobody knows that outside the Czech Republic. I'm not Czech. I'm not Japanese either, but I found the Japanese for 'bouquet of flowers' is 'hana no hanataba'. What I like about that is that it's symmetrical but not by letter. It's symmetrical by group, except that it isn't quite that either. You've got 'hana' either side of the word 'no', but the 'hana' on the right-hand side of it has some more syllables. So it's a distorted symmetry, which seemed very appropriate for the shape of the piece. Anyway, 'hana no hanataba' sounds much better than 'bouquet of flowers'. But really it's 'String Quartet No. 3'.

CD: Do you think writing for string quartet places an extreme lens on the pure stuff of music?

JA: Yes, I do think so. Why that is, I have no idea. The way I hear the quartet as a medium is like the way Scarlatti treated the keyboard. In other words, it's sufficiently neutral enough to offer you many imaginary sonic worlds. It can be chameleon-like and change into an imaginary trumpet, or an imaginary set of guitars, or an imaginary folk band, or an imaginary eighteenth-century ensemble and so on.

It's very good for projecting sonic fantasy and therefore one's focusing on the sheer stuff of the registers, the pitches, the rhythms, what all that does, because that's all you've got; there's nothing else. The other thing about the quartet medium is that in a sense it's just me, the player, and the listeners. It's a more private medium, in a way. It's a medium which has a history of being quite intense, and composers tend to say the essence of things in string quartets. I certainly feel I use it that way. I use writing my quartets to explore things I don't know – a sort of laboratory mentality. Very exciting, from my point of view. I like doing them because they turbocharge my music for a few years after that.

CD: With the third movement, the first word that I wrote here was just 'extraordinary'. [Laughter]

JA: Thank you!

CD: There's stillness, then incredible energy, and then stillness again. Around about bar 190 onwards, where we get these pizzicato textures. We've had crotchety stuff, and then we've got the violins pootling along on the top, and underneath we've got the viola and the cello coming in with these sudden pizzicati. It struck me that there was a little bit of the spirit of the Angel's music from *Saint François*.

JA: Oh I see what you mean. I hadn't thought of that. The essence of that passage is a polymetric thing. There is metric phrasing in the first and second violins, in 5/8. That's quite consistently in fives. The pizzicato punctuation in the cello and viola, on the other hand, seems to be more in 3/8, with the downbeat of the 3/8, to make matters slightly more saucy, on the second beat of bar 192. The cello is always lower than the viola. I think that we hear downbeats much easier on a lower note or chord.

CD: Yes, it's a kind of foot stamp.

JA: So it's like saying, 'And *one*, two, and *one*, two.' Over the next 20 bars I make up as many variations of that as I can, each of which ends with a sforzando *arco* chord. That eventually turns out to be key in getting us back to B, which is where we started the movement. It's a little like planning a car trip: you don't always want to take the quickest way. As a creative artist, efficiency is not always, in spite of what some people say, the first option.

CD: The scenic route via a nice country pub.

JA: Precisely. In this case, it was quite a challenge knowing how to get from bar 190 to what I thought would be a recapitulatory feel of the music in B, like at the opening of the movement. First of all in terms of speed and texture, and then also in terms of the pitch content. What happens, if you look at the first two violins, is that they gradually get more and more tremolos between two notes. These get longer and faster, until they just dissolve into trills. It's an old Beethoven trick. You get so fast that you get a hovering trill, and he does that in the last movement of Op. 111. When that hovering tremolo is reached in my movement, one can again have long tones as the music now appears slow. That was the textural way I got from very fast to very slow. Then I had to do it with pitch and metre as well. So these are all, let's say, little games that one plays with the listener.

CD: Texturally, it's like the way that in certain situations in mathematics, positive infinity can tend towards negative infinity. So it's going so fast that it finds stasis.

JA: Yes, it's very like that. Since you've mentioned the character of the third movement, there was a conscious task I wanted to set myself. The challenge was to write the main slow movement of the piece and the main fast movement of the piece in the same movement. So it's a very long movement – about eight and a half minutes. It's by far the longest movement in the work. I wrote this movement in order from the first bar to the last, which is by no means always the case.

The harmonic substance of the third movement is focused upon what I term a 'spectral minor triad'. I will admit that I've always had a slight prejudice against the old minor triad in tonality. I didn't like the sound of it, I now realise, although that seems a silly thing to say about what can be a perfectly beautiful sound. I always liked the sound of the major triad more. Some acoustician will say it's because the major triad is much closer to the overtone series and all that. One way that people have analysed the emotional associations, let's say, of minor tonality in Western music is that it's so close to the overtone series but it contains one very significant alteration – the minor third – which produces a psychological reaction. That's probably true. But I don't enjoy the sound of it. [Laughter]

CD: That clearly was the case with Messiaen as well. The minor triad is so rare in his music.

JA: Well it's the distinction between Messiaen and Jehan Alain. When Jehan Alain is using the octatonic mode, in his *Trois Danses* for example, he's got far more minor triads in it.

CD: The same thing with Stravinsky as well. The *Symphony of Psalms* is all octatonic, but has a much more minor sensibility to it than Messiaen has, especially in the first movement.

JA: That's true, yes.

CD: So how did you find a minor triad that you like?

JA: I'd been wondering whether there was a way in which you could have an acoustic minor triad that was really consonant, nearly as consonant as the major triad, but I couldn't find it. Then I saw that it was under my nose all along. I was thinking about going back to the harmonic series and seeing if there was anything in there. I had written out a harmonic series on E. I landed on B-natural. The reason for that is that, on my original chart, B-flat is opposite B-natural. There were 12 slots, as originally there were going to be 12 movements, and the idea was this would be the halfway point. The 12 movements became pairs of keys in movements (see Figure 10). So there are six movements, not 12, and some of them don't have two keys, while the last movement has about five. As so often, I never go along with regular schemes – I immediately get bored. Anyway, the B-natural was originally the furthest away from B-flat I felt I could get, so they're polar opposites in movement three, which was the first I composed. That's why I was thinking the movement was going to be B, whether it was the third or sixth movement in the piece.

CD: But the harmonic area was fixed regardless of where the movement ended up?

JA: Yes. Now, if you go up the E harmonic series, to harmonics six, seven and nine, and you're on E, those notes would be B, D-quarter-flat and F-sharp. I had always said that I did not use the major third distorted by plus or minus a microtone, because it would sound out of tune. I was also careful about the minor third because I knew that between harmonics six and seven it's there the whole time. So this triad has those intervals that I used not to employ. That's to say between D-quarter-flat and F-sharp, we have a major third stretched, which I previously thought could only sound wrong. Then I'd found out with this triad that it can sound right to my ears. The F-sharp and the B is a perfect fifth, so that offers a frame for it, with this strange pitch in the middle. It sounds beautiful.

There was a piece by Per Nørgård called *Night-Symphonies, Day Breaks*, which takes, as its main chord, C, E-quarter-flat and G. The idea there was to have an uncertain third that didn't know whether it was major or minor but is exactly halfway between the two. I remember Per saying at the time that this summed up his attitude towards politics, that he was rather centre-inclined and didn't want to be at either extreme. I like that piece, but it was not the sound I wanted. This is a quite different sound. I keep talking about the third movement being in B – but the B and other pitches at the opening are overtones of E, so that's where you get your ambiguity.

CD: Rather than uncertainty between major and minor, its pushing out the other side of minor towards something with a hint of pentatonic.

JA: In a way, yes. Now this is where I suddenly started to get interested. First of all, the physical sound of this new triad I found really very sensual. There is a very immediate attraction to this sound. Then too, the first place you're going to go away from such a triad is not to the dominant, not to the perfect fifth above at all, but of course to the fourth, to E, because it's derived from a harmonic series on E, and that's going to be very strongly implied. That triad keeps naturally inclining towards E in this movement, and other partials of the E harmonic series.

All this triggered an automatic resemblance to a composer and a piece I was not thinking of in connection with this work, Sibelius's *Tapiola*. The key of B minor is around somewhere in most of *Tapiola*, but it's always with a strong element of E major. It's very distinctive. It's using the same thing as I'm doing in my third movement, using normal tuning, whereas I'm approximating Just intonation tuning. At the first performances, the JACK Quartet really got that tuning right. We found we were getting all kinds of resonances and difference tones, which are very rich on string instruments. At the end of the third movement, we began to find in rehearsals that the difference tones between the

D-quarter-flat in the cello and the E on the viola were extremely loud. For this ending, the lowest string of the cello is tuned down a semitone to get the low tonic B right down in the bass. All this produces really low resonances, all kinds of combination tones, which made it sound as though there was a much bigger bass that isn't there. I was very excited by that and I saved it for the end of the movement.

CD: It's a remarkable sound.

JA: I think a lot about registers. I start this third movement bang in the middle with the clearest possible statement of what it's about – the triad of B, D quarter-flat and F-sharp. It says in the score, 'inhale', 'exhale'. I ask them to do that. I thought of this harmony as having a balance of tension and release and so on, that cadencing back into that chord at the start of each bar felt like a release of something. So the breathing pattern just clarifies that. The next problem was how to get out of it. In a sense, Sibelius offered me the clue because once I'd realised there was this automatic resemblance to *Tapiola*, then all I had to do was think of this mode as freely as he would have thought of his. You alter pitches from it, you focus on different areas of it. So it proved quite easy to modulate away from it – I just had to use notes as pivots to other modes. However, I found that quite substantial areas, especially of the slow parts of the piece, could be pretty much in that mode and just oscillate around it, which of course is exactly what Sibelius does in *Tapiola*.

CD: So this flattened minor, as it were, provides you with the opportunity for an entirely new set of harmonic ambiguities to explore.

JA: I've become very interested in how to create ambiguity in the listening and composing process with very simple means. When I was rehearsing with the JACK, they definitely had the sense of areas pulling against each other and sliding back and forth ambiguously, until the end of the movement, where it's quite clear that I land on B. Except there's some ambiguity even there, because there's such a strong element of E in that B – everything being played is an overtone of E. If you hear it live, it has what might be a very low E as a difference tone. It was a lot of fun to play around with these things. I'd not thought of doing that the day before I started that movement, beyond asking why I couldn't find a minor triad that I like. [Laughter]

I wanted to have this feeling that you'd heard these sounds before, but not quite like this. It's familiar, but there's something slightly different about it.

CD: Like a familiar landscape photographed with a filter.

JA: Yes, especially as the other thing I like is just one note being tuned differently may change the whole colour of a familiar triad. I always felt uneasy with spectral music, which this isn't, when there were multitudes of quarter-tones. I began to find that a little indiscriminate. In the hands of a good composer like Murail, extraordinary, but with others it can be difficult to get shading and variety from music with too many quarter-tones.

CD: If it's going to be Christmas every day, it stops being Christmas.

JA: Exactly.

CD: Does all of the third movement use that quarter-tone flattened B minor?

JA: The slow passages generally are in this new type of B minor, as it were, and the rest of the movement tends to modulate away and avoid B as a note, in order to get contrast going. That's particularly true of the fast passages, which move substantially away from it. All kinds of other pitches occur, which are not E either. Since E and B are paired in the tonic sections, obviously I avoid those notes elsewhere. It's common sense really, but you have to have a way back into them. It's a little like finding your way around the Hampton Court maze.

In the finale of the Quartet, where I used this spectral minor triad quite a bit, there are several bits where they all play that triad melodically at the unison, and you really can hear the tuning. For example: C-sharp, E-quarter-flat, G-sharp. The JACK could actually play it in tune with each other, at fast speed. You do like people to be able to play pieces. Well, the JACK are amazing players, of course!

CD: Given the difficulty of knowing what some things will sound like outside your head, how on earth did you come up with the conclusion to the Quartet? It is a truly extraordinary sound, which I would say, if you played it to most people, they would assume that it was a string quartet with some kind of electronic trickery.

JA: That's what I intended. I like the endings of pieces to throw up a different sonic dimension, if possible. It can be rather satisfying psychologically to suddenly find that something else happens near the end which completely changes things.

CD: Opening a new door.

JA: Also, I wanted it to sound bigger than a quartet, which I think it does. There was also a private joke with a couple of composer colleagues who have a big allergy to the string-quartet medium. One of the objections they point to is the fact that there's no strong bass, because you have a cello that doesn't go lower than two octaves below middle C: you can't have big resonant basses. Many people have complained that the low C string of the cello sounds too boxy, that it doesn't have a full enough sonority. In truth, for that string to really resonate more, the whole instrument should be considerably longer... Anyway, obviously the cello is no double bass – that's the point, so the ensemble has a bass-register problem and you've got to sort it out. There's also this big octave gap between viola and cello. Percy Grainger says this is why he never wrote a string quartet. He found that gap objectionable, whereas he didn't think that the saxophone family had such a gap, but we'd got it wrong with the string family. Typical Grainger, a slightly odd theory. [Laughter] Anyway, I thought it would be nice to have a final section in my Third Quartet where the bass is so rich that it sounds as though there really is a double bass. The end of the third movement already hints at that idea, but the end of the whole Quartet also involved a little bit of self-reference, a follow-up I'd always wanted to do to a much earlier piece.

CD: Is this *Ring Dance?* That's what I wrote when I heard it.

JA: *Ring Dance*, exactly. Initially I thought I'd end the Quartet fast, but that was not going to work for this piece for a number of reasons. The balance of slow music against fast was getting a bit too fast-heavy, so I needed more slow music, but the context was very loud. Then I thought of having a coda with only very loud, slow chords. This would be the follow-up to *Ring Dance* – some 30 years later. The Quartet has non-tempered pitches, though, which is one thing I never used in *Ring Dance*. So there are two devices. The cello has a lot of low double-stops, particularly towards the end of the piece, with open C and G strings. That will give you a difference tone of C an octave below the C string. It can sound thunderous.

I'd noticed this clearly when I first heard the two-cello transcription of *Ring Dance*. I decided to end the Quartet with that double-stopping of the two lowest cello strings, giving the deep low C (which is the lowest on the piano) as a resultant tone. In the Quartet I added some resonances above to interact with that sound. The main decision was to focus on F-quarter-flat. That pitch doesn't feature in an overtone series on C until very high up. In a harmonic series on C, the F in the middle register should be a quarter-sharp, the 11th harmonic. Instead, I decided to have an F-sharp normally tuned and have an F immediately below it, a quarter-tone flat so that you get one of my favourite intervals, a three-quarter-tone. The F-quarter-flat is introduced, by the way, at a moment where there's a strong focus on the cello's G string – which has F-quarter-flat as its 7th harmonic. Then I add the low cello C below it. The F-quarter-flat is consonant with G, but dissonant with C as it's not a harmonic of that note.

The whole passage was about playing with different intervals and resonances so that they gradually ground their way towards a pitch which had not featured in the movement, or in the whole Quartet, as being a tonic at all, which was that C. The Quartet ends on C.

So finally, after 30 years, I paid my debt to *Ring Dance*, as it were. I was very frustrated when I finished *Ring Dance* to find absolutely no use for it in anything else I composed. I couldn't see what to do with this strange thing. It was a bit of a relief finally to find a way of following it up. If the music sounds exuberant or pretty fierce, that's because there was a sense of enormous exhilaration and release to me at finding that ending.

CD: It's got a kind of radiance but it's stark, or honest radiance.

JA: A roughness – the roughness of rubbing the strings is important to that ending.

CD: It sounds like there's something producing white noise, like there's whistling going on. There's also the growling, and so it just sounds like there's a whole load of additional stuff which is nothing to do with a string quartet.

JA: I was just trying to see if I could make the Quartet become as un-quartet-like as possible. I was hoping to suggest electronics, all kinds of resonances, difference tones, extra bass notes that aren't there. Anything to make that Quartet leap out into another region, really.

CD: It's also about as far from the opening as you can get.

JA: Very far. You know that phrase of Nielsen, about how he composed? He always said, 'You never know where you'll end up.' That's always my experience of it. What I really like is if I imagine an ending and then what comes up is something else that I hadn't foreseen, but seems more exciting. Endings should seem right in retrospect, but not totally foreseeable in advance. You want that nice combination of surprise but rightness in some way, depending on the ending. That was very important for the end of this Quartet, which had been a very big harmonic adventure for me.

The other thing is that there are several movements that don't use any macrotones, and several that use them a lot. That was important as a way of defining this circle of keys in different ways through the whole work. The other gambit, which the fourth movement uses, was to explore the possibility of defining a tonic using noise. So there are a lot of bow-pressure changes and movements of bowing position, but not much development of pitch. The tonic G is there most of the time and only very simple, mostly open string intervals going around it. I was trying see if it's possible to colour the tonic by means of noise or noises or instabilities, but feel that it's still there as a tonic, as a recognisable home. That interested me. And you don't do that in conventional Western tonality. [Laughter]

CD: So there are very different approaches in each movement.

JA: Yes, I'm interested in having variety within a certain continuity. I like having areas where something happens, contrasted with other areas where it doesn't. For example, one sound that occurs quite a lot in the piece is over-bowing of different sorts. Nowhere, though, do I have a whole movement that's just that sound. In the second and fifth movements, I don't use any extended techniques of any sort. I had very grand plans for my fifth movement which turned out to be nonsense, because when I had finished the fourth movement, all my instincts told me to make movement five a variation of movement two, but a variation of a sort that I have always disapproved of in others: reversal. I've often been frustrated by composers who just run parts of their music backwards: it's not a musical thing to do and often produces rubbish.

So I decided to play with symmetry. What you get is not the second movement backwards, though it opens as if that might be the case. Increasingly it deviates from literal symmetry, in a variety of ways. This relates to something Grisey says in his treatise on time, *Tempus ex Machina*, where he talks about the fallacy of notationally symmetrical rhythms. He points out that our memory doesn't work that way. So, for example, if you take Messiaen's famous non-retrogradable rhythms, they don't necessarily sound symmetrical at all.

CD: No, they can't do really.

JA: The simplest one is: crotchet, quaver, crotchet. You're either going to think of it as 'one-two-three, one-two', or 'one-two, one-two-three'. In other words, by group: the quaver will seem to attach itself either to the crotchet that starts or the crotchet that ends. The musical context might determine which, but you certainly won't hear that rhythm as symmetrical.

CD: And even then, when you get those examples in the *Traité*, like the one you just gave, you don't know that the second crotchet is a crotchet. Where does it end?

JA: Exactly. You have to get another impulse after it to know that, so at that point the whole rhythm becomes non-symmetrical anyway. Grisey suggests that the way to create real musical symmetry might be to do it by grouping, not by exact note values. I thought that was interesting and that it might be possible in the case of a whole movement, to have some of it reverse literally, have some of it with the sections in reverse order but not played backwards, and some of it just recomposed. The order of the sections gets increasingly wrong as the fifth movement proceeds, so what we end with is something that was around the middle of the second movement, now varied and extended.

CD: That's also a reflection of how memory works. With musical dictation, once you get beyond a certain length, you may remember it, but you're going to start making errors, and then you might get the order of things wrong.

JA: There was a very funny episode when I was 16 or 17. I was given an oral test. The A Level boards used to send out a cassette of tests that you could give your students.

CD: Yes, I remember those.

JA: In one test an oboe played a long flowing melody – and that, as I later realised, was deliberately misleading, because the original melody is played on violins. The oboe played a melody so long and asymmetrical that I only just managed to write it down. It turned out, when I heard it about two years later in a totally different context, that I did already know this melody. It was from the opening of the third movement of Nielsen's 'Inextinguishable' Symphony, with the first two notes of the melody omitted. It was totally out of context and on the wrong instrument, so I didn't recognise it. Anyhow, in trying to do that dictation, I noticed exactly what you're saying. The only way of writing that long melody down was to isolate it gradually into groups. I could write out the opening, but I couldn't remember what happened after a certain point. One then had to forget the opening to concentrate on the rest of it. That taught me a lot about how events, musically, can be processed by the mind. In this fifth movement of my Quartet, I was thinking of that example and what it did to my memory as I was trying desperately to write it down. It's a question of playing with expectation as well as memory.

CD: Which is at the heart of composition.

JA: Indeed. Now Grisey uses the word 'anamorphosis' to describe what he envisaged. He never composed a piece that did this, as far as I know. I wish he had. Anyway, you take a musical image and you distort it in order to play with memory. Anamorphic distortion interests me a great deal visually, so I thought of the fifth movement as at times a quasi-anamorphic distortion of the second movement, playing with the memory of the listener. That seemed to me to be a much more meaningful way of varying the fifth movement. I was also thinking of John Cage's quote from Schoenberg. So many of Cage's pieces are called 'variations' because he was very influenced by Schoenberg's dictum that variation was a form of repetition with some things altered and others not. That's exactly what I was trying to do with the fifth movement.

CD: How did that relate to the harmonic circle?

JA: It meant that this lovely scheme I started with for the whole Quartet had been blown to smithereens. [Laughter] Movement five now had exactly the same tonics as movement two. At that point, movement six was left in a position of having a lot of keys to sweep up, meaning that the movement was going to be very varied, which I wanted the finale to be anyway.

CD: One thing that strikes me about the key clock is that several of the movements are using microtonal tunings, but you don't have that in your set of keys. Were you not tempted to have that?

JA: No. I think because the intonation problems, practically, that it raised would be enormous. You would then have to be able to predict that people would not only play the tonic precisely, but, say, the perfect fourth or fifth above it, very precisely – all that in non-tempered tuning. It would lead to a rather utopic situation. Who knows? I might do that in another piece, but at the moment my feeling is that I wouldn't, because I like precision in my tuning.

CD: Why not tune down?

JA: Oh, it sounds awful. Very often, if you tune the string down, it just starts drifting back up again. The resonance board is used to being at the normal pitch. I've seen that happen many times. You have an instrument that has been tuned irregularly for weeks, and then it will stick. Then, of course, you won't be able to use it for any other tuning, which is the problem. I know several quartets who carry around spare instruments to play Scelsi's Fourth Quartet, which has very extreme scordatura, but you can't use your best cello for it because the A string of the cello is a minor third too high. The physical tension that creates is enormous. So you really have to prepare the instrument for weeks ahead to do that. The price you pay for scordatura is too extreme, but perhaps it may soon be possible for players to do it properly. What I wrote in either the Second or Third Quartet would not have been playable 30 years ago, in my view. A year after I finished it, my Second Quartet was being played very accurately by students at Tanglewood. I never thought that would be possible for decades! So things change, and students are very open to trying new things. Many of their teachers now have done this for some time. The Arditti are long established in the field, and the JACK Quartet do all kinds of tuning to the nearest cent virtually, and so on. So one day it may be possible for me to do a scheme like this with tonics that are not in normal tuning and to get all the notes absolutely perfectly accurate.

At the Wigmore Hall dress rehearsal for the Third Quartet's premiere, the JACK Quartet's relatively new second violin arrived early, and was practising intonation intervals, just to warm himself up, for about half an hour. I've never heard such exact intonation, one interval after another. It's amazing what players can do now, so give it another 20 or 15 years maybe – or just another five, for all I know – and I could write even more complex intonation.

CD: Other than the very end, we've not really touched on the sixth movement.

JA: That deliberately has certain reminiscences from earlier movements. Not quotes, but the string monody near the start, with the chord sustained, is a reminiscence of the third movement. There are other things that recall other movements. The dancey stuff in the sixth movement is more like some of the second movement, but now with special tuning which you didn't get in the second movement. Things like that. It relates to various earlier things and also has its own personality, then comes up with this coda, which is very much something you have not heard before in the work. The sixth movement was written last because I had to know, by then, what was left to use in terms of pitches and textures that had not appeared. The big thing that wasn't yet really explored was the bass, so that comes in in a big way at the end. It was done contextually. Having done that, I don't think the next quartet will be like this. And I do have ideas for the next one... [Laughter]

Conversation Seventeen

Advocacy

Anderson's work as an advocate for all sorts of music has surfaced in passing at numerous points in these conversations. Whether as Artistic Director of the Philharmonia Orchestra's 'Music of Today' programme for a decade, advice on programming in numerous other settings or through numerous talks, interviews and articles about fellow composers, his straightforward love of all kinds of music is compelling. Rather than detail the specifics of such work, this conversation explores some of the issues and principles involved with advocacy. It starts with dialogue about the intellectualisation of composers and their ability, or otherwise, to articulate. It moves, via some observations on perception, to exploring good and bad practice in speaking to audiences. The benefits of unexpected encounters with works lead to musings about the effort of listening, contemporaneous reception of great masterpieces and changing perceptions of composers.

CD: Many composers, not least yourself, are very articulate when talking not just about their own works, but music and aesthetic issues in general. However, others are not. I've been heavily involved with research degrees at the Conservatoire for many years and we have a large number of composers, so I've spent many hours supporting them in articulating, through words, the research that resides within their music. Some find that more difficult than others. What concerns me, though, is that it has almost become an expectation now that a composer has to have a PhD to be taken seriously. Is there a danger of an over-intellectualisation of composition? Or, more accurately, where is the space for somebody who is purely instinctive, or is a Satie-esque composer, or a compositional equivalent of Le Douanier Rousseau?[1]

---

[1] Henri Rousseau (1844–1910), primitivist painter.

JA: I do worry about that. In one case, there was a composer who was already getting quite a lot of stuff played and wanted to study a PhD with me. After a certain point I had to say to that composer, 'I don't think you need this at the moment. Continue doing what you're doing, and perhaps come back later.' Since then, they've become a very successful opera composer. It depends on who you are. In that particular case, I just didn't think it was going to help that composer then. Somebody like György Kurtág finds any verbal articulation extremely difficult. He's a very instinctive composer who's got a very passionate commitment to what he does, but he doesn't like to talk about it.

CD: You find this with performers as well sometimes. When I ran the University concert series at Sheffield, we had a very big name come along, a front-line, major-label performer. This person is known as being a wonderful communicator when they're playing, so I encouraged them to say some stuff during the concert. It was awful. They just did not know how to do it. They had nothing of any insight or use at all. A wonderful performer, very nice person, but they needed to keep their mouth shut. I'd gone to countless Music in the Round concerts, where the form was that, say, Peter Cropper from the Lindsay String Quartet would lounge back in his chair and introduce a piece in an apparently off-the-cuff but always engaging and insightful way. It was something that really informed the listening, so I naively thought everybody should do this. Then I heard this other person and realised it can be profoundly off-putting if done badly!

JA: I don't think every composer should do it either. I am all for composers being able to write English and talk well, but I'm also very aware that there are large areas of musical activity that are almost impossible to verbalise. I so often find contemporary choreographers more stimulating about the way they approach the material that they are working with, physically, than composers. What's wonderful about choreographers, one of the reasons they are so inventive with their materials, is that they often are not comfortable communicating any other way. They pour that into the dance.

CD: And yet, there is an appetite from the public for a bridge towards any art form, an encouraging hand.

JA: Part of the problem is the rather obvious one of knowing what to say. For example, Anthony Burgess made a shorter version of Joyce's *Finnegans Wake*, basically to reduce it to a length that most people might be able to cope with, given the toughness and oddity of the language. He writes that the premise of the book is very simple, with the philosopher Vico and the idea of the four ages of the universe, which are the four books of the *Wake*. Then there's a family, and there are two sons, and there's a daughter, and there's a wife and a husband. The husband's having a big nightmare, and that's most of the book. Then he wakes up. I remember thinking when I tried to trudge through that aged 15 that if that's what this book is about, why doesn't it just say so, and why would anyone bother making a vast book about such a boring story? I owe it to Cage who, when he was talking about his *Roaratorio*, said that the story of *Finnegans Wake* isn't what that book is about at all, because if it were, what would the fuss be about? The problem is, the communicator thinks that the general public only understand stories, and books are stories, so they've got to tell them the story of the book and reduce it not only to a manageable length, but to a manageable narrative. Doing so takes all the *Finnegans Wake*-iness out of *Finnegans Wake*. It's not exactly *Finnegans Wake* for dummies, but it's getting on that way.

Anthony Burgess was a great novelist, but, as communicators, if we're trying to be the intermediary between the music and the public, we have to really be wary that we do not do what he did to *Finnegans Wake*: it retarded my appreciation of that book by years.

CD: There are also those who try to make things needlessly complex. I had to read Descartes for my philosophy subsid. as a student. I wrestled with the impenetrable introduction to my edition, wondering how on earth I would get my head round this thing, then was delighted to discover that Descartes is wonderfully lucid and clear.

JA: There are many similar instances. I will scream the next time I hear somebody introducing a 12-note piece of Schoenberg by playing people the 12-note row. For the general public, it's not going to mean a thing, and they're not going to be able to hear it in the music. So what exactly are you trying to prove? All you're doing, in fact, is reinforcing prejudices that people still have about Schoenberg, that it's all pre-calculated, mathematical, horrible music.

CD: When I've had to analyse any serial piece with students – I did a little bit of this recently when we looked at *Agon* – I say, 'Ok, I want you to analyse this. Come back next week with stuff to say about it, but you're not allowed to mention the series.'

JA: Yes, excellent.

CD: Otherwise, it's as useless as telling them to go away and find all the G minor chords in Mozart's Fortieth.

JA: And who is that going to help?

CD: The fact that it's in G minor tells us very little about the piece. I used to do a Case Studies class with second-year students and the first thing we'd do is listen to a bit of one of the pieces, usually a Bach cantata, a different one each year. I tell them to imagine I had not been in the room, and then to tell me what they've heard, but without using any technical information, none of what they were taught in harmony or musicianship in the first year. Just tell me what the music sounds like. They find it very difficult.

JA: It's very hard, yes.

CD: It's the hardest thing to do, and yet it's the most common thing they will be expected to do as musicians, to talk intelligently about music. People will expect it, but those people won't necessarily know the terminology. Of course, one of the first things the students say is that it's fugal. I point out it's a technical term, but, even if we allowed it, just about any piece of Bach's music has a fugue, or what might very loosely be construed as fugal writing, so that hardly narrows it down. They need to tell me what this particular fugue sounds like.

JA: That's very close to how I would normally speak to the general public about music. It's very important, learning to articulate what you really do hear, without hiding behind terms like 'fugal'. Your point is that if you can't use the word 'fugal', you have to say something which gives somebody a way to understand what you mean by it. It's a little like having to translate into a different language, isn't it?

CD: It is, and it's also a reminder to yourself of how most people experience things, and with most pieces, how I would first experience them. I know some people do things differently, but when I first hear a piece of music, I try to just hear it. I try not to analyse it as I'm listening. There are things that you notice that you can't help, but I'm not sitting there, trying to work out whether it's in sonata form or anything like that. I'm just trying to listen to the music.

JA: For about the last three or four years, I've been doing some work at the Guildhall with Professor John Sloboda about listening to new music. We offer a facility, effectively, to composers at the Guildhall, when they're having a new piece played, to get some feedback on what those who heard it think. Not whether they liked it or not, but in terms of things like how many sections they thought it had, if they thought it had any, and how long did they think the piece was? A very interesting question, by the way.

CD: Oh, yes. Having been at the premiere of Finnissy's *The History of Photography in Sound*, and thought the final piece of this vast cycle, 'Etched bright with sunlight', was a lovely, shimmering coda of about 10 minutes, I dropped the disc in shock when the Nicolas Hodges recording arrived and I discovered it actually lasts around half an hour![2]

JA: The subjective reaction to duration is fascinating, and that was also borne out in this research with John Sloboda. The audiences are often asked about what they thought the piece was about. If there was a programme, did they hear any relation between the programme and what they heard? All those kinds of things. Now, inevitably, a lot of the audience that turns up to hear student concerts are, of course, other students, but you usually also get people from outside, friends and family, who aren't musicians. All that goes into the mix. So we do get a decent spread. We found the data very interesting. We don't have a standard questionnaire. The composer compiles the questionnaire. We check over, making sure the questions are clear, or checking if there's any additional question they've forgotten to ask; the questionnaire is also vetted by an ethics committee, as is essential in such contexts. It's handed out with the programme for people to fill in if they wish. It's all anonymous. We try to provide a situation where it requires very little effort to communicate with the composer. There are no conclusions of any general sort, but I notice that some of the most lively and valuable responses appear not to come from musicians.

CD: They will often have a far more open mind, which is why what is communicated or not about an unfamiliar piece is so important.

JA: Intermediaries have a big responsibility not to do something which will positively hinder. Ernest Newman was asked to introduce the first broadcast of the performance of Schoenberg's Orchestral Variations, a piece he hated.[3] He started by saying, 'It will last for twenty minutes and you may feel that you might be better employed elsewhere.' He then went on to say that he didn't understand this music, couldn't make head or tail of it, and that nobody else he knew could either. Nevertheless, he concluded, Schoenberg is clearly a sincere musician, so just be patient and indulge him.[4] Well, who the hell is going to want to listen to a piece of music if it's introduced like that? That's an extreme case, but it's not as unusual as you would think.

---

[2] Michael Finnissy, *Etched Bright with Sunlight*, Nicolas Hodges (piano), recorded 1999/2000, St George's Bristol, Metronome MET CD 1058 (CD). The piece lasts 29' 27" on this recording. A complete performance of *The History of Photography in Sound* lasts around five and a half hours.

[3] Ernest Newman (1858–1969) was one of the leading British music critics of the first half of the twentieth century.

[4] See Jenny Doctor, *The BBC and Ultra-Modern Music, 1922–1936* (Cambridge: Cambridge University Press, 1999), p. 251.

CD: It's so frustrating when people are apologetic about any music. I can understand the temptation, but I learnt from observing Peter Hill talking that his enthusiasm for and confidence in the music shines through. He never thinks people might not like it. I realised that if you just show your enthusiasm for a piece, people will take it or leave it, but usually they will take it.

JA: I went to a performance Rattle did of the Schoenberg Orchestral Variations 10 years ago, at the Proms. It got a huge standing ovation, absolutely massive, and that is one of Schoenberg's most dissonant pieces. Of course, it was with Rattle and the Berlin Philharmonic and it did sound gorgeous, but nobody particularly seemed to notice that it was anything other than a big piece of symphonic music in a particular idiom. And they palpably enjoyed that.

CD: When I was first going out with Liz, my wife, we went to a couple of concerts where Webern's pieces were played, first of all at a music department concert and then a Music in the Round concert with The Lindsays. Both concerts were packed, the Webern was just part of everything else and was enthusiastically received. A couple of months after these concerts, Webern came up in conversation with a bunch of musos, and Liz was astonished to discover that he was supposed to be difficult. As far as she was concerned it was colourful, creative music and it had been received rapturously. It really astonished her that there was any kind of problem with his music at all.

JA: One of the biggest prejudices against twentieth-century music as a whole, and contemporary music, remains among the self-appointed middle people who don't think that the audience can cope. Meaning probably that they themselves can't.

CD: Yes, the patronising approach to it all. It's dangerous trying to predict what people will like. An insidious myth has arisen in some circles that, because much classical music was written for privileged people in specific situations, and because much of it requires many years of hard training to perform it really well, the music itself is elitist and only for a privileged elite. The middle of the last century saw a much needed push for the serious consideration of a wider range of music, whether jazz, pop, rock or traditional/folk. I enjoy listening to and playing those types of music.

JA: So do I, as is reflected in part by the range of music mentioned in our conversations.

CD: The trouble is that some people seem to regard it as a competition, rather than it all being music. Some also think people will only be interested in 'their' music, the inference being that they will not understand or be enthused by other music. I once had someone tell me that classical music wasn't for working-class people and they shouldn't be made to study it at school. This person went to a private school and Cambridge, incidentally. He was rather dumbfounded when I pointed out that I come from a working-class background, didn't regard myself as a class traitor for listening to Beethoven or Stravinsky and found his remarks deeply offensive. That patronising, divisive attitude has been taken up by some cultural theorists and educationalists, and has been used at times as a figleaf for slashing the funding for music provision when what's needed is much more support to provide access for those on low incomes.

JA: That is vitally important. In my experience, listeners from many different backgrounds will listen sympathetically and are very open. I've had wonderful experiences talking with audiences and playing them all kinds of stuff. I also think that the big multinationals might be jolly surprised by what would happen if they tried to mass promote a piece like, say, Jonathan Harvey's *Mortuos Plango*. It could easily be a hit if they ever thought of it. What happened to Górecki's Third Symphony could certainly happen to that. It could easily happen, for that matter, to quite a lot of other contemporary music. It's true that a certain abruptness and disjunction was cultivated in a certain period of music, but that hasn't prevented Stockhausen being massive among pop people. If you look on YouTube, you see the reactions when somebody puts up *Gesang der Jünglinge*. There are still quite a lot of people saying, 'This just freaked me out', and 'This is just nuts.' And why not? It's very interesting to see that a piece already 65 years old can still provoke that reaction. On the other hand, there are a lot of reactions that are really very heart-warming, saying, 'Never heard anything like this before, love it and I'm going to look up more like it.' What's nice is that now people don't have to ask where they can find it, because it's all there. In that sense, the Internet is helping enormously.

CD: The temptation, particularly in financially tough times, is to play safe, but Rattle showed with the CBSO in the early 1980s that the exact opposite is the case.

JA: In the middle of when I was Composer-in-Residence with the London Philharmonic Orchestra, Jude Kelly and Gillian Moore decided to mount a festival partly based on Alex Ross's book, *The Rest is Noise*.[5] In fact, that was just a useful tag line, because Mr Ross's book is a very personal view of that period of music.

CD: As would be anyone's book, to be fair.

---

[5]   Alex Ross, *The Rest is Noise* (London: Harper Perennial, 2009). Gillian Moore is Director of Music at The Southbank and at this time Jude Kelly was Artistic Director.

JA: Quite. It has its points and it's lively, though there are huge areas of music, like Sibelius and Nielsen and all sorts of contemporary composers that are either barely mentioned, or neglected. Anyway, the London Philharmonic Orchestra decided that they would be part of that scheme, and it served as a wonderful excuse to play a large amount of twentieth-century music. The repertoire covered was wider than in that book and was a very good survey of contemporary and twentieth-century music in many ways. The London Sinfonietta were also heavily involved. They had Lachenmann over several times, for example, they had a huge amount of Schoenberg, Webern, Stravinsky and Bartók, as well as quite a lot of jazz, Ferneyhough and all sorts of different stuff, and the audiences were very full. If you put on something, you're convinced by it, it's of good quality, you let people know properly that it's happening, and you play it really well – I must emphasise that last criterion – people will not only turn up, they'll respond fully. I don't see, however, why people should be only fed that diet or a Beethoven diet or anything else. An exaggerated diet in any way is going to risk turning people off. The Proms is proof that a wide range of high-quality musical performances will generate one of the most open-minded concert audiences in the world.

It may be that some of the more eccentric pronouncements of contemporary art composers, involving Sirius or whatever,[6] have not helped. Nonetheless, we tend to forget that outreach in this country was started by new music and with the composers. The idea that composers just sit there not caring who listens to their music is certainly not true of any composer I've ever come across. Mr Ferneyhough grouped around him players who like to perform his work. He found circumstances so that he could be played, and played well. He didn't just write the music and shut the door on people. Michael Finnissy we know is an expert pianist and was touring for many years with dance projects and all kinds of things.

CD: And Finnissy has also composed things like *East London Heys* with amateurs in mind.

JA: Yes, and he's done community pieces. He's done a lot of work for many years with CoMA[7] and so on. We all know how much Olly Knussen has done to promote new music to the public, and Judith Weir is doing brilliantly in her post as Master of the Queen's Music. Personally, I love talking with audiences, either before, during or after concerts. I'm really happy to do it. I like introducing people to all kinds of music, particularly contemporary music. There's a pleasure in finding the right phrase or the right style of introduction to get an audience

---

[6]   Stockhausen claimed to have come from Sirius.
[7]   Contemporary Music for All.

that might even be actively resistant to it, to disabuse them of that prejudice, and get them excited, listening to it and enjoying it.

I've dealt enough with audiences to know that you can easily get across even a supposedly complicated piece of contemporary music without using any technical jargon. This relates to my dad's need to communicate his scientific discoveries in plain English across the radio to people, so that they could understand just how central to their lives not overusing antibiotics was, for example, or what the real dangers of a salmonella epidemic were or were not. He needed to be able to express that in everyday language so that people could understand what was going on. It was essential. He said to me early on, 'You don't need to condescend to the audience. Communicate properly.'

CD: Well, if you can get people like Brian Cox explaining things to do with quantum physics or whatever, there's really no excuse not to convey stuff about music.

JA: None whatsoever. I believe in the public funding of the arts. Let me say that absolutely unambiguously. It's a wonderful thing. If only people realised that the amount of public funding it takes to create what could be a very healthy arts scene is peanuts in terms of gross national expenditure. It's almost a fake problem. However, I also believe that if the public are paying, they should absolutely have the right to see it and to listen to it, whether it's orchestras, the Arts Council, the BBC or anyone else doing it. The trouble with YouTube is getting people to know what's there, because so much is. That's where the BBC is very powerful because they have access to national channels of communication that are well recognised. If the BBC endorses something and puts it out, a lot of people, potentially, will know about it much more readily than they can if something is being put on YouTube. Nonetheless, there are many wonderful things on YouTube. When you look at the number of hits and views and so on that some very challenging contemporary art music, and the arts generally, get on YouTube, you realise that a substantial potential audience is out there, and that increasingly its being gotten through to in ways that it wasn't before. Personally, I rejoice in that.

CD: Yes, that said, the proliferation of TV and radio channels theoretically means that there is enough space for everyone to access whatever music they want, whether that's contemporary music, Baroque, free jazz or whatever, or any other content for that matter. The danger is that it can lead to ghettoisation, meaning that people don't come across stuff beyond fairly narrow parameters. You don't trip over things in the same way.

JA: Tripping over things is so important. It's important in life generally, but it's vital in culture. If you see a poster of an artist you didn't know by accident in the middle of the street, that can startle you and change your life. If you turn on the television or the radio and you hear a fragment of music that you've never heard before, we all know that can change your perception of music, art or whatever. This is one of the reasons, by the way, why I still believe in libraries, because the act of browsing physically is terribly important. You're looking for Stockhausen, but you come across something else, or you're looking for Ferneyhough and you come across Grainger, or it could be the other way around, maybe! Michael Finnissy was once amused by my finding a score of his amongst the oversize scores in Central Music Library near Victoria Station: it was filed exactly between Ferneyhough and Grainger. He loved that... Anyhow, browsing is vital to the experience of discovering a world you had no idea existed. You can't do it if such things are kept off of the shelves and kept off of the airwaves and kept off of the TV. You just cannot.

CD: No, and there aren't the high street shops these days, so you're forced to buy things online, and your online retailer tells you what you're going to like.

JA: The whole thing about the physical library is it's a very organised randomness. The organisation is by alphabet or by topic, but it's not by style. You don't put all the modern music scores in a library together. There's a strong potential to be surprised. That's also very important in a live concert. There was a wonderful series which was only being done occasionally when I was a kid called 'The Innocent Ear'. Robert Simpson pioneered it. The idea was to put on music, but they only said what the piece was after it had finished.

CD: Rob Cowan sometimes does that with a single piece.

JA: I wish people would try advertising concerts without saying what music was to be played. I love going to a Prom without knowing what I'm about to hear. On many nights, you can just buy a ticket and go into the arena. I've had wonderful experiences like that. I can't understand why people would be afraid of music they don't know.

CD: No. It has puzzled me as well. The only thing I can think is that music involves time and effort. Depending on what mood they're in and knowing how powerfully music can affect them, they're not sure that they necessarily want to be taken into those kinds of places.

JA: Which is fair enough.

CD: There's a point that I make in my first-year lecture called 'A Brief History of Recorded Sound'. I start with notation, incidentally, and go right up to Blu-ray audio and downloads, but I end by giving a demonstration on a phonograph, essentially a 1930s equivalent to an iPod, showing the sheer amount of effort that listening involved. I've got *Enigma Variations* or the Elgar Cello Concerto, or Beethoven Five, and you have to crank it up, you have to change the needle. Every single time you get your disc out, you put it on, it plays for its four and a half minutes and then you have to turn it over, do the whole cranking and needle-changing again before you carry on listening to the development section of Beethoven Five or whatever it might be. The point is this is not going to be something that's in the background. You're not going to go to all that effort in order to ignore it. Now there's the notion coming out of Kant, that the frame of art separates it from the everyday noise – the separation from the everyday enables us to enter into the art. With music increasingly becoming part of the everyday noise, that potentially affects what it is as an art form. There's nothing that can be done about this. It's just a fact, but it's something that not enough musicians pay attention to. I challenge the students to spend 24 hours, at some point in their first year, not listening to any electronically reproduced music anywhere.

JA: An interesting experience.

CD: On the radio, on their hi-fi, MP3 player, phone, on a doorbell, in a lift, on TV, round the supermarket.

JA: You would have to make quite an effort.

CD: Yes, it is really hard. Recording came in nearly a century and a half ago, but basically, we're talking much less than a century for it to become really prevalent and almost inescapable.

JA: It's less than a century. Of course, there were musicians in pubs and all that long before that, but you could always ask the musician to stop.

CD: Also, that music was being played by a person. This is the notion of music played without a person present to create it.

JA: Yes, it's different. I know that one of the people most worried about this as a composer was Nono in his later years. One of the reasons he took to writing those very still and often very quiet and static late pieces was because he was very worried people were losing the capacity to listen carefully. That's why he calls his opera *Prometeo* 'A Tragedy of Hearing'. He was very worried that our listening faculties were being much blunted by society and mechanical reproduction. I'm not sure that writing lots of very quiet slow music is the answer. Nono wanted to do that, he was free to do it, and sometimes he did it rather wonderfully (as in his late work *Caminantes... Ayocoucho*), but I don't think he was sorting out society's ills by doing it. The trouble is that while I absolutely agree with what you've just said, I'm not sure what composers can do about it.

CD: There's nothing that can be done about it. It's just something that people need to be aware of, that music, as a thing, has been fundamentally changed by the advent of recording. People's relationship with it is fundamentally different from what it was 100 years ago.

JA: Surely, that does encourage the attitude of music as being basically just a kind of background entertainment noise or sound. I'm sure it does. However, it's been a very long time now since people started predicting the death of the public concert, and it hasn't yet died. I'm always fascinated by the live event, even when what you're playing them is a tape of *Gesang der Jünglinge* or something like that. Except for going to church or synagogue, or whatever religion, it's one of the very few big public activities where people get together and, apparently, nothing is happening physically. They're just sitting there, listening. I find that a very special thing.

CD: It is easy to see the temptation for promoters to think that, in order to cultivate that audience, they should avoid things that are difficult or challenging, not realising that things that are 'easy' are less compelling. For a shared experience to be more than just a lot of people in a room together it needs to be meaningful.

JA: A lot of nonsense is talked about music people think is marketable, because they think it sounds smooth, pretty, audience-appealing, friendly. In my experience, if you shove an uninitiated audience into a big piece by Xenakis they will get very excited and respond positively, because these days they have heard all kinds of harsher noises from all kinds of rock and music on TV and goodness knows what. Some self-styled radicals think that they are opposing society's conventions by scratching a violin or whatever. It's not opposing anyone's expectations. On the contrary, it could be argued that some areas of society have stereotyped contemporary music as using any sounds like that and that by writing such things, you are actually fulfilling their image of what a contemporary composer is. That occurred to me for the first time when I heard Lachenmann's music played at Darmstadt in '88. It was a disturbing experience, not on the surface, because everyone applauded the pieces, they liked them. Everyone there expected Lachenmann to sound like that and they would have been booing if he hadn't. That struck me as a not entirely healthy situation, given that Lachenmann has said elsewhere that he doesn't wish to fulfil anyone's expectations. But I love his music, regardless.

I would love a musical arena where people drop all these *a prioris*. In Tanglewood one time there was a pre-concert talk before Sandy Goehr's *Colossos or Panic* was played by the Boston Symphony Orchestra. An audience member said to Sandy, 'Don't you see that what we want is Beethoven's Tenth Symphony? We don't want all this other stuff. All we want from you lot is another symphony by Beethoven. Why can't you provide it?' Goehr said, wisely, that there's nothing he'd rather do but even if he'd written Beethoven's Tenth Symphony, he wouldn't know it and neither would the audience. Of course, at the time that Beethoven's Ninth Symphony was premiered, people didn't realise they'd heard what we think of as Beethoven's Ninth Symphony. They didn't think it was rubbish, no, but the reviews said it was very complicated and awfully long, and it would take many hearings to really appreciate the worth of this piece. They didn't say, 'This is one of mankind's greatest achievements of all time.' There was no thought like that, in any of the reviews, whatsoever. So I think Sandy's reply was right to the concert lover, frankly. We will never know. Nobody hearing *The Rite of Spring* realised they had heard what we think *The Rite of Spring* has been. They didn't say, 'This is the most important thing since *Tristan*.' People are always looking for the X, Y, Z of our day, but Stravinsky wasn't sitting down to write the most important piece in the history of music since *Tristan* or Beethoven Nine, although in fact it ended up being that. You don't. You can't. It's a total nonsense. So promoting contemporary music and indeed writing it is a much more complicated and ambiguous thing. No one in Prague in 1925 would have said that the most important living Czech composer was Janáček. They would certainly have said he's an interesting figure, but most people would have said Suk, or possibly one of the others like Ostrčil, because that was reliable, well written and conventionally approved. Janáček was this fascinating oddball figure whom they certainly valued by then, but the most important composer of that period? Forget it. We think of him that way *now*.

CD: I did some work on recordings and piano rolls and, of course, in terms of solo piano recordings, there are many more piano rolls, by a factor of about six or seven to one, than there are acoustic recordings. Masses of stuff. So, in the period before 1925, before we get electric recording, if we discount Chopin, and it's a fairly close-run thing with Chopin, who would you say, in terms of piano repertoire, is the most recorded French composer?

JA: It's not Debussy or Ravel?

CD: No, not even remotely close. It's Chaminade. In the States there were Chaminade societies. She was by far the best-known French composer outside of France. She was forging an international career for herself and she was out in the States for much of the time, but very easily dismissed and given this label of salon composer. It's possible her gender may have played a part in this dismissal. Now I'm not saying that she should be rated alongside Chausson or Debussy necessarily, but maybe she should. There are interesting things in Chaminade beyond those we generally hear, some very good songs and things like that. As so often with women composers, there are other things, even an opera, that we never get to hear, so it's impossible to make a proper assessment.

JA: I'll look out some more Chaminade. Anyone involved in programming or performing concerts need to remember that great music doesn't just become great of its own accord. Someone needs to bring it to light. If you don't bother doing that, it's not only sad, it is verging on the irresponsible.

Figure 11   Julian Anderson with Edward Gardner and the BBC Symphony Orchestra,
The Barbican, London, 21 October 2017, photograph by John Fallas

Conversation Eighteen

Partnerships

The final conversation charts the working relationships behind works spanning nearly two decades. It starts with Anderson's residency with the City of Birmingham Symphony Orchestra, looking specifically at *Imagin'd Corners* and the various partnerships involved in developing the electronics for *Book of Hours*. The conversation then moves on to the factors influencing *The Discovery of Heaven*, written for an orchestra Anderson knew well, the London Philharmonic Orchestra. A third orchestral relationship is explored with *Incantesimi*, commissioned by Sir Simon Rattle for the Berlin Philharmonic, before the conversation turns to music written for soloists, with *Prayer* for violist Lawrence Power and *Sensation* for Pierre-Laurent Aimard. Anderson reveals how the first movement of *Sensation* to be composed acted as the catalyst not just for the rest of that work, but a new relationship with the piano.

— ◆ —

CD: Any compositional career is built on partnerships. I wonder if we might have a look at some different types of partnerships, along with the resulting pieces. Two notable ones in your career so far would be the formal residency with the City of Birmingham Symphony Orchestra and the association and later residency with the London Philharmonic Orchestra that ultimately resulted in *The Discovery of Heaven*. Could we start with an overview of the working arrangement – hinterland, if you like – of each?

JA: The conditions of the Birmingham residency involved not just the orchestra, but also the chorus and the BCMG.[1] It was that special set-up where they all

---

[1]   Birmingham Contemporary Music Group

worked together in the same building the whole time. As you know, the NMC disc of my music is in fact my Birmingham residency.[2] If I was working with the BCMG I'd go into the CBSO Centre and see the orchestra rehearsing there. I was constantly going between the groups. I had very fruitful relations with the managers of both the CBSO – Stephen Maddock, who knows more music than it would be possible to believe – and the BCMG, which Steven and Jackie Newbould ran brilliantly; both they and Stephen Maddock knew all about how to work with composers. Sakari Oramo was chief conductor at that time and I was very influenced by his musical taste – our musical enthusiasms overlap. Obviously, we had Sibelius in common, but many other things too – Nielsen, contemporary Finnish music, Busoni, Janáček, Kurtág – and we got on very well. As you know, Sibelius and aspects of Finnish early twentieth-century culture play a part in the *Symphony* anyway, which is dedicated to Sakari.

CD: And how about the LPO?

JA: I first worked with them in 2002, when Vladimir Jurowski conducted them in *Khorovod*. He did it on one rehearsal plus the day and it was a fantastic performance. They did it amazingly well. Jurowski and I started discussing repertoire, and it turns out we share an interest in what you might call late nineteenth-, early twentieth-century 'lost' repertoire: Suk, Enescu, Janáček, Nielsen, Myaskovsky. People who are very provocative and exciting composers, but who are just a little bit oblique to what is considered the canon. Even now, Nielsen is not somehow accepted in the way that he should be, even though there are lots of symphony cycles on CD.

Also in 2002, the LPO did *The Stations of the Sun* very well under Daniel Harding, and they played *The Crazed Moon* in 2003 with Tadaaki Otaka, so the orchestra knew my work. Then Tim Walker came along as manager, and it became clear that Jurowski was going to be the next music director after Kurt Masur. Tim Walker and I also got on very well. The LPO appointed me Composer in Residence for four years, ending in 2015. The commission for *The Discovery of Heaven* came about as part of that appointment in 2011–12.

CD: Looking more closely at your CBSO residency, the first fruit of that was *Imagin'd Corners*, which not only showcases the orchestra, but has a particular focus on the horns.

JA: Well one of my brothers learnt the horn for a while, so I'd heard it practised in the home and had nice memories of that. I knew bits of horn repertoire very well from early on in my childhood.

[2] NMC D121. It features *Eden, Imagin'd Corners, Four American Choruses, Symphony* and *Book of Hours*.

CD: And *Imagin'd Corners* isn't your only work where horns do interesting things, is it?

JA: The second part of the *Diptych* has a lot of antics for the horns at the end off stage, and there are other pieces since where horns feature in a big way even if they're not soloistic. That said, the horn parts in *Imagin'd Corners* are not very elaborate in terms of what's required, less than in a Strauss tone poem or a Mahler symphony. The piece is only 11 minutes long. They don't play in all of the piece because they're moving around, but when they play, they're doing something very specific. It's ambiguous: these are and are not solo parts. This was my first residency with a full-size orchestra and I was trying to get to know them. They played the Strauss *Alpine Symphony* in the first concert I heard in Birmingham's Symphony Hall after I was named Composer-in-Residence. They made full use of the hall's acoustic baffles, with the horn calls going back and forth. It was a marvellous sound.

CD: And it is very much a piece that uses space.

JA: The thing that really interests me about space is not only the feeling of music coming from different sides, which is exciting, but also that if you put people off stage and they play very loudly, it still sounds loud even though it may be quiet. You sense that it is being played loudly, however quiet the volume. There is a difference, psychologically, between a sound that is actually quiet and a sound that is very loud but is far away and merely sounds quiet. The latter does not, psychologically, sound quiet. So if a horn calls loudly from a distance, you can tell that it's clearly very loud really, and it doesn't sound the same way. There was a project in 1991–92, which I never finished, called *Noises Off*, where the whole ensemble was going to be off stage in different places outside of the auditorium. I had the idea to do it for somewhere like the Queen Elizabeth Hall, with players behind the main entrance doors to the hall which would be opened and closed by hand, as well as in the backstage areas. I won't bother to finish that because more recently Benedict Mason has independently been very thorough in exploring what you can do with putting instruments in different areas of the entire hall, off stage, backstage, upstairs, outside and much more. So he's the master of that medium of extended spatiality, as it were, and I happily leave it to him.

However, the fact that I thought of the *Noises Off* project shows you that I have always been eager to explore the psychological effect of space in my music. I suspect this originally comes from my enthusiasm for Thea Musgrave, who's been an influence on my music in several regards. I particularly admire her Concerto for Orchestra, the Clarinet Concerto, the Horn Concerto, the *Memento Vitae* commemorating Beethoven and the choral work *Rorate Coeli*. The spatial and musical dramas of those pieces – the way the horn soloist moves around the stage in the that concerto, for example, or the way she successfully intensifies the drama in layers of harmonic and textural activity in *Memento Vitae* and the Concerto for Orchestra – all this has certainly affected my orchestral writing which has a similar propensity for dramatic forms and a certain amount of movement on- and off-stage. In *The Bearded Lady*, the oboe or clarinet is chased off stage by the piano in this little drama, and then plays a bit from a distance, though at that point the clarinet, or the oboe, depending on which version you play, changes instrument. The clarinet plays a bass clarinet or basset horn, and the oboe plays a cor anglais, so the spatial distance changes the actual timbre in some way. In *Imagin'd Corners*, the opening is based on the idea that *ff* off stage is equal to *p* or *pp* on stage, which is why the first thing you hear is a very loud note from one horn on stage, then a loud chord from all the horns off stage and finally on-stage pianissimo muted strings. The off-stage horns are only just louder than that muted string sound on stage. I like that paradox, and the whole opening is based on that idea.

CD: Isn't this also where an alphorn comes into things?

JA: Yes, I have a great love of alphorns generally – the horn being an out of doors instrument and therefore a spatial instrument par excellence. I have a particular interest in Romanian folk music and their traditions of alphorn-playing. There are three instruments: one is called a bucium, which is shorter than the Swiss alphorn, another is called the tulnic, which is even shorter than the bucium, and finally the shortest of all, called trimbitza. They all go higher up the harmonic series than the Swiss alphorn, even beyond partial 16, so you get many strange forms of intonations. I first heard them in Barrie Gavin and Bert Lloyd's documentary called *The Miraculous Circumstance* made in 1981 for the Bartók centenary.[3] Seeing that incredible film – so richly evocative, so strikingly colourful and carefully documenting living folk traditions – was a life-changing experience. By chance I saw it again eight years later when they (finally) repeated it on BBC2, and it was like recovering a very precious memory. As I have said before in these conversations, almost everything from *Khorovod* to *The Stations of the Sun* came out of that experience. Bert Lloyd and Barrie Gavin filmed bucium players, who are almost always women, in the mountainous region of Maramures, Romania. The alphorns are made of wood. You have to soak a wooden trumpet to make it sound well. There was a wonderful shot of the women gathering by the mountain stream, in Maramures, rotating the alphorns, soaking them with the stream water, blowing trial notes on them and exchanging gossip. It was a marvellous total sound: a mountain stream and these alphorns being tried out with these women's voices. I used it in a now withdrawn student tape piece, roughly 10 minutes long, called *Bucium*, which was included

---

[3]   Barrie Gavin (director), *The Miraculous Circumstance*, broadcast on BBC Two, 21 March 1981.

in my final undergraduate portfolio at the Royal College. I thought there should be *musique concrète* with pitches, so I used the sample of a bucium sound for many recordings. I got permission from Bert Lloyd's widow, Charlotte, to use his recordings and it was based entirely on them.

CD: You withdrew the tape piece, though.

JA: Yes, but the last section of *Imagin'd Corners* is an instrumental simulation of the opening of *Bucium*. It uses a particular Romanian alphorn effect where they do yelps down to a pitch. You have these yelps on the horns going down to a G again and again in the final section of *Imagin'd Corners*, and I'd used that sampled alphorn sound repeatedly in the opening section of the tape piece. If I were to play you the two, you would hear immediately it's almost the same.

So, the sounds of the bucium and tulnic feature in a big way in *Imagin'd Corners*. This is one of the reasons why I have a problem, by the way, with Ligeti's use of horn harmonics in his Horn Concerto and elsewhere in his output. They always seem to be presented to sound out-of-tune. That's not at all how I use them. I've always used them to sound as though that's the real tuning. There is a flat E-flat off stage at the start of *Imagin'd Corners*, and one of the viola players said to me, 'I think we're flat on our E-flat, and I know why. It's because the horns are playing a natural seventh.' I listened to the broadcast and the violas are indeed a bit flat. You can tell they're trying to get as flat as the horns. I found the difference between the flat seventh, the natural seventh on the off-stage horns and the normal tuned seventh on stage on the strings was acceptable if the horns were very far away. It was as if the distance factor neutralised the differences.

CD: A sort of Doppler effect?

JA: Yes. At the opening of that piece you hear the difference, but not very much. If they were on stage playing that you'd really hear the difference.

CD: *Imagin'd Corners* and *Symphony* were for the CBSO, but *Book of Hours*, which was part of the same residency, was for Birmingham Contemporary Music Group.

JA: Yes, the idea was that I'd focus on the orchestra first and last, but also write for BCMG and the chorus. At one point I was thinking of writing some kind of piece that would involve the musicians enacting the walk from the CBSO Centre to Symphony Hall in the ICC.[4] The set-up is so amazing but we never did that.

CD: You broke out of the ensemble by using electronics instead.

---

4   International Conference Centre.

JA: I had wanted to do a piece involving electronics ever since July 2000, when Magnus Lindberg showed me, on a Mac laptop, the then latest software from IRCAM, which was able to do a lot of things that I'd wanted to be able to do at home. I'd given up electronics in 1990, saying to Lawrence Casserley, who ran the studio at the Royal College, that I wouldn't do any more electronics until you could get all the contents of that studio on to a portable computer that I could carry around in a briefcase. It was actually only 10 years later – though none of us could have anticipated that.

Eric de Visscher was then running IRCAM and he suggested that I should come on their one-month course for composers. It was a crash course where you work 18 hours a day for a month to get to know software, and so I did this in the summer of 2002. I lived off banana crêpes and a few bistros, so when I got back I was on a long diet! I went on a couple of visits to IRCAM before that to see workshops and things on the software, and to talk to various people about what was possible. This confirmed my view that this was the right time to start up again in electronics.

CD: So then you brought what you learnt back to Birmingham.

JA: Well, at the end of the time at IRCAM I still didn't know how to use the software properly! I had to get a trainer in Birmingham, which was my dear friend Lamberto Coccioli, whom you know.[5]

CD: Yes, my colleague, so that was another partnership to throw into the mix.

JA: Lamberto introduced me to some non-IRCAM software, which enriched the palette of *Book of Hours* significantly. I made a rule that if I couldn't make the sound entirely without help, I wouldn't use it. Now that's all very well, but unless you have several years of experience, that's not going to work. It is a restriction and you need restrictions in working with electronics, as too much is possible. At the same time, it wasn't a fully realistic aspiration.

CD: Isn't that almost like saying you would only write a note for a trombone or flute or whatever that you can play yourself?

JA: In a way, yes. I began every day for about three years with an hour of playing around with the software, whichever software. It was a lot of work. Later I also had help from Richard Polfreman in London. We spent a week going through the sounds I'd made and improving them, making new ones together, etc. Even then I remade many of them when I got back home, because now I knew exactly how to do so. It was that kind of collaboration. In other words, it was very hands-on

---

[5]   Lamberto Coccioli is Associate Principal and Professor of Music and Technology at Royal Birmingham Conservatoire.

in my case; it was not at all the case of an assistant making the sounds for me or anything like that, really not. Those sounds were made by me, with the necessary help and guidance for which I'm extremely grateful.

CD: Lamberto did tell me that you were unusual in knowing precisely what you wanted the electronics to do.

JA: I had seen too many composers assume the back-seat driver position and I didn't think it was right, to be honest with you. I just felt I'd got to be able to understand what was going on and do as much of it as possible myself. Every sound sample I made, from the shortest to the longest, was submitted to Lamberto's judgement. I said to him, 'Don't squirm. If you think it sounds cheesy, you must say.' I needed to know whether somebody currently active in electro-acoustics thought these sounds would convince. It was all going fine until we came to the big electronic interlude in Part II, which lasts about three minutes. With the first version I took to him (and I'd already made several versions before that one!), he said, 'No, it won't do.' I was trying to synthesise the sound of a very large metal percussion instrument being banged, scratched, bounced, hit, scraped along the floor and so on. Lamberto said, 'It sounds like very bad guitar strumming. It will ruin the whole interlude, and quite possibly the whole work.' He wasn't advising me how to rectify those things, he just told me to try again. We went through another version and he still said no. In each case, he was quite right. You have to step outside and assess it as a neutral person. Finally, the proverbial third time lucky, after hundreds of hours of work, I came up with a version that was really violent and raw: I feared it would be unbearable in performance, it was so intense, but it was just what I had meant all along. Lamberto immediately said, 'That's it! That will work and I know exactly how that's going to function in the piece.' So Lamberto was very helpful. That kind of objective, factual criticism is vital if you're working in an area unfamiliar to you.

CD: With the CBSO, it was a matter of becoming acquainted with the orchestra and various associated ensembles and people in Birmingham. However, when you wrote *The Discovery of Heaven* for the London Philharmonic, you already had those relationships to a degree.

JA: Yes, I already knew the London Philharmonic quite well, as I explained earlier. *The Discovery of Heaven* was certainly partly influenced by that, or by the luxury – and it is a luxury – of knowing players for that long and having also sung with them as a member of the London Philharmonic Choir for some years. The other thing, of course, is that I had already written *Alleluia* for them before I was resident composer.

CD: Did all that make it easier to write for them?

JA: On the one hand, I knew the players and the LPO sound well. On the other, I wasn't immediately sure what I wanted to compose for them when I started what became *The Discovery of Heaven*. I'd written Act I of *Thebans* (or at least I thought I had – I later threw it away), but I couldn't immediately work out what to write for the LPO.

CD: So how did you get past that?

JA: When I'm at a loss, I often read books or look at pictures. Not because I want to write programme music, but it generally helps unblock me. I reread, not initially for anything to do with the orchestral piece, Harry Mulisch's epic novel, *The Discovery of Heaven*. I thought, 'God, that would make the most marvellous opera', but I was already writing an opera, so I thought again and realised it could be an orchestral piece, in the sense that the panoramas of the novel really offer a huge amount of contrast. I was trying to write something that is not symphonic, but an orchestral suite. I love the Tchaikovsky suites for orchestra – another thing people don't play enough – and there are also wonderful suites for orchestra by Enescu, too. But if you call it an orchestral suite, nobody will play it, so I gave it a title which I hope is more suggestive. I got bored with the novel eventually, as you often do when you're writing pieces based on literature, but it provided enough of a structure.

CD: So the novel is just a point of departure, rather than this being a storybook piece?

JA: In Mulisch's novel there's the contrast between action that happens in Heaven – where two angels are dialoguing – and actions that happen on Earth at different times of history, including, and this is one interest of mine, Amsterdam in the late '60s and early '70s. I know several of the people who were involved in the Dutch incidents that are referred to in that novel. There's a reference to a famous political concert at the Theater Carré, involving Louis Andriessen, Reinbert de Leeuw and Peter Schat. I'd spoken to Reinbert about the political demonstration concert at the Carré and what that whole period meant to that group when they were starting out.

CD: Do you feel close to The Hague School and all that?

JA: Yes, in part. As I've already mentioned, I first went over there sometime in 1986 and heard an early performance of Andriessen's *De Stijl* by Karlslaag. I enjoyed the directness and energy of the new Dutch music, its lack of fuss and its engagement with popular musics. But I also have my reservations about The Hague School. Their claims are sometimes a bit dogmatic. Nevertheless, some wonderfully fresh music has come from Holland, and I love working with Dutch players. I felt *The Discovery of Heaven* to be a homage in some way to Provo

Dutch culture. In an interview Peter Schat remarked that Holland became Provo land, only nobody admits it. He then made a list of the attributes of Holland before '66 and the repressive social atmosphere of the previous time. It reminded me alarmingly of things in UK society. I thought a lot about the political situation when I was writing *The Discovery of Heaven*.[6]

Another aspect of *The Discovery of Heaven* was that I wanted to express solidarity with young people everywhere, their aspirations, and their commitment to maintaining freedom. It's partly a political piece, though I didn't emphasise that because I dislike preaching. In any case there were enough complications for people to understand in the title and its relevance in Mulisch's book without that. I don't like telling people how to think. If I read about somebody's noble politics in a programme note, I get very sceptical.

For many years, having strong political views, I didn't put them into the music because I didn't really want to. There's a self-righteousness that steals over people when they start writing political pieces, that they feel they've stood up for something. As Auden points out, it usually just pleases you and your friends and makes you feel rather conceited. He rightly points out that is not a healthy emotion for a creative artist.

CD: This is one of the traits that the film *Team America* lampoons – it's essentially equal opportunities in its satire as it attacks everyone. It points out the absurdity of the gung-ho, militaristic approach, but it also targets the self-importance of Hollywood actors parading their conscience about such things and their naivety about some of the political realities.

JA: That's a bit like *Bowling for Columbine* also, which I thought was a very good film. So, it was very gingerly that I approached this kind of thing, and therefore the Mulisch was a useful channel for it. Of course, Mulisch was Provo, so I knew which side of the line he, Jan van Vlijmen, Louis Andriessen, Peter Schat and Reinbert de Leeuw were on. Broadly speaking, I was in favour of what they achieved in Holland, which was very healthy, until it more recently came under attack from neo-conservatism. I felt it was time to say something about all this, but in such a way that it's not the be all and end all of the piece.

CD: How does it manifest itself in the piece?

JA: The work is built on contrasts which do not resolve. The second movement of *The Discovery of Heaven* is called 'In the Street', a title borrowed from Janáček's piano sonata, 'From the Street'.[7] The first movement of my piece is about as

---

[6]   See Peter Schat, *Interview 2002 part 1*, available on youtube.com [last accessed 1 November 2019].
[7]   *1. X. 1905* (Piano Sonata), known as 'From the Street'.

remote from political matters as you apparently can be. In a sense, the whole work is about incompatibilities. The first movement is an experiment in synthesising on the orchestra the sound of the Japanese mouth organ called the shō. It relates to my love of Japanese *gagaku*. I'm interested in dialoguing with various musical traditions, as you know. I call it 'tourism', because it's inescapable, especially since the Internet came along. But it's always happened. I'm not Japanese, but I've loved *gagaku* since I was in my teens and know quite a lot about it. That seems to me fair.

CD: Well, the alternative is parochialism.

JA: Jane Fulcher's fascinating book, *The Composer as Intellectual*, points out the composers of Messiaen's and Jolivet's generation were changed positively by their engagement with non-Western musics, refusing to treat them as in any way 'inferior' or 'exotic', but taking them very seriously in their own right.[8] Messiaen became a far more open composer because of that. That's admirable, and I also sympathise with it.

I analysed recordings of the shō, and I realised it on the orchestra in different ways, different modes, the modes of attack, the kind of cluster chords. Not only on the strings and clusters, as Messiaen does in his *Sept Haïkaï*, but also on the wind, or combinations of the two. I analysed the breath attack of the shō, and synthesised noise on the orchestra as well: there are bits where you get scratch-tones on the strings, etc. There's also a strange sense of time, because with the shō you often circular breathe or you inhale and exhale through the instrument; the sound can go on forever. As that happens, it ebbs and flows. The sense of time direction to my ears is ambiguous. I was very attracted by that, so what keeps happening in the first movement of *The Discovery of Heaven* is the music builds up and then it just stops. There's one passage where a texture is going on and I simply erased it and put a gap of about two bars. Then it starts up again, and I just put a note to the conductor: 'Carry on as if nothing happened.' I like that, that sense of drifting time, circular time.

Messiaen did these wonderful analyses of Debussy. Do you remember what he says about Debussy's rhythmic language in the *Traité*? It's something I'd never thought of. He said that what makes Debussy unusual is the deliberate confrontation of very long durations with very short ones, side by side, and nobody had ever done that before. I'd never thought of that, but he's totally right.

CD: Of course, while Messiaen says Debussy was the first to do that...

JA: That's debatable.

---

8   Jane Fulcher, *The Composer as Intellectual: Music and Ideology in France, 1914–1940* (New York: Oxford University Press, 2005). See esp. pp. 299–305.

CD: Well, to start with, there's Pérotin.

JA: Interesting idea. I was going to say Chopin, because there are passages of his music which you could analyse that way.

CD: There are, yes, and Messiaen certainly knew his Chopin, he was his favourite piano composer, so it's curious he identifies this with Debussy rather than Chopin, but maybe it's a matter of degree.

JA: He singles out for particular attention Debussy's willingness to confront streams of very short note values with very long ones, and this is what creates the suspension of metrical time to the listener's ear when you hear a Debussy piece. The combination of those things means you cannot work out what the pulse is, because the fast values are too short relative to the long values being too long: you can't hear the proportional relationship.

I began seeing that in other musics too, and I decided to base the first movement of *Discovery* on that premise. The first thing you hear is a long note and then you get a flurry of very short ones. That's like the model for the whole thing. You only get very long or very short notes. The movement ends in a kind of reverse situation – a very long note followed by an extremely short one. That, also, is an accidental nod in the direction of the ending of *Gruppen*, which famously, after all the flamboyance, winds down to a single horn note on E-flat. After being held for really quite a long time, it just goes up to a very short G – which is such a strange way to end such a flamboyant piece. It's rather like a shrug. I always wanted to do a little homage of that.

I wanted to give that a meaning and a context by confronting it with opposites in the second and third movements of *The Discovery of Heaven*. The second movement is like walking down different parts of Amsterdam at different times of year and seeing what you meet.

CD: So there's not a linear 'storytelling' to any of this?

JA: No, the ideas have no logical succession, necessarily. There is an overall build-up to a street demo feeling at the end of the movement, which gets quite violent. That is continued into the last movement, 'Hymns', which follows without a break. The idea of that was to see if I could damage my own music. I got that idea from Miró's *Burnt Canvases*. Miró was Catalan and very political, of course. There was a wonderful Tate retrospective of Miró in 2011.[9] In one series of later paintings, he painted quite typical late Miró and then he assaulted them. He poured petrol all over them, walked all over them, cut them, burnt them. They're called 'toiles brûlées', and I thought that was something incredible, to

---

[9]   *Miró: The Ladder of Escape*, Tate Modern: Exhibition, 14 April–11 September 2011.

see somebody take considerable care to paint these marvellous works of art, and then actually damage them.

CD: That's a very different thing from the approach by some in the '60s of destroying objects – paintings, pianos, violins or whatever – created by others.

JA: The bravery of the Miró works struck me very positively, so I wrote this long musical line which is sustained mainly on the brass and is quite diatonic, hymn-like. It rolls on and on. I then printed that out and literally took a pen and slashed it. I did it quickly, just like an artist would. I'd never worked that way before. Then I just took the slashes and said, 'Alright, that will be time. I'll put that there, I'll put that there, that will be there.' I made each of them a different sound, short sounds, that would attack and try to destroy the hymn. That then raises a parallel with the side drum trying to destroy the lyricism in Nielsen's Fifth Symphony, a piece I've always loved. I thought I could try and do something a bit like that. In my case, what happens is the hymn music, in order to win over, does not have a big, glorious G major victory, like in the Nielsen, but has to change in order to win over the violence. It has to get faster, in fact, more violent. It gradually accelerates until eventually what was a note that would have lasted, say, 20 seconds in the first few pages is now lasting a 16th note at crotchet equals 160. It becomes almost unplayable at that point. I couldn't resolve the conflict between the hymn-type melodies and the noises, so I just left that passage and went elsewhere. Incidentally, that first section of the third movement contains more extended techniques and noise sounds than my music generally does. That's not an area I've used much, but there I needed it.

CD: It's striking, though, that Thebans was percolating at this time, and the openings of Act I and especially Act III essentially start in the realm of noise, also using extended techniques, but with a completely different sentiment and musical intent.

JA: Yes, in Thebans the noises in Act III are really the sounds of the sacred wood outside Athens. In The Discovery of Heaven, eventually the noises become concentrated into two or three very sharp eruptions. As that's happening, a much calmer music takes over, but it is not, in my view, any resolution of anything. That, I have to confess, since he's now dead, was also something to do with Jonathan Harvey, to whom the whole piece is dedicated – it was written as a present for Jonathan, who was dying at that time, and none of us knew how long he'd survive. He was a lovely man, special, luminous. The coda is, in my hearing of the piece, very intimate. But at the end it just breaks off. What's been a very smooth, arhythmic texture in the strings gradually becomes equal crotchets. When it does that, I just put a double bar line in and stopped. There's no resolution; the work remains open.

Discovery is full of contradictions. The Miró canvases helped me with that because they're so anti-synthetic. They're full of loose ends and I like that.

CD: We've spoken about works where there's a close relationship with an ensemble that goes beyond the piece in question. That's not the case with something like *Incantesimi*, which was written for Rattle and the Berlin Phil. How did that work?

JA: Well, Rattle is one of those conductors who has remained heavily involved with new music. Many conductors start off in new music because it's an area where work is needed. Then, if they get their lucky break, some drop it and just do standard rep. Happily, many conductors have a genuine love of new music and continue to champion it throughout their career. He's one of several famous conductors who play new music as a matter of course. This is becoming much more common now among younger conductors.

CD: And Rattle's predecessor, Abbado.

JA: Another very fine example, true. So there's a background in the Berlin Phil of playing quite a lot of new music. Nonetheless, the way Rattle chose to mark leaving that job was exceptional. He commissioned many composers to write shortish pieces, of between about five and 10 minutes, as well as touring *Le Grand Macabre*, the Ligeti opera. That's really something. Of course, I was delighted to be asked to do one of these. It was put in lovely programmes of Brahms, Dvořák and Beethoven – standard repertoire, which is fine by me. As it happens, the premiere was in a programme with two pieces I've loved for much of my life and feel very close to for different reasons: Beethoven's Fourth Piano Concerto, which is my favourite Beethoven piano concerto, and the Dvořák *Slavonic Dances* in the second half. I don't think the interaction between folk and art music in the Dvořák is as tarted up as people say. It's honest and they're very earthy, distinctive pieces with a strong flavour, as the best Dvořák does have. I've always liked him much more than Smetana for that reason. The music seems to me more direct. Of course, Janáček in that sense is from Dvořák, not from Smetana so much.

CD: Both Rattle and the Berlin Phil are far from unknown quantities, so how did you approach the commission?

JA: I met Rattle. We talked about the playing qualities of the orchestra and I asked him about various players. He spoke with great admiration of the whole orchestra and we went over the various sections in more detail. When it came to the wind, one of the names which came up was that of the cor anglais player, Dominik Wollenweber. Rattle alerted me to his prowess on the instrument, and once I had heard him I needed no persuading because that guy's tone is just fantastic, something like the best soprano saxophone you ever heard crossed with the best oboe you ever heard. I watched him playing on YouTube and thought immediately, 'I must do something for that player.' I've always loved cor anglais.

CD: It has a big role in *Thebans*, doesn't it?

JA: Yes, it was Antigone's instrument, so I'd written a lot of big lines for it in *Thebans* and I was very happy to do more with the cor anglais. I immediately had the notion of doing a piece which had five musical ideas going around at once, but not necessarily all together. They rotate around each other, circling around like planets in a model of the solar system, you know, an orrery. I love all that and I'm very interested in astronomy, in an amateurish way. In saying five ideas, I was thinking of the Finale of Mozart's 'Jupiter' Symphony, but unlike that work, in my piece the music is not a fugue. I wanted to have this feeling of the ideas in dialogue with each other, circling around each other and in constantly different relationships to each other. Some ideas would be texture, some would be melody, some would be chords, all kinds of things, from something almost thematic to something that's just a chord type. Among the five ideas there is the cor anglais melody, which generally starts with a minor third and then a major second, so can therefore be a bit pentatonic in feeling. Another idea is an ascending major ninth with a fall after it – that's usually on the high strings. That worked in combination with the cor anglais pattern, and could also work well on its own, going into a canon and echo with itself or heterophony with different variants of the fall written over each other at different speeds.

CD: How is the piece structured in relation to these ideas?[10]

JA: My original thought was that towards the end all five would come together in a big climax. I tried writing such a passage and it was totally opaque, you couldn't hear anything. Eventually I worked out that each zone of the piece would have a different focus on one of these ideas, and what happens at the end is the idea of the ascending ninth with the falling melody after it becomes hugely intensified on the whole orchestra. I wanted a sudden onrush just at the point the piece is ending. The last thing you hear is the cor anglais, but then it just fades from view very quickly. The end is deliberately somewhat inconclusive and open, as so often.

The piece had, as with the Violin Concerto, no preformed shape. I worked with those ideas like a very slow-motion juggler, juggling five objects in the air, seeing which one was the one next to come around. It was written straight into full score, which is not my norm these days. Like Nielsen used to say, I felt as though I'd crept inside the instruments.

---

[10] See Conversation Six, 'Composing (or not)' for discussion of an early sketch for *Incantesimi*.

In the middle of composing it, I had a triplet figuration at one point that suddenly developed into a whole new fast section – very fast. I didn't know anything about that before I composed it. I tried to write something incredibly fast and feather-light, a little bit of a post-Mendelssohn scherzo, swift but very quiet.

CD: You've said you didn't know anything about the scherzo section and you've said things of a similar vein at various points in these conversations. Non-composers might be surprised at this notion of the material having a sort of life of its own, that at times you don't have a conscious sense of why the material is doing what it's doing or where it's going. Given that so much musicological work is from the premise, presumption even, of understanding the composer's intentions, the creative rationale behind the piece, it seems from the outside to be a very odd relationship with the music you are creating.

JA: Francis Bacon said that one of the things that started him off doing his mature paintings was that he made an accidental mark on canvas with his brush, and found it more interesting than what he was trying to paint. It's very necessary, as an artist, to be reactive to those moments where something completely out of the blue comes up that you cannot explain or understand. It's important to be responsive enough to the creative moment to let something fly off somewhere you didn't plan.

That's not to say that it's always right. For example, in *Sensation* there was a section which came up unexpectedly, but it didn't work and I had to chuck three or four pages, go back and write something else that worked better. You have to know when it's rubbish or when it's a really good idea, or indeed when it's just a rewritten memory of something else you've heard. Having said that, all music comes from somewhere, and rewritten memories can be found in such a large amount of great pieces that I don't see any evil in that, provided you're not plagiarising anyone.

CD: 'Rewritten Memories' would be a good name for a piece.

JA: But I do see what you mean, that it is hard to understand how these almost chance accidents can generate music. But then it's also hard to understand when I'm making the music!

CD: We've spoken thus far about big ensemble pieces, but I wonder about the relationships involved where a piece is for an individual, such as with the viola piece *Prayer*.

JA: I'd wanted to write a viola solo piece for a very long time.

CD: It's your instrument, of course.

JA: Not really. Only in the sense that as a teenager I frequently dropped it and made the most horrible noise on it... but yes, I knew it. More seriously, there's this amazing viola player with the Nash Ensemble called Lawrence Power. The idea was I'd write a piece for him, but it was also a birthday present for Ginny Macbeth, a wonderful person who I've been working with since 2006 and who has become a dear friend as well as a good professional colleague. She's a music publicist, but is something far more than that. She's somebody who helps musicians get across the divide between our profession and the public. That divide is often the newspapers and the media generally, and Ginny is brilliant at dealing with it. She really understands musicians. She's highly musical and deeply cultured, very sophisticated at handling the problem of how to promote music and composing in particular, which is terribly difficult for the general public to understand because you can't see it happen. You can't see the person compose, but you can see a person perform, so it's more difficult to put composing across to the media.

CD: Mind you, it does remind me of that Monty Python sketch with novel-writing from Dorset, where there's a sports-style commentary on Thomas Hardy writing a novel.[11]

JA: That's a marvellous sketch, you're quite right. I once did a day in the De La Warr Pavilion in Sussex when I was composer-in-residence with the now-defunct chamber orchestra Sinfonia 21. I was asked whether I would be willing, using computer technology, to sit in a room and compose a piece that day, which would be premiered by six string players of Sinfonia 21 in the evening. People came and watched this piece gradually taking shape on the screen. The piece itself is not, as they say, a survivor, but it was an interesting experience.

CD: Was this recorded for posterity at all?

JA: There isn't a video, which I now regret, not out of vanity, but because it is quite an unusual thing to have a piece written over about eight hours where, bit by bit, you can see it grow. It's the only way you can show people what decisions are involved in composing a piece of music.

Anyway, Ginny Macbeth's job is to get composers and musicians across to the public, and she manages to do that very effectively without compromise. She never goes way over the top, saying they're the greatest composer since Beethoven or some nonsense like that. She's very subtle but persistent. Consequently, she's become a trusted ally and when she had an important birthday I wanted to write her a piece. Amelia Freedman at the Nash heard about this and suggested

[11] 'Novel Writing' on the 1973 album *The Monty Python Matching Tie and Handkerchief* (Charisma, CAS 1080).

I wrote it for Lawrence Power. So, very happily, that's what I did. I got very interested in the idea of praying. This relates to my string orchestra piece *Past Hymns*, which is also to do with the fervour of petitioning God. One of the things I always enjoyed about the Jewish religion is the attitude to prayer, which is quite different to that of Christianity. You don't just say, 'We're not worthy,' and all that. You petition God, you criticise or even attack him. There's a very big Jewish tradition of it. I remember, Bernstein was very worried when he wrote the *Kaddish* Symphony, which has such passages for the narrator. He was worried people would take offence because the narrator's address to the creator is sometimes critical. Then a Hebrew scholar pointed out to him that this is absolutely allowed, it's encouraged. The Jewish attitude towards prayer chimes very much with my own feelings of what a prayer is like. My viola piece *Prayer*, therefore, does have some inflections of Jewish modality in it as well, and it is not a gentle work – far from it.

I needed to have a moment of revelation where all the straining that goes on in the piece, constantly climbing up and urging itself on, suddenly vanishes to reveal a glimpse of something quite different, serene. It had to be reached by a sense of effort. There is a cadenza about two-thirds of the way through the piece, which goes up into very high harmonics: the rhetoric of the rest of the piece is simply abandoned. It's very still and I explore micro-intervals of Just intonation. I focus finally on an enlarged major second between two open string harmonics: it's a double-stop C and very flat B-flat-flat. It's a very strange interval, totally outside of the tempered system. Then the music abruptly abandons that register and returns to the rougher music.

In composing the work I also thought a lot about Lawrence Power's huge capacity for making a dramatic statement on the viola.

CD: More recently you have written the piano piece *Sensation* for another remarkable virtuoso, Pierre-Laurent Aimard.

JA: Yes, the title could be in French or in English, which is one of its attractions for me.

CD: And on top of working in both languages, it also potentially has a double meaning.

JA: The starting point for the piece was an idea of doing a set of pieces about the five senses. In fact there are six movements, so that didn't quite follow through, but the idea of it being about sense and sense perception is predominant. It starts with a movement which is extremely quiet. The fact that whole work is called *Sensation* but starts with a very quiet movement felt like a good oblique way making it clear that this work is not about the showy kind of sensation.

CD: For someone who composes at the piano, aside from the four Etudes, which are all brief, and a small handful of other short pieces, the instrument has been pretty conspicuous by its absence in your output.

JA: Before this project I just did not feel that I'd quite got inside the piano. I'm not meaning to say that the piano pieces I've written before are no good, but somehow I felt I wasn't writing idiomatically enough for it. Two pianists had been in touch before this. One was Robert Levin, with whom I was on the faculty at Harvard, and we've talked for years about me writing a really large-scale piano piece, modelled after something like the *Piano Fantasy* of Copland or the *Night Fantasies* of Carter, something like that. Certainly something in the American big-piano tradition. I had always thought that the piece for Robert Levin would be a Sonata: but I haven't written it yet. A bit before that, Stephen Osborne and the BBC Scottish Symphony Orchestra got in touch about me writing a piano concerto. I was interested, but felt I wasn't ready to tackle it yet. Eventually I agreed but it took me a while. I couldn't think what to do with piano and orchestra, or the piano itself.

In August 2015, things came to a head in a very unexpected way. It's another one of those serendipitous things we were talking about before. I started to write a piano piece, which I thought was going to be about two hours of work. I knew it was going to be a short piece based on a particular idea. I wrote, and when I next looked at my watch I'd been at my desk five hours non-stop and I'd got about four or five bars done. [Laughter]

Nine days later, at 15 hours' work a day, I had this piece finished, which was way in excess of what I thought it would take to compose. It is not a complicated piece to look at on the page. I realised I was getting very interested in the piano as a resonator, and the piano as an acoustic object, and in the piano culturally, in everything that the piano can be, which is everything else, in fact. That's what interests me about piano music: the piano has a history of being an imaginary everything else, imaginary other instruments. And because of the pedal, you've also got the resonance question, and therefore imaginary acoustics come into it. The piece is called 'She Hears'. It was prompted by reading the biography by Christopher Grogan of Imogen Holst.[12] I've come across her music repeatedly and been hugely impressed; she uses a personally distinctive form of modality which is quite unlike other British composers of that period. I'm quite indignant she wasn't more esteemed by others, but tragically also by herself because she didn't take herself as seriously as a composer as she should have done.

There was a kind of friendship between Imogen Holst, a spinster living in Aldeburgh, and Oskar Kokoschka, a product of Viennese café society. It

---

[12] Christopher Grogan (ed.), *Imogen Holst: A Life in Music*, revised edition (Woodbridge: Boydell, 2010).

seems a strange juxtaposition, but they were very friendly, and he admired and respected her enormously, especially her devotion to listening, which was quite as important to her as any money, or any food. On the back of a picture that he gave to her called 'King David' he wrote an inscription: 'For Imogen/She Hears.' I was very touched by that, and that became the title of my piece.

I decided it would be quiet, slow music, and it would probably be best on piano. It was a strange experience writing it. Every note had to be precisely that note, in that place, in that register only. I spent hours in each progression finding just that right one. Mostly the chords are four parts, and, although it's not stylistically connected, technically 'She Hears' was very much connected to my love and study of Bach chorales as a kid. I think of each voice part in 'She Hears' as having its own trajectory.

CD: It sounds a bit like you were doing a kind of musical Battleships, trying to find where your notes lay.

JA: Yes. I was addicted to that game as a kid. I wasn't very good at it but I was addicted. [Laughter] That's a brilliant metaphor because composing often is like Battleships, it really is. It has the same feeling of there being an answer out there, but you've got to find it. You've got to somehow work it out. So I wrote the piece and very soon after that I had the idea of a cycle of five pieces. In fact, it was jointly commissioned by the Aldeburgh Festival for Pierre-Laurent Aimard and by the Santa Fe Chamber Music Festival, who had also co-commissioned the Second Quartet. Then I wrote *Van Gogh Blue* right after that and, to my great surprise, the fourth movement of *Van Gogh Blue* was a transcription of 'She Hears' note for note – a few things added, but it's there.

That turned out to be very time-consuming because I could hear in my head what it should sound like, but to find how to realise that on an ensemble was very hard. I'd have probably written the fourth movement of *Van Gogh* much quicker if it had been a new piece rather than a transcription! That proved my feeling, given how much recomposition had to go on in that transcription, that perhaps 'She Hears' really was pianistic.

Just after *Van Gogh Blue* was finished, I wrote another piano piece about touch, a homage to Aimard for his range of pianistic touch. It's called 'Toucher', in the infinitive. That was also partly reference to a particular tradition of French pianism, the *jeu perlé*.

CD: Which goes back to Saint-Saëns.

JA: It goes back to Saint-Saëns and even before that. It's Roger Nichols who educated me in this. I listened for many years to his programmes when he was on the radio quite a lot in the '80s and his books are very perceptive.

CD: Oh, absolutely. I've learnt a lot also from the way that he writes, quite apart from the marvellous insights.

JA: It was Roger who pointed out that in *Visions de l'Amen* Messiaen had very cleverly combined two completely different French piano traditions of play in the two pianos. The melodic and harmonic part Messiaen wrote for himself is a warmer, sensuous tradition of the singing line and the sensuous chord. The Saint-Saëns tradition was the Loriod part: birds, and bells, dense figuration, and all that. Of course, it's more complicated than that in practice, but there's a lot of truth in this. Loriod's playing is at least partly in that *jeu perlé* tradition. Although he is hugely versatile as a performer, there's an element of that in Aimard's playing too.

CD: Well, he's one of the principal inheritors of Loriod's approach to playing.

JA: But he has so many other aspects, too. I was thinking about that fantastic energy he has, the agile suppleness of his playing. There's lyricism, always with a slight edge to it, and a wonderful range of colours. *Toucher* focuses on the contrast between very fast short notes and very long resonances – the same idea from Messiaen's analysis of Debussy as used for the first movement of *The Discovery of Heaven*. It works well with the piano because those are two things that the piano can idiomatically do. It can play very short notes because of the hammers, or you can play a long chord either holding it or putting the pedal down, so it feeds into the acoustic nature of the instrument to use those temporal extremes. That piece also uses the third pedal very extensively as the mediator between different kinds of durations. The third pedal is for medium-long individual durations, the sustaining pedal is very long reverberation with every string resonating, and no pedal at all means very short notes, though, of course, with the third pedal, you can have both at once. That was a very useful way of combining two segregated streams of music. There is a gradual converging into a middle-register chorale, which starts in the outer extremes and gradually progresses to a more normal middle register. As that's happening, there are much faster figurations that start exclusively in one register (the treble) and gradually spread to every register. So there's two registral processes going on, and at the point where they meet in the middle the piece stops. Or rather, I then added an intervention with the normal sustaining pedal, which I hadn't used otherwise in the piece. The first really sustained sound in the piece is a 12-tone chord that is split into several note groups. This is 12-note in the sense of Obukhov, not in the sense of Schoenberg.

Sensation therefore also begins to show my debt to, and study of, Nicolas Obukhov's music. I knew that Aimard would be playing several pieces of Obukhov at Aldeburgh, pieces that I very much like and that I've studied. That also seemed a meaningful connection between me, the piano and Aimard, as it were, Obukhov being behind so much of Messiaen somehow, and a fascinating figure in his own right.

As well as Messiaen and Loriod and later Boulez, Aimard also studied with Maria Curcio, whose teaching is very different to the Messiaen–Loriod line. I also wanted to pay a little bit of indirect tribute to Aimard's long connections with Boulez. In 2015 he'd asked me to talk at Aldeburgh on the Boulez Third Sonata, which I did with the fantastic pianist Florent Boffard. Boffard had got permission from Sacher and Boulez to play the unpublished movements of that, one of which turns out to be an outstandingly fine piece of piano music, possibly the best piano music Boulez ever wrote. The lack of publication I can only assume is because the piece is not in the style of the rest of the Sonata, but is in a style more akin to Szymanowski. It's a very lush, overripe, trill-ridden sort of hothouse piece, which is perhaps out of place in the rest of the Sonata, and I think he sensed it didn't really belong. It's quite big, by the way, and a fabulous masterpiece. It must be published and recorded, it's incredible. I enjoyed doing that, so when composing *Sensation* I thought I'd like to do a tribute to the Boulez tradition, and to Aimard's place in that. So I decided to make a piece that was about that tradition but made from the material that that tradition abhors, namely triads. So the whole of the third piece, called 'Sightlines', consists of very fast lines converging or diverging. These are all based on triads. Either you just get streams of triads or a triad arpeggiated and interlaced with others. At first it's very fast and purely monodic. Eventually it develops into frenetic two-point counterpoint – this is only in the last page – which culminates in an eruption which covers, in the smallest possible space, all 12 major and minor triads arpeggiated in both hands at once. It's verging on the unplayable. It's the nearest to a completely out-of-control passage I've ever written. It looks quite precise and simple on paper, but when you hear it live it just sounds as if there's almost no harmony at all. I found it fascinating to see if you could take the simplest, most common musical sound you find in pop music or any music, commercial music, just the triad, and push it into an area where it's almost producing white noise. I had a lot of fun with that.

CD: At that point you had three pieces. When did it move away from being five pieces for the five senses?

JA: By the stage I was writing the fourth piece, the five senses idea was becoming a little bit boring. I was really making a piano cycle which was sensory-based, but not necessarily with five movements. Next I wanted to do a nocturne, something about the perfumes of the night. I remember very much going for long walks at night outside Avignon when I was on the Messiaen course in 1987, with the smell of sage, the wonderful smell of plants and the humidity of the nights there, which is such a special atmosphere. I've always loved nocturnes, so this is my homage to that genre. It's called 'Nuits' in the plural, and it enshrines and also interrogates the nocturne, rather as my *Symphony* did the genre of symphony. I thought of the night as being full of insects and animals sending out signals. The first half is without pedal and is full of insects and birds. It starts with a very lyrical but nervy song of a bird, an abstracted night bird, a little like a nightingale, but not in any literal sense. This high melody is combined with very short punctuations, like frogs, in the extreme bass register. Pierre-Laurent was also playing *Catalogue d'oiseaux* in Aldeburgh, so that was a bit in my mind. I transcribed several frog choruses from recordings, producing chords which repeatedly interrupt the melody.

That became the first half of the piece, which is without pedal. Traditionally you put the pedal down in nocturnes. There's much more to night music than that, so I reserved the pedal until halfway through this piece. Towards the end of the first half I start adding more octaves, which leads to the explosion of octaves in the middle of the work, where the pedal comes down for the first time and I'm dealing with the acoustic resonance of the piano. Stravinsky is right when he says that octaves are peculiarly pianistic.

I became fascinated by double octave doubling at the piano; or single octave doubling, the different registers and resonances of octaves, combining octaves with different chords, etc., all kinds of ways in which you can create imaginary spaces, imaginary acoustics using the octave and the sustaining pedal. It's one of the ways that the piano, this most immobile, immovable and heavy of instruments, can suddenly change its acoustics. It can seem to fly from a cathedral acoustic into a forest acoustic and then into the driest acoustic imaginable.

At that point, I'd found the starting point for my piano concerto. It was in writing the fourth piece, in effect I began sketching the concerto, which is called *The Imaginary Museum* – about the virtual relocation of the piano to different kinds of imaginary acoustic space: a cave, a mountain, an ocean, all kinds of different places, evoked by purely acoustic means, no electronics.

CD: So this is the piano evoking entire sensory worlds, not just taste or smell or touch, or even a painting-style tableau, but its ability to transport the mind in a vivid way.

JA: Absolutely. The rediscovery of the octave in 'Nuits' catapulted the piece into this exploration of acoustical space. Once the pedal does come down, it's very rarely raised for the rest of the work. The two parts of that movement are opposites of each other, if you see what I mean. The second half is dominated by filigree – tremolos, trills, roulades and arpeggios, which are more the stuff of piano nocturnes, but are placed here in a deliberately overripe and hyperactive context.

CD: And aren't there two endings, depending on whether or not it is played on its own?

JA: Yes, at the end the tune from the start is reprised. It's not exact, it has tremolos decorating it, above and below, but it's recalled as it gradually descends to the end. There are indeed two endings. If you're playing the fourth piece on its own, a final little frog call, without pedal, finishes it off. If you are playing the fifth piece, then there's a transition passage at top speed, which is the hardest in the whole work. It starts out as very quiet parallel octaves in the bottom register of the piano, and gradually ascends. As it does so, it changes interval, going through all the intervals in one way or another. It starts with the indication 'as fast as possible', and then halfway through it says '*Noch schneller*' [even faster], which is a quote from that Schumann piano work where he says, '*so schnell wie möglich*' [as quickly as possible] and then says, '*Noch schneller*' further on. In *Sensation*, this virtuosic transition takes about three pages of frenetic activity to get to the top of the piano. To sum the whole thing up, there's one final bar which is just a black-and-white note *glissando* from the bottom of the piano right to the top in one gesture as a single rapid *glissando*, which is effectively saying you can do this several ways: You can climb up the piano gradually with an elaborate filigree over three and a half pages with different interval cycles and so on, or you can just rip from the bottom to the top of the piano in a single *glissando*. [Laughter] And that catapults us into the fifth movement, 'Alba', which is therefore the pendant to 'Nuits' and is a celebration of dawn.

CD: As in the mediaeval alba or dawn song.

JA: Yes, the alba was the warning song to lovers, not only saying, 'Dawn is approaching, you must leave'...

CD: In the sense of Act II of *Tristan* and or *Cinq rechants*.

JA: Precisely. It can be that, but the alba could also be the celebration of dawn itself, of sunlight and the first rays of sun. I've always loved dawn and always wanted to do a piece about it. This is a pendant or parallel to 'She Hears' at the start of the cycle. It has the same time signature as the first piece, alternating 3/4 and 4/4, with chords only on the downbeat of whichever bar. That was the restriction I had for both pieces. Later in 'Alba' I started adding grace notes on the beat, which deforms the metre still further, confusing one's sense of durations. As that happens, the chords start very much right at the top register of the piano and gradually spread to the whole of the piano, again with the pedal predominantly down the whole time, because the music is building up bell resonances. Once that's got to a kind of limit, I added, spontaneously, a coda sixth movement, which was meant to be a little harmonic and melodic summary of the whole of *Sensation*. It has little fragments of music separated by increasingly long silences. It's very intimate – the nearest to normal piano music, perhaps, in the whole work. There are a lot of false relations, as my harmony's always full of that.

Finally, it comes to a cadential point of rest, which was a problem. I rewrote that piece about 10 times before I was happy with it. If only these two pages of piano music survived from my output, I think people could still have an idea of what I was up to... It had to be that concentrated.

CD: Your musical genome, as it were.

JA: I know that sounds ridiculous, but that is how I felt about it.

CD: In a way, it's you signing the piece.

JA: Perhaps... As a whole cycle, *Sensation* is a bit extreme: 'She Hears' could virtually be put in for a Grade 4 or Grade 5 Associated Board exam, whereas pieces like 'Sightlines' or 'Nuits' are highly virtuosic; and there's pretty much every degree of difficulty in between. That range excites me. I like sharp contrasts and a rich vocabulary. Where this is heading, I've no idea, and I don't want to know. I never think about that. Perhaps I feel I'm in more control of musical means now than I was, say, 30 years ago. I'll always love taking risks, and in *Sensations*, through the range of contrasts, textures and moods, I think that continues.

CD: So you now have greater certainty, and yet, at the same time, you haven't the faintest idea where all this is going.

JA: No. It's better that way.

CD: And that's possibly a perfect place to end.

JA: Maybe.

Coda

Multiple Choices

CD: Looking at your catalogue, at times you seem to have had multiple projects at once.

JA: Not now, but from 1988 to 1994, yes, there were. Now I write one piece at a time, but it's normal to think about other things to come.

CD: *Harmony* clearly came in the middle of the opera and things like that.

JA: Yes, but it was based upon music from the opera. Funnily enough, just now, I have two very different pieces on the go, though I'm only focusing on one of them. There's a guitar piece [*Catalan Peasant with Guitar*] and a new ensemble piece [*Van Gogh Blue*]. The guitar piece is the one I'm concentrating on. Writing for the guitar is hard: the fingering is such a nightmare. I've had to learn the guitar in order to compose it. I'm enjoying it, but it's very difficult.

CD: Six strings to get wrong?[1]

JA: Yes, and I keep mis-numbering them! So sometimes I work on the ensemble piece to get a break from that problem, but I'll only work intensively on the ensemble piece once the guitar piece is finished. So it's still just one piece at a time really, and I've worked that way since 1994. But of course my mind is constantly thinking ahead, bouncing ideas about for other things. That's a remnant of the period from 1988 to 1994 when I had six pieces on the go at once. I never do that now.

---

[1]   A reference to JA's tendency to mis-number strings on string instruments.

CD: While you're working on a piece, some of that is relatively simple, just getting notes down on a page. You say there are ideas bouncing around your head. Is your mind conceiving other things while doing some of the more mechanical bits of writing?

JA: Oh, sure. The mechanical part is the copying – usually. I say that because, as already explained, in some cases major new ideas have cropped up at the fair-copying stage – as in *The Crazed Moon* and elsewhere. So even at the fair-copy stage, occasionally, fresh things can suddenly crop up.

CD: But, otherwise, the copying is mechanical so your mind is free?

JA: Yes. Sometimes, when it's a purely mechanical copying task, I put on talking books. It can be relaxing. David Attenborough's autobiography, *Finnegans Wake* on CD, Thoreau's *Walden* and Naxos audio books are good. I've read a lot of literature this way. I didn't know until recently that Stravinsky was sometimes read to by Robert Craft when he was orchestrating. Then he'd suddenly say, 'Wait a minute.' Ten minutes, perhaps, would pass with him concentrating on a problem, and then he'd suddenly say, 'So, what happened?' and Craft would continue reading. I don't have to say, 'Hold on a minute', I just put the CD on pause. Mr Attenborough will wait... But it could be three days before I put him back on again because if a major new idea has occurred to me while copying I go with that totally. At that point, composing starts again and I can't listen to anything.

I don't know whether this is true of other composers, but when I'm composing – and I compose partly at the piano and partly at the desk, I go between the two – I often play bits of music I'm interested in at the piano, from memory. If a passage I'm working on reminds me of a bit of Nielsen's Fifth, or something from Messiaen, or Pérotin or Xenakis, I'll bash that out on the keyboard. Somehow I need other music when I'm composing – but only certain music. It's not because the musical passages in my works really sound anything like those in the other composers' music stylistically. It's something else, some kind of free association... I can't explain this. It may just be as simple as starting on a minor third, say C and A above middle C. If I put that down I might be reminded of the opening, for example, of Nielsen's Fifth, which starts with those pitches on the violas. That's a very remarkable opening, suggesting uncertainty and drift, yet it's not chromatic at all. That's very suggestive compositionally to me, so perhaps I'll play it. So from time to time I play little fragments of other music when I'm composing.

CD: Maybe that's a little bit like Messiaen putting a reminder in his diary, 'Pack these scores', before leaving Paris to compose for the summer.

JA: Could be. When I read about that in his diaries I sympathised. Why wouldn't one want to learn from other composers? One feeds off other music. It's like taking a composition lesson from Claude Le Jeune, or Sibelius, or Xenakis, or Nielsen, and saying, 'How did you get out of that?' That kind of thing. Also, the feel of sounds under the fingers is very important for composing. And I find it physically pleasurable to be able to take a bit of Beethoven or Crawford Seeger, or whoever, and just play that, perhaps badly, but I'll play it – you take physical ownership of it somehow in your fingers. You can play with the sounds, play them in an order the composer didn't write, or transpose them a bit, and before you know where you are you're composing something new. The French composer and scholar Thomas Lacôte showed me Messiaen's sketch for the long monodic sixth movement of *Quartet for the End of Time*. Messiaen makes a list of favourite melodic figures all jumbled up on the left-hand page – a French folk song, bits of Grieg's *Peer Gynt*, some plainchant, whatever. On the right-hand page you have the sketch for the sixth movement. It sounds completely like Messiaen, but now you can hear how he's transformed these favourite musics into something personal and strong. This isn't postmodernism, it's just common sense. If Messiaen could do that, why can't we all?

Chronology

1967	Born in London. Learns piano, flute and percussion at school, sings in choir.
1977–80	Listens frequently to BBC Radio 3. Learns to read full scores through borrowing from the local library. First attempts at composing (piano pieces, wind quintet, percussion ensemble, orchestral pieces).
1981	Attends Westminster School (until end of 1985). Composition tuition from Assistant Director of Music John Baird. German lessons and informal tuition from Richard Stokes, Head of German, who introduces JA to Carter's Second String Quartet and Aribert Reimann's *Lear*.
March	Visits the British Music Information Centre. Director Roger Wright introduces JA to Oliver Knussen there. Starts listening to France Musique at home, hearing new music by Xenakis, Jolas, Takemitsu, Taira, Grisey, Murail, Rădulescu, Lévinas, Ohana, Sciarrino, Lachenmann, among others.
November	Attends rehearsals and concert by Pierre Boulez and the BBC Symphony Orchestra of Boulez's *Pli selon pli* at the Royal Festival Hall. Introduced to Boulez by violinist John Crawford, who is in the orchestra's strings.
December	Meets George Benjamin.
1982	*SING* for 24 voices (begun in December 1981).
July	First public performance of a very short composition for unaccompanied choir (school choir conducted by Charles Brett).

Other works composed at this period (none performed):
Eros for flute, clarinet and violin.
Phainetai moi kenos isos theoisin for tenor and ensemble (words: Sappho).

1983   *Rounds* for small ensemble, *The Descent into Hell* for choir. Begins first composition using spectral techniques: *Eos* for strings and percussion.

December   Hears the broadcast world premiere on France Musique of Messiaen's *Saint François d'Assise*.

1984   *Ashes* (later retitled *Phoenix*) for amplified flute.

February   Meets the composer and writer Bayan Northcott.

May   Meets Tristan Murail in London at a concert by Music Projects/London.

June   *Ashes* premiered by Daniel Glaser at school concert.

1984–85   *Light Music* (String Quartet No. 1) completed, partly based on material from *Eos* and, like it, a spectral composition. Meets Jonathan Harvey, Adrian Jack and Sinan Savaskan.

September   On Knussen's recommendation, begins regular composition lessons with John Lambert.

1986
March   Meets Olivier Messiaen at BBC SO rehearsals of three scenes from *Saint François d'Assise*.

May?   Short trip to Holland where JA hears an early concert performance of Andriessen's *De Stijl*.

July   Short trip to Darmstadt International Summer Courses for New Music for about three days, where he meets Horațiu Rădulescu and Eric Tanguy.

Autumn   Short visit to Paris, hears Grisey's *Partiels* played by Ensemble L'Itinéraire/Yves Prin where he is introduced to Gérard Grisey. Meets Maurice Ohana (first in London, then in Paris), who introduces him to pianist and musicologist Dr Caroline Rae.

1987   *L'Espace (avec Jehan, Claude et Jean-Christophe)* for large ensemble (version for large orchestra including 4 bass flutes, 2 contrabass clarinets, 2 electric guitars, etc., begun the following year), *In* for saxophone and percussion, *Ring Dance* for 2 violins.

March   Messiaen Festival at the Royal Academy of Music in London (two weeks of concerts, rehearsals, workshops, lectures, etc. in the presence of Messiaen and Yvonne Loriod). JA attends every event.

April–June Private lessons with Tristan Murail in Paris. Attends concerts and lectures at IRCAM, Radio France, etc. Meets and hears seminars by Kaija Saariaho, Helmut Lachenmann, Harry Halbreich, Denys Bouliane, Philippe Hurel, Michael Obst, Edison Denisov, Marco Stroppa, Edward Dudley Hughes. Attends analysis classes by Robert Piencikowski at IRCAM on Berio's *Coro* and Lachenmann's *Mouvement (-vor der Erstarrung)*. Several visits to Horațiu Rădulescu in Versailles.

July   Attends analysis course by Olivier Messiaen at the Centre Acanthes, Avignon.

September   Starts studies at the Royal College of Music (composition and tonal techniques: John Lambert; analysis/history: Roderick Swanston and Jeremy Dale Roberts; electronics: Lawrence Casserley; attends conducting classes by Edwin Roxburgh).

October/   First published articles on music in *Music and Musicians*: 'New
November   Music in Paris' and 'Olivier Messiaen's Analysis Course at the Centre Acanthes'.

October   First broadcast talk: 'Messiaen's *Saint François d'Assise* – an intro- duction' for BBC Radio 3's Music Weekly.
                In first performed at Sussex University by David Coggins (sax.) and JA (perc.)

1987–92   Numerous visits to France and Germany to hear new-music concerts and study contemporary French, Italian and German new music.

1988   Starts work on *Khorovod* and *Dark Night* (later retitled *Diptych*), both of which are composed over the next few years.

May   RCM Composers Exchange Visit with the composers of the Musikhögskolan in Stockholm. Composition consultation with Sven-David Sandström. *Ring Dance* for 2 violins premiered at Royal Conservatoire of Music in Stockholm.

July	Attends Darmstadt Summer Courses for New Music: lectures, concerts and seminars by (among others) Klaus Huber, Younghi Paagh-Paan, Helmut Lachenmann, Walter Zimmerman, Brian Ferneyhough, Christopher Fox, Clarence Barlow, N.A. Huber, Anatol Vieru, Aurel Stroe, Horaţiu Rădulescu, Chris Dench, etc. In addition, meets Friedrich Hommel (Director of the Ferienkurse), Walter Maas, Rodney Sharman, Fabrice Fitch, Fabien Lévy, James Clapperton, Andrew Toovey, etc.
December	Meets Richard Causton and David Robert Coleman.
1989	
Autumn	'La musique spectrale dans le contexte' and 'Tristan Murail: development d'un style' published in Paris musical review *Entretemps* (Numéro Grisey/Murail).
1990	Completes *Diptych* for orchestra. *Litany* for wordless choir (withdrawn), *Bucium* for tape (based on the sound of the Romanian alphorn). Graduates from the RCM with First Class Honours on BMus (London) degree.
June	Organises RCM Festival of New Music: recitals, workshops, lectures and seminars; concerts conducted by Leslie Larkum and JA.
July	Composition classes with György Ligeti and Marco Stroppa at the International Bartók Seminar, Szombathely, Hungary.
August	Composition course with Per Nørgård at Dartington International Summer School. *Litany* for choir premiered by BBC Singers/John Poole at Dartington.
October	Begins postgraduate studies in composition with Alexander Goehr at Cambridge University.
1991	
February	First visit to Denmark, guest lecturing on 'Spectral Music – history and techniques' at the Royal Conservatory in Copenhagen (to the composition class of Ib Nørholm) and the Aarhus Conservatory (to the classes of Per Nørgård and Karl Aage Rasmussen).
March	Organises Cambridge Festival of Contemporary Music, including concerts conducted by Thomas Adès, JA and a piano recital by Nicolas Hodges.

June	Second RCM Festival of Contemporary Music (JA conducts Takemitsu's *Rain Spell*).
August	*Pavillons en l'Air* (second movement of *Diptych*, commissioned as separate piece in version for small orchestra by the Dartington International Summer School) premiered by Diego Masson and the Dartington Festival Orchestra. JA attends composition classes by Vinko Globokar at Dartington.
October	MPhil in Composition from Cambridge University.
1991–92	*Diptych* wins Royal Philharmonic Society Prize for Young Composers. Freelance work as librarian and teacher, including at the Royal Ballet School where JA observes many rehearsals for Balanchine's choreography of *Agon*.
1992	*Seadrift* for soprano, flute, clarinet and piano.
July	Attends Britten–Pears Course in Contemporary Composition and Performance (organised by Oliver Knussen and Colin Matthews).
September	First published composition: *Pavillons en l'Air* (second part of *Diptych*) signed as standalone piece by Editions Salabert, Paris.
October	Continuation of studies with Alexander Goehr (until June 1995).
1993	*Liens* for string sextet and soprano (texts by Rimbaud and Apollinaire) commissioned by A.I.E.C. Sextuor, Lille (work subsequently withdrawn), *Tiramisù* for ensemble commissioned by Adrian Jack for the MusICA concerts, *Scherzo with trains* for 4 clarinets commissioned by Joy Farrall.
June/ August	Benjamin Britten Memorial Scholar at the Tanglewood Music Center, USA, where a fragment of *Khorovod* is performed.
October	*Liens* premiered by A.I.E.C. Sextuor with Marianne Pousseur (soprano) in Lille.
December	*Scherzo with trains* premiered by Joy Farrall and others at Wigmore Hall.
1994	*Khorovod* for ensemble completed (commissioned by London Sinfonietta), *The Bearded Lady* for oboe and piano (commissioned by Nicholas Daniel), *The Colour of Pomegranates* (commissioned by the Park Lane Group).

January	*Tiramisù* premiered by the Cambridge New Music Players/Paul Hoskins, who tour it in various venues over the next two years.
February	*Seadrift* and *Tiramisù* performed at a concert of the London Sinfonietta/Oliver Knussen at the Barbican.
June	*Seadrift* performed at the Aldeburgh Festival by London Sinfonietta/Diego Masson. First professional orchestral performance: *Pavillons en l'Air* performed by Tokyo Metropolitan Symphony Orchestra/Kazufumi Yamashita at Suntory Hall, Tokyo as part of Tōru Takemitsu's Suntory International Program for Music Composition (initiative: Magnus Lindberg).
September	JA appointed Constant and Kit Lambert Fellow at the RCM (until July 1996).
October	*The Bearded Lady* for oboe and piano premiered by Nicholas Daniel and Julius Drake at Wigmore Hall.
November	*The Bearded Lady* premiered in clarinet and piano version at West Road, Cambridge by Stuart Stratford and Richard Ormrod.
December	*Khorovod* premiered by London Sinfonietta/Markus Stenz.
1995	*I'm nobody, who are you?* for baritone, violin and piano (commissioned by Cheltenham International Festival).
January	*The Colour of Pomegranates* premiered at the Park Lane Group. Final revisions to *Diptych*.
February	*Khorovod* performed at Ars Musica, Brussels by Sinfonia 21/Martyn Brabbins.
March	Death of John Lambert. *Diptych* premiered by BBC SO/Oliver Knussen as part of the Talking Music festival at the Barbican, together with performances of *Seadrift* and *The Bearded Lady* by the Nash Ensemble/Martyn Brabbins.
June	*I'm nobody, who are you?* premiered at Pitville Pump Room, Cheltenham (William Dazeley, Julius Drake, Priya Mitchell).
August	*Khorovod* (final version) premiered at the BBC Proms by London Sinfonietta/Markus Stenz. Signs general agreement with Faber Music Ltd.
September	Appointed to composition staff of the RCM.

1996–97   *Past Hymns* for string orchestra, *Poetry Nearing Silence* for 7 players, *The Crazed Moon* for orchestra.

1997
January   *Past Hymns* premiered at St John's, Smith Square by Sinfonia 21/ Martyn Brabbins, followed by Arts Council Network UK tour (10 performances).

March   *Poetry Nearing Silence* premiered at the Purcell Room, London by Nash Ensemble/Martyn Brabbins.

July   *The Crazed Moon* premiered at the Cheltenham Festival by the BBC National Orchestra of Wales/Tadaaki Otaka.

October   *Khorovod* (US premiere) by the Los Angeles Philharmonic/Oliver Knussen.

1997–98   *The Stations of the Sun* for orchestra.
Composer in Residence with the chamber orchestra Sinfonia 21, which lasts until it ceases operations in 2003.

1998
July   *The Stations of the Sun* premiered at the BBC Proms by BBC SO/ Sir Andrew Davis. Meets Sir Richard Rodney Bennett.

September   First visit to New York, where *Khorovod* is performed by the Juilliard New Music Ensemble/Joel Sachs.

1999   *Towards Poetry* (ballet based on newly extended version of *Poetry Nearing Silence* to choreography by Mark Baldwin), *O Sing Unto the Lord*, anthem.

Spring   *Towards Poetry* premiered and toured by Royal Ballet on their Dance Bites Tour. Reprised later in the year at Sadler's Wells, London.

November   *O Sing Unto the Lord* premiered by combined choirs of Westminster Cathedral, Westminster Abbey and St Paul's Cathedral/James O'Donnell on St Cecilia's Day.

1999–2000   *Alhambra Fantasy* for ensemble.

2000
February   *Alhambra Fantasy* premiered by London Sinfonietta/Oliver Knussen at Queen Elizabeth Hall (London) and toured to Festival Présences, Radio France, Paris.

September	Composer in Residence to the City of Birmingham Symphony Orchestra (until July 2005).
2000	Head of Composition at the RCM.
November	Death of stepfather.
2001–02	*The Bird Sings with its Fingers* for small orchestra. *Shir Hashirim* for soprano and orchestra. *Imagin'd Corners* for horns and orchestra.
2002	
March	*Imagin'd Corners* premiered by CBSO/Sakari Oramo at Symphony Hall, Birmingham.
April	Studies at IRCAM, Paris to learn software for *Book of Hours*.
September	Artistic Director of the Philharmonia Orchestra's concert series Music of Today at the South Bank Centre, London (until July 2011). JA programmes and introduces composers on stage during each concert. Numerous UK and world premieres.
2002–03	*Symphony* for orchestra.
2003	
June	Month-long stage at IRCAM, Paris in connection with electronics for *Book of Hours*.
December	*Symphony* premiered by CBSO/Sakari Oramo at Symphony Hall, Birmingham.
2004–05	*Book of Hours* for ensemble and live electronics.
2004	JA appointed Fanny P. Mason Professor of Music at Harvard University (until July 2007).
2005	*Eden* for orchestra. Joins London Philharmonic Choir as member of the bass section (until end 2012).
February	*Book of Hours* premiered by Birmingham Contemporary Music Group/Oliver Knussen at CBSO Centre, Birmingham.
March	Featured composer at Musica Nova Festival, Helsinki (performances of nine compositions, including Finnish premieres of *Symphony*, *The Bearded Lady* and *The Bird Sings with its Fingers*).

July	*Eden* premiered by CBSO/Martyn Brabbins at Cheltenham Town Hall as part of the Cheltenham International Festival.
2005–06	*Heaven is Shy of Earth* for mezzo-soprano, chorus and orchestra.
2006	
March	Death of father.
August	*Heaven is Shy of Earth* premiered at 2006 BBC Proms by BBC Symphony Orchestra & Chorus/Angelika Kirchschlager (mezzo-soprano)/Sir Andrew Davis.
September	First commercial recordings: monographic CDs on Ondine and NMC Recordings.
2005–07	Daniel Lewis Young Composer Fellow at the Cleveland Orchestra.
2007– present	Professor of Music and Composer in Residence at Guildhall School of Music and Drama.
2007	
September	Gramophone Contemporary Award for Ondine CD.
2006–09	*Fantasias* for orchestra.
2009	*The Comedy of Change* for ensemble.
September	*The Comedy of Change* concert premiere by Asko-Schönberg Ensemble/Oliver Knussen, subsequent tour with *Comedy* and *Book of Hours*, same players/Reinbert de Leeuw. *The Comedy of Change* premiered in Plymouth as ballet by Rambert Dance Company with choreography by Mark Baldwin, followed by UK tour through 2009–10.
November	*Fantasias* premiered by Cleveland Orchestra/Jonathan Nott.
2009–10	*Bell Mass* for choir and organ.
2010	
June	*Bell Mass* – liturgical and concert premieres by Choir of Westminster Abbey/James O'Donnell.
August	*Fantasias* (UK premiere) by National Youth Orchestra/Semyon Bychkov on UK tour finishing at the BBC Proms (Royal Albert Hall, televised). Teaches Advanced Composition Class at the Dartington International Summer School.

2011–14	*Thebans*, opera in three Acts for soloists, chorus and orchestra, commissioned by English National Opera.
2011	Composer in Residence with the London Philharmonic Orchestra (until 2015). *The Discovery of Heaven* for orchestra.
2012–13	Visiting Professor of Composition at Edinburgh University.
2012 **March**	*The Discovery of Heaven* premiered by LPO/Ryan Wigglesworth.
2013	Composer in Residence at the Wigmore Hall (London, until 2016).
June	String Quartet No. 1 'Light Music' (1984–85) premiered by Arditti String Quartet at Aldeburgh Festival.
November	Portrait day of concerts and talks at Wigmore Hall (performances of nine compositions, also music by Sciarrino, Abrahamsen and Grisey).
2014	String Quartet No. 2 'Dreihundert Weihnachtslieder'.
May	*Thebans* premiered by ENO/Edward Gardner (seven performances) in a production by Pierre Audi.
June	String Quartet No. 2 'Dreihundert Weihnachtslieder' premiered by Arditti String Quartet at Wigmore Hall (London).
August	Exclusive contract with Schott Music Ltd.
2014–15	*In lieblicher Bläue* for violin and orchestra, *Van Gogh Blue* for ensemble, *Catalan Peasant with Guitar* for guitar. Meetings with Julian Bream.
2015 **March**	*In lieblicher Bläue* premiered by LPO/Carolin Widmann (violin)/ Vladimir Jurowski.
May	*Thebans* (German premiere) by Bonn Opera/Johannes Pell (director: Pierre Audi; same production as London 2014).
June	Series of talks on the music of Boulez at the Aldeburgh Festival for his ninetieth birthday, including UK premiere by Florent Boffard of unpublished movements from Boulez's Third Piano Sonata.

November	*Catalan Peasant with Guitar* premiered by Laura Snowden at Wigmore Hall.
	Van Gogh Blue premiered by Nash Ensemble/Alexandre Bloch at Wigmore Hall.
	Ring Dance re-premiere by Nash Ensemble at Wigmore Hall (first performance since 1988).
2015–16	*Incantesimi* for orchestra, *Sensation* for piano.
2016	
June	*Incantesimi* premiered by Berlin Philharmonic/Sir Simon Rattle, followed by European tour.
	Composer in Residence at the Aldeburgh Festival (performances of 10 compositions, Hesse Memorial Lecture at the Festival and presents concerts of Messiaen, Hardanger fiddle Music, etc.).
	Sensation premiered by Pierre-Laurent Aimard at Aldeburgh Festival.
2016–17	*The Imaginary Museum* for piano and orchestra, *Magnificat* (text: Latin Vulgate) for unaccompanied choir, *Nunc Dimittis* (text: Latin Vulgate) for unaccompanied choir.
2017	
March	*Ring Dance* new version for 2 cellos premiered by Cellophony at King's Place (London).
June	*Nunc Dimittis* premiered by Gonville & Caius College Choir/ Geoffrey Webber.
July	*The Imaginary Museum* premiered by BBC Scottish Symphony Orchestra/Steven Osborne (piano)/Ilan Volkov at BBC Proms (Royal Albert Hall).
August	Teaches Composition Class at Tanglewood Music Center.
October	BBC Symphony Orchestra Total Immersion on Julian Anderson's music.
	Research Conference 'Heaven Is Shy of Earth: Julian Anderson at 50' at Guildhall School of Music and Drama.
	Talks, films, concerts of ensemble, choral and orchestral pieces at the Barbican Centre, performed by musicians from Guildhall School of Music and Drama, the BBC Singers and the BBC Symphony Orchestra, with conductors Richard Baker, Edward Gardner, Nicholas Kok and Jack Sheen.

November	*Magnificat* premiered by ORA/Suzi Digby at LSO St Luke's.
2017–18	String Quartet No. 3 'hana no hanataba', *Capriccio in memory of Steve Stucky* for piano, *Evening Canticles* for choir.
2018 **April**	String Quartet No. 3 'hana no hanataba' premiered by JACK Quartet at Wigmore Hall with subsequent European tour.
May	LPO CD of *In lieblicher Bläue* wins *BBC Music Magazine* Award.
June	Featured composer at the SICPP Festival, New England Conservatory, Boston, directed by Stephen Drury. Talks, seminars, workshops; public performances of 15 pieces. US premiere of String Quartet No. 3 'hana no hanataba' by Fromm Quartet at Tanglewood Music Festival.
July	Death of Oliver Knussen.
2018–19	*Litanies* for cello and orchestra, *Landscapes* for cello solo.
2019 **May**	*Evening Canticles* premiered by Choir of St John's College, Cambridge/Andrew Nethsingha.
November	*Landscapes* premiered by Anssi Karttunen at Villa Mairea, Finland.
2019–20	New work for orchestra (in progress), new work for 8 unaccompanied voices (in progress).
2020 **February**	*Litanies* premiered by Orchestre national de France/Anssi Karttunen (cello)/Pascal Rophé as part of Festival Présences, Radio France, Paris (subsequent performances in Birmingham, Hong Kong, Oslo, Stockholm, etc.).
June	*SING* (1982) premiered by BBC Singers/Sofi Jeannin at Aldeburgh Festival.
August	New work for orchestra premiered by BBC SO/Semyon Bychkov at BBC Proms (Royal Albert Hall). New work for 8 unaccompanied voices premiered at Tanglewood Music Festival.

List of Personae

Our conversations naturally refer to numerous people. The following list is intended to aid the reader to orient some of these names. It only includes contemporary figures, reflecting contact in day-to-day life, though some have since died, and generally omits those people mentioned just once and where it is immediately clear who they are. Some are well known, others less so, but we hope these brief descriptions are a useful reference. We sincerely apologise to anyone whose name has been accidentally omitted from this list, and for any inadvertent errors or omissions within each short entry.

Abrahamsen, Hans – Danish composer, winner of the 2016 Grawemeyer Award in Music Composition

Adès, Thomas – composer, conductor, pianist, writer, Artistic Director of the Aldeburgh Festival (1999–2008), Artistic Partner of the Boston Symphony Orchestra (since 2016), winner of the 2000 Grawemeyer Award in Music Composition

Aimard, Pierre-Laurent – French pianist, Artistic Director of the Aldeburgh Festival (2009–16)

Andriessen, Louis – Dutch composer, writer, teacher. Winner of the 2011 Grawemeyer Award in Music Composition

Arditti, Irvine – violinist, founder and leader of the Arditti String Quartet, which specialises in twentieth-century and contemporary music

Asbury, Stefan – conductor, teacher

Attia, Kader – French conceptual artist

Audi, Pierre – theatre/artistic director, founder of the Almeida Theatre in Islington (London), Artistic Director of Dutch National Opera (1988–2018), Artistic Director of the Park Avenue Armoury in New York (since 2015), Artistic Director of the Aix-en-Provence Festival (since 2018)

Baird, John – composer, Head of Music at Westminster School (1983–96)

Baldwin, Mark – choreographer, Artistic Director of the Rambert Dance Company (2002–18)

Balmer, Yves – French musicologist specialising in modern French music, Professor of music analysis at Conservatoire de Paris (since 2008)

Benjamin, Sir George – composer, conductor, Prince Consort Professor of Composition at the Royal College of Music (1985–2001). Henry Purcell Professor of Composition at King's College, London (since 2001)

Bennett, Sir Richard Rodney – composer, pianist, singer

Bernas, Richard – conductor, percussionist, founder of Music Projects, London

Berry, John – clarinettist, arts administrator, theatre producer, Director of English National Opera (2005–15), founder of the theatre company Scenario 2

Blackford, Richard – composer, Head of Music at the Royal Ballet School (1990–95), Composer in Residence to the Brno Philharmonic (2007)

Brett, Charles – countertenor, Director of Music at Westminster School (1976–83), Professor at the Royal Academy of Music (1988–2003)

Causton, Richard – composer, Reader in Composition at Cambridge University

Clayton, Nicky – neuroscientist

Coccioli, Lamberto – composer, music technologist, administrator, Associate Principal of the Royal Birmingham Conservatoire

Cooper, Adam – dancer, choreographer, actor, theatre director

Cowan, Rob – music broadcaster, writer

Crisp, Clement – dance critic for the *Financial Times* (since 1957)

Crossley, Paul – pianist, Artistic Director of the London Sinfonietta (1988–94)

Daniel, Nicholas – oboist, conductor, founder member of Britten Sinfonia

Davis, Sir Andrew – conductor, Music Director of Chicago Lyric Opera, Conductor Laureate of the BBC Symphony Orchestra

Drummond, John – television director, arts administrator, Director of the BBC Promenade Concerts (1985–95)

Dufourt, Hugues – French composer and philosopher, who devised the term 'spectral music'

Elder, Sir Mark – conductor, Music Director of English National Opera (1979–93) and of the Hallé (since 2000)

Fallas, John – musicologist, writer

Ferneyhough, Brian – composer, writer, teacher, Professor of Composition at Stanford University, California (since 2000)

Finn, Jonathan – software developer, singer, co-creator of Sibelius Software

Finnissy, Michael – composer, pianist, Chair of Composition at Southampton University (since 1999)

Freedman, Amelia – founder and Artistic Director of the Nash Ensemble, Artistic Director of the Bath International Festival (1986–1993). Head of Classical Music at the South Bank Centre, London (1995–2006). Artistic Director of Bath Mozartfest (since 1995) and Bath Bachfest (since 2011)

Gardner, Edward – conductor, Music Director of English National Opera (2006–2015), Chief Guest Conductor, City of Birmingham Symphony Orchestra (2011–15), Principal Conductor of the Bergen Philharmonic (since 2015) and of the London Philharmonic Orchestra (from 2021)

Gavin, Barrie – film director specialising in music, winner of the Golden Harp Award for his documentary about Bartók's folk music collecting, *The Miraculous Circumstance* (1981)

Goehr, Alexander – composer, writer, teacher, Professor of Music at Cambridge University (1976–99)

Grisey, Gérard – French composer, theorist, teacher, Professor of Composition at the Paris Conservatoire until his premature death in 1998 at the age of 52

Gutman, Stephen – pianist, teacher

Halsey, Simon – choral conductor, Director of the London Symphony Chorus

Hamer, Laura – musical scholar, Staff Tutor in Music at the Open University (since 2018)

Harvey, Jonathan – composer, Professor of Composition at Sussex University

Hetzer, Christof – German stage and costume designer

Hill, David – choral conductor, organist, Music Director of the Bach Choir (since 1998)

Hill, Peter – pianist, scholar, biographer of Olivier Messiaen, Emeritus Professor of Music at The University of Sheffield

Hodges, Nicolas – pianist, teacher

Holloway, Robin – composer, writer, Professor of Composition at Cambridge University (until 2011)

Hoskins, Paul – conductor, Director of Music at Rambert Dance Company (1996–2018)

Howat, Roy – pianist, scholar specialising in modern French music, Keyboard Research Fellow at the Royal Academy of Music and Research Fellow at the Royal Conservatoire of Scotland

Jack, Adrian – composer, writer, broadcaster, formerly of the Radio 3 Music Department and founder-director of the concert series MusICA

Jolas, Betsy – French composer, teacher, Professor of Composition and Analysis at the Paris Conservatoire (1975–96)

Jurowski, Vladimir – Russian conductor, Principal Conductor of the London Philharmonic Orchestra (2006–21), Music Director of the Bavarian State Opera (from 2021)

Kalman, Jean – French lighting designer
Kelly, Jude – theatre director, producer, former Director of the South Bank Centre
Kingsbury, Martin – founding director, Faber Music
Knussen, Oliver – composer, conductor, teacher, Artistic Director of the Aldeburgh Festival (1983–98) and of the new music program at the Tanglewood Summer School (1986–93)

Lachenmann, Helmut – German composer, cultural theorist, teacher
Lacôte, Thomas – composer, organist, scholar, Professor at the Paris Conservatoire
Lambert, John – composer, pianist, organist, pedagogue
Levin, Robert – pianist, conductor, composer, scholar, Professor of Music at Harvard University (1993–2014)
Lewis, George – composer, musicologist, trombonist, installation artist, teacher. Edward H Case Professor of American Music at Columbia University (since 2004) where he is now Vice-Chair of the Department of Music
Lindberg, Magnus – composer, conductor, pianist
Loriod, Jeanne – French performer on the electronic ondes Martenot, sister of Yvonne Loriod
Loriod, Yvonne – French pianist, composer, second wife of Olivier Messiaen

Macbeth, Ginny – music publicist, founder of MacBeth Media Relations
Maddock, Stephen – music administrator, chief executive, City of Birmingham Symphony Orchestra (since 1999)
Martland, Steve – composer, died prematurely in 2013 at the age of 59
Masson, Diego – French conductor, founder of the Ensemble Musique Vivante in Paris
Matthews, Colin – composer, teacher, founder NMC recordings, Prince Consort Professor of Composition at the Royal College of Music (since 2000), Honorary Professor at the University of Nottingham (since 2005)
McGuinness, Frank – playwright, teacher, Professor of Creative Writing at University College, Dublin (since 2007)
Meecham, Paul – arts administrator, Managing Director of the London Sinfonietta (1991–97), currently President of the Utah Symphony (since 2016)
Moore, Gillian – music educator, arts administrator, Artistic Director of the London Sinfonietta (1998–2008), currently Director of Music at the South Bank Centre, London
Murail, Tristan – French composer, teacher, performer on the ondes Martenot, Professor of Music at Columbia University (1997–2010)
Myers, Thalia – pianist, pedagogue

Newbould, Jackie – arts administrator, General Manager of the Birmingham Contemporary Music Group (until 2016)

Newbould, Steven – arts administrator, Artistic Director of the Birmingham Contemporary Music Group (until 2016)

Newman, Chris – composer, painter, writer, performance artist

Nichols, Roger – writer and scholar specialising in modern French music

Nørgård, Per – Danish composer, writer, inventor of the 'infinity series'

Northcott, Bayan – composer, writer, Chief Music Critic of *The Independent* (1986–2009)

Nott, Jonathan – conductor, Music Director of the Bamberg Symphony Orchestra (2000–16) and of the Orchestre de la Suisse Romande (since 2017)

O'Donnell, James – organist, choral conductor, Director of Music at Westminster Cathedral (1988–99) and Westminster Abbey (since 1999)

Okabe, Shinichiro – Japanese composer, analyst, Professor at Meiji Gakuin University (since 2001)

Oramo, Sakari – Finnish conductor, Chief Conductor of the City of Birmingham Symphony Orchestra (1998–2008) and of the BBC Symphony Orchestra (since 2013)

Osborne, Stephen – pianist

Otaka, Tadaaki – Japanese conductor, Principal Conductor of the BBC National Orchestra of Wales (1987–95) and of the Osaka Philharmonic Orchestra (since 2016)

Payne, Anthony – composer, writer

Plaistow, Stephen – pianist, writer, broadcaster, Head of New Music at the BBC (until 1989)

Polfreman, Richard – music technologist

Power, Lawrence – violist, member of the Nash Ensemble, Visiting Professor of the Royal College of Music

Pye, Tom – set and costume designer

Rădulescu, Horațiu – Romanian composer and theorist, much involved with spectral composition

Rattle, Sir Simon – conductor, Chief Conductor of the City of Birmingham Symphony Orchestra (1979–97), of the Berlin Philharmonic (2002–18) and of the London Symphony Orchestra (since 2017)

Saariaho, Kaija – Finnish composer and teacher, who has lived in France since 1982, winner of the 2003 Grawemeyer Award in Music Composition

Savaskan, Sinan – composer, Head of Academic Music at Westminster School since 1995, Composer in Residence to the Octandre Ensemble

Seymour, Lynn – ballerina, choreographer

Sloboda, John – music scholar, psychologist of music, Professor of Psychology at Keele University (until 2008), Research Professor at the Guildhall School of Music and Drama (since 2009)

Smaczny, Jan – scholar, broadcaster specialising in Czech music, Emeritus Professor of Music at Queen's University, Belfast

Stenz, Markus – German conductor, Music Director of the London Sinfonietta (1994–98), of the Gürzenich Orchester (2003–14) and the Netherlands Radio Philharmonic Orchestra (2012–19)

Stokes, Richard – translator, scholar and teacher, Head of German at Westminster School (until 2010), currently Professor of Lieder at the Royal Academy of Music

Stroppa, Marco – composer, theorist, Head of Research at IRCAM, Paris (1987–90), Professor of Composition at Stuttgart University (since 1999)

Suckling, Martin – composer, violinist, Lecturer in Music at York University (since 2012)

Tchamkerten, Jacques – Swiss scholar, organist, performer on the ondes Martenot

Trapani, Chris – American composer, Visiting Assistant Professor of Composition at the University of Texas at Austin (since 2018)

Turnage, Mark-Anthony – composer, Professor of Composition at the Royal College of Music (since 2004)

Walker, Timothy – arts administrator, Chief Executive and Artistic Director of the London Philharmonic Orchestra (since 2002)

Weir, Judith – composer, Master of the Queen's Music (since 2014)

Whitehouse, Richard – music critic

Widmann, Carolin – German violinist

Wright, Peter – dancer, choreographer, Artistic Director of the Birmingham Royal Ballet (until 1995)

Wright, Roger – arts administrator, Director of the British Music Information Centre (1978–87), Senior Producer of the BBC Symphony Orchestra (1987–89), Artistic Administrator of the Cleveland Orchestra (1989–92), Executive Director and Vice President of Deutsche Grammophon (1992–97), Controller of BBC Radio 3 (1998–2014) and Director of the BBC Promenade Concerts (2007–14), Chief Executive of Aldeburgh Music and Snape Maltings (since 2014)

Glossary of Musical Terms

Note: This book deals with music (in particular, my own music) as a part of culture and society, not in isolation from them. As such, neither book nor music is aimed at specialists. Detailed discussion of musical issues, and of many musical pieces, is nevertheless included within the text of the book. Some of these discussions include technical musical terms. It was decided to include this Glossary of many such terms, both those in common musical use and some more specialised ones. An abiding concern, dating back to my childhood, has been the worrying use of jargon (in both music and life generally) to alienate any but the most devoted initiates. I have never believed that any worthwhile human activity cannot, with due care, be explained in plain language, and am suspicious when those involved refuse to do so. In order to avoid disrupting the flow of the conversations in this book, many musical terms are not explained there, but here.

Two more caveats: a) the definitions which follow are mine and reflect my usage of these concepts. This is deliberate, and although I have tried factually to back up the assertions in this Glossary, this is not an academic dictionary (of which there are plenty already). I make no apology for the personal angle taken on these matters, which I hope makes the Glossary more relevant to the book and more lively to read, whatever your background. (A few touches of humour perform the same function. As Hans Keller said, 'I only joke when I'm in dead earnest.')

b) In order to save space, unlike in the main text, nothing here is provided with references to published articles or to any books other than musical scores.

All the music referred to in the Glossary, whether well known or not, is available at the time of writing (January 2020) on YouTube, often with the musical score moving in synch. If you don't know the composer or work mentioned, please take the opportunity to give it a try.

Words in **bold** within an entry are defined under an entry elsewhere in the Glossary.

J.A.

acoustic beats

When two **frequencies** are very close in pitch – and therefore close in frequency – they produce a beating vibration at the speed of the difference in frequency between them. For example, a frequency of 440 Hertz put in close proximity to a frequency of 442 Hertz will produce acoustic beats of 2 Hertz (or two vibrations per second). If the distance between two frequencies becomes sufficiently large, they no longer produce beats but **difference tones** which, unlike beats, are not physically present but merely heard in listeners' ears.

acoustics

From the Ancient Greek 'acou-o' meaning 'I hear'.

The scientific study of sounds and their interaction. Acoustical terminology is regrettably full of confusing redundancies, with multiple terms for the same phenomena. For example, the terms **harmonic series**, 'overtone series', 'harmonic spectrum', 'overtone spectrum' all refer to the same phenomenon; **difference tones**, 'sum and difference tones', 'combination tones' and 'resultant tones' all refer to the same phenomena, etc.

See also **psycho-acoustics**.

aleatoric music/aleatoricism

From the Latin 'alea' meaning 'dice'.

Music in which certain details are left to chance or the player's choice. For example, Lutosławski's Second Symphony opens with all the brass playing precisely notated rhythms which are, however, not co-ordinated with one another. The result is a dense and unpredictable texture. The aleatoric element here is in the rhythms, which are unco-ordinated (whereas in traditional Western music the rhythms are usually co-ordinated). The pitches, however, are fully determined in this example. In other aleatoric music, the pitches might also be left to chance, or the order of sections in a work, etc.

See also **open form**.

beats *see* **acoustic beats**.

blocs sonores

French, literally 'sound blocks'; *see* **chord multiplication**.

brush bowing

Also known as *spazzolare* (Italian, meaning 'to brush'). A string-playing technique in which the player vertically brushes the strings with the bow, rather than applying the usual horizontal bowing action – for which reason the technique is also sometimes called 'vertical bowing'. The result is an imprecise mixture of bow noise and pitch.

See also **extended techniques**.

canon

A device found in **counterpoint**. A melodic line played by one part is imitated by one or more other parts, each part usually entering substantially before the previous part has completed the melodic line. If imitating part(s) enter(s) at the same pitch as the initial melodic line, this is called a **unison** canon.

See also **heterophony**.

cantus firmus

From the Latin 'cantus' meaning 'song', and 'firmus' meaning 'strong' or 'constant'.

A very slow melody underpinning a musical work (or a section of it), much used in medieval and Renaissance music. It is often a plainsong or else a popular song. Because of its extreme slowness, a *cantus firmus* is not usually clearly perceived in the music using this technique: it forms the background to a more rapidly moving musical texture in the foreground. However, in the *Benedictus* of John Taverner's *Missa Gloria Tibi Trinitas* (c.1525), at the words 'in nomine Domini' ('in the name of the Lord') the composer places the *cantus firmus* in an unusually high register and at a faster speed, so the *cantus* is heard very clearly. This 'in nomine' type of *cantus firmus* was much admired and subsequently imitated by several subsequent generations of British composers in works they named *In Nomine*. Some of the last *In Nomine* compositions were composed by Henry Purcell, after which the device fell into disuse. After 1955, both *cantus firmus* in general and the 'in nomine' composition in particular were revived by (among others) Sir Peter Maxwell Davies, most of whose output was composed using these devices, most extensively in his opera *Taverner* (which quotes the *Missa Gloria Tibi Trinitas* by Taverner, and is based upon an account of his life). More recently, *cantus firmus* technique and especially the 'in nomine' variety of it have been widely revived by composers of many different styles and nationalities, though as with Maxwell Davies the resultant music rarely sounds in any way medieval or Renaissance in musical style.

chord multiplication

A **twelve-note** row is divided up into smaller note groups of between one and five notes each. Each of these are then transposed onto each other, producing what Boulez terms *blocs sonores*: blocks of sounds which look like chords, on paper, but are in fact simply modes of limited numbers of notes which may be played in any register or order. Chord multiplication was discovered by Boulez while composing *Le Marteau sans maître* as a means of escaping the rigid pitch systems of **serialism** and twelve-note technique. It is used in every Boulez piece after about 1954, and has been adopted by composers influenced by his work.

chromatic scale

The twelve pitches per **octave** of **equal temperament**.

402

cluster
A very closely spaced bunch of notes, usually played together to form a distinct musical sonority. They may be **chromatic, diatonic** or **microtonal**. A chromatic cluster is built from adjacent semitones (the smallest interval of Western tuning); a diatonic cluster is built from adjacent notes in a diatonic scale; a microtonal cluster is built from an interval smaller than the semitone, such as **quarter-tones** or eighth-tones. Clusters made sporadic historic appearances in Western music, often for pictorial reasons. An early example is the opening of Rebel's *Les Elements* (c.1720), where clusters are used to depict chaos; a low organ cluster is used in Verdi's *Otello* (1887) for similarly atmospheric reasons. In piano music by Cowell, Ornstein and Ives (dating from 1900 to 1930), clusters are used for either percussive effects or evoking natural phenomena such as storms or thunder. Much used in Bartók (Fourth String Quartet (1928), *Music for Strings, Percussion and Celesta* (1936)), after 1945 they were especially prominent in composers from Eastern European countries, such as Ligeti, Lutosławski, Penderecki and Xenakis. The fashion for chromatic or microtonal clusters reached its height in the mid-1960s, since when they have been used much more rarely (although they are still heard in scores for thriller movies and the like). Diatonic clusters, however, are still in wide use, notably in **minimalist** music.

combination tones *see* **difference tones.**

consecutives
Pitches moving in exact parallel motion in more than one part. Forbidden in traditional **counterpoint.**

counterpoint
The art of combining melodies, sometimes in imitation of each other, sometimes not. Devices of counterpoint include **canon** and fugue.

diatonic
Music using the simplest and most consonant intervals or modes of the tempered scale, for example, the white notes of the piano keyboard.

difference tones/sum tones/resultant tones
Two **frequencies** may, if sufficiently far apart from each other in pitch and placed in close physical proximity at sufficient volume, produce the sensation of a third tone in the ear of the listener. The frequency of this third tone is determined by the numerical difference between the two original frequencies. Sometimes the extra tone may be determined by the addition of the two original frequencies. Still more tones may be produced either by the addition or subtraction of the **harmonics** of the two original tones, or else by the difference between one resultant tone and one of the two original tones. Unlike **beats,**

which are physically present and may be measured with acoustical equipment, difference tones are not physically present but are produced in the listener's ear only. Otherwise they are similar to beats, though not the result of frequencies at closely similar pitches.

See also **ring modulation**.

equal temperament

The normal tuning used in Western music since around 1750, and in most instrumental popular or rock music until very recently. It arose because the various previous attempts at tuning constantly resulted in rendering certain chords and keys almost unusably out of tune. Equal temperament rationalised these problems by dividing the octave into 12 equal parts, called **semitones**, and basing all other chords and intervals exclusively on these 12 pitches, which are also known as the **chromatic scale**. This rationalised tuning has enormous benefits in that all intervals sound the same at any pitch transposition, facilitating movement and rapid change in music. The downside of this tuning is that most of its intervals are distant from the pure tuning of intervals found in the harmonic series. Equal temperament is therefore very far from **Just intonation**.

Keyboard instruments such as pianos and synthesisers are generally tuned in this temperament (or else, in as close as possible a simulation of it). Since rock and popular music generally use commercial synthesisers tuned this way, and due to the mass exploitation of that music across the world, in the past 50 years equal temperament has become overwhelmingly (and to some, disquietingly) the most common tuning heard on the planet.

Whether or not in reaction against this trend, modern/contemporary art music and some recent pop music has much explored various alternative tunings. Numerous contemporary art composers create music using all manner of other temperaments (as is reflected in several items in this Glossary and in many conversations in this book). In pop music, various figures, most noticeably Jacob Collier, have recently begun to explore such alternative tunings and have even created hit songs using them.

electronic music

Music created using exclusively or mainly electronic tone-generating devices. In the 1950s the Electronic Studio of Cologne Radio was set up to explore such possibilities, in distinction to the *musique concrète* of French Radio which created works using recordings of real sounds. The supposed opposition between electronic music and *musique concrète* gradually became irrelevant as works emerged which mixed the two techniques seamlessly. The earliest prominent example of this fusion was Stockhausen's *Gesang der Jünglinge* (1955–56). Thereafter, *concrète* composers also employed electronic sound with increasing frequency, and Stockhausen also began to devise minutely accurate and realistic electronic simulations of instrumental sounds (as in the tape part of his *Kontakte*). In numerous subsequent electro-acoustic works it becomes very hard to discern what is electronically generated and what is *concrète*. İlhan Mimaroğlu's *Agony* and François Bayle's *Toupie dans le Ciel* are both purely electronic – the former goes out of its way to disguise the fact, whereas the latter deliberately flaunts the fact to evoke the image of the title (meaning 'spinning top in heaven'). Composers prominent in electronic music, in addition to those mentioned above, include Peter Zinovieff, Daphne Oram, Eliane Radigue, Jonathan Harvey, Else Marie Pade, Herbert Eimert, Bernd Alois Zimmermann, John Cage, etc.

extended techniques

The use of performing techniques not usually employed in the playing of a Western musical instrument; for example, bowing the wooden body of the violin rather than its strings (as would normally be the case), or breathing tonelessly down a brass instrument (instead of blowing a precise pitch); or *spazzolare* on strings. Many of these techniques result either in unstable or fragile pitches, or some variety of unpitched **noise**. Many are also quieter than normal playing techniques. Composers who have used such techniques extensively in their compositions include George Crumb, Heinz Holliger, Vinko Globokar, George Lewis, Salvatore Sciarrino, Helmut Lachenmann, Chaya Czernowin and numerous younger composers. Extended techniques require special notation as well as specialised training for their successful performance. Composers using such techniques need to work closely with players of the instruments concerned, or else be expert performers themselves, in order to ensure no harm is done to the instrument in the performance of their chosen extended technique.

See also **brush bowing**.

frequencies

Sound is measured as waves, comprising vibrations per second. These are also known as 'frequencies' or as 'cycles per second'. The unit of sound frequencies is Hertz: a frequency of 440 Hertz = 440 wave cycles per second (and gives the pitch A to which an orchestra usually tunes). The higher the number of cycles per second, the higher the perceived pitch.

frequency modulation spectra

A pair of **frequencies** are modulated against each other: the 'carrier' frequency is modulated by the 'modulator'. An index controls the extent of the modulation.

The result is a complex sound which can be especially useful in simulating the sonorities of bells or of brass instruments. Often used in computer music, the computer form of this technique was accidentally discovered in the late 1960s by John Chowning, who was attempting to get a computer to simulate a note with vibrato around it. The note in this experiment was effectively the 'carrier' frequency; the vibrato rate was the 'modulator' frequency. What emerged from the computer, however, was not a vibrato note, but a richly complex bell-like sonority. Chowning subsequently patented this computer technique. It was commercially exploited by the firm Yamaha to create many commercial synthesisers, of which the most famous were the DX- and TX- varieties marketed in the 1980s and 1990s. It is still much used in the computer generation of sounds.

glissando

A gradual glide from one pitch to another. In contrast to a *portamento*, a *glissando* starts as soon as the first pitch is played and lasts until the new pitch is reached. *Glissandi* were originally used by composers as an onomatopoeic sound effect (often in passages evoking thunder, or other natural sounds). From the 1920s onwards they became increasingly common as a serious component in the musical substance (Prokofiev's Symphony No. 3, Varèse's *Amériques*). From around 1915 Australian composer and pianist Percy Grainger devised a type of 'free music' which consisted entirely of continuously gliding tones, and from 1940 onwards built electric 'free music machines' to perform such music. *Glissandi* play a major part in the musical syntax of Xenakis, especially in his works from 1954 to 1970, and featured frequently in the music of Penderecki, Lutosławski, Ligeti and others in the 1960s.

grand rights

Performing rights applying to the performances of music in theatres or as part of a theatrical or dance spectacle; for example, opera, ballet, incidental theatre music. Grand rights, unlike normal performing rights, are not collected by performing-rights agencies, but agreed individually by the theatre concerned and the composer of the music (or their publisher). They amount to a percentage cut of the box-office takings of the performance(s) concerned.

harmonic series

Also known as the overtone series, or the harmonic spectrum. The harmonic series is both simple and very common. It comprises a fundamental tone and its whole-number multiples, in the proportions 1:2:3:4:5:6:7:8:9, etc. ad infinitum, the tones being known as **harmonics** (or **partials**, or **overtones**). In pitch terms, the result is an ascending series of intervals which get smaller and smaller to the ear, and which increasingly lie outside **equal temperament**. The first interval is the octave, the second is the perfect 5th, then the perfect 4th, then the major 3rd, then the minor 3rd, etc. Most Western concert instruments with definite pitch – strings, brass, woodwind, piano, harp, etc. – have **spectra** which resonate in this manner. For those who read music, the following figure gives the first 16 harmonics of the overtone series to the nearest **quarter-tone** (each harmonic is numbered, the fundamental being also known as the 1st harmonic; the accidentals in front of harmonic 7, 11, 13 are quarter-tones):

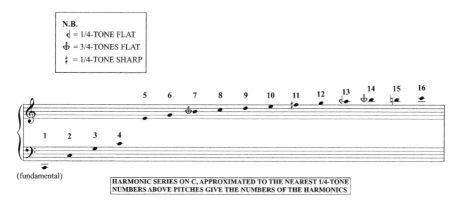

A couple of important consequences follow on from this:

1. Each harmonic of the overtone series has its own overtone series contained within the harmonic series itself. The overtones of the 2nd harmonic (in the example above, the pitch C below middle C) would be harmonics 2, 4, 6, 8, 10, 12, 14, 16, etc.; the overtones of harmonic 3 would be harmonics 3, 6, 9, 12, 15, etc.; and so on, ad infinitum. The harmonic series, therefore, is self-reflexive: it reproduces itself on every part of itself. This explains its very special and resonant character: every part of it is reinforcing every other part.

2. The lower harmonics (harmonics 1–6) produce a basic unit of Western tonal harmony: the major triad. By focusing on these lower harmonics, the harmony of Western tonality built a language on the simplest and most consonant intervals.

In acoustic reality, even these lowest harmonics are not included precisely within equal temperament, though they are close enough to it for common usage. A tuning system which attempts to reproduce the exact intervallic properties of the harmonic series is known as one approaching **Just intonation** – the more exactly it reproduces the intervals of the harmonic series, the more 'Just' the tuning is.

harmonic spectrum
Another term for **harmonic series**.

harmonics
The component parts of the **harmonic series**, also known as **partials, overtones,** etc.

heterophony
From the Greek 'heteros' meaning 'different', and 'pho-né' meaning 'sound'.

407

Several variants of the same melody played simultaneously, like having a theme and its variations all at once. A simple instance of this may be heard at the opening of Oliver Knussen's *Flourish with Fireworks*, where a fanfare figure is repeatedly played in several different rhythms at the same time, producing an orchestral echo effect. Heterophony as a term may also be used to describe the use of closely similar but non-identical melodies or musical parts unfolding at the same time.

Heterophony is often found in many traditional musics (for example, Indonesian gamelan, Japanese *gagaku*, Ethiopian Jewish worship and Hebridean psalm-singing), but was also employed in later Beethoven (the 1st movement and the double fugue in the finale of the Ninth Symphony, parts of the *Missa Solemnis* and several passages in his late string quartets) and some Brahms (Fourth Symphony). It was revived by twentieth-century composers such as Enescu and Bartók, who encountered it via folk-music traditions. After 1945 heterophony was much exploited by Messiaen (*Turangalîla-Symphonie*, 9th movement) and his pupils Boulez (*Rituel, Notations, Sur Incises*), Amy (*Diaphonies*), Éloy (*Etude III*), Grisey (*Modulations, Transitoires*), Benjamin (*Upon Silence, Sudden Time*), as well as by composers as varied as Tippett (*The Rose Lake*, String Quartet No. 5), Zygmunt Krauze (*Aus Aller Welt Stammende*) and many others. Modern Romanian composers have made a special feature of folk-inspired heterophony in their music; for example, Ştefan Niculescu (*Ison II*), Aurel Stroe (*Canto II*) and Horaţiu Rădulescu (*Capricorn's Nostalgic Crickets* and *Mirabilia Mundi*). It is often a feature of other contemporary composers inspired by folk and traditional musics, such as Michael Finnissy (*English Country Tunes, Red Earth*).

Heterophony may also be produced by the technique of **canon** when all musical parts share the same sequence of pitches (as in a canon at the unison) but differ from each other in rhythm, as happens throughout Ligeti's *Lontano*. Ligeti's Requiem makes use of many forms of heterophony. The device is especially prominent in the 'Kyrie' movement of the Requiem and is also much used in his *Atmosphères*, in both of which it contributes significantly to the surreal reverberation textures exploited in Kubrik's masterly use of these pieces for many parts in his film *2001: A Space Odyssey*.

hocket

From the Old French 'hocquet' meaning 'hiccup'.

A melody is split up note by note among a number of musical parts, such that each only plays one note of the melody at a time. Found in much Western medieval music, and also found (though not under this name) in many traditional musics, especially Central African vocal and instrumental music from the sub-Saharan regions. It has featured in much concert music composed since about 1946 (Messiaen *Turangalîla-Symphonie*, 7th and 9th movements), and is especially prominent in certain works of Birtwistle (*Tragoedia, Carmen Arcadiae*).

hybrid non-repeating scales *see* **multi-register scales**.

irrational rhythms
A confusing term seemingly invented by Messiaen to describe rhythms subdividing the basic beat of the music into prime numbers 3, 5, 7, 11, 13, 17, etc. (or multiples of these). Such divisions of the basic beat enable composers to use a varied range of speeds simultaneously. The term is misleading as there is nothing 'irrational' about the rhythms in the mathematical sense.

isorhythm
A melody or musical part constructed from the simultaneous use of both pitch and rhythm *ostinati*, where the number of pitches circling is different from the number of rhythms. The pitches and rhythms therefore go in and out of phase with one another as the isorhythm progresses through a work. Much medieval music uses isorhythm (Machaut *Hocquetus David*), and the practice was revived by composers from 1930 onwards (Messiaen *La Nativité du Seigneur*, *Quartet for the End of Time*, and many works of Birtwistle, Maxwell Davies, Boulez, etc.).

just intonation
The tuning of musical intervals as close as possible to those found in the **harmonic series**.
   Various tunings have been proposed to achieve this, of which the most current in Western music prior to 1750 was **meantone tuning**.

macrotones/macrotonality
Any intervals larger than the tempered **semitone** but not in **equal temperament**.
   A term I believed I had devised around 2002 to describe the use of such intervals and to keep them distinct from **microtones**. It turned out that others independently were using the term macrotone for designating such intervals – perhaps unsurprisingly, as it is the logical name for them, despite which the term is still not in wide use (though the intervals are).
   Macrotonality refers specifically to a system I devised from around 1999 onwards, to control and articulate the use of such intervals in a musical context. It is explained in the appendix immediately following this Glossary, and is used in most of my pieces since 2002.

meantone tuning
A variety of tuning much used up to about 1750 which brings the twelve notes of the **chromatic** scale and their resultant larger intervals close to the tuning of the **harmonic series**. In so doing it makes some chords and keys almost unplayably out of tune, for which reason it was gradually abandoned in favour of **equal temperament**.
   See also **just intonation**.

microtones
Any musical intervals smaller than the **semitone**.

MIDI
Musical Instrument Digital Interface: a code agreed in 1983 between manufacturers of digital musical instruments enabling different synthesisers and computers to share musical information. All digital instruments are programmed to read this code. MIDI is also used as a shorthand expression for the computer playback of musical scores by notation software.

minimalism
Music built from the predominant use of hypnotic repetition, steady pulse and slowly changing diatonic harmony. Anticipated in the works of Carl Orff from the late 1930s onwards (*Carmina Burana, Antigone, Trionfo di Afrodite*), true minimalism emerged in the US from around 1964 in the music of La Monte Young, Riley, Reich, Glass and others, in reaction to the obsessive avoidance of repetition, steady pulse and diatonic harmony in the **serialism** of the immediately preceding era. From around 1970, the influence of minimalism spread to affect composers in Holland (Andriessen, de Bondt, Wagenaar), the UK (Bedford, Cardew, Nyman, Skempton, Colin Matthews), Estonia (Pärt), Japan (Kondo), Australia (Sculthorpe) and Poland (Górecki, Kilar), etc. Since the successful premiere of Adams's opera *Nixon in China* in 1987, the influence of minimalism has spread across much of the globe.

mode
A collection of pitches from which all or some of a piece's harmony and melody is built. Like **twelve-note technique**, mode and modality are terms too widely used and complicated to be explained here more than very briefly (the reader is encouraged to look up the many websites explaining these terms). Here are a few key points about modes in music, especially modern and contemporary music:

1. If the mode is just a collection of pitches which may be played in any order or combination, it is the same as an unordered **pitch set**. The chords produced by Boulez's **chord multiplication** are just such modes, which accounts for the curiously static modal feel of much of his work since 1954 or so. Much music since 1920 freely uses such modes, whether **diatonic** or **chromatic**. Most **minimalism** uses diatonic modes in this way.

2. More usually in the music – and not just Western music – a mode is not simply a collection of pitches playable in any order, but implies a hierarchy between the pitches, i.e. some are more important and used more often or at more crucial points in the music than others. The modes of plainchant are of this second type – each uses all the white notes of the (piano) keyboard, but each has a principal tone, plus another tone often

410

used to go to that principal tone at the melody's conclusion. The ragas of Hindustani music are of this type as well, often having quite complicated rules for the order in which the notes may be played, their relationship to each other, etc. The diatonic major and minor scales of Western tonality are also of this second type of mode, including a main note (or 'tonic') which determines the key of the music, a secondary tone – confusingly termed the 'dominant' – which is the next most important note, and a 'leading note' which normally rises up to the tonic, etc.

multiphonics
Normally, an individual woodwind or brass instrument may only play single sounds at any one time. Multiphonics are sounds produced by non-standard playing techniques on such instruments (such as unusual fingerings or lip positions, or singing into the instrument while playing, etc.). They have a chord-like presence of more than one sound simultaneously. The result doesn't sound like a chord, as the frequencies are often outside normal tunings and not all have the same loudness. Multiphonics are frequently described as sounding 'electronic'. Such sounds have been exploited for a long time by jazz performers such as Ornette Coleman and John Coltrane. In so-called classical concert music, multiphonics have been exploited mainly since around 1960, when they began to be explored by such composers as Szalonek and Bartolozzi. They feature especially in the music of Holliger, Sciarrino, Ferneyhough, Lachenmann, Dillon, Czernowin, and composers of spectral music such as Grisey, Murail and Rădulescu.

An interesting extension of such sounds may be found in their use for sound samples in electro-acoustic music: *Pashanti* (1979) by David Evan Jones uses oboe and clarinet multiphonics for its spectral content but gives these sounds such different attacks and durations that their sonic origin is not evident on hearing the music. The striking feature of multiphonics on woodwind and brass is precisely that they transcend the basic sound world of the instrument so drastically that the resulting sounds appear not to belong to those instruments at all. Having said which, by now (2020) such sounds are so common as to have even featured in mainstream movie scores (usually for moments of unease, terror, sci-fi, mystery, etc.) so that, rather like clusters, they are in danger of becoming clichéd.

multi-register scales
Modes spread over several registers and/or octaves. Each register or octave may have different pitches, or may have pitches which only occur within that register, as well as pitches common to other registers. Each register of such a mode is also distinguished by having its own main tones, secondary tones, etc. Such modes are often found in various traditional musics. My ensemble work *Khorovod*

(1989–95) is built entirely upon such modes, as are many of my subsequent works. Whether rightly or wrongly, I have also analysed music by other twentieth-composers as having been written this way, especially Stravinsky, Bartók, Webern from the Symphony Op. 21 onwards, and some Messiaen, Boulez, Stockhausen, Reich, Andriessen, Saariaho and Benjamin. For example, I believe that the many polyphonic levels of superimposed *ostinati* in 'The Procession of the Sage' from part 1 of Stravinsky's *The Rite of Spring* are heard as parts of a single large multi-register scale, whether the composer intended this or not. (As yet there is no generally accepted theory of how such passages are heard or how they were conceived by the composer.)

musique concrète
Music which uses only or predominantly recordings of sounds from real life (hence the term 'concrete'), which are manipulated, altered, distorted, reversed, sped up, slowed down, filtered, etc. The principal pioneers of this were Pierre Schaeffer and his Groupe de Recherches Musicales in Paris, founded in 1948.

    See also **electronic music.**

neo-Romanticism
Music written in the past 60 years which revives certain features of music composed between 1830 and 1910. Prominent examples include *Scenes and Arias* by Maw, *Scenes from Schumann* by Holloway, *Final Alice* by Del Tredici and certain works by composers as varied as Henze, Rochberg, Penderecki, Glanert, Gruber, Rihm, Takemitsu, Knussen, Tower, Read Thomas, Schuller, Dusapin, Lindberg, Schnittke, MacMillan and many others. Among the features from Romantic music often revived in neo-Romantic composers are **diatonic** and/or **chromatic** tonal harmony, richly varied and sometimes lush orchestral colours, dramatic and expressive gestures, large-scale formal patterns of climax and relaxation, etc. Such features became more prominent in music generally after 1970, and may be found in the orchestral *Notations* of Boulez, despite his stated opposition to neo-Romanticism, or in *Gondwana* by Murail, supposedly a composer of **spectral music**, or in *Ignis Noster* by James Dillon, who is usually associated with **new complexity**. In reality, neo-Romantic features may swim in and out of music by a wide range of composers, which does not necessarily mean that either they or their music are to be termed neo-Romantic. For this reason, the category has become increasingly vague and may be found even less helpful than such labels generally aren't.

neumes
From the ancient Greek 'pneuma' meaning 'breath'.

    A catalogue of basic melodic shapes, usually in units from one to five notes in length. Such shapes were initially represented by short squiggles on plain paper (giving the reader the general contour of a melody, but not its precise pitches), and later by clumps of lozenge-shaped notes on musical staves to indicate precise pitches. Neumes underpin the entire repertoire of both plainchant and medieval music. They have been much revived by composers since around 1920. The standard reference book for plainchant, the *Liber Usualis*, opens with a catalogue of neumes.

new complexity
A term coined independently by the music critics Harry Halbreich and Richard Toop to describe the music of some composers active after 1970 who have written using repeatedly extreme density of rhythm, pitch, dynamic and register changes, etc. The notation of such music often uses slow speeds so that fast articulations have to be notated in very small note values, giving the music a strikingly wild appearance in the musical score (anyone wishing to confirm this may Google-images-search *La Terre Est Un Homme* by Brian Ferneyhough). Music composed using these features may involve such a density of conflicting performance instructions that it is at times not literally possible to perform exactly what is written – something has to be approximated or left out. There are ample precedents for this in musical history. The choral parts of Ligeti's Requiem (especially its Kyrie second movement) are acknowledged by the composer to be not literally singable as notated; as Ligeti often pointed out, the filigree string parts near the end of Wagner's *Die Walküre* are not literally playable; the very fast low runs in the double basses in the 'Storm' movement of Beethoven's 'Pastoral' Symphony are surely not intended to be played fully accurately, being a simulation of rumbling thunder; many areas of Xenakis's music feature parts not literally playable in every detail (for example, the opening piano cadenza of his *Eonta*); and some of the wilder **polyrhythms** in Chopin verge on the unplayable (as in some of his Ballades and Etudes). By now (2020), several generations of performers have emerged who are expert at playing new complexity: the Arditti and JACK Quartets, and pianists Nic Hodges and Ian Pace, the flautist Mario Caroli, the bass clarinettist Harry Sparnaay, are prominent examples of such performers. Composers associated with this tendency include Brian Ferneyhough, Michael Finnissy, James Dillon, Chris Dench, Richard Barrett, James Erber, Klaus K. Hübler, Claus-Steffen Mahnkopf, among others.

new simplicity
A term used at various stages and in various countries since the early 1960s to describe music at the opposite pole from that referred to in the previous entry. As far as I can discover, the term was first used in Denmark around 1964 to refer to music of radically stripped down, unflinchingly clear musical textures – a characteristic which has remained typical of much Danish music ever since. Apparently initiated by Henning Christiansen's *Constructions*, the tendency soon spread to the music of Pelle Gudmundsen-Holmgreen, Poul Ruders, Hans Abrahamsen

and Bent Sørensen. The term was later independently applied to a different group of composers working in Germany in the 1970s, including Clarence Barlow, Walter Zimmermann, John McGuire, Gerald Barry, Claude Vivier, Chris Newman and others; it has since been applied to various UK composers, notably Howard Skempton. In almost all cases, a composer of new simplicity reduces many aspects of musical texture to a minimum, concentrating upon essentials or even upon seemingly obvious musical facts with the aim of refreshing musical syntax and listening habits. As Gudmundsen-Holmgreen remarked, this is not done out of any wish to be provocative, but to produce fresh musical perceptions. New simplicity is a quite distinct tendency from **minimalism**, despite sharing several characteristics with it.

noise
An acoustical phenomenon is termed a 'noise' if it exhibits permanent instability of its frequencies, such that within the sound's range any frequency is equally likely to be present at any time and any amplitude. Waves of the sea, gusts of wind, the rattle of a side drum, the hiss of a champagne bottle just after opening are all examples of acoustical noise.

non-repeating scales *see* **multi-register scales.**

non-tempered tunings
Any pitches or tuning not found in **equal temperament.**
    See also **microtones** and **macrotones/macrotonality.**

note row *see* **twelve-note music.**

octave
If you start on any pitch in **equal temperament** and go up (or down) all twelve **semitones** of the **chromatic scale**, you will end up at a higher (or lower) version of the same pitch at which you started: this is known as the octave of the original pitch, because it is also eight white notes up (or down) on the piano keyboard.

open form
Music in which the sequence of some or all sections is left open to the choice of the performers. Such works often have no set start or end, as in Stockhausen's *Piano Piece XI* (1957). Performances of such pieces may differ very widely in both duration and moment-to-moment details.
    See also **aleatoric music.**

ostinato **(plural:** *ostinati***)**
A repeated pattern of either rhythms or pitches, or both.
    See also **isorhythm.**

overtones
Another term for **harmonics**.

overtone series
Another term for the **harmonic series**.

partials
Another term for **harmonics**.

particell
Also known as the 'short score', this is a musical sketch containing only the essence of the piece being composed on as few musical staves as possible, often without any indications of the instruments which may be playing the music, or even their dynamics. Short scores are used by composers in order to get down the trajectory for a large work, or a large passage of it, as swiftly as possible without having to work out all of its details. Many composers use this sketching device, and such sketches may have crucial subsequent importance in editing a score so as to produce an *Urtext* edition.

pentatonic
A **mode** of five different pitches which may be played in any order or combination. Most often applied to the black keys of the piano keyboard. Many famous traditional melodies use only the black notes of the piano, for example *Auld Lang Syne*.

performing rights
A sum of money paid to the composer of a work by the organisation performing the work or promoting the concert in which it features, without which licence the work may not be performed. Traditionally, performing rights are divided up equally between the composer and their publisher (unless their music is self-published, in which case 100 per cent of the rights are paid to the composer). Performing rights are payable to a composer upon their signing up with a Rights Collection Agency such as the PRS in the UK, SACEM in France or STIM in Sweden. In the UK and EU, performing rights are payable for any performance of a composer's works during the composer's lifetime, and for 70 years after the composer's death to the heirs of the composer's estate.

pitch set
Pretty much what it says: any set or group of pitches. If the pitches may be used by the composer in any order, they are termed an 'unordered set'. If a particular order of the pitches is significant or even rigidly adhered to, they are termed an 'ordered set'. Unordered sets are probably the most commonly used pitch device in so-called classical concert music at the moment: almost everyone, from **minimalists** to **new complexity** composers, has passages using unordered sets.

Unordered sets are very similar to **modes**, but usually have no prioritisation among their pitches, whereas in modes some pitches may be more important than others.

polyphony
From Ancient Greek 'poly' meaning 'many' and 'phoné' meaning sound.

The combination of different melodies or musical textures simultaneously. Often used interchangeably with **counterpoint**, but arguably wrongly as the term polyphony covers a much wider range of phenomena, including for example the accidental coincidence of more than one music. Apparently Gustav Mahler, delighted while on holiday in the Austrian alps by hearing musical bands from several different neighbouring villages all playing at the same time in different keys and speeds, exclaimed 'That is real polyphony!' He would certainly never have said 'That is real counterpoint!' as he knew that counterpoint is a conscious and deliberate combination of musical parts, and thus could never be a matter of accident. When Charles Ives simulates the impression of several bands playing different pieces at the same time, he is writing a variety of polyphony. On this basis, it could be argued that a texture employing *cantus firmus* technique is polyphonic rather than contrapuntal. In short, counterpoint combines melodies carefully into a new and deliberate whole; polyphony includes this, but enlarges on it by allowing sharp or total difference between the parts or musics involved.

In practice, you should expect to see these terms used fairly interchangeably by musicians, but the above distinction is worth bearing in mind.

polyrhythm
A combination of at least two different rhythms simultaneously, especially those of different length from one another.

portamento
Gliding from one pitch to another, not continuously as in a *glissando*, but shortly before the end of the first pitch, usually to add expressive intensity to the arrival of the next pitch.

psycho-acoustics
The study of the way the brain perceives sounds. Psycho-acoustics has been of much interest to composers since around 1965, including Stockhausen, Boulez, Berio, Reich, Riley and especially composers of **electronic** and **spectral music**.

quarter-tones
A variety of **microtone** in which the **semitone** is divided into two equal parts – hence the name.

resultant tones *see* **difference tones.**

ring modulation
Adding and subtracting two or more **frequencies** (and perhaps their **harmonics**) to produce **difference** and **sum tones** which, unlike the purely acoustic form of these phenomena, are part of the actual resultant sound spectrum, rather than being purely auditory illusions. The first ring modulators were built in the 1950s and the sound quickly became one of the most popular in **electronic music.** Several major works, notably Stockhausen's *Mantra*, exploit this technique almost exclusively. In popular culture, ring modulation achieved worldwide fame through the BBC's sci-fi series *Doctor Who*, in which the voices of the Daleks were produced by ring-modulating the human voice with a low frequency.

scales, non-repeating/multi-register *see* **multi-register scales.**

semitone
The smallest common interval in Western concert music. There are 12 semitones in each register or octave. All other intervals in Western concert music are built from multiples of semitones; for example, the minor third occupies a distance of three semitones.
   See **equal temperament.**

serial music/serialism
This is a later development of **twelve-note music,** largely from 1945 onwards, in which the use of rows to determine the order and content of pitches and harmonies is extended to using rows of rhythms, rows of dynamic values, and rows of any other type of sonic material. Such rows are termed 'series', and the resultant music is therefore known as 'serial music'. Possibilities of using rhythmic series as well as pitch ones were hinted at in a few works composed before 1945 (Fritz Heinrich Klein's *Die Maschine* from 1921). Fully fledged serial music emerged in the music of Babbitt and Messiaen roughly simultaneously after World War II. Such ideas were subsequently developed in the music of Boulez, Nono, Stockhausen, Berio and many others. The most famous and still-performed examples of this music include *Structures Books I and II, Le Marteau sans Maître* and *Pli selon pli* by Boulez, Stockhausen's *Gruppen* for three orchestras and his *Piano Pieces*, Nono's *Il Canto Sospeso* and Berio's *Sequenza* cycle. The era of strict serialism was brief, and reactions against it not slow to set in. Cage's introduction of chance operations and theatrical absurdity into concert music was one such reaction; **minimalism** was another; **neo-Romanticism** and **spectral music** were others.

sonata form
One of the most common forms of Western classical music, especially from about 1760 onwards.
   A first theme in the home key (or tonic) is followed by a transition to a second,

contrasting theme, often in the dominant (the key a perfect fifth away from the tonic). All the music so far is called the 'exposition'. It is immediately repeated (though these repeats are sometimes optional). The next section, called the 'development', takes the music through rapidly changing keys and harmonic areas, and breaks both first and second themes into fragments. After that comes the 'recapitulation', which is essentially the same as the 'exposition' except that the second theme is heard in the tonic. There may follow a coda in which more development occurs (this is especially a feature of Beethoven's music), ending in the tonic.

The first movements of most symphonies are in sonata form or some variant of it. The form isn't hard to follow, and it can be fascinating to hear how differently this form is treated by Haydn, Mozart, Beethoven, Schubert, Schumann, Brahms, Bruckner, Tchaikovsky, Schoenberg, Sibelius, Nielsen, Shostakovich and more recent composers.

The essential feature of sonata form is the contrast between themes being stated (in the exposition and recapitulation) and themes being developed or fragmented (everywhere else). The harmonic contrast in sonata form is similarly between passages of relative stability (the exposition and recapitulation) and passages of increasing instability (everywhere else). Schoenberg focused upon passages of harmonic instability and increasing fragmentation of themes so much that he ended up devising **twelve-note technique** in which everything is derived from a single theme (or row) which is constantly changed and developed: as he often said, in his music 'everything is development'.

spectrum (plural: spectra)
The spectrum of a sound is a list of its component **frequencies** and their respective loudness (termed their 'amplitude'), plus the way both of these change over time. Both of these determine how the sound is perceived.

spectral music/spectralism
A musical tendency which emerged from the late 1960s onwards, in which composers attempt to use the acoustic substance of sounds – sound **spectra** – as the basis of the harmony, melody, textures and form of their music. A simple example occurs at the start of Grisey's ensemble piece *Partiels* (1975), in which the **frequencies** from the spectrum of a low trombone note are re-created on the other instruments. The term was not coined until 1979 by the French composer Hugues Dufourt, prior to which various other terms were being used for composers of this type (for example, Rădulescu's term 'plasmatic music' and Grisey's term 'liminal music', etc.). In practice, spectral music uses not merely sound spectra as its source material but also **psycho-acoustics** – the way we perceive sounds – and the acoustical relationships among different sounds. Many spectral pieces therefore also explore degrees of change over time, and with that the varying degrees of predictability or unpredictability in the music. Aside

from those composers already mentioned, composers whose names have been at one or other time associated with spectralism include Scelsi, Stockhausen, Ligeti, Risset, Nørgård, Saariaho, Lindberg, Lévinas, Haas, Benjamin, Vivier, Grosskopf, Harvey, Causton, Dumitrescu, Avram, Fineberg, Hillborg, Suckling and numerous younger composers. Until about 2000, spectral music had relatively little prominent exposure internationally, but since then it has become very well known, with numerous composers being influenced by aspects of it, leading international festivals and conductors performing such music, and even some mainstream films using it (for example, the 2010 Paramount feature *Shutter Island*, starring Leonardo DiCaprio).

Like **minimalism**, with which it shares some features (for example, the uses of both consonance and repetition), spectral music was spurred on by a reaction against the rigidity of **serial music**.

sum tones *see* **difference tones.**

twelve-note music/twelve-note technique
Music composed using a specific order of the 12 notes of the **chromatic scale**, sometimes misleadingly referred to as **serial music**. The technique is too elaborate to explain in detail here (there are plenty of decent websites and YouTube videos doing so). The following is a very brief summary of the basics.

The composer devises an order of the 12 notes (possibly from intuitive preliminary sketching) to use as the basis of their piece. This order of 12 notes is generally called the original 'row' of the work. In basic twelve-note technique, the composer uses the original row, or its inversion (in which all the intervals of the original row are turned upside down), or its retrograde (the original row in reverse), or its retrograde inverted. These four basic forms of the row are deployed throughout the work to form all the melody and harmony of the music. In addition to being used at the same starting pitch as the original row, all rows may also be transposed so as to start on any of the 12 pitches of **equal temperament.**

The origins of this technique are much contested. Varieties of it emerged in Russia around 1910–14 in the music of Scriabin, Obukhov, Golishev and Lourié. Schoenberg is generally credited with devising this technique in the early 1920s, despite both the above Russian precedents (which he is unlikely to have heard) and the more serious precedents of it in the *Altenberg Lieder* composed by his student Berg in 1912, in which many of the above premises and numerous others laid out in Schoenberg's writings on the topic after 1923 are already present. Schoenberg certainly did know the Berg work, as he conducted the first performance of it (or rather of two songs from it, selected against Berg's wishes from the whole set of five) in 1913. At no point did Schoenberg publicly acknowledge this important anticipation of his technique in Berg's music. Schoenberg was also very insistent that his technique had precedence over that evolved just before by another Viennese composer, Hauer, whose variety of the technique differs from Schoenberg's in numerous ways. In particular, Hauer generally divided his twelve-note rows into pairs of six-note **modes** whose pitches may occur in any order (he termed these 'tropes'; offshoots of this technique were to be much exploited later by Stravinsky, Krenek, Perle, Knussen and numerous others). By contrast, in classical twelve-note technique as advocated by Schoenberg the order of the whole row is regarded as inviolable.

Having said which, Schoenberg himself generally broke most of the rules he laid out for this technique in any work he composed using it. For example, his *Variations for Orchestra* Op. 31, the first large-scale work he composed in twelve-note technique, opens with an Introduction gradually unfolding 12 different pitches, but in the literal order they are introduced (for the record: B flat–G–E–C sharp–F sharp–B, etc.) they are not the twelve-note row of the piece, which is only presented clearly for the first time in the second section of the work, the Theme. (For those who wish to know, what's really happening in the Introduction to this work is that two forms of the row – the original row and its inversion starting a minor third lower – are being introduced simultaneously; but since they are both played at once or in close alternation, the effect to the listener is of a quite different note order being played.)

A remaining issue with twelve-note techniques and their offshoots: usually it is not possible to hear the mechanisms of twelve-note music when listening to it. That's to say, the musical reality of such works does not usually allow or even encourage the listener to perceive any of their underlying pitch structuring. As already hinted, even in much Schoenberg, the basic row is rarely audible as such. This results in two other problems:

- much of the written literature surrounding such music deals not with how it sounds but how it was composed, which is of neither interest nor relevance to most listeners;

- since there's little else for listeners to read about this music, other than vague descriptions or else biographies of the composers' lives, there remains a serious lack of helpful verbal communication for even sympathetic and interested listeners to this music.

Both of these consequences, plus under-prepared performances, have greatly hindered the public reception of such music, and have laid it open to charges of elitism and inaccessibility. This is unjust to the greatest music using this technique (such as most works by Schoenberg, Berg and Webern, the later Stravinsky, and much more recent music). Bad twelve-note music exists just as much as any other kind of bad music, however, and a lack of discrimination at times in the promotion of this music has also damaged the public reception of it.

See also **equal temperament, pitch set, serialism.**

unison

When two or more musical parts meet on the same pitch at the same **octave**, they are said to be at the unison.

Urtext

From the German 'ur' meaning 'original' and 'text' meaning 'text'.

A published musical score in which the editor has attempted to arrive at a version of the music as close as possible to that originally intended by the composer, using autograph manuscripts, first editions, instrumental parts and other usually archival material. Such editions generally come with extensive footnotes and a critical commentary enabling the performer of the music to see how the editor decided upon the printed music. The extent to which such editions truly restore the composer's original intentions remains a matter of dispute. The following example illustrates some typical issues arising with *Urtext* and similar scores. Dr Paul Wingfield's path-breaking new edition of Janáček's *Glagolitic Mass* (Universal Edition, 1993) aims to restore the music to its 'first version', placing the last movement of the work at the start, and making numerous changes to the musical text on the basis of manuscript and rehearsal sources. Janáček immediately revised the work, either during or following its first performances, and the only edition of the score published during his lifetime (the standard vocal score) placed the final movement at the end alone, the designated first movement (entitled 'Úvod', meaning 'Introduction' in Czech) at the start, and did not include most of the other changes printed by Wingfield. The rationale behind these decisions is thoroughly and responsibly explained in Wingfield's Preface to the full score and in his book about the work (Cambridge University Press, 1993). Since then, Dr Wingfield has also re-edited the final version of the work, thus ensuring that both versions remain available in circulation.

vertical bowing *see* **brush bowing**.

Macrotonality

A modal vocabulary based upon non-tempered intervals larger than the semitone.

BASIC RULES

1. The smallest interval allowed is the semitone. The smallest non-tempered interval allowed is a ¾-tone (i.e. a semitone enlarged by a quarter-tone). Thus this vocabulary is the opposite of microtonality (the use of intervals smaller than the semitone) – hence the name macrotonality.

2. All modes are drawn from the harmonic series, harmonics 7–14, approximated to the nearest quarter-tone. Numbers above pitches give the number of the harmonic concerned. The fundamental frequency of each harmonic series is three octaves below harmonic No. 8 (the boxed pitches).

3. The following intervals are banned on their own, either in chords or closely adjacent melodic lines:
   - the quarter-tone (banned regardless of context);
   - the octave plus or minus a quarter-tone (similarly);
   - the perfect fifth plus or minus a quarter-tone (sometimes allowed in chords with at least one other interval present);
   - the major third minus a quarter-tone (similarly).

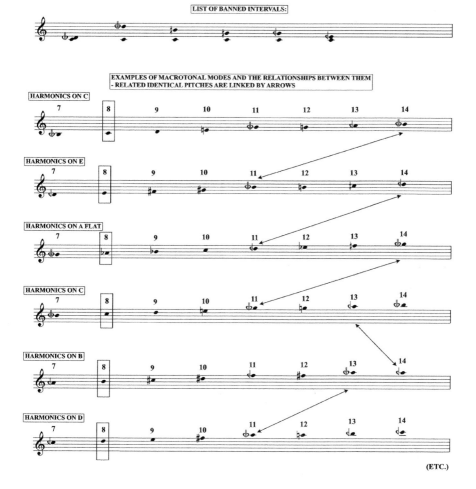

(ETC.)

Catalogue of Published Works by Julian Anderson

This worklist was drawn up by John Fallas and revised in consultation with the composer.

SING (1981–82, rev. 2019) for chamber choir

String Quartet No. 1 'Light Music' (1984–85, as *Light Music*; published 2013 under current title)

Ring Dance (1987; published 2015) for 2 violins
   arranged for 2 cellos (2015)
   (*arrangement in preparation* for 2 violas)

Diptych (1988–90) for orchestra

Khorovod (1988–94, rev. 1995) for 15 players

Seadrift (1988–93) for soprano and 3 players

Scherzo (with trains) (1993) for 4 clarinets

Tiramisù (1993–94, rev. 1995) for 10 players

The Bearded Lady (1994) for oboe (doubling cor anglais) and piano
   arranged for clarinet and piano (1994)

The Colour of Pomegranates (1994) for alto flute and piano

I'm nobody, who are you? (1995) for tenor/high baritone, violin and piano

Past Hymns (1996) for string orchestra

Poetry Nearing Silence (1996–97) for 7 players

The Crazed Moon (1996–97) for orchestra

Bach Machine (1997) for 3 players

Somewhere near Cluj (1998) for solo piano

The Stations of the Sun (1997–98) for orchestra

Piano Etudes Nos 1–4 (1995–99)

Towards Poetry (1999; extended version for dance of *Poetry Nearing Silence*) for 7 players

O sing unto the Lord (1999) for SATB choir
Alhambra Fantasy (1998–2000) for 16 players
The Bird Sings with its Fingers (2000) for chamber orchestra
Shir Hashirim (2001) for soprano and chamber orchestra
Imagin'd Corners (2001–02) for orchestra with 5 obbligato horns
Quasi una passacaglia (2002) for solo piano
Steps (2003) for solo piano
I saw Eternity (2003) for SATB choir a cappella
Symphony (2002–03) for orchestra
Four American Choruses (2002–03) for SATB chorus a cappella
Old Bells (2004) for solo piano
Book of Hours (2002–04) for 19 players and electronics
Eden (2004–05) for orchestra
My beloved spake (2006) for SATB choir and organ
Heaven is Shy of Earth (2005–06; 'Gloria (with Bird)' added 2010) for mezzo-
    soprano, choir and orchestra
Alleluia (2007) for choir and orchestra
Lucretius (2008) for soprano and percussion
Prayer (2009) for solo viola
Fantasias (2006–09) for orchestra
The Comedy of Change (2009) for 12 players
Bell Mass (2010) for double SATB choir and organ
Transferable Resistance (2010) for brass ensemble
The Discovery of Heaven (2011) for orchestra
Another Prayer (2012) for solo violin
Harmony (2013) for choir and orchestra
Thebans (2010–14), opera in 3 acts
String Quartet No. 2 '300 Weihnachtslieder' (2014)
In lieblicher Bläue (2014–15), poem for violin and orchestra
Catalan Peasant with Guitar (2015) for solo guitar
Van Gogh Blue (2015) for 8 players
Sensation (2015–16) for solo piano
Incantesimi (2015–16) for orchestra
Magnificat (2016) for unaccompanied choir
Nunc dimittis (2016–17) for unaccompanied choir
The Imaginary Museum (2016–17), concerto for piano and orchestra
Capriccio (2017) for solo piano
Tombeau (2017) for soprano, violin, cello and piano
String Quartet No. 3 'hana no hanataba' (2017–18)
Evening Canticles (St John's Service) (2018) for choir and organ
Fanfare SC-GH (2018) for 2 trumpets
Litanies (2018–19) for cello and orchestra

List of Recordings of Julian Anderson's Music

The recordings are listed chronologically by date of release. The second section lists the works recorded in alphabetical order with numbers referring to the entries for the recordings in the first section.

I. LIST OF RECORDINGS

1. Somewhere near Cluj
Thalia Myers (piano)
Recorded Challow Park, Wantage, Oxon, 15–16 February 1999
Released 1999, NMC NMC D057, also on NMC D069 and NMC D207
Part of *Spectrum*

2. O sing unto the Lord
The Choir of New College Oxford – Edward Higginbottom (director)
Recorded Douai Abbey, Berkshire, 13–15 July 2005
Released 2006, Avie AV2085
Also includes choral works by Dove, Grier, Holloway, Jackson, Joubert, MacMillan, O'Regan, Weir, Wigglesworth and Wishart

3. Khorovod[a]; The Stations of the Sun[b]; The Crazed Moon[b]; Alhambra Fantasy[a]; Diptych[b]
London Sinfonietta[a], BBC Symphony Orchestra[b] – Oliver Knussen
Recorded: Watford Colosseum, December 2001[a]; BBC Maida Vale Studio 1, January 2000[b]
Released 2006, Ondine ODE 1012–2

4. Eden[a]; Imagin'd Corners[b]; Four American Choruses[c]; Symphony[d]; Book of Hours[e]
City of Birmingham Symphony Orchestra[a,b,d], City of Birmingham Symphony Chorus[c], Birmingham Contemporary Music Group[e], Lamberto Coccioli/Scott Wilson (live electronics)[e] – Martyn Brabbins[a], Sakari Oramo[b,d], Simon Halsey[c], Oliver Knussen[e] (conductors)
Recorded: Cheltenham Town Hall, 1 July 2005 (live)[a], Symphony Hall Birmingham, 19 January 2006[b], Hawksyard Priory, Lichfield, 20–21 February 2005[c], Symphony Hall Birmingham, 4 December 2003[d], Royal Northern College of Music, Manchester, 29 January 2005[e]
Released 2006, NMC NMC D121

5. Quasi una passacaglia
London Sinfonietta – George Benjamin (conductor)
Live recording, Purcell Room, London, 12 June 2002
Released 2006, London Sinfonietta SINFCD12004
Part of *Snapshots: Fiftieth birthday tributes for Oliver Knussen*

6. Lucretius
Claire Booth (soprano), Owen Gunnell (percussion)
Recorded Hall One, King's Place, London, 21 August–17 September 2008
Released 2009, NMC NMC D150 (4 CDs)
Part of *The NMC Songbook*

7. The Comedy of Change
The New York Philharmonic – Alan Gilbert (conductor)
Live recording, Peter Norton Symphony Space, New York, 18 December 2010
Released 2011, New York Philharmonic NYP20110107
Also includes works by Lindberg, Grisey, Matheson and Yim

8. Piano Etudes Nos 1–3
Clare Hammond (piano)
Recorded Cosmo Rodeswald Hall, University of Manchester, 3–4 January 2011
Released 2012, Prima Facie PFCD006
Also includes piano works by Grange, Hellawell, Hesketh and Swayne

9. Fantasias[a]; The Crazed Moon[b]; The Discovery of Heaven[c]
London Philharmonic Orchestra – Vladimir Jurowski[a,b], Ryan Wigglesworth[c] (conductors)
Live recordings: Royal Festival Hall, London, 3 December 2011[a], 19 March 2011[b], 24 March 2012[c]
Released 2013, London Philharmonic Orchestra LPO – 0074

10. Piano Etude No. 1
Peter Hill (piano)
Recorded Reid Concert Hall, University of Edinburgh, 23 March/6 April 2014
Released 2014, Delphian DCD34141
Also includes piano works by Messiaen, Ravel, Dutilleux, Stockhausen and George Benjamin

11. In lieblicher Bläue[a]; Alleluia[b]; The Stations of the Sun[c]
Carolin Widmann (violin)[a], London Philharmonic Choir[b], London Philharmonic Orchestra – Vladimir Jurowski (conductor)
Live recordings: Royal Festival Hall, London, 14 March 2015[a], 1 March 2014[b], 7 December 2013[c]
Released 2016, London Philharmonic Orchestra LPO – 0089

12. My beloved spake; Bell Mass; O sing unto the Lord; I saw Eternity; Four American Choruses; Nunc dimittis
Choir of Gonville & Caius College, Cambridge, Michael How & Luke Fitzgerald (organ scholars), Geoffrey Webber (director and solo organ)
Recorded Chapel of Merton College, Oxford, 2–4 July 2017
Released 2018, Delphian DCD34202
Also includes Frescobaldi *Toccata quarta*

13. The Comedy of Change[a]; Heaven is Shy of Earth[b]
Susan Bickley (mezzo-soprano)[b], London Sinfonietta[a], BBC Symphony Orchestra and Chorus[b] – Oliver Knussen (conductor)
Live recordings: Queen Elizabeth Hall, London, 31 March 2010[a], Barbican Hall, London, 26 November 2010[b]
Released 2018, Ondine ODE 1313–2

14. Capriccio
Gloria Cheng (piano)
Recorded 2018
Released 2018, Bridge Records Bridge 9509
Part of *Garlands for Steven Stucky*

15. Fanfare: SC-GH
Sam Pierce, Bradley Jones (trumpets)
Recorded Duke's Hall, Royal Academy of Music, London, 12 July 2018
Released 2019, Somm Recordings SOMMCD 0196
Also includes works by Alwyn, Arnold, Balfour Gardiner, Arthur Benjamin, Chagrin, Elgar, Howells, Parry, Quilter, Stanford, Virgil Thomson and Walton

16. Poetry Nearing Silence[a]; Van Gogh Blue[b]; Ring Dance[c]; The Bearded Lady[d]; The Colour of Pomegranates[e]; Prayer[f]; Another Prayer[g]
Philippa Davies (alto flute)[e], Richard Hosford (clarinet)[d], Benjamin Nabarro (violin)[c,g], Michael Gurevich (violin)[c], Lawrence Power (viola)[f], Ian Brown (piano)[d,e], Nash Ensemble[a,b] – Martyn Brabbins (conductor)
Recorded Menuhin Hall, Yehudi Menuhin School, Cobham, Kent, 1–3 April 2019
Released 2019, NMC NMC D256

II. LIST OF WORKS RECORDED

Bibliography

Aguila, Jésus, *Le Domaine musical: Pierre Boulez et vingt ans de création contemporaine* (Paris: Fayard, 1992).

Anderson, E.S., 'Origin of Transferable Drug-Resistance Factors in the Enterobacteriaceae' *British Medical Journal* 2 (27 November 1965), 1289–91.

Anderson, Julian, 'Dans le contexte', *Entretemps* 8 (1989), 13–23.

Anderson, Julian, 'De Sables à Vues aériennes: Le développement d'un style', *Entretemps* 8 (1989), 123–37.

Anderson, Julian, 'Harmonic Practices in Oliver Knussen's Music since 1988: Part I', *Tempo* 221 (2002), 2–13.

Anderson, Julian, 'Harmonic Practices in Oliver Knussen's Music since 1988: Part II', *Tempo* 223 (2003), 16–41.

Anderson, Julian, 'Messiaen and the Notion of Influence', *Tempo* 63/247 (January 2009), 2–18.

Anderson, Julian, 'Sibelius and Contemporary Music', in *The Cambridge Companion to Sibelius*, ed. Daniel M. Grimley (Cambridge: Cambridge University Press, 2004), pp. 196–216.

Anderson, Julian, 'The Orchestral Music', in Henrietta Brougham, Christopher Fox and Ian Pace (eds), *Uncommon Ground: The Music of Michael Finnissy* (Aldershot: Ashgate, 1997).

Anderson, Julian, 'Timbre, Process and *accords fixes*: Dutilleux and his Younger French Contemporaries', *Contemporary Music Review* 29/5 (2010), 447–61.

Apel, Willi (ed.), *French Secular Music of the Late Fourteenth Century*, foreword by Paul Hindemith (Cambridge, Massachusetts: The Mediaeval Academy of America, 1950).

Babbitt, Milton, 'Who Cares if You Listen?', *High Fidelity* 8 (February 1958), 38–40, 126–27.

Balmer, Yves, Thomas Lacôte and Christopher Brent Murray, *Le modèle et l'invention: Olivier Messiaen et la technique de l'emprunt* (Lyon: Symètrie, 2017).

Barraqué, Jean, 'Propos Impromtu', in Laurent Feneyrou (ed.), *Jean Barraqué: Écrits* (Paris: Publications de la Sorbonne, 2001).

Boulez, Pierre, *Boulez on Music Today*, trans. Susan Bradshaw and Richard Rodney Bennett (London: Faber, 1971).

Boulez, Pierre, *Penser la musique aujourd'hui* (Paris: Gonthier, 1963).

Bouliane, Denys – see LeBaron, Anne.

Britten, Benjamin, 'On Receiving the First Aspen Award', speech given on 31 July 1964 at Aspen Music Festival, Colorado. The speech is reproduced in full on the festival website: http://www.aspenmusicfestival.com/benjamin-britten (accessed 30 September 2017).

Budd, Robert, *Penicillin: Triumph and Tragedy* (Oxford: Oxford University Press, 2007).

Canetti, Elias, *Crowds and Power*, trans. Carol Stewart (London: Victor Gollancz, 1962). First published as *Masse und Macht* (Munich: C. Hanser, 1960).

Carpenter, Humphrey, *The Envy of the World: Fifty Years of the BBC Third Programme* (London: Weidenfeld & Nicolson, 1996).

Cooper, Martin, *French Music: From the Death of Berlioz to the Death of Fauré* (London: Oxford University Press, 1951).

Craft, Robert, 'Amorous in Amherst', *The New York Review of Books* (23 April 1987), reproduced in Robert Craft, *Down a Path of Wonder: Memoirs of Stravinsky, Schoenberg and other Cultural Figures* (Norfolk: Naxos Books, 2006), pp. 399–413.

Czechoslovakia: Romanesque and Gothic Illuminated Manuscripts (Paris: UNESCO, 1959).

Decroupet, Pascal (ed.), *Pierre Boulez, Le Marteau sans maître: Facsimile of the Draft Store and the First Fair Copy of the Full Score*. A Publication of the Paul Sacher Foundation (Mainz: Schott, 2005).

Dingle, Christopher, 'La statue reste sur son piédestal: Messiaen's *La Transfiguration* and Vatican II', *Tempo* 212 (April 2000), 8–11.

Dingle, Christopher and Nigel Simeone, *Olivier Messiaen: Music, Art and Literature* (Aldershot: Ashgate, 2007).

Dingle, Christopher, *Messiaen's Final Works* (Farnham: Ashgate, 2013).

Dingle, Christopher, *The Life of Messiaen* (Cambridge: Cambridge University Press, 2007).

Doctor, Jenny, *The BBC and Ultra-Modern Music, 1922–1936* (Cambridge: Cambridge University Press, 1999).

Dufourt, Hugues, 'Musique spectrale: pour une pratique des formes de l'énergie', *Bicéphale* 3 (1981), 85–89.

Eisen, Cliff, 'Mozart, Wolfgang Amadeus', in Christopher John Murray (ed.), *Encyclopedia of the Romantic Era, 1760–1850, Volume 2* (New York: Fitzroy Dearborn, 2004)

Ford, Andrew, *Composer to Composer: conversations about contemporary music* (London: Quartet Books, 1993).

Forte, Allen and Steve E. Gilbert, *An Introduction to Schenkerian Analysis* (New York: W.W. Norton, 1982).

Fry, Stephen, *Moab is my Washpot* (London: Hutchinson, 1997).

Fulcher, *The Composer as Intellectual: Music and Ideology in France, 1914–1940* (New York: Oxford University Press, 2005).

Grant, M.J., *Serial Music, Serial Aesthetics: Compositional Theory in Post-War Europe* (Cambridge: Cambridge University Press, 2001).

Grogan, Christopher (ed.), *Imogen Holst: A Life in Music*, rev. edn (Woodbridge: Boydell, 2010).

Hall, Patricia, *Berg's Wozzeck*. Studies in Musical Genesis, Structure, and Interpretation (New York: Oxford University Press, 2011).

Haskell, Henry (ed.), *The Attentive Listener: Three Centuries of Music Criticism* (Princeton, New Jersey: Princeton University Press, 1996).

Heinemann, Stephen, 'Pitch-Class Set Multiplication in Theory and Practice', *Music Theory Spectrum*, Vol. 20, No. 1 (1998), 72–96.

Heyworth, Peter, 'Messiaen's St Francis', *The Observer*, 4 December 1983, 34.

Hill, Peter and Nigel Simeone, *Messiaen*, trans. Lucie Kayas (Paris: Fayard, 2008).

Hillier, Paul, 'I felt a controlling hand taking over', *The Guardian* (28 September 2007), available at http://www.theguardian.com [accessed 13 February 2017].

Hutton, Ronald, *The Stations of the Sun: A History of the Ritual Year in Britain* (Oxford: Oxford University Press, 1996).

Janáček, Leoš, 'Wells and fountains', reproduced in *Janáček: Leaves from His Life*, ed. and trans. Vilem and Margaret Tausky (London: Kahn & Averill, 1982).

Gilbert E. Kaplan, 'Mahler and Tradition: Is There or Isn't There? Gilbert E. Kaplan and Peter Franklin in Search of One', *Musical Times*, Vol. 133, No. 1797 (November 1992), 559–63.

Keller, Hans, *The Great Haydn Quartets: Their Interpretation* (London: Dent, 1993).

Kennedy, Michael, *The Works of Ralph Vaughan Williams* (London: Oxford University Press, 1964).

Koechlin, Charles, *Traité de l'orchestration*, 4 vols (Paris: Max Eschig, 1954–59).

Krenek, Ernst, *Studies in Counterpoint Based on the Twelve-Tone Technique* (New York: G. Schirmer, 1940).

LeBaron, Anne and Denys Bouliane, 'Darmstadt 1980', *Perspectives of New Music*, Vol. 29, No. 1/2 (Autumn 1980–Summer 1981), 420–41.

Lockspeiser, Edward, *Debussy: His Life and Mind – Volume II 1902–1918* (London: Cassell, 1965).

Messiaen, Olivier, *Technique de mon langage musical*, 2 vols (Paris: Alphonse Leduc, 1944; single-volume edition, 1999); published in English as *The Technique of*

My Musical Language, 2 vols, trans. John Satterfield (Paris: Alphonse Leduc, 1956; single-volume edition, 2001).

Messiaen, Olivier, *Traité de rythme, de couleur et d'ornithologie*, 8 vols (Paris: Alphonse Leduc, 1994–2002).

Morton, Lawrence, 'Footnote to Stravinsky Studies: *Le Sacre du Printemps*', *Tempo* 128 (March 1979), 9–16.

Mozart, Leopold, *A Treatise on the Fundamental Principles of Violin Playing*, trans. E. Knocker (Oxford: Oxford University Press, 1948).

Myers, Rollo H., *Modern French Music: From Fauré to Boulez* (New York: Praeger, 1971).

Palmer, Andrew, *Encounters with British Composers* (Woodbridge: Boydell, 2015).

Pavić, Milorad, *Dictionary of the Khazars: A Lexicon Novel*, trans. Christina Pribicevic-Zoric (New York: Alfred A. Knopf, 1988).

Pavić, Milorad, *Landscape Painted with Tea*, trans. Christina Pribicevic-Zoric (New York: Alfred A. Knopf, 1990).

Peyser, Joan, 'Wolpe: A Thoroughly Modern Maverick; About Stefan Wolpe', *New York Times*, 6 February 1972, D17.

Phillips, Tom, *The Heart of A Humument* (Stuttgart and London: Hansjörg Mayer and Talfourd, 1985).

Ponsonby, Robert, *Musical Heroes: A Personal View of Music and the Musical World over Sixty Years* (London: Giles de la Mare, 2009).

Queneau, Raymond, *Cent mille milliards de poèmes* (Paris: Éditions Gallimard, 1961).

Rae, John, *Delusions of Grandeur: A Headmaster's Life 1966–86* (London: HarperCollins, 1993).

Reaney, Gilbert (ed.), *Corpus Mensurabilis Musicæ 11: Early Fifteenth-Century Music*, 7 vols (The American Institute of Musicology, 1955–83).

Retallack, Joan (ed.), *Musiccage: Cage Muses on Words, Art, Music* (Hanover and London: Wesleyan University Press/University Press of New England, 1996).

Ross, Alex, *The Rest is Noise* (London: Harper Perennial, 2009).

Salzer, Felix, *Structural Hearing: Tonal Coherence in Music* (New York: Boni, 1952).

Schaeffer, Pierre, *Solfège de l'objet sonore trois microsillons d'exemples sonores illustrant le: traité des objets musicaux* (Paris: Editions du Seuil, 1966).

Schloezer, Boris de, 'Igor Strawinsky', in *La Revue Musicale*, 5/2 (1 December 1923), 107–09.

Stravinsky, Vera and Robert Craft, *Stravinsky in Pictures and Documents* (New York: Simon & Schuster, 1978).

Stucky, Steven, *Lutosławski and his Music* (Cambridge: Cambridge University Press, 2009).

Sudek, Josef, *Janáček Hukvaldy* (Prague: Supraphon, 1971).

Swann, M.M., K.L. Baxter, H.I. Field et al., *Report of the Joint Committee on the Use of Antibiotics in Animal Husbandry and Veterinary Medicine* (Cmnd 4190) (London: HMSO, 1969).

Taruskin, Richard, *Stravinsky and the Russian Traditions, Volume One: A Biography of the Works Through Mavra* (Berkeley: University of California Press, 1996).

Taruskin, Richard, *Text and Act: Essays on Music and Performance* (Oxford: Oxford University Press, 1995).

Tchamkerten, Jacques, 'From *Fête des Belles Eaux* to *Saint François d'Assise*: the evolution of the writing for ondes Martenot in the music of Olivier Messiaen', in Christopher Dingle and Nigel Simeone, *Olivier Messiaen: Music, Art and Literature* (Aldershot: Ashgate, 2007).

Tucker, Anthony, 'E S Anderson', *The Guardian* (22 March 2006); available online at: https://www.theguardian.com/society/2006/mar/22/health.science.

Unsigned, 'Mechanical Amusement', *The Times* (7 September 1910), 9.

Villars, Chris (ed.), *Morton Feldman says: selected interviews and lectures 1964–1987* (London: Hyphen Press, 2006).

Whittall, Arnold, 'Measure of Authenticity: The Macrotonal Music of Julian Anderson', *The Musical Quarterly* 156/1930 (Spring 2015), 7–22.

Discography

[Arom, Simha], *Liturgies Juives d'Ethiopie*, rec. by Simha Arom and Avi Nahmias, Jerusalem, 1986, Maison des Cultures du Monde W 260013 (CD).

Bach, J.S., *Cello Suites*, Pablo Casals (cello), rec. Abbey Road Studios, London, 23 and 25 November 1936 and Paris, 2–3 June 1938 and 13–16 June 1939, HMV DB 3671/3; DB 3399/401; DB 3402/4; DB 6538/40; DB 6541/4; DB 3674/7 (78s).

Bach, J.S., *The Complete Cantatas*, Helmuth Rilling, Hänssler HAEN98630 (71 CDs).

Bach, J.S., *The Sacred Cantatas*, Leonhardt Consort & Concentus musicus Wien, Nikolaus Harnoncourt & Gustav Leonhardt (conductors), Warner 2564699437 (60 CDs).

Bach, J.S., *St Matthew Passion*, Ex Cathedra Choir & Baroque Orchestra, Jeffrey Skidmore (conductor), Orchid Classics ORC100007 (2 CDs).

Basie, Count, *Li'l Darlin'* in *The Atomic Mr Basie*, Count Basie Orchestra, Count Basie (piano and conductor), rec. New York 1957, Roulette Records SRCP 3000 (LP)

Beethoven, Ludwig van, *Missa Solemnis*, Charlotte Margiono (soprano), Catherine Robbin (mezzo-soprano), William Kendall (tenor), Alastair Miles (bass), Monteverdi Choir, Orchestre Revolutionnaire et Romantique, John Eliot Gardiner (conductor), rec. All Saints' Church, Tooting, London, November 1989, Archiv Produktion 429 779–2 (CD).

Berg, Alban, *Wozzeck*, excerpts, Richard Bitterauf (Wozzeck), BBC Symphony Orchestra and Wireless Chorus, Adrian Boult (conductor), live rec. Queen's Hall, London, 14 March 1934, Ponto PO-1053 (2 CDs).

Boulez, Pierre, *Le Marteau sans maître*, Marie-Thérèse Cahn (chant), Pierre Boulez (conductor), live rec. Petit Théâtre Marigny, Paris, 21 March 1956, Véga C35 A67 (10" vinyl).

Boulez, Pierre, *Le Marteau sans maître*, Jeanne Deroubaix (chant), Pierre Boulez (conductor), rec. [date and location unknown] released 1964, Adès 14.008 (LP), Accord 4769209 (4 CDs).

435

Boulez, Pierre, *Le Marteau sans maître*, Yvonne Minton (chant), Pierre Boulez (conductor), rec. ?1973, CBS 73213 (LP).

Boulez, Pierre, *Le Marteau sans maître*, Hilary Summers (chant), Pierre Boulez (conductor), rec. IRCAM, Paris, September 2002, DG 00289 477 5327 (CD).

Boulez, Pierre, *Le Marteau sans maître*, Margery Mackay (chant), Robert Craft (conductor), released 1958, Columbia Masterworks ML 5275 (LP).

Britten, Benjamin, *War Requiem*, Galina Vishnevskaya, Peter Pears, Dietrich Fischer-Dieskau, The Bach Choir, London Symphony Orchestra Chorus, Highgate School Choir, Melos Ensemble, London Symphony Orchestra, Benjamin Britten (conductor), rec. Kingsway Hall, London, January 1963, Decca SET 252/3 (2 LPs); 478 5433 (2 CDs + Blu-ray).

Britten, Benjamin, *War Requiem*, Elisabeth Söderström, Robert Tear, Thomas Allen, Boys of Christ Church Cathedral, Oxford, CBSO Chorus, City of Birmingham Symphony Orchestra, Simon Rattle (conductor), location unknown, rec. 1983, EMI CDS 7 47034 8 (2 CDs).

Cardew, Cornelius, *The Great Learning*, The Scratch Orchestra, rec. Chappell Recording Studios, London, 15–16 February 1971, Deutsche Grammophon 2538 216 (LP).

Carter, Elliott, Concerto for Orchestra, London Sinfonietta, Oliver Knussen (conductor), rec. Henry Wood Hall, London, 15–16 February 1991, Virgin Classics 0777 7592712 2 (CD).

Carter, Elliott, *Symphonia: Sum Fluxae Pretium Spei*, BBC Symphony Orchestra, Oliver Knussen (conductor), rec. Henry Wood Hall, London, August 1998, Deutsche Grammophon 459 660–2 (CD).

Chaurasia, Pandit Hariprasad, *Raga Jait*, Pandit Hariprasad Chaurasia (flute), Fazal Qureshi (tabla), live rec. Kufa Gallery, London, 28 June 1990, Navras Records NRCD 0007 (CD).

Crawford Seeger, Ruth, *Ruth Crawford Seeger Portrait*, New London Chamber Choir, Schönberg Ensemble, Lucy Shelton (soprano), Reinbert de Leeuw (piano), James Wood (conductor), Oliver Knussen (conductor), rec. Amsterdam and London, 1996–7, Deutsche Grammophon DG 0289 449 9252 6 (CD).

Elgar, Edward, *Cockaigne Overture*, The Symphony Orchestra, rec. (?)Hayes, 28 February 1917, HMV 2–0728 [HO2498af] (78s); Music & Arts CD-1257 (4) (4 CDs).

Elgar, Edward, *Cockaigne Overture*, Royal Albert Hall Orchestra, rec. Queen's Hall, London, 27 April 1926, HMV D 1110–11 [CR 332–5] (78s); EMI 50999 0 95694 2 3 (9 CDs).

Elgar, Edward, *Cockaigne Overture*, BBC Symphony Orchestra, rec. No. 1 Studio, Abbey Road, London, 11 April 1933, HMV 2b 4174–6/DB 1935–6 (78s); EMI 50999 0 95694 2 3 (9 CDs).

Finnissy, Michael, *Etched Bright with Sunlight*, Nicolas Hodges (piano), rec. 1999/2000, St George's Bristol, Metronome MET CD 1058 (CD).

Flanders, Michael and Donald Swann, *At the Drop of a Hat*, live rec. Fortune Theatre, London, 21 February 1957, Parlophone PMC 1033 (LP).

Flanders, Michael and Donald Swann, *At the Drop of Another Hat*, live rec. Haymarket Theatre, London, 2 October 1963, Parlophone PMC 1216 (LP).

Flanders, Michael and Donald Swann, *The Bestiary of Flanders and Swann*, rec. London 1963, Parlophone PMC 1164 (LP).

[Florentz, Jean-Louis], *L'Assomption à Däbrä Gännät: L'Église Orthodoxe Éthiopienne de Jérusalem*, recorded by Jean-Louis Florentz, Jerusalem, July–September 1987, Radio France Ocora 560027/28 (2 CDs).

Haendel, George Friedrich [sic], *Water Music & Fireworks*, Le Concert Spirituel, Hervé Niquet (conductor), rec. l'Arsenal de Metz, France, September 2002, Glossa GCDSA 921616 (SACD).

Haydn, Joseph, *The Complete Symphonies*, Philharmonia Hungarica, Antal Doráti, Decca 478 1221 (33 CDs).

Haydn, Joseph, *The Complete Symphonies*, Vienna Chamber Orchestra, Ernst Märzendorfer, Scribendum SC818 (33 CDs).

Haydn, Joseph, *The Virtual Haydn: complete works for solo keyboard*, Tom Beghin (keyboards), rec. McGill University April 2007 to March 2009, Naxos NBD0001–04 (4 Blu-ray discs); 8.501203 (12 CDs + DVD).

Hildegard of Bingen, 'A feather on the breath of God', Gothic Voices with Emma Kirkby, directed by Christopher Page, rec. Church of St Jude-on-the-Hill, Hampstead, London, 14 September 1981, Hyperion CDA66039 (CD).

Holst, Imogen, *String Chamber Music*, Simon Hewitt Jones violin, David Worswick violin, Tom Hankey viola, Oliver Coates cello, Thomas Hewitt Jones cello, Daniel Swain piano, rec. All Saints Church, West Dulwich, August 2007, NMC NMC D236.

Janáček, Leoš, *Katya Kabanova*, Cheryl Barker (Katya), Jane Henschel (Kabanicha), Robert Brubaker (Boris Grigoryevich), Welsh National Opera, Carlo Rizzi (conductor), rec. Brangwyn Hall, Swansea, 11–15 December 2006, Chandos CHAN 3145(2) (2 CDs).

Lambert, John, *The Music of John Lambert, 1926–1995: Solos and Ensembles*, Anthony Aarons (trumpet), Charles Ramirez (guitar), Albion Guitar Quartet, Sounds Positive, Bingham String Quartet, David Sutton-Anderson (conductor), NMC NMC D026 (CD).

Lewis, George, *The Will to Adorn*, International Contemporary Ensemble, George Lewis (trombone), Steve Schick (conductor), David Fulmer (conductor), rec. 2011–16, Tundra New Focus Recordings TUN005 (CD).

Mahler, Gustav, Symphony No. 5, New York Philharmonic Orchestra, Leonard Bernstein (conductor), 7 January 1963, Philharmonic Hall (now Avery Fisher

Hall), Lincoln Center, New York, Columbia M2S 698 (LP); Sony Classical SX12K 89499 (12 CDs).

Mahler, Gustav, Symphony No. 5, Members of the New York Philharmonic, Leonard Bernstein (conductor), live rec. 8 June 1968, at the Mass on the day of burial of Robert Francis Kennedy, St Patrick's Cathedral, New York City, Sony Classical SX12K 89499 (12 CDs).

Mahler, Gustav, Symphony No. 5, Wiener Philharmoniker, Leonard Bernstein (conductor), live rec. September 1987, Alte Oper, Frankfurt am Main, Deutsche Grammophon 423 608–2 (CD).

Mahler, Gustav, 'Adagietto' from Symphony No. 5, Concertgebouw Orchestra of Amsterdam, Willem Mengelberg (conductor), rec. May 1926, Concertgebouw, Amsterdam, Matrices WAX 1548 and 1549; Columbia L1798 (78s); Naxos 8.110855 (CD).

Mahler, Gustav, Symphony No. 5, Philharmonic-Symphony Orchestra of New York, Bruno Walter (conductor), rec. 20 February 1947, Carnegie Hall, New York, Matrices XCO-37365–373880; Columbia 12666-D–12637-D (M-718) (78s); Naxos 8.110896 (CD).

Martel, Caroline (director), *Le Chant des Ondes* (Les Films du Paradoxe, 2012), DVD EDV 311 (DVD).

Messiaen, Olivier, *Chronochromie*, Cleveland Orchestra, Pierre Boulez (conductor), rec. Masonic Auditorium, Cleveland, March 1993, Deutsche Grammophon 445 827–2 (CD).

Messiaen, Olivier, *Chronochromie*, BBC Symphony Orchestra, Antal Doráti (conductor), rec. No. 1 Studio, Abbey Road, London, 27 September and 11–16 October 1964, HMV ASD 369 (LP).

Messiaen, Olivier, *Oiseaux exotiques*, Yvonne Loriod (piano), Orchestre du Domaine Musical, Rudolf Albert (conductor), live rec. (world premiere) Petit Théâtre Marigny, Paris, 10 March 1956, Véga C 30 A 65 (LP), Accord 4769209 (4 CDs); Accord 480 1045 (7 CDs).

Messiaen, Olivier, *Oiseaux exotiques*, Yvonne Loriod (piano), Symphonieorchester des Bayerischen Rundfunks, Pierre Boulez (conductor), live rec. Herkulessaal der Residenz, Munich, 17 April 1964, Col Legno WWE 2 CD 20084–2 (CD).

Messiaen, Olivier, *Oiseaux exotiques*, Philippe Entremont (piano), Cleveland Orchestra, Pierre Boulez (conductor), live rec. Severance Hall, Cleveland, Ohio, 19 and 21 November 1970, Musical Arts Association, TCO 093–75 (CD).

Messiaen, Olivier, *Oiseaux exotiques*, Yvonne Loriod (piano), Ensemble InterContemporain, Pierre Boulez (conductor), live rec. Théâtre des Champs-Élysées, Paris, 26 November 1988, Disques Montaignes XXIIII (CD).

Messiaen, Olivier, *The Piano Music of Olivier Messiaen*, Peter Hill (piano), rec. Rosslyn Hill Unitarian Chapel, 21–22 February and 25–26 September 1985, Unicorn Kanchana DKP(CD)9078 (CD).

Messiaen, Olivier, *Quatuor pour le fin du Temps*, Olivier Messiaen (piano), Jean Pasquier (violin), André Vacellier (clarinet), Étienne Pasquier (cello), rec. Scuola Cantorum, 1956; Club Français du Disque – Musicdisc 30 RC 719 (LP); Accord 461 744–2 (CD); Accord 480 1045 (CD).

Messiaen, Olivier, *Saint François d'Assise*, Philippe Rouillon (Saint François), Maria Orán (L'Ange), Groot Omroepkoor, Nederlands Kamerkoor, Radio Symfonie Orkest, Radio Kamer Orkest, Kent Nagano (conductor), live rec. Muziekcentrum Vredenburg, Utrecht, 28 September 1986, KRO KK 8802 (4 CDs).

Messiaen, Olivier, *La Transfiguration de Notre-Seigneur Jésus-Christ*, Yvonne Loriod (piano), Arturo Muruzabal (cello), Martine van der Loo (flute), Harmen de Boer (clarinet), Peter Prommel (marimba), Ruud Stotÿn (vibraphone), Henk de Vlieger (xylorimba), Koor van de BRT Bruxelles, Groot Omroepkoor and Radio Symfonie Orkest Hilversum, Reinbert de Leeuw (conductor), rec. Concertgebouw, Amsterdam, 29 June 1991, Auvidi Montaigne MO 782040 (2 CDs).

Messiaen, Olivier, *Vingt Regards sur l'Enfant-Jésus*, Peter Hill (piano), rec. St Paul's New Southgate, 16–20 September 1991, Unicorn Kanchana DKP (CD), 9122/23 (2 CDs).

Messiaen, Olivier, *Vingt Regards sur l'Enfant-Jésus*, Yvonne Loriod (piano), rec. Paris, 13 March 1956, Véga C 30 A 60/61/62 (3 LPs); Universal/Decca 4817069 (13 CDs).

Messiaen, Olivier, *Vingt Regards sur l'Enfant-Jésus*, Yvonne Loriod (piano), rec. Église Notre-Dame du Liban, Paris, October 1973, Erato OME 1 (8 LPs); Warner 2564 69986–5 (2 CDs).

Messiaen, Olivier, *Vingt Regards sur l'Enfant-Jésus*, Yvonne Loriod (piano), live rec. Radio Bremen, 27 October 1985, Schwann AMS 5201 (2 LPs).

Monteverdi, Claudio, *Combattimento di Tancredi e Clorinda*, Rolando Villazón (tenor), Patrizia Ciofi (soprano), Topi Lehtipuu (tenor), Le Concert d'Astrée, Emmanuelle Haïm (direction), rec. Paris, November 2005, Virgin Classics 0946 363350 2 5 (CD).

Monty Python, *The Monty Python Matching Tie and Handkerchief*, rec. 1973, Charisma CAS 1080 (LP).

[Munrow, David], *The Art of Courtly Love*, The Early Music Consort of London, David Munrow (director), rec. 1971 and 1973, EMI/His Master's Voice SLS 863 (3 LPs).

Murail, Tristan, *Gondwana*, Orchestre National de France, Yves Prin (conductor), live rec. 20 December 1980, Radio-France, Adda/Salabert Trajectoires SCD8902 (CD).

Musgrave, Thea, Concerto for Orchestra, Clarinet Concerto, Horn Concerto, *Monologue, Excursions*, Scottish National Orchestra, London Symphony Orchestra, Gervase de Peyer (clarinet), Barry Tuckwell (horn), Malcolm

Williamson (piano), Thea Musgrave (piano and conductor), Norman del Mar (conductor), Alexander Gibson (conductor), rec. London and Glasgow 1970–73, Lyrita Recorded Edition, SRCD.253

Nørgård, Per, *Unity Behind Trinity: Three Organ Works,* Jens Christiansen (organ), rec. 1990, Copenhagen, Kontrapunkt 32081.

Payne, Roger, *Songs of the Humpback Whale,* released 1970, CRM Records SWR 11 (LP).

Roché, Jean C., *Oiseaux Méditerranéens,* n.d., SRL J.C. Roché et Cie LPL 2409 1Y (LP).

Saariaho, Kaija, *Works for Orchestra,* Los Angeles Philharmonic Orchestra, Finnish Radio Symphony Orchestra, Orchestre de Paris, Avanti! Chamber Orchestra, Tapiola Chamber Choir, Petri Alanko (alto flute), Anssi Karttunen (cello), Riikka Rantanen (contralto), Gabriel Suovanen (baritone), Petteri Salomaa (baritone), Esa-Pekka Salonen (conductor), Christoph Eschenbach (conductor), Hannu Lintu (conductor), Jukka-Pekka Sasaste (conductor), ONDINE ODE 1113–2Q.

Schoenberg, Arnold, *Pierrot Lunaire,* Cleo Laine (sprechtstimme), Nash Ensemble, Elgar Howarth (conductor), rec. ?1974, RCA Red Seal LRL1 5058 (LP).

Sibelius, Jean, Symphony No. 5 in E flat major (original version), Lahti Symphony Orchestra, Osmo Vänskä (conductor), rec. Church of the Cross (Ristinkirkko), Lahti, Finland, 11–12 May 1995, BIS BIS-CD-800 (CD).

Stockhausen, Karlheinz, *Stimmung,* Theatre of Voices, Paul Hillier (director), rec. September 2006, Stavnsholtkirken, Copenhagen, Harmonia Mundi HMU80 7408 (SACD).

Stravinsky, Igor, *The Firebird* and *Les Noces,* The Royal Ballet, Orchestra of the Royal Opera House, John Carewe (conductor), rec. 1996, The Royal Opera House, Covent Garden, Opus Arte OA0833D (DVD).

Stravinsky, Igor, *L'Histoire du Soldat (Suite),* Israel Baker (violin), Roy D'Antonio (clarinet), Don Christlieb (bassoon), Charles Brady (cornet), Robert Marsteller (trombone), Richard Kelley (bass), William Kraft (percussion), Igor Stravinsky (conductor), rec. American Legion Hall, Hollywood, California, 10/13 February 1961, Columbia Masterworks MS 6272/ML5672 (LP); Sony SM3K 46291 (3 CDs); Sony 88875026162 (57 CDs).

Stravinsky, Igor, *The Rite of Spring,* Minneapolis Symphony Orchestra, Antal Doráti (conductor), rec. Northrop Auditorium, Minneapolis, 1953, Mercury MG 50030 (LP).

Stravinsky, Igor, *Le Sacre du printemps; The Firebird,* Mariinsky Ballet and Orchestra, Valery Gergiev (conductor), rec. Mariinsky Theatre, St Petersburg, June 2008, BelAir Classiques, BAC041 (DVD); BAC441 (Blu-ray).

Thomas, Dylan, *Under Milk Wood,* Richard Burton, etc., rec. London, 24 January 1954, Argo RG 21/22 (2 LPs); Naxos AudioBooks NA288712 (CD).

Thomas, Dylan, *Under Milk Wood*, Dylan Thomas, etc., rec. Poetry Center, New York, 14 May 1953, Caedmon TC 2005 (2 LPs); reissued on CD as part of Dylan Thomas, *The Caedmon Collection*, Caedmon UACD 95(11) (11 CDs).

Vaughan, Sarah, *Sassie Swings the Tivoli*, live rec. Copenhagen, 18 July 1963, produced by Quincy Jones, Mercury 20011 SMCL (LP).

Varèse, Edgar, *Déserts* (world première), Orchestre National de France, Hermann Scherchen (conductor), rec. Théâtre des Champs-Élysées, Paris, 2 December 1954, on *Archives Hermann Scherchen (de Purcell a Varèse)*, Tahra TAH 599–600 (CD).

Wagner, Richard, *Orchestral Works*, Jane Eaglen (soprano), London Classical Players, Roger Norrington (conductor), rec. 1994, EMI CDC 5 55479–2 (CD).

Index